# Basic Marketing Research

## Customer Insights and Managerial Action

### 9th Edition

Tom J. Brown
Oklahoma State University

Tracy A. Suter
The University of Tulsa

Gilbert A. Churchill, Jr.
University of Wisconsin — Madison

Australia • Brazil • Mexico • Singapore • United Kingdom • United States

**_Basic Marketing Research_, Ninth edition**
**Tom J. Brown, Tracy A. Suter and**
**Gilbert A. Churchill. Jr.,**

Vice President, General Manager, Social Science
& Qualitative Business: Erin Joyner

Product Director: Mike Schenk

Product Manager: Heather Mooney

Project Manager: Julie Dierig

Content Developer: Erica Longenbach

Product Assistant: Allie Janneck

Marketing Manager: Katie Jergens

Digital Content Specialist: David

Digital Production Project Manager:
Timothy Christy

Manufacturing Planner: Ron Montgomery

Sr. Art Director: Michelle Kunkler

Intellectual Property

    Analyst: Diane Garrity

    Project Manager: Sarah Shainwald

Cover Image Credits: iStockphoto.com/
Sezeryadigar; iStockphoto.com/peterhowell

Production Management and Composition:
Lumina Datamatics, Inc

For product information and technology assistance, contact us at
**Cengage Learning Customer & Sales Support, 1-800-354-9706**

For permission to use material from this text or product,
submit all requests online at **www.cengage.com/permissions**
Further permissions questions can be emailed to
**permissionrequest@cengage.com**

Library of Congress Control Number: 2017944243

Student Edition ISBN: 978-1-337-10029-8

**Cengage Learning**
20 Channel Center Street
Boston, MA 02210
USA

Cengage Learning is a leading provider of customized learning solutions
with employees residing in nearly 40 different countries and sales in more
than 125 countries around the world. Find your local representative at
**www.cengage.com.**

Cengage Learning products are represented in Canada by
Nelson Education, Ltd.

To learn more about Cengage Learning Solutions, visit **www.cengage.com**

Purchase any of our products at your local college store or at our
preferred online store **www.cengagebrain.com**

Printed in the United States of America
Print Number: 01     Print Year: 2017

To *DiAnn, Drew, Taylor, Avery, and Brady* (Tom J. Brown)

To *Kristen, Camille, and Emma* (Tracy A. Suter)

To our grandchildren
*Kayla Marie*
*Johnathan Winston*
*Kelsey Lynn*
*Sean Jeffrey*
*Ethan Thomas*
*Averie Mae*
(Gilbert A. Churchill, Jr.)

# Brief Contents

# Contents

## Part 1   Introduction to Marketing Research and Problem Definition   *3*

### Chapter 1   The Role of Marketing Research   *4*

### Chapter 2   The Research Process and Ethical Concerns   *15*

### Chapter 3   Problem Formulation   *27*

## Part 2  Working with Existing Information to Solve Problems  *57*

# Part 3   Collecting Primary Data to Solve Problems   *111*

# Part 4    Analyzing Data    *239*

# Part 5    Reporting the Results    *283*

# Chapter 20    The Written Research Report    *302*

# Preface

*Basic Marketing Research: Customer Insights and Managerial Action,* 9th edition, provides an introductory look at marketing research for undergraduate students, managerially oriented graduate students, or anyone who wants an appreciation of the marketing research process. Our goal was to produce a readable book that overviews the datagathering and information-generating functions from the perspective of both researchers who gather the information and marketing managers who use the information.

Marketing research can be a complex topic. New types and sources of data are flowing into the organization at an increasing pace, making the process of information generation all the more complex. In this environment, marketing managers need to consider all relevant sources of data, whether the data already exist or must be collected. As industry trends have changed, we have attempted to keep our book relevant and engaging. For example, earlier editions of this book focused heavily on gathering and analyzing survey data; we still retain a great deal of information about how to gather such data effectively. We have continued the shift in emphasis, however, that we began in earlier editions toward the process of working with existing data when they are available. A great deal of attention and resources in industry are shifting to the analysis of the greatly multiplying sources of data available to firms.

*Basic Marketing Research: Customer Insights and Managerial Action* provides a framework for the choices and decisions that marketing analysts must make as they gather and analyze data. This is important, because decisions made in one stage of the research process have consequences for other stages. Both managers and marketing researchers need to appreciate the interactions among the parts of the research process so they can have confidence in a particular research result.

## Organization

*Basic Marketing Research: Customer Insights and Managerial Action,* 8th edition, is intended to serve both aspiring researchers and managers by breaking down the marketing research process into the basic stages that should be followed when answering a research question. The process, which we reproduce at the end of this Preface, has four general stages:

1. Problem Definition
2. Data Collection
3. Data Analysis
4. Information Reporting

Each of these stages can be further broken down into different topics, making the material much more digestible for readers. For example, we use eleven chapters to discuss the data collection process, beginning first with the retrieval of existing data from a firm's decision support system, then on to the retrieval of existing data from external secondary data sources, and then—if necessary—on to the collection of primary data. We have organized the book in this fashion to emphasize the key decisions that managers must make in their hunt for useful information. If managers know what information they need (a key aspect of problem definition), the key decisions involve locating sources for the needed information. In the research industry, greater attention and resources are being turned toward the use of secondary data (that is, data that already exist) to solve problems. This book recognizes that trend by including a separate section on working with existing information to solve problems, including a chapter on working with "big data." We still devote a substantial portion of the book, however, to the generation of primary data with an eye toward collecting data with high degrees of validity.

## Key Features

*Basic Marketing Research: Customer Insights and Managerial Action* has several special features to enhance the teaching and learning experience. The general approach used to discuss topics is to provide readers with the pros and cons of the various methods used to address a research problem and then to develop an appreciation of why these advantages and disadvantages arise. Our hope is that managers and researchers will be able to creatively apply and critically evaluate the procedures of marketing research. Other important features include the following.

**Learning Objectives.** A set of learning objectives in each chapter highlights the most important topics covered in the chapter. The learning objectives are discussed and are then reinforced point by point in the chapter summary.

**Manager's Focus.** These short features provide insights into how the information in that particular chapter or section is relevant to marketing managers. The goal is to emphasize the role of marketing managers in the research process and to offer guidelines for achieving the most usable results. Jon Austin, who teaches marketing research at Cedarville University and has a strong background working with clients in industry, provided the inspiration—and most of the writing—for the "Manager's Focus" entries.

The manager's focus discussions highlight one of the key distinctions of this book—we favor managerial usefulness and understanding over deep technical sophistication. It's not that we don't appreciate the "nuts and bolts" of topics such as big data integration and analysis, sampling, and sophisticated statistical analysis. We just believe that in a beginning course—covering everything from exploratory research to big data analytics to behavioral customer insights to primary data collection to statistical analysis—it's a lot more important to communicate the basic uses of marketing research, key decisions along the way, when and why to apply certain analysis techniques, and how to interpret the results of an analysis. Deeper knowledge about most of the topics in the book is readily available in advanced courses and textbooks.

**Key Terms with Definitions.** A running glossary appears throughout the text. Key terms in each chapter are boldfaced, and their definitions appear in the margin where the terms are discussed. A complete **Glossary** is also included at the end of the text.

**Research Windows.** The Research Windows provide a view of what is happening in the world of marketing research, describe what is happening at specific companies, and offer some specific how-to tips. They serve to engage the readers' interest in the chapter topic and to provide further depth of information. Some examples include "Marketing Research Company Job Titles and Mean Compensation" (Chapter 1); "Online Focus Groups and Webcam Interviews for Better Understanding Traveler Decision Making" (Chapter 4); "Data, Data Everywhere: Target, Big Data, and You" (Chapter 6); "How Key Ingredient Used A/B Tests to Design Web Site" (Chapter 8); and "'Driving' Towards Golfer Insights at PING" (Chapter 10).

**The Qualtrics Research Suite.** This feature was built for marketing researchers by marketing researchers. Enclosed with each new copy of Basic Marketing Research 9e, is an access code that gives you access to a tool that makes survey creation easy enough for a beginner while at the same time sophisticated enough for the most demanding academic or corporate researcher. Qualtrics allows you to create and deploy surveys, and provides data for analysis. Qualtrics access requires the code provided in the access card available with each new copy of the book. It may be accessed at https://www.qualtrics.com/support/.

**Ethics as a Foundational Discussion.** "Bad" research can violate participant trust. Researchers who use the research process as a sales tactic, a process known as sugging, harbor potential mistrust between research participants and the researcher. Advocating for a particular position or point-of-view at the expense of seeking honest insights, a practice called advocacy research, is outside of the scope of what marketing research intends to accomplish. Both of these topics as well as a deeper dive into three types of ethical reasoning are discussed early. The purpose of marketing research is research. The purpose is not sales or promotion. This message is foundational to Basic Marketing Research.

**Seeking the "what" and the "why."** "Big data" is a topic of considerable discussion in the marketing domain and business in general. The same is true of behavioral analytics. Each gives greater and greater consideration for what consumers have done and are doing as evidenced by their purchase and related behaviors. Behavioral data are critically important in modern business practices, but sometimes a researcher also wants to know why consumers participated in a particular behavior. In this case "big data" may not be the best tool for the job. Basic Marketing Research gives consideration for both by recognizing the value of what and why questions. What questions can be considered in the "Working with Existing Data" portion of the text while why questions are asked and answered in the "Collecting Primary Data" portion. Both types of considerations are brought together in the end to give a full and complete picture of data from multiple sources.

**A Tangible, Applied Example.** It is quite common for students to ask professors for a high-quality example of a student project from a past semester. If the students can see a top-notch, peer-produced model, they can produce top-notch work themselves. We have provided just such an example by including data collection instruments from multiple data sources, oral presentation slides, and a written research report as a tangible example of the type of research project that can be completed over the course of a semester. This eliminates the guesswork about what a professor might seek from his/her students when planning for students to work with firms in their communities to both assist the organization and learn by doing marketing research.

**MindTap: Empower Your Students** MindTap is a platform that propels students from memorization to mastery. It gives you complete control of your course, so you can provide engaging content, challenge every learner, and build student confidence. Customize interactive syllabi to emphasize priority topics, then add your own material or notes to the eBook as desired. This outcomes-driven application gives you the tools needed to empower students and boost both understanding and performance.

- **Access Everything You Need in One Place** Cut down on prep with the preloaded and organized MindTap course materials. Teach more efficiently with interactive multimedia, assignments, quizzes, and more. Give your students the power to read, listen, and study on their phones, so they can learn on their terms.

- **Empower Students to Reach their Potential** Twelve distinct metrics give you actionable insights into student engagement. Identify topics troubling your entire class and instantly communicate with those struggling. Students can track their scores to stay motivated towards their goals. Together, you can be unstoppable.

- **Control Your Course—and Your Content** Get the flexibility to reorder textbook chapters, add your own notes, and embed a variety of content including Open

Educational Resources (OER). Personalize course content to your students' needs. They can even read your notes, add their own, and highlight key text to aid their learning.

- **Get a Dedicated Team, Whenever You Need Them** MindTap isn't just a tool, it's backed by a personalized team eager to support you. We can help set up your course and tailor it to your specific objectives, so you'll be ready to make an impact from day one. Know we'll be standing by to help you and your students until the final day of the term.

**Data.** Data are provided for the Avery Fitness Center project. These data allow readers to perform the analyses discussed in Chapters 17 and 18. Readers might also want to conduct the analyses used to produce the AFC Research Report we provide as part of Chapter 20. These data are available to adopters on the text web site (go to www .cengagebrain.com and enter the ISBN found on the back cover of your book to locate this text's materials). We have updated the presentation, however, to reflect that data are often drawn from different sources (both communication- and observation-based sources) and merged in order to gain greater insights.

**Changes to the Ninth Edition.** This ninth edition of *Basic Marketing Research: Customer Insights and Managerial Action* brings with it several changes. Instructors will appreciate several features of this new edition. (1) The format of the book is changing to meet the needs of students. This edition is available in digital format, OR digital plus softcover paper version. Both options are available at attractive price points for students. (2) To stay current with industry practice, the authors have added or updated important content, including (a) A/B tests, with multiple examples, as one form of field experiment; (b) updated content on big data as applied to marketing analytics, predictive analytics, social media considerations, and data visualization; (c) recognition of the use of technology for techniques like online bulletin board focus groups and webcam interviews, (d) new content necessary to appreciate the ability to combine data from multiple sources (e.g., existing internal behavioral data on customers merged with new survey data) to generate answers to problems, including new content on aggregating data, merging data, and the new sources of error that arise; and (e) an ongoing example in the analysis chapters that demonstrates the merging of data from various sources. Although the world of research is becoming more complicated, the authors successfully walk the tightrope of providing enough information for students to focus and stay current with general industry trends without weighting them down with a scatter approach. As with previous editions, the authors aim to provide students with the information they need to conduct a start-to-finish project. This is consistent with the authors' strengths as marketing research professors and

active participants in literally hundreds of real-world research projects.

# Acknowledgments

This book has benefited immensely from the many helpful comments received along the way from interested colleagues. We especially want to acknowledge the following people who reviewed the manuscript for this or one of the earlier editions. While much of the credit for the strength of this book is theirs, the blame for any weaknesses is strictly ours. Thank you, one and all, for your most perceptive and helpful comments.

| | |
|---|---|
| David Andrus | Richard H. Kolbe |
| Joseph Ballenger | Elizabeth K. La Fleur |
| Stephen Batory | Ron Lennon |
| Edward Bond | Subhash Lonial |
| Donald Bradley | Daulatram Lund |
| Terry Childers | Douglas Mac Lachlan |
| James S. Chow | Tridib Mazumdar |
| C. Anthony Di Benedetto | Kristy McManus |
| Elizabeth Ferrell | Craig Marty |
| Danielle Foster | Sanjay S. Mehta |
| Jule Gassenheimer | Donald J. Messmer |
| Myron Glassman | Sangkil Moon |
| Andrea Godfrey | Robbie Mullins |
| Ronald Goldsmith | Stacy Neier |
| David Gourley | Thomas Noordewier |
| Dhruv Grewal | Astrid Proboll |
| Thomas S. Gruca | Pradeep A. Rau |
| D.S. Halfhill | Steve Remington |
| Eddie Hand | Debra Ringold |
| James E. Hansz | Deborah Roedder |
| Doug Hausknecht | Abhijit Roy |
| Jeff Hopper | Daniel Rutledge |
| Vince Howe | Paul Sauer |
| Mariea Hoy | Ye Sheng |
| Glen Jarboe | L. J. Shrum |
| Leonard Jensen | Bruce Stern |
| John Roland Jones | Rodney Stump |
| Wesley H. Jones | R. Sukumar |
| Marcia Kasieta | John H. Summey |
| Ram Kesavan | Ron Taylor |
| Susan King | Michael Tsiros |

| | |
|---|---|
| Leon Tyler | Konya Weber |
| David Urban | Joe Welch |
| Gerrit H. van Bruggen | R. Dale Wilson |

I want to thank my colleagues in the Spears School of Business at Oklahoma State University, as well as my colleagues at other schools, for their continuing support and friendship. Many people have helped with this book in a variety of ways over the years, including Darrell Bartholomew, Tyler Bell, Janet Christopher, Steve Locy, John Phillips, Jerry Rackley, and Amy Sallee—thank you! Jon Austin (Cedarville University) did an amazing job with the "Manager's Focus" features placed throughout the book. Thanks also to the editorial and production staffs at Cengage Learning for their efforts on the book: Heather Mooney, Julie Dierig, Jenny Ziegler, Diane Garrity, and Erica Longenbach.

I also want to thank the hundreds of students that have enjoyed (well, maybe *endured* is the better word) my marketing research courses over the years. I never grow tired of teaching this material, and the projects that we conduct help me to continue to learn about the process of gathering and interpreting data to address real marketing situations. Those projects greatly influence my thinking about marketing research and, by extension, the contents of this book.

Many thanks also to my friend and colleague, Tracy Suter. Your insights and wisdom are demonstrated throughout the book and supplemental materials. Thousands of students and instructors have benefited from your efforts. Thank you for participating with me in this continuing process.

I am grateful to Gil Churchill for giving me the opportunity to work with him on this book in the first place. For readers who don't know, this is the ninth edition of a book Gil wrote years ago for undergraduate students. We've changed the contents over the years to make the material even more accessible to students and to keep up with changes in the industry, but without his initial efforts we wouldn't have this book. Watching Gil for a few years at the University of Wisconsin was a privilege, and I learned a great deal from his example.

Projects like this require lots of time and effort, and my family has graciously allowed me the space to work on it. My wife, DiAnn, has always been a lovely source of inspiration. DiAnn, I love you completely—you continue to thrill me. I also thank our children, Drew, Taylor, Avery, and Brady, for their love and for the wonderful way they help keep my attention where it really needs to be. Finally, I thank God for His blessings and the joy of knowing Him.

**Tom J. Brown**
*Stillwater, Oklahoma*

I want to begin by thanking Tom Brown, my dear friend and colleague at Oklahoma State University. You continue to provide a terrific example of doing the right things the right way for the right reasons. I value such an approach and greatly appreciate that you do, too.

Next, I want to thank our colleagues, students, and alumni associated with the Spears School at Oklahoma State and the Collins College at The University of Tulsa. Of particular note is alumnus Dean (it's a name not a title as he told us) Headley. It was Dean's Marketing Research course as an undergraduate student that provided the initial spark of interest in this topic for me. That spark carried through graduate school, the early stages of my career, and then textbook coauthorship. Dean provided us, as undergraduate students, the chance to collect real data for a real firm. That initial opportunity to conduct marketing research is something I pay forward each semester.

Next, I want to thank a variety of people in the academic community who have been rock-solid in their advice, friendship, guidance, and support over the years: David Bednar, Scot Burton, O.C. Ferrell, Charles Futrell, Tom Jensen, Steve Kopp, Dave Kurtz, John Mowen, Alvin Williams, and Alex Zablah. Your experience, insight, and willingness to listen have always been, and will always be, greatly valued. The same is true of Erica Longenbach and Heather Mooney at Cengage Learning. Your patience and perseverance are incredible.

Finally, you don't have to know me very well or talk with me very long before you realize the joy in my life comes from a handful of critically important relationships. To my Lord and Savior, I am blessed beyond measure and thankful beyond belief. To my beautiful bride, Kristen, I love you more today than yesterday. Your support is unwavering. To our terrific daughters, Camille and Emma, I am still in anxious anticipation of the future. I love, cherish, and appreciate all of you.

**Tracy A. Suter**
*Tulsa, Oklahoma*

My colleagues at the University of Wisconsin have my thanks for the intellectual stimulation and psychological support they have always provided.

I also wish to thank Janet Christopher, who did most of the typing as well as many other things on earlier editions of this book. She was efficient in her efforts and patient with mine. I also wish to thank students Beth Bubon, Joseph Kuester, Jayashree Mahajan, Jennifer Markkanen, Kay Powers, and David Szymanski for their help with many of the tasks involved in completing this book. I would like to thank the editorial and production staff of Cengage Learning for their professional efforts on my behalf.

Finally, I once again owe a special debt of thanks to my wife, Helen, and our children. Their unyielding support and generous love not only made this book possible but also worth doing in the first place.

**Gilbert A. Churchill, Jr.**
*Madison, Wisconsin*

# About the Authors

**Tom J. Brown** is Noble Foundation Chair in Marketing Strategy and professor of marketing in the Spears School of Business at Oklahoma State University. In addition, he serves as Director of the Center for Customer Interface Excellence, also in the Spears School. He received his Ph.D. from the University of Wisconsin-Madison. Professor Brown teaches marketing research and has supervised hundreds of student research projects for industry clients ranging from not-for-profit service organizations to Fortune 500 companies.

Professor Brown is a past recipient of the Sheth Foundation Best Paper Award in the *Journal of the Academy of Marketing Science*. In addition, he received a Richard D. Irwin Foundation Doctoral Dissertation Fellowship while at the University of Wisconsin, the Kenneth D. and Leitner Greiner Teaching Award, and the Regents Distinguished Research Award, both at Oklahoma State University.

Professor Brown's scholarly articles have appeared in a variety of outlets, including *Journal of Marketing Research, Journal of Marketing, Journal of Consumer Research, Journal of the Academy of Marketing Science, Journal of Applied Psychology, Journal of Retailing, Cornell Hotel and Restaurant Administration Quarterly, Journal of Service Research,* and others. His current research interests include organizational frontline research (e.g., customer orientation of frontline employees; customer influences on frontline employees) and causes and effects of corporate associations (e.g., reputation, identity). He is cofounder of the Corporate Associations/Identity Research Group as well as the Organizational Frontlines Research Symposia series. He is active in the American Marketing Association, having co-chaired multiple national conferences, co-hosted the AMA/Sheth Doctoral Consortium, and served as president of the Academic Council. In addition, he actively serves in a leadership role at Sunnybrook Christian Church.

**Tracy A. Suter** received his Ph.D. from the University of Arkansas. Prior to joining the management and marketing faculty at The University of Tulsa, he served as a faculty member in the Department of Marketing and School of Entrepreneurship at Oklahoma State University and as a marketing faculty at the University of Southern Mississippi. Professor Suter teaches a wide range of courses with emphasis on marketing research and applied creativity. Each semester undergraduate marketing research students complete real-world research projects for area for-profit and not-for-profit firms under his guidance. These service-learning projects now number in the hundreds completed.

Professor Suter's research interests include public policy, the use of new technologies in marketing, and consumer-to-consumer communities. He has published in journals such as the *Journal of Business Research, Journal of Public Policy & Marketing,* and *Journal of Retailing* among many others. He also serves on two editorial review boards of academic journals and is a frequent reviewer for other journals and conferences.

Professor Suter is currently the first holder of the David and Leslie Lawson Chair at Tulsa and is the former Daniel White Jordan Chair at Oklahoma State. He has received numerous awards for both research and teaching activities including the University of Arkansas Award for Excellence in Teaching, the Sherwin-Williams Distinguished Teaching Competition Award given by the Society for Marketing Advances, and the Kenneth D. and Leitner Greiner Outstanding Teaching, Regents Distinguished Teaching, and President's Outstanding Faculty Awards, all at Oklahoma State University. Tracy is frequently asked to speak to doctoral students and other academic groups about teaching excellence.

**Gilbert A. Churchill, Jr.,** received his D.B.A. from Indiana University in 1966 and joined the University of Wisconsin faculty upon graduation. Professor Churchill was named Distinguished Marketing Educator by the American Marketing Association in 1986, the second individual so honored. This lifetime achievement award recognizes and honors a living marketing educator for distinguished service and outstanding contributions in the field of marketing education. Professor Churchill was also awarded the Academy of Marketing Science's lifetime achievement award in 1993 for his significant scholarly contributions. In 1996, he received the Paul D. Converse Award, which is given to the most influential marketing scholars, as judged by a national jury drawn from universities, businesses, and government. Also in 1996, the Marketing Research Group of the American Marketing Association established the Gilbert A. Churchill, Jr., lifetime achievement award, which is to be given each year to a person judged to have made significant lifetime contributions to marketing research. In 2002, he received the Charles Coolidge Parlin lifetime achievement award from the American Marketing Association for his substantial contributions to the ongoing advancement of marketing research practice.

Dr. Churchill is a past recipient of the yearly William O'Dell Award for an outstanding article in the *Journal of Marketing Research*. He has also been a finalist for the award five additional times. He is a co-author of the most and third-most influential articles of the past century in sales management, as judged by a panel of experts in the field. His articles have appeared in such publications as the *Journal of Marketing Research, Journal of Marketing, Journal of Consumer Research, Journal of Retailing, Journal of Business Research, Decision Sciences, Technometrics, and Organizational Behavior and Human Performance.*

In addition to *Basic Marketing Research*, Professor Churchill is the coauthor of several other books, including *Marketing Research: Methodological Foundations,* 11th ed. (Mason, OH: Southwestern, 2015); *Marketing: Creating Value for Customers,* 2nd ed. (Burr Ridge, IL: Irwin/McGraw-Hill, 1998); *Sales Force Management: Planning, Implementation, and Control,* 6th ed. (Burr Ridge, IL: Irwin/McGraw-Hill, 2000); and *Sales force Performance* (Lexington, MA: Lexington Books, 1984). He is a former editor of the *Journal ofMarketing Research* and has served on the editorial boards of the *Journal of Marketing Research* and *Journal of Marketing,* among others. Professor Churchill is a past recipient of the Lawrence J. Larson Excellence in Teaching Award.

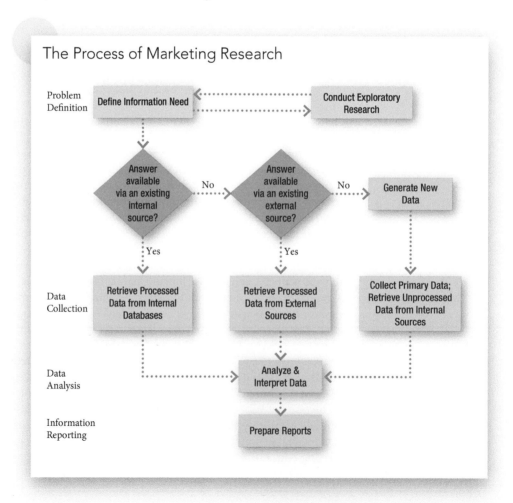

## The Process of Marketing Research

# Basic Marketing Research

## Customer Insights and Managerial Action

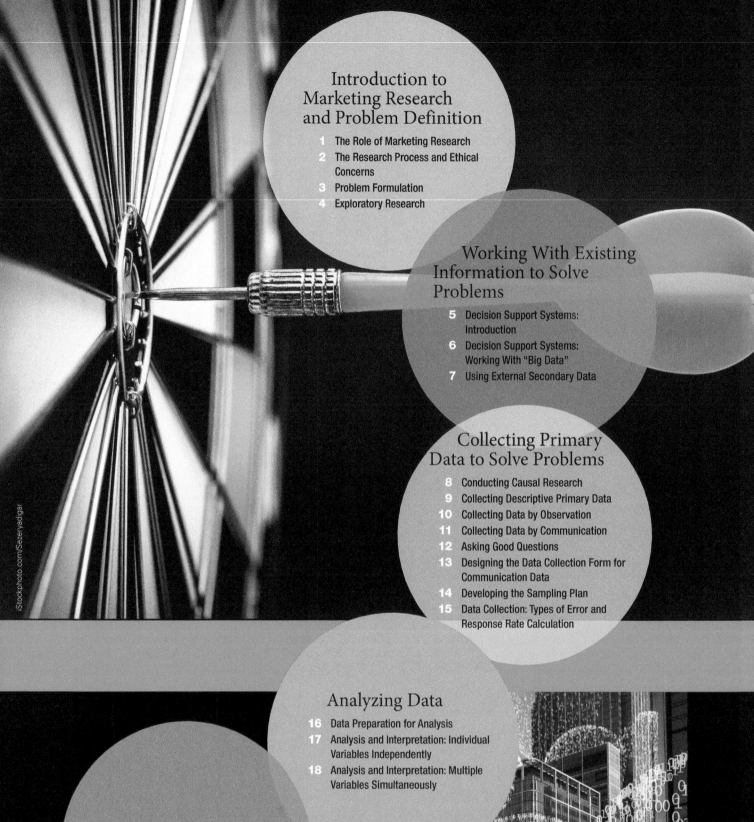

iStockphoto.com/Sezeryadigar

Stockphoto.com/peterhowell

# Part 1

# Introduction to Marketing Research and Problem Definition

iStockphoto.com/mrcmos

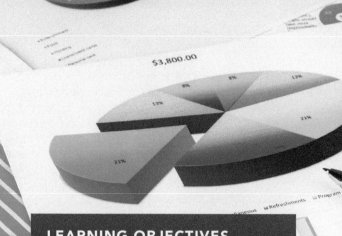

# CHAPTER 1

# The Role of Marketing Research

Billion Photos/Shutterstock.com

## LEARNING OBJECTIVES

▶ Define marketing research.

▶ Discuss different kinds of firms that conduct marketing research.

▶ List some of the skills that are important for careers in marketing research.

▶ List three reasons for studying marketing research.

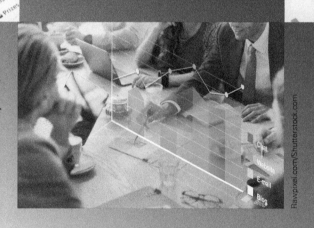

Rawpixel.com/Shutterstock.com

## [ INTRODUCTION ]

Marketing research is a much broader and more common activity than many people realize. Most of us have completed online surveys, filled out questionnaires, or participated in other obvious forms of marketing research. Did you know, however, that using social media, activating location services on your phone, or visiting web sites also makes you a participant in the ever-expanding world of marketing research? In this book, we'll present a variety of examples of how marketing research is being used to improve the marketing process for companies—and for their customers. And modern marketing research isn't just for large organizations with deep pockets. Sophisticated technologies are becoming broadly available, and the cost of conducting useful marketing research is now within the reach of almost any company. A word of caution, however: Things are advancing so rapidly that, by the time you read this, even more new and exciting approaches to gathering and using data will have hit the scene. This is an exciting time for information detectives—and we are delighted to be able to offer you a guided tour through the basics of the marketing research process.

Before we get started, we'd like to establish an important ground rule. The tools we teach should be used in ways that ultimately help deliver satisfactory products, services, and experiences to your customers. You've probably heard that marketing is about creating exchanges between individuals or firms that leave both sides better

4

off than if no exchange had occurred. We believe strongly in this principle. Marketing is an honorable, worthy endeavor when this principle guides your efforts, including your efforts to better understand your customers and the marketplace.

OK, let's get started. In this chapter, we introduce the broad role of marketing research within a company or organization. In addition, we identify different types of companies that conduct marketing research, briefly discuss job opportunities in marketing research, and present three important reasons that individuals across a wide range of industries should develop a working knowledge of marketing research.

## 1-1 The Problem: Marketers Need Information

All businesses or organizations share a common problem: They need information in order to develop and deliver products and/or services that can satisfy their customers' needs. Consider the following examples.[1]

**Example** *Electronic Arts (EA) partnered with A/B testing company Optimizely on the latest release of EA's popular SimCity game. EA had various options for the placement, color, and display of a direct promotional discount on the preorder webpage of the game. Optimizely also included an option that removed the promotional offer altogether. Counterintuitively, the preorder page with no discount, an option EA had not previously considered, drove 43% more purchases than all other tested options. In total EA sold 1.6 million copies of SimCity, and about half were digital downloads.*

**Example** *City blocks on geographical maps often define neighborhoods and retail districts within a city. But what about the areas where people gather regardless of residential versus commercial zoning distinctions? The Livehoods Project at Carnegie Mellon University looks to understand the hidden structures of cities by analyzing social media services like tweets and check-ins. The restaurants, shops, and music stages define an area where people hang out instead of a Census tract or map. The outcome is locations within a city that have social meaning to its residents instead of mere municipal borders.*

**Example** *The Weather Channel uses television, its web site, and mobile apps to provide viewers with important weather forecasts and other content, such as road conditions and health information for allergy sufferers. It was interested in working with third-party publishers and advertisers to determine how changes in weather impact consumer buying decisions, especially apparel, food, and seasonal offerings. Partnering with Qualtrics, a web-based research and survey design firm, The Weather Channel was able to design research studies that provided real-time geographic, behavioral, and weather-related data directly to advertisers. In turn, these advertisers were able to determine the types of content that were most relevant to The Weather Channel's audience.*

**Example** *Researchers from Procter & Gamble (P&G) conducted home visits in more than 100 Vietnamese homes. Among other things, the researchers found new uses for some of their existing brands. For example, the company now promotes Ambi Pur (sold in the United States as Febreze) as a deodorant for motorbike helmets. The need for such a product intensified a few years ago when helmet usage became mandatory in Vietnam, a very humid country in which motorbikes are a key form of transportation.*

**Example** *Sanofi-Avantis is a large pharmaceuticals company headquartered in Paris. Working with existing data on pregnant women in developing countries, their director of vaccine operations in Southeast Asia discovered that midwives had become an important element in the distribution channel for infant vaccines.*

**Example** *John Deere tractor sales took off internationally due in part to the introduction of the 8R tractor line. To guide the development of the new tractor, the company interviewed growers from around the world. The resulting tractor was highly versatile, with more than 7,800 different configurations sold. After introducing the new line, the company began interviewing its customers—1,500 of them—as it began to work on the next new line of tractors.*

As these examples illustrate, different companies need different kinds of information, and the information they need can be gathered in diverse ways. Salespeople use the results of marketing research studies to help sell their products. Politicians use marketing research in the form of polling data to plan campaign strategies. Media companies use research to better understand their readers/viewers so that they can sell advertising spots to other companies. Even churches use marketing research to determine when to hold services. The point is that marketing research is an essential activity that can take many forms, but its basic function is to gather information that is needed to help managers make better decisions.

As we emphasized earlier, the goal of marketing is to create exchanges with customers that satisfy the needs of both the customer and the marketer. Marketing managers generally focus their efforts on several key elements—the product or service, its price, its placement or the channels in which it is distributed, its promotion, the tangible elements at the point of contact, and the processes and people involved in making the exchange or delivering the service. The goal is to develop a marketing strategy that combines the marketing mix elements so that customers are satisfied and the organization stays in business over the long run.

> The goal of marketing is to create exchanges with customers that satisfy the needs of both the customer and the marketer.

Many factors in the marketing environment affect the success of the marketing effort. Unfortunately, many of these factors are not under the marketer's control, including other social actors (competitors, suppliers, governmental agencies, customers themselves, and so on) and societal trends in the external environment (economic, political and legal, social, natural, technological, and competitive trends; see Exhibit 1.1). As a result, marketing managers have an urgent need for information—and marketing research is responsible for providing it. Marketing research is the firm's formal communication link with the environment. More formally, **marketing research** is the process of gathering and interpreting data for use in developing, implementing, and monitoring the firm's marketing plans.

**marketing research**
The process of gathering and interpreting data for use in developing, implementing, and monitoring the firm's marketing plans.

Marketing research is involved with all phases of the information management process, including (1) specifying what information is needed, (2) gathering the relevant data from internal and external sources, (3) analyzing and interpreting the data, and (4) communicating the results to the appropriate audiences. In fact, we use these stages as the general outline of this book.

Another way of looking at the function of marketing research, however, is to consider how management uses it. Some marketing research is used for planning, some for problem solving, and some for control. When used for planning, it deals largely with determining which marketing opportunities are worthwhile and which are not. Also, when good opportunities are uncovered, marketing research provides estimates of their size and scope to help managers allocate resources correctly. Problem-solving marketing research tends to focus on tactical decisions with respect to the elements of the marketing mix. Control-oriented marketing research helps management isolate trouble spots and generally monitor ongoing operations. Exhibit 1.2 provides a general list of the kinds of questions marketing research can address with regard to planning, problem solving, and control decisions.

Solid marketing research is becoming increasingly important as the world continues as a global economy. That's why companies as diverse as P&G and John Deere have invested heavily in research in international markets. For example, marketing research helped McDonald's adjust its positioning as attitudes toward the company changed in the United Kingdom. When the company first crossed the Atlantic in the mid-1970s, customers appreciated its American origins and the novelty of fast, efficiently prepared food. The company's

**Exhibit 1.1** ▶ The Environments Affecting Marketing

**Exhibit 1.2** ▶ Examples of Questions Marketing Research Can Help Answer

I.   Planning
   A.   What kinds of people buy our products? Where do they live? How much do they earn? How many of them are there?
   B.   Are the markets for our existing products increasing or decreasing? Are there promising markets that we have not yet reached?
   C.   Do our customers have other needs that we can meet? What new products or services can we develop to meet these needs?
   D.   Are the channels of distribution for our products changing? Are new types of marketing institutions likely to evolve?

II.  Problem Solving
   A.   Product
      1.   Which of various product designs is likely to be the most successful?
      2.   What kind of packaging should we use?
   B.   Price
      1.   What price should we charge for our products?
      2.   As production costs decline, should we lower our prices or try to develop higher-quality products?
   C.   Place
      1.   Where, and by whom, should our products be sold?
      2.   How should we design our online store?
   D.   Promotion
      1.   How much should we spend on promotion? How should it be allocated to products and to geographic areas?
      2.   What combination of media—newspapers, radio, television, magazines, the Internet—should we use?

III. Control
   A.   What is our market share overall? In each geographic area? By each customer type?
   B.   Are customers satisfied with our products? How is our record for service? Are there many returns?
   C.   How does the public perceive our company? What is our reputation with the trade?
   D.   How do our products compare with direct competitors?

first UK ad slogan announced, "There's a difference at McDonald's you'll enjoy." Within a few years, however, research showed that UK consumers were describing McDonald's as inflexible and arrogant—a negative take on the efficiency that consumers associated with the company's American heritage. As a result, McDonald's adjusted its ad campaigns to use softer messages depicting McDonald's at the center of UK family life. During 2015, 3.7 million people per day visited a McDonald's restaurant in the United Kingdom.[2]

## 1-2 Who Does Marketing Research?

Although individuals and organizations have practiced marketing research for centuries—the need for information has always existed—the formal practice of marketing research can be traced to 1879. That is the year when advertising agency N. W. Ayer & Son collected data on expected grain production from state officials and publishers across the United States for a client who produced agricultural machinery. The agency constructed a crude market survey by states and counties; this was probably the first real instance of marketing research in the United States.[3]

The Curtis Publishing Company is generally given credit for establishing the first formal marketing research department back in 1911. The Nielsen Company, still a world leader in the marketing research industry, began operation in 1923. The notion of marketing research as an important business function really took off around the end of World War II as competition for customers heightened.

Today, three major categories of firms conduct marketing research: (1) producers of products and services, (2) advertising agencies, and (3) marketing research companies.

## Manager's Focus

No matter what type of organization completes a marketing research project—internal researchers of a product/service producer or external researchers at an advertising agency or research company—it is always seeking to meet the information needs of marketing managers. The quality of the organization's work will have a direct effect on the integrity of the marketing intelligence available to managers. Managers sometimes fail to realize the roles they play that significantly influence the quality of the work researchers perform on their behalf.

As a future marketing manager, how will your behavior affect the quality of marketing researchers' work? Think carefully about that question for a moment. What could you do for researchers to enhance their efforts? What behaviors on your part might limit or hinder the performance of quality marketing research?

One key role is informational in nature. To serve your needs well, researchers will need to fully understand your marketing situation. Put simply, they need to know what you already know. Who are your target customers? What is your marketing strategy? What are your competitors doing? What has been learned through prior marketing research studies or other market intelligence-gathering activities? What decisions are being considered now? What issues are unclear to you now? Under what political constraints are you operating within your organization? What failures and successes have occurred in the past?

Managers are often reluctant to admit what they don't know or how their efforts have failed in the past, but disclosure of these various types of information can have a profound impact on researchers' abilities to tailor their work to address managers' unique needs. In other words, successful marketing research depends on a series of information exchanges between researchers and managers (many other such exchanges will be discussed in later Manager's Focus sections). For this to occur, managers and researchers must develop relationships based on trust and mutual respect. By developing expertise in marketing research in this course, you will be better prepared to develop and nurture these essential relationships in your future career as a manager.

### 1-2a COMPANIES THAT PRODUCE OR SELL PRODUCTS AND SERVICES

Marketing research began to grow significantly when firms found they could no longer sell all they could produce. Instead, they had to gauge market needs and produce accordingly. Marketing research was called on to estimate these needs. As consumers began to have more choices in the marketplace, marketing began to assume a more dominant role and production a less important one. The marketing concept emerged and along with it a reorganization of the marketing effort. Many marketing research departments were born in these reorganizations.

Although some companies choose to outsource marketing research (and some choose to ignore it altogether, unfortunately), many firms have one or more people assigned specifically to marketing research. Marketing research departments are common among industrial and consumer manufacturing companies. These companies conduct research designed to develop and market the products they manufacture. For example, companies such as the Goodyear Tire and Rubber Company, Kraft Foods, The Hershey Company, and the Oscar Meyer Company have their own marketing research departments.

Other types of companies also have marketing research departments. Publishers and broadcasters, for example, do a good deal of research. They attempt to measure the size of the market reached by their message and construct a demographic profile of this audience. These data are then used to sell advertising space or time. Digitally focused companies such as Microsoft and Google run large internal research departments. Large retailers such as Walmart and JC Penney have operated marketing research departments to gather information about consumer preferences, store image, and the like. Financial institutions such as banks and brokerage houses do research involving forecasting, measurement of market potentials, determination of market characteristics, market-share analyses, sales analyses, location analyses, and product-mix studies. For example, one major home mortgage lender wanted to understand how to best serve first-time home buyers. The research team conducted one-on-one interviews followed by concept tests that allowed the company to better understand the needs of these buyers.

> Many firms have one or more people assigned specifically to the marketing research activity.

## 1-2b ADVERTISING AGENCIES

As you might imagine, advertising agencies often conduct research designed to help create effective advertising campaigns and to assess their effectiveness with target audiences. They might test alternative approaches to the wording or art used in an ad or investigate the effectiveness of a particular celebrity spokesperson. Much agency research is aimed at gauging consumer awareness of brands during and after advertising campaigns. Many agencies also do marketing research for their clients to determine the market potential of a proposed new product or the client's market share.

Ad agencies sometimes conduct research to better understand consumer interests and behaviors in order to serve their corporate clients. For example, when Boden, a UK-based clothing company with annual sales of $500 million, sought to enter the crowded US women's fashion market, it hired AMP, a Boston-based ad agency, to assist. AMP took a two-phased research approach. First, AMP sought to thoroughly understand the drivers and motivations of women's purchase decisions and emotional connection to Boden via exploratory research. Second, AMP conducted a national online survey to assess the current state of Boden's brand, including perceptions, purchase intent, and likelihood to recommend among other things. Taken together, these two studies led to creative strategies

and media recommendations far beyond Boden's traditional catalog-driven approach. The subsequent Splash of Happy campaign saw a 71% increase in brand awareness and a sales increase of 8% year over year.[4]

## 1-2c MARKETING RESEARCH COMPANIES

Many companies specialize in conducting marketing research. In the United States, marketing research is an $11.2 billion industry—that's about $35 spent on research each year for every man, woman, and child in the United States.[5] Worldwide, total revenues for the marketing research industry exceed **$22.5** billion.[6] (And these numbers don't reflect the research done by producers and advertising agencies.)

Most marketing research firms are relatively small organizations, but they can have a large influence on the companies that hire them. As an example, consider H²R Market Research located in Springfield, Missouri. The company does a tremendous amount of research for the Herschend Family Entertainment (HFE) Corporation, which owns or manages theme parks and tourist attractions across the United States, including Dollywood (Pigeon Forge, Tennessee) and Silver Dollar City (Branson, Missouri). Research Window 1.1 presents an overview of the kinds of research H²R Market Research conducts for HFE.

## research window 1.1

### *Marketing Research at Herschend Family Entertainment Properties*

H²R Market Research conducts the research for each of the properties owned or managed by Herschend Family Entertainment (HFE) Corporation across the United States, including the Silver Dollar City, Dollywood, and

Wild Adventures theme parks. H²R Market Research uses one of the most comprehensive databases of primary and secondary entertainment-related research in the entertainment industry. This library of guest, theme

*(continued)*

## research window 1.1   *(continued)*

park, tourism, and consumer information is largely the foundation of HFE's long-term strategic plans and marketing strategies.

**Guest Research, Profiling, Analysis, and Consumer Insights** H²R has an ongoing, in-house guest survey program designed to gather customer demographics, geographic origin, behavior, and level of satisfaction. These surveys are conducted in person, by telephone, or over the Internet. H²R processes, analyzes, and produces reports on the resulting database of guest information seasonally and by customer segment. In addition to measuring each customer segment's size and attendance trends, the company also uses this information to analyze the impact of capital additions and the economic impact by customer segment. Likewise, in an effort to understand guests' needs and wants on a much deeper level, H²R Market Research uses a variety of qualitative and quantitative methodologies designed to discern guests' functional and emotional needs. This enables each of the HFE properties to better predict the impact of market and marketing changes, in addition to helping them better connect with consumers.

**Market Area Research, Profiling, and Analysis** H²R also regularly conducts research designed to provide insights about the geographic area in which each of the properties is located. Among other things, such research identifies destination trends and provides a better understanding of the types of tourists who are visiting the area but *not* visiting the HFE properties. The information gathered includes general tourist demographic profiles, visitor counts, resident market size and demographics, market performance, and census data.

**Research and Analysis Designed to Address a Specific Issue** In addition to these regularly scheduled research activities, H²R frequently invests in research and analysis designed to answer specific marketing or management questions. For example, these efforts have produced reports with titles such as "Consumer Insights Evaluation," "Estimates of Market Potential," "New Product Concept Evaluations," "Assessment of the Bluegrass and BBQ Festival Visitor," and "Guest Psychographic Profiles Assessed Using PRIZM." The results of

such studies led to the introduction of The Grand Exposition section of the Silver Dollar City theme park. According to Brad Thomas, the general manager, "In conducting extensive research with moms, they told us they want more rides they can ride together as a family. So instead of adding one new major ride, we decided to add 10 new family rides that bring the park's ride capacity up more than 50 percent." The results of these types of studies have led to the creation and development of most new shows and attractions added at Silver Dollar City over the past five years.

**Competitive Research** Competitive research is another avenue of research for H²R. The company monitors both local competition and competitive destinations and has developed a large database of top-50 theme park information. This database includes theme park attendance history, pricing history, history of capital additions and estimated capital investments, overnight domestic leisure visitors to each park's home market, resident population, resident income, resident age, year the park opened, size of the park, number of coasters installed, and other variables. The information is used to estimate the influence of these types of factors on park attendance. For example, Dollywood might want to determine the relationship between the length of a roller coaster, the number of roller coasters at a park, or the overall size of the park on theme park attendance. Using such information can help H²R provide better insight to decision makers within the property concerning the design and layout of the park.

**Other Research and Statistical Analysis** Other research and analysis activities that are frequently used include lifetime value analysis, factor analysis, hierarchical cluster analysis, discriminant analysis, and regression forecasting models. Such statistical analyses help in the understanding of the potential value (or lack thereof) of specific customer segments or market programs being considered.

### Tracking Consumer and Leisure Trends

H²R closely monitors trends from a variety of industries in an effort to evolve with their customers' changing needs, wants, and behaviors. The company tracks things as demographic and behavioral trends of guests,

guests' ages, party composition, last visit, incomes, and attendance at other Herschend Family Entertainment properties. Such changes influence the creation of future strategic decisions and marketing plans.

Consumer trends are also of great concern. H²R tracks changes in social, demographic, technological, economic, and commerce trends by reviewing books, periodicals, social media, blogs, and syndicated research studies and by attending conferences on these topics. The company also pays attention to trends in the theme park industry. In addition to the attendance, pricing, and capital trends mentioned above, H²R

researches stock prices of publicly traded theme parks, consolidation in the industry, new theme park queue-line technologies being introduced, new types of ride technologies, and marketing promotions.

These are just a few of the trends being followed by H²R for the HFE properties. Literally hundreds of resources are evaluated and analyzed every year for the purpose of determining how such trends might impact the company.

**Source:** H²R Market Research.

Some marketing research firms are large global companies. Exhibit 1.3 shows the names, home countries, and revenues of the 10 largest marketing research firms in the world. Some firms provide standardized ("syndicated") research; they collect certain information on a regular basis and then sell it to clients. For example, Nielsen provides product-movement data for grocery stores and drugstores as well as a wide variety of data for other types of clients. Syndicated research is not custom designed, except in the limited sense that the firm will perform special analyses for a client from the data it regularly collects. Other firms, though, specialize in custom-designed research. Some of

these firms provide only a field service, such as data collection or data analysis, while others are full-service suppliers that help the client with all phases of a project. For example, GfK provides full-service customized research services, conducting studies from start to finish using a range of techniques.

Other organizations that provide or conduct marketing research include government agencies, trade associations, and universities. Government agencies provide much marketing information in the form of published statistics. In fact, the federal government is the largest producer of marketing facts through its various censuses and other

**Exhibit 1.3 ▶** The World's 10 Largest Marketing Research Firms

| RANK/ORGANIZATION | PARENT COUNTRY | WORLDWIDE RESEARCH REVENUE (U.S. $ IN MILLIONS) |
|---|---|---|
| 1. Nielsen Holdings N.V. | United States | 6,172.0 |
| 2. Kantar | United Kingdom | 3,710.0 |
| 3. IMS Health Inc. | United States | 2,921.0 |
| 4. Ipsos SA | France | 1,980.9 |
| 5. GfK SE | Germany | 1,712.6 |
| 6. IRI | United States | 981.0 |
| 7. dunnhumby | United Kingdom | 970.5 |
| 8. Westat | United States | 509.6 |
| 9. INTAGE Holdings Inc. | Japan | 375.7 |
| 10. comScore | United States | 368.8 |

Source: Developed from information in (2016, October). The 2016 AMA gold global top 25 report. *Marketing News*, pp. 36–52. This report describes the services provided by the 25 largest global research organizations.

publications. Trade associations often collect and share data gathered from members. Much university-sponsored research of interest to marketers is produced by the marketing faculty or by the bureaus of business research found in many schools of business. Faculty research is often reported in marketing journals, while research bureaus often publish monographs.

## 1-3  Job Opportunities in Marketing Research

Employment opportunities for those interested in a career in marketing research continue to be good. The U.S. Bureau of Labor Statistics reports that employment for marketing research analysts is expected to grow faster than the average for all occupations—a 19% projected growth rate—through the year 2024.[7] Why? Because the demand for information continues to

grow—and so will the demand for individuals who can collect, analyze, and interpret this information.

### 1-3a  TYPES OF JOBS IN MARKETING RESEARCH

A marketing researcher—whether internal or external to the firm—might perform many different kinds of tasks. Depending on whether you work for a producer, an advertising agency, a marketing research firm, or some other type of organization, the type and scope of jobs available can vary greatly. In smaller companies, researchers are likely to be exposed to a greater variety of tasks, simply out of necessity. In larger firms, the work tends to be more specialized for each employee. The responsibilities of a marketing researcher could range from simple analyses of questionnaire responses to the management of a large research department. Research Window 1.2 lists some common job titles with mean (average) compensation for

## research window 1.2

### Marketing Research Company Job Titles and Mean Compensation

| Market Research Company Job Titles | Total Compensation ($) |
|---|---|
| Owner / Partner | 200,206 |
| President / CEO / COO | 234,232 |
| Senior Vice President or Vice President | 176,926 |
| Director of Research | 114,000 |
| Group Head / Manager | 102,080 |
| Senior Project Director / Manager | 85,493 |
| Project Director / Manager | 71,210 |
| Senior Research Analyst | 67,859 |
| Research Analyst | 52,938 |
| Statistician | 86,556 |
| Business Development | 111,929 |
| Senior Research Associate | 66,794 |
| Research Associate | 50,542 |
| Field Manager / Director | 77,476 |
| Field Associate | 47,833 |
| Facility Manager | 59,800 |
| Marketing / Communication Manager | 87,900 |
| Business Development / Sales Director | 118,457 |
| Sales / Account Representative | 123,735 |
| Administrator / Coordinator | 40,000 |
| Other | 83,042 |

**Source:** (2016). Market research salaries by job title. *Quirk's Marketing Research Review*. Retrieved from www.quirks.com. Compensation data in the table are based on the responses of 1,496 marketing research company employees who subscribe to Quirk's in an online survey conducted between May 12 and June 9, 2015.

marketing research company employees based on a recent survey by Quirk's Marketing Research Media.

In consumer goods companies, the typical entry-level position is research analyst, often for a specific brand. While learning the characteristics and details of the industry, the analyst will receive on-the-job training from a research manager. The usual career path for an analyst is to advance to senior analyst, then research supervisor, and on to research manager.

At marketing research companies, the typical entry-level position might be a trainee position, in which the researcher will spend some time conducting interviews, assisting with analyses, or any number of other activities. The goal is to expose trainees to the processes the firm follows so that when they advance in the company, they will be familiar enough with the firm's capabilities to respond intelligently to clients' needs for research information.

The requirements for entering the marketing research field include human relations, communication, conceptual, and analytical skills. Marketing researchers need to be able to interact effectively with others, and they need to be good communicators—both orally and in writing. They need to understand business in general and marketing processes in particular. When dealing with brand, advertising, sales, or other types of managers, they need to have some understanding of the issues facing these managers. Marketing researchers also should have basic numerical and statistical skills: they must be comfortable with numbers and with the techniques of marketing research. And as companies begin to work with the increasingly larger datasets that are rapidly becoming available, there will be an increasing demand for analysts capable of working with the technologies required to capture, store, and analyze these data.

For marketing researchers working for producers, it is not uncommon to switch from research to product or brand management at some point in the career path. One advantage these employees possess is that after working so closely with marketing intelligence, they often know more about the customers, the industry, and the competitors than anyone else in the company with the same years of experience. Note, though, that to make this switch, you'll need to develop more knowledge about marketing and business in general than those who plan to focus exclusively on marketing research.

Successful marketing researchers tend to be proactive rather than reactive. That is, they tend to identify and lead the direction in which the individual studies and overall programs will go, rather than simply responding to explicit requests for information. Successful marketing researchers realize that marketing research is conducted for one primary reason—to help managers make better marketing decisions.

## 1-4 Why Study Marketing Research?

Most business schools offer courses in marketing research, and many require students who are completing majors in marketing to take a marketing-research course. Why?

There are at least three important reasons for a business student to be exposed to marketing research training. First, some students will discover that marketing research can be rewarding and fun. For these students, initial training in how to be an "information detective" may lead to a career in marketing research. These students usually develop an immediate appreciation for the power and responsibility involved in taking preexisting or new data and converting them into information that can be used by marketing managers to make important decisions. Thus, for some students at least, the study of marketing research will be directly relevant to their careers.

Most students will not go on to careers in marketing research; why should they study the topic? We are all consumers of marketing and public opinion research on an almost daily basis. The second important reason for studying marketing research, therefore, is to learn to be a *smart* consumer of marketing research results. Businesspeople are increasingly exposed to research results, usually by someone trying to convince them to do something. Suppliers use research to promote the virtues of their particular products and services; advertising agencies use research to encourage a company to promote a product in particular media vehicles; product managers inside a firm use research to demonstrate the likely demand for the products they are developing to get further funding. Effective managers, however, do not take research results at face value but instead ask the right questions to determine the likely validity of the results.

A third key reason for studying marketing research is to gain an appreciation of the process—what it can and cannot do. As a manager, you will need to know what to expect marketing research to be able to deliver. The process of gathering data and generating information is full of opportunities for error to slip into the results. Thus, no research is perfect, and managers must take this into account when making decisions. Managers also need to understand what they are asking of researchers when requesting marketing research. The process is detailed, time consuming, and requires a lot of thought and effort. As a result, marketing research is costly to an organization and should *not* be undertaken on trivial issues or to support decisions that have already been made.

# Summary

## Learning Objective 1

**Define marketing research.**

Marketing research is the process of gathering and interpreting data for use in developing, implementing, and monitoring the firm's marketing plans.

## Learning Objective 2

**Discuss different kinds of firms that conduct marketing research.**

Producers and sellers of products and services often have marketing research departments that gather information relevant to the particular products and services sold and the industry in which they operate.

Advertising agencies often conduct research, primarily to test advertising and measure its effectiveness. Marketing research companies are in business to conduct research; some focus on very specific topics or aspects of the research process, while others are more general in focus.

## Learning Objective 3

**List some of the skills that are important for careers in marketing research.**

Most positions in marketing research require analytical, communication, and human-relations skills. In addition, marketing researchers must be comfortable working with numbers and statistical techniques, and they must be familiar with a great variety of marketing research methods.

## Learning Objective 4

**List three reasons for studying marketing research.**

(1) Some students pursue careers in marketing research; (2) almost everyone is a consumer of marketing research in one way or another and needs to be able to know how to evaluate the likely validity of the research; and (3) managers must understand what marketing research can and cannot do, as well as what is involved in the process of conducting research.

## Key Term

marketing research (page 6)

## Review Questions

1. How is marketing research defined? What are the key elements of this definition?

2. Who does marketing research? What are the primary kinds of research done by each enterprise?

3. Why did marketing research begin to experience real growth after World War II?

4. In a large research department, who would be responsible for specifying the objective of a research project? For deciding on specific procedures to be followed? For designing the questionnaire? For analyzing the results? For reporting the results to top management?

5. What are the necessary skills for employment in a junior or entry-level marketing research position? Do the skills change as one changes job levels?

6. If so, what new skills are necessary at the higher levels?

7. Why is it important to study marketing research?

# Endnotes

1. For more information on these examples, see Ha, A. (2013, June 14). Optimizely explains how it boosted SimCity pre-order revenue. *TechCrunch*. Retrieved from http://www.techcrunch.com; Wilson, M. (2012, April 19). A map of your city's invisible neighborhoods, according to foursquare. *Fast Company*. Retrieved from http://www.fastcompany.com; The Weather Channel Qualtrics site intercept case study. Retrieved from http://www.qualtrics.com; (July 9–15, 2012), P&G woos the hearts, minds, and schools of Vietnam. *Bloomberg Businessweek*, pp. 19–21; Dan Briody, D. (2011, September). Big data: Harnessing a game-changing asset. *Economist Intelligence Unit*, 12. Retrieved from http://www.sas.com; Gruley, B., & Singh, S. D. (2012, July 9–12) Big green profit machine. *Bloomberg Businessweek*, 44–49.

2. McDonald's reports fourth quarter and full year 2015 results (2016, January 25) Retrieved from http://www.mcdonalds.co.uk

3. Lockley, L. C. (1974). History and development of marketing research. In Robert Ferber (Ed.), *Handbook of marketing research* (p. 4). McGraw-Hill.

4. Boden. Retrieved from http://ampagency.com/case-studies/boden/

5. Bowers, D. (2016, June). The 2016 AMA gold top 50 report. *Marketing*, 40.

6. American Marketing Association. (2016, October). The 2016 AMA gold global top 25 report. *Marketing News*.

7. Bureau of Labor Statistics, U.S. Department of Labor. Market research analysts. *Occupational outlook handbook, 2016–17 edition*, Retrieved from http://www.bls.gov/ooh/business-and-financial/market-research-analysts.htm

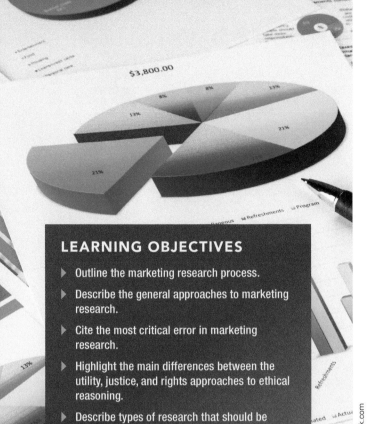

Billion Photos/Shutterstock.com

Rawpixel.com/Shutterstock.com

# CHAPTER 2

# The Research Process and Ethical Concerns

## LEARNING OBJECTIVES

▶ Outline the marketing research process.

▶ Describe the general approaches to marketing research.

▶ Cite the most critical error in marketing research.

▶ Highlight the main differences between the utility, justice, and rights approaches to ethical reasoning.

▶ Describe types of research that should be avoided.

## [ INTRODUCTION ]

Chapter 1 highlighted problems marketing research can be used to solve. It emphasized that marketing research is a firm's communication link with the environment and can help marketing managers in planning, problem solving, and control. Although every company has its own way of using marketing research, in this chapter we describe the general marketing research process (see Exhibit 2.1). As a researcher, sometimes you'll gather and use existing processed data from internal sources. In other cases, you'll gather or purchase the processed data you need from external sources. Other times, however, the data you need won't have been gathered by anyone and it will be your job to collect new-to-the-world data (or maybe to gather unprocessed internal data and turn it into useful information). In all cases, however, there is a general process that managers should follow as they seek information.

## 2-1 The Marketing Research Process

The marketing research process outlined in Exhibit 2.1 provides an overview of the general sequence of activities undertaken to provide information needed for decision making. Initially, the information need must be carefully defined, a process that often involves exploratory research. The next stage involves capturing the data necessary for satisfying the information need. This can be accomplished by

**Exhibit 2.1 ▶** The Marketing Research Process

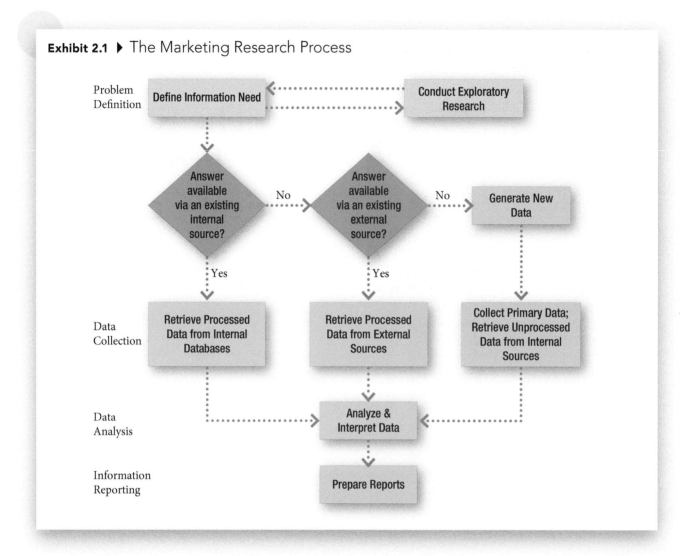

using existing data from inside or outside the firm or by collecting new data of various types for the problem at hand. Once data capture is complete, the focus shifts to data analysis and interpretation. The final stage in the process involves communicating the results to the appropriate managers so that they can make informed decisions. As you might imagine, researchers deal with many issues in each stage. Exhibit 2.2 lists some of the typical questions needing answers at each stage.

The remaining chapters in this book describe in detail each of the stages in the research process. In this chapter, we provide a quick overview. Let's start with the single most important step in the process, problem definition.

### 2-1a   PROBLEM DEFINITION (CHAPTERS 3 AND 4)

Only when a problem or opportunity has been precisely defined can research be designed to provide the needed information to address it. Part of the process of problem definition includes specifying the manager's *decision problem* and one or more *research problems* to be addressed. You

simply can't move further until the decision problem and the research problem(s) can be stated explicitly. Once you've pinned down the problem, you are in position to prepare the *research request agreement,* a document that clearly states the research problem(s) to be addressed in a research project.

If relatively little is known about the phenomenon to be investigated, *exploratory research* is often used to clarify the issues. Typically, exploratory research is used when the problem to be solved is broad or vague. It may involve reviewing published data, interviewing knowledgeable people, conducting focus groups, investigating trade literature that discusses similar cases, analyzing the reams of data held in a company's databases, or any of a variety of other activities. One of the most important characteristics of exploratory research is its flexibility. When you don't know very much about the problem, you rely on intuition and might try several types of exploratory research to get a better grasp on the issues. The most important outcome of exploratory research at this stage is a clear understanding of exactly what information managers need to make important decisions. With this knowledge, researchers and managers can agree on the research request agreement.

**Exhibit 2.2** ▶ Questions Typically Addressed at the Various Stages of the Research Process

| STAGE IN THE PROCESS | TYPICAL QUESTIONS |
| --- | --- |
| Problem Definition | What is the purpose of the study? To solve a problem? Identify an opportunity? |
| | Is additional background information necessary? |
| | What is the source of the problem (planned change or unplanned change)? |
| | Is the research intended to provide information (discovery oriented) or to make a decision (strategy oriented)? What information is needed to make the decision? |
| | How will the information be used? Should research be conducted? |
| | How much is already known? |
| | What type(s) of exploratory research should be conducted to clarify the problem? |
| | Can a hypothesis be formulated? |
| Data Capture | Can existing data be retrieved from internal sources? Has the data been cataloged and organized? |
| | Can existing data be retrieved from external sources? |
| | What is to be measured? How? |
| | What is the source of the data to be collected? |
| | Can observation techniques be used to gather data? |
| | Should electronic or mechanical means be used to make the observations? |
| | Can objective answers be obtained by asking people? |
| | How should people be questioned? |
| | Should questionnaires be administered in person, over the phone, through the mail, or online? |
| | Should structured or unstructured items be used to collect the data? |
| | Should the purpose of the study be made known to the respondents? |
| | What specific behaviors should be recorded? |
| | What criteria define the target population? |
| | Is a list of population elements available? |
| | Is a probability sample desirable? |
| | How large should the sample be? Should insights from the entire population be sought instead? |
| | Who will gather the data? |
| | How long will the data gathering take? |
| Data Analysis | Who will handle the editing of the data? How will the data be coded? |
| | How will data from different sources be aggregated? |
| | What analysis techniques will be used? |
| Prepare the Research | Who will read the report? |
| Report (Information Reporting) | What is their technical level of sophistication? |
| | What is their involvement with the project? Are managerial recommendations called for? What will be the format of the written report? Is an oral report necessary? |
| | How should the oral report be structured? |

## 2-1b DATA CAPTURE: EXISTING DATA (CHAPTERS 5 THROUGH 7)

Broadly speaking, there are two ways marketing research gathers marketing intelligence: (1) by collecting data to address specific problems or (2) by putting systems in place that provide marketing intelligence on an ongoing basis. Each approach has its merits; most companies would benefit from using both ways.

Look at the differences between the two approaches this way: Both sources of marketing intelligence illuminate the darkness, but collecting data on specific problems is like a flashlight, while collecting ongoing data is like a candle.[1] A marketing research project can shed intense, focused light on a particular issue at a particular time. In contrast, a continuous marketing information system rarely shows all the details of a particular situation, but its glow is broad and steady.

Much of the data that marketing managers need to make routine decisions may already exist inside a company's databases. Companies with well-developed *decision support systems* (DSS) might routinely track sales of their products by region, salesperson, product line, and any other way they can break it down as a means of determining the success of various marketing plans. And companies are getting much better at finding value within "big data," data sets from sensors placed in products, GPS location data sent by electronic equipment (e.g., cell phones), online searches, social media data, calling center audio recordings, e-mails from customers, and the list goes on. Regardless of the particular internal source, if the information needed to solve a problem is held by the company in processed form (e.g., cataloged, organized), the data are retrieved and prepared for data analysis.

Many times, however, the problem goes beyond the scope of regularly collected internal data. The next step is to consider whether or not the data are available from an existing external source. Such sources might include the government (e.g., census data), trade associations, published sources, or commercial sources—organizations that specialize in collecting and selling third-party data to those who need it. If the external data fit the problem at hand and come from a credible source, you'll probably want to use those data rather than to pay to capture your own data on the topic.

## 2-1c DATA CAPTURE: PRIMARY DATA (CHAPTERS 8 THROUGH 15)

Sometimes the information you need is specific to a particular issue, and the data you need to address the problem aren't readily available from internal or external sources. In those cases, your job is to collect new-to-the-world data to address the problem. This often means collecting data from customers, prospects, employees, the general public, or any other group that has the information you need. Such new data are usually referred to as primary data. It's also possible that you can create usable information from unprocessed internal data—companies routinely collect and save tons of data even if they don't know how or when they'll use them. Importantly, once you process these data and begin to use them they can become part of your internal databases, available for use as part of the company's decision support system.

> Collecting data on specific problems is like a flashlight, while collecting ongoing data is like a candle.

Generating new data is generally a time-consuming, expensive process—that's why the model we presented earlier in Exhibit 2.1 indicates that new data should only be generated if the information cannot be obtained from the company's internal sources or from external sources. Once a problem is well-defined and clearly stated in the research request agreement, descriptive or causal research can be conducted. Sometimes researchers also conduct exploratory research at this stage to further refine the issues at hand. They do this in order to guide descriptive or causal research or to provide richer insights in specific situations.

*Causal research* uses experiments to identify cause-and-effect relationships between variables. Using test markets to determine which version of a product to offer, which package design to use, which advertising campaign is most effective, which price to charge, and so on are examples of causal research. Many online companies use A/B tests (i.e., simple experiments) to determine the best means of marketing products and services. Although causal research, especially in the online context, is growing in importance, descriptive research is a more common means of gathering primary data for many companies.

As the name suggests, *descriptive research* focuses on describing a population, often emphasizing the frequency with which something occurs or the extent to which two variables are related to one another. There are lots of questions to be answered when conducting descriptive research, including: Should the data be collected by observation or questionnaire? How should these observations be made—personally or electronically? How should the questions be administered—in person, over the telephone, through the mail, or with an online survey?

Once you've settled on the study method, design the actual observation form or questionnaire for the project. Suppose you decide to use a questionnaire. Should it include a fixed set of questions and alternative answers, or should the responses be open ended to allow respondents to reply in their own words? Should the purpose be made clear to the respondents, or should the study objectives be disguised? Should some type of rating scale be used? What type?

After determining how the needed information will be collected, decide what group will be observed or questioned. Depending on the study, the *population* might be preschoolers, sports car drivers, Pennsylvanians, or tennis players. The particular subset of the population chosen for study is known as a *sample*. In designing the sample, you must specify (1) the *sampling frame*, which is the list of population elements from which the sample will be drawn; (2) the type of sampling plan to be used; and (3) the sample size. There are two basic types of sampling plans. In a *probability sample*, which is the preferred category, each member of the population has a known, nonzero chance

## Manager's Focus

In this chapter, we provide a road map of what you will be studying throughout the remainder of this book. Later chapters will place strong emphasis on issues that should be considered when designing projects and the steps researchers must complete to perform quality research. At this point, we simply want to remind you of why it is essential for you as a marketing manager to have a strong background in these areas. Without this knowledge, you will be completely dependent on the recommendations of others as you attempt to evaluate proposed research projects and the quality of the information produced by completed studies. *In other words,* *you will be placing your career in the hands of others—a risky proposition at best.* Armed with research expertise, however, you will be a formidable force in the marketing efforts of your organization. You will be an effective independent consumer of research services and an invaluable sounding board as research providers seek feedback on the methods they propose using on your behalf. In an information-driven marketplace, managers who comprehend the role of marketing research and the limitations and strengths of the information generated by different techniques are indispensable to an organization.

---

of being selected. This allows us to determine, at a certain margin of sampling error, what would have been true for the whole population if we had information from or about all elements. With a *nonprobability sample,* however, the researchers choose, in one way or another, which individuals or groups will be part of the study. The results apply only to the sample—they can't safely be projected to the population.

### 2-1d DATA ANALYSIS (CHAPTERS 16 THROUGH 18)

You might retrieve a mountain of existing internal or external data or collect primary data from many thousands of respondents, but those data are useless unless you analyze and interpret them correctly in light of the problem at hand. Data analysis generally involves several steps. For new data gathered by asking people questions, individual responses must be scanned to be sure that they are complete and consistent and that the instructions were followed. This process is called *editing.* After being edited, the responses must be *coded,* which involves assigning numbers to each of the answers so that they can be analyzed by a computer. When data involve observations of behavior over time (e.g., purchases of a product based on scanner data), decisions must be made about appropriate time units for *aggregation.* There is also the issue of *merging* data when they come from different sources. Once the data have been edited, coded, aggregated, and/or merged, they are ready to be analyzed.

Most analysis is quite straightforward, involving frequency counts (i.e., how many people answered a question a particular way, often reported as a percentage) or simple descriptive statistics (e.g., means and standard deviations). Sometimes the research calls for cross-tabulation, which allows a deeper look at the data by looking for differences or relationships across groups. Suppose, for instance, that researchers asked women if they have purchased a certain new cosmetic. The responses (i.e., percentage who have purchased) may be cross-classified by age group, income level, and so forth. We give you enough information about these and other kinds of analyses so that you can use a statistics software package to produce your own analyses.

### 2-1e INFORMATION REPORTING (CHAPTERS 19 AND 20)

The written research report is the document you'll submit to management that summarizes your research results and conclusions. This is all that many executives will see of the research effort, and it becomes the standard by which the research is judged. Thus, the research report must be clear and accurate because no matter how well you've performed all the previous steps in the research, the project will be no more successful than the research report. In addition, in many cases you'll get the opportunity to do a research presentation as well. This is really important: The written research report and oral presentation are critical to whether or not the research ultimately will be used.

### 2-1f THE GOAL: MINIMIZE TOTAL ERROR

There is one more thing to consider about the research process we've outlined. No one has ever designed a perfect decision support system or conducted a perfect marketing research project (especially when it comes to collecting new primary data). Even the best projects contain error of one kind or another; it can enter at any stage of the process. The goal is to minimize total error in the marketing research process, not any particular type. It's really dangerous to focus on just one or two kinds of error and forget

**Exhibit 2.3** ▶ Questionable Ethical Decision Making in Marketing Research

- A promotions company hired by an automobile dealership sent letters to local residents inviting them to a special "market test" at the dealership the following weekend. Recipients were led to believe that their help was needed for research purposes. Inquiries with the dealership and the promotions company eventually revealed that the only "research" being conducted involved how many people they could get into the dealership to take a test drive and—they hoped—buy a car. An employee of the promotions company admitted that they do this because it works.

- A few years ago, a well-known soft drink company was feeling pressure to increase sales. Its managers decided to focus on bumping up sales through the Burger King restaurant chain. Managers at Burger King were willing to sponsor a multimillion-dollar promotion for one of the soft drink company's new products if a two-week market test indicated that a sales promotion effort was effective at increasing sales of value meals in a particular market. Results for the first week were not good—and unless the test results improved substantially, Burger King indicated that it wouldn't go forward with a planned national promotion of the new product. Representatives from the soft drink company proceeded to give $9,000 in cash to kids' clubs and other nonprofits in the market to be used to buy hundreds of value meals. These behind-the-scenes efforts added enough value meals to the total consumed in the test market to help convince Burger King to go forward with the national promotion. Not surprisingly, the national promotion was later deemed a disappointment. The artificially inflated sales during the soft drink company's cash infusion could not be maintained after the market test period ended.

about the others, although that happens all too frequently. If you'll think carefully about the questions we presented earlier in Exhibit 2.2, you'll be better prepared to minimize the different kinds of error.

> Error can enter at any stage of the process.

## 2-2 Marketing Research Ethics

Marketing researchers must make many decisions over the course of a single research project. Throughout the process, researchers must consider the ethics of the choices they make.

**Ethics** are the moral principles and values that govern the way an individual or a group conducts its activities. Ethics apply to all situations in which there can be actual or potential harm of any kind (e.g., economic, physical, or mental) to an individual or a group. **Marketing ethics** are the principles, values, and standards of conduct followed by marketers. Exhibit 2.3 provides two examples of instances in which companies demonstrated questionable (at best) ethical decision making with respect to marketing research.

Many researchers (and managers as well) often fail to think about whether it is morally acceptable to proceed in a particular way. Many think that if an action is legal, it is ethical. It's not that simple, however. There can be

**ethics** Moral principles and values that govern the way an individual or a group conducts its activities.

**marketing ethics** The principles, values, and standards of conduct followed by marketers. Marketing researchers must make many decisions over the course of a single research project. Throughout the process, researchers must consider the ethics involved in the choices they make.

differences between what is ethical and what is legal. Even among those who understand this, many don't seem to evaluate the ethical implications of their decisions. Some researchers probably don't care; others may find it easier to ignore such considerations because doing the right thing isn't always easy.

Marketing researchers must recognize that their jobs depend a great deal on the goodwill of the public. "Bad" research that violates the trust of study participants will only make it more difficult and costly to approach, recruit, and survey participants. Even researchers who don't care whether their actions are right or wrong ought to be concerned about such issues from a business perspective. Good ethics is good business—one reason that marketing and public opinion research associations have developed codes of ethics to guide member behavior. Exhibit 2.4 contains the 10 basic principles of the Code of Conduct for the Market Research Society, a leading trade association based in London. Drawn from a much longer document, this is just one example—other organizations have similar codes of conduct for members. Professional marketing researchers care deeply about ethical considerations.

## 2-3 Three Methods of Ethical Reasoning

In judging whether a proposed action is ethical or not, we need to adopt one or more moral reasoning frameworks. In this section, we'll briefly overview three frameworks: the utility, justice, and rights approaches.

**Exhibit 2.4 ▶** The Principles of the Market Research Society (MRS) Code of Conduct

1. Researchers shall ensure that participation in their activities is based on voluntary informed consent.
2. Researchers shall be straightforward and honest in all their professional and business relationships.
3. Researchers shall be transparent as to the subject and purpose of data collection.
4. Researchers shall respect the confidentiality of information collected in their professional activities.
5. Researchers shall respect the rights and well-being of all individuals.
6. Researchers shall ensure that participants are not harmed or adversely affected by their professional activities.
7. Researchers shall balance the needs of individuals, clients, and their professional activities.
8. Researchers shall exercise independent professional judgement in the design, conduct and reporting of their professional activities.
9. Researchers shall ensure that their professional activities are conducted by persons with appropriate training, qualifications and experience.
10. Researchers shall protect the reputation and integrity of the profession.

Source: Code of Conduct, Market Research Society, (September 2014), 3. Retrieved from www.mrs.org.uk, January 3, 2017.

The **utility approach** method focuses on society as the unit of analysis and stresses the consequences of an act on all those directly or indirectly affected by it. The utility approach holds that the correct course of action is the one that promotes "the greatest good for the greatest number." As a result, you would need to take into account all benefits and costs to all persons affected by the proposed action—in effect, to society as a whole. If the benefits outweigh the costs, then the act is considered to be ethical and morally acceptable. Determining all the relevant costs and benefits can be extremely difficult, however. And because society is the unit of analysis, it is entirely possible that one or more individuals or groups may bear most of the costs, while other individuals or groups enjoy most of the benefits.

Take a look at Exhibit 2.4 and imagine that you have been hired to conduct research on how consumers shop for vegetables and other produce in a grocery store. Was the decision to use video cameras to record consumers' behaviors in the store—without their knowledge—an ethical decision? Using the utility approach, we attempt to add up the benefits (e.g., knowing how consumers *really* behave when it comes to reading nutrition labels as a starting point for developing better ways of communicating this important information); better understanding of the purchase process so that the company can ultimately sell more produce, thereby employing more workers and putting more money into the economy; and the costs (e.g., violation of shoppers' privacy and their ability to choose whether or not to participate in the research; the

**utility approach**
A method of ethical or moral reasoning that focuses on society and the net consequences that an action may have. If the net result of benefits minus costs is positive, the act is considered ethical; if the net result is negative, the act is considered unethical.

**justice approach**
A method of ethical or moral reasoning that focuses on the degree to which benefits and costs are fairly distributed across individuals and groups. If the benefits and costs of a proposed action are fairly distributed, an action is considered to be ethical.

costs of doing the research). Considering only these potential costs and benefits, most people would probably say that the action was ethical from a utility perspective: the potential benefits to the company and society from the information gained seem to outweigh the costs borne by the consumers who participated in the study without their knowledge, as well as the cost of the actual research.

The **justice approach** to ethical reasoning considers whether or not the costs and benefits of a proposed action are distributed fairly among individuals and groups. Who decides what amounts to a "fair" distribution of benefits or costs? Essentially, it boils down to societal consensus—what is generally accepted by most people in a society—about what is equitable. If the benefits and costs of an action are fairly distributed, then the action would be considered morally acceptable under the justice approach.

Now, back to the grocery store. To the extent that the knowledge gained from the research has the potential to benefit most people in the society—including those shoppers that participated in the study along with the company that paid for the research—through improved eating habits (for consumers) and improved profits (for the firm), we could probably argue that the benefits were more or less fairly distributed. (By the way, we should note that a "fair" distribution is not necessarily an "equal" distribution. In this situation, the company itself and its workers may enjoy a greater share of the benefits, but they also took on a greater share of the costs and risks.) On the other hand, suppose that the company conducted the research for the sole purpose of figuring out how to sell more products without regard for its customers or their needs. If the people who pay important costs (e.g., loss of privacy, knowledge of their participation) see none of the benefits, then the action would likely be judged as unethical from the justice approach.

Finally, let's consider the **rights approach** to ethical decision making. Both the utility and justice approaches focus on the consequences of behaviors. Under the rights approach, however, a proposed action is right or wrong in and of itself—there is less concern about an action's consequences. Researchers following the rights method of ethical reasoning focus on the individual's welfare and rights. They believe that every individual has a right to be treated in ways that ensure the person's dignity, respect, and autonomy. Probably most people in the United States would argue, for example, that every person has a right to be safe, to be informed, to choose, and to be heard.

What about the research with grocery store customers? When we focus on the rights of the individuals who are being studied without their knowledge or permission, it seems fairly easy to judge the research to be unethical under the rights approach. And this highlights one of the

**rights approach** A method of ethical or moral reasoning that focuses on the welfare of the individual and that uses means, intentions, and features of an act itself in judging its ethicality. If any individual's rights are violated, the act is considered unethical.

difficulties of applying the rights approach: In general, it is more difficult to judge an action as ethical under this approach because it is nearly impossible to ensure that every right of every relevant individual or group has not been violated.

As a practical matter, it's not always easy to apply these models to marketing research decisions. As a researcher, though, you'll have to decide whether or not a particular action is ethical and whether or not to proceed. For many people, there is a natural tendency toward the rights approach, with its focus on individual rights. Still, as we saw with the grocery-store example, society can often benefit through the (temporary) violation of basic rights, such as the right to be informed and to choose to participate in research. The goal of marketing research is to discover the truth about a phenomenon or situation—in the grocery store, we might not be able to observe true consumer behaviors if we tell people that they are being observed, for example.

As we have seen, the frameworks will not always lead to the same conclusion. Exhibit 2.5 offers some practical guidelines for what to do when the answer isn't obvious. The important point is that researchers must consider the ethical ramifications of their actions.

**Exhibit 2.5** ▶ Applying the Ethical Frameworks in Practice

You have been hired to help a large producer of leafy vegetables understand how consumers shop for produce in grocery stores. The company is considering different methods of packaging its produce, especially with respect to how best to display nutritional content. Company managers believe that if more people understand the nutritional value of their products (as well as those of other producers) consumers will begin to make better decisions about the foods that they and their children eat. To accomplish this, however, they need to fully understand how consumers actually behave within the grocery store environment (e.g., how much time they spend reading nutritional information, comparing different types of vegetables, selecting particular vegetables for purchase). Because you suspect that shoppers will change their shopping behaviors if they know that they are being observed, you have decided to place small cameras in strategic locations in the produce sections of four participating grocery stores and record consumer behaviors over a two-week period.

• Is this decision ethical using the utility approach to ethical reasoning?
• Is this decision ethical using the justice approach to ethical reasoning?
• Is this decision ethical using the rights approach to ethical reasoning?

**Three Approaches to Ethical Analysis**

| | KEY ISSUE | LEVEL OF ANALYSIS | LIKELIHOOD OF AN ACTION BEING JUDGED ETHICAL |
|---|---|---|---|
| The UTILITY Approach | Do benefits outweigh costs? | Society | Most |
| The JUSTICE Approach | Are costs and benefits distributed fairly? | Society | |
| The RIGHTS Approach | Are any rights being violated | Individual | Least |

## Manager's Focus

One of the most important areas for ethical consideration is the confidentiality required in the relationship between marketing researcher and client. But confidentiality is a two-way street. Obviously, researchers need to keep confidential the highly sensitive information clients provide to them. But what about the information research firms provide to clients? For example, due to the highly competitive nature of their industry, research companies often seek to differentiate themselves by developing proprietary research techniques. To obtain an account, they must reveal to prospective clients what they do. In addition, when research firms bid for a project by submitting a research proposal, they are revealing their unique ideas of what should be done for the client. We have personally experienced a situation in which a client announced that a competitor submitted a superior proposal, but they preferred working with us, so the client asked us to implement our competitor's proposed project. Disclosing a research provider's intellectual property to another company is just as unethical as a research company disclosing a client's confidential information. We have stated before that successful collaboration between managers and researchers is based on mutual trust. As a manager, your ethical conduct will be vital in establishing trusting relationships with research providers.

## 2-4  Research to Avoid

Although the process of marketing research has many benefits, it is not a perfect process, even when used appropriately. Sometimes, however, researchers choose actions that are inappropriate or even unethical. Stealing competitors' documents in the name of competitive intelligence, falsifying data or results to please a client or manager, conducting **advocacy research** in which the goal is to support a particular position with pseudoscientific results rather than to search for the truth, and attempting to sell products or services or ideas after telling respondents you are conducting marketing research, a process known as **sugging**, are all blatantly unethical uses of marketing research (Exhibit 2.6 provides more details about sugging). Unfortunately, these offenses and many others occur all too often.

> **advocacy research** Research conducted to support a position rather than to find the truth about an issue.
>
> **sugging** Attempting to sell products or services or ideas under the guise of marketing research.

Besides unethical research, there are other types of research that should be avoided. Sometimes a manager or client will have preset ideas about a particular situation, and his or her position may not change, regardless of what your research results suggest. When this is the case, research would be a waste of the firm's resources. It's even worse when the manager takes it a step further to "suggest" what the results ought to be, which amounts to advocacy research and is clearly unethical. Conducting a project for this manager has very little upside for the researcher. If the results work out as expected, you get no credit; if they don't work out, you get all the blame. The manager may be

---

**Exhibit 2.6** ▶ Practical Guidelines for Ethical Analysis

| ETHICAL TEST | PRACTICAL ETHICAL GUIDELINE |
|---|---|
| Common Sense | If proposed course of action violates your "common sense," don't do it. |
| One's Best Self | If the proposed course of action is not consistent with your perception of yourself at your "best," don't engage in it. |
| Making Something Public | If you would not be comfortable with people knowing you did something, don't do it. |
| Ventilation | Expose your proposed course of action to others' opinions. Don't keep your ethical dilemma to yourself. Get a second opinion. |
| Purified Idea | Don't think that others, such as an accountant or lawyer, can "purify" your proposed action by saying they think it is okay. You will still be held responsible. |
| Big Four | Don't compromise your action or decision by greed, speed, laziness, or haziness. |
| Gag Test | If you "gag" at the prospect of carrying out a proposed course of action, don't do it. |

Source: Archie B. Carroll and Ann K. Buchholtz, *Business and Society: Ethics and Stakeholder Management*, 7th ed. (Cincinnati, OH: South-Western College Publishers, 2009), p. 309.

**Exhibit 2.7** ▶ Sugging: Sales Under the Guise of Research

**How Is "Sugging" Different From Legitimate Survey, Opinion and Marketing Research?**

Selling, in any form, is different. Whether conducted by telephone, by mail, by fax or via the internet, sales-related activities are not research. The purpose of a sales call, email, fax or mail solicitation is to encourage members of the public to purchase a good or service. Conversely, the purpose of research (in any form – via telephone, mail, in-person interview, door-to-door, mall or focus group) is to gather information and opinions from members of the public to measure public opinions of products and services or social and political issues. Occasionally, survey research companies will offer a gift to the respondent in appreciation of his or her cooperation. Such a gift could be a cash donation to a charity, a product sample, or a nominal monetary award. But, sales or solicitation is not acceptable or permitted in legitimate and professionally conducted research. In fact, if a research company attempts to sell anything while conducting research, they would be in violation of the MRA Code of Marketing Research Standards, and may be in violation of federal law (e.g., the FTC Act, or the Telemarketing Sales Rule).

**How Is "Sugging" A Violation of Privacy?**

Under survey, opinion and marketing research practices, research companies will never divulge your identity, personal information or individual answers unless you give them permission to do so. In addition, they will never sell or give your name or phone number to anyone else. No one will ever contact you as a result of your participation except perhaps to validate that you did in fact participate. Conversely, sales calls disguised as research calls may be using your information for list generation, may sell that information to third parties and/or may be used to contact you to conduct a sale.

**How Can You Tell If It Is Real Research?**

Overall, there are three easy questions that *you* should ask to determine whether the telephone call, mail piece or e-mail is a legitimate survey:

1. "Are you selling anything?"
2. "Will my participation in this survey result in anyone contacting me to try to sell me anything?"
3. "Will my name and personal information be sold or dispensed to anyone who will contact me to try to sell me anything?"

    A legitimate research company will answer no to all of these questions.

Source: From "Sales Under the Guise of Research (Sugging)," Marketing Research Association, January 13, 2015. Retrieved from www.marketingresearch.org on January 3, 2017.

## Manager's Focus

Research has discovered important differences in orientation between managers and research providers. Managers tend to prefer research that confirms what they already believe to be true about the marketing situation. Researchers, in contrast, often value unexpected research findings that may be suggestive of new environmental opportunities or threats. When research disconfirms a manager's expectations, the tendency is to not believe the results or to blame the unexpected results on flawed research. As a marketing manager, it is important for you to recognize the possible confirmation bias you might bring to the research process. By developing a strong understanding of the methods presented in this book, you will be in a much better position to decide whether particular unexpected results are likely based on errors in the research or might reflect true results that you simply hadn't expected. This ability will make you a valuable asset to your marketing team.

setting you up as an alibi in case the advertising campaign fails or the new product never catches on (e.g., "But the research results were all positive. . ."). This is a manager to avoid, if possible.

Research should also be avoided when resources, such as time and budget, to do the research appropriately are lacking. This may seem strange, in that some research ought to be better than none at all, but this isn't always the case. The danger is that managers will use preliminary or exploratory research as justification for important decisions. Not all research has to be expensive or time consuming, but important decisions should be supported by adequate research. Too often, managers are willing to take shortcuts.

> *Feeling pressed for time, these managers typically ask researchers to run a few focus groups, make 100 telephone calls to test a concept, or undertake one of the many other popular conventional techniques we refer to as "death wish" research. These techniques seem reasonable to the time-challenged because they're quick, low-cost, and often corroborate what the marketer already thought. They may take less time and cost less money, but death wish research techniques offer little in the way of value. What companies usually get is more misinformation than information, which then contributes to the failure of marketing programs. As a result, not surprisingly, executives' confidence in marketing research has declined.[2]*

Even when done correctly, marketing research may not be a good idea in some situations. For example, the benefits of marketing research must always be weighed against the risks of tipping off a competitor, who can then rush into the market with a similar product at perhaps a better price or with an added product advantage. And when a product is truly innovative, it is difficult for consumers to judge whether or not they will ultimately buy and use the product. Some companies will forgo test marketing if there is little financial risk associated with a new product introduction. The best strategy is to examine the potential benefits from the research and to make sure they exceed the anticipated costs, both financial and otherwise.

# Summary

## Learning Objective 1

**Outline the marketing research process.**

There are four general stages in the marketing research process: (1) problem definition, (2) data capture, (3) data analysis, and (4) information reporting. There are three potential types of data sources that should be considered sequentially in light of a specific information need. These are (1) existing data from internal sources, (2) existing data from external sources, and (3) new data from individuals or unprocessed data from internal sources.

## Learning Objective 2

**Describe the general approaches to marketing research.**

There are two general approaches to marketing research: (1) the collection of data to address specific problems and (2) the development of decision support systems that provide marketing intelligence on an ongoing basis. The first approach can be compared to a flashlight that provides a great deal of light directed at a specific point. The second approach is like a candle that offers a steady glow but doesn't provide great illumination of any particular point.

## Learning Objective 3

**Cite the most critical error in marketing research.**

Total error, rather than the size of an error that occurs in any single stage, is the most critical error in research work.

## Learning Objective 4

**Highlight the main differences between the utility, justice, and rights approaches to ethical reasoning.**

The utility approach focuses on society as the unit of analysis and stresses the consequences of an act on all those directly or indirectly affected by it. If the benefits of the act to society exceed its costs, the act is ethical; if the net benefits are negative, the act is unethical. The justice approach considers the degree to which costs and benefits are fairly distributed, based on societal consensus. If the costs and benefits are equitably distributed, the action is ethical. The rights approach focuses on the individual as the unit of analysis and specifically on the rights to which every individual is entitled. Activities that violate an individual's basic rights are considered unethical.

## Learning Objective 5

**Describe types of research that should be avoided.**

Several types of research should be avoided, including unethical research (e.g., sugging, advocacy research); research to support a decision that has already been made; research for which adequate resources are unavailable; and research in which the costs involved outweigh the benefits to be obtained.

## Key Terms

ethics (page 20)

marketing ethics (page 20)

utility approach (page 21)

justice approach (page 21)

rights approach (page 22)

advocacy research (page 23)

sugging (page 23)

## Review Questions

1. What is the research process?

2. What are the various forms of data capture?

3. What is the most important error in research? Explain.

4. What are the main differences between the utility, justice, and rights approaches to ethical reasoning?

5. Why is it important to consider marketing research ethics?

# Endnotes

1.  Williams, R. J. (1966, January). Marketing intelligence systems: A DEW line for marketing men. *Business Management*, 32.

2.  Clancy, K. J., & Krieg, P. C. (2001, Winter). Surviving death wish research. *Marketing Research: A Magazine of Management & Applications*, 13, 9.

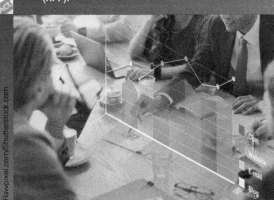

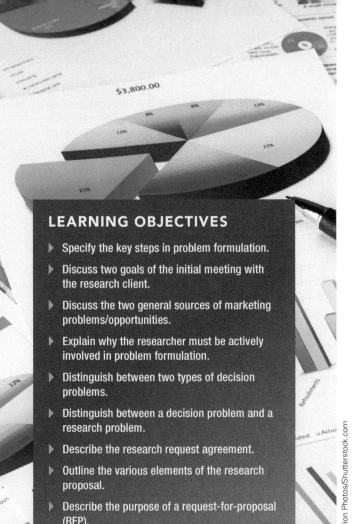

CHAPTER 3

# Problem Formulation

## LEARNING OBJECTIVES

▸ Specify the key steps in problem formulation.

▸ Discuss two goals of the initial meeting with the research client.

▸ Discuss the two general sources of marketing problems/opportunities.

▸ Explain why the researcher must be actively involved in problem formulation.

▸ Distinguish between two types of decision problems.

▸ Distinguish between a decision problem and a research problem.

▸ Describe the research request agreement.

▸ Outline the various elements of the research proposal.

▸ Describe the purpose of a request-for-proposal (RFP).

Billion Photos/Shutterstock.com

Rawpixel.com/Shutterstock.com

## [ INTRODUCTION ]

Defining the marketing research problem correctly is a really big deal. Far too many technically competent research studies produce valid results that aren't very useful because researchers asked all the wrong questions. The Coca-Cola Company found this out the hard way when it introduced New Coke—based on millions of dollars of perfectly wonderful, but ultimately off-target, research—back in the 1980s.

To set the stage, Coca-Cola's market share had shrunk from 60% in the mid-1940s to less than 24% in 1983. At the same time, Pepsi, the product's chief rival, had continued to gain market share. Coca-Cola managers could easily see there was a problem. Stung by Pepsi-Cola's "Pepsi Challenge" promotional campaign, which showed consumers consistently preferring the taste of Pepsi to Coke in blind taste tests, company researchers, managers, and executives became convinced that Coca-Cola had a "taste problem."[1]

The company's researchers proceeded to conduct extensive marketing research—including 190,000 blind taste tests with consumers, costing $4 million—to compare the taste of a new version of Coca-Cola with that of Pepsi and regular Coke. The new formulation was preferred by a majority of consumers. Further research demonstrated that the results held—in fact, were stronger—when consumers were allowed to glimpse the labels to see what they were tasting. Managers were confident that they had developed a product that would successfully solve the taste problem. On the basis of the

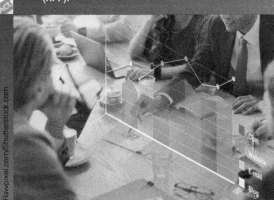

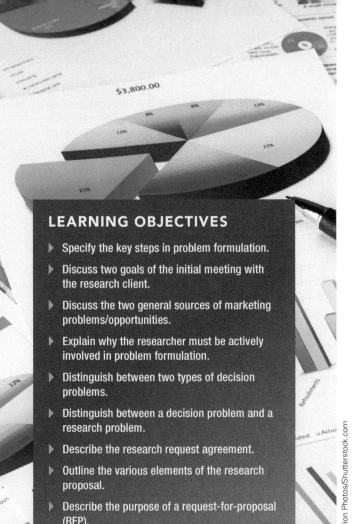

research, the company introduced New Coke to the world in April 1984, replacing the original formula.

The decision to replace the original product with New Coke turned out to be a huge misstep. The company reversed course less than three months later and brought back the original Coca-Cola flavor. What happened? The research was technically sound; it is quite likely that people actually preferred the sweeter taste of New Coke, all else equal. The bigger issue for many consumers, however, was the idea that the original Coca-Cola—with a century's worth of history and imagery—was being discontinued. Although Coca-Cola managers recognized in advance that some consumers would probably not accept a change in the brand, they continued to focus on the "taste problem."

Here's another example: Some years ago, after much hard work to develop a cigarette with an acceptable taste but no visible smoke, RJR Nabisco launched Eclipse. Unfortunately, smokers didn't care to buy the product; they liked the smoke of a cigarette. Cigarette smoke was a problem only for non-smokers—and they, by definition, were not the company's target market. The company's $100 million development effort went to correct something its customers didn't view as a problem by developing a product they didn't want.[2]

## 3-1  Problems Versus Opportunities

When we talk about "defining the problem" or "problem formulation," we simply mean a process of trying to identify specific areas where additional information is needed about the marketing environment. A manager might face a situation that is obviously negative for the organization. For example, a retailer might experience sharply reduced revenues compared with earlier periods, a civic organization might face a chronic shortage of volunteers, or an entrepreneur might lack evidence of market demand to persuade investors to "buy in" to her idea for a new kind of product. These kinds of situations are normally thought of as "problems." On the other hand, a manager might face a situation with potentially positive results for the organization (e.g., the organization's research department has invented a new chemical compound that promises to revolutionize the product category, or brand managers think they have identified a market segment of consumers whose needs are not being met adequately by competitors). One of us once worked with a company whose biggest problem was determining what to do next with all of the money it was making! Although these don't sound much like problems, managers still need information about whether to exploit these opportunities, and if so, how.

We think it is better to think of problems and opportunities as two sides of the same coin. Regardless of perspective, both situations require good information about the marketing environment before managers make important decisions. And today's opportunity is tomorrow's problem if a company fails to take advantage of the opportunity while its competitors do. Similarly, a company that successfully deals with a problem before its competitors has created an opportunity to move ahead in the industry. For these reasons, we usually refer to a "problem" as something that needs information, regardless of whether the organization originally viewed the situation as a problem or an opportunity.

## 3-2  The Problem Formulation Process

How can a company avoid the trap of researching the wrong problem? The best way is to delay research until the problem is properly defined. Too often, researchers jump ahead and write a proposal describing the methods they will use to conduct the research. Instead, in cooperation with managers, you'll want to take the necessary time to fully understand the situation. Many times, this involves conducting fairly extensive exploratory research to pin down the issues at hand. Even well-designed and executed research can't rescue a project (and the resulting business decisions and consequences) if you fail to define the problem correctly.

> How can a company avoid the trap of researching the wrong problem?

Exhibit 3.1 presents the key steps in problem formulation. Defining the problem is among the most difficult—and certainly most important—aspects of the entire marketing research process. The difficulty is primarily due to the uniqueness of every situation a manager may encounter. Although we provide some fairly specific directions, problem formulation involves more art than science, and it must be approached with great care.

### 3-2a  STEP ONE: MEET WITH THE CLIENT

The first step toward defining the problem correctly is to meet with the manager(s) who are requesting marketing research. Do this as early as possible for two important reasons. First, it's important that managers and researchers are able to trust and communicate openly with each other. This won't happen until you begin to know one another and build a relationship. To the extent possible, researchers need to keep the client engaged and actively participating in the process, especially during problem formulation, but also at later stages.

The second reason to meet with the client is straightforward. You need to get as much information as possible from the manager with respect to the problem/opportunity at hand. In particular, you need a clear understanding of the problem from the manager's viewpoint, along with all relevant background information. The broader context is critical, as many people will become very focused on a specific task (e.g., "I need a taste test") versus the

**Exhibit 3.1 ▶ Key Steps in Problem Formulation**

**Meet with the client** to obtain (a) management statement of problem/opportunity, (b) background information, (c) management objectives for research, and (d) possible managerial actions to result from research.

**Clarify the problem/opportunity** by questioning managerial assumptions and gathering additional information from managers and/or others as needed. Perform exploratory research as necessary.

**State the manager's decision problem,** including source (planned change or unplanned change in environment), type (discovery- or strategy-oriented), and scope (one-time or recurring).

**Develop a full range of possible research problems** that would address the manager's decision problem.

**Select research problem(s)** that best address the manager's decision problem, based on an evaluation of likely costs and benefits of each possible research problem.

**Prepare and submit the research request agreement** to the client. Revise in consultation with the client.

---

broader issue (i.e., "We're losing market share"). Without the broader issue in mind, you can accidentally go down a very specific and possibly incorrect path.

Here are some questions that are appropriate at this point.

- What is the problem or opportunity you're facing right now? Can or should this be defined more broadly? Can it be defined more narrowly?

- What caused you to notice the problem? Is there any other evidence or information that you have?

- Why do you think this situation has occurred? (Ask "Why?" five times to dive deeper into the possible causes.)

- What is likely to happen if nothing changes in the next 12 months?

- Is this likely to be an ongoing problem? Do you need to gather relevant information on a continuous basis?

- What do you hope to accomplish by using marketing research?

- What actions will you take depending upon the answers?

### Planned Change versus Unplanned Change

In general, there are only two basic sources of marketing problems: (1) unplanned changes in the marketing environment and (2) planned changes in the marketing environment. Understanding the problem's basic source will provide clues about the nature of the problem and the type of research that is needed.

Sometimes problems/opportunities show up unexpectedly due to changes in the external environment. How a firm responds to new technology or a new product introduced by a competitor or a change in demographics or lifestyles largely determines whether the change turns out to be a problem or an opportunity. For example, a great

deal of marketing research is conducted to track changes in consumer preferences.

A slightly different form of unplanned change involves serendipity, or chance ideas. An unexpected new idea might come from a customer in a complaint letter. Marie Moody, founder of Stella & Chewy's, a maker of premium pet foods, learned to listen carefully to customer complaints after finally agreeing to use opaque—rather than transparent—packaging on frozen pet foods in response to complaints. Consumers were choosing other brands because they could see ice crystals on the Stella & Chewy's products. Customers responded favorably, and sales began to soar.[3]

In still other cases, companies have performed basic research in their laboratories and produced chemicals or compounds that they don't know what to do with—until someone stumbles upon a way to use them. A chemist working in a Procter and Gamble (P&G) lab, for instance, developed a new compound (hydro-xypropyl beta cyclodextrin; thankfully known as HPBCD for short); unfortunately, there was no obvious use for it. The chemist, who happened to be a heavy smoker, went home one evening to a wife who was curious about why his clothes no longer smelled like smoke. It turned out that HPBCD has one amazing quality—the compound removes odors from clothing and other objects. This was a breakthrough; marketing research results for years had shown that consumers desired a product that would remove and not simply mask bad odors. Within a short period of time, P&G introduced Febreze to the U.S. marketplace.[4]

Not all change is unanticipated, though; much of it is planned. Most firms want to increase their business, and they develop various marketing actions to do so. These actions include the development and introduction of new products, improved distribution, more effective pricing, and promotion. Planned change is oriented more toward the future and is proactive; unplanned change tends to be oriented more toward the past and is often reactive. Planned change is change that the firm wishes to bring about—the basic issue is how.

Marriott has traditionally been one of the better companies at identifying new opportunities in the tourism and hospitality industry. When the company recognized a need for a hotel geared toward business travelers, researchers proceeded to conduct research with business travelers to determine the features that were most desired, a process that resulted in the Courtyards by Marriott hotel chain. This is an excellent example of research to implement a planned change.

### 3-2b STEP TWO: CLARIFY THE PROBLEM/OPPORTUNITY

During the first step in problem formulation, the researcher's primary task is to listen carefully as managers provide their perspective on the problem, its background and source (planned versus unplanned change), and what they hope to learn through marketing research. Step 2 involves helping managers get precisely to the heart of the problem. This may seem odd at first—after all, shouldn't managers have a better understanding of the problem than the researcher? It's not a good idea, however, to let a manager perform her own diagnosis and prescribe the treatment as well. Further, many managers focus too

quickly on a specific issue when it may not be the real cause of a current problem. Your job as a researcher is to serve as a consultant to help determine root causes and clear paths of action.

Sometimes it's necessary to challenge managers on their preexisting assumptions. For example, in the case of a new service that hasn't lived up to revenue expectations, may be consumers never really needed that service. Sometimes it also helps to probe managers as to why the problem is important: "Why do you want to measure customer satisfaction? Have you seen signs that customers may not be satisfied? Are you concerned about a new competitor that has entered the market? Are you planning to upgrade service and want a baseline measure of current satisfaction?" The point isn't to put a manager on the spot; the point is to help the manager understand the true nature of the problem. Asking hard questions is much easier if you've demonstrated your professionalism and have developed a rapport with the client.

One of the most important things you can do for a manager is to provide a different perspective. Many managers, particularly those who have been with a company for a long time, are afflicted with "normal thinking." That is,

**Exhibit 3.2 ▶ The Problem With "Normal Thinking"**

There is an old story of a factory worker who left the factory each night pushing a wheelbarrow piled high with scrap materials. At the factory gate, the security guard would tip his hat, say "Good evening," and wonder to himself why anybody would want to take that stuff home. But because the scraps held no value to the company, the guard let him pass each night. Years later, after both the security guard and the factory worker had left the company, the former guard happened to meet the worker. After they exchanged greetings, the guard leaned over to the worker and said, "Say, now that we're both retired, there's something I've just got to know. What did you want with all that trash you took home every night?" The worker looked at him and smiled. "I didn't want the trash," he said. "I was stealing wheelbarrows!"

they look at the business in routine ways. In many ways, this is a good thing; the presence of normal operating procedures allows greater efficiency through the development of standards and routines.

Normal thinking often can get in the way of understanding the true nature of a problem, however. It's your job as a researcher to provide a new perspective, even though the client may not appreciate it at first. Exhibit 3.2 offers an example to help you begin thinking creatively. The security guard was guilty of normal thinking—he failed to consider alternative perspectives.

Bringing a new perspective to a problem may sound like a good idea, but how do you actually do it? How could the Coca-Cola Company have known to define its problem a bit more broadly than simply one of taste? To be honest, it's tough. Because researchers don't deal with a manager's issues on a daily basis, they are automatically less likely to fall victim to normal thinking, so that's a good start. And in most cases, it's a good idea to conduct exploratory research, particularly when managers have seen evidence of a problem (e.g., falling sales revenue, increasing complaints from customers) but don't know the underlying causes. Exploratory research is often very helpful in pinpointing the problem.

> **strategy-oriented decision problem** A decision problem that typically seeks to answer "how" questions about a problem/opportunity. The focus is generally on selecting alternative courses of action.

### 3-2c STEP THREE: STATE THE MANAGER'S DECISION PROBLEM

After working through the first two steps, you should be able to state the manager's **decision problem**, which is simply the basic problem/opportunity facing the manager for which marketing research is intended to provide answers. A well-stated decision problem takes the manager's perspective, it is as simple as possible, and it takes the form of a question. For example, consider a new restaurant near a university campus that has been open for six months but has yet to make a profit. Costs have been held as low as possible; however, sales revenue simply hasn't materialized as quickly as expected. While the owner no doubt has many questions about her business, its lack of success, and how to move forward successfully, her initial decision problem might best take the form, "Why are store revenues so low?" This situation was certainly unanticipated, so the problem has originated from unplanned change.

> **decision problem** The problem facing the decision maker for which the research is intended to provide answers.
>
> **discovery-oriented decision problem** A decision problem that typically seeks to answer "what" or "why" questions about a problem/opportunity. The focus is generally on generating useful information.

The decision problem facing the restaurant owner is an example of a **discovery-oriented decision problem**. Discovery-oriented problems are common with unplanned changes in the marketing environment. In these situations, managers often simply need basic information ("What is going on and why?"). The researcher provides facts that decision makers can use in formulating strategies to deal with the unanticipated situation. For example, you could provide information about customer satisfaction (perhaps the restaurant doesn't consistently offer a quality product), or the overall awareness level among the target market (maybe most people don't know about the restaurant), or consumer perceptions of competing restaurants (perhaps a nearby restaurant is perceived as a better value for the money). In each case, you can offer facts that help shed light on the basic problem.

Note, however, that discovery-oriented research rarely solves a problem in the sense of providing actionable results. This form of research simply aims to provide some of the insights and building blocks necessary for managers to make better decisions.

Discovery-oriented decision problems may also apply to situations of planned change, particularly in early stages of planning when the issue is to identify possible courses of action (as opposed to choosing a preferred course of action). In this situation, key questions are likely to include "What options are available?" or "Why might this option be effective?"

A second form of manager's decision problem, the **strategy-oriented decision problem**, aims squarely at making decisions. This type of decision problem is commonly used with planned change, with an emphasis on how the planned change should be implemented. It is also appropriate for problems originating from unplanned change, provided that enough is known about the situation (perhaps through discovery-oriented research) in order to make decisions. Suppose that initial research for the restaurant indicated that only 38% of the potential customers in its target market were aware that it existed. An appropriate decision problem at this point might be "How do we increase awareness?" Researchers might determine the effectiveness of two proposed advertising campaigns at generating awareness. Notice that the output from the research process in this situation will be a recommendation about which of two specific alternatives to choose. The key distinction between discovery-oriented and strategy-oriented decision problems is that strategy-oriented research provides actionable results.

If possible, you should attempt to conduct strategy-oriented research because the results are designed to provide a clear decision about how to move forward. Providing additional "facts" through discovery research doesn't necessarily get managers much closer to a good decision. Still, there are times when discovery-oriented research is absolutely

> Providing additional "facts" doesn't necessarily get managers much closer to a good decision.

essential, particularly when managers are confronted with unplanned changes in the environment.

There's one other important consideration when developing the manager's decision problem. The researcher, working with managers, must decide whether this is a one-time information need (e.g., choosing a new location or brand logo for the restaurant) or if the information will be needed at regular intervals in the future (e.g., tracking customer satisfaction or target market awareness over time). Sometimes, the information that marketing managers need is very specific and applies only to a given context, and the decision problem should be specified as a one-time project. When the information will be needed regularly in the process of managing and marketing the enterprise, the decision problem should be specified as a recurring project. The decision about whether an information need is one-time or recurring is not trivial. The good news, however, is that the correct answer should become clear by talking with your client.

**research problem**
A restatement of the decision problem in research terms.

### 3-2d STEP FOUR: DEVELOP POSSIBLE RESEARCH PROBLEMS

The manager's decision problem describes the manager's view of the problem/ opportunity. A **research problem** is a restatement of the decision problem in research terms, from the researcher's perspective. A research problem states specifically what research can be done to provide answers to the decision problem.

Consider again the restaurant owner facing the discovery-oriented decision problem of "Why are store revenues so low?" As is true of most discovery-oriented problems, there are lots of actions you can take that would provide insight into the problem, including:

- Investigate current customer satisfaction.

- Assess target market perceptions of the restaurant and its competitors.

- Determine target market awareness.

## Manager's Focus

One of the most common criticisms managers have of marketing research studies is that the findings are not "actionable." By this, they mean that it is not clear what step(s) should be taken in response to the research. While this may be a fair assessment of many research studies, managers often share more responsibility for this outcome than they realize. There are several ways managers might "short circuit" the problem definition process and thereby limit the usefulness of research findings.

For example, managers at times believe the marketing problem is adequately defined in the request-for-proposal (RFP) they issued. Before granting a contract for a project, however, managers are understandably protective of confidential information, so they may not have revealed certain issues that might have led the marketing research firm to define the problem differently and possibly propose different methods. After a research firm's proposal has been accepted, managers too commonly consider the process to have been completed. And so they delegate subsequent interactions with the research firm to the internal marketing research staff or lower-level managers who may not be as knowledgeable about the marketing issues confronting the organization. Such behavior can result in a decision problem that may not reflect all of the complexities of the actual marketing situation.

As you will see in this chapter and the next one, it is often necessary to complete some preliminary (or exploratory) research before the marketing problem can be fully or adequately defined. This means that at the time a research provider has been selected, the problem formulation stage may be only partially completed. Even though the research proposal has been accepted, you should realize that the final research methods may need to be adjusted based on what is learned from the exploratory research and the corresponding re-specification of the decision problem. Therefore, as a marketing manager, it is essential that you stay engaged in the problem formulation process until you and the research provider agree that it has been properly finalized. By doing this, you will dramatically increase the odds that the completed project will give you the guidance you need (i.e., will be actionable).

Here's something else: If your research provider is willing to proceed on the basis of the marketing problem as specified in the RFP, you should consider replacing that provider with one that recognizes its responsibility to guide you through the problem formulation stage. Helping you properly formulate the problem is one of the most important services provided by a research firm because research based on a poorly defined problem will likely lead you down the wrong path.

**Exhibit 3.3** ▶ Examples of the Relationship Between Decision Problems and Research Problems

| DECISION PROBLEMS | POSSIBLE RESEARCH PROBLEMS |
| --- | --- |
| **Discovery-Oriented (What? Why?)**<br>Why are store revenues so low? | Investigate current customer satisfaction.<br>Assess target market perceptions of store and competitors.<br>Determine target market awareness. |
| What needs do our customers have that currently are not being met? | Investigate customer lifestyles.<br>Determine customer problems with existing products.<br>Measure customer satisfaction. |
| **Strategy-Oriented (How?)**<br>How do we increase store traffic? | Investigate effectiveness of different sales promotions.<br>Determine consumer response to two proposed ad campaigns.<br>Measure consumer preferences for new store layouts. |
| How should we introduce a new product? | Run test market to determine consumer preferences for different package sizes.<br>Determine if at least 80% of test market purchasers are satisfied with product.<br>Determine if product sampling promotion leads to 15% initial purchase rate. |

Each of these possible research problems begins with an action word and describes information to be uncovered that might help solve the decision problem. At this stage, your primary task is to develop the full range of research problems for a given decision problem. Exhibit 3.3 provides examples of the relationship between decision problems and research problems.

With strategy-oriented decision problems, there are typically fewer possible research problems because the focus has shifted to making a choice among selected alternatives. At least, that's the way it's supposed to work. When the restaurant owner shifted to the strategy-oriented decision problem, "How do we increase awareness?" there were still several strategic options available, including improved signage, increased levels of sales promotion, the introduction of an advertising campaign, and so on. Research problems might have included "Determine which style of lettering is most readable on outdoor signage," "Investigate the effectiveness of alternative coupon designs," or "Determine consumer response to two proposed advertising campaigns." Presumably, the manager's experience, the available budget, and/or discovery-oriented research led her to decide that advertising was the best area to consider for further research. (Don't forget that defining the problem is often more art than science.)

Where do you get ideas about possible research problems? Usually, they come from the client during the process of clarifying the problem. Sometimes, however, you'll uncover new ideas through exploratory research or as a result of your own experience. In any case, the key point at this stage of problem formulation is to specify the full range of potential research problems.

3-2e **STEP FIVE: SELECT RESEARCH PROBLEM(S) TO BE ADDRESSED**

There are often many possible research problems that would provide useful information, especially with discovery-oriented decision problems. Even strategy-oriented problems will sometimes have many associated research problems. The trick is to figure out which research problem(s) to pursue, given resource constraints. Only in rare cases will decision makers fund research on all possible research problems. As a result, you'll need to carefully review each of the research problems in terms of the trade-off between the information to be obtained versus the costs of obtaining that information. The costs may include money, time, and effort.

For example, we noted three of the possible research problems for the restaurant owner facing the discovery-oriented decision problem, "Why are store revenues so low?" Investigating customer satisfaction will require gathering information from current customers. Assessing target market perceptions of the store and its competitors, as well as determining the target market's overall awareness of the store, require collecting data from the target market, many of whom are not current customers. To address all three research problems would be costly. In this situation, you would work closely with the owner to determine the most likely problem area(s) and, in turn, the most profitable areas of research. (Again, more art than science.) If you've done a thorough job at previous stages in the problem definition process, the selection of research problems should be relatively straightforward.

It is important to stress at this point that it is better to address one or two research problems fully than to try to tackle multiple issues and do a half-baked job on each. Our experience is that novice researchers tend to believe that they can accomplish much more in a single project than is actually possible. You just can't do all the research you want to do because of budget considerations, which makes the choice of research problem(s) so critical.

3-2f    **STEP SIX: PREPARE THE RESEARCH REQUEST AGREEMENT**

When working with internal managers or external clients, the written research request agreement will make your life as a researcher much easier. The **research request agreement** summarizes the problem formulation process to make certain that the client and the researcher agree about the research problems to be addressed. A good research request agreement includes the following items:

1. **Background:** The events that led to the manager's decision problem. While the events may not directly affect the research that is conducted, they help the researcher understand the nature of the problem more deeply.
2. **Decision problem:** The underlying question confronting the manager. A brief discussion of the source of the problem (i.e., planned versus unplanned change) should be included, along with a discussion of (a) whether the problem is discovery-oriented or

> **research request agreement** A document prepared by the researcher after meeting with the decision maker that summarizes the problem and the information that is needed to address it.

strategy-oriented and (b) whether this is a onetime or recurring information need.

3. **Research problem(s):** The range of research problems that would provide input to the decision problem. An overview of costs and benefits of each research problem should be included. The final choice of research problem(s) to be addressed must be indicated and justified.
4. **Use:** The way each piece of information will be used. For discovery-oriented decision problems, indicate key information to be obtained and how managers will use the information. For strategy-oriented decision problems, indicate the way the information will be used to help make the action decision. Supplying logical reasons for each piece of the research ensures that the research problem(s) make sense in light of the decision problem.
5. **Population and subgroups:** The groups from whom the information must be gathered. Specifying these groups helps the researcher design an appropriate sample for the research project.
6. **Logistics:** Approximate estimates of the time and money available to conduct the research. Both of these factors will affect the techniques finally chosen.

The research request agreement should be submitted to the decision maker for his or her approval. If possible, it is best to get that approval in writing with a signature directly on the agreement. Research Window 3.1 presents the research request agreement between a research group and a nonprofit organization seeking a onetime marketing research project on the topic of domestic violence.

## research window 3.1

### Research Request Agreement Presented to Family Crisis Services, Inc., by Research Partners, Ltd.

#### Background

Family Crisis Services, Inc. (FCS), was formed in 1979 as a nonprofit agency to offer services to individuals. Funded by the United Way, the state's Office of Attorney General, the Federal Office for Victims of Crime, and by private donations from groups and individuals, the organization's goal is to provide comprehensive, confidential treatment and counseling to families in crisis due to domestic violence, sexual assault, and/or child abuse or neglect.

FCS offers various services to the local community, including sheltering for victims of domestic violence, a

help line, counseling and consultation, a relief nursery, parenting education, community education on domestic violence, and a sexual assault response team. All services are offered to victims without consideration of individuals' ability to pay.

Despite the fact that university students make up about half of the population of the city in which FCS is located, the FCS director has noted that students rarely use the services offered by the organization. This is unfortunate because national statistics suggest that a significant number of college students are affected by domestic violence at some point during their college career. The director is concerned that most students may not know that FCS exists and that its services are available to them when needed. In addition, FCS relies on volunteers to deliver many of its client support services. Perhaps more university students would volunteer their services if they knew of the existence of FCS and the services it provides. FCS has done no prior formal marketing research.

### Decision Problem

**"Why aren't more students using the services of FCS?"** The director desires to fulfill the organization's goals for all local residents, including university students. This is a discovery-oriented decision problem that has arisen from an unplanned change in the marketing environment—the unexpectedly low number of university-student clients. At this point, a one-time project is proposed.

### Research Problems

There are several different research problems that might be addressed; each would offer insights into the general decision problem. This section discusses the most promising of these research problems and provides the rationale for selecting two of them for further attention.

**(Research Problem 1) Investigate student awareness of the services offered by FCS.** The director has already noted that he believes that lack of awareness is the likely reason that so few university students utilize the services of FCS. Awareness is relatively straightforward to measure, student respondents can be readily accessed, and costs would probably be low.

**(Research Problem 2) Determine the incidence level of domestic violence among local university students.** Another possibility is that domestic violence is simply not very common in the local area among students. This seems unlikely to be true, but establishing that the problem exists might be a good first step. One difficulty is likely to be establishing a common understanding of what constitutes "domestic violence," but researchers should be able to offer a relatively clear definition of the concept before assessing the incidence level. A more difficult hurdle is the sensitivity of the issue to respondents

who have experienced domestic violence or to those who will simply consider the questions to be "too personal."

**(Research Problem 3) Determine student satisfaction with the services provided by FCS.** If students have turned to FCS for help in the past but have been disappointed in the services offered, they likely will not return—and they'll probably share their experiences with others. Given the director's belief that few students have sought help and the difficulty of finding prior student clients due to confidentiality requirements, the costs of pursuing this research problem would likely be quite high.

**(Research Problem 4) Determine student awareness for any organization providing services to victims of domestic violence.** It is conceivable that students' needs for assistance with domestic violence issues are being met by other organizations, either on campus, in the community, or in students' hometowns. If this is the case, the director's fears that students don't know where to go for help may be unfounded. This research problem might be easily combined with Research Problem 1 or 2 because it would require the same general population of university students. As with these research problems, the costs would be relatively low.

**(Research Problem 5) Investigate student perceptions of the FCS office location.** Even if students are aware of the services offered by the organization, perhaps its location makes it less likely that students would go to FCS for help. Although this could be an important issue, the research team believes that this is secondary to the basic awareness issue. In addition, unless the researchers can effectively describe the location to respondents, the sample would need to be drawn from among students who have actually visited the office. According to the director, there just aren't many of these.

**(Research Problem 6) Determine which media outlets university students are most likely to use.** If an awareness problem exists among students, FCS may need to rethink its promotion strategy. Knowing which traditional and new media vehicles (newspapers, radio stations, television stations, social networks, video channels, podcasts, etc.) are routinely used by students could inform future decisions about advertising and other forms of promotion. Given the number

*(continued)*

# research window 3.1    (*continued*)

of options available, collecting this information could take significant time with each student respondent, and the accuracy of the information would be questionable. It is difficult for individuals to communicate perceptual processes such as attention to all the different media they encounter in their daily lives. Plus, it is possible that awareness is not the issue at all, which would make the information obtained from pursuing this research problem less valuable.

### Research Problems Selected

After reviewing these research problems (and others), the research team has concluded that Research Problems 1 and 4 offer the greatest value in terms of providing information that is likely to address the decision problem. Each involves collecting information from the same population (see the following); including both issues should not make the data collection forms too long.

### Use

The key information to be obtained will include (a) unaided awareness and recognition of FCS as an entity providing services for victims of domestic violence, and (b) unaided awareness for any other organizations providing similar services. The FCS director plans to use the results to determine the degree to which a problem exists in terms of student awareness and to help make decisions about increasing communications with students.

### Population and Subgroups

Although the population will be formally defined in the research proposal, the researchers intend to collect data from local university students. FCS clients have primarily been women; most respondents should be women, but a small proportion of men (say, 20% of the sample) should be included. Because Research Partners, Ltd. is donating its services (see next), the sample size will be limited to 200 to 250 individuals.

### Logistics

The project should be completed in approximately three months. As a nonprofit organization, FCS has limited funds available that can be dedicated to marketing research. Research Partners, Ltd., has agreed to donate its services, although the director has agreed to cover out-of-pocket expenses.

**Source:** The contributions of student researchers Jeff Blood, Trey Curtis, Kelsey Gillen, Amie Kreger, David Pittman, and Matt Smith are gratefully acknowledged.

## 3-3   The Research Proposal

Once the problem has been defined and research problem(s) agreed upon, you can turn your attention to the specifics of conducting the research. Much of the remainder of this book addresses these issues in detail. In this section, though, we provide a quick overview of the contents of the research proposal. This proposal specifies the techniques, along with estimated costs, to be used in implementing the research, whether a one-time project or the development of (or addition to) a decision support system.

Notice that in the research request agreement, we paid little attention to research methods, other than a general specification of the population to be studied. That all changes, however, with the preparation of the formal **research proposal**, which lays out the proposed method of conducting the research. The research proposal also provides another opportunity to make sure the research

> **research proposal**
> A written statement that describes the marketing problem, the purpose of the study, and a detailed outline of the research methodology.

will provide the information needed to address the decision maker's problem.

Some research proposals are very long and detailed, running 20 pages or more. Others are much shorter. Regardless of their length, however, most proposals should contain the following elements. Pay close attention to the level of detail required by the client company; this will normally be apparent from a review of the request-for-proposal developed by the client. (We discuss this in the following section.)

### 3-3a   PROBLEM DEFINITION AND BACKGROUND

This section presents a short summary of the information contained in the research request agreement, including the background of the problem, the manager's decision problem, and the specific research problem(s) to be addressed by the project or system. It is often a good idea to include a few words justifying the particular research problem(s) under study.

## 3-3b RESEARCH DESIGN AND DATA SOURCES

The type of research (exploratory, descriptive, causal), type of data to be sought, and the proposed sources of those data are discussed in this section. A brief explanation of how the necessary information or data will be gathered (e.g., surveys, experiments, library sources) is given. Sources refer to where the information is located, whether in government publications, company records, actual people, and so forth. The relevance of all techniques (qualitative and quantitative) should be discussed. The nature of the problem will probably indicate the types of techniques to be employed, such as online surveys, in-depth interviews, or focus groups.

## 3-3c SAMPLING PLAN

The sampling plan starts with a detailed description of the population to be studied, then states the desired sample size (including the rationale or calculations used for obtaining the sample size), discusses the sampling method, identifies the sampling frame, and discusses how item non-response and missing data are to be handled. The reason for using the type of sample proposed must be justified.

## 3-3d DATA COLLECTION FORMS

This section provides information about any forms to be used to gather primary data. For surveys, this involves either a questionnaire or an interview schedule. For other research, the forms could include inventory forms, guidebooks for focus groups, observation checklists, and so forth. You'll need to state how these instruments have been or will be validated and provide any available evidence of their reliability and validity. The data collection form itself, in its proposed final format, will be included in an appendix (see Section H).

## 3-3e ANALYSIS

The analysis discusses editing and proofreading of questionnaires, coding instructions, and the type of data analysis, including any specialized statistical techniques. Most importantly, you will include an outline of the tables and figures that will appear in the report (i.e., dummy tables). These tables and figures will likely be included in an appendix (see Section H).

## 3-3f TIME SCHEDULE

The time schedule is a detailed outline of the plan to complete the study. The study should be divided into workable pieces. Then, consider the persons involved in each phase, their qualifications and experience, and so

forth, and estimate the time for the job. Some jobs may overlap. This plan will help in estimating the time required.

**Timeline**

1. Preliminary investigation — Jan. 10 to Jan. 22
2. Final test of questionnaire — Jan. 24 to Jan. 29
3. Sample selection — Jan. 31 to Feb. 5
4. Mail questionnaires and field follow-up — Feb. 7 to Apr. 2
5. Analysis and preparation of final report — Apr. 4 to May 2

## 3-3g PERSONNEL REQUIREMENTS AND COST ESTIMATE

These provide a complete list of all personnel who will be required, indicating exact jobs, time duration, and expected rate of pay. Assignments should indicate each person's responsibility and authority. Personnel requirements are combined with time on different phases to estimate total personnel costs. Estimates on travel, materials, supplies, analysis, computer charges, and any other costs must also be included. If an overhead charge is required, it should be calculated and added to the subtotal of the preceding items.

## 3-3h APPENDICES

This section will include data collection forms (including script for telephone interviewers, recruiting messages for online surveys, and cover letters for written formats), any technical information or statistical information that would have interrupted the flow of the text, and dummy tables or figures included in the analysis plan.

Once the decision maker has read and approved the proposal, he or she should formalize acceptance of it by signing and dating the document.

## 3-4 Choosing a Research Supplier

In Chapter 1, we noted that many companies have formal marketing research departments. Some companies don't, however, instead preferring to hire marketing research companies to provide the information they need. Even companies with an internal marketing research department sometimes require the services of outside companies.

Using research suppliers has many advantages. If the research workload tends to vary over the course of the year, the firm may find it less expensive to hire suppliers to conduct specific projects when needed than to staff an entire in-house department. In addition, the skills required for various projects may differ. By hiring outside suppliers, the firm can match the project to the vendor with the greatest expertise in the particular area under investigation. Another important advantage is the degree of objectivity that an outside research supplier can bring to a project.

Although it has become increasingly common to outsource marketing research, many managers are uncertain as to how to select a research supplier. The first step is to decide when research is really necessary. Although there is no simple formula for assessing this need, most managers turn to research when they are unsure about their own judgment and other information sources seem inadequate. Before contacting research suppliers, it is important to identify the most critical areas of uncertainty and the issues that would benefit most from research.

Once you've determined the most critical area for research, you are ready to find the right supplier for the job. If your company has a particular research provider in mind, perhaps because of prior relationships or recommendations from others, it would be normal to move on to discussions with that provider, leading to a research request agreement and later the research proposal. If the company does not have a particular provider in mind or by policy must receive proposals from multiple research vendors, a request-for-proposal will often be issued to a number of research providers who might be interested in taking on the project.

A **request-for-proposal (RFP)** is simply a document that describes, as specifically as possible, the nature of the problem for which

**request-for-proposal (RFP)**
A document that describes, as specifically as possible, the nature of the problem for which research is sought and that asks providers to offer proposals, including cost estimates, about how they would perform the job.

research is sought and that asks providers to offer proposals, including cost estimates, about how they would perform the job. The RFP should be structured in such a way that it will be easy to compare the proposals from different providers. Asking for specific information about each step of the research process is a good way to accomplish this, particularly when the company issuing the RFP has been thorough in describing the kind of information and project it is seeking.

Experts suggest that managers seek proposals from at least three companies. In general, the most important asset of a research firm is the expertise of the research professional(s) who will be involved in the design, day-to-day supervision, and interpretation of the research. It pays to talk with these people before selecting a vendor.

After reading the proposals and meeting key personnel, you'll want to perform a comparative analysis. You will use the proposals to evaluate each vendor's understanding of the problem, how each will address it, and the cost and time estimates of each.

One way for firms to work with marketing research suppliers is to form long-term partnering relationships with a few select firms. In such arrangements, the client and research firms work together on an ongoing basis on those projects for which the research firm has the necessary expertise, instead of the client relying on project-by-project bids to select suppliers for specific projects.

## Manager's Focus

Academic researchers have examined various factors that influence whether or not managers use specific marketing research information when making decisions. One significant factor is the extent to which the manager trusts the research provider. The effect of trust on information use is particularly strong when managers lack the research expertise necessary to evaluate the actual quality of the marketing research information. This may seem like a reasonable response. There is some evidence, however, that suggests that research providers sometimes get complacent about how they conduct their research when they are in a long-term

relationship with a client. Because they believe it is unlikely that they will be replaced, research providers may lack the drive to ensure that the project is conducted, analyzed, and interpreted carefully. As a result, a manager's trust in an existing research provider can blind the manager to quality issues. It is in your own best interest to learn how to determine the quality of a proposed or completed research project rather than to rely on a general (and possibly unwarranted) belief about the trustworthiness of the researcher who provided it. As we've said before, helping you develop this ability is a central objective of this book.

# Summary

## Learning Objective 1

**Specify the key steps in problem formulation.**

The six key steps are (1) meet with the client, (2) clarify the problem/opportunity, (3) state the manager's decision problem, (4) develop a full range of possible research problems, (5) select research problem(s) to be addressed, and (6) prepare and submit a research request agreement.

## Learning Objective 2

**Discuss two goals of the initial meeting with the research client.**

The two goals are to (1) develop rapport and open communication lines and (2) obtain as much information as possible about the problem/opportunity.

## Learning Objective 3

**Discuss the two general sources of marketing problems/opportunities.**

The two sources of marketing problems are (1) unanticipated change and (2) planned change. Research on planned change tends to be proactive, while research on unanticipated, or unplanned, change tends to be reactive.

## Learning Objective 4

**Explain why the researcher must be actively involved in problem formulation.**

Researchers play a key role in problem formulation because they bring a new perspective to the problem opportunity situation. Managers often fall into routine ways of seeing the business and its environment; researchers can help them get to the heart of the problem.

## Learning Objective 5

**Distinguish between two types of decision problems.**

A decision problem is the basic problem or opportunity facing the manager. Discovery-oriented decision problems typically ask "what" or "why" and generate information that can be used by managers to make important decisions. Strategy-oriented decision problems are usually directed at "how" planned change should be implemented and focus on making decisions.

## Learning Objective 6

**Distinguish between a decision problem and a research problem.**

A decision problem is the problem/opportunity as seen by managers. Research problems restate the decision problem in research terms, from the researcher's perspective.

## Learning Objective 7

**Describe the research request agreement.**

The research request agreement summarizes the problem formulation process in written form and is submitted to managers for approval. It includes the following sections: origin, decision problem, research problem(s), use, targets and their subgroups, and logistics.

## Learning Objective 8

**Outline the various elements of the research proposal.**

Most research proposals contain the following elements: tentative project title, statement of the marketing problem, purpose and limits of the project, outline, data sources and research methodology, estimate of time and personnel requirements, and cost estimates.

## Learning Objective 9

**Describe the purpose of a request-for-proposal (RFP).**

A company issues a request-for-proposal in order to solicit proposals from research providers. The RFP should be specific enough to allow easy comparisons across vendors.

## Key Terms

decision problem (page 31)

discovery-oriented decision problem (page 31)

strategy-oriented decision problem (page 31)

research problem (page 32)

research request agreement (page 34)

research proposal (page 36)

request-for-proposal (RFP) (page 38)

## Review Questions

1. What does it mean when we say that problems and opportunities are two sides of the same coin?

2. What are the sources of marketing problems or opportunities? Are different sources typically associated with different research objectives? Explain.

3. What is "normal thinking"? Why is it a problem when defining the marketing problem/opportunity?

4. What is the basic nature of a decision problem?

5. What are the fundamental characteristics of the two types of decision problems?

6. What is a research problem? Why is it important to develop the full range of possible research problems?

7. What is involved in a research request agreement? What is included in the written statement?

8. How does the research proposal differ from the research request agreement?

9. What factors should be considered when choosing a research supplier?

10. What are the benefits of using a request-for-proposal?

# Endnotes

1. Allen, F. (1994). *Secret formula*. New York, NY: Harper Collins, 401.
2. Edwards, C. (1999, June 13). A look at the century's hyped products. *Chicago Tribune*, Sec. 5, p. 12.
3. Moody, N. (2009, December 24). How to profit from complaints. *Fortune Small Business. Retrieved* from http://money.cnn.com
4. Duhigg, C. *The power of habit: Why we do what we do in life and business.* New York, NY: Random House, pp. 38–39.

# Exploratory Research

## LEARNING OBJECTIVES

▶ Describe the basic uses of exploratory research.

▶ Specify the key characteristics of exploratory research.

▶ Discuss the various types of exploratory research and describe each.

▶ Identify the key person in a focus group.

▶ Discuss two major pitfalls to avoid with focus groups (or any other form of exploratory research).

## [ INTRODUCTION ]

The main purpose of **exploratory research** is to gain insights and ideas so that problems and opportunities can be more clearly defined. Consider the following decision problem confronting a brand manager: "Why has market share for Brand X slipped during the most recent quarter?" You simply can't proceed on a problem this broad without further guidance. In Chapter 3, we noted that a key part of problem definition is identifying specific research problems that might be addressed. This is a central role for exploratory research, which can be used to identify the areas where research is likely to be most useful. For example, suppose that a quick analysis of the company's database revealed that over the same time frame sales for another brand in the company's product line had skyrocketed, suggesting that Brand X sales might have been cannibalized by the second brand. Or maybe a focus group with consumers showed that a product recently introduced by a competitor was preferred to Brand X on important attributes. Or, what if a quick online survey revealed that current users of Brand X were less than thrilled with its recent performance, suggesting that product quality had slipped? The insights obtained from any of these exploratory approaches (or others) would be useful for directing researchers toward important research problems to be pursued.

> **exploratory research** Research conducted to gain ideas and insights to better define the problem or opportunity confronting a manager.

Notice that none of these examples of exploratory research leads to a conclusive answer. When conducted correctly, exploratory research should provide a better understanding of the situation—but this kind of research is not designed to come up with final answers and decisions. At the end of the exploratory phase, researchers hope to know more about the situation and have an idea about which potential avenues for research (research problems) are likely to yield the most useful information. The most formal outcome that *might* be achieved from exploratory research is one or more hypotheses about the key aspects of a situation. A **hypothesis** is an educated guess about how two or more things are related.

There are other uses for exploratory research, too. For example, exploratory research can be used to increase your familiarity with a problem, especially when you are new to the company and/or problem. For example, when you work with a company for the first time you'll need to develop a working knowledge of the industry, company, and specific problem area. Exploratory research is effective for this.

An exploratory study can also be used to clarify concepts. For instance, if management is considering a change in service policy intended to increase dealer satisfaction, an exploratory study could be used to (1) clarify what is meant by dealer satisfaction and (2) develop a method by which dealer satisfaction could be measured.

So, exploratory research can be used for

- Better formulating the manager's decision problem
- Increasing the researcher's familiarity with the problem
- Clarifying concepts

**hypothesis** A statement that specifies how two or more measurable variables are related.

In general, exploratory research is appropriate for any problem about which little is known. It becomes the foundation for a good study. Exploratory studies are typically small scale and quite flexible.

### Small Scale

Regardless of the particular methods you use, exploratory studies should almost always be relatively small in size. You simply can't afford to devote the bulk of the research budget to exploratory research. What would be the point, anyway? Answers and decisions will flow from other types of research, not from exploratory research. Having said this, however, we want to emphasize that enough resources must be devoted to exploratory research to ensure that the problem has been adequately defined. Sometimes that may mean spending a little more money on the exploratory phase than originally planned, but it's usually money well spent.

### Flexibility

Exploratory studies are very flexible with regard to the methods used for gaining insight and developing hypotheses. Basically, anything goes. Exploratory studies rarely use detailed questionnaires or involve probability sampling plans. Instead, researchers frequently use multiple methods, perhaps changing methods as they learn more about the problem. You need to follow your intuition in an exploratory study. While exploratory research may be conducted in a variety of ways, literature searches, data mining, depth interviews, focus groups, case analyses, and projective methods are among the most common approaches (see Exhibit 4.1).

**Exhibit 4.1** ▶ Types of Exploratory Studies

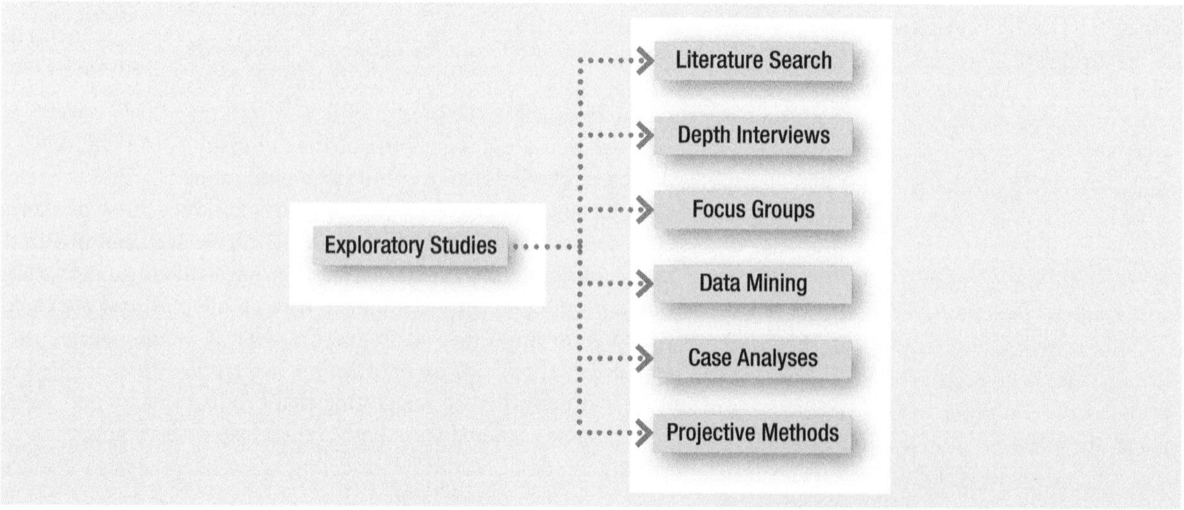

## 4-1 Literature Search

One of the quickest and least costly ways to conduct exploratory research is to do a **literature search**. Almost all marketing research projects should start here. There is an incredible amount of information available in libraries, through online sources, in commercial databases, and so on. The literature search may involve conceptual literature, trade literature, or published statistics from research firms or governmental agencies.

A few years ago, Miller Business Systems, Inc., was able to respond effectively to a competitive threat because of its ongoing effort to review trade literature. Using published industry sources, the company developed profiles of its competitors, which it then kept in its database. The company regularly scanned the database to monitor competitive actions. Based on this information, the company noticed that a competitor had hired nine furniture salespeople in a 10-day period. This was a tip-off to a probable push by the competitor in the office-furniture market. Miller was able to schedule its salespeople to make extra sales calls and hold on to their accounts.[1] As another example, researchers who supply research for Silver Dollar City, the theme park located in Branson, Missouri, regularly monitor all sorts of literature for insights into customers, markets, and competitors (see Research Window 1.1 in Chapter 1).

Sometimes conceptual literature is more valuable than trade literature. For example, a firm with concerns about customer satisfaction might begin its exploratory research by reviewing academic studies and industry reports on the topic, with an eye toward uncovering factors that have been shown to drive satisfaction. The issue of how to measure customer satisfaction could be researched at the same time.

Remember our earlier example with declining sales for Brand X? Initial insights into this problem could easily be obtained by analyzing published data and trade literature. We might learn, for example, whether the problem was an industry problem (everyone's sales are down) or a firm problem (other firms' sales have held steady or even increased). The results of the exploratory literature search could then be used to define one (maybe two) particular research problems that can be addressed with much greater confidence and focus.

It is important to remember that in a literature search, as with all other kinds of exploratory research, the major emphasis is on the discovery of ideas and tentative explanations of the phenomenon and not on drawing conclusions. Finding answers and drawing conclusions are better left to more formal research.

> **literature search**
> A search of statistics, trade journal articles, other articles, magazines, newspapers, books, and/or online sources for data or insight into the problem at hand.
>
> **depth interview**
> Interviews with people knowledgeable about the general subject being investigated.

## 4-2 Depth Interviews

**Depth interviews** (sometimes referred to as "in-depth interviews") attempt to draw from the knowledge and experience of people who know something about the issue driving the research. For example, a San Francisco builder once did depth interviews with architects and designers to try to better understand the builder traits that tended to turn off potential home buyers. Some of the answers included bad manners, workers who tracked dirt across carpets, and beat-up construction trucks parked in homeowners' driveways. Based on this information, the company bought a new truck, had its estimators wear jackets and ties, and made sure its work crews were impeccably polite. In less than two years, the company's annual revenue more than quintupled.

Anyone who knows anything about the issue at hand is a potential candidate for a depth interview. This could include current customers, members of the target market, executives and managers of the company, sales representatives, wholesalers, retailers, and so on. For example, a children's book publisher gained valuable information about a recent sales decline by talking with librarians and schoolteachers. These discussions indicated that more and more people were using library facilities, while book sales were decreasing. The increase in library usage was, in turn, traced to an increase in federal funds that had enabled libraries to buy more books for their children's

### Manager's Focus

If you or somebody else in the company aren't already doing it, it's important that you implement an environmental scanning process within your organization. It doesn't have to be formal, but you really need some means of scanning publicly available information about your industry, your customers, and so on. You'll want to make every effort to obtain marketing intelligence from existing sources before any new marketing research studies are conducted. Literature searches are efficient ways of gathering market intelligence, some of which might even be fed into your organization's databases (see Chapter 5). Even smaller companies with limited budgets should have personnel who regularly monitor the available literature for relevant market information that can be distributed to decision makers.

collections. Similarly, some years back, Ford Motor Company designed a medium-duty truck intended for beverage distribution, among other things, after seeking feedback from fleet owners, mechanics, and drivers.

As with other types of exploratory research, depth interviews are quite flexible. Participants are selected based on their likely ability to provide usable information. It's important to include people with differing points of view and opinions. Sometimes the questions asked are the same across respondents, and sometimes they differ. There's no need for a formal questionnaire at this point, unless it is short and/or designed to start or guide the conversation. The questions should be general, allowing flexibility in how participants answer.

As the name suggests, the point of a depth interview is to encourage the respondent to offer as much information as possible. As a result, sometimes depth interviews can last for an hour or more. Be sure to keep an audio or video recording of the interview, assuming that the participant agrees.

At first glance, depth interviews seem similar to the personal interview method of collecting descriptive research data (discussed later in this book). Depth interviews are used to collect exploratory information, don't require a random sample, and are usually informal. On the other hand, personal interviews are used to collect descriptive data (which we'll describe in great detail later in Chapters 9 through 15), usually use random samples of well-defined populations, and are very formal in terms of the questions and answers included.

## 4-3  Focus Groups

Focus group interviews are a popular form of exploratory research. In a **focus group**, a small number of individuals are brought together to talk about some topic of interest to the focus group sponsor. The discussion is directed by a **moderator** who attempts to guide the discussion, making it as inclusive as possible of all participants. As a result, participants hear others' ideas and can respond with their own ideas.

Group interaction is the distinguishing aspect of a focus group, compared with a set of individual depth interviews. It is also the primary advantage of focus groups over most other exploratory techniques. Because of their interactive nature, ideas sometimes drop "out of the blue" during a focus group discussion. Further, ideas can be fully developed because of the snowballing effect: A comment by one individual can trigger a chain of responses from other participants. The presence of other people and the opportunity to listen to their comments often encourages even very shy participants to express their thoughts and feelings. As a result, responses are

**focus group**
An interview conducted among a small number of individuals simultaneously; the interview relies more on group discussion than on directed questions to generate data.

**moderator** The individual that meets with focus group participants and guides the session.

often more spontaneous and less conventional than they might be in a depth interview.

> Group interaction is the distinguishing aspect of a focus group, compared with a set of individual depth interviews.

### Characteristics of Focus Groups

Although focus groups vary in size, most consist of 8 to 12 members. Smaller groups are too easily dominated by one or two members; with larger groups, frustration and boredom can set in, as individuals have to wait their turn to respond or get involved. The typical focus group session lasts from one-and-a-half to two hours.

Respondents are usually selected so that the groups are relatively homogeneous. That is, the goal is to include people who are more or less like one another. This promotes better discussion as people realize that they have things in common with other participants. It also helps prevent individuals from being intimidated by other participants. For example, perceived differences in social status or other socioeconomic factors might discourage

## Manager's Focus

As a manager, you must think carefully before using focus groups. Focus groups can be helpful in the right circumstances, but there are several alternative exploratory research techniques available, and you should select one or more that best fit the types of questions you are trying to address. In our opinion, focus groups are used far more often than they ought to be. Research firms too often recommend focus groups simply because they specialize in them, not because they are the most appropriate exploratory tool. Relatively few firms have the expertise necessary to competently perform the entire range of exploratory methods. Therefore, when you need exploratory information, you should interview prospective firms by asking them to thoroughly discuss the advantages and disadvantages of alternative exploratory methods as they apply to your current information needs. You should then select the firm that speaks most authoritatively about alternative approaches and presents a compelling case for why a particular technique best fits the questions you are addressing. Under no circumstances should you select a firm or a method simply because it is used frequently by other organizations.

some people from speaking at all while encouraging others to dominate the discussion. Keeping everyone involved in the discussion is one of the key roles of the moderator.

Most firms conducting focus groups use screening interviews to find focus group participants. Clients will normally have specific criteria for the kinds of participants they want. In fact, under normal circumstances, the more specific the criteria, the more useful the results will be. As a result, it is critical to recruit participants who meet the requested criteria. This isn't always easy, because the more specific the screening criteria, the more difficult it is to identify and recruit participants. Increasing the incentives provided to participants should increase the likelihood that they'll show up and participate, but it's no guarantee. And increasing the incentives also increases the chances that some people will claim that they meet the screening criteria just to receive the incentives. These "professional" focus group participants must be avoided.

Given that the participants in any one group should be reasonably homogeneous, how can a firm be sure that the full range of opinions will be represented? The best way is to hold multiple groups. That way, the characteristics of the participants can vary across groups. Ideas discovered in one group session can be introduced in later group sessions for reaction. A typical project might have less than five groups, but some may have up to 12 or more. The issue is whether the later groups are generating additional insights. When they show diminishing returns, the groups should be stopped. When Visa was considering and developing a new brand mark, they conducted 58 focus groups across seven different countries! Groups were formed based on location, gender, and whether or not the participant primarily used Visa products.

Focus groups take one of two basic forms: *traditional focus groups* that meet face-to-face, often at facilities designed especially for focus groups, or *online focus groups* that use Web-based technology to "meet." Massachusetts WIC (Women, Infants and Children) program, working in conjunction with Market Street Research, Inc. (MSR), conducted 24 traditional, in-person focus groups in English and Spanish with Caucasian, Puerto Rican, Dominican, and African American mothers on the national issue of overweight children. Traditional focus groups were a good methodology for this project because it allowed WIC and MSR to explore mothers' feelings about this sensitive issue while also enabling insights to be heard from traditionally underrepresented populations, such as Spanish-speaking immigrants who faced a unique set of challenges.[2] For traditional focus groups, the typical setup includes a conference room with nice furniture and fixtures that can comfortably hold the participants. Often, a one-way mirror is placed at one end of the conference room, with space behind the mirror to house audiovisual equipment for recording the focus group interview as well as seating for researchers, clients, and/or advertising agency representatives.

With online focus groups, participants meet electronically using one or more of the many types of technologies that allow multiple individuals to participate simultaneously over the Web. Such approaches offer tremendous speed and cost benefits, particularly when using an established online panel of respondents. There are other advantages of online focus groups as well, including the ability to form groups composed of people from far-flung locations or to deal with sensitive topics. Online focus groups can be an effective tool for producing useful exploratory insights. Market Street Research, Inc., maintains expertise in online and traditional focus groups. Research Window 4.1 details another focus group example, but this time online was the best approach coupled with webcam interviews.

## research window 4.1

### Online Focus Groups and Webcam Interviews for Better Understanding Traveler Decision Making

The travel and hospitality industry, especially the hotel and accommodations portion of it, continues to be challenged by home-sharing outlets like Airbnb and Vacation Rental By Owner (VRBO) as more and more consumers seek unique vacation experiences known previously only to locals. Changing guest tastes have made the sea of hotel chains within a downtown district secondary options instead of primary choices. If consumers use standard hotel room booking, they flock to online travel agencies and third-party booking engines such as Expedia or Booking.com or even aggregator sites like Kayak or Travelocity. Where are travelers not flocking? [NameYourFavoriteHotelBrand].com.

Branding firm Sullivan and qualitative research firm 20|20 Research partnered to study the modern traveler and share these and other interesting findings in their "Where They Go. Why They Stay" traveler

*(continued)*

## research window 4.1    (*continued*)

decision-making report. 20|20 Research is an industry leader in applying technological advances to marketing research with specific expertise in qualitative techniques. Two such techniques were used here: online discussion forums (20|20 specializes in online focus groups and bulletin board focus groups allowing for both synchronous and asynchronous participation) and webcam interviews. 20|20 interacted with 25 respondents as they researched and ultimately selected where they intended to stay for an upcoming pleasure trip.

The 25 respondents were evenly divided by gender (13 females, 12 males) from across the United States. Their ages ranged from 27 to 54 with incomes ranging from $60,000 to $125,000 annually. This group also included a subset (10 of the 25) who belonged to travel-based loyalty programs. Their travel planning behavior was monitored throughout. They were asked open-ended focus group-style questions and were interviewed by webcam during follow-up conversations, all while planning their next vacation destination.

We provide specific findings below. But first, consider two counterintuitive surprises: (1) Not one person visited a hotel's branded web site among the 10 to 14 different places where they sought information, reviews, and pricing, and (2) Reddit was a consistent source for seeking travel advice and also asking for insight at the specific neighborhood level in the cities they planned to visit. According to Lauren Walsh, Sullivan's chief marketing officer, "Before this, if you had asked me if Reddit is a place people go to for travel advice, I never would have thought to say yes."

Hotel marketers should be aware that many of the travel planning decisions do not include the properties they own, online or off. Not surprisingly, most everyone started with a Google search. A popular search phrase was "hotels near [destination]." If a hotel brand was not included in that initial search, it did not get full consideration moving forward. What seemed to matter most

was the experience sought or planned (family vacation, romantic getaway, girls' weekend, etc.). If hotels did not emphasize those types of experiences or highlight the uniqueness of their locations, it was another opportunity missed.

In sum, four key insights stand out. First, would-be travelers ranked location above amenities, price, and ratings. They especially wanted to see linkages to the local community, including cultural landmarks and neighborhoods of interest. They sought immersive experiences. Second, social influencers make a major impact on booking decisions. These influencers did more than simply write reviews; they also answered specific destination-relevant questions on Reddit.

Third, 46% of travelers book accommodations on a booking engine. "Search is the front line on where people are seeking information to stay," Walsh said. This means that offline real estate is just as important as SEO-driven online real estate. On that front, the third-party aggregators are winning. Finally, these travelers gave no consideration to branding or loyalty or direct bookings. When asked if they were ready to book, brands were not a consideration. When asked where they would book, brands were likewise not a consideration. And then, when they ultimately did book, they did not type Hilton.com, Hyatt.com, or Marriott.com. The report suggests that search, experiences, and uniqueness ruled the day.

**Sources:** Birkner, C. (2016, Dec. 14). "Hotel websites don't matter—and 3 other insights on travel booking trends," *AdWeek*. Retrieved from http://www.adweek.com/brand-marketing/hotel-websites-dont-matter-and-3-other-insights-travel-booking-trends-175093/; Ting, D. (2016, Dec. 15). "What hotel CMOs need to know about Google, Metasearch and Reddit." *Skift*, Retrieved from https://skift.com/2016/12/15/what-hotel-cmos-need-to-know-about-google-metasearch-and-reddit/; Walsh, L. (2016, Dec. 14). "An inside look at traveler decision-making," *Sullivan*. Retrieved from http://www.sullivannyc.com/ideas/inside-look-traveler-decision-making/

Are online focus groups as effective as traditional focus groups? Remember that the key advantage of a focus group compared with other types of exploratory research is the synergy obtained by having multiple participants interviewed simultaneously. When participants meet together, experience each other's presence, and feed off one another's comments, the desired synergy can be maximized. Online focus groups can be incredibly useful, but even with the latest technologies, electronic interaction is necessarily

more limited, making it difficult to effectively duplicate the true value of focus group research online. Still, online focus groups can provide valuable exploratory data, and the cost benefits are so great that many companies now use this approach. The trick is to obtain maximum value while overcoming the limitations. Exhibit 4.2 presents some best practice suggestions for conducting online focus groups.

In general, focus groups are less expensive to conduct than are individual depth interviews, mostly because multiple

**Exhibit 4.2 ▶** Tips for Running an Online Focus Group

**Tips for Running an Online Focus Group**

- Because communication is more difficult (compared with face-to-face), keep the number of participants at eight or fewer in any particular session.
- Keep the length of the sessions to 90 minutes or less.
- Use the most sophisticated technology that is available across the participants in a group. For groups of current or potential customers, you may be limited to text or voice using a program such as Skype.
- Use technology if at all possible in order to get a sense of nonverbal language.
- Be proficient in the use of the chosen technology, or have technical help available for possible glitches.
- Make certain there is a separate, clear communication channel with focus group observers (e.g., client, agency, other researchers) so they can connect with the moderator during the session.
- Work diligently at the beginning of the session to create a "connection" and rapport across participants.
- Establish ground rules early for participants about how and when to communicate. Include a simple initial task that requires each participant to communicate with the group.
- Maintain participant engagement by changing tasks somewhat frequently, especially when there is no video connection across the group.

respondents are handled simultaneously. That's not to say that they are inexpensive, however. By the time you hire an experienced moderator to conduct the session and write the report, rent a facility, and pay incentives to participants, a focus group has become costly. And that's just one focus group; add a series of focus groups and the costs can really rise.

### The Role of the Moderator

The moderator in the focus group plays the single most important—and most difficult—role in the process. For one thing, the moderator typically translates the study objectives into a guidebook. The **moderator's guidebook** lists the general (and specific) issues to be addressed during the session, placing them in the general order in which the topics should arise. In general, the funnel approach is used, in which the moderator introduces broad general topics or tasks first, and then the conversation begins to focus on the key issues under study.

To develop the guidebook and conduct a focus group effectively, the moderator needs to understand the background of the problem and the most important information the client hopes to obtain from the research process. The moderator also needs to understand the overall plan for the use of focus groups: how many will be held, whether the focus groups will be held face-to-face or online, how many participants will be in each, what kinds of people will be involved, and how the sessions might be structured to build on one another.

The moderator must lead the discussion so that all objectives of the study are met and that interaction among the group members is stimulated. The focus group session

**moderator's guidebook** An ordered list of the general (and specific) issues to be addressed during a focus group; the issues normally should move from general to specific.

cannot be allowed to dissolve into a series of individual depth interviews in which the participants each take turns responding to a predetermined set of questions. As a result, the moderator's role is extremely delicate. It requires someone who is intimately familiar with the purpose and objectives of the research and at the same time possesses good interpersonal communication skills. One important measure of a focus group's success is whether the participants talk to each other, rather than the moderator. Some of the key qualifications moderators must have are described in Exhibit 4.3.

### The Dark Side of Focus Groups

Despite their benefits, focus groups must be approached with care. As with other forms of exploratory research, focus groups should be used to generate ideas and insights to help clarify problem definition. They are not designed to provide final answers; it's a risky strategy to implement decisions based solely on focus group results unless the insights generated are crystal clear.

When interpreting focus group results, it is important to be as objective as possible. And that's not an easy thing to do. When managers bring preconceived ideas about what they want or expect to see, it's no surprise when they find evidence in one or more of the group discussions that supports their position. Because executives have the ability to observe the discussions through one-way mirrors, follow along with an online session, or review recordings of the sessions, focus groups are more susceptible to executive biases than most other exploratory techniques. These biases may not be intentional, but they can still be

**Exhibit 4.3** ▶ Nine Characteristics of Good Focus Group Moderators

**Superior Listening Ability**

It is essential that the moderator listen to what the participants are saying. A moderator must not miss the participants' comments because of lack of attention or misunderstanding. The effective moderator knows how to paraphrase, to restate the comments of a participant when necessary, and to ensure that the content of the comments is clear.

**Excellent Short-Term Auditory Memory**

The moderator must be able to remember comments that participants make early in a group and then correlate them with comments made later by the same or other participants. A participant might say that she rarely watches her weight, for example, but then later indicate that she always drinks diet soft drinks. The moderator should remember the first comment and be able to relate it to the later one so that the reason for her diet soft drink consumption is clarified.

**Well Organized**

The best moderators see things in logical sequence from general to specific and keep similar topics organized together. A good moderator guide should be constructed logically, as should the final report. An effective moderator can keep track of all the details associated with managing the focus group process so that nothing "falls through the cracks" that impacts negatively on the overall quality of the groups.

**A Quick Learner**

Moderators become intimately involved in a large number of different subject areas— and for only a very short time in each. An effective moderator is able to quickly learn enough about a subject to develop an effective moderator guide and conduct successful group sessions. Moderators normally have only a short period of time to study subject areas on which they will be conducting groups. Therefore, the most effective moderators can identify the key points in any topic area and focus on them so that they know enough to listen and/or probe for the nuances that make the difference between an extremely informative and an average group discussion.

**High Energy Level**

Focus groups can be very boring both for the participants and for the client observers. When the tenor of a group gets very laid back and lifeless, it dramatically lowers the quality of the information the participants generate. The best moderators find a way to inject energy and enthusiasm into the group so that both the participants and the observers are energized throughout the session. This ability tends to be most important during the second group of an evening (the 8 to 10 o'clock session) when observers and participants are frequently tired because of the late hour and can become listless if they are not motivated to keep their energy and interest levels high. The moderators must also keep a high energy level so that the discussion is very productive to the end.

**Personable**

The most effective moderators are those who can develop an instant rapport with participants, who then become actively involved in the discussion to please the moderator. Participants who don't establish rapport with the moderator are much less likely to "open up" during the discussion, and the output from the group is not as good.

**Well-Above-Average Intelligence**

This is a vital characteristic of the effective moderator because no one can plan for every contingency that may occur in a focus group session. Moderators must be able to think on their feet to process the information that the group is generating and then determine what line of questioning will most effectively generate further information needed to achieve the research objectives.

Source: Greenbaum, T. L. *The Handbook for Focus Group Research*, 2nd ed. 77–78.

harmful. And many managers find it too easy to use focus group data to intentionally support their positions. As one observer put it, "The primary function of focus groups is often to validate the sellers' own beliefs about their product."[3] Consider the company who introduced a new product for teenage girls based on focus group research:

*Following a series of focus groups the company concluded that what teenage girls wanted was technologically enhanced nail polish. This was a happy coincidence as technologically enhanced nail polish was precisely what the company produced![4]*

Another example: A few years ago, the president of a restaurant chain based in the southwestern United States gave a presentation about his company's marketing efforts. He discussed how focus groups had been used to test an

## Manager's Focus

We emphasize throughout this chapter that managers must be very careful not to misuse exploratory research findings. The findings from focus group interviews are among those most frequently misused by managers, even by managers who should know better. We once observed the president of an advertising and marketing research consulting firm announce that his company was launching a new service because "the focus group findings were all positive." Focus groups, when used properly, are uniquely capable of capitalizing on group dynamics to generate new ideas or insights that would not emerge if respondents were interviewed separately and could not help build on other people's ideas. It is important to always remember that these ideas and insights can be very useful in helping you create new marketing strategies. But exploratory techniques should not be used to make final decisions about implementing a particular marketing strategy. You need other kinds of research (descriptive or causal) to make decisions, especially decisions like this that are central to the company's or brand's future success.

upcoming advertising campaign. In fact, he had observed at least one of the focus groups and could recall the words of one particular focus group participant, which (not surprisingly) happened to express his own feelings about the campaign very well.

### Nominal Groups

Before we move on to other forms of exploratory research, let's consider **nominal groups**, which are a variation of focus group interviews and share many of their characteristics. The primary difference is that nominal groups require written responses by participants before open-group discussion. It was noted earlier that smaller groups can be too easily dominated by one or two members or that larger groups can lead to frustration or boredom as individuals wait to respond or get involved. Nominal groups hope to ensure that these issues are avoided, regardless of group size, by asking people to think and write before speaking. Here's how a nominal group interview works.

First, the moderator proposes the question or topic for discussion. Once it is clear that all participants fully understand the issue, participants are invited to think about and then record their thoughts on paper. Second,

**nominal groups**
A group interview technique that initially limits respondent interaction while attempting to maximize input from individual group members.

**data mining** The use of powerful analytic technologies to quickly and thoroughly explore mountains of data to obtain useful information.

the moderator asks respondents one by one to reveal their written responses. Often, the moderator will write the individual responses for all group members to see. Individuals are encouraged to record new ideas stimulated by the sharing from others. At the same time, verbal discussion between group members is discouraged until after all participants have had a chance to reveal their ideas. Next, the complete set of individual responses is reviewed by the group and the moderator. Discussions center on clarification of existing thoughts and elimination of duplication. Finally, group members are asked to prioritize the group's ideas. The ideas with the highest priority, as agreed upon by the group, are now the focus of the group discussion.

Nominal groups limit respondent interaction initially in an effort to maximize individual input. Like focus groups, it is a terrific technique for generating new ideas. In fact, nominal groups can produce more, and more varied, ideas than focus groups due to their concentration on individual participation. It also minimizes any potential concerns of "group think," domination by a few individuals, or the lack of involvement by respondents who are generally more quiet or shy.[5]

## 4-4 Data Mining

Most of the techniques we discuss in this chapter can be described as qualitative in nature. That is, they produce data that are subjective and must be interpreted carefully, taking into account the context in which they were generated. The data themselves usually involve words and themes to be interpreted, not numbers to be crunched. Not all exploratory research is qualitative in nature, however. In particular, when data analysts begin to sift through the vast amounts of data held in a company's databases looking for patterns among variables, they are performing an increasingly common and important form of exploratory research. Although we'll have much more to say about databases, decision support systems, and "big data" in Chapters 5 and 6, it's important to recognize the important exploratory uses of quantitative data analysis.

The technical term for searching for statistical patterns in datasets is **data mining**, which has been defined as the use of "powerful analytic technologies to quickly and thoroughly explore mountains of data, isolating the valuable, useful information."[6] Businesses hope data mining will allow them to boost sales and profits by better understanding their customers and/or improving the performance of the products and services they offer. For example, coaches in the National Basketball Association (NBA) have used data mining to sort through game statistics to determine their most productive combinations of players and measure the effectiveness of individual players. Similarly, the movie *Moneyball* depicts how statisticians have changed the scouting process for selecting players for some Major League Baseball teams by scouring statistics looking for key insights that lead to better overall performance for the team.

> Businesses hope data mining will allow them to boost sales and profits by better understanding their customers and/or improving the performance of the products and services they offer.

Have you ever sent flowers to your mother for Mother's Day? 1-800-Flowers.com used data mining to discover that professional, suburban mothers were a key demographic for their continued growth: These women accounted for a large portion of the company's business because they tended to order flowers for their own mothers as well as for their mothers-in-law.[7] The company used this insight to better design a successful holiday promotion. This example, by the way, represents a very common use of exploratory data mining, to examine associations between variables held in a company's database.

Note, however, that even when the results appear immediately actionable (for example, designing a promotion to appeal to professional, suburban mothers for Mother's Day purchases), when data mining is used to discover new insights, it is still an exploratory tool that generates hypotheses that can be validated in future work. And data mining must be used with a clear understanding of the data being analyzed. One analyst working with Costco purchase data discovered that people who purchased meat were likely to also purchase eggs. He also discovered that people who purchased soft drinks were also very likely to purchase eggs. The same held true for people purchasing frozen foods. This was a puzzling result; were eggs becoming so popular that they were being prepared with almost every meal? A closer look revealed that all of the data came from a one-week period in March. It turns out that lots of people purchase eggs in the week before Easter![8]

## 4-5  Case Analyses

**Case analysis** involves the study of selected examples or cases of the phenomenon about which insights are needed. You might examine existing records, observe the phenomenon as it occurs, conduct unstructured interviews, or use any of a variety of other approaches to analyze what is happening in a given situation.

For example, the Inside Consumer Experience research project installed 13 cameras each in two nursing homes in The Netherlands to record food intake during the evening meals. One nursing home was simply observed. The other started with observation,

| |
|---|
| **case analysis** |
| Intensive study of selected examples of the phenomenon of interest. |

then changes were implemented based upon what was learned. More social interaction between participants and staff was instituted. The furnishings in the dining room and the ways meals were presented were improved. Meal preparation now included at least 60% organic products. The results revealed that food intake increased in the second group.[9]

Case analyses can be performed in lots of different ways. We once performed careful observation of the service delivery process in an endodontist's office (including observing a root canal, in progress) as a means of gathering exploratory data about key aspects of the processes that drive patient satisfaction. We sat in the waiting area, detailing the surrounding environment and observing patients interact with staff before and after procedures. We noted the location and appearance of the building and spoke with the endodontist and his staff to obtain needed input. In short, we wanted to learn as much as we could about the process by focusing on this particular case; our approach involved observation and interviews, as well as examining the printed materials patients received.

When conducting case analyses (or any other type of exploratory research), it's important to record all relevant data, not just data that support any initial hypotheses that researchers or managers have already formed. The success of the case analysis approach depends upon the researcher's ability to interpret the diverse mass of information collected across cases. The researcher must be able to sort through the data and see the "big picture," insights that apply across multiple cases, not just details that apply only to individual cases. Finally, as with all other forms of exploratory research, the goal is to gain insights, not to test explanations.

Case analyses seem to be especially effective for generating insights when the cases chosen reflect recent changes in behavior. For example, the way a market adjusts to the entrance of a new competitor can reveal a great deal about the industry's structure. Similarly, a company can probably

## Manager's Focus

"Best practices" studies have become popular methods by which businesses benchmark against highly successful companies. While they can provide valuable results, it is also possible for managers to misunderstand the underlying reasons for successful performance when they analyze only the highest-performing organizations. As a manager, you are probably more likely to pinpoint the underlying drivers of relative success and failure in an industry if you compare and contrast organizations representing the whole spectrum of market performance.

learn more from a long-time customer that has defected to a competitor than it can from a long-time customer who stays with the company.

Cases that reflect extremes of behavior are also great to study. A researcher once worked with a company to improve the productivity of its sales force. By carefully studying several of the company best and worst salespeople, the researcher discovered an important difference between the high and low performers. The best salespeople were checking the stock of retailers and pointing out items on which they were low; the low performers were

> **ethnography** The detailed observation of consumers during their ordinary daily lives using direct observations, interviews, and video and audio recordings.

not taking the time to do this. Similarly, to determine the factors responsible for the differences in unit sales across a company's sales territories, you'll probably learn more by comparing the best and worst territories than by looking at all territories.

## Ethnography

An increasingly popular form of case analysis is **ethnography**. These procedures, which have been adapted from anthropology, involve the detached and prolonged observation of consumers' emotional responses, cognitions, and behaviors during

---

## research window 4.2

### What Is Ethnographic Marketing Research?

Ethnographic market research (EMR) helps companies understand the consumer in terms of cultural trends, lifestyle factors, attitudes, and how social context influences product selection and usage. Traditionally, when businesses want to determine how consumers feel about a product or service, they employ focus groups. These groups meet in a room and discuss the topic at hand. In contrast, what EMR does is take away the room, remove artificial settings, and throw open the door to the real world. Using anthropology as its foundation, EMR uses a variety of techniques and forums to present a complete picture of consumers and how products and services fit into their daily lives.

#### On-Site

On-site ethnographic research sessions take place wherever the consumer uses the product or service—in a restaurant, store, office, or even car. Conducting place-based research allows the researcher to interview and observe as the behavior is carried out and provides an opportunity for follow-up questions as needed.

#### In-Home

In-home EMR sessions are similar to on-site events, but they are limited to the home environment. They can include one or multiple family members and often last for several hours. The researcher is immersed in the home environment and observes, asks questions, and listens to obtain insight into consumer trends, reactions, problems. Consumers go about solving those product- or service-based dilemmas. In-home sessions provide businesses with insight into how to improve products, what new items are needed and how changing needs affect usage.

#### Virtual

Virtual EMR sessions are conducted online and require the participants to carry out a variety of tasks, usually over a period of days or weeks. Consumers might be asked to write essays on a product- or service-related topic, select pictures, or even film themselves. This full immersion process is designed to reveal a 360-degree image of the consumers' attitudes, emotions, and perceptions.

#### Peer Parties

Peer parties mirror the traditional focus group, in that multiple consumers join to discuss a product or service, answer questions, and provide feedback. The two formats differ in that the EMR peer party event takes place in a residence and participants know each other. The relaxed, festive atmosphere is intended to bring forth feedback and insight that would otherwise be less likely to surface. A researcher moderator assists in guiding the conversation, but otherwise remains in the background.

#### Cross-Cultural and Organizational Analysis

Increasingly, businesses operate across multiple borders and within varying cultures. Cross-cultural and organizational analysis identifies obstacles the parent company might encounter in foreign countries and assists in redefining how specific corporate cultures or products might need to be altered for maximum success and productivity.

**Source:** Shear, J. "What is ethnographic marketing research?" (n.d.). Retrieved from http://smallbusiness.chron.com

their ordinary daily lives. Unlike anthropologists, however, who might live in the group being studied for months or years, ethnographers use a combination of direct observations, interviews, and video and audio recordings to make their observations more quickly. Research Window 4.2 provides more insights into the use of ethnographic research.

Like other methods of case analysis, ethnography is useful as an exploratory research tool because it allows insights based on real behavior, rather than on what people say. For example, an academic researcher conducted a 16-month ethnography of households and the brands in their kitchen pantries. She used interviews and observation, as well as projective techniques such as sentence completion and a drawing task (see next section), to gain an understanding of the perception of brands in consumer households.

One family that she studied (a couple in their forties and their 14-year-old son) clearly demonstrated the insights that can be generated through ethnography. The family's kitchen has an old-fashioned "general store" look, and they prefer that their groceries simply blend into the background. In fact, they often remove products from their original packaging and place them in more discreet containers. They also place the flashier brands that the son purchases out of general view. When asked about the importance they place on food brands, the couple made comments such as, "I really don't pay attention to brands," "We aren't brand loyal," and "I don't have any real preferences for brands." Based on these answers, a marketer conducting traditional research may have expected this family to be completely unaffected by brand names and packaging.

Observation of the family, however, made it evident that they bought many of the same brands over and over again. In particular, the family bought the Dominick's store brand for many of its food choices. The couple describes this brand as "not flashy," "discreet," and "subtle." While consciously attempting to avoid nearly all things related to branding, the couple was unknowingly becoming very loyal to a brand that they valued for its ability to simply blend in, evidence that consumers' expressed beliefs do not always indicate their purchasing behaviors.[10]

Despite the popularity of ethnography and other forms of case analysis, we need to offer some words of caution about their (mis)use. As with other forms of exploratory research, the usefulness of the technique for generating insights depends on the quality and objectivity of the analysis. Interpreting rich, qualitative data is very difficult to do. Remaining objective about the results (that is, not allowing preconceived ideas and expectations to influence the interpretation) may be even harder to do. And we can't resist reemphasizing another point: Exploratory methods should be used to generate insights to focus problem definition and, maybe, to help develop hypotheses. They are not useful for discerning final answers and making decisions, although some researchers attempt to use them for that purpose.

## 4-6    Projective Methods

Sometimes individuals have difficulty expressing their true feelings, beliefs, and behaviors. Consumers won't describe many of their motives and reasons for choice because a truthful description would be damaging to their egos, especially when they feel pressure to think, feel, or behave in certain ways. Sometimes they just can't put their feelings or motivations into words—or maybe they don't even know why they do what they do. Yet marketers need to understand what motivates consumers and how they really feel about phenomena in order to create truly satisfactory exchanges with their customers. Asking direct questions, however, can sometimes produce answers that are either useless or misleading.

Researchers have tried to overcome subjects' reluctance to discuss their feelings and/or to provide truthful answers through the use of **projective methods**. Projective methods encourage respondents to reveal their own feelings, thoughts, and behaviors by shifting the focus away from the individual through the use of indirect tasks. The basic assumption is that people's reactions to the indirect tasks are indicators of their basic beliefs and feelings.

Researchers have used many different types of projective methods, ranging from asking people to describe what a brand would be like if it came to life to asking respondents to draw or select pictures of the kinds of people who would use certain products. Among the most common techniques are word association, sentence completion, storytelling, and role playing.

### Word Association

With **word association**, subjects respond to a list of words with the first word that comes to mind. The test words are intermixed with neutral words to conceal the purpose of the study. Suppose that a research team is doing a study on people's feelings about protecting the natural environment. Some of the key words that might be used for a word association task could include *traffic, lakes, smokestacks,* and *city,* mixed in with words such as *margarine, blue jeans,* and *refrigerator.*

Responses to each of the key terms are recorded word for word and later analyzed for their meaning.

**projective methods**
Methods that encourage respondents to reveal their own feelings, thoughts, and behaviors by shifting the focus away from the individual through the use of indirect tasks.

**word association**
A projective method in which participants are asked to respond to a list of words with the first word that comes to mind.

The responses are usually judged in three ways: by the frequency with which any word is given as a response, by the average amount of time that elapses before a response is given, and by the number of respondents who do not respond at all to a test word after a reasonable period of time. An individual's pattern of responses, along with the details of the response to each question, are then used to assess the person's attitudes or feelings on the subject.

## Sentence Completion

**Sentence completion** requires that the respondent complete a number of sentences with the first thoughts that come to mind. The responses are recorded word for word and are later analyzed.

While the analysis of qualitative responses is subjective, sometimes the results are clear enough that there would be good agreement in their interpretation. Consider the following sentence prompts (responses written in italics):

- People who are concerned about ecology *care about the future.*

- A person who does not use our lakes for recreation is *being thoughtful about the ecosystem.*

- When I think of living in a city, I *can't help but think of the smog over LA.*

Compare those responses to these of another person:

- People who are concerned about ecology *are just tree-huggers who want to run up my taxes.*

- A person who does not use our lakes for recreation is *a person who doesn't enjoy water sports.*

- When I think of living in a city, *I think about cruising my car downtown on Saturday night!*

Presumably, these two respondents could easily be characterized as belonging to segments of consumers who are more and less ecologically concerned.

One advantage of sentence completion over word association is that respondents can be provided with a more directed stimulus. There should be just enough direction to evoke some association with the concept of interest. The researcher needs to be careful not to convey the purpose of the study or provoke the "socially acceptable" response. Obviously, you'll need some skill to develop a good sentence-completion or word-association test.

## Storytelling

The **storytelling** approach often relies on pictorial material such as cartoons, photographs, or drawings. Basically,

**sentence completion**
A projective method in which respondents are directed to complete a number of sentences with the first words that come to mind.

**storytelling**
A projective method of data collection relying on a picture stimulus such as a cartoon, photograph, or drawing, about which the subject is asked to tell a story.

**role playing**
A projective method in which a researcher will introduce a scenario or context and ask respondents to play the role of a person in the scenario.

respondents are asked to tell stories about the pictures. The pictures can be of anything that might somehow lead to relevant insights about the problem/opportunity at hand. The way an individual responds to the pictures or drawings helps researchers interpret that individual's values, beliefs, attitudes, and personality.

With respect to the environmentalism example, the stimulus might be a picture of a city, and the respondent might be asked to describe what it would be like to live there. The analysis of the individual's response would then focus on the emphasis given to pollution in its various forms. If no mention were made of traffic congestion, dirty air, noise, and so on, the person would be classified as displaying little concern for pollution and its control.

## Role Playing

The **role playing** technique is similar in many ways to storytelling. With role playing, however, the researcher will introduce a scenario or context and ask respondents to play the role of a person in the scenario. The researcher might ask how "people you know" or "the average person" or "people like you" or even how the respondents themselves would react in the situation. As with other projective methods, the goal is to get a glimpse into respondents' own feelings, beliefs, actions, and so on, by shifting the focus away from them and onto the task itself.

Suppose, for example, that the environmentalism researchers wanted exploratory feedback on city residents' likely reactions to a number of pollution control efforts being considered by local officials. Rather than ask residents direct questions about whether or not they are in favor of— or would abide by—new regulations about carpooling or time of day restrictions on lawn mowing, the researchers might instead use a scenario in which the regulations were being introduced in another city. They could then ask the research participants how a resident of that city is likely to feel and respond to the regulations. In the process of describing the anger, feelings of being hassled, frustration, willingness to obey the law, or positive feelings of being able to "do my part" likely to be felt by residents of the other city, the respondents will reveal a great deal about their own feelings.

The usual concerns about the difficulty of data analysis and interpretation apply to projective methods, just as they apply to other forms of exploratory research. And, as always, researchers must keep in mind that no form of exploratory research, including projective methods, is designed to get final answers or make decisions.

# Summary

## Learning Objective 1

**Describe the basic uses of exploratory research.**
Exploratory research is used primarily to help formulate the manager's decision problem. It is also useful for developing hypotheses, gaining familiarity with a phenomenon, and /or clarifying concepts. In general, exploratory research is appropriate for any problem about which little is known. The output from exploratory research is ideas and insights, not answers.

## Learning Objective 2

**Specify the key characteristics of exploratory research.**
Exploratory studies are typically small scale and are very flexible; anything goes.

## Learning Objective 3

**Discuss the various types of exploratory research and describe each.**
Common types of exploratory research include literature searches, depth interviews, focus groups, data mining, case analyses, and projective methods. Literature searches involve reviewing conceptual and trade literature or published statistics. Depth interviews attempt to tap the knowledge and experience of those familiar with the general subject being investigated. Focus groups involve a discussion among a small number of individuals, normally 8 to 12, simultaneously.

Data mining involves exploratory statistical analysis of a company's databases looking for useful patterns. With case analyses, researchers study selected cases of the phenomenon under investigation; ethnographic research is a popular example. Finally, projective methods encourage respondents to reveal their own feelings, thoughts, and behaviors by shifting the focus away from the individual through the use of indirect tasks.

## Learning Objective 4

**Identify the key person in a focus group.**
The moderator is key to the successful functioning of a focus group. The moderator must not only lead the discussion so that all objectives of the study are met but must also do so in such a way that interaction among group members is stimulated and promoted.

## Learning Objective 5

**Discuss two major pitfalls to avoid with focus groups (or any other form of exploratory research).**
Researchers and managers must consciously work to remain as objective as possible when reviewing and interpreting exploratory data. It is very easy to see what you expect or want to see in qualitative data. The second pitfall to avoid is to use exploratory research to obtain answers and decisions rather than the ideas, insights, and hypotheses that these techniques were designed to deliver.

## Key Terms

exploratory research (page 41)
hypothesis (page 42)
literature search (page 43)
depth interviews (page 43)
focus group (page 44)
moderator (page 44)
moderator's guidebook (page 47)
nominal groups (page 49)
data mining (page 49)
case analysis (page 50)
ethnography (page 51)
projective methods (page 52)
word association (page 52)
sentence completion (page 53)
storytelling (page 53)
role playing (page 53)

## Review Questions

1. What are the basic uses for exploratory research?

2. What are the key characteristics of exploratory research?

3. What is a literature search? What kinds of literature might be searched?

4. What are the characteristics of a depth interview? Who should be interviewed?

5. How does a focus group with 8 to 12 people differ from a series of depth interviews with 8 to 12 people? How does a focus group differ from a nominal group?

6. What characteristics should a good focus group moderator possess? Why is each important?

7. How might focus groups be misused?

8. In what types of situations would data mining be useful?

9. What are two common approaches to the use of case analyses?

10. What is the basic point of projective methods? What are some popular approaches?

# Endnotes

1.  Galante, S. P. (1986, March 3). More firms quiz customers for clues about competition. *The Wall Street Journal*, 17. See also L'egare, T. (1996, Spring). Acting on customer feedback, *Marketing Research: A Magazine of Management & Applications* 8, 46–51.

2.  Interview with Ingrid Steblea, Vice President, Research, Market Street Research, Inc.

3.  Gross, D. (2003, Oct. 10). Lies, damn lies, and focus groups. *Slate*. Retrieved from http://slate.msn.com

4.  Hodgson, P. (2004, June 1). Focus groups: Is consumer research losing its focus? *Userfocus*. Retrieved from http://www.userfocus.co.uk

5.  de Ruyter, K. (1996, Jan.). Focus versus nominal group interviews: A comparative analysis. *Marketing Intelligence and Planning*, 14, No. 6, 44–50; Retrieved from http://www.proquest.com

6.  Kant-ardzic, M. M. & Zurada, J., Eds. (2005). *Next generation of data-mining applications*. Hoboken, N.J.: John Wiley & Sons, 1.

7.  "1-800-flowers.com customer connection blooms with SAS business analytics," Retrieved from http://www.sas.com

8.  Linoff, G. (2012, March). "Experience? Software? Common sense?" *JMPFOREWARD*, 9–10. Retrieved from http://www.jmp.com

9.  Verkerk, A. (2013, Feb. 14). Behavioral research blog: Two examples of on-site observational studies with elderly people, *Noldus*, Retrieved from http://info.noldus.com/bid/91123/Two-examples-of-on-site-observational-studies-with-elderly-people

10. Coupland, J. C. (2005, June). Invisible brands: An ethnography of households and the brands in their kitchen pantries, *Journal of Consumer Research*, 106–118. Retrieved from Business Source Elite database.

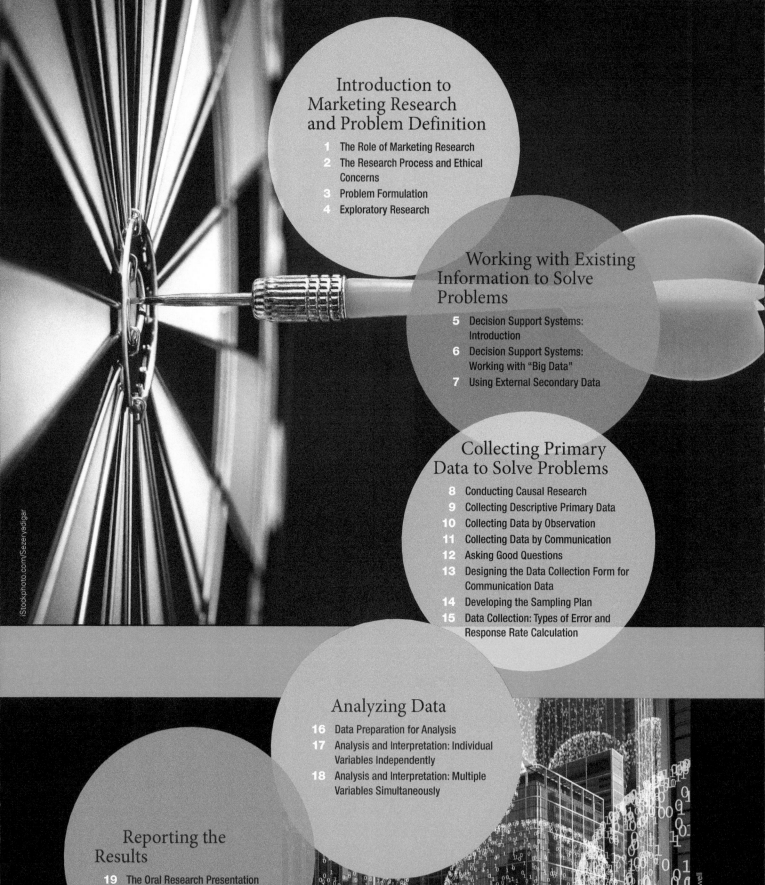

# Part 2

# Working with Existing Information to Solve Problems

Billion Photos/Shutterstock.com

# CHAPTER 5

# Decision Support Systems: Introduction

## LEARNING OBJECTIVES

▶ Define the difference between secondary data and primary data.

▶ List the advantages and disadvantages of working with secondary data.

▶ Define what is meant by a marketing information system (MIS) and a decision support system (DSS).

▶ Identify the components of a decision support system.

▶ Discuss knowledge management.

Rawpixel.com/Shutterstock.com

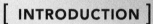

## [ INTRODUCTION ]

A fundamental purpose of marketing research is to help managers make decisions they face each day in their various areas of responsibility. Marketing managers need information to carry out the firm's marketing activities. Marketing information can take the form of customer purchasing patterns, assessment of demand for a firm's products, preferences among product design alternatives, sales revenue from different geographic areas, or customer satisfaction with products and services, just to name a few.

We noted earlier that there are two basic ways marketing research can gather marketing intelligence: (1) by conducting projects to address specific problems (we'll refer to this as the *project approach*) or (2) by putting systems in place that provide data on an ongoing basis (this will be the *systems approach*). Much of this book deals with gathering specific information from individual consumers or firm employees to address particular issues. In this chapter, however, we focus on information systems that provide a steady stream of existing data that managers can use to make decisions. In Chapter 6, we'll address the explosion of "big data" that is expanding the breadth and depth of data available to managers at a breathtaking pace. As a preview, Research Window 5.1 showcases some of the ways existing data can be better understood with modern visualization tools.

## research window 5.1

### *"Big Data" Visualized: More Than One Billion Served*

The concept of "big data" has gained increasing attention over the last several years. As more and more firms capture data from e-commerce sites, purchase transactions, and mobile computing, the next important wave is determining how best to make sense of it all. Tableau Software was built on two very simple premises: Databases should be converted to charts, graphs, interactive maps, and the like, and special programming skills need not be necessary to generate custom reports and interactive visualizations of the data. With the help of Tableau, data analysis through data visualization has never been simpler and more insightful.

Tableau works best with spreadsheet-type data—classic rows and columns. From there, dragging and dropping leads to visual organization. If you are curious about the number of bank closures since 2000, an interactive map of the United States can be created to show bank closures by state and year with data from the FDIC. Perhaps you want to know which country has the greatest infant mortality rate. Data from the UN Interagency Group on Mortality Estimation can produce a world map superimposed with a bar chart revealing that West Africa has the highest number of infant deaths. If a lighter topic with a bit more levity is your interest, all the spells uttered in the seven-part *Harry Potter* series can be charted with direct, interactive reference to the book, passage, and character verbalizing the spell.

Tableau Public, a free edition, can handle data sets consisting of 100,000 rows of data, while the Professional Edition notes unlimited data availability. To date, more than 300,000 users have produced in excess of 800,000 interactive visualization graphs that have been viewed more than one billion times using Tableau Public. All manner of visualized data—line graphs, column charts, and so on—across topics like business and real estate, health and science, and travel and lifestyle have been created. This leads one to believe that the types of data Tableau can summarize visually are practically limitless.

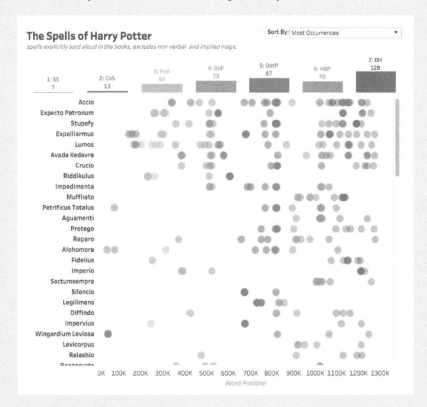

**Sources:** Denne, S. (2011, Nov. 23). "Big-data success stories: Tableau software," Retrieved from http://blogs.wsj.com /venturecapital/2011/11/23/big-data-success-stories-tableau-software; Dan, H. (2017, Jan. 16). "Your tableau public vizzes have reached one billion views!" Retrieved from https://public.tableau.com/en-us/s/blog/2017/01/your-tableau-public-vizzes-have -reached-one-billion-views.

Before we go any further, however, we need to introduce the notion of secondary data, because secondary data make up most of the data held in data systems used in marketing research.

## 5-1   Secondary Data

Sometimes the data that marketers need to make decisions already exist inside or outside the organization. Data that have already been collected, often for some other purpose or by some other organization, are known as **secondary data**. Sometimes, however, the information that a manager needs doesn't exist anywhere and must be gathered from individuals inside or outside the firm. These new-to-the-world data collected for the purpose at hand are known as **primary data**. (And—just to confuse the issue a little—note that primary data collected for a particular purpose become secondary data if they can be used for another purpose. All information in a database was primary data at some point.)

Here's a quick example to help you understand the difference in these two types of data. If Maytag conducted an online survey on the demographic characteristics of washing machine purchasers to determine who buys the various sizes and styles of front- and top-loading washing machines, this would be primary data. If, instead, the company used its existing files and compiled the same data from warranty cards its customers had returned (i.e., *internal* data) or if it used already published industry statistics on appliance, specifically washing machine, buyers (i.e., *external* data), the information would be considered secondary data.

When a problem or opportunity has been carefully defined, the first consideration should be whether or not the information needed to address the issue already exists, either from the company's internal decision support system or from external sources (take a look back at Exhibit 2.1 that describes the marketing research process). The general rule is that primary data should be collected only if secondary data are unavailable from internal or external sources. There are an amazing number of secondary sources; we'll describe some of these in the following chapters. As a quick example, the US Census Bureau collects a wealth of information about the US population, households, businesses, and a whole host of other things. This information is readily available for use as secondary data for such tasks as market analysis.

Successful research projects should begin with a careful search for existing secondary data. Some types of marketing research rely almost exclusively on secondary data. It is important to know what is available in secondary sources, not just to avoid "reinventing the wheel" but also because

**secondary data**
Data that have already been collected, often for some other purpose or by some other organization.

**primary data**
Information collected specifically for the investigation at hand.

secondary data can possess some significant advantages over primary data. They have their disadvantages, too.

### 5-1a   ADVANTAGES AND DISADVANTAGES OF SECONDARY DATA

The most significant advantages of secondary data are the time and money they can save. If the information being sought is available as secondary data, the researcher can simply retrieve the data from internal or external sources and proceed to data analysis and/or interpretation. Relative to collecting primary data on the topic, this should take much less time and involve little cost. With secondary data, the original compiler of the information has already paid the expenses incurred in collecting the data. Even if there is a charge for using the data (unlike statistics compiled by government or some trade associations, commercial data are not free), the cost is usually much less than if the firm collected the information itself.

Secondary data are not without potential problems, however. Two problems that commonly arise with secondary data are (1) they do not completely fit the problem and (2) they are not totally accurate. Because secondary data were collected for other purposes, they may not fit the problem as defined. In some cases, the fit will be so poor that the data are completely inappropriate. Usually, poor fit is due to one or more of the following problems: different units of measurement, different class definitions, or the age of the data.

The size of a retail store, for instance, can be expressed in terms of gross sales, profits, square feet, and number of employees. Consumer income can be expressed by individual, family, household, and spending unit. If you need individual-level income but only household income is available, it may be necessary to collect primary data to get the information you need. Even if the units are consistent, you may find the class boundaries presented are often different from those you need. For example, if you need individual income measured in fairly small increments (say, 0 to $4,999, $5,000 to $9,999), it won't help much if the available secondary data provides individual income using wider boundaries (0 to $19,999, $20,000 to $39,999, etc.). It's also possible that secondary data are out of date. The time from data collection to data dissemination is often long. For example, government census data have great value while current, but this value decreases rapidly with time. Remember, the broad U.S. Census of the population is conducted only once every 10 years.

The other common problem with secondary data is that it is sometimes difficult (or impossible) to judge their accuracy. As you'll learn throughout this book, there are lots of sources of error possible in the collection, analysis, and presentation of marketing information. When a researcher is collecting primary data, firsthand knowledge helps in gauging the accuracy of the information being collected. But when using secondary data, the task of assessing accuracy is more difficult. It helps to consider the source of the data, the sponsor of the research, and the general quality of the data collection methods and presentation.

Secondary data can be secured from either a primary source or a secondary source. A **primary source** is the source that originated the data. A **secondary source** is a source that in turn took the data from a primary source. When possible, always use the primary source of secondary data. Take this recent headline as an example, "We're Seriously Underestimating the Virtual-Reality Market." The headline alone would suggest that, at a minimum, virtual reality (VR) should be the focus of the article's discussion. Upon reading the first paragraph you learn that VR is not the sole focus. Instead, it's a combination of virtual and augmented reality (AR). You also learn that AR and VR combined is expected to be a $150 billion industry in five years. Consulting the primary source and author of the original study, you learn that AR is forecasted to be worth $120 billion, leaving VR to be worth only $30 billion.[1] Technically, the secondary source headline is not incorrect. We could still be underestimating the VR market; however, since AR is expected to be four times larger than VR, doesn't the primary source provide a more interesting discovery?

A second way to judge the accuracy of secondary data is to pay attention to which organization sponsored the research. Consider the following example: According to the results of a survey, almost one-third of the respondents have talked to a doctor about a treatment they saw advertised, and about 75% of the respondents said ads for prescription drugs showed both the risks and benefits of the medicine.[2] The results were released at a time when the U.S. Food and Drug Administration was preparing new guidelines for advertising prescription drugs directly to consumers. The survey was sponsored by *Prevention* magazine, which makes money in part by selling advertising to prescription drug companies. Does the presence of a business interest mean that the research doesn't accurately reflect consumer attitudes and behaviors? No, but it does mean that you need to look very closely at how the data were collected. Research that has been collected in such a way that the results will support a particular position is often referred to as **advocacy research**. Again, not all data collected or sponsored by an interested party should automatically be rejected as advocacy research. But pay attention.

A third way to gauge the accuracy of secondary data is to look for evidence that the research was done properly. For example, a user needs to understand how the data were collected. A primary source should provide a detailed description of the data collection process, including definitions, data collection forms, method of sampling, and so forth. If it doesn't, be careful! Such omissions may indicate sloppy methods (at best) or advocacy research (at worst). When the details are provided, examine them thoroughly. You'll need to be familiar with the research process and the potential sources of error in order to gauge the quality of secondary data. The remainder of this book provides much of the needed insight for evaluating secondary data.

5-1b ## TYPES OF INTERNAL SECONDARY DATA

There are many types of internal secondary data. In this section, we'll discuss some of the standard types of internal data that have been input into data systems for decades, in some cases. In Chapter 6, we'll identify some of the newer sources that have been coming online in recent years with the onslaught of data availability.

For most companies, the sales and cost data compiled in the normal accounting cycle represent promising internal secondary data for many research problems—such as evaluation of past marketing strategy or assessment of the firm's competitive position in the industry. Transaction data serve as the building blocks for overall company sales performance, often broken down by customer, product, geographic region, salesperson, channel, and so on. In business-to-business contexts, the sales invoice is a gold mine of information, usually containing all or part of the following information:

- Customer name and location

- Product(s) or service(s) sold

- Volume and dollar amount of the transaction

- Salesperson (or agent) responsible for the sale

- End use of the product sold

- Location of customer facility where product is to be shipped and/or used

- Customer's industry, class of trade, and/or channel of distribution

- Terms of sale and applicable discount

- Freight paid and/or to be collected

- Shipment point for the order

- Transportation used in shipment

At the retail level, register transaction receipts don't often contain this much information, but as we'll learn in later chapters, more and more companies are learning to

**primary source** The originating source of secondary data.

**secondary source** A source of secondary data that did not originate the data but rather secured them from another source.

**advocacy research** Research conducted to support a position rather than to find the truth about an issue.

gather increasing amounts of information about individual customers and their transactions with the firm. For one thing, it's relatively easy to track online transactions, tying them together by credit card numbers or customer numbers. And many customers voluntarily tie themselves to their purchases when they use shopping cards to receive discounts at various retailers.

There are lots of other useful sources of internal secondary data. Customer inquiries, complaints, or other communications can be filed away in a company's databases, whether they come in over the telephone, through e-mail, via online chats, forums or social media, or in person. Many companies routinely track customer satisfaction at the product level. Other documents provide different sorts of information. Some of these are listed in Exhibit 5.1.

Even something as simple as a product registration card can be used for marketing intelligence. Years ago, when the Skil Corporation launched a cordless power screwdriver, management was surprised to find that a substantial proportion of the new screwdrivers were being sold to elderly people, based on information obtained from registration cards. Although marketing managers had positioned the product for the "do-it-yourself" target market, the ease of use made the product attractive to older consumers. The company began advertising in publications targeting older Americans.[3]

## Exhibit 5.1 ▶ Some Useful Sources of Internal Secondary Data

| SOURCE | INFORMATION PROVIDED |
|---|---|
| Cash register receipts | • Type (cash or credit) and dollar amount of transaction by department by salesperson |
| Online account information | • Type (credit or online money transfers) and dollar amount of transaction by department by web/mobile entity |
| Location services | • Placement and time of mobile telephone use at retail outlets |
| Salesperson's call reports | • Customers and prospects called on (company and individual seen; planned or unplanned calls)<br>• Products discussed<br>• Orders obtained<br>• Customer's product needs and usage<br>• Other significant information about customers<br>• Distribution of salesperson's time among customer calls, travel, and office work<br>• Sales-related activities: meetings, conventions |
| Salesperson's expense accounts | • Expenses by day, by item (hotel, meals, travel, etc.) |
| Individual customer (and prospect) records | • Name and location and customer number<br>• Number of contacts by company salespersons (agents)<br>• Sales by company (in dollars and/or units, by product or service, by location of customer facility)<br>• Customer's industry, class of trade, and/or trade channel<br>• Estimated total annual usage of each product or service sold by the company<br>• Estimated annual purchases from the company of each such product or service<br>• Location (in terms of company sales territory) |
| Financial records | • Sales revenue (by products, geographic markets, customers, class of trade, unit of sales organization, etc.)<br>• Direct sales expenses (similarly classified)<br>• Overhead sales costs (similarly classified)<br>• Profits (similarly classified) |
| Credit memos | • Returns and allowances |
| Warranty cards | • Indirect measures of dealer sales<br>• Customer service |

> Even something as simple as a product registration card can be used for marketing intelligence.

With our definition and overview of secondary data out of the way, we're ready to shift our attention to the systems approach to marketing research. These systems use a great deal of internal secondary data in the process of helping marketing managers make more informed decisions.

## 5-2  The Systems Approach

Much of the information that marketing managers need for decision making is predictable, can be organized inside a company's database systems, and can be made readily available to managers on an ongoing basis. This is the big advantage of the systems approach over the project approach: Current information needed for normal operations is available when managers need it. The big disadvantage of the systems approach? Managers are limited to the information available in the database.

### 5-2a  THE EVOLUTION AND DESIGN OF INFORMATION SYSTEMS

The earliest attempts at providing a steady flow of information for marketing managers (the candlelight glow of the systems approach versus the flashlight beam of the project approach) were **marketing information systems (MIS)**. An MIS data system produces regular, standardized reports based on data held in an organization's database(s). The key word in this definition is *regular,* because the emphasis in an MIS is to produce information on a steady basis. Once an MIS is designed and implemented, managers receive regular reports as they are issued and distributed.

**marketing information system (MIS)**
A set of procedures and methods for the regular, planned collection, analysis, and presentation of information for use in making marketing decisions.

**decision support system (DSS)**
A system that combines data, models for guiding decisions, and a user interface that allows users to interact with the system to produce customized information.

The trick, of course, is to identify, in advance, the data that managers will need and to ensure that those data get in the system. An MIS is only as good as its design.

Most of the data managers need for the ongoing management of an organization are fairly straightforward, especially when the marketing environment is stable. As a result, under normal circumstances, an MIS—with its standardized reports—is sufficient. Managers receive information they need, make decisions based on that information, and the organization moves forward. The information from daily, weekly, or monthly reports inform the standard operations of the firm. What happens, however, when the marketing environment is more dynamic and managers need data at irregular intervals or need to drill down more deeply into the available data?

The next generation of information systems offered managers greater access to the information held in a company's database. In contrast to an MIS, which emphasizes standardized reports at regular intervals, a **decision support system (DSS)** includes software that allows managers to more fully employ the available information to assist in making decisions. A DSS system combines data, models for guiding decisions, and a user interface that allows users to interact with the system to produce customized information. Thus, besides storing information and producing standardized reports, the DSS allows managers to access the database and to produce the information they need, when they need it. The DSS includes models for analyzing the data in the system—for example, creating tables or graphs of key data and seeing how a forecast changes when assumptions change.

Good information systems thus have two key outputs: (a) the standardized, up-to-the-minute reports needed for day-to-day operations and (b) custom reports that can easily be produced by managers when needed. In addition, the information system should incorporate features that make it easy to use in an interactive mode by people who aren't tech savvy. These include

## Manager's Focus

We have emphasized several times how important it is for you to learn how to evaluate the quality of marketing research information. You should make use of secondary data when they are available and relevant to your marketing efforts. However, you should *never* use secondary data without first scrutinizing its quality. At times, managers can be too trusting of secondary data, assuming its quality must have been verified before it

was put into the decision support system or published. The knowledge about research methods you acquire from this book will enable you to better judge the appropriateness of the methods originally used to generate the secondary data. When you have the expertise to make these assessments, you can have much greater confidence as you make decisions based on the vast array of market intelligence available.

graphical interfaces and menu-driven procedures for analyzing results. For example, Exhibit 5.2 provides an example of a **marketing dashboard**, which is one way of visually presenting relevant marketing information to a manager. Meant to approximate an automobile's dashboard, a marketing dashboard is designed to provide interactive visualization of a company's key summary measures. Note from the exhibit the wide range of information available to the manager. The standardization allows for a quick snapshot of current results. Just as important, the data can be rearranged, broken down by various variables, or otherwise "drilled down" in real time by a manager who needs more information. Again, this ability to interact with the system to create customized information is the true value of a decision-support system.

**marketing dashboard** A visual display of relevant marketing information designed to provide interactive access to a company's key marketing metrics.

Ideally, the information system will provide the intelligence that marketers need for making decisions. To accomplish this, system designers start with a detailed analysis of each decision maker who might use the system. They attempt to understand each manager's decision-making responsibilities, capabilities, and style. They identify the types of decisions each decision maker routinely makes, the types of information needed to make those decisions, the types of information the individual receives regularly, and the special studies that are needed periodically. The analysis also considers the improvements decision makers would like in the current information system, not only in the types of information they receive, but also in the form in which they receive it. Next, systems designers specify the data to be input into the system, how to secure and store the data, how to access

**Exhibit 5.2 ▶ Example of a Marketing Dashboard**

and combine the data, and what the report formats will look like. Only after these analysis and design steps are completed can the system be constructed. Programmers write and document the programs, making data retrieval as efficient as possible in terms of computer time and memory. When all the procedures are debugged, it is put online so managers with authorized access can view the dashboards or request reports.

## 5-2b CUSTOMER RELATIONSHIP MANAGEMENT

One of the most important uses of a DSS in marketing is customer relationship management. **Customer relationship management (CRM)** refers to a system that attempts to gather all relevant information about a company's customers—everything from demographic data to sales data to service records and more. The goal is to better understand customers' needs and behaviors and to put this information in the hands of those who interact with customers. Numerous companies have developed sophisticated software packages for handling the technical side of CRM; in fact, the software has become the focus of CRM for many people. The better understanding, however, is that CRM is a process designed to aid marketers in identifying and solving customer needs. The software supports this function and can be part of the larger DSS of the organization. Research Window 5.2 provides more information about CRM.

> **customer relationship management (CRM)** A system that gathers all relevant information about a company's customers and makes it available to the employees that interact with the customers.

---

## research window 5.2

### CRM Definition and Solutions

#### What is CRM?

Customer Relationship Management, or CRM, is a strategy used to learn more about customers' needs and behaviors in order to develop stronger relationships with them. Good customer relationships are at the heart of business success. There are many technological components to CRM, but thinking about CRM in primarily technological terms is a mistake. The more useful way to think about CRM is as a strategic process that will help you better understand your customers' needs and how you can meet those needs and enhance your bottom line at the same time. This strategy depends on bringing together lots of pieces of information about customers and market trends so you can sell and market your products and services more effectively.

#### What is the goal of CRM?

The idea of CRM is that it helps businesses use technology and human resources to gain insight into the behavior of customers and the value of those customers. With an effective CRM strategy, a business can increase revenues by:

- providing services and products that are exactly what your customers want

- offering better customer service

- cross selling products more effectively

- helping sales staff close deals faster

- retaining existing customers and discovering new ones

#### That sounds rosy. How does it happen?

It doesn't happen by simply buying software and installing it. For CRM to be truly effective, an organization must first understand who its customers are and what their value is over a lifetime. The company must then determine what the needs of its customers are and how best to meet those needs. For example, many financial institutions keep track of customers' life stages in order to market appropriate banking products like mortgages or IRAs to them at the right time to fit their needs.

Next, the organization must look into all of the different ways information about customers comes into a business, where and how this data is stored, and how it is currently used. One company, for instance, may interact with customers in a myriad of different ways, including mail campaigns, web sites, brick-and-mortar stores, call centers, mobile sales force staff and marketing and advertising efforts. CRM systems link up each of these points. This collected data flows between operational systems (like sales and inventory systems) and analytical systems that can help sort through these records for patterns. Company analysts can then comb through the data to obtain a holistic view of each

*(continued)*

## research window 5.2   (*continued*)

customer and pinpoint areas where better services are needed. For example, if someone has a mortgage, a business loan, an individual retirement account (IRA), and a large commercial checking account with one bank, it behooves the bank to treat this person well each time it has any contact with him or her.

### Are there any indications of the need for a CRM project?

You need CRM when it is clear you don't have an accurate view of who your customers are and what their needs or desires are or will be at any given stage in their lives. If you are losing customers to a competitor, that's a clear indication that you should improve your understanding of your customers.

### How long will it take to get CRM in place?

It depends. If you decide to go with a hosted CRM solution from an application service provider and you are planning to use the software for a specific department like sales, the deployment should be relatively quick—perhaps 30 to 90 days. However, if you are deploying either a hosted application or an on-premise package (involving the purchase of software licenses upfront) on an enterprise-wide basis (that involves different departments like sales, marketing, and operations), you should expect the implementation and training to take months, if not years. The time it takes to put together a well-conceived CRM project depends on the complexity of the project and its components and how well you manage the project.

### How much does CRM cost?

Again, it depends. A hosted sales automation application can cost from $65 to $150 a month for a basic sales automation package. If you want more sophisticated functionality and a greater level of support, you pay a lot more. An enterprise on-premise CRM package can cost anywhere between several thousand to several millions of dollars, depending again on how many functions you purchase and how many computers or "seats" have access to the software. For instance, one company or department might purchase an e-mail marketing management application or a sales force automation application, while a larger firm might want to purchase an integrated package that includes a database as well as applications for marketing, sales,

and customer service and support (via call centers and online). Obviously, the integrated software package is much more expensive.

### What are the keys to successful CRM implementation?

- Develop your customer-focused strategy first before considering what kind of technology you need.

- Break your CRM project down into manageable pieces by setting up pilot programs and short-term milestones. Start with a pilot project that incorporates all the necessary departments but is small enough and flexible enough to allow tinkering along the way.

- Make sure your CRM plans include a scalable architecture framework. Think carefully about what is best for your enterprise: a solution that ties together "best of breed" software from several vendors via web services or an integrated package of software from one vendor.

- Don't underestimate how much data you might collect (there will be *lots*) and make sure that if you need to expand systems you'll be able to.

- Be thoughtful about what data is collected and stored. The impulse will be to grab and then store *every* piece of data you can, but there is often no reason to store data. Storing useless data wastes time and money.

### What causes CRM projects to fail?

Many things. From the beginning, lack of a communication between everyone in the customer relationship chain can lead to an incomplete picture of the customer. Poor communication can lead to technology being implemented without proper support or buy-in from users. For example, if the sales force isn't completely sold on the system's benefits, they may not input the kind of demographic data that is essential to the program's success. One Fortune 500 company is on its fourth try at a CRM implementation because it did not do a good job at getting buy-in from its sale force beforehand and then training sales staff once the software was available.

---

**Source:** Excerpted from Wailgum, T. (2007, Mar. 6). "CRM definition and solutions." Retrieved from www.cio.com

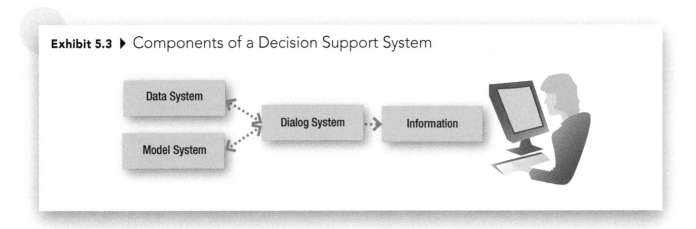

**Exhibit 5.3 ▶** Components of a Decision Support System

## 5-3 Components of Decision Support Systems

As noted above, MIS and DSS have evolved into useful tools for marketing decision makers. Let's focus a bit more attention now on the various parts of a DSS. There are three basic components of a DSS: (1) the data system, (2) the model system, and (3) the dialog system. All three components can be seen in Exhibit 5.3; using these three components yields managerial information as shown to the right of the figure. Further explanation of the components themselves is provided in the following sections.

### 5-3a THE DATA SYSTEM

The **data system** in a DSS includes the processes used to capture and store data coming from marketing, finance, and manufacturing, as well as information coming from any number of external or internal sources. The typical data system has modules containing customer information, general economic and demographic information, competitor information, and industry information, including market trends.

> **data system** The part of a decision support system that includes the processes used to capture and the methods used to store data coming from a number of external and internal sources. It is the creation of a database.

The growth in computing power and the emergence of increasingly sophisticated data processing capabilities have led to the development of huge databases within companies. In the past, a business's databases were limited to relatively current information; many new ones contain historical information as well. At this point, companies are capturing any and all data possible, even when they don't know how they may eventually use the data. Walmart has developed a data warehouse to store over 1 petabyte of online data (a petabyte equals a little over 1 million gigabytes), according to Stephen O'Sullivan, senior director of global e-commerce at WalmartLabs. The company, which has been notoriously secretive about its data, won't disclose the size of the larger warehouse holding transaction data from its 11,600-plus stores in 27 countries, but O'Sullivan did note that there is "a lot more data" compared with the online warehouse.[4] The company uses the information to select products that need replenishment, analyze seasonal buying patterns, examine customer buying trends, select markdowns, react to merchandise volume and movement, and more.

As the number of commercial databases and corporate information systems has expanded, so too has public concern over the issue of privacy. The concern is twofold: First, to what degree is an individual's right to privacy being violated in the generation and sharing of these databases? When people register on online merchant sites or apply for store shopping cards, they usually agree to allow the company to collect certain data about them (even if they don't read the fine print). But what about companies that track your shopping behaviors on their web sites by logging the IP address of your computer or companies that connect your shopping in their brick-and-mortar stores by tying together purchases made with the same credit card number? You might be amazed at what companies can know about you and your behavior. To the degree that companies use this information to deliver more and better products and services that meet your particular needs, this is probably a good thing. Sharing information with others, though, begins to raise concerns for many people.

The second concern for us with companies maintaining data about their customers is the ability to safeguard the data from those who would use the information for illegal purposes. Research Window 5.3 describes common ways that criminals might gain access to private information held in company databases—and not all of these can be blamed on the company's lack of security. In several cases, consumers themselves allow their private information to be compromised. As even well-known companies like Amazon, eBay, and Apple's iCloud fall victim to security breaches, data security will continue to be a critical issue for information system managers.[5]

## Manager's Focus

Market orientation is an organizational culture of generating and disseminating market intelligence and responding appropriately to that intelligence. The key to success, however, is performing these processes on an organization-wide basis. One of your responsibilities as a marketing manager is to create a culture in which all key personnel recognize and fulfill their responsibilities of continually gathering relevant market intelligence and entering it into the organization's system. Many boundary-spanning employees obtain a wealth of valuable information through regular interaction with current or prospective customers, but all too often they are not given adequate incentives to make this information available to others in the organization. We once observed a large company, for example, that commissioned a marketing research study to reproduce some essential market intelligence that its sales representatives already possessed but were not disseminating to decision makers. Conducting marketing research is both expensive and time consuming and should be avoided when the needed information can be obtained more quickly and at a fraction of the cost from existing sources within the organization.

Assuming that the privacy of the database can be assured, the key criterion for adding a particular piece of data to a database is whether it is useful for making decisions. The basic task of a DSS is to capture relevant marketing data in reasonable detail and to put those data in a truly accessible form. It is crucial that the database management capabilities built into the system are able to organize the data in the way that a particular manager needs it.

**model system**
The part of a decision support system that includes all the routines that allow the user to manipulate the data so as to conduct the kind of analysis the individual desires. It is the collection of analytical tools to interpret the database.

### 5-3b  THE MODEL SYSTEM

The **model system** in a DSS includes all the computerized routines that allow the user to do the analyses that he or she wants. Whenever managers look at data, they have a preconceived idea of how something works and, therefore, what is interesting and worthwhile in the data. Most managers also want to manipulate data to gain a better understanding of a marketing issue. Routines for manipulating the data can range from summing a set of numbers to conducting a complex statistical analysis to finding an optimization strategy using some kind of nonlinear programming routine. Still, the most common procedures are the simple ones: counting the cases that fall into different groups; summing, averaging, computing ratios; building tables; and so on.

The BayCare Health System, an alliance of not-for-profit community hospitals in west central Florida, developed a DSS designed to provide

## Manager's Focus

Managers are sometimes too quick to file away marketing research reports once the current information need has been met. These managers fail to recognize how these reports can be a valuable source of internal secondary data when facing new business situations. Sometimes managers do this because they have taken "ownership" of the information and don't want to share it with other managers in the organization who might benefit from it when addressing various marketing issues. This tendency is particularly pronounced among managers who initiate marketing research studies to confirm what they believe to be true or to provide political cover for decisions they want to make or have already made. For example, in the middle of a project a client once told us, "I have already implemented my decision. If the results support what I did, I will broadcast them throughout the company. But, if they don't, I'll bury them so deeply nobody will ever see them."

When you are a manager and you commission marketing research studies, be sure to take the necessary steps to make certain your organization gets maximum benefit from its investment. Instead of squirreling away marketing research reports, you should work with the information technology staff to feed the findings into your information systems to make them available for use by anyone in your organization.

## research window 5.3

### Data Security Breaches: Selected Points of Focus and Incident Classification Patterns

**Phishing** A form of social engineering in which an attacker uses fraudulent electronic communication (typically an e-mail) to lure the recipient into divulging information. Most appear to come from a legitimate entity and contain authentic-looking content. The attack often incorporates a fraudulent web site component or malicious attachment.

**Credentials** Stolen credentials, hacking and malware actions refer to instances in which an attacker gains access to a system or device protected by username and password authentication.

**Web App Attacks** Exploitation of code-level vulnerabilities in a web application, including overcoming authentication mechanisms.

**Point-of-Sale Intrusions** Remote attacks on retail transactions, particularly point-of-sale terminals and card readers.

**Insider and Privilege Misuse** Unapproved or malicious use of firm resources by insiders (i.e., employees), outsiders (due to collusion with insiders), or partners (those granted privileges by insiders).

**Physical Theft and Loss** Any circumstance where an information asset is misplaced or missing whether accidentally or through malice.

**Crimeware** The involvement of financially motivated malware.

**Payment Card Skimmers** The implantation of skimming devices on payment systems like ATMs, gas pumps, point-of-sale terminals, and the like, for the purpose of reading magnetic stripe data from payment cards.

**Cyber-Espionage** Incidents undertaken by state-affiliated participants exhibiting espionage motives by gaining unauthorized access to networks and related systems.

**Source:** Excerpted from *2016 Data Breach Investigations Report*, Verizon, 2016, retrieved from www.verizonenterprise .com 17–20, A27–A52.

---

managers (corporate and medical) with key information for making decisions about specific health care programs for the communities it served. The system tracks a large number of indicators, ranging from community socio-economic indicators to behavioral risk factors, and it has been used to identify specific problem areas among the communities covered by the program. For example, several communities with unusually high levels of deaths due to stroke were identified. When follow-up research indicated the problem of lack of transportation among the elderly, minority, and low-income populations in these areas, a mobile medical unit was developed to deliver medical services and prevention/education services to the affected groups.[6]

Researchers are creating more sophisticated models for manipulating data, often for relatively specific purposes. For example, DSSs have been developed to enable brand managers to make better marketing-mix decisions for their brands, to help bankers make stronger credit management decisions, to guide managers when they make new product development decisions, to assess alternative marketing plans for motion pictures before they are released, and to match donor livers to the most suitable transplant patients.[7] New uses for modeling data to help make important decisions are being developed every day.

### 5-3c THE DIALOG SYSTEM

The element of a DSS that clearly separates it from an MIS is its **dialog system**, also called a language system. Dialog systems provide managers who are not programmers themselves with the user interface to explore databases by using analytical tools to produce reports that satisfy their own particular information needs. The reports might include tables or figures; individual managers can specify the format. The dialog systems are sometimes

**dialog system**
The part of a decision support system that permits users to explore the databases by employing the system models to produce reports that satisfy their particular information needs. It is the user interface of the decision support system, which is also called a language system.

## Manager's Focus

Having a superior information system can be instrumental to the success of an organization. Whether or not your future organization develops and implements an exceptional MIS or DSS will be as dependent on your actions as a marketing administrator as it will be on the efforts of the information technology staff. Specifically, *you* and the other marketing managers will need to (1) make the information system a strategic priority and (2) authorize the financial resources necessary to support a truly effective system.

Most businesses are relatively small, so you may become a manager in a smaller company with limited financial resources. If this is the case, will the principles presented in this chapter be applicable to you? We

believe the answer is an emphatic "Yes!" Managers in smaller companies often view the establishment of an MIS, much less a DSS, to be beyond their reach. Consequently, they make many decisions based on limited information, and many smaller businesses ultimately fail due to poorly conceived marketing strategies. Small business managers would be well advised to do what they can to establish an MIS, even if it does not rival the sophistication of those developed by large corporations. At a minimum, they should have one employee dedicated to systematically gathering relevant market intelligence and making it available in a useable format to the decision makers within the company.

---

menu driven, requiring only a few clicks of a mouse or a tap on a tablet screen. Regardless of how the manager interacts with the system, the point is that managers can do it themselves without relying on others to prepare the particular report that they need. This allows them to target the information they want and not be overwhelmed with irrelevant data. They can ask a question and then, on the basis of the answer, ask a subsequent question, and then another, and another, and so on.

> Dialog systems provide managers with the user interface to explore the databases.

As the availability of online databases and sophisticated model systems has increased, so too has the need for better dialog systems. Dialog systems put data at the decision maker's fingertips. While that sounds simple enough, it is actually a difficult task because of the large amount of data available, the speed with which they hit a company, and the variety of sources from which they come.

## 5-4  Knowledge Management

The level of sophistication in the design and uses of decision support systems opens up access to so much data that higher-level management of information becomes critical. An executive in charge of information can ensure that it is used in support of strategic thinking. In many

organizations, this function is now the responsibility of a chief information officer, or CIO.

The CIO's major role is to run the company's information and computer systems like a business. The CIO serves as the liaison between the firm's top management and its information systems department. He or she is responsible for planning, coordinating, and controlling the use of the firm's information resources and is much more concerned with the firm's outlook than with the daily activities of the department. CIOs typically know more about the business in general than the managers of the information system departments who are often stronger technically. In many cases, the managers of the information system department report directly to the CIO. Research Window 5.4 discusses the CIO's role at Domino's Pizza.

A growing number of companies are extending the idea of information systems management to include management of the knowledge that resides inside its employees' heads. Often referred to as organizational knowledge, one of an organization's greatest assets can be what its people know about customers, its products and processes, and its marketplace. However, few companies yet have a way to make that information widely available to those who can use it. **Knowledge management (KM)** is an effort to systematically collect organizational knowledge and make it accessible to others. Exhibit 5.4 offers an illustration of how knowledge management might work on the golf course.

When Arjan van Unnik, formerly head of knowledge management at Royal Dutch Shell, wanted to boost knowledge management, he sought the natural early

**knowledge management (KM)**

The systematic collection of employee knowledge about customers, products and processes, and the marketplace.

**Exhibit 5.4 ▶** Knowledge Management on the Golf Course

Think of a golf caddie as a simplified example of a knowledge worker. Good caddies do more than carry clubs and track down wayward balls. When asked, a good caddie will give advice to golfers, such as, "The wind makes the ninth hole play 15 yards longer." Accurate advice may lead to a bigger tip at the end of the day. On the flip side, the golfer—having derived a benefit from the caddie's advice—may be more likely to play that course again. If a good caddie is willing to share what he knows with other caddies, then they all may eventually earn bigger tips. How would knowledge management (KM) work to make this happen? The caddie master may decide to reward caddies for sharing their tips by offering them credits for pro shop merchandise. Once the best advice is collected, the course manager would publish the information in notebooks (or make it available on PDAs), and distribute them to all the caddies. The end result of a well-designed KM program is that everyone wins. In this case, caddies get bigger tips and deals on merchandise, golfers play better because they benefit from the collective experience of caddies, and the course owners win because better scores lead to more repeat business.

Source: Excerpted from Levinson, M. (2007, Mar. 7). "Knowledge Management Definition and Solutions." Retrieved from http://www.cio.com

adopters within the organization to help convince the others. He began promoting knowledge to employees, and about 20% really bought into the idea. "That gave us fertile ground to kick off the community," van Unnik commented. Over the first seven years of the knowledge management program, the proportion of employees participating in the system grew exponentially; over half the company's 30,000 employees had registered on the company's knowledge portal.

The usefulness of a knowledge management system depends on the willingness of company employees to share information. One means of promoting such sharing of information is to simply make the process as simple as possible. At Halliburton, employees can jot down insights using pencil and paper and pass them along to the knowledge management staff to be entered in the system. "This lowers the barrier of entry," according to Halliburton's director of knowledge management.

### 5-4a LIMITATIONS OF THE SYSTEMS APPROACH

At first, the systems approach was regarded as the solution for information problems inside the firm. The reality, however, often fell short of the promise. Effective MIS or DSS systems are often difficult to implement, for several reasons. People tend to resist change, and adding an information system can lead to lots of changes. Also, many decision makers don't want to tell others what factors they use and how they combine them to make decisions; without such disclosure, it is next to impossible to design systems that will give them the information they need.

Even when managers are willing to disclose their decision-making process and information needs, there are problems. Different managers often pay attention to different things and, thus, have different data needs. Very few formats are optimal for a variety of users. Either the developers have to design with "compromises" that are

satisfactory for most users, but not really best for anyone, or they have to customize the system to meet each manager's needs, one at a time.

The costs and time required to build information systems are often underestimated, because managers fail to grasp the size of the task and the changes in organizational structure, key personnel, and electronic data-processing systems that are required. By the time the information systems can be developed, the managers for whom they are designed have often moved on to other jobs or organizations, or the economic and competitive environments around which they were designed have changed. As a result, these information systems are sometimes out of date soon after implementation. In some cases, the whole process has to start all over again.

There is one final problem with the systems approach, and it's a big one: Managers are limited to the data available in the system. No matter how colorful the dashboard is or how easy the system is to use, if the right kinds of data are not collected in the first place, the system will be ineffective for guiding a current marketing decision. To some extent, this problem is unavoidable; managers are constantly learning new things and applying them to their businesses. Before we know the value of various kinds of information, it is unlikely that we will include them in our databases. Sometimes, however, limited data availability indicates that information systems managers may not have done a thorough job of identifying the kinds of data that managers need to make good decisions.

### 5-4b INTELLIGENCE GATHERING IN THE ORGANIZATION OF THE FUTURE

Although one might expect they would, the explosion in databases and the emergence of DSSs have not eliminated traditional marketing research projects for gathering

## research window 5.4

### *Insights from Kevin Vasconi, Executive Vice President and Chief Information Officer of Domino's Pizza*

For a CIO, data management is at the core of what they do. This is certainly true for Kevin Vasconi of Domino's. After a successful career in the automotive industry, Vasconi joined Domino's as it continues its push into online ordering and running 75% of its nearly 10,000 franchise's point-of-sales (POS) system through one global entry point.

A single, common, global POS entry has many advantages. First, it allows for greater efficiencies as individual franchise owners are not each setting up their own systems. This is no small issue with so many franchises and over such diverse geographic locations. Second, it allows for various parts of an operation—from e-commerce to supply chain—to be interconnected. This level of integration helps with everything from ordering to inventory management efficiencies. Third, and often overlooked, it allows for experimentation and testing.

On the e-commerce front, Domino's generates about 50% of sales transactions through online orders in the United States. Over 50% of all orders in Northern Europe, specifically the UK, Australia, Japan, and South Korea are received online. The growth drivers of this online ordering system are mobile devices where Domino's mobile apps for iPhone and Android are ranked either first or second in their respective e-commerce category. Given this growth, Domino's will experiment with promotions through what is called A/B testing to maximize this distribution channel.

For Domino's, this form of testing involves setting up two web sites; one (e.g., the "A") is its standard site while the other is a special promotion (e.g., the "B").

As consumers visit the web site, some see the standard offering, while others are directed to the special promotion. Click-stream and related behaviors, including purchase behavior, are then recorded and compared to see the customer impact of receiving a special offer or not.

Constant testing is important to ensure that these various mobile and online platforms function as intended. If an individual store experiences heavy call volume on a Friday or Saturday night, the e-commerce platform can handle the excess capacity better than an individual employee taking phone orders. At no time is this more evident than Super Bowl weekend, when Domino's has sold as many as 1.2 million pizzas (or 17 million slices). Prior to a big weekend, or even a Super Sunday, Domino's will test things like: Are credit cards transactions processing correctly? Is the mobile app set to receive orders without concern? All aspects of a CIO's IT department are investigated as a big pizza-buying event draws near.

The role of a CIO is relatively new compared to other C-suite functions like CEO, CFO, or COO, but Domino's is a perfect example of why they have become so important in such a short amount of time.

---

**Source:** "How Domino's runs a pizza 'IT war room,'" *The Financial Times.* Retrieved from https://www.ft.com /content/62eb7e35-eda0-3621-8de5-d70421f3a4fb? ft_site=next; Liddle, A. J. (2012, Oct. 12). "IT in 3: Domino's pizza CIO discusses strategy." Retrieved from http://www .nrn.com/latest-headlines/it-3-dominos-pizza-cio-discusses-it -strategy; "Domino's 101: Basic Facts." Retrieved from https://biz.dominos.com/web/public/about-dominos/fun-facts

---

marketing intelligence. For one thing, many of the project-oriented techniques discussed in this book are used to generate the information that goes into the databases that businesses use in their DSSs. Thus, the value of the insights gained from these databases depends directly on the quality of the underlying data, and users need to be able to assess their quality. For another, while DSSs provide valuable input for broad strategic decisions, allow managers to stay in tune with what is happening in their external environments, and serve as excellent early warning systems, they sometimes do not provide enough information about what to do in specific instances, such as when the firm is faced with introducing a new product, changing

distribution channels, evaluating a promotional campaign, and so on. When actionable information is required to address specific marketing problems or opportunities, the research project will likely continue to play a major role.

In sum, both traditional (or project-based) approaches and systems-based approaches to gathering information will always be important. In an increasingly competitive world, information is vital, and a company's ability to obtain and analyze information will largely determine its future. In the following chapters, we continue the discussion of systems-based approaches; in later chapters, we'll focus on gathering primary data through research projects.

# Summary

## Learning Objective 1

**Define the difference between secondary data and primary data.**
Secondary data are data that have already been collected, often for some other purpose or by some other organization. Primary data are data collected specifically for the investigation at hand.

## Learning Objective 2

**List the advantages and disadvantages of working with secondary data.**
The most significant advantages offered by secondary data are time savings and money savings for the researcher. Two disadvantages that commonly arise when secondary data are used are (1) they do not completely fit the problem and (2) they are not completely accurate.

## Learning Objective 3

**Define what is meant by a marketing information system (MIS) and a decision support system (DSS).**
A marketing information system is a set of procedures and methods for the regular, planned collection, analysis, and presentation of information for use in making marketing decisions. A decision support system combines data, models for guiding decisions, and a user interface that allows users to interact with the system to produce customized information.

## Learning Objective 4

**Identify the components of a decision support system.**
A decision support system has three major components: the data system, the model system, and the dialog system. The data system collects and stores data from internal and external sources. It creates the database. The model system consists of routines that allow the user to manipulate data in order to analyze them as desired. It is the analytical component. The dialog system serves as the user interface permitting marketers to use the system models to produce reports based on criteria they specify themselves. It is the output component.

## Learning Objective 5

**Discuss knowledge management.**
Some of an organization's greatest assets are what its people know about customers, its products and processes, and its marketplace. Knowledge management is an effort to systematically collect organizational knowledge from employees and make it accessible to others.

## Key Terms

secondary data (page 60)
primary data (page 60)
primary source (page 61)
secondary source (page 61)
advocacy research (page 61)
marketing information systems (MIS) (page 63)
decision support system (DSS) (page 63)
marketing dashboard (page 64)
customer relationship management (CRM) (page 65)
data system (page 67)
model system (page 68)
dialog system (page 69)
knowledge management (KM) (page 70)

## Review Questions

1. How does a project emphasis in marketing research differ from a systems emphasis?

2. What are the main advantages and disadvantages of secondary data? Do these apply equally to internal and external secondary data?

3. What are the main differences between a marketing information system and a decision support system?

4. In a decision support system, what is a data system? A model system? A dialog system? Which of these is most important? Why?

5. How does knowledge management expand the concept of an information system? What additional kinds of marketing intelligence can it provide?

# Endnotes

1. Aguirre, S. (2015, May 26). "We're seriously underestimating the virtual-reality market." *Recode*, Retrieved from http://www.recode.net/2015/5/26/11562926/were-seriously-underestimating-the-virtual-reality-market; Merel, T. (2015, April 6). "Augmented and virtual reality to hit $150 billion, disrupting mobile by 2020," *TechCrunch*, Retrieved from https://techcrunch.com/2015/04/06/augmented-and-virtual-reality-to-hit-150-billion-by-2020/

2. Goetzl, D. (1999, June 28). "Second magazine study touts value of DTC drug ads." *Advertising Age*, 22.

3. Wood, W. (1988, Sept.) "Targeting: It's in the cards, " *Marketing & Media Decisions*, 121–122.

4. Higginbotham, S. (2012, March 23) "WalmartLabs is building big data tools—and will then open source them." Retrieved from http://gigaom.com; Walmart store demographic information retrieved from http://stock.walmart.com

5. Perlroth, N. (2012, Jan. 18). "Web attacks may rattle consumers." *New York Times*. Retrieved from ProQuest.com

6. Studnicki, J., Murphy, F. V., Malvey, D., Costello, R. A., Luther, S. L., & Werner, D. C. (2002, Winter). "Toward a population health delivery system: First steps in performance measurement." *Health Care Management Review*, 76–95.

7. For more information, see Wierenga, B. & Van Bruggen, G. H. (2001, May–June). "Developing a customized decision-support system for brand managers." *Interfaces*, S128S145; Kanungo, S. Sharma, S., & Jain, P. K. (2001). "Evaluation of a decision support system for credit management Decisions," *Decision Support Systems*, 30, 419–436; Thieme, R. J., Song, M., & Calantone, R. J. (2000, Nov.). "Artificial neural network decision support systems for new product development project selection." *Journal of Marketing Research*, 499–507; Eliashberg, J., Jonker, J., Sawhney, M. S., & Wierenga, B. (2000, Summer). "MOVIEMOD: An implementable decision-support system for prerelease market evaluation of motion pictures." *Marketing Science*, 226–243; and Cruz-Ramirez, M., Herras-Martinez, C., Fernandez, J. C., Briceno, J., & de la Mata, M. (2012, Oct. 16). "Multi-objective evolutionary algorithm for donor-recipient decision system in liver transplants." *European Journal of Operational Research*. Retrieved from ProQuest.com

8. Paul, L. G. (2003, Dec. 1). "Why three heads are better than one (how to create a know-it-all company)." *CIO Magazine*. Retrieved from http://www.cio.com

9. Paul, L. G. "Why Three Heads Are Better Than One."

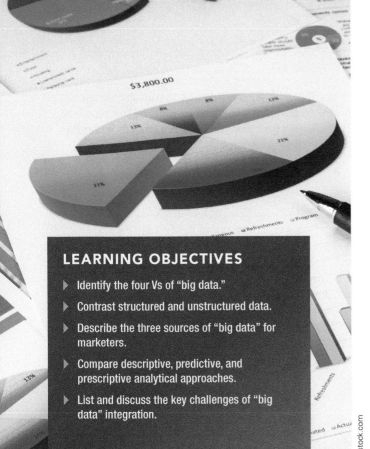

Billion Photos/Shutterstock.com

# CHAPTER 6

# Decision Support Systems: Working With "Big Data"

Rawpixel.com/Shutterstock.com

## [ INTRODUCTION ]

Most people have heard expressions like "looking for a polar bear in a snowstorm" or "finding a needle in a haystack." A snowstorm is distracting and chaotic, allowing even the largest polar bear to blend seamlessly into the white snow. A haystack is large and unorganized, making it easy for a small, narrow needle to remain hidden among the hay straws. So it is with big data. Companies are collecting data in incredible quantities. Transaction data at retail, location data on mobile devices, and click-stream data on web sites and apps, including social media platforms, are constantly being collected by firms worldwide. There are proverbial snowstorms and haystacks of data piling up in companies across the globe. The challenge: finding a big polar bear or tiny needle that provides insight to the data collector that competitors do not have.[1]

## 6-1   The Four Vs: Volume, Velocity, Variety, and Veracity

To begin, let's first establish a framework for understanding the key elements of big data. It is generally accepted that big data is multidimensional.[2] The first dimension is **volume**—the sheer amount of data being collected. To help demonstrate the volume dimension, let's consider some examples starting with daily Facebook activity. It has been estimated that we send 10 billion messages, click the Like button 4.5 billion times, and upload 350 million new pictures daily. This produces zettabytes of data. "How big is a zettabyte?" you might ask. One zettabyte can hold 250 billion DVDs. To look at it another way, the New York Stock Exchange (NYSE) collects about a terabyte of structured trading data every day.[3] A terabyte could hold 1,000 copies of *Encyclopedia Britannica*. So, Facebook's zettabytes dwarfs NYSE's terabyte activity everyday. If we consider all the data generated in the world between the beginning of time and the year 2000, it is the same amount we now generate every minute![4]

The second dimension—**velocity**—refers to the pace of data flow into and out of a firm. In some respects, velocity can ebb and flow by industry. For instance, banks and airlines have more data than firms in other industries due to the transactional nature of their businesses.[5] For them, it is difficult to keep pace with the inflow of data, the quality of the data, and the opportunity to make sense of it all. Walmart has data inflows of over 1 million customer transactions per hour. That's over 168 million per week or some 700 million per month! How do firms manage such massive data flows? When *The Economist* conducted a survey of business leaders regarding big data and asked how difficult it was to access their organizations' data in a timely manner, 55% of them said, "Difficult." In short, too much of a good thing can be overwhelming.

The third dimension—**variety**—might be the most challenging issue of all. Market researchers once were limited to whether or not survey questions were open-ended, allowing a respondent to answer freely, or closed-ended, providing a respondent with a set of possible responses and asking them to merely pick from among them. Open-ended responses may be difficult to interpret, but at least there's a straightforward process for doing so. The sources of big data are highly variable: Data can take the form of survey responses, transaction details, social media references, location data, or many other forms. By looking at examples, an analyst would generally know what to expect from survey data. Systems could be established to catalog and categorize survey data—and even transactional data—but it's a lot less clear how to analyze social media data, GPS location data, or the other new forms of data that are flooding into firms. Going forward, determining

**volume** The sheer amount of data being collected in "big data" systems.

**velocity** The pace of data flow, both into and out of a firm.

**variety** The combination of structured and unstructured data collected in "big data" systems.

**veracity** The accuracy and trustworthiness of data collected in "big data" systems.

**big data** The process of capturing, merging, and analyzing large and varied data sets for the purpose of understanding current business practices and seeking new opportunities to enhance future performance.

(1) which combinations of data are most valuable and (2) how the wide variety of data types might be combined are key challenges for marketing research analysts and information systems professionals.

> Data can take the form of survey responses, transaction details, social media references, location data, or many other forms.

Finally, data are potentially messy and filled with inaccuracies. Consider social media posts containing misspellings, nonuniform abbreviations, typos, slang terminology, and no general filter. This fourth and final dimension is referred to as the **veracity** of the data. The challenge of mistakes in the data is that they can breed mistakes in the information derived from analyzing these data. In such an instance, veracity would be low. The challenge then is developing high veracity—accurate and trustworthy—data sources and systems. That old chestnut of garbage in, garbage out still applies.

Taken together, to capture high volumes of data with great velocity, of high variety, and of unquestionable veracity is the essence of the phrase "big data." More specifically, we define **big data** as the process of capturing, merging, and analyzing large and varied data sets for the purpose of understanding current business practices and seeking new opportunities to enhance future performance. Big data is not just about generating the inputs but establishing the processes to yield insightful outcomes. Joe Solimando of Disney's Consumer Products group said it this way, "Big data calls for a lot more creativity in how you use data. You have to be way more creative about where you look for business value: If I combined this data with this data, what could it tell me?"[6]

## 6-2   The Fifth V: Value

A recent study of hundreds of C-level executives (e.g., Chief Executive Officers, Chief Operating Officers, Chief Information Officers), business unit leaders, and IT decision makers across 18 countries provided some interesting findings about business value in big data.[7] Here are some highlights:

- 91% report that they are already using tools to manage and analyze big data

- 75% report that their company will make additional investments to improve their ability to analyze data within the next 12 months

- 73% report that they have leveraged data to increase revenue

- 57% of those used data to increase an existing revenue stream

- 43% of those used data to create new revenue streams

These findings suggest that firms using big data are finding value in doing so. But before we delve too quickly into the increased revenue opportunities, let's take a quick look at the costs. Major software companies, including IBM and Microsoft, have spent more than $15 billion buying software firms specializing in data management and analytics.[8] In turn, they are selling these software solutions to other firms who are investing tens of millions of dollars to discover the value inherent in big data. Increasing revenue is one thing, but return on investment is quite another. So, to say that firms are finding value suggests that the increased revenue through existing revenue streams or the creation of new revenue streams makes the investment pay off. Consulting company McKinsey predicts that a retailer using big data to its fullest potential can increase operating margins by 60%.[9] Let's consider some examples of how firms in various industries have realized value.

### Improving Customer Retention Rates

Assurant is a financial services firm specializing in payment protection insurance. One of the main priorities of its call center is to retain customers calling to cancel insurance. In an industry where retention rates max out at 16%, it was important for Assurant to seek ways to keep more customers, especially its most profitable customers. Call center experts suggested that the best way to improve customer retention was to cut down on wait times. In fact, the goal was to answer 80% of customer calls in 20 seconds or less. A reduction in wait time, they said, was directly related to increased customer satisfaction. However, the data suggested an alternative. A minimal increase in wait times would allow for better call routing so that customers and customer service representatives could be better matched in terms of rapport and mutual understanding. Assurant implemented this increased wait time/call matching approach and achieved customer retention rates in the high 40% range.[10]

### Dealing With Negative Word of Mouth

Best Western International (BWI) manages over 4,000 hotels worldwide. Like many hotel chains, BWI solicits survey responses from guests following a hotel stay. As a part of this system, hotel managers are provided feedback once the survey responses have been analyzed and reported. But what if a guest posts a negative review via social media or a travel web site? Feedback between a guest and a hotel is one thing; publicly available reviews on a web site are quite another. To address this issue, BWI partnered with Medallia to create a system to harness this unsolicited, unstructured data.[11] If a guest leaves a negative review via Facebook, Twitter, or a travel site like TripAdvisor, the system collects the review, matches it to the specific hotel, and alerts the hotel manager of the review. The manager can then read the review and respond accordingly via the social media or travel site. The goal is to address the issue swiftly before any long-term damage is done.[12]

### Enhancing Health Care

Big data, its management, and its analysis must be done in a way that avoids perceptions of Big Brother. Kaiser Permanente understands this and has invested an estimated $6 billion for an integrated electronic health records system. According to Carol Cain, senior director of clinical information services for the Kaiser Permanente Care Management Institute, the issue isn't the health records but rather the data that can be captured, stored, managed, and analyzed from them. Such data leads to information that can identify and close gaps in health care. If an individual patient allows Kaiser to link its supermarket loyalty card to the system, the patient will not receive a warning message with the purchase of a candy bar, but will be helped with medication adherence once a prescription is filled. The system, currently home to 9 million patient health records, also works well on a group level. A recent discovery by the analytics department found a relationship between lack of access to parks and rates of obesity in Oakland, CA. As a response, Kaiser invested in building parks in some communities and partnered with schools and the YMCA to aid health through proactive lifestyle opportunities.[13]

### Reducing Carbon Footprints

One of the logical applications of big data at UPS was fleet optimization. With 19.1 million package and document deliveries daily and nearly 5 billion per year through its 108,000 vehicles, even small fleet changes make a big impact. Adjustments to delivery routes, reductions in engine idle time, and predictive vehicle maintenance leading to greater operating efficiency has saved UPS over 39 million gallons of fuel while also avoiding 364 million delivery miles. The next frontier? The UPS airplane fleet.[14]

### Creating Personalized Promotions

Major retailers have been realizing the value of big data for decades. Sears Holdings needed an opportunity to do the same. The good news: It collected huge amounts of customer, product, and promotion data. The bad news: The data were fragmented. Instead of having data centrally available, they were stored by brand—Sears data, Craftsman data, Lands' End data, and so on. Step one for Sears was to consolidate its various brands and the data collected from each to make data analysis more readily available and cross-branded. Step two was to maximize these new analytical results to create personalized promotions at the customer level. Now, Sears had always been able to generate personalized promotions, but each took about eight weeks. By that time, promotional effectiveness was unclear. Under this new system, the same promotions can be produced in one week or even faster and are much more precisely tailored to the current needs of the customer.[15] For an example of how another major retailer, Target, used personalized promotions, see Research Window 6.1.

## research window 6.1

### Target, Big Data, and You

**Bringing it all together: Guest ID**

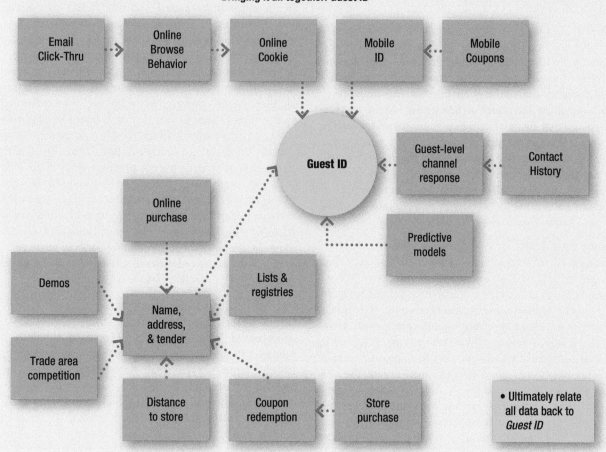

If you do much shopping at Target, there's a good chance that the Minneapolis-based retailer knows a lot more about you than you think they know—and a lot more than you may want them to know.

Several years ago, a group of marketing managers approached Andrew Pole, a statistician in the company's analytics group, with an interesting question. Would it be possible, they asked, to identify Target customers who were expecting babies based on the data about those customers held in the company's databases? For Pole, with graduate degrees in statistics and economics and a unique interest in using data to understand people and their behaviors, this was an intriguing challenge.

Why would Target marketing managers care so much about the family planning status of its female customers? It turns out that having a baby is such a life-altering event that even long-established purchase routines are interrupted. Not only do families with new babies need thousands of dollars' worth of baby food, clothes, furniture, formula, diapers, and the like, the presence of a new little one can change a lot of other shopping habits as well. Leisurely shopping trips to multiple stores to buy the *just perfect* foods, clothing, and household items are replaced with hurried visits to the nearest store that can provide *good enough* items to survive until the next shopping trip. And that's where Target comes in.

As a general retailer, Target offers products across a wide range of categories. Need a jar of baby food and a loaf of bread? No problem. How about freshly ground coffee (to battle sleep deprivation) and a box of detergent for cleaning baby's clothing? Target can handle those as well. There is great incentive for Target and other retailers to capture attention and change buying habits during this special time in a family's life.

Target is among the growing number of companies that have learned to use big data to their advantage. They just happened to get very good at it—thanks to Pole and his colleagues—well before most other companies did. Working with the treasure trove of data that millions of its customers provide on a daily basis, Target analysts identify patterns in the data that allow them to predict which customers will need particular kinds of products. Instead of developing "one-size-fits-all" promotional campaigns, Target wants to pinpoint its offerings at the individual or household level—and the analysis of big data allows them to do this with a high level of accuracy and success. What kinds of data? How does it work?

Starting a little over a decade ago, Target began building a vast data warehouse that assigned every shopper an identification code—known internally as the "Guest ID number"—that kept tabs on how each person shopped. When a customer used a Target-issued credit card, handed over a frequent-buyer tag at the register, redeemed a coupon that was mailed to them, filled out a survey, mailed in a refund, phoned the customer help line, opened an e-mail from Target, visited Target.com, or purchased anything online, the company's computers took note. A record of each purchase was linked to that shopper's Guest ID number along with information on everything else they'd ever bought.

Also linked to that Guest ID number was demographic information that Target collected or purchased from other firms, including the shopper's age, whether they were married or had kids, which part of town they lived in, how long it took them to drive to the store, an estimate of how much money they earned, if they'd moved recently, which web sites they visited, the credit cards they carried, and their home and mobile phone numbers (Duhigg, *The Power of Habit*, pp. 187–188).

So, just how well-informed is Target? Current estimates suggest that the company can tie about 50% of in-store purchases and virtually all of online purchases to particular customers. As illustrated in the figure below, which is from a presentation given by Andrew Pole, the key information connector is the Guest ID. Data from internal records and external sources are connected to the unique Guest ID.

Having the data is one thing; knowing what to do with them is another. This is why analysts such as Pole are in high demand. To develop an algorithm that would allow Target to assign a pregnancy likelihood score to the women in its database, Pole and his colleagues first examined very closely the purchases of women who had registered with Target's baby shower registry. (Expectant mothers sometimes register with Target or other retailers so that friends and family can purchase baby gifts identified by the parents and added to their wish lists. As part of the process of registering, women are asked to provide their due dates.) By analyzing these purchases, the statisticians were able to identify particular types of products that these mothers-to-be were purchasing at different stages of their pregnancies. For example, one analyst observed that women tended to begin purchasing more unscented lotions around the start of the second trimester. Soon, Pole was able to piece together a predictive analysis based on about 25 products that allowed him to predict which women were expecting, the stage of their pregnancies, and the approximate due date.

Armed with this information, Target applied the analysis to all the women in its database, calculating a pregnancy likelihood score for each. Soon they had a list of tens of thousands of women who were very likely pregnant. Because they could estimate the stage of the pregnancy, the company was able to accurately target the right kinds of promotional offers at the right times. Note that these were already Target customers; the goal was to get the women into the stores for a greater proportion of their purchases at a time when new purchasing habits were being developed.

How successful was the program? Target isn't going to share that information with the general public, but the company has seen substantial success over the past decade. And there's anecdotal evidence on the predictive accuracy of this particular program. One father was

(*continued*)

## research window 6.1 *(continued)*

incensed to learn that Target had sent his teen daughter advertisements for baby furniture and maternity clothing. Speaking with a store manager, he wondered aloud if the company was trying to encourage his daughter to get pregnant. When the store manager called the father back a few days later to apologize (again), the father sheepishly admitted that his daughter was indeed expecting, something he hadn't known earlier. Target did, however.

As with any predictive analysis, not all predictions are accurate, and sometimes the wrong promotions end up with the wrong people. At least one Target customer has mistakenly received the "We Heard You Said 'Yes'" brochure from Target with an invitation to register

with the company's wedding registry before he or she actually received a proposal.

**Source for illustration:** Avinash Kaushik, retrieved from https://plus.google.com/u/1/+avinash/posts/f5K1ueN9Tk1#+avinash/posts/f5K1ueN9Tk1 on October 27, 2012; see also Charles Duhigg, *The Power of Habit*, 2012, p. 189.

**Sources:** Charles Duhigg, *The Power of Habit*, 2012 (New York: Random House); Sean Deale, "Target's Predictive Analytics Misfires Again," April 17, 2012, downloaded from http://www.instoretrends.com/index.php/2012/04/17/target-marketing-wedding-misfire-blunder/on October 25, 2012; and Charles Duhigg, "How Companies Learn Your Secrets," *The New York Times*, February 16, 2012, downloaded from http://www.nytimes.com on February 20, 2012.

## 6-3 Marketplace Sources of "Big Data"

To this point, we have established what "big data" is and provided a few examples of how it has been used. Now, let's be more specific about the role of "big data" from purely business, marketing, and consumer insights perspectives. First, you should recognize that the potential for high volume, velocity, variety, veracity, and value of data are not limited to business markets. Data are infinitely available in many aspects of scientific and governmental endeavors. Fields as diverse as astronomy, biology, environmental sciences, genomics, meteorology, and physics collect massive amounts of data. The Big Data Research and Development Initiative established 84 different big data programs across six different federal government departments to explore important problems facing the US government.[16] Even so, our focus here is on business and, more specifically, marketing. For a look at how big data are reinvigorating the marketing function within organizations, we turn to Don Schultz, a leading observer (and sometime critic) of marketing research as commonly applied in industry (see Research Window 6.2).

Firms investing in the capture, storage, and analysis of large and varied data sets are forward-looking and cutting edge. While some companies have moved ahead in this process, the majority are at the beginning stages. To demonstrate, Exhibit 6.1 shows not only what the past has been for marketing researchers but also what the future holds as researchers seek greater consumer insights. Many of the topics listed in this exhibit, including observational

> **structured data**
> Data that can be written into rows on a spreadsheet or database based on standard column headings.

and survey data, will be discussed in later chapters. This discussion will begin by establishing a distinction between structured and unstructured data sources and continue with a description of several key sources of data. Clearly, some of these sources are not being fully used by most companies, but we, and others, predict they will be fully used in the not-too-distant future.

### 6-3a STRUCTURED DATA

Transactional data collected by banks, airlines, and retailers are easily structured. Think of **structured data** as filling in rows of data on a spreadsheet. The columns are labeled with headings, such as first name, last name, address, telephone number, purchase amount, model number purchased, and so forth. If a column heading can be described, a row entry can be written. This is far from new. When customers complete warranty cards, for instance, all their contact information as well as the purchase date and serial number of the product can be entered into a database. When a customer makes a purchase, the transactional information can also be written to a database. When a person completes profile information to join a social media site, the profile information can be written to a database. If it can be captured in rows and columns, it can be structured.

### 6-3b UNSTRUCTURED DATA

By contrast, if a blogger writes a movie review about the latest feature film to hit theaters or, better yet, a blogger films a movie review for her YouTube channel, how are

## research window 6.2

### The Decline and Resurgence of Marketing Research: An Interview With Don Schultz

*Don E. Schultz is professor emeritus-in-service, Department of Integrated Marketing Communications, at the Medill School, Northwestern University. He has received numerous teaching awards, worked with countless corporate clients, and was named by* Sales and Marketing Management *magazine as one of the most influential people in America.*

**Q: You've often been accused of saying that research has contributed to the decline of marketing's importance. Is that still true?**

It is true. I have been a frequent critic of market and marketing research, and I think you can only do that if you've been actively engaged in the area. And, I have been for nearly 40 years now. So yes, I do think that market research has often harmed marketing more than it has helped.

When modern marketing first began in the 1950s, academics and professionals alike bought into the 4Ps … that is, the belief that marketing systems could be codified as product, price, place (distribution), and promotion. If you got those four elements right, customers would magically appear on your firm's doorstep. Over the years, as the 4Ps gained more acceptance and appeal, an inside-out view of marketing developed. Market research contributed to that supply-chain, inside-out view of marketing by encouraging the belief that the marketer controlled the entire system and, thus, controlled customers. Customers or prospects were merely pawns in the grand "game of marketing." Since actual consumer marketplace behaviors were difficult to obtain, researchers built consumer behavior models that attempted to predict what consumers would do based on various marketing inputs and activities. Those models were mostly based on attitudinal data … that is, the belief that psychological variables such as awareness, attitudes, beliefs, and the like could be used to predict how customers would or should respond to various marketing activities. Since it was very difficult to measure actual consumer behaviors then, surrogates such as The Hierarchy of Effects model, positioning, AIDA (attention, interest, demand, and action), impact of exposure frequency, and the like were used to attempt to predict what consumers might do under various marketing or communication conditions. The marketing people,

having nothing better, bought into those models. These models were often complex, seemingly sophisticated, and required research people to develop and explain them. It was a "golden age of research," some might say.

The only problem, as soon as actual marketplace behavioral data became available that showed what consumers were actually doing, it became obvious that many of the models simply couldn't survive the light of day. They sounded good but often didn't produce the results for which they were intended. So, because marketers couldn't predict, much less measure marketplace results, senior managers began to question the entire process. And, since marketing had hooked its future primarily to the 4th P, promotion, if the advertising and promotion predictions couldn't be justified or measured, the credibility of the system began to be questioned. Marketing lost its seat at the strategy table. And, since market research was primarily a supplier to the marketing group, their influence declined as well.

That's still the case in many organizations today. Predictions don't pan out, so the predictors have no credibility and the systems they have developed are challenged.

**Q: You said market research was having a resurgence though. How is that happening?**

Over the past decade or so, actual marketplace consumer behavior has become more and more available. That has come from increasing amounts of actual consumer behavior in the form of scanner shopping panels, loyalty programs, the infamous "cookies" on computer streams, and the increasing interactivity of consumers and customers on the Internet and through other electronic systems. Today, consumers generate, and marketers are able to capture more and more actual consumer behavioral data. That has enabled a number of marketing organizations to move from "inside-out," that is one-way, outbound marketing and communication to "outside-in" interactive systems in which much more is known about individual customers i.e, what they saw, where they shopped, how they bought, all data that provides a better view of customers at the individual, rather than at the aggregate, level.

The increase in actual consumer behavioral data has enabled market researchers to move from prediction to

*(continued)*

# research window 6.2    (*continued*)

explanation. That's what we're now calling "customer insights." The research task becomes more of explaining why customers do what they do, than trying to predict what they might do in the future. These explanations, made available through new techniques, such as ethnography, neuroscience, and very complex consumer analytic algorithms, all have contributed to the new importance of market research within the organization. In truth, market research today is likely leading marketing and marketing activities rather than the other way around. In my view, that can only mean market and marketing research will become more, rather than less, important in the future.

**Q: That seems like a rather rosy picture of the future of market research. Is that your view now?**

While market research is gaining more importance now, there are some major issues that researchers are going to have to cope with, not tomorrow, but today. While researchers are capable of dealing with the current marketplace, there are three big areas of change that I think will impact them in the future.

One: Our research tools were all built to develop a "predictive" model of consumer behavior. We relied on attitudinal data in which the marketing organization controlled all the variables relevant in the 4Ps approach. Marketers controlled the product, the pricing, the distribution, and even the promotion. If you control all the variables, prediction becomes much easier. But, when you don't control them, as we are increasingly seeing in the interactive marketplace, prediction becomes almost impossible and explanation takes the lead. But, market researchers have not developed the explanatory tools that are necessary today. They have continued to refine the predictive tools of the past. In short, market researchers are going to need a whole new toolbox of research techniques including such things as network models, massive database analytic tools, longer-term explanatory models, rather than simple input and return methodologies that are in place today.

Two: We'll need new data-gathering techniques. Historically, the individual survey form has been the research technique of choice. That works well when individual decisions drive consumer behavior but, in communal societies, such as China, India, Brazil, Indonesia, and the like, it is the group that is important,

not the individual. Plus, people in emerging markets are not accustomed to being questioned or surveyed. They often refuse the interview and, when the interview is granted, their answers often reflect more of a desire to please the interviewer rather than to provide a relevant answer. And, increasingly, neural science is challenging the entire "questionnaire" approach to market research. That means market research people of the future must be better at listening than talking. Data is all around us. People are talking continuously on the Internet and through social media. Researchers must improve their "listening skills" by scraping the Web, building up communities of like-minded consumers, generating web-based "opinion posts," and the like. Unobtrusive and customer-volunteered data are the key research concepts for the future but they are only nascent today.

Three: Re-thinking statistical analysis and quantitative research. Today, almost every research tool is based on trying to fit responses into a normal curve. To find the mean, mode, and median. The "big middle group" that supposedly signifies a "relevant" market. That's because today, market research is focused on breaking down the total market into groups that would be what are called "markets," i.e., Moms, car buyers, obese people, Millennials ... in short, marketer aggregated groups that would be suitable for efficient marketing efforts. Increasingly, however, we're learning that the market is made up of individuals, all unique, all different, all with their unique needs, desires, and requirements. When we start to think of people rather than markets, all our statistical tools become quite limited, if not obsolete. The "normal curve" is no longer relevant. Mashing everyone together is no longer the primary goal of research. That simply means we will need new analytical forms and formats to deal with people in all their variations and aberrations. People, not markets, will be the critical element in the future for market research.

**Q: That sounds like market research has a great future. Are you advising students to enter this field rather than the managerial areas such as product or brand management, advertising agencies, or the media?**

Yes, definitely. I believe we are entering another "golden age" of market and marketing research. If you're curious, creative, and want to invent the future, market research is probably the best place to be in marketing.

**Exhibit 6.1  ▶  Sources of Data by Era**

| | HISTORICAL ERA | CURRENT ERA | FUTURE ERA |
|---|---|---|---|
| Data Type | • Survey Data | • Survey Data | • Personal and Mechanical Observational Data |
| | • Personal Observational Data | • Personal and Mechanical Observational Data | • Social Data |
| | • Limited Transactional Data | • Transactional Data | • Mobile Data<br>• Omni-channel Transactional Data<br>• Survey Data |
| Data Format | • Structured | • Structured and Some Unstructured | • Structured and Unstructured |
| Data Lag Time | • Weeks to Months | • Days to Weeks | • Real Time to Days |
| Data Volume | • Low | • Medium to High | • Extremely High |
| Data Velocity | • Low Flow | • Medium to High Flow | • High Flow |
| | • Inward | • Inward and Outward | • Inward and Outward |
| Data Variety | • Low | • Medium to High | • High |
| Data Veracity | • Medium to High | • Medium | • Low to Medium |
| Data Analytics | • Descriptive | • Descriptive and Predictive | • Descriptive and Real-Time Predictive |

the contents of the review captured? This simple illustration attempts to make a clear distinction between structured and **unstructured data**, or data that take the form of social media comments, blog posts, other text-based communication, photos, video, audio, or any other form that is not easily arranged in structured format. While writing the movie review, the blogger certainly isn't filling in the blanks on an online form, so her remarks do not fit nicely in the rows and columns of a spreadsheet or database. As media elements like photos, video, and audio are introduced, the challenge only escalates. However, this is the challenge marketers must face and overcome, and insights come in a wide variety of forms.

**unstructured data**
Data that take the form of social media comments, blog posts, other text-based communication, photos, video, audio, or any other form that is not easily arranged in structured format.

**social data**
Unstructured data available from social media and social networking Web-based platforms.

### Social Data

Much attention is given to social media and networking tools such as Facebook, Twitter, Google+, YouTube, Instagram, LinkedIn, Tumblr, Snapchat, Pinterest—and whatever latest, greatest social media platform has emerged since we wrote this chapter. While the appeal of social media and networking is staggering, there are two areas that stand out above the rest: (1) the Voice of the Customer (VoC)

impact[17] and (2) the establishment of a customer's social networks. VoC data are largely *unstructured* posts on social media networks that can inform managers of customers' experiences and expectations, demographics, psychographics, their likes, dislikes, and anything they elect to willfully share. If a customer offers an unrequested opinion about a product or service via social media, that word-of-mouth communication—whether positive, negative, or neutral—has greater reach and longevity than traditional forms of word-of-mouth. The reach component is especially true if the customer has an extensive social network in place. These peer-to-peer (P2P) or consumer-to-consumer (C2C) social network communities provide a great deal of insight not only into the nature of connections but also into who leads and who follows.

Social network analysis is a popular tool for studying social connections. Designed as a hub-and-spoke system, the leader is identified as a system hub, while multiple followers are nodes on the spokes. The more spokes any hub contains, the more influence that leader has within the social network. According to Accenture, "The unprecedented adoption of social networking is spawning a breed of super-influencers who can make or break a product, service or brand in record time. More than two-thirds of consumers search and read about brands on social media sites."[18] Companies that have harnessed the ability to listen to customers' voices have a data-driven advantage relative to competitors.

> Social networking is spawning a breed of super-influencers who can make or break a product, service or brand in record time.

### Mobile Data

Currently, almost 70% of all US adults have mobile access to the Web through either a smartphone or tablet computer.[19] While tablet computing is newer, smartphones have greatly increased market penetration. Although people primarily use these phones for texting (to communicate with members of their social networks) and taking photos (to share via social media), there is a growing trend of mobile phone use during in-store shopping. During the most recent holiday season, 76% of US residents used their mobile devices for seasonal shopping, and 84% planned to search Amazon.com before shopping or purchasing elsewhere.[20] The web sites or apps hosting the pricing and product review information can capture that the queries are coming from mobile devices as opposed to desktop or laptop computers. This insight has a role to play in web site design (e.g., optimizing for mobile use via faster loading) and potential redirection of mobile searchers to mobile mirror sites instead of the main search site.

Another important component of mobile data is location-based services. Mapping services, location sharing, and location data from call records open the possibility of location-based marketing in real time. In 2010, Starbucks and L'Oreal were the first brands to test location-based messaging with consumers in the United Kingdom who received geo-targeted text messages. The program was designed to set up an opportunity for the over 1 million British consumers who opted -in to be reached when they were within the more than 800 *geofences* created for Starbucks across Britain. Participants who entered a particular geofence received a mobile coupon for Starbucks if they had expressed an interest in food and drink at the time of signing up. Early data indicated that 65% of customers who were part of the program made a Starbucks purchase; 60% found the location-based messages to be "cool and innovative."[21]

### Omni-Channel Transactional Data

If you're interested in purchasing a simple product like a SD card for quick electronic storage, you have many options. You can visit a consumer electronics store. You can search for SD cards on a retail web site using your home computer and purchase online—and then decide if you'd like to pick it up at the store or have it mailed to you. You can follow

**mobile data**
Both structured and unstructured data available from mobile telephones, including smartphones and other mobile devices like tablet computers.

**omni-channel transactional data**
A collective term for all the different purchasing options a consumer has available, including store-based retailers, e-commerce sites, mobile purchasing, in-store pickup, home delivery, and so on.

an e-mail message from a retailer on your mobile phone to a discount on an SD card and then purchase it on your mobile device. The options seem endless. Brick-and-mortar, e-commerce, mobile, in-store pick-up, home delivery—welcome to omni-channel retailing.[22] Retailers such as Apple and Best Buy recognize that transactional data is available at each of these purchase points. If you are at an Apple Store and use the same credit card that is registered with your iTunes account, your in-store purchase behavior is linked to your Web-based purchase behavior. If you elect to receive news and other iTunes information via your Apple ID, your e-mail address and iPhone number are linked to your credit card. Said differently, data in one context is linked to data in another context, and another, and another, until Apple gets a 360-degree view of your purchasing patterns. This allows the company to provide individualized messages to you based on your purchase history at any of its many storefronts.

## 6-4 Big Data Analysis

One big data story has been told and retold to the point that we probably should not repeat it … but here we go anyway. The story, legend has it, originated in the *Financial Times of London* in the mid 1990s. At its core, it's a simple story: A large US supermarket chain discovered, through analyzing a large transactional data set, that when customers bought diapers they also bought beer. To exploit this relationship, the chain moved the beer next to the diapers on the shelf to support or even enhance the buying pattern. As is true with most legendary stories, the more the tale was retold, the taller the tale became. Customers became men in general then young fathers specifically. Afternoon purchases morphed into after-work purchases from one day a week to two; light shopping on Thursdays, weekly shopping on Saturdays. There was even a reason given for the relationship: Young fathers deserved a reward for their willingness to buy diapers and spend the weekend with their infants.

Now, this was not a typical combination, like milk and breakfast cereal, for example, an unsurprising purchase relationship; here were two things that did not logically fit together. The legend grew, as did a group of naysayers. Some said the reason the investigation began in the first place was based on observations by convenience store clerks. Others said it was made up to sell data analysis products and services, while still others said they could also find such a relationship but it was so weak that it was not worth mentioning. To ultimately put the issue to rest, here are the facts (as we understand them): A group at Teradata analyzed 1.2 million single ticket transactions from 25 Osco Drug stores. The analysis uncovered that between 5:00 and 7:00 p.m. consumers bought beer and diapers. Osco management was made aware of this relationship, knew that moving the beer closer to the diapers was an alternative, but elected not to move the products together on the store shelves. So, big data analysis did find a relationship but management chose not to exploit it. Sometimes truth is duller than legend.[23]

This is but one example of how analytical techniques can be applied to large data sets to describe consumer behavior, predict future consumption actions, or prescribe courses of action for a firm and its management. Exhibit 6.2 provides another example. This exhibit contains a psychographic profile of people who have "liked" Frito-Lay on Facebook. The analysis is based on millions of Facebook users worldwide who allow their data to be shared with MicroStrategy's Wisdom analysis software. The results, which can be

**Exhibit 6.2** ▶ Psychographic Profiles of Frito-Lay "Fans" in Wisdom Professional

| PROFILE | FANS | % | AFFINITY |
|---|---|---|---|
| Deal Hunters | 7,246 | 11% | 10.9 |
| Budget Shoppers | 9,641 | 15% | 9.8 |
| Game Lovers | 28,047 | 44% | 8.4 |
| Pet Lovers | 8,272 | 13% | 8.4 |
| Politics—Republicans | 8,531 | 13% | 7.1 |
| Do-It-Yourselfers | 10,282 | 16% | 6.6 |
| Parents of Young Kids | 3,227 | 5% | 6.3 |
| Social Activists | 28,159 | 44% | 4.1 |
| Brand Conscious | 9,431 | 15% | 4.0 |
| Health and Beauty Conscious | 20,515 | 32% | 3.9 |
| Politics—Democrats | 9,217 | 15% | 3.6 |
| Car Lovers | 9,000 | 14% | 3.6 |
| TV Fans | 25,457 | 40% | 3.3 |
| Food Lovers | 18,081 | 28% | 3.2 |
| Travel Lovers | 17,656 | 28% | 3.1 |
| Techies | 8,406 | 13% | 3.1 |
| Religious People | 6,168 | 10% | 2.7 |
| Comedy Lovers | 6,266 | 10% | 2.4 |
| Movie Lovers | 17,320 | 27% | 2.4 |
| Music Lovers | 18,236 | 29% | 2.0 |
| Outdoor Enthusiasts | 4,056 | 6% | 1.9 |
| Brides-To-Be | 1,517 | 2% | 1.8 |
| Sports Lovers | 12,186 | 19% | 1.6 |
| Book Lovers | 8,458 | 13% | 1.5 |
| Art Connoisseurs | 7,098 | 11% | 1.3 |
| Party-goers | 764 | 1% | 1.0 |
| Frequent Travelers | 1,010 | 2% | 1.0 |
| Environmentally Aware | 157 | 0% | — 1.1 |

Source: From report produced on October 18, 2012, using Wisdom Professional, courtesy of MicroStrategy.

prepared for just about any brand or organization within seconds, provide a snapshot view of how the brand or organization is being evaluated among various lifestyle categories. Over 7,000 people (about 11% of the Frito-Lay fans in the overall data set at the time the data were pulled) could be characterized as "deal hunters" based on their Facebook activity. "Affinity" reflects the attachment of the different psychographic categories to Frito-Lay relative to everyone in the Wisdom database. Deal hunters were 10.9 times more likely to "like" Frito-Lay than the overall population.

Below we provide further examples of different analytic approaches. While these sets of examples are not intended to be exhaustive, they should establish a solid basis for what is possible in the modern era.

## Descriptive Analysis

The beer and diapers example falls under a large set of **descriptive analysis** techniques known as data mining, a set of techniques used to extract patterns from large data sets. Association rule learning, a data mining technique, was used to conduct a market basket analysis on the 1.2 million single ticket transactions. The technique sought to discover and describe interesting relationships within all of the shopping carts (i.e., market baskets) of Osco Drug consumers. As noted, shoppers putting both milk and breakfast cereal in their baskets is an expected association; a shopper putting in both beer and diapers is not.

Data fusion is another descriptive analysis technique. The goal is to integrate and analyze data from various sources as opposed to relying on only a single source. An example might be combining real-time sales data with real-time social media mentions in order to better understand customer sentiment toward an advertising campaign. If only the sales data were used, it might provide insight, but the inclusion of the social media data adds a dimension of potential depth of understanding.

Both of these examples are relatively straightforward sets of relationships, but what if the relationships are less obvious or harder to discover? Neural networks analysis is a descriptive analysis technique used for finding nonlinear patterns in the data, based on biological neural networks. Neural networks analysis can be used to find patterns when relationships are not closely affiliated. Pattern recognition has been useful in the past, including identifying high profitability customers who could leave for a competitor or identifying fraudulent insurance claims made by otherwise consistent policyholders. On the surface, both groups appear to be loyal customers, so being able to identify the patterns that might lead to profitable customers leaving or consistent customers committing fraud are both harder to discover and particularly valuable.

Finally, a growing area of descriptive analysis is visualization. The Tableau example in Chapter 5 (Research Window 5.1) recognizes the value of creating charts, graphs,

> **descriptive analysis** Designed to enhance understanding of available data to benefit firm performance.
>
> **predictive analysis** Designed to aid both explanatory and forecasting abilities for the betterment of the firm.

images, maps, diagrams, and the like to allow for better communication and better understanding of the data. Data visualizations could be as simple as word clouds on a web site or histograms of Internet traffic from sites like Alexa.com or Google Trends. In total, all these descriptive analysis techniques are designed to understand business performance.[24]

## Predictive Analysis

As the name implies, **predictive analysis** differs from descriptive analysis in that predictive analysis focuses on future-oriented, potential behaviors as opposed to merely classifying past behaviors. Target's ability to identify and reach pregnant women for specialized promotions is one example of predictive analysis (see Research Window 6.1). Predictive analysis tries to uncover explanatory and predictive models of business performance based on the relationship between data inputs and business outcomes. Here is a set of techniques that have predictive capabilities.

The first technique, regression analysis, can be used with both big data and standard data sets. It involves seeing how an outcome might change when one or more key variables change. Intended largely for forecasting in this context, regression analysis can be used in instances such as determining if a customer can be cross-sold or up-sold a product at the point of purchase. We'll discuss regression analysis in greater depth later. For now, recognize that a change in an outcome variable (e.g., cross-selling) can be impacted by any number of things. Regression would be used, in this context, to predict the most likely variables that produce the change in the outcome variable (i.e., positively impacting the cross-sell).

Time series analysis is another predictive analysis technique that can be used with big data and standard data. Its goal is to discover data-based trends by analyzing sequences of data over successive times to not only recognize the data pattern but forecast how the data will extend into the future. Seasonal or cyclical data are natural candidates for time series analysis. Research Window 6.3 notes how Google has applied time series analysis to predict flu symptoms, something that health care providers can draw on to adequately prepare patients for flu season.

The final type of predictive analysis we'd like to discuss is simulation. A simulation takes multiple random samples from the existing big data set to run thousands of "what if" analyses, each with different assumptions about market conditions and other marketplace dynamics. As a forecasting tool, the outcomes of these simulations provide a distribution of likelihoods that each set of assumptions will lead to a set of marketplace responses. One of the more noteworthy simulation tools—Monte Carlo simulations—has been used extensively by AT&T Labs to predict future traffic growth on its networks. The more AT&T can learn about usage patterns of its current network for the

## research window 6.3

### *Google.org Flu Trends*

We know that Google is a technology juggernaut. Born of the Dot-Com boom, Google is a relatively young company with a near ubiquitous presence. Curious about Abraham Lincoln's height? Google it. Need to know the square footage of the Museum of Modern Art? Google it. Feeling flu-like symptoms coming on? Lots of people Google that, too.

According to the Pew Research Center, 59 percent of U.S. adults look for health-related information online. Moreover, this trend has been fairly steady dating back to 2002. Since Google is the most popular search engine, it stands to reason that Google would receive a bulk of those queries. Google.org, the philanthropic arm of Google, attempts to mix historical influenza data along with real-time search data to predict country- and region-specific flu activity around the world.

As Google.org notes, "Each week, millions of users around the world search for health information online. As you might expect, there are more flu-related searches during flu season, more allergy-related searches during allergy season, and more sunburn-related searches during the summer." In the case of the flu, Google.org has worked with representatives from the Centers for Disease Control and Prevention (CDC) to predict the potential of seasonal and pandemic influenza outbreaks that led to tens of millions of respiratory illnesses and 250,000–500,000 deaths worldwide per year.

Citing a study published in the journal *Nature* (2009), Google time-series search and real-time search data were used to predict (a) a sharp rise in early February 2008 of influenza-like illness (ILI), (b) the peak of ILI in early March 2008, (c) a rapid decline in late March 2008, and (d) a leveling-off of flu season in mid-May 2008. Historical data from the CDC was also shown to demonstrate and confirm the remarkable accuracy of the Google predictions.

Following its forecasting ability of flu trends, Google.org has set its sights on predicting dengue

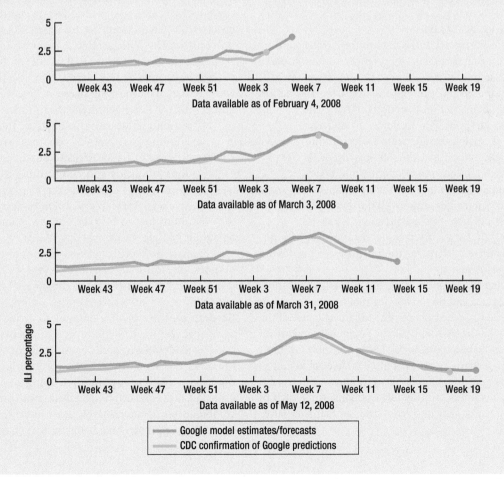

*(continued)*

## research window 6.3   (*continued*)

trends, a mosquito-transmitted viral disease with symptoms including sudden fever and acute joint pain. Early returns matching its predictive capacity to historical data from Brazil's Ministry of Health again demonstrate remarkable accuracy. Google.org is also partnering with UNICEF by way of a $1 million grant and dispatched Google engineers to identify, map, and contain the Zika virus outbreak.

Coupling Google's presence as a dominant search engine with its ability to find the patterns in the data creates opportunities for prediction and forecasting in health care and a wide variety of other industries. It also demonstrates a public health benefit of predictive analytics.

**Sources:** Google Flu Trends, accessed November 19, 2012, at http:// www.google.org/flutrends/; Google Dengue Trends, accessed November 19, 2012, at http://www.google.org /denguetrends/intl /en_us/; Fighting the Zika Virus, accessed February 13, 2017, at http://google.org/special-programs /#content-fighting-the-zika-virus; Jeremy Ginsberg, Matthew H. Mohebbi, Rajan S. Patel, Lynnette Brammer, Mark S. Smolinski, and Larry Brilliant (2009), "Detecting Influenza Epidemics Using Search Engine Query Data, *Nature*, Vol. 457 (February), 1012–1014, reprint accessed at http://static .googleusercontent.com/external_content/untrusted_dlcp /research .google.com/en/us/archive/papers/detecting -influenza-epidemics.pdf on November 19, 2012; Susannah Fox (2012), "Pew Internet: Health," November 13, accessed November 19, 2012, from http://pewinternet.org /Commentary/2011/November/Pew-Internet-Health.aspx.

purposes of predicting future usage patterns, the better it can manage its current network resources and plan for future network expansion. For other perspectives on the future of a broad set of "big data" outcomes from other industry experts, see Exhibit 6.3.[25]

### Prescriptive Analysis

Once marketing analysts understand the current context via descriptive analysis and can predict a future outcome with some degree of confidence via predictive analysis, the next step is to recommend the best course of action among the firm's various options. That's the role of **prescriptive analysis**. For instance, a company might use predictive techniques to forecast future consumer behaviors and then follow up with prescriptive techniques to efficiently and effectively manage scheduling, production, inventory management, and supply chain dynamics to meet the predicted future demand. As such, prescriptive analysis is used to determine a set of high-value alternative actions for the purposes of improving business performance.[26]

A key element of prescriptive analysis is *optimization*. The marketplace can be so complex that a manager might be challenged to adequately consider all the choices, all the alternatives, all the trade-offs, all the potential problems, all the potential benefits, and so on. Using optimization tools allows managers to uncover potential courses of action as well as possible interactions between those actions and the likely constraints limiting those actions. After each of these combinations is considered, the optimal alternative is provided.

> **prescriptive analysis** Designed to optimize the various courses of action available to enhance firm performance.

IBM Research is actively investigating all three forms of big data analysis. Its "Smarter Planet" approach is helping to make the complexities of the analysis more accessible to managers who want to learn more about analytics in general. Using sports as the backdrop, IBM explains that *descriptive analysis* is nothing new to coaches or players wanting to learn about on-field or on-court results. The difference is the scale, or size and scope, of data availability. Instead of studying the last period, last game, or last season, big data allows for the study of data over multiple seasons. Even then, the individual must rely on his or her own intuition or interpretation abilities to gain any real insight. *Predictive analysis* allows a coach or player to quickly understand and estimate outcomes across various scenarios and conditions. In Grand Slam tennis, IBM's Slamtracker has applied predictive analysis to years' worth of data about every point played by every player (some 39 million data points). Before each match, IBM's Keys to the Match system analyzes historic head-to-head stats of both competitors, including stats against players with comparable styles of play to predict the top three keys to winning the match for each.[27] In terms of optimization, Major League Baseball uses *prescriptive analysis* to create its schedule each year. Between stadium commitments, travel and hotel considerations, sponsorship relationships, and all the other factors and trade-offs confronting a team and the league, establishing multiple 162-game schedules is no small task. Prescriptive analysis can consider all the combinations of alternatives and prescribe the optimal scheduling approach on a team-by-team basis.[28]

**Exhibit 6.3** ▶ The Future of "Big Data:" The Good and the Bad Results From the Pew Internet and American Life Project

A group of "digital stakeholders" was asked to make predictions about the future of Big Data. Here are some of their responses:

**The Positive Perspective**

Media and regulators are demonizing Big Data and its supposed threat to privacy. Such moral panics have occurred often thanks to changes in technology. But the moral of the story remains: there is value to be found in this data, value in our newfound publicness. Google's founders have urged government regulators not to require them to quickly delete searches because, in their patterns and anomalies, they have found the ability to track the outbreak of the flu before health officials could, and they believe that by similarly tracking a pandemic, millions of lives could be saved. Demonizing data, big or small, is demonizing knowledge, and that is never wise. (Jeff Jarvis)

Big Data is the new oil. The companies, governments, and organizations that are able to mine this resource will have an enormous advantage over those that don't. With speed, agility, and innovation determining the winners and losers, Big Data allows us to move from a mind-set of "measure twice, cut once" to one of "place small bets fast." (Bryan Trogdon)

Big Data allows us to see patterns we have never seen before. This will clearly show us interdependence and connections that will lead to a new way of looking at everything. It will let us see the "real-time" cause and effect of our actions. (Tiffany Shlain)

Big Data gives me hope about the possibilities of technology. Transparency, accountability, and the "wisdom of the crowd" are all possible with the advent of Big Data combined with the tools to access and analyze the data in real time. (Tom Hood)

**The Negative Perspective**

Big Data will yield some successes and a lot of failures, and most people will continue merely to muddle along, hoping not to be mugged too frequently by the well-intentioned (or not) entrepreneurs and bureaucrats who delight in trying to use this shiny new toy to fix the world. (Anonymous)

We can now make catastrophic miscalculations in nanoseconds and broadcast them universally. We have lost the balance inherent in "lag time." (Marcia Richards Suelzer)

Big Data will generate misinformation and will be manipulated by people or institutions to display the findings they want. The general public will not understand the underlying conflicts and will naively trust the output. This is already happening and will only get worse as Big Data continues to evolve. (Anonymous)

Better information is seldom the solution to any real-world social problem. It may be the solution to lots of business problems, but it's unlikely that the benefits will accrue to the public. We're more likely to lose privacy and freedom from the rise of Big Data. (Barry Parr)

**Source:** Janna Quitney Anderson and Lee Rainie, "Big Data: Experts Say New Forms of Information Analysis Will Help People Be More Nimble and Adaptive, but Worry Over Humans' Capacity to Understand and Use These New Tools Well," July 20, 2012. Downloaded from http://www.pewinternet.org on July 25, 2012.

## 6-5 Key Challenges of "Big Data" Integration

By now we trust you are gaining a better understanding of the role and potential of big data as a source for understanding, forecasting, and optimization—but plenty of challenges remain. In Chapter 5 we discussed the role of individual privacy. That is certainly an important challenge all individuals and firms must consider. As Exhibit 6.4 demonstrates, challenges can become opportunities if you are willing to be open-minded. Below are some other key challenges that are less customer focused and more firm focused.

### Access to and Retrieval of Data

Access and retrieval issues take on at least two forms: (1) the ability to make use of the structured data to enhance decision making and (2) the ability to merge unstructured and structured data. Consider the small, local grocer with a barcode scanner at every register. The store manager or owner has a wealth of transaction data for each customer who passes through a check-out line. While those data might link to a larger decision support system for ease of in-store price changes or simple reordering reports, does it provide the necessary insights for merchandising ideas via market basket analysis? What about personalized promotions using the store's loyalty program? If a customer enters a Facebook status update about the great service a butcher provided in the meat department, can that be combined with the barcode data? Transactional data are terrific, but so many more insights are available to the decision maker who can access the data or retrieve the data necessary for maximum impact. Too many managers fail to take advantage of full data integration.

**Exhibit 6.4 ▶** Big Data and the Individual Consumer

*Scott Yara is EMC Greenplum Senior Vice President for Products and an expert in the business applications of Big Data. Here is his vision for how individuals might soon benefit from the use of Big Data:*

"Let's say you're a young woman who lives in a condo in the suburbs and works in an office downtown," Yara says. "When it's time to go to work, you instruct your condo when to wash the dishes, when to start a load of laundry, when to open or shut the windows depending on the weather."

Then you're at the office, Yara says. Your washing machine sends you a text that says it's out of detergent and can't do the load you requested. The text includes a coupon for detergent at the store where you most often shop (based on a credit card spending algorithm). It beeps you when you're near the store (based on geo location data and smart car sensors) so you don't forget. Your refrigerator texts to say you're low on lettuce so if you plan to have a salad with dinner tonight (based on the menus you programmed into the fridge) you should pick up the veggie when you get the laundry detergent. Maybe there is a two-for-one coupon included for your favorite salad dressing.

Or maybe you're planning a trip or wondering about your bank balance or thinking about phone services. When you call up the airline or your bank or your telephone company you won't be irritated to learn they don't have your latest purchase history or account details available. Those simple things will start to become much more commonplace and over time the services themselves will seem more personalized to you.

Source: Terry Brown, "The Sweet Sound of Big Data," undated, downloaded from http://www.emc.com on August 10, 2012, p. 4.

## Analytic Skills

According to one recent analysis, big data are getting bigger—60% growth per year—while employee analytic skills are lagging: 62% of employees lack the analytical skills to turn data into information.[29] The McKinsey Global Institute predicts that demand for analysts will exceed supply by 140,000 to 190,000 jobs in the coming years and that the need for additional managers and analysts will top 1.5 million people.[30] Supporting both of these points, a survey of senior executives revealed that when asked to select their organization's biggest data challenges, 45% said, "We have too much data and too few resources to manage them"; 30% responded, "We do not have the right skills within the organization to manage data effectively"; and 22% answered, "We don't have the right analytical skills to know how to use the data effectively."[31] Opportunities abound for those who are willing to enhance their analytic skills.

## Firm Integration of Big Data

There's one other challenge facing organizations as they expand into a big data world—and it's an enormous one. Think ahead a couple of years and imagine that your employer, a major health care provider, is moving further down the path of digitizing patient data and integrating those data with dozens of other data sets held internally or by other members of the health care system. To accomplish this task, the firm's information technology (IT) department has merged the data sources, some structured (e.g., measurable statistics including height, weight, blood pressure readings, the different aspects of a patient's cholesterol screening) and some unstructured (e.g., patients' open-ended descriptions of symptoms, video of surgical procedures, patients' social media comments about the care received) using Hadoop, an open source big data solution. All you have to do is to train all the organization's employees on how to use the system and the insights will rain down on the firm. Patient data will become enhanced treatment information, treatment information will lead to better decision making by doctors, and hospital or clinic performance will exceed all expectations. It sounds like a fairy-tale ending—because it is.

In the United States alone, there are over 50 million patient databases (and we're only talking about one industry). The technical integration of these databases is no small task—but new solutions for the technical aspects of integration are arriving with greater frequency.[32] The bigger data integration problem, in our estimation, will be on the human side. Analysts and managers must find the insights hidden in all of those newly integrated data sets, turning mounds of data into meaningful information. And employees in all corners of the organization must learn to collect the right kinds of data and to work with the information generated by the big data system. Employee receptivity to new systems or supplier support of new systems can't be taken for granted. From enterprise resource planning (ERP) to customer relationship management (CRM), history suggests that three out of five new system installations fail.[33] There are many aspects of firm integration that must be considered before big data can reap big results.

# Manager's Focus

To borrow a phrase from the fictional character Forrest Gump, social media and mobile devices "goes together like peas and carrots." Interestingly, this creates both opportunities and concerns that marketing managers should consider fully.

An individual using the camera function of a smartphone has a perfect way of capturing a moment with a digital image. Posting it to one of many popular social media sites is a perfect way for that individual to share the moment. Using the location function of the social media site's status update allows the mobile photographer a chance to both remember exactly where the moment took place and share this news with others.

A manager could collect the profile information of the mobile photographer along with the photo and the location. The managerial challenge can be summarized with another famous quote from Mr. Gump, "Life is like a box of chocolates. You never know what you're gonna get."

We hear of the great promise presented by "big data." We hear about the potential of personalizing content at the individual level and maximizing segmentation efforts for the firm. We hear about companies collecting remarkable volumes of data but we also hear about firms collecting both more data than is needed and more data than can be adequately managed. Worse, we hear about firms collecting data they neither know how to use nor are willing to delete. So, just because the data is getable, should it be gotten? Is the profile information helpful to collect? Does the accompanying photo add value, especially as a form of unstructured data? Does having location data meet a need or fill a void?

As a future manager considering the allure of "big data," be reminded that many of the rules of traditional data collection still apply; foremost among them: Know exactly how each piece of data is going to be used before collecting it. Becoming awash in "useless" data is reminiscent of another famous Gump line, "Stupid is as stupid does."

# Summary

## Learning Objective 1

**Identify the four Vs of "big data."**
"Big data" is multidimensional. The first V is volume or the sheer amount of data being collected, the second V is velocity, which refers to the pace of inward and outward data flow, the third V is variety for the wide array of data types available to a firm, and the fourth V is veracity in reference to the accuracy and trustworthiness of the data.

## Learning Objective 2

**Contrast structured and unstructured data.**
Structured data can be easily contained in classic rows and columns of spreadsheets and databases. Examples of structured data include customer profile data. By contrast, unstructured data does not follow a complete-the-form or fill-in-the-blank convention, making it much harder to manage. Examples of unstructured data include photos, video, and audio captured from the Web.

## Learning Objective 3

**Describe the three sources of "big data" for marketers.**
As the third V suggests, data comes in a wide variety of forms. Historical data sources, like survey and observational data, are still available. The most widely acknowledged and newest sources of data are from social media, mobile devices, and multiple purchasing channels, also known as omni-channel transactional data.

## Learning Objective 4

**Compare descriptive, predictive, and prescriptive analytical approaches.**
Descriptive analysis is designed to enhance understanding of available data to benefit firm performance. Predictive analysis is designed to aid both explanatory and forecasting abilities for the betterment of the firm. Finally, prescriptive analysis is designed to optimize the various courses of action available to enhance firm performance.

## Learning Objective 5

**List and discuss the key challenges of "big data" integration.**
Three key challenges to "big data" integration include access to and retrieval of quality data, lack of sufficient analytical skills within the firm, and issues related to firm integration of both within and between firms.

The first and third challenges bring the importance of the four Vs into focus. Volume, velocity, variety, and veracity each add to those challenges, while the second challenge is one that could require both employee and potential employee training to address the challenge for the industry in total.

## Key Terms

volume (page 76)
velocity (page 76)
variety (page 76)
veracity (page 76)
big data (page 76)
structured data (page 80)
unstructured data (page 83)
social data (page 83)
mobile data (page 84)
omni-channel transactional data (page 84)
descriptive analysis (page 86)
predictive analysis (page 86)
prescriptive analysis (page 88)

## Review Questions

1. Which of the four Vs—volume, velocity, variety, or veracity—creates the biggest challenge to marketing managers intent on "finding a needle in a haystack"?

2. How might a marketing manager obtain value from "big data" that is different from value obtained from traditional data sources?

3. Compare and contrast structured versus unstructured data. Using Facebook as an example, would data available from Facebook to a marketer be structured, unstructured, or both?

4. In terms of marketplace sources of "big data," what is social data? Mobile data? Omni-channel transactional data?

5. What are the main differences between descriptive, predictive, and prescriptive analyses?

6. What are the three main challenges marketing managers face when attempting to integrate "big data" into the firm?

# Endnotes

1. The "needle in a haystack" analogy originated in a white paper: Sun, H. and Heller. P. (2012, August). "Oracle information architecture: An architect's guide to big data." Retrieved from http://www.oracle.com/technetwork/topics/entarch/articles/oea-big-data-guide-1522052.pdf.

2. Laney, D. (2001, February). "3D data management: Controlling data volume, velocity, and variety." Application Delivery Strategies, META Group. Retrieved from http://blogs.gartner.com/doug-laney/files/2012/01/ad949-3D-Data-Management-Controlling-Data-Volume-Velocity-and-Variety.pdf. Marr, B. (2015, March 19). "Why only one of the 5 Vs of big data really matters." Retrieved from http://www.ibmbigdatahub.com/blog/why-only-one-5-vs-big-data-really-matters.

3. Conner, M. (2012, July 18). "Data on big data," Retrieved from http://marciaconner.com/blog/data-on-big-data/.

4. Arthur, C. (2011, June 29). "What's a zettabyte? By 2015, the Internet will know, says Cisco." *The Guardian*. Retrieved from http://www.guardian.co.uk/technology/blog/2011/jun/29/zettabyte-data-internet-cisco. Marr, B. (2015, March 19). "Why only one of the 5 Vs of big data really matters." Retrieved from http://www.ibmbigdatahub.com/blog/why-only-one-5-vs-big-data-really-matters.

5. (2011, Sept.). "Big data: Harnessing a game-changing asset." *The Economist*. Retrieved from http://www.sas.com/resources/asset/SAS_BigData_final.pdf.

6. (n.d.) "Big data: Big opportunities to create business value." Information Intelligence Group of EMC, Retrieved from www.emc.com.

7. (2012, June). "Global survey: Is big data producing big returns?" *Avanade*, Retrieved from http://www.avanade.com/Documents/Research%20and%20Insights/avanade-big-data-executive-summary-2012.pdf.

8. "Data, data everywhere." (2010, Feb. 25). *The Economist*. Retrieved from http://www.economist.com/node/15557443.

9. (2011, June). "Big data: The next frontier for innovation, competition, and productivity." McKinsey Global Institute, McKinsey & Company. Retrieved from http://www.mckinsey.com/~/media/McKinsey/dotcom/Insights %20and%20pubs/MGI/Research/Technology%20and%20Innovation/Big%20Data/MGI_big_data_full_report.ashx.

10. Pearlson, K. (2011, Jan.). "Analytics versus intuition." International Institute for Analytics. Retrieved from http://iianalytics.com/2011/01/analytics-versus-intuition/.

11. "Best Western uses Medallia to drive guest loyalty." Medallia Resources. Retrieved from http://www.medallia.com/resources/item/guest-loyalty-case-study/.

12. Thompson, B. (2012, Oct. 5). "From big data to big decisions: Three ways analytics can improve the retail experience." *Customer Think*. Retrieved from http://www.customerthinkcom/article/from_big_data_to_big_decisions_3_ways_analytics_can_improve_retail _experience.

13. Versel, N. (2013, March 7). "Big data helps Kaiser close healthcare gaps." Retrieved from http://www.informationweek.com/healthcare/electronic-medical-records/big-data-helps-kaiser-close-healthcare-g/240150269.

14. Bloom, A. (2015, May 25). "20 examples of ROI and results with big data." *Pivotal*. Retrieved from https://content.pivotal.io/blog/20-examples-of-roi-and-results-with-big-data.

15. Brynjolfsson, E., & McAfee, A. (2012, Sept. 11). "Big data's management revolution." *Harvard Business Review*. Retrieved from http://blogs.hbr.org/cs/2012/09/big_datas_management_revolutio.html.

16. Kalil, T. (2012, March 29). "Big data is a big deal," Office of Science and Technology Policy. Retrieved from http://www.whitehouse.gov/blog/2012/03/29/big-data-big-deal.

17. Campbell, D. "VoC and social media make great partners." OpinionLab. Retrieved from www.opinionlab.com/voc-and-social-media-make-great-partners/.

18. (2012, May 1). "Winning the intensifying battle for customers." *Accenture*. Retrieved from http://www.accenture.com/SiteCollectionDocuments/PDF /Accenture-Communications-Next-generation-Customer-Analytics-Big-Data.pdf.

19. Mediati, N. (2015, Nov. 1). "Pew survey shows 68 percent of US adults now own a smartphone." *PCWorld*. Retrieved from http://www.pcworld.com/article/2999631/phones/pew-survey-shows-68-percent-of-americans-now-own-a-smartphone.html.

20. Pearson, B. (2016, Dec.) "Holiday spending to exceed $1 trillion and 11 other surprising data points of Christmas." *Forbes*. Retrieved from https://www.forbes.com/sites/bryanpearson/2016/12/22/holiday-spending-to-exceed-1-trillion-and-11-other-surprising-data-points-of-christmas/2/#2c5a316a35b9.

21. Butcher, D. (2010, Oct. 15). "Starbucks breaks first location-based mobile campaign with major carrier." *Mobile Marketer*. Retrieved from http://www.mobilemarketer.com/cms/news/database-crm/7754.html.

22. Dorf, D. (2012, Oct. 26). "Analytics in an omni-channel world." *Insight-Driven Retailing*. Retrieved from https://blogs.oracle.com/retail/entry/analytics_in_an_omni_channel.

23. J. Power, D. J. (2002, Nov. 10). "Ask Dan." *DSS News*. Retrieved from http://www.dssresources.com/newsletters/66.php. Burleson Consulting. (2008, March 3). "All about beer and diapers." *Oracle Tips by Burleson Consulting*. Retrieved from http://www.dba-oracle.com/oracle_tips_beer_diapers_data_warehouse.htm.

24. (2011, June). "Big data: The next frontier for innovation, competition, and productivity." McKinsey Global Institute, McKinsey & Company. Retrieved from http://www.mckinsey.com/~/media/McKinsey/dotcom/Insights%20and%20pubs/MGI/Research/Technology%20and%20Innovation/Big%20Data/MGI_big_data_full_report.ashx. Lustig, I., Dietrich, B., Johnson, C., & Dziekan, C. "Analytics journey," *Analytics Magazine*, November/December 2010. Retrieved from http://www.analytics-magazine.org/november-december-2010/54-the-analytics-journey.html.

25. "Big data: The next frontier for innovation, competition, and productivity." (2011, June). McKinsey Global Institute, McKinsey & Company. Retrieved from http://www.mckinsey.com/~/media/McKinsey/dotcom /Insights%20and%20pubs/MGI /Research/Technology%20and% 20Innovation/Big%20Data/MGI_big_data_full_report.ashx. Feuer, M. D., Woodward, S. L., Kim, I., Palacharla, P., Wang, X., Bihon, D. ... Chiu, A. L. "Simulations of a service velocity network employing regenerator site concentration." AT&T Labs. Retrieved from http://www.research.att.com/export/sites/att_labs/techdocs/TD_100677.pdf.

26. Lustig, I., Dietrich, B., Johnson, C., & Dziekan, C. "Analytics journey." *Analytics Magazine*, November/December 2010. Retrieved from http://www.analytics-magazine.org/november-december-2010/54-the-analytics-journey.html.

27. "IBM slamtracker." *The Championships, Wimbledon 2013.* Retrieved from http://www.wimbledon.com/en_GB/slamtracker /index.html.

28. Johnson, C. (2012, Aug. 8). "Advancing analytics to predict specific needs." *Building a Smarter Planet.* Retrieved from http://asmarterplanet.com/blog/2012/08/advancing_analytics .html.

29. "Big data does not make better decisions. Analytical skills do." *Overcoming the insight deficit.* Retrieved from http:// www.executiveboard.com/exbd/information-technology/ insight-deficit/index.page.

30. (2011, June). "Big data: The next frontier for innovation, competition, and productivity." McKinsey Global Institute, McKinsey & Company. Retrieved from http://www.mckinsey .com/~/media/McKinsey/dotcom/Insights%20and%20pubs /MGI/Research/Technology%20and%20Innovation/Big%20 Data/MGI _big_data_full_report.ashx.

31. "Big data: Harnessing a game-changing asset." (2011, Sept.). *The Economist.* Retrieved from http://www.sas.com /resources/asset/SAS_BigData_final.pdf.

32. Bizer, C., Boncz, P., Brodie, M. L., & Erling, O. (2011, Dec.) "The meaningful use of big data: Four perspectives—four challenges." *SIGMOD Record,* Vol. 40 (No. 4). Retrieved from www.sigmod.org/publications/sigmod-record/1112/pdfs/10 .report.bizer.pdf.

33. Simon, P. (2010, Feb.). *Why new systems fail: An insider's guide to successful IT projects.* Course Technology PTR.

# Using External Secondary Data

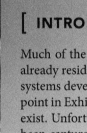

## LEARNING OBJECTIVES

▸ Describe the process of searching for published external secondary data.

▸ List three common uses of the information supplied by standardized marketing information services.

▸ Define geodemography.

▸ Describe the use of diary panels and scanner data for assessing product sales.

▸ Discuss the purpose and operation of people meters and portable people meters.

▸ Define single-source data.

## [ INTRODUCTION ]

Much of the data that marketing managers need to make decisions already resides inside the organization, often in the decision support systems developed for just that purpose. That's why the first decision point in Exhibit 2.1 is to determine if relevant internal secondary data exist. Unfortunately, many decisions require information that hasn't been captured internally. In these cases, managers should next look to external sources for the relevant data. Much of the time, good data can be obtained from published sources. Although a cost is often associated with obtaining these data, that cost is generally much less compared to collecting primary data on the topic. In the first portion of this chapter, we suggest a process for searching for published information.

Sometimes companies need very specific information that generally can't be obtained from published sources. Many standardized marketing information services are available to provide specific information to marketing researchers. These commercial services are more expensive than using published information, but still less expensive than collecting primary data. Data suppliers sell to multiple companies, allowing the costs of collecting, editing, coding, and analyzing data to be shared. Because multiple companies must be able to use the data, however, the data and how they are to be collected must be standardized. As a result, such data is not always a perfect fit for a company, the primary disadvantage of standardized marketing information. In this chapter, we describe main types and sources of standardized marketing information.

## 7-1  External Secondary Data From Published Sources

Although most people underestimate what is available, there is likely to be relevant external secondary data on almost any problem a marketer might confront. The fundamental problem is not the availability of external secondary data, but rather identifying and accessing it. Even researchers who have an idea of how much valuable secondary data exists may not know how to find the data. Exhibit 7.1 provides guidelines for getting started on a search of secondary data on a particular topic.[1]

### Step 1

The first step is to identify what you want to know and what you already know about your topic. This may include relevant facts, names of researchers or organizations associated with the topic, key papers and other publications with which you are already familiar, and any other information you may have.

### Step 2

A useful second step is to develop a list of key terms and authors. These terms and names will provide access to secondary sources. Unless you have a very specific topic of interest, it is better to keep this initial list long and quite general.

### Step 3

In Step 3, you are ready to begin the search. Numerous online database sources are useful for this process; Exhibit 7.2 describes some of the best of these. For example, Hoover's Online provides a wealth of information about companies and their products for 85 million companies and 900 industries; some of the information is available at no cost. Exhibit 7.3 contains information about the electronic securities industry. If you need information about a particular industry, don't forget to visit the web sites of its trade associations. Many trade associations gather detailed information relevant to the operations of an industry. So, if you needed more information about the electronic securities industry, for example, you might start with http://www.esaweb.org/, the web site for the Electronic Securities Association.

**Exhibit 7.1** ▶ How to Get Started When Searching Published Sources of Secondary Data

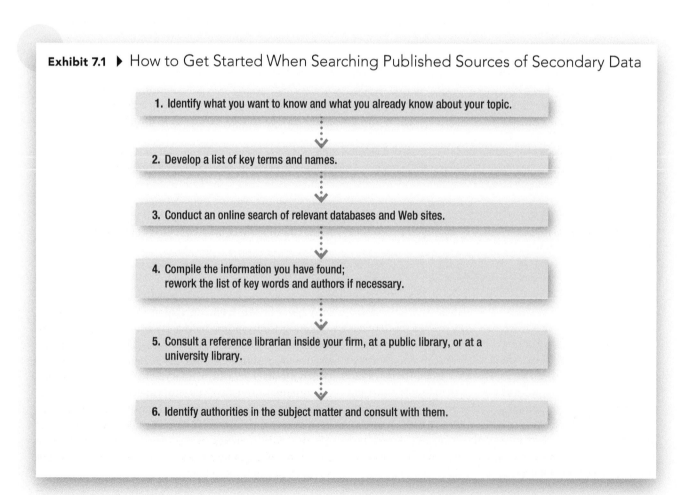

1. Identify what you want to know and what you already know about your topic.

2. Develop a list of key terms and names.

3. Conduct an online search of relevant databases and Web sites.

4. Compile the information you have found; rework the list of key words and authors if necessary.

5. Consult a reference librarian inside your firm, at a public library, or at a university library.

6. Identify authorities in the subject matter and consult with them.

**Exhibit 7.2** ▶ Key Online Sources of Secondary Data for Business Purposes

The availability of business information has grown exponentially with the Internet. Finding appropriate resources can be daunting. The following list identifies key business resources, both free and subscription-based, that are widely available in both public and academic libraries.

**Free web resources**

Census (www.census.gov)—The Census Bureau supplies demographic, economic, and business data down to the county and city levels.

EDGAR (www.sec.gov/edgar.shtml)—The Electronic Data Gathering, Analysis, and Retrieval (EDGAR) system contains almost all financial, ownership, and operations documents filed with the US Securities and Exchange Commission (SEC) by public companies.

Yahoo! Finance (finance.yahoo.com)—Offers news and information, including original video programming, stock quotes, stock exchange rates, corporate press releases, and financial reports.

**Subscription-based web resources** (These resources may be available at no cost through university and public libraries)

Hoover's Online (Hoover's Inc., www.hoovers.com)—Includes company overviews, histories, and products/operations on more than 100 million contacts, 85 million companies, and 900 industries. (Basic company information is available from the free web site.)

IBIS*World* (www.ibisworld.com)—Contains over 1,000 current US industry profiles based on the North American Industry Classification System (NAICS).

ReferenceUSA (resource.referenceusa.com)—Search for US companies' directory information using many criteria, including geographic location, SIC, size of company, and so on.

NetAdvantage (netadvantage.standardandpoors.com)—Provides financial data on public companies, stock quotes, and industry surveys. (Also available in print format)

General Business/Company Information: Various subscription databases provide articles from journals, magazines, and newspapers providing news and analysis of companies and industries. Popular examples: *ABI/Inform (ProQuest)*, *Business Source (EBSCO)*, *Factiva (Dow Jones & Company)*.

**Subscription-based print resources** (Commonly found in print, but also available as online subscription)

Industry Ratios—Used for benchmarking, industry ratios resources will generally provide average industry asset size for companies in the industry. Different resources will cover various industries. Popular examples: *Almanac of Business and Industrial Financial Ratios (CCH Inc)*, *Industry Norms and Key Business Ratios (Dun & Bradstreet Corp)*, *RMA Annual Statement Studies (Risk Management Association)*

Value Line Investment Survey—A weekly stock analysis newsletter containing company financial data and price forecasts in three sections: Ratings and Reports, Summary and Index, and Selection and Opinion. Web site (www.valueline.com) provides some free material.

Source: Information initially aggregated by Professors Steven Locy and Victor Baeza of the Edmon Low Library at Oklahoma State University, updated February 2017.

### Step 4

Next, compile the literature you have found. Is it relevant to your needs? You may be overwhelmed by information at this point, or you may have found little that is relevant. If you need more information, rework your list of key words and authors and expand your search to include a few more years and a few additional sources. Once again, evaluate your findings. By the end of Step 4, you should have a clear idea of the nature of the information you are seeking and sufficient background to use more specialized sources.

### Step 5

One very useful specialized source is a reference librarian. Reference librarians are specialists who have been trained to know the contents of many of the key information sources in a library and on the Web, as well as how to search those sources most effectively. A reference librarian can usually uncover information that is relevant to your current problem. The reference librarian will need your help, however, in the form of a carefully constructed list of key words or topics. Remember, a reference librarian cannot be of much help until you provide specific details about what you want to know.

**Exhibit 7.3** ▶ Sources of Data on the Electronic Security Systems Industry

**ELECTRONIC SECURITY SYSTEMS**

*See also:* INDUSTRIAL SECURITY PROGRAMS

**DIRECTORIES**

*Automotive Burglary Protection and Mechanical Equipment Directory.* Underwriters Laboratories, Inc. Lists manufacturers authorized to use UL label.

*National Burglar and Fire Alarm Association Members Services Directory.* National Burglar and Fire Alarm Association. Names and addresses of about 4,000 alarm security companies. Formerly *National Burglar and Fire Alarm Association–Directory of Members.*

*Security Distributing and Marketing-Security Products and Services Locator.* Cahners Business Information. Formerly *SDM: Security Distributing and Marketing–Security Products and Services Directory.*

*Security: Product Service Suppliers Guide.* Cahners Business Information. Includes computer and information protection products. Formerly *Security–World Product Directory.*

**HANDBOOKS AND MANUALS**

*Burglar Alarm Sales and Installation.* Entrepreneur Media, Inc. A practical guide to starting a burglar alarm service. Covers profit potential, start-up costs, market size evaluation, owner's time required, pricing, accounting, advertising, promotion, and the like. (Start-Up Business Guide No. E1091). *Effective Physical Security: Design, Equipment, and Operations,* second ed. Lawrence J. Fennelly, editor. (1996). Butterworth-Heinemann. Contains chapters written by various US security equipment specialists. Covers architectural considerations, locks, safes, alarms, intrusion detection systems, closed circuit television, identification systems, and so on.

**PERIODICALS AND NEWSLETTERS**

*9-1-1 Magazine: Public Safety Communications and Response.* Official Publications, Inc. Covers technical information and applications for public safety communications personnel.

*Security Distributing and Marketing.* Cahners Business Information. Covers applications, merchandising, new technology and management.

*Security Management.* American Society for Industrial Security. Articles cover the protection of corporate assets, including personnel property and information security.

*Security Systems Administration.* Cygnus Business Media.

*Security: The Magazine for Buyers of Security Products, Systems and Service.* Cahners Business Information.

**TRADE/PROFESSIONAL ASSOCIATIONS**

ASIS International (American Society for Industrial Security). 1625 Prince St., Alexandria, VA 22314-2818. Phone: (703) 519-6200. Fax (703) 519-6299. URL: http://www.asisonline.org.

Automatic Fire Alarm Association. P.O. Box 951807, Lake Mary, FL 32795-1807. Phone: (407) 322-6288. Fax (407) 322-7488. URL: http://www.afaa.org.

Central Station Alarm Association, 440 Maple Ave., Suite 201, Vienna, VA 22180-4723. Phone (703) 242-4670. Fax (703) 242-4675 E-mail: communications@csaaul.org.

National Burglar & Fire Alarm Association. 8300 Colesville Rd., Ste. 750, Silver Spring, MD 20910. Phone: (301) 907-3202. Fax (301) 907-7897 E-mail: staff@alarm.org. URL: http://www.alarm.org.

Source: Linda D. Hall, ed., (2005). *Encyclopedia of Business Information Sources,* 20th Ed. Detroit: Thomson Gale, 305–307.

## Step 6

If you encounter roadblocks, consult an authority. Identify some individual or organization that might know about the topic. Business consultants, financial analysts, trade association staff, faculty at universities, government officials, and business executives can often be useful information sources.

## 7-2 Standardized Marketing Information—Profiling Customers

Published external secondary data are useful when they are available, but much of the time researchers need information that is more specific than that available in published format. In those situations, researchers often turn to providers of standardized marketing information. As we noted earlier, these companies gather key information and then sell it to other companies who need it. In the following sections, we describe types of **standardized marketing information**, starting with research that helps companies profile their customers and prospects.

Market segmentation is common among businesses seeking to improve their marketing efforts. Effective segmentation demands that firms group their customers into relatively homogeneous segments, tailoring marketing programs to individual groups and thereby making the programs more effective. A common segmentation base for firms selling industrial goods takes into account the industry designation(s) of its customers, most typically by means of the North American Industry Classification System (NAICS) codes. The NAICS codes are a system developed by the US Census Bureau for organizing business information reporting on topics such as employment, value added in manufacturing, capital expenditures, and total sales. In the NAICS system, major industry sectors are given a two-digit code, and the types of businesses making up the industry are given additional digits. Exhibit 7.4 demonstrates how the utility industry is coded using the NAICS system.

One source of standardized marketing information for profiling customers that is especially popular among industrial goods and service suppliers is the Dun & Bradstreet global commercial database. This information service provides information on over 131 million active companies located throughout the world. The data, which can be broken out by NAICS codes, allow sales management to construct sales prospect files, define sales territories and measure territory potentials, and isolate potential new customers with particular characteristics. They allow advertising management to select potential customers by size and location; to analyze and select the media to reach them; to build, maintain, and structure current mailing lists;

**Exhibit 7.4** ▶ NAICS Codes for Utility Industries

| | |
|---|---|
| 22 | Utilities |
| 221 | Utilities |
| 2211 | Electric Power Generation, Transmission and Distribution |
| 22111 | Electric Power Generation |
| 221111 | Hydroelectric Power Generation |
| 221112 | Fossil Fuel Electric Power Generation |
| 221113 | Nuclear Electric Power Generation |
| 221114 | Solar Electric Power Generation |
| 221115 | Wind Electric Power Generation |
| 221116 | Geothermal Electric Power Generation |
| 221117 | Biomass Electric Power Generation |
| 221118 | Other Electric Power Generation |
| 22112 | Electric Power Transmission, Control, and Distribution |
| 221121 | Electric Bulk Power Transmission and Control |
| 221122 | Electric Power Distribution |
| 2212 | Natural Gas Distribution |
| 22121 | Natural Gas Distribution |
| 221210 | Natural Gas Distribution |
| 2213 | Water, Sewage, and Other Systems |
| 22131 | Water Supply and Irrigation Systems |
| 221310 | Water Supply and Irrigation Systems |
| 22132 | Sewage Treatment Facilities |
| 221320 | Sewage Treatment Facilities |
| 22133 | Steam and Air-Conditioning Supply |
| 221330 | Steam and Air-Conditioning Supply |

Source: "2-6 digit 2012 Code Files." Retrieved from http://www.census.gov/cgi-bin/sssd/naics/naicsrch?chart=2012.

to generate sales leads qualified by size, location, and quality; and to locate new markets for testing. Finally, they allow marketing research professionals to assess market potential by territory, to measure market penetration in terms of numbers of prospects and numbers of customers, and to make comparative analyses of overall performance by districts and sales territories and in individual industries.

Firms selling consumer goods have traditionally targeted groups of customers rather than individual customers. **Geodemographers**, as they are typically called, combine census data with their own survey data or data gathered from other sources, such as motor vehicle registrations or credit transactions, to produce customized products for their clients. These data are often combined with geographic data, using mapping

**standardized marketing information**
Secondary data collected by companies that sell the data to multiple companies, allowing the costs of collecting, editing, coding, and analyzing them to be shared. The data are standardized so that multiple companies can use them rather than customized for a specific company.

**Exhibit 7.5** ▶ Sample Geodemographic Map of Birmingham, AL

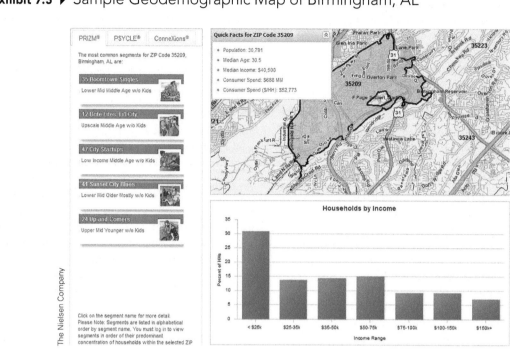

The Nielsen Company

software (often referred to as a geographic information system, or GIS), that allow a user to draw a map showing average data for the region and then zoom closer to look at particular towns in more detail. In a classic example, Chase used geodemography with mapping analysis to determine that only two-thirds of one branch's customers lived in its trade area, with the other customers working in the area but living elsewhere. Further analysis indicated that many of the customers who lived out of the area worked at nearby medical centers and that, as a group, the remote customers might represent more than a half billion dollars in potential deposits. They also discovered that a competing bank was actually in a better location to attract this potential business. Based on the GIS analysis, Chase was able to identify options for relocating the existing branch.[2]

Another thing that geodemographers do is regularly update the census data through statistical extrapolation. The data can consequently be used with much more confidence during the years between censuses. Another value-added

**geodemography**
The availability of demographic, consumer behavior, and lifestyle data by arbitrary geographic boundaries that are typically quite small.

feature that influenced industry success has been the analysis of census data. Firms supplying geodemographic information have cluster-analyzed the census-produced data to produce "homogeneous groups" that describe the US population. Exhibit 7.5 shows some results.

For example, Nielsen's PRIZM (Potential Ratings for Zip Markets) system uses scores of demographic considerations to classify residential neighborhoods. This system breaks down US neighborhoods into 66 segments based on consumer behavior and lifestyle. Each segment has a name that theoretically describes the type of people living there, such as The Cosmopolitans, Upward Bound, Boomtown Singles, Shotguns & Pickups, and Gray Power.

## 7-3 Standardized Marketing Information—Measuring Product Sales and Market Share

Firms need to have an accurate assessment of their progress if they are to succeed in an increasingly competitive environment. One way to accomplish this is to review internal records and determine how much they have sold into the distribution channel (wholesalers, distributors, retailers, and the like). Knowing how much product has been shipped to wholesalers and retailers doesn't provide

> Effective segmentation demands that firms group their customers into relatively homogeneous segments.

a timely understanding of how the product is doing with consumers, however. Furthermore, simply totaling sales invoices offers no information at all about how a company's product is doing relative to products from other companies. Historically, there are several ways of measuring sales to final consumers, including the use of household diary panels, as well as scanner data at the store level.

## 7-3a DIARY PANELS

Diary panels are an important source of information about products purchased by households. Whether recorded on paper or reported online, the key feature of a diary panel is that a representative group of individuals or households keeps track of purchases made or products consumed over a given period of time. In this way, purchasing and/or consumption behavior can be extrapolated to the larger population.

Specifically, the NPD Group tracks a number of purchase and consumption trends in the United States. For example, the National Eating Trends (NET) service has operated a household diary panel since 1980. Participants keep a daily record of all food and drink consumed by all household members, whether inside the home or purchased outside the home. In this way, the company can track a variety of characteristics, including market share, of interest to the food and beverage industry. The NPD Group also offers results from an online consumer panel of nearly 2 million members covering a wide range of products. The company uses weekly surveys to capture purchase data from panel members.

## 7-3b SCANNERS

Another way to assess product sales and market share is to work with retailers, rather than a consumer panel, to get the data. In working with retailers, the usual approach is to use scanners that record point-of-sale product purchases.

**scanner** An electronic device that automatically reads the bar code imprinted on a product, looks up the price in an attached computer, and instantly prints the description and price of the item on the cash register receipt.

Although old-fashioned store audits are still used in some US stores and in stores in many international markets (see Exhibit 7.6 for details about how a store audit works), the vast majority of consumer products in the United States are now tracked via scanner.

Most retail products have a unique bar code identifying the company associated with the product as well as the product itself. The code, first used in the United States in 1974, is imprinted on the product or on a tag or label attached to the product. As the bar code is read by a fixed or handheld **scanner**, the scanner identifies the number, looks up the price in the attached computer, and immediately prints the description and price of the item on the cash register receipt. At the same time, the computer can keep track of the movement of every item scanned. Where scanning is available, sales data (units sold, price) are collected from a retailer's system. The research provider takes these data and matches the code to a description in order to make the information more useful. Scanners are so pervasive that the majority of retail sales information today is based on scanner data.

In addition, other data sources can be combined with this information. For example, suppose that you or your research provider collected information about whether a product had been featured in a promotional display or in advertising. You might also collect information about historical pricing for the product and compare it to the current pricing. In all of these cases, you would attempt to take the "causal" data and see whether it is related to changes in product sales, thereby assessing the effectiveness of various marketing actions such as short-term promotions, pricing changes, new product introductions, and unexpected events like product recalls or shortages. The effect of scanners on standardized marketing research has been profound.

---

**Exhibit 7.6 ▶** Conducting a Store Audit to Measure Product Sales

Here's how a store audit works. The research firm sends field workers, called auditors, to a select group of retail stores at fixed intervals. On each visit, the auditors take a complete inventory of all products designated for the audit. The auditors also note the merchandise moving into the store by checking wholesale invoices, warehouse withdrawal records, and direct shipments from manufacturers. Sales to consumers are then determined by the following calculation:

Beginning inventory

+ Net purchases (from wholesalers and manufacturers)

− Ending inventory

= Sales

The store audit was pioneered by the Nielsen Company and served as the backbone of the Nielsen Retail Index for many years. The method is still used to measure sales in stores and markets where scanner data are not available.

## 7-4    Standardized Marketing Information—Measuring Advertising Exposure and Effectiveness

Most suppliers of industrial goods advertise heavily in trade publications. To sell space effectively, trade publications typically sponsor readership studies and make them available to potential advertisers. Suppliers of consumer goods and services also have access to media-sponsored readership studies. In addition, a number of services have evolved to measure consumer exposure to the various media.

> Most suppliers of industrial goods advertise most heavily in trade publications.

### 7-4a    TELEVISION AND RADIO

The Nielsen television ratings produced by the Nielsen Company are probably the most familiar form of media research to most people. Almost everyone has heard of Nielsen ratings and their impact on which television shows are canceled by the networks and which are allowed to continue. Nielsen ratings are designed to provide estimates of the size and nature of the audience for individual television programs.

Data needed to compute Nielsen ratings are gathered in a variety of ways. **People meters** attempt to measure not only the channel to which a set is tuned, but also who in the household is watching. Each family member has his or her own viewing number. Whoever turns on the set, sits down to watch, or changes the channel is supposed to enter his or her number into the people meter. Information from the approximately 20,000 household Nielsen people meter (NPM) panel is transmitted to a central computer for processing. In addition, Nielsen supplements people meter data with approximately two million consumer diaries across the United States during certain times of the year.

Through the data provided by these basic records, Nielsen develops estimates of the number and percentage of all households viewing a given program. Additionally, Nielsen breaks down these aggregate ratings by numerous socioeconomic and demographic characteristics, including territory, education level of head of household, household income, occupation of head of household, household size, and so on. These breakdowns assist the television networks in selling advertising on particular programs, while assisting advertisers with choosing programs that reach households with the desired characteristics.

Advertisers buying radio time are also interested in the size and demographic composition of the audiences they

**people meter** A device used to measure when a television is on, to what channel it is tuned, and who in the household is watching it.

**portable people meter** A pager-like device carried with a person or worn on a person's clothing used to measure when a person is listening to a radio station or watching a television broadcast outside their home.

will be reaching. Radio-listening statistics are typically gathered using diaries that are placed in a panel of households. Nielsen Audio (formerly Arbitron), for example, generates telephone numbers randomly to ensure it is reaching households with unlisted numbers and sends diaries to household members who agree to participate. In contrast with television ratings, radio ratings are typically broken down by age and gender and focus on individual rather than household behavior,

Nielsen Audio also uses a **portable people meter** (PPM) in many markets as a means of tracking audiences more accurately. The PPM is about the size of a pager and is carried (or worn on clothing) by consumers throughout the day. The devices sense inaudible codes embedded into programming by radio and television broadcasters (including cable television) so that an accurate record can be made of actual exposure to media, including out-of-home broadcasts via smartphone screens or at sports bars, for example. The PPMs are even equipped with motion sensors to verify that the device has been moved (presumably carried by the respondent).

Each night, participants recharge the unit in a base station that also automatically sends collected data back to a central computer for processing. As of mid 2017, about 80,000 PPMs were in use.[3]

### 7-4b    PRINT MEDIA

Several services measure exposure to, and readership of, print media. One of the oldest is the GfK MRI's Starch Advertising Research program, which measures the effectiveness of magazine advertisements. In 2010, the company measured 144,000 ads from 3,150 issues of over 180 national magazines published in the United States. For each magazine issue, respondents are asked to indicate the degree to which they have read each of the ads (i.e., remembered seeing the ad; saw the advertiser's name; read any of the ad; read all of the ad) and to respond to other questions about the ads, including:

- Ad readership levels: noted, associated, "read any" and "read most" ratings

- Action taken

- Brand disposition

- Purchase behavior or intention

- Publication and advertising engagement

- Demographics: age, gender, education, marital status, children in household, race, ethnicity, household income

Starch Readership Reports provide insights into ad readership; they also gauge reader interest and reactions to a magazine's editorial content and advertising. An important feature is the ability to compare readership scores for a particular ad against (a) the other ads in the issue, and (b) ads of similar size, color, and product category. This helps make Starch scores effectively assess the impact of changes in theme, copy, layout, use of color, and so on.[4]

## 7-4c INTERNET

Advertisers also need information about consumers' online activities, which continue to grow. At last count, only 13% of Americans were not online.[5] It's easy to count the number of times that a site or banner ad has been accessed, along with revenues from online transactions. As with other forms of media, however, it's more complicated to determine the demographics of those accessing a web site—and this is important for decisions about which web sites to choose for advertising purposes.

In the United States and certain other countries worldwide, the Nielsen Company offers Digital Voice, a popular syndicated service that assesses Internet usage. Panel members provide basic information about themselves and other household members (e.g., date of birth, gender, occupation, education level, and annual income) and then install a computer app that tracks their Internet usage and reports it to Nielsen. In addition, they also receive surveys from time to time as they visit particular web sites. In exchange, panel participants are registered in lotteries to win cash prizes that are awarded monthly. Regular reports from the service detail a web site's audience size and composition, time spent at the site, and so on. Exhibit 7.7 lists comScore's top-10 multi-platform properties based on the number of different Internet users who visited the brand's site(s) during a recent one-month period. For example, over 246 million people visited the top brand, Google, during the month. In second place, Facebook attracted over 209 million visitors. More importantly for marketers, Nielsen and comScore can determine the types of consumers—based on their demographics and online activity—who visit different web sites.[6]

Another area of Internet-oriented measurement is media consumption over mobile devices, including smartphones and tablets. Several companies offer syndicated research reporting on mobile media usage and audience composition. For instance, comScore's Mobile Metrix service includes a large panel of mobile device users whose usage is tracked by comScore and combined with census-level data to provide a comprehensive look into mobile media consumption. Flurry Analytics, a part of the Yahoo! Developer Network, currently offers a free analytics service that allows companies to track usage and a variety of additional metrics for their apps on mobile devices.

Just as it's important to know which customers are viewing your web site online via computer or mobile connections, companies have learned that understanding the effectiveness of their social media campaigns is also important. As a result, several large research providers—including

**Exhibit 7.7 ▶ Top 10 Multi-Platform Properties (Desktop and Mobile) for December 2016 (Total United States–Home and Work Locations)**

| PROPERTY | UNIQUE VISITORS/VIEWERS |
|---|---|
| 1 Google Sites | 246,699,000 |
| 2 Facebook | 209,121,000 |
| 3 Yahoo Sites | 206,389,000 |
| 4 Microsoft Sites | 190,235,000 |
| 5 Amazon Sites | 189,003,000 |
| 6 Comcast NBCUniversal | 164,821,000 |
| 7 CBS Interactive | 163,060,000 |
| 8 AOL | 156,593,000 |
| 9 Apple | 153,289,000 |
| 10 Time Network (U.S.) | 128,767,000 |

Read as: During December 2016, 246.7 million unique US people visited Google web sites.

Source: "Latest Rankings: Digital Media." Retrieved from https://www.comscore.com/Insights/Rankings.

comScore, WebTrends, and Nielsen—offer tools for assessing a brand's reach and impact with consumers via Twitter, Facebook, YouTube, and other social media sites. As we learned in Chapter 6, the ability to analyze massive amounts of data, including consumer remarks in social media, is rapidly changing the nature of consumer research.

## 7-4d CROSS-PLATFORM SERVICES

Analyzing advertising exposure and effectiveness in each of the individual media outlets (e.g., television, radio, magazine, newspaper, online, mobile, social network) is crucial for gauging their effectiveness. Recognizing that a single advertising campaign will often appear simultaneously across a wide spectrum of media, several research providers attempt to deliver an overall assessment of a marketing campaign's effectiveness across multiple media platforms.

The Simmons National Consumer Study (offered by Experian) uses a national probability sample of about 25,000 consumers and serves as a comprehensive data source allowing the cross-referencing of product usage and media exposure. The company's research encompasses both Hispanic and non-Hispanic households. Using stratified sampling, participants are sent a survey booklet that collects information about household usage of an extensive list of about 8,000 brands of products and services. In addition, each household member receives a personal survey booklet that collects extensive media usage measures across roughly 1,000 media properties as well as personal information on demographics and lifestyle, shopping behavior, and so on. The National Consumer Study is staged year-round, so client companies can observe changes in response to their brands over time. By taking into account both media habits and product usage, the data allow companies to better segment, target, and communicate to the most promising groups.[7]

GfK MRI offers syndicated data on household exposure to various media and household consumption of various products and services. Its annual survey of nearly 26,000 representative US adult respondents takes place in two phases. The first stage involves in-home personal interviews to detail media usage, demographics, and lifestyle characteristics. Because researchers talk face to face with respondents, they are able to get very detailed information about the types of media that respondents have used and can remember from the days immediately preceding the interview. In the second stage, interviewers leave a booklet with respondents to assess personal and household usage of approximately 550 product and service categories and 6,000 brands. The booklet is returned to the company, often directly to the interviewer. The key benefit of the GfK MRI study (and the Simmons study as well) is that the results can be projected to national populations. The key disadvantage to both studies, however, is that the results rely upon consumer self-reported media behavior rather than an objective measure of that behavior.

Several companies can overcome the problem of self-reports of media usage, at least in part. Recall that unobtrusive mechanical processes that can be incredibly accurate often measure media exposure. For example, comScore tracks mobile web site usage automatically among its panel members. The company also tracks a variety of other types of media usage as well, including television (the company retrieves data from millions of set-top cable television boxes) and Web usage. By going across media, the company can thus report advertising exposure (and lots of other things as well) for panel members. WebTrends offers a similar product that is based on their mobile, Web, and social media analytics. The Nielsen Company combines television viewership data from its people meters with online activity from its Digital Voice panel. In each of these cross-platform syndicated offerings, the behavioral data are much more accurate than the self-reported data of the survey-based tools described above. On the other hand, the survey-based approaches are based on representative samples and take a much wider range of media into account.

Without doubt, cross-platform research can play an increasingly important role as researchers begin to harness the different sources of data (internal and external) that are becoming available. As an example, Artie Bulgrin, ESPN's Senior Vice President for Global Research and Analytics noted that cross-platform measurement and big data represent two distinct paths. His suggestion is to combine the two instead of using big data as a replacement, which is happening often as big data becomes increasingly popular. ESPN wants to learn a variety of things from the cross-platform efforts data, including analyzing the mix of channels people view to deeper understanding regarding the time spent with various media modes.[8]

## Manager's Focus

Although the fees for standardized marketing information services are lower than the costs of conducting customized marketing research, they can still represent a significant financial investment for your organization. Therefore, you need to carefully evaluate the likely usefulness of any standardized information before purchasing it. The steps for defining a marketing problem are as pertinent to assessing the relevance of standardized marketing information services as they are to designing a primary marketing research study. A key distinction here, however, is that the provider of standardized information services will not guide you through the problem formulation process. Learning to navigate the problem formulation steps yourself is one reason this book is relevant to you as a manager.

Some standardized information services are available on a subscription basis. You may find yourself, therefore, in situations where your organization already purchases certain types of standardized marketing information on an ongoing basis. In such circumstances, it is a good idea to periodically audit the degree to which your organization actually uses the information it is receiving. This review may reveal that your organization is not taking advantage of its resources, which may prompt you to better use the standardized marketing information you already have. The audit might also lead you to conclude the information is unnecessary. Once again, if you have carefully defined the marketing problems you are facing, you will be in a good position to determine whether subscriptions to standardized marketing information services should be continued or terminated.

### 7-4e STRIVING TOWARD NIRVANA: SINGLE-SOURCE DATA

Step back for a moment from all the details of external secondary data and providers of standardized marketing information. Think about the kinds of information that marketers would like to have available to them as they market their products and services. In a perfect world, they would know everything about their customers' individual characteristics (e.g., their needs, attitudes, demographic characteristics, product knowledge, purchase intentions) and their behaviors in response to the various marketing actions that marketing managers can control. Exhibit 7.8 illustrates this idea.

Although it isn't possible to have complete information about every customer—to say nothing of consumers' exposure to marketing actions and their resulting behaviors—marketing researchers have worked for decades to create systems that tie together as much of this information as possible. Combining all of the relevant data at the individual consumer or household level produces what has become known as **single-source data**.

Much of the single-source data in industry is tightly controlled by retailers. As we've seen, a large retailer can tie the vast majority of purchases in its stores to particular households via shopping cards or store-based credit cards and point-of-purchase scanner data. To obtain a shopping card, the applicant provides certain demographic information that can then be attached to actual purchasing behavior. And the company controls the basic elements of the marketing mix, including prices, coupons sent to the customer, and so on. As a result, the retailer can use the single-source data to make important marketing decisions. Many retailers have—or could have—similar systems.

Many companies that want the advantages of single-source data, however, are not in a position to capture proprietary data. For example, suppose that Toyota wanted to understand how its advertising campaigns affected purchase of its new Camry among particular market segments. Shopping cards and scanner data simply aren't going to help. Big data analytics and a new approach to single-source data, however, might do the trick.

Consider the TRAnalytics service offered by TiVo Research and Analytics, a wholly owned subsidiary of TiVo. Using household-level media exposure captured by TiVo and cable television set-top boxes, combined with household purchase behavior obtained from retailers and other vendors across a wide variety of categories, the service can provide clients precise information about products that are purchased by households viewing particular programs or in response to particular advertisements. For example, Scripps Network Interactive recently became a client after discovering that several of its television networks (e.g., The Food Network, HGTV, The Travel Channel) scored very high among households who had actually purchased new automobiles. The service is capable of combining automobile purchase data obtained from the Experian Automotive North American Vehicle Database with minute-by-minute television viewing behavior for about a million different households, making it possible to connect purchasers of specific makes and models to particular networks and programs. Such fine-grained

> **single-source data** Data that allow researchers to link together purchase behavior, household characteristics, and advertising exposure at the household level.

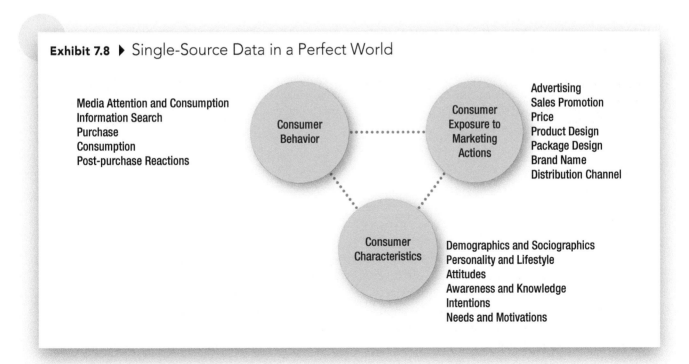

**Exhibit 7.8** ▶ Single-Source Data in a Perfect World

Media Attention and Consumption
Information Search
Purchase
Consumption
Post-purchase Reactions

Consumer Behavior

Consumer Exposure to Marketing Actions

Advertising
Sales Promotion
Price
Product Design
Package Design
Brand Name
Distribution Channel

Consumer Characteristics

Demographics and Sociographics
Personality and Lifestyle
Attitudes
Awareness and Knowledge
Intentions
Needs and Motivations

## Manager's Focus

Because the providers of standardized marketing information services present themselves as experts in specific fields and can legitimately claim that other organizations are already purchasing their services, it would be easy for you as a manager to conclude that the information they provide is of high quality. But this is not necessarily the case, especially since the criteria for determining quality and appropriateness differ across marketing situations.

Remember, the providers of standardized marketing information services do not collect data specifically for your organization. Representatives of these information suppliers have—at best—a limited understanding of your unique marketing problems and corresponding marketing intelligence needs. As a result, the burden is on you to evaluate the quality of standardized marketing information before purchasing it. Standardized

marketing information services are nothing more than commercial sources of secondary data. Researchers should feel free to ask a variety of important questions to help evaluate the quality of standardized marketing information (secondary data). These questions will help you assess the extent to which the information (a) fits your specific needs and (b) is accurate.

When you evaluate the accuracy of secondary data, include an assessment of "the general evidence of quality." This involves a careful review of the ability of the secondary marketing information service to collect the data and the appropriateness of the methods it uses. Don't be afraid to ask questions; legitimate providers of sound marketing information have nothing to hide. Beware of "super-secret" methods and sources that can't be shared. There's really no need for much mystery in the process of data collection, just sound methods and hard work.

information gives Scripps a tremendous advantage as it approaches potential automotive advertisers for its programs. Similar single-source data are available in other categories as well.[9]

A quick look at Exhibit 7.8 will confirm, however, that single-source data systems such as large retailer proprietary systems and the syndicated TRAnalytics system aren't complete, in the sense that no existing system captures all the data that marketers would like to tie to particular consumers or households. (That's why we titled this section "Striving Toward Nirvana"; we aren't there yet.) A complete system would require augmenting the available secondary data on things like media exposure and purchase behavior with primary data on consumer knowledge, attitudes, motivations, information search, post-purchase reactions, and so forth. Even if the relevant

data could be identified, the costs of collecting it would be prohibitive.

And there's one other thing. For the most part, managers are understandably focused more on how particular marketing actions produce purchase behavior than on the underlying explanation of why those actions produced purchase behavior for those particular customers. Scholars develop theories about why things work the way they do; practitioners tend to care more about discovering which actions produce which results under which conditions for which customers. As such, the emerging approaches to single-source data hold great promise. As we've noted elsewhere, there is a great need for managers and researchers who understand the potential value of the data that are increasingly available and can work to combine those data sources in ways that provide insight.

# Summary

## Learning Objective 1

**Describe the process of searching for published external secondary data.**

There are a number of steps involved in a search for published secondary data. These include identifying the information need. developing a list of key terms and names, conducting an online search for the information, compiling the information obtained and refining the list of key words and authors if necessary, consulting reference librarians for additional information, and identifying and consulting with authorities on the topic.

## Learning Objective 2

**List three common uses of the information supplied by standardized marketing information services.**

The information supplied by standardized marketing information services is commonly used to (1) profile customers, (2) measure product sales and market share, and (3) measure advertising exposure and effectiveness.

## Learning Objective 3

**Define geodemography.**

Geodemography refers to the availability of demographic, consumer behavior, and lifestyle data by arbitrary geographic boundaries that are typically small.

## Learning Objective 4

**Describe the use of diary panels and scanner data for assessing product sales.**

The key feature of a diary panel, whether recorded on paper or reported online, is that a representative group of individuals or households keeps track of purchases made or products consumed over a given period of time. Scanner data are produced by an electronic device that automatically reads the bar code imprinted on a product. Sales data are recorded when the product is scanned at the point of sale. These data are often made available to producers as a means of gauging product sales at retail.

## Learning Objective 5

**Discuss the purpose and operation of people meters and portable people meters.**

People meters attempt to measure which household members are watching which television channels at what times. Each member of the family has his or her own viewing number. Whoever turns on the set, sits down to watch, or changes the channel is supposed to enter his or her number into the people meter, which is an electronic device that stores and transmits this information to a central computer for processing. Portable people meters are pager-like devices that household meters carry with them (or wear on their clothes) to measure radio listenership or out-of-home television viewership.

## Learning Objective 6

**Define single-source measurement.**

Single-source measurement refers to organizations that have the capability to monitor product-purchase data and advertising-exposure data by household and to relate that information to the demographic characteristics of the household.

## Key Terms

standardized marketing information (page 99)
geodemographers (page 100)
scanner (page 101)
people meters (page 102)
portable people meters (page 102)
single-source data (page 105)

## Review Questions

1. Why should researchers look for published sources of secondary data before searching for standardized marketing information?
2. What is "standardized" about standardized marketing information?
3. What does it mean to "profile" customers or prospects? Why would a company need this information?
4. What is the purpose of geodemography?
5. Given that companies know their revenues, why do they also need standardized information about product sales and market share?
6. How does a diary panel work?
7. Why can the effect of scanners on standardized marketing information be described as "profound"?
8. How are people meters used to assess television viewership?
9. How are portable people meters used to assess radio listenership?
10. How might a company assess the success of its online advertising?
11. What are cross-platform services? Why might they be important?
12. What is single-source data?

# Endnotes

1. The figure and surrounding discussion are adapted from Stewart, D. W., & Kamins, M. A. (1993). *Secondary research: Information sources and methods*, 2nd ed. Thousand Oaks, CA: Sage.

2. "Customer Profile: Chase Manhattan Bank." Retrieved from http://www.cbe.wwu.edu.

3. De Los Santos, G. (2016, Dec. 21). "Nielsen to increase portable people meter sample size by 10% across 48 radio metro areas." *Nielsen Press Room*. Retrieved from http://www.nielsen.com/us/en/press-room/2016/nielsen-to-increase-portable-people-meter-sample-size-by-10-percent-across-48-radio-metro-areas.html.

4. "Starch syndicated." Retrieved from http://www.gfkmri.com/Products/Starch/StarchSyndicated.aspx.

5. Anderson, M., & Perrin, A. (2016, Sept. 7). "13% of Americans don't use the internet.  Who are they?" Retrieved from http://www.pewresearch.org/fact-tank/2016/09/07/some-americans-dont-use-the-internet-who-are-they/.

6. "Latest Rankings: Digital Media." Retrieved from https://www.comscore.com/Insights/Rankings. See also the *Digital Voice* web site, http://digitalvoice.nielsen.com/content/digitalvoice/us/en/home.html.

7. Information retrieved from http://www.experian.com/simmons-research/consumer-study-details.html.

8. Warc, (2015, July 15). "ESPN backs cross-platform research." Retrieved from https://www.warc.com/LatestNews/News/ESPN_backs_crossplatform_research.news?ID=35135.

9. "TiVo Research and Analytics (TRA) signs Scripps Networks Interactive to a research and analytics deal," Retrieved from http://pr.tivo.com/press-releases. See also the company's web site, http://www.traglobal.com.

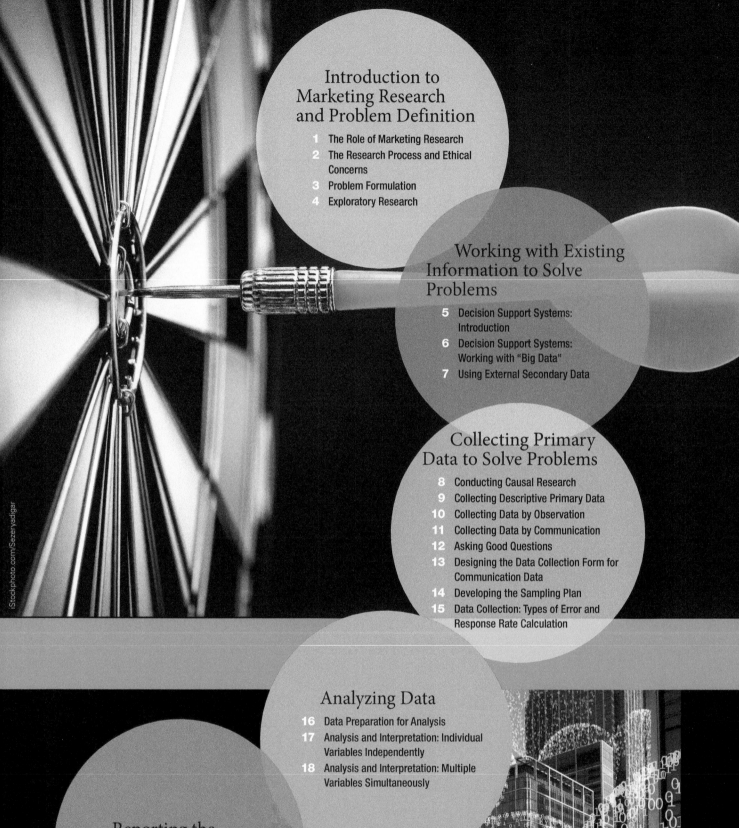

# Part 3

# Collecting Primary Data to Solve Problems

iStockphoto.com/mrcmos

CHAPTER **8**

# Conducting Causal Research

Bilion Photos/Shutterstock.com

## LEARNING OBJECTIVES

▸ Discuss the three general types of primary data research.

▸ Clarify the difference between laboratory experiments and field experiments.

▸ Explain which of the two types of experiments has greater internal validity and which has greater external validity.

▸ Describe the use of an A/B test.

▸ List the three major considerations in test marketing.

▸ Distinguish between a standard test market and a controlled test market.

▸ Discuss the advantages and disadvantages of simulated test marketing.

## [ INTRODUCTION ]

You've carefully defined the decision problem. You've gathered all the existing internal data you can find that are relevant to the decision that needs to be made. You've searched for published secondary data and tried to find syndicated research—but you still don't have the information you need to make your decision.

Now what?

This situation isn't all that unusual. Many research problems call for data that simply do not currently exist. We introduced the notion of *primary data* in Chapter 5. Recall that primary data are new-to-the-world data collected specifically for the current purpose. The truth is that unless you are facing a straightforward, recurring issue, the odds are pretty high that you're going to need to capture new data to provide solutions for many marketing problems. This chapter is the first in a series of chapters devoted to helping you become effective at gathering new data. As we've mentioned before, even if you never go on to a research career, we at least want you to understand the process and be able to evaluate research that others have conducted.

Rawpixel.com/Shutterstock.com

Take a look back at Exhibit 2.1. Our decision model has now placed us in the "generate new data" domain (i.e., the third column of the exhibit). Using one or more of three general approaches to collecting new data (i.e., exploratory, descriptive, or causal research), the task is now to collect relevant data from individuals. We briefly discuss these three categories of research in the next section and then spend the remainder of the chapter detailing the use of causal research. We'll address descriptive research in great detail in the following chapters.

## 8-1 Three Approaches to Generating New Data

In Chapter 4, we discussed several different varieties of exploratory research. Recall that the goal of exploratory research is to discover ideas and insights in the process of defining the decision problem. A soft-drink manufacturer faced with an unexpected drop in sales might conduct an exploratory study to generate possible explanations (i.e., hypotheses) that can be confirmed or refuted by further research.

Given that the main point of exploratory research is to provide insights that help define the decision problem, why bring it up now in our discussion of generating new data? There are a couple of reasons. First, exploratory data meet our definition of primary data; they are new-to-the-world data that are typically gathered with a particular purpose in mind. The second reason for considering exploratory research at this point in the process is that some companies and researchers use exploratory techniques almost exclusively in gathering new data. They find the answers they are seeking in their exploratory data, make decisions based on this information, and proceed on to other issues. And this may surprise you—but much of the time, the combination of managers' business instincts and exploratory research results will lead to reasonable decisions. It's a process that we can't endorse, however, when a bad decision would be costly.

**Descriptive research** is typically concerned with describing a group on various characteristics (e.g., brand attitude, preferences, demographic variables) or the relationship between characteristics (e.g., is brand attitude different for men versus women?). An investigation of the trends in the consumption of soft drinks with respect to such characteristics as age, sex, and geographic location is a descriptive study. Descriptive research is very common, can be carried out using a survey or by gathering behavioral data, and sometimes involves drawing a sample from a larger population. Descriptive research is what you probably thought of when you heard the phrase *marketing research.*

**Causal research** is concerned with determining cause-and-effect relationships. Causal studies typically take the form of experiments, because experiments are best suited for determining cause and effect. For instance, a soft-drink manufacturer may want to determine which of several sales promotions is most effective. One way to proceed would be to use different sales promotions (e.g., coupons) in different geographic areas and investigate which approach generated the highest sales. If the study was designed properly, the company might have evidence

to suggest that one or the other promotional approach caused the higher rate of sales.

So, what's the best type of research for a particular situation? Most, but not all, projects involve exploratory research in the process of defining the problem and developing insights and hypotheses about what is happening (in the case of unplanned changes in the marketing environment) or what might happen (in the case of planned change in the marketing environment). Unless researchers arrive at an answer to a low-risk decision problem in the midst of their exploratory research—or can gather enough relevant secondary data to make the decision—marketing research projects often proceed to a descriptive data collection phase. Descriptive research should be conducted, however, only when researchers know what the key issues are and what questions need to be asked. And when a company needs precise answers about the effects of various proposed marketing actions on important outcomes, managers use causal research.

These three basic approaches to generating new data can be viewed as stages in a continuous process. Exhibit 8.1 shows the interrelationships. Exploratory studies are often seen as the initial step. Consider, for example, the following problem: "Brand *X*'s share of the soft drink market is slipping. Why?" This statement is too broad to serve as a guide for detailed descriptive or causal research. Exploratory research should be used to gather insights and develop research problems that would help solve the manager's decision problem. The research problems, which would be based on hypotheses about why market share is decreasing, would then serve as specific guides for descriptive or causal studies.

Suppose the tentative explanation that emerged from the exploratory research was that the particular brand of soft drink was being viewed in the marketplace as "old-fashioned" or "not exciting anymore." In a descriptive research project, researchers could draw a random sample of people who consume soft drinks and have them rate various brands of soft drinks (including Brand *X*, of course) along key dimensions to determine exactly how Brand *X* stacks up against other brands in the category. Using descriptive research, researchers might also determine which attributes of soft drinks are most closely associated with consumer attitudes and self-reported purchasing behaviors for Brand *X*. In short, through descriptive research we could learn a whole lot about how Brand *X* is perceived in the marketplace and how it compares to competing brands on important product attributes.

If the descriptive study's results demonstrated that the brand no longer scored well on key attributes with consumers, managers might decide to bolster it with a new advertising campaign. But spending substantial amounts of advertising money to revive fading brands is

**descriptive research** Research in which the major emphasis is on describing characteristics of a group or the extent to which variables are related.

**causal research** Type of research in which the major emphasis is on determining cause-and-effect relationships.

**Exhibit 8.1** ▶ Relationships Among Types of Primary Data Research

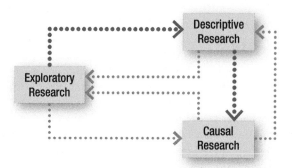

risky business. Is there a way to determine, in advance, if the new campaign will be effective at changing the brand's image? The researchers might choose to test the effectiveness of the proposed campaign through a test market study, a key form of causal research.

Although we've presented the different types of research as if they must proceed in order, that's not always the case. Sometimes managers will get results from descriptive or causal projects that lead to more questions. Then these questions, in turn, lead to more exploratory research. The smaller arrows in Exhibit 8.1 demonstrate the different ways in which the types of research can be interrelated. We present the basics of causal research in this chapter, including several examples of how marketing researchers apply the concept of experimentation in practice.

## 8-2    Causal Research

Everyone is familiar with the general notion of causality, the idea that one thing leads to the occurrence of another. The scientific notion of causality is fairly complex, however, and a detailed discussion of it is beyond the scope of this book. An important point to recognize from the start is that we can never really prove that one thing causes another.

> An important point to recognize from the start is that we can never really prove that one thing causes another

### 8-2a    ESTABLISHING CAUSALITY

In order to say that one thing "caused" another, three conditions must be met: (1) There must be consistent variation between the cause and the effect, (2) the time order

of the cause and the effect must be correct, and (3) other explanations must be eliminated.

### Consistent Variation

Suppose that an auto manufacturer wanted to test the relationship between customer satisfaction with its dealerships and the company's market share in different areas. If dealership satisfaction leads to higher market share (this is our hypothesis), we will find the following: In territories where our dealers receive high marks for customer satisfaction, we should have higher market shares than in territories with poor levels of customer satisfaction. If we find, however, that there is no relationship between dealership satisfaction and market share (if dealerships with higher levels of customer satisfaction don't have higher market shares), we would conclude that either our hypothesis is faulty or that there are additional factors involved.

If market share increases as dealership satisfaction increases across the dealerships that we are studying, we have found evidence of consistent variation. The cause-and-effect variables change in a consistent way. The pattern of change is also consistent with our expectations, or our theory, about what ought to occur.

A consistent pattern of variation or relationship between two variables is not enough to conclude that one caused the other, however. All we can conclude is that the correlation makes the hypothesis more likely; it doesn't prove it. We are always inferring, rather than proving, that a causal relationship exists. In the same way, the lack of an association between two variables is not enough to conclude that one variable didn't cause the other. This is because sometimes other variables can be related to the cause-and-effect variables in a way that hides the true relationship between them.

### Time Order

This one is easy: Causes cannot come after effects. Suppose that the auto manufacturer studied the relationship between dealership customer satisfaction and market share over time and found the following consistent pattern: Within 24 months after a substantial increase in market share, customer satisfaction ratings increased. As before, there is consistent variation between the proposed cause-and-effect variables. However, our proposed causal variable (customer satisfaction with the dealership) has occurred after our proposed effect variable (market share), which disproves our hypothesis. Instead, we might develop a new hypothesis that improving market share may lead to greater resources to provide a higher quality customer experience at the dealership. The situation is actually a little more complicated than this (it is technically possible for causes and effects to occur simultaneously or for two variables to each cause the other), but the main idea remains the same: Causes cannot come after effects.

### Elimination of Other Explanations

The final condition for establishing causality is the most difficult to meet—and it's the reason we cannot *prove* that one thing causes another. To fully establish causality, you must eliminate all other possible causes for the outcome variable. This may mean physically holding other factors constant in a lab experiment (more on this a little later), or it may mean adjusting the results to remove the effects of other possible causal factors. Here's the kicker: Even if we've held constant or accounted for all the other possible causes we can think of, we can *never* be certain that there's not another potential cause that we don't know about yet.

Let's go back to the automobile manufacturer who was trying to determine whether dealership satisfaction influences market share. Establishing a relationship between customer satisfaction and market share and that the changes in market share followed the changes in dealership quality would successfully achieve the first two conditions for determining causality. We would also need to demonstrate that pricing strategies, new models of cars, competitive actions, the overall economic environment in different regions, and so on, didn't cause the changes in market share. Even if we hold some of these things constant (no price incentives in the markets under study during the test period) and control others by measuring them and accounting for them statistically (competitors' pricing strategies), we still can't prove that there isn't one or more additional variable that might have caused the changes in market share.

Does this mean that we shouldn't bother trying to establish causal relationships? Not at all. Even though we can't prove with certainty that a change in one variable produces a change in another, our research can help narrow down the likely causal relationship between two variables by eliminating other possible causes. With descriptive research, we typically do this by measuring the other variables and attempting to control their effects on the outcome variable via statistical techniques. With causal research, we use experiments to work toward establishing possible causal relationships.

8-2b ## EXPERIMENTS AS CAUSAL RESEARCH

An **experiment** can provide more convincing evidence of causal relationships than an exploratory or descriptive study can because of the control it gives investigators. In an experiment, a researcher manipulates, or sets the levels of, one or more proposed causal variables (independent variables) to examine the effect on one or more outcome variables (dependent variables). The researcher does so while attempting to account for the effects of all other possible causal variables, usually by holding them constant. Because we are able to control the levels of the independent variable(s), we can be more confident that the relationships we discover are real.

There are two basic types of experiments—laboratory experiments and field experiments. Each has advantages and disadvantages researchers need to be familiar with.

### Laboratory Experiments

A **laboratory experiment** is one in which we create a situation with the desired conditions, then manipulate some variables while controlling others. By holding other variables constant while manipulating the independent variable(s), we can observe and measure what happens to the dependent variables while the effect of other factors is minimized.

Here's an example of a lab experiment. Researchers used an experiment to better understand "trip chaining," the practice of driving to more than one retail shop on the same shopping trip (as opposed to making separate trips to each retailer). The researchers believed that consumers prefer to drive short distances between retailers (that is, the retailers are "clustered") rather than to drive longer distances between retailers ("non-clustered" retailers)—even when the total distance traveled from home, to the retailers, and back home again was the same. To test this hypothesis, the researchers developed detailed maps and driving directions for both clustered and non-clustered trip chains and presented them to undergraduate students who agreed to serve as experimental subjects. Street names were changed and some streets removed from the maps presented to subjects; in this way, prior knowledge of the geographic area could be controlled. Students saw both the clustered and the non-clustered manipulations of trip chains and then indicated which would be their preferred

> **experiment** Scientific investigation in which an investigator manipulates one or more independent variables and observes the degree to which the dependent variables change.
>
> **laboratory experiment** Research investigation in which investigators create a situation with exact conditions in order to control some variables and manipulate others.

route. Confirming the researchers' hypothesis, 74% chose the clustered route.[1]

In some ways, the task presented to subjects was similar to that confronting consumers in real life. For example, when we shop for various items, we must choose which routes to take. In other respects, however, the study wasn't as realistic: These were not the real consumers living in the real geographic area represented on the maps.

Because we are able to produce a somewhat "sterile" environment in which outside variables are held constant, lab experiments generally have relatively high degrees of internal validity. **Internal validity** refers to our ability to know that changes in the dependent variable are due to the experimental variable and not to other factors. This is important; marketing managers need to know whether or not changes in the experimental variable (degree of clustering) actually produced the observed changes in the outcome variable (consumer preference) so that they can formulate a marketing strategy.

### Field Experiments

A **field experiment** is a research study in a realistic or natural situation, although it, too, involves the manipulation of one or more variables under as carefully controlled conditions as possible. Field experiments differ from lab experiments mostly in terms of environment.

The researchers studying consumer preferences for clustered (versus non-clustered) trip chains also conducted a field experiment. In this case, the experiment was conducted with residents who actually lived in the area that had been mapped for subjects in the lab experiment. For the field study, however, researchers used a telephone survey and based the study on the subjects' home address and the locations of actual retailers in the area. Asked to imagine that they needed to make trips to the two kinds of retailers, subjects then chose between two alternative routes (one that was clustered and one that was non-clustered). As in the lab study experiment, even though the overall travel distance for each option was about the same, subjects preferred the clustered trip chain compared with the non-clustered trip chain.

Note the differences in the two studies. In the field experiment, no attempt was made to set up special conditions. Manipulation of the experimental variable—the degree to which the trip chain was clustered or not—was imposed in a natural environment. The laboratory experiment, on the other hand, was contrived. Subjects were not real consumers considering real shopping trips that they might make to real retailers located in their real home environments.

**internal validity**
The degree to which an outcome can be attributed to an experimental variable and not to other factors.

**field experiment**
Research study in a realistic situation in which one or more independent variables are manipulated by the experimenter under as carefully controlled conditions as the situation will permit.

**external validity**
The degree to which the results of an experiment can be generalized, or extended, to other situations.

**A/B test** A field experiment in which two versions (i.e., A and B) of some marketing element are randomly assigned to subjects and then compared on outcomes of interest.

Field studies usually have higher degrees of external validity than do lab studies. **External validity** refers to the extent to which the results of an experiment can be generalized, or extended, to other situations. Field studies have higher external validity because of the more realistic conditions of the experiment. In our example, real consumers reported their preferences about shopping behavior in their own geographic area. Note, however, that external validity and internal validity work against one another: Having greater external validity means giving up a degree of internal validity and vice versa. For example, to gain greater internal validity, we must hold more elements in the situation constant across conditions, and this makes the experiment less realistic, thereby lowering external validity. Similarly, if we want more external validity, the more realistic environment that is required serves to decrease internal validity.

So, which type of validity is more important? The answer is that both types are important. Both internal and external validity are matters of degree rather than all-or-nothing propositions. A study with little internal validity is worthless; on the other hand, a study with little external validity won't help a marketing manager very much either. One possible strategy is to conduct both types of experiments. The laboratory experiment can be used to establish the basic cause-and-effect relationship between one or more independent variables and the dependent variable(s), and the field experiment can be used to confirm the effect in a more natural environment, thus providing some evidence of external validity.

Field experiments are growing in popularity, most likely due to their higher levels of external validity and the ease with which certain types can be implemented in online settings. The following sections present two important types of field experiments, A/B testing and market testing.

## 8-3    Field Experiments in Marketing: A/B Testing

An **A/B test** is a simple field experiment in which two versions (i.e., A and B) of some marketing element are randomly assigned to subjects in the field and then compared on outcomes of interest. A/B testing (also called *split testing*) is commonly used in online settings as a means of optimizing the performance of company web sites. For example, managers at Bionic Gloves, an online retailer specializing in a range of different types of gloves, were concerned about shopping cart abandonment—too many of their shoppers were exiting the web site after adding items to their online shopping carts, never returning to complete the transaction. Researchers decided to use an A/B test to determine if the "gift card code" or "special offer code" boxes that appeared on the existing checkout page might somehow be causing shoppers to leave the site. They created a new version of the checkout page that was identical to the original, except that it included neither of the boxes for special code numbers. Over the course of 48 days, 1,400 visitors were randomly assigned to either the A (original) or B (revised) version of the checkout page. The result: The new version of the checkout page (i.e., no boxes for special codes) increased revenues by nearly 25%. The researchers speculated that when shoppers saw the boxes for special codes they left the web site to hunt for the promotional codes—then many of them simply didn't return.[2]

Now let's take a closer look at the study conducted for Bionic Gloves. Because the study was conducted in a live setting, with real consumers spending real dollars in real situations, this clearly qualifies as a field experiment (as opposed to a lab experiment). Despite being conducted in the field, however, this study held relatively high levels of internal validity to go along with its high external validity because of the tightly controlled nature of the online context. The manipulation of the checkout page (i.e., the original page with special code boxes versus the new checkout page without the boxes) served as the independent variable, with revenues generated serving as the dependent variable.

Sometimes A/B tests are conducted in offline settings, and sometimes they can be much more complicated than the test conducted for Bionic Gloves. Still, simple tests are routinely performed, most following a structure similar to that shown in Exhibit 8.2. Multiple companies provide analytic software for implementing and analyzing data from A/B tests. Many companies rely on Google Analytics, the platform used by the online recipe company Key Ingredient, as outlined in Research Window 8.1.

With A/B testing, sometimes the difference between outcomes of versions tested is very small. For Key Ingredient, the proposed new version of its web site reduced the mean number of pageviews by only 4%, but this would have been enough of a difference to greatly affect the performance of the company. A study conducted by Amazon once confirmed that a new algorithm for making purchase recommendations was superior to an older algorithm, producing an increase in revenue of 3%. For Amazon, 3% amounts to several hundred million US dollars.[3]

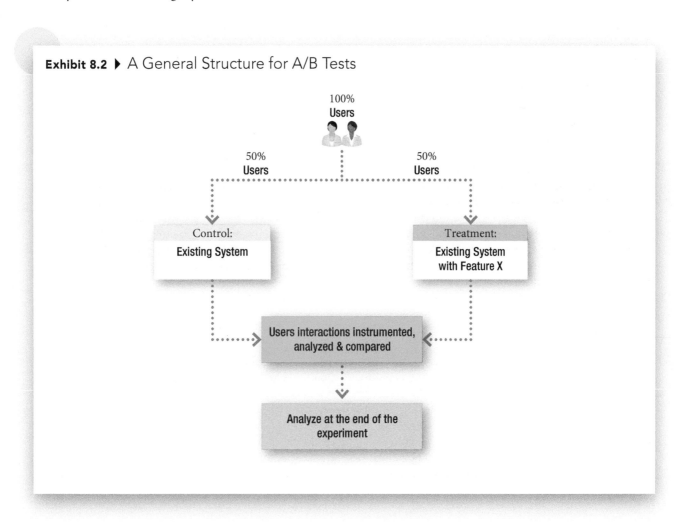

**Exhibit 8.2 ▶** A General Structure for A/B Tests

## research window 8.1

### How Key Ingredient Used A/B Tests to Design Web Site

Key Ingredient was founded in 2005 in Austin, Texas, with the goal of helping people succeed in cooking every day. Since that time, Key Ingredient has become an important digital cooking ecosystem, with an organic, shareable, free-to-use, online collection of more than two million recipes. Key Ingredient is accessible on the Web and through the Android and iOS mobile platforms.

Like many Web-based companies, Key Ingredient makes most of its revenue through advertising. As a result, getting visitors to stay on the web site longer and click on more pages is a critical driver of results and revenue. "Pageviews" has become a commonly used—and very important—web site metric, because the more pages viewed, the more ads shown, and the more advertising revenues earned.

In late 2015, Key Ingredient was considering a change in the background color of its web site homepage—from gray to white—to better appeal to members of the booming millennial market. Managers believed that a cleaner, more modern approach to design might help attract and retain this important demographic. They thought that switching from a gray background to a white background might be a more attractive design choice for this audience, potentially leading to more pageviews (and revenue). In fact, managers had great confidence that the new design was superior to the original. Before they implemented the change, however, managers decided to test their ideas.

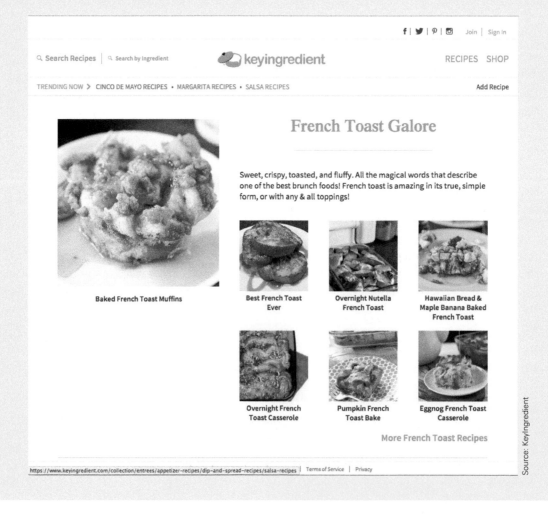

Source: KeyIngredient

### About the Experiment

To test the new design, researchers within the company implemented an A/B test. Some managers expressed concern that the new design might alienate existing users, many of whom were not in the millennial demographic. If they were right, a drop in pageviews would mean that even if millennials liked the design, the negative effect from other users had overwhelmed any positive effects from millennials. Managers were confident that the new design would be preferred, but they ran the A/B test anyway as part of their routine approach to such proposed changes.

For the actual test, two versions of the homepage were prepared that differed only in terms of background (i.e., gray versus white; the independent variable—see below). For two weeks, each visitor to the company's web site ($n = 17, 398$) was randomly assigned to one of the two experimental conditions and the number of pages viewed during each session was recorded (i.e., average number pageviews was the dependent variable).

### The Results

At the conclusion of the two-week experiment, users exposed to the original gray background viewed an average of 5.59 pages per session. Those exposed to the new white background viewed an average of 5.38 pages per session—a decrease of nearly 4%. (That may not sound like much, but a decrease in pageviews of this magnitude would have resulted in substantial lost revenue for Key Ingredient.)

Bottom line: The field experiment saved the company from making a decision favored by managers that would have directly affected the company's profitability. The experiment allowed the company to explore, test, and ultimately reject a bad idea—even one that was "obvious" on the surface to managers.

## 8-4 Field Experiments in Marketing: Market Testing

**Market testing** (sometimes called **test marketing**) involves the use of a controlled experiment done in a limited but carefully selected section of the marketplace. Market testing is often used to predict the sales or profit outcomes of one or more proposed marketing actions. Very often, the action in question is the marketing of a new product or service. Even if a company has performed previous tests of the product concept, the product package, the advertising copy, and so on, the test market is still the final gauge of consumer acceptance of the product. For example, fast food restaurants routinely will test new menu items in selected markets before making a decision about a national roll-out. McDonald's used test markets to determine that demand existed for its higher-end McCafé coffee offerings before beginning the commercialization process on a larger scale. At present, the company is testing a new breakfast Happy Meal for kids in select stores.[4]

Test marketing is not restricted to testing the sales potential of new products; it has been used to examine the effectiveness of almost every element of the marketing mix. Market tests have been used to measure the effectiveness of new displays, the responsiveness of sales to shelf-space changes, the impact of changes in retail prices on market shares, the price elasticity of demand for products, the effect of different commercials on sales of products, the differential effects of price and advertising on demand, and even changes in the channel of distribution.

### 8-4a KEY ISSUES IN MARKET TESTING

#### Cost

Cost is a big issue in test marketing. Cost can include everything from hardware and software costs in setting up virtual test markets to the costs associated with doing live tests in the field (e.g., product distribution, in-store shelf maintenance, and a host of other expenses). It is expensive to set up virtual test markets—but it is much more expensive to run tests in the field where you have to incur the usual costs of getting a new product in the channel of distribution—including the cost of developing and producing the actual product.

> **market testing (test marketing)**
> A controlled experiment done in a limited but carefully selected sector of the marketplace.

#### Time

The time required for an adequate test market can also be substantial. Altria spent three years testing a new cigarette called Marlboro Ultra Smooth—which was

> Market testing is often used to predict the sales or profit outcomes of one or more proposed marketing actions

## Manager's Focus

In Chapter 4, we cautioned you to avoid using focus group interviews until you are convinced that doing so is truly the most appropriate way of gathering exploratory data. You should understand that descriptive research—especially surveys—can be overused in much the same way as focus groups. Much of the time, researchers are quick to recommend them—and managers readily approve them—without carefully considering whether there might be a more appropriate way to collect the needed information. As a manager, you should specifically discuss with researchers whether a given situation would be best addressed with descriptive research or causal research. Managers are too often willing to make decisions based on associations found in surveys (because they are relatively simple to obtain) and too seldom insist on research that will enable them to infer cause-and-effect relationships. The danger of this common approach can be seen in the following example.

A friend, whose identity will be kept anonymous, was the CEO of a company that grew produce items that were marketed through grocery stores. When developing new packaging for a product, the CEO hired the services of a marketing research consultant. The consultant completed a series of focus group interviews in which questions were asked about the features of packages that consumers found to be most desirable. Based on this information, several prototype packages were designed. In personal interview surveys, consumers evaluated the alternative package designs, and the one most preferred by the target consumer groups was selected. After the new packaged items arrived in supermarkets, the company was dismayed to discover that consumers were not buying them. The CEO visited stores to observe consumers' buying processes. He repeatedly witnessed consumers picking up the new packages, looking them over, placing them back down, and ultimately buying a competitor's brand. When he asked consumers why they had chosen not to buy his brand, most of them told him that while the new packages were attractive in appearance, they did not permit the consumer to see the produce inside. The CEO was embarrassed to realize that he and his research consultant never bothered to test for actual market response before implementing the new package.

Managers must recognize that descriptive survey data generally are a poor substitute for market tests when trying to gauge how the target market will respond to changes in marketing strategy. Consumers' responses to questions on surveys do not always correspond well with their actual behavior in the marketplace.

---

designed to be safer than regular cigarettes—before deciding to discontinue the product due to lack of demand. Chick-fil-A tested a spicy chicken sandwich for two-and-a-half years in Baltimore, Maryland, before rolling it out nationwide.[5]

Many times, though, we simply don't have the luxury of spending years in test markets (which is unfortunate, because a test market's accuracy increases with time). Virtual test markets can be completed much more quickly and inexpensively, but their accuracy decreases substantially because of the simulated nature of the context—these are more like lab experiments than field experiments in many ways. We'll discuss the different types of test markets a little later.

### Control

The problems associated with control show up in several ways. First, there are the control problems in the experiment itself. What specific test markets will be used? How will product distribution be organized in those markets? Can the firm get wholesalers and retailers to cooperate? Can the test markets and control cities be matched sufficiently to rule out market characteristics as the primary reason for different sales results?

One of the problems with market testing is the possibility that competitors can see a company's new product before it is fully commercialized. With many market tests, there are few secrets. When a Frito-Lay assistant brand manager would fly to a test-market city in Iowa to follow up with test sites selling the company's new Baked Lays product, the gate attendant at the small airport would routinely tell her which other snack foods companies had also had representatives in town to check the progress of the new product. In addition, competitors can, and do, sabotage marketing experiments by cutting the prices of their own products or by gobbling up quantities of the test marketer's product—thereby creating excitement and false confidence on the part of the test marketer.

Test marketing has been called the most dangerous game in all of marketing because so many things can misfire, as shown by the examples in Exhibit 8.3. Some of these misfires represent mistakes made by the company testing the new product (including the failure to test the product

**Exhibit 8.3** ▶ (Mis)adventures in Market Testing

- Procter & Gamble once developed a new liquid bleach, Vibrant, to compete with Clorox brand bleach. Days after putting the new product into a standard test market in Portland, Maine, virtually all households in the test market area had received a free gallon of Clorox bleach, completely skewing the results of the market test.

- When asked, consumers will often indicate a desire for healthier menu selections at fast-food restaurants. In response, some time ago, McDonald's developed and introduced the McLean Deluxe into all of its US locations without doing its normal market testing. The product never caught on and was later discontinued.

- A few years ago, a company developed a temporary hair-coloring product that consumers used by inserting a block of solid hair dye into a special comb. It failed miserably. On hot days when people perspired, the hair dye ran down their necks and foreheads if they had applied a little too much. Apparently, no one bothered to test the product in conditions where people might perspire.

- Frito-Lay test-marketed its Max potato, corn, and tortilla chips containing the Olestra fat substitutes in Grand Junction, Colorado; Eau Claire, Wisconsin; and Cedar Rapids, Iowa. A television crew sampled the chips and succumbed to diarrhea and then broadcast a report about it, creating lots of bad publicity for the chips.

- When Procter & Gamble introduced its Always brand sanitary napkin in a test market in Minnesota, Kimberly-Clark Corporation and Johnson & Johnson countered with free products, lots of coupons, and big dealer discounts, which caused Always not to do as well as expected.

- When a large packaged-goods company set out to introduce a squirtable soft drink concentrate for children, it held focus groups to monitor user reaction. In the sessions, children squirted the product neatly into cups. Yet once at home, few could resist the temptation to decorate their parents' floors and walls with colorful liquid. After a flood of parental complaints, the product was withdrawn from development.

Sources: "War-Gaming with P&G's A.G. Lafley," *Fortune*, April 8, 2013; Bret Thorn, "Lesson Learned: Menu Miscues," *Nation's Restaurant News*, May 20, 2002, downloaded via ProQuest, June 23, 2005; Ann Lynn and Michael Lynn, "Experiments and Quasi-Experiments: Methods for Evaluating Marketing Options," *Cornell Hotel and Restaurant Administration Quarterly*, April 2003, downloaded via ProQuest on June 16, 2005; Annetta Miller and Karen Springen, "Will Fake Fat Play in Peoria?" *Newsweek*, June 3, 1996, p. 50; Kathleen Deveny, "Failure of Its Oven Lovin' Cookie Dough Shows Pillsbury Pitfalls of New Products," *The Wall Street Journal*, June 17, 1993, pp. B1 and B8; Jack Neff, "Is Testing the Answer?" *Advertising Age*, July 9, 2001, p. 13; Annetta Miller and Dody Tsiantor, "A Test for Market Research," *Newsweek* 110, December 28, 1987, pp. 32–33; Leslie Brennan, "Test Marketing Put to the Test," *Sales and Marketing Management* 138, March 1987, pp. 65–68; Kevin Wiggins, "Simulated Test Marketing Winning Acceptance," *Marketing News* 19, March 1, 1985, pp. 15 and 19; Eleanor Johnson Tracy, "Testing Time for Test Marketing," *Fortune* 110, October 29, 1984, pp. 75–76; Damon Darden, "Faced with More Competition, P&G Sees New Products as Crucial to Earnings Growth," *The Wall Street Journal*, September 13, 1983, pp. 37 and 53; Lynn G. Reiling, "Consumer Misuse Mars Sampling for Sunlight Dishwashing Liquid," *Marketing News* 16, September 3, 1982, pp. 1 and 12; Betty Morris, "New Campbell Entry Sets Off a Big Spaghetti Sauce Battle," *The Wall Street Journal*, December 2, 1982, p. 31; and Roger Recklefs, "Success Comes Hard in the Tricky Business of Creating Products," *The Wall Street Journal*, August 23, 1978, pp. 1 and 27

in the first place) and some demonstrate competitive reactions. Others simply reflect the true value of a market test: The ability to spot problems early, before they become even more costly and embarrassing.

**8-4b    TYPES OF TEST MARKETS**

There are three general categories of test markets: standard, controlled, and simulated. In a **standard test market**, such as those we've been describing, a company develops a product and then attempts to sell it through the normal distribution channels in a number of test-market cities. The product's potential success can be gauged, and different elements of the marketing mix for the product can be experimentally varied with an eye toward developing the best marketing mix combination for the

**standard test market** A test market in which the company sells the product through its normal distribution channels.

product. The key feature of a standard test market is that the producer must sell the product to distributors, wholesalers, and/or retailers just as it would any other product in the test markets chosen.

What makes some cities better than others for standard test markets? Several factors are involved. The proposed test-market city needs to be demographically representative of the larger market in which the product will ultimately be sold. Most popular test-market cities are reasonably representative of the overall population, although some are more representative than others. If the product is geared more toward a specific segment of the population, however, then markets should be chosen with high representation of that segment. For example, for products targeted toward Hispanic consumers,

## Manager's Focus

As a manager, you need to be fully aware of the risks inherent in standard market tests. The obvious goal of such testing is to get an advantage over your competitors. Implementing your marketing strategy in selected markets will make your company vulnerable to a variety of competitive responses, however. So, when deciding whether or not to use a standard market test, an important decision criterion is the degree to which your company has some type of reasonable protection. This can come from the legal system (e.g., trademarks, copyrights, patents) or barriers to market entry such as the need for large capital investments, long product development time frames, or dominant brand equity that would enable your company to overcome any

threat imposed by a competitor that attempted to steal your idea and beat you to the market with it. In the absence of such protection, it may be in your company's best interest to use an alternative, such as a simulated market test. Due to competitive risk factors, even companies as large and dominant as Procter & Gamble have limited their use of standard market tests and have increased their use of more secure approaches.

In most situations, if it's financially feasible, you should employ some type of market test before implementing a new or revised marketing strategy. Because managing a market test can be a complex undertaking, it is often wise to hire a firm that specializes in market tests to handle the process for you.

---

test markets with higher proportions of Hispanic residents are obviously desirable.

Popular standard test-market cities also possess other features prized by researchers. The test market should be large enough that it has its own media outlets (e.g., newspapers and radio and television stations), which allow tests of advertising and promotion. It must also be large enough to have a sufficient number of the right kind of retail outlets. When Taco Bell was looking for a test market for its Grilled Stuft Burrito, for example, it was important to find a market with a good mix of company and franchise-owned restaurants. Fresno, California, was selected.[6] It is also important that test markets be geographically isolated from other cities in order to avoid "spillover" effects from nearby markets where testing is not taking place. Such spillover effects might include advertising and other promotion or a significant percentage of consumers in the test market traveling outside the test market to shop.

In a **controlled test market** (sometimes called a forced-distribution test market), the entire test program is conducted by an outside service such as GameChanger or Integrated Research Associates. The service establishes relationships with retailers and can therefore guarantee distribution. If a company wants to test the performance of a new type of air freshener, for example, it will produce the product, get it to the research company, write a check—and wait for the results. With no concerns about getting retailers to put the product on their shelves, a

**controlled test market** An entire test program conducted by an outside service in a market in which it can guarantee distribution.

**simulated test market (STM)** A study in which consumer ratings are obtained along with likely or actual purchase data often obtained in a simulated store environment; the data are fed into computer models to produce sales and market share predictions.

company can know in short order (sometimes within a couple of weeks) how actual consumers will respond to the new product. Often, they can also gather additional attitudinal data from the consumers.

This all sounds good, but there's an important catch: Not all companies that produce new products can guarantee that those products will get distribution that quickly—or at all—in the marketplace. Even if a company has enough market power to get distribution, controlled test markets are usually performed much faster than standard market tests. Although the results can be reasonably accurate, they typically aren't as accurate as a standard test market.

A third type of market testing is the **simulated test market (STM)**. A simulated test market differs from standard and controlled test markets in that consumers do not purchase the product (or service) being tested from a retail store. In fact, in many cases, the product has not even been put into production. Instead, researchers will typically recruit consumers to participate in the simulated study. Consumers are shown the new product or product concept and asked to rate its features. They may be shown commercials for it and for competitors' products. All the information is fed into a computer model, which has equations for the repeat purchase and market share likely to be achieved by the test model. The key to successful simulation is the equations built into the computer model. Nielsen's BASES simulation approach, an industry leader, reports accuracy within 9% for first year sales forecasts.[7]

**Exhibit 8.4** ▶ Shopping for Ketchup in a Virtual Store

Source: Peter Breen, "Shaping Retail: The Use of Virtual Store Simulations in Marketing Research and Beyond," undated, the In-Store Marketing Institute, p. 5 (photo credited to Decision Insight).

Increasingly, simulated test markets are taking the form of **virtual test markets** that allow experimental subjects to "interact" with products as they view retailer store shelves—and sometimes whole stores—electronically, rather than physically. How does that work? Exhibit 8.4 presents a display that subjects might see if they click a bottle of Heinz Tomato Ketchup on a virtual store shelf. This process is meant to simulate the process of taking the bottle off the shelf, examining it, and potentially adding it to a shopping cart. Because the shopping experience in a virtual test market is completely controlled by the researcher, just about any element of the marketing mix can be manipulated and effects on important outcomes can be measured. In many ways, virtual test markets are laboratory experiments and, as a result, benefit from higher degrees of internal validity than do other forms of market testing.

**virtual test market**
A simulated test market in which subjects "interact" with products and stores electronically, rather than physically.

Virtual test markets also share the key disadvantage of lab studies as well. When "shoppers" examine products, prices, and promotions in virtual "stores," there is less certainty that the results of causal research studies will transfer to the marketplace (lowered external validity).

## Comparing the Three Types of Test Markets

Marketers who need to test-market a new product or to fine-tune an element of a marketing program must choose which type of test market to use. Each of the approaches has advantages and disadvantages.

One advantage of simulated test markets is the protection they provide from competitors. They are also good for assessing trial- and repeat-purchasing behavior. They are faster than full-scale tests and are particularly good for spotting weak products, which allows firms to avoid full-scale testing of these products. Plus, of the three

**Exhibit 8.5** ▶ Relative Advantages and Disadvantages of Different Types of Test Markets

| RANK/ORGANIZATION | SIMULATED | CONTROLLED | STANDARD |
|---|---|---|---|
| Speed | *** | ** | * |
| Cost | *** | ** | * |
| Security | *** | ** | * |
| Validity | | | |
|    Internal | *** | ** | * |
|    External | * | ** | *** |
| Prediction accuracy | * | ** | *** |

*** = most favorable; * = least favorable

forms we've discussed, simulated test markets are the least expensive. The primary disadvantage of simulated test markets is that they do not provide any information about the firm's ability to secure trade support for the product or about what competitive reaction is likely to be. As a result, they are more suited for evaluating product extensions than for examining the likely success of radically different new products.

Controlled test markets are more expensive than simulated test markets, but they are less costly than standard test markets. One reason they cost less is that the research supplier provides distribution and handles all aspects of display, pricing, and so on. This perfect implementation of the marketing plan also represents one of the weaknesses of the controlled test market. Acceptance or rejection of the new product by the trade in the marketplace is typically critical to the success of any new product. A controlled test market guarantees acceptance by the trade for the duration of the test, but acceptance will not be guaranteed during the actual marketing of the product. When a new product fits in nicely with a company's existing line, for which it already has distribution, the controlled test market is a fairly good indicator. When the product

is new or represents a radical departure for the manufacturer, the question of trade support is much more problematic, and the controlled test is much less useful under these circumstances.

The traditional, or standard, test market provides a more natural environment than either the simulated or the controlled test market and, as a result, offers the greatest degree of prediction accuracy. This advantage must be balanced against some important disadvantages, however. Standard test markets are the most expensive, take the most time, and are the most likely to tip off competitors compared with the other approaches. Even so, the standard test market may be a logical choice when (1) it is important for the firm to test its ability to actually sell to the trade and get distribution for the product; (2) the capital investment is significant and the firm needs a prolonged test market to accurately assess its capital needs or its technical ability to manufacture the product; and/or (3) the company is entering new territory and needs to build its experience base so that it can play for real, but it wants to learn how to do so on a limited scale. The relative advantages and disadvantages of the three basic types of test markets are shown in Exhibit 8.5.

# Summary

## Learning Objective 1

**Discuss the three general types of primary data collection.**

The three general types of primary data collection are exploratory research, descriptive research, and causal research. The major emphasis in exploratory research is on the discovery of ideas and insights. Descriptive research is typically concerned with describing characteristics of a group or the extent to which variables are related. A causal research design is concerned with determining cause-and-effect relationships.

## Learning Objective 2

**Clarify the difference between laboratory experiments and field experiments.**

Laboratory experiments differ from field experiments primarily in terms of environment. The researcher creates a setting for a laboratory experiment; a field experiment is conducted in a natural setting. Both types, however, involve control and manipulation of one or more presumed causal factors.

## Learning Objective 3

**Explain which of the two types of experiments has greater internal validity and which has greater external validity.**

The laboratory experiment typically has greater internal validity because it allows greater control of the variables. Field experiments are generally considered more externally valid, meaning that their results are better able to be generalized to other situations.

## Learning Objective 4

**Describe the use of an A/B test.**

An A/B test, also known as a split test, is a unique form of field experiment most characteristically used in online environments. Such tests are used to better balance internal and external validity by firms controlling web- or mobile-based variables (internal validity) while functioning in the real, digital world (external validity).

## Learning Objective 5

**List the three major considerations in test marketing.**

Three of the more important issues in test marketing are cost, time, and control.

## Learning Objective 6

**Distinguish between a standard test market and a controlled test market.**

A standard test market is one in which companies sell the product through their normal distribution channels. In a controlled test market, the entire program is conducted by an outside service. The service pays retailers for shelf space and therefore can guarantee distribution to those stores that represent a predetermined percentage of the marketer's total store sales volume.

## Learning Objective 7

**Discuss the advantages and disadvantages of simulated test marketing.**

Simulated test-marketing studies, including virtual test markets, provide the following advantages: (1) They protect a marketer from competitors, (2) they are faster and cheaper than full-scale tests, and (3) they are particularly good for spotting weak products. However, they do have disadvantages in that they cannot provide any information about the firm's ability to secure trade support for a product or indicate what competitive reaction is likely to be.

## Key Terms

Descriptive research (page 113)

Causal research (page 113)

experiment (page 115)

laboratory experiment (page 115)

Internal validity (page 116)

field experiment (page 116)

External validity (page 116)

A/B test (page 116)

Market testing (test marketing) (page 119)

standard test market (page 121)

controlled test market (page 122)

simulated test market (STM) (page 122)

virtual test markets (page 123)

## Review Questions

1. What are the three basic types of research used to collect primary data? What is the basic purpose of each?

2. Why is exploratory research considered to be a basic type of primary data research?

3. What is the general sequence in which the three basic types of research are employed?

4. Is it possible to establish that one thing causes another? Why or why not?

5. What is an experiment?

6. What is the difference between a lab study and a field study?

7. What is the difference between internal validity and external validity? Which form of validity is more important?

8. What is an A/B test? What is the general structure for performing such a test?

9. What is market testing? What are the three basic types of test markets?

10. Under what conditions is a standard test market a better choice than either simulated or controlled test markets?

# Endnotes

1. Brooks, C. M., Kaufmann, P. J., & Lichtenstein, D. R. (2008). Trip chaining behavior in multi-destination shopping trips: A field experiment and laboratory replication. *Journal of Retailing, 84* (1), 29–38.

2. (March 13, 2015). Promo code box on your shopping cart page could be bleeding dollars. A/B test it. Retrieved from https://vwo.com/blog/promo-code-box-ecommerce-website-bleeding-dollars-ab-test/

3. (2002, May/June). Test and learn. *Marketing Management, 22;* Kohavi, R., Longbotham, R., Sommerfield, D., & Henne, R. M. (2009). Controlled experiments on the Web: Survey and practical guide. *Data Mining and Knowledge Discovery, 18,* 140–181. Retrieved from http://www.exp-platform.com; Kohavi, R., Deng, A., Frasca, B., Longbotham, R., Walker, T., & Xu, Y. (2012). Trustworthy online controlled experiments: Five puzzling outcomes explained. Retrieved from http://www.exp-platform.com

4. Duggan, W. (2016, September 26). McDonald's Happy Meal undergoes biggest change in 30 years. *Benzinga.* Retrieved from EBSCOhost (www.ebscohost.com); (2008, July 9). McDonalds rolls out coffee bar buildout concept at select restaurants in southwest. *Financial Wire.* Retrieved from ProQuest (www.proquest.com).

5. O'Connell, V. (2008, June 23). Altria drops new filter cigarettes in strategic setback," *The Wall Street Journal.* Retrieved from Pro-Quest (http://www.proquest.com); Cho, H. (2010, July 25). Baltimore a valuable test market for Chick-fil-A. *The Baltimore Sun.* Retrieved from http://articles.baltimoresun.com

6. Wright, D. A. (2001, May 21). The perfect place for a test market. *The Business Journal,* 12.

7. Retrieved from http://www.nielsen.com/us/en/solutions/product-development.html

# Collecting Descriptive Primary Data

## LEARNING OBJECTIVES

▸ Cite three major purposes of descriptive research.

▸ List the six specifications of a descriptive study.

▸ Discuss the difference between cross-sectional and longitudinal designs.

▸ Explain what is meant by a panel in marketing research, and explain the difference between a continuous panel and a discontinuous panel.

▸ Describe the emphasis in sample surveys.

▸ List the kinds of demographic and socioeconomic characteristics that interest marketers.

▸ Cite the three main approaches used to measure awareness.

▸ Give an important reason that marketers are interested in people's motives.

Billion Photos/Shutterstock.com

Rawpixel.com/Shutterstock.com

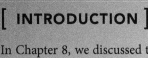

## [ INTRODUCTION ]

In Chapter 8, we discussed the use of causal research to collect primary data. Under most circumstances, though, managers don't necessarily need to "prove" that one variable causes another. Instead, they are perfectly content to look for relationships among variables (e.g., are women more satisfied with our brand compared with men?) or to simply examine the degree to which certain groups possess certain characteristics (e.g., what percentage of our target market are aware that our service exists?). Descriptive research is the right choice for these situations.

Our first task is to more fully explain descriptive research and some different forms that it can take. Then we discuss several different categories of primary data, noting that the usual goal is to understand and predict customers' behaviors. This chapter is the first of several that present the different stages in the process of collecting primary data using descriptive research.

## 9-1 Descriptive Research Designs

Descriptive research is very common in business and other aspects of life. In fact, most of the marketing research that you have heard about or participated in before taking a research course can be categorized as descriptive research. With a descriptive research design, we are usually trying to describe some group of people or other entities.

Researchers typically use descriptive research for the following purposes:

1. **To describe the characteristics of certain groups.** For example, a research group gathered information from individuals who had eaten at a particular barbecue restaurant chain in a Midwestern US city to help managers develop a profile of the "average user" with respect to income, sex, age, and so on. The managers were surprised to learn that about half of their customers were women; they had started with the mistaken belief that a clear majority of their customers were men.

2. **To determine the proportion of people who behave in a certain way.** We might be interested, for example, in estimating the proportion of people within a specified radius of a proposed shopping complex who currently shop or intend to shop at the center. Most behavioral data (see Chapter 10) are collected via descriptive research. For example, when a shopper makes a purchase at most retailers, the purchase behavior is recorded as part of scanner data.

3. **To make specific predictions.** We might want to predict the level of sales for a certain brand for each of the next five years so that we could plan for the hiring and training of new sales representatives.

Descriptive research can be used to accomplish a wide variety of research objectives. However, descriptive data become useful for solving problems only when the process is guided by one or more specific research problems, much thought and effort, and quite often exploratory research to clarify the problem and develop hypotheses. A descriptive study design is very different from an exploratory study design, though. While exploratory studies are flexible in nature, descriptive studies are much more systematic and rigid. They require a clear specification of the *who, what, when, where, why,* and *how* of the research.

Suppose a chain of electronics stores is planning to open a new store and wants you to investigate how customers choose particular stores for shopping. Here are a few of the questions—there are many more—that you'll need to answer before data collection for the descriptive study can begin.

- **Who** should be considered a customer? Anyone who enters the store? Someone who makes a purchase? Should we work at the individual or household level?

- **What** characteristics of customers should be measured? Are we interested in their age and gender or in where they live and how they came to know about the store?

- **When** will we measure characteristics of the customers? While they are shopping or later? Should the

study take place during the first weeks of operation of the store, or should it be delayed six months?

- **Where** will we measure the customers? Should it be in the store, immediately outside the store, or should we attempt to contact them at home?

- **Why** do we want to measure them in the first place? Are we going to use these measurements to plan promotional strategy? Are we going to use these measurements as a basis for deciding where to place other stores?

- **How** should we measure the customers? Do we use a questionnaire, or should we observe their purchasing behavior? If we use a questionnaire, what form will it take? How will it be administered?

Some of the answers to these questions will be fairly obvious; others, however, won't be. You might not have answers until after much thought or even after a small pilot or exploratory study. Here's the important point: You should delay data collection until you have clear answers about *who, what, when, where, why,* and *how.*

## 9-1a TWO TYPES OF DESCRIPTIVE STUDIES

Exhibit 9.1 provides an overview of various types of descriptive studies. The basic distinction is between cross-sectional designs, which are the most common, and longitudinal designs. Typically, a **cross-sectional study** involves researching a sample of elements from the population of interest. Characteristics of the elements, or sample members, are measured only once. For example, a retailer might send an online survey to a sample of recent customers to determine how satisfied they were with a new store layout. It's a one-time survey with a sample that won't be contacted again for research purposes.

A **longitudinal study**, on the other hand, involves a panel, which is a fixed sample of elements. The elements may be stores, dealers, individuals, or other entities. The panel, or sample, remains relatively constant through time, although members may be added to replace dropouts or to keep it representative. The sample members in a panel are measured repeatedly, in contrast with the one-time measurement in a cross-sectional study. Both cross-sectional and longitudinal studies have weaknesses and advantages.

### Longitudinal Analysis: Consumer Panels
There are two types of panels: continuous panels (sometimes called true panels) and discontinuous panels (sometimes called omnibus panels). **Continuous panels** rely on repeated

---

**cross-sectional study** Investigation involving a sample of elements selected from the population of interest that are measured at a single point in time.

**longitudinal study** Investigation involving a fixed sample of elements that is measured repeatedly through time.

**continuous panel** A fixed sample of respondents who are measured repeatedly over time with respect to the same variables.

**Exhibit 9.1** ▶ Classification of Descriptive Studies

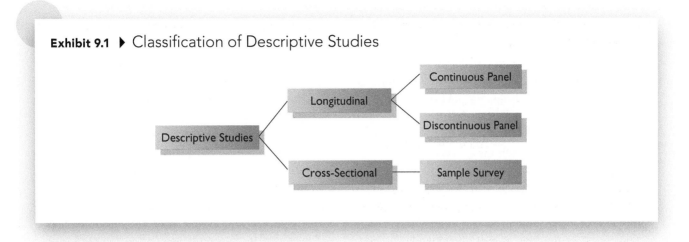

measurements of the same variables from the same people. For example, NPD maintains a panel of over 50,000 consumers who regularly upload their shopping receipts through a special application on their phones. And they have a panel of over 2 million consumers who have agreed to allow the company to electronically monitor their e-mail accounts to capture receipts for online purchases. Because NPD also has other information about these consumers in its database, the company can offer its clients very useful information about what kinds of consumers are purchasing their products. Notice that the same people (i.e., the consumers) are providing the same measurements (i.e., product purchase information) over time, making this a continuous panel.

With a **discontinuous panel**, the information collected from panel members varies. At one time, it may be attitudes with respect to a new product. At another time, the panel members might be asked to evaluate alternative advertising copy. As an example, Ipsos offers discontinuous panels in dozens of countries around the world and collects data using online surveys, telephone surveys, and /or personal interviews. In many countries, the omnibus survey is fielded weekly, with results available in a matter of days.

The advantages and disadvantages of both types of panels compared with cross-sectional studies are about the same. For example, panels are probably the best format for collecting detailed demographic information, such as respondents' incomes, ages, education levels, and occupations. Cross-sectional studies are limited in this respect, because respondents being contacted for the first and only time are rarely willing to give lengthy, time-consuming interviews. Panel members are usually compensated for their participation so interviews can be longer and more involved, or there can be several interviews. The sponsoring firm can afford to spend more

**discontinuous panel** A fixed sample of respondents who are measured repeatedly over time but on variables that change from measurement to measurement.

time and effort securing accurate classification information because this information can be used in a number of studies.

Panel data are also believed to be more accurate than cross-sectional data, especially when it comes to measuring things like purchasing behavior and watching and listening to media outlets. With cross-sectional designs, respondents are asked to remember and report their past behaviors, a process that inevitably leads to error because people tend to forget. In a panel, on the other hand, behavior can often be recorded as it occurs so less reliance is placed on memory. When other behaviors, such as television viewing, are of interest, actual viewing behaviors can be recorded electronically as they occur, thus minimizing the possibility that they will be forgotten or distorted.

The main disadvantage of panels is that they are nonrepresentative and/or nonrandom. The agreement to participate involves a commitment on the part of the designated sample member, and many individuals do not want to make this commitment. They don't want to be bothered with testing products, evaluating advertising copy, or carefully reporting purchases. Because these activities require a sizable time commitment, families in which both husband and wife work, for example, may be less well represented than those in which one partner works and the other is at home. Even when the companies who run these panels attempt to match the composition of the panel with the demographics of the target population, the results still cannot be projected to the population because the participants were not randomly drawn from the population (see Chapter 14).

Most consumer panels have cooperation rates of 50% or less—and that's among households that agreed to participate in the panel. A large percentage of consumers choose not to join a panel in the first place. As might be expected,

## Manager's Focus

The benefits of longitudinal analysis (monitoring consumer processes over time) should be immediately obvious to you as a marketing manager. Using the panel services of marketing research companies, however, is only one way of achieving these benefits. Companies as diverse as John Deere, Kellogg's, and ESPN have established proprietary online panels with which they can continuously monitor specific variables over time (use as continuous panels) or measure a variety of variables on an *ad hoc* basis (use as discontinuous panels). Because they obtain panel data on a regular basis, maintaining their own panels enables them to reduce costs while increasing the speed with which they can access the panel. This approach, however, is more feasible for larger companies that have the necessary financial and technological resources. It also helps when your products and services have an inherent appeal to consumers or business customers so that they can enjoy serving on the panel.

If you think broadly, you may begin to recognize other ways various organizations obtain longitudinal data. For example, many supermarkets have programs for which they provide pricing incentives to customers who register their purchases using a store card. This enables them to track purchases for customers on an ongoing basis. Similarly, online merchants, both large and small, employ a variety of technologies that enable them to monitor online behavior and measure such variables as web site access rates, conversion rates, and repeat purchases. It is also important that the information uncovered should feed into the organization's decision support system to maximize its usefulness to managers. Throughout your career, you'll always want to think creatively about how to leverage existing technology to acquire relevant data, including longitudinal data when possible.

cooperation rates tend to be higher when consumers find the topic interesting or when less work is required of them.

The better ongoing panel operations select prospective participants very systematically. They attempt to generate and maintain panels that are representative of the total population of interest (although they will still be nonrandom). Quite often, to create a representative panel, they will use quota samples, in which the proportion of sample members possessing a certain characteristic is approximately the same as the proportion possessing that characteristic in the general population. As a very simplified example of this, consider an organization that wants to study sports-car owners. If the organization knows that in the general population of interest, 52% are men and 48% are women, then it will want its quota sample to reflect that percentage.

### Cross-Sectional Analysis: Sample Survey

Despite the advantages of longitudinal analysis, in practice the cross-sectional design is probably the more important descriptive design. The cross-sectional study has two key features that distinguish it from longitudinal studies. First, it provides a snapshot of the variables of interest at a single point in time, as opposed to a series of pictures that, when pieced together, provide a movie of the situation and the changes that occur. Second, in the cross-sectional study, the sample of elements is typically selected to be representative of some known universe, or population. Therefore, a

**sample survey**
Cross-sectional study in which the sample is selected to be representative of the target population and in which the emphasis is on the generation of summary statistics, such as averages and percentages.

great deal of emphasis is placed on selecting sample members, usually with a probability sampling plan. That is one reason the technique is often called a **sample survey**.

A cross-sectional sample survey offers two strong advantages over panel designs. For one thing, very specific populations can be targeted and members of those populations recruited to participate in the survey. Targeted recruitment is possible with consumer panels, but only using the data that have been collected about the participating individuals or households. For example, if a retail store located in a midsized city in the northeastern United States decided to conduct a satisfaction study among its customers, unless the store has created its own panel, it is highly unlikely that an existing panel is going to be as efficient as simply sampling from its customer database and using a sample survey.

A second advantage of sample surveys is the ability to use a probability sampling plan that will allow the results of the sample to be projected to the overall population. As we'll discuss later, this is a very important issue because managers are more concerned about answers that apply to everyone in the population rather than answers that apply only to the people who provided the information.

Although sample surveys are very commonly used, they have several disadvantages. For one thing, surveys are expensive in terms of time and money. Depending upon the depth and sophistication of the survey and the sampling plan, it might be months before hypotheses can be

## Manager's Focus

One of the limitations of sample surveys is that they are often developed too quickly, without enough preliminary effort to fully understand the issues being studied (without sufficient exploratory research). And poor surveys are usually produced by people who haven't been trained in the art and science of questionnaire design. Managers sometimes (often?) think that they can develop their own questionnaires because "anyone can ask questions." It just isn't that simple. Well-done performances of any kind (ballet, theater, sports—even hair styling) look easy to those observing the performance. The performer, however, understands the amount of training, effort, and experience required to make it look so easy. We urge managers to resist temptation and enlist the services of a professional marketing researcher (inside or outside the firm) to create survey instruments. Even better, find one that routinely employs exploratory research techniques, especially literature searches and depth interviews, as part of the process of developing questionnaires.

---

tested; good surveys aren't just thrown together, as you'll learn in upcoming chapters. Although some types of exploratory research can have little or no cost, collecting descriptive research is often an expensive proposition.

Survey research also requires a good deal of technical skill. As a result, you'll either need to possess the technical skills required at each stage of the process or have access to technical consultants. Only rarely will a person be able both to develop an attitude scale and to design a complex probability sample.

## 9-2 Types of Primary Data

Let's step back for a moment from the details of descriptive research. Regardless of whether you choose to collect data using a longitudinal panel or sample survey (or conduct causal research, for that matter), the data that marketing researchers collect typically fall into one of the following categories: (1) behavior, (2) demographic/socioeconomic characteristics, (3) psychological/lifestyle characteristics, (4) attitudes, (5) awareness/knowledge, (6) intentions, and (7) motivation. Exhibit 9.2 presents these seven types of data.

### 9-2a BEHAVIOR

Exhibit 9.2 organizes these seven types of data in an important way. **Behavior** concerns what individuals or organizations have done or are doing. Marketers typically are most concerned about consumers' behaviors, such as viewing promotions, gathering information online, shopping at stores, purchasing products and services (in-store or online), using products after purchase, talking to others about their experiences, and so on. Marketing analytics capture many of these consumer behaviors and managers routinely use these behavioral data to make important decisions. They do this for good reason: As we'll see a little later, behavioral data are often more accurate and objective

**behavior** What subjects have done or are doing.

than are other kinds of data because they can be observed and recorded by researchers or—even better—by electrical/mechanical devices. Plus, it's a long-standing adage that the best predictor of future behavior is past behavior. Behavioral data are so important that we placed them in the center of Exhibit 9.2.

Behavioral data can be obtained by observing behaviors or by asking consumers to remember and report their behaviors. As we note elsewhere, however, asking people to report their behaviors can lead to more forms of bias because it depends on respondents' ability to accurately remember and report those behaviors. Even so, asking about specific behaviors performed during a specific time frame can yield solid information.

Behavioral data are becoming increasingly available through various technologies (scanners and the Web). With the advent of new technologies, managers have at their disposal an increasing number of innovative and effective ways of tracking consumer behavior. As a result, companies are increasingly placing a higher priority on tracking the behavior of target markets. Because of Web analytics, the process of tracking behavioral information via the Web, a revolution is occurring regarding behavioral data access.

> Companies are increasingly placing a higher priority on tracking the behavior of target markets.

There are a couple of important limitations of behavioral data, however. For one thing, sometimes there are no behavioral data available to solve a marketing problem. Many of the types of data shown in Exhibit 9.2 simply cannot be observed. A marketer who has developed a new service offering has no purchase data on which to predict the likely success of the service once it is offered to customers. At least initially, she must rely on consumer feedback in the form of attitude measures or purchase intentions based on

**Exhibit 9.2** ▶ Seven Types of Primary Data

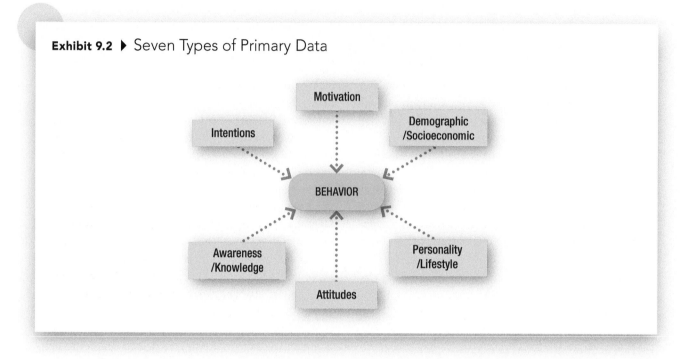

a description of the service concept. A second major limitation of behavioral data is that they offer no direct insights into *why* consumers performed those behaviors. Maybe it doesn't matter to some managers why some groups of consumers are more likely to spread negative word-of-mouth than others, but truly understanding the drivers of these behaviors and others allows for much better decisions, both now and in the future. Focusing only on behavior will cause managers to miss important customer insights. Still, we recognize the importance of behavioral data in Exhibit 9.2 by connecting all the different categories of data to behavior.

### 9-2b DEMOGRAPHIC/SOCIOECONOMIC CHARACTERISTICS

Primary data of great interest to marketers are the respondent's demographic and socioeconomic characteristics, such as age, education, occupation, marital status, gender, income, and social class. These variables are often used to cross-classify the collected data to help interpret the consumers' responses. Suppose we are interested in people's attitudes toward sustainability. We might find that attitudes toward green marketing are related to the respondents' level of education or are different for men and women. Similarly, marketers frequently ask whether the consumption of particular products (SUVs, disposable diapers, vacation golf packages) is related to a person's age, education, income, and so on.

Demographic variables are often used as a basis for market segmentation. For example, gender has been used to segment categories as diverse as cigarettes (Marlboro versus Virginia Slims), razors (Gillette Fusion versus Venus), and athletic shoes (Foot Locker versus Lady Foot Locker). Lots of

**personality** Normal patterns of behavior exhibited by an individual; the attributes, traits, and mannerisms that distinguish one individual from another.

**lifestyle** How individuals live, what interests them, their values, and what they like.

other demographic and socioeconomic variables have been used as well.

### 9-2c PERSONALITY/LIFESTYLE CHARACTERISTICS

Other primary data of interest to marketers are the respondent's psychological and lifestyle characteristics in the form of personality traits, activities, interests, and values. **Personality** refers to the basic dispositions exhibited by an individual—the attributes, traits, and mannerisms that distinguish one individual from another. We often characterize people by the personality traits—aggressiveness, dominance, friendliness, sociability—they display.

Marketers are interested in personality because it seems as if it would affect the way consumers and others in the marketing process behave. Many marketers maintain, for example, that personality can affect a consumer's choice of stores or products or an individual's response to an advertisement or point-of-purchase display. Similarly, they believe that salespeople or frontline service workers who are extroverted or customer-oriented are more likely to be successful. Although the empirical evidence regarding the ability of personality to predict consumption behavior or salesperson success is weak, personality remains a popular variable with marketing researchers.

Lifestyle analysis (sometimes called psychographic analysis) rests on the premise that a company can plan more effective strategies to reach its target market if it knows more about its customers' **lifestyles** in terms of how they live, what interests them, their values, and what they like. For example, Frito-Lay conducted research that identified two broad categories of snackers that

## Manager's Focus

Effective marketing decision making requires accurately predicting how consumers or organizational buyers will behave in response to alternative marketing actions. How will organizational buyers respond if we increase our prices? If we change the positioning emphasis of our advertisements, how will our target consumers react? How will existing and prospective organizational customers respond if we add a new model to our product line? If we increase the quality of our product and market it through more exclusive retail outlets, how will target consumers react? Making these types of predictions involves modeling *consumer* or *organizational buyer behavior*. A hypothesis specifies how two or more *measurable variables* are related. When you read this, you may have wondered "what exactly are 'measurable variables'?" We begin to answer that question in this chapter by describing some of the general types of variables commonly measured in marketing research studies. As a manager, you need to (a) determine which variables are most relevant to your marketing situation and (b) formulate hypotheses about how the variables are related to one another. Don't forget that exploratory research can help you gain useful insights in these areas. They can help you identify which characteristics, attitudes, knowledge issues, motivations, and so on, appear to correspond with one another and ultimately with buyers' behavior. These hypothesized relationships represent a working model of buyer behavior pertaining to your marketing circumstances.

The relationships between variables are much easier for you to recognize if you have a strong understanding of *buyer behavior theory*. This is why you may have taken (or may take in the future) a *buyer behavior* (or consumer behavior) course. Studying buyer behavior theory is really just a form of exploratory research. Specifically, it's an extensive literature search in which you examine how different buyer-related variables have been found to correspond with one another in previous research contexts. Through this secondary research process, you will learn about many generalizable models of buyer behavior that represent possible relationships between variables in the specific marketing situations you will face as a manager.

With an understanding of buyer behavior theory, you will become a much more effective user of marketing research services. As a manager, you'll draw on your prior managerial experiences, your understanding of buyer behavior theory, and the findings of exploratory research performed on your behalf in order to formulate sound hypotheses (a buyer behavior model) pertaining to your organization's marketing problems. Once you have decided on your hypothesized model, you will need to employ your marketing research expertise to select and work with a research supplier to complete descriptive and/or causal research to test your hypotheses. The goal, however, is not to merely confirm or disconfirm your hypotheses—it's to achieve marketing success by developing a thorough understanding of the issues that drive your target customers' behaviors.

it called "compromisers" and "indulgers." The compromisers were typically female and more likely to exercise, read health and fitness magazines, be concerned about nutrition, and read product labels. Frito-Lay appeals to this group with its Baked Lay's potato chip, a reduced-fat snack. Frito-Lay's traditional potato chips are targeted to the other psychographic category, the indulgers, who were mostly male, in their late teens and early twenties, snack heavily, feel unconcerned about what they eat, and hesitate to sacrifice taste for a reduction in fat.[1]

### 9-2d    ATTITUDES

An **attitude** refers to an individual's overall evaluation of a specific object or idea. Attitudes are important in marketing because they are

> **attitude** An individual's overall evaluation of something.

generally thought to lead to behaviors. In general, if a person has a positive attitude toward a product or brand, then the person is more likely to buy that product or to choose that brand. Because attitudes influence behavior in this way, marketers want to shape attitudes or target people with favorable attitudes. As a result, marketers often want to learn people's attitudes toward product categories, brands, products, services, web sites, retailers, and a whole host of other things.

Here's a quick example of measuring brand attitude. YouGov offers daily tracking of brand attitude and other variables through its BrandIndex service. Using a continuous panel, the London-based company tracks thousands of brands in the United Kingdom, the United States, and several other regions around the world. Panel members are asked a variety of questions, including the following "general impression" measure to assess overall brand attitude: "Which of the following brands do you have a generally POSITIVE/NEGATIVE feeling about?" The daily score for a company is produced by taking the percentage of people who report a positive impression of the company and subtracting the percentage who report a negative impression. Exhibit 9.3 presents a recent report for Lay's, one of the key Frito-Lay brands. As shown at the bottom of the dashboard report, the overall attitude toward Lay's was the second highest in the snack-food industry in the United States (behind only Ritz) at that time.

There are a number of other important variables that marketers often measure that are similar to attitudes. For example, companies care a great deal about the quality of their products and services, as perceived by their customers.

**Exhibit 9.3 ▸** Attitude Toward Lay's from YouGov BrandIndex

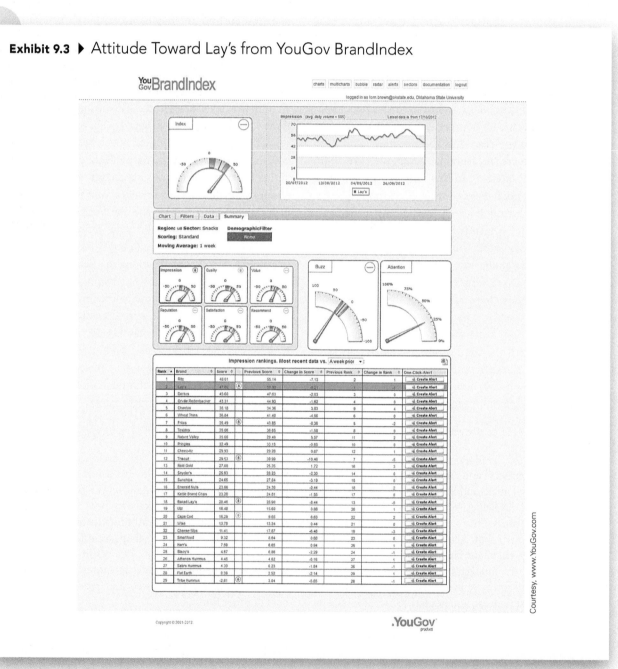

Source: From report produced on October 31, 2016, using BrandIndex, courtesy YouGov.

We also routinely measure customer satisfaction as a critical post-purchase response. These concepts (and others) share an important similarity with attitudes: They are based on how an individual evaluates some target object or idea.

## 9-2e  AWARENESS/KNOWLEDGE

**Awareness/knowledge** as used in marketing research refers to what respondents do and do not know or believe about some product, brand, company, advertisement, and so on. For instance, marketers are always interested in judging the effectiveness of ads in television, radio, magazine, billboard, and Web banners. One measure of effectiveness is the product awareness generated by the ad, using one of the three approaches illustrated in Exhibit 9.4.

All three tests of memory (unaided recall, aided recall, and recognition) are aimed at assessing the respondent's awareness of, and knowledge about, the ad. We assume that different levels of performance on these measures reflect differences in the extent to which consumers have cognitively processed (in detail or just superficially) the ad, the brand name, the featured attributes, and so on. Consumers have retained more knowledge from the ad when they can name the brand in an unaided recall test compared to a recall test when they have been given hints.

> **awareness /knowledge** Insight into, or understanding of facts about, some object or phenomenon.

Both measures of recall reflect more knowledge and retention than simple recognition.

One way to measure the short-term success of an ad is "day-after recall" (or DAR), which involves a survey taken the day following the airing of a new ad (such as the day after the Super Bowl). Ad agencies can compare the day-after recall scores for an ad to their database of prior scores for other ads to project sales for the product being advertised.

Increasingly, psychologists and advertising researchers are exploring the idea that consumers do not have to explicitly remember an ad for that ad to have an impact on their behavior. For example, after airing an ad for Adidas, you could use "implicit" or indirect tests of memory. Rather than asking, "Do you remember any recent ads for athletic shoes or Adidas?" you might instead ask consumers to list brand names of athletic shoes, shoes affiliated with athlete spokespersons, and so on, to assess the number of times the Adidas brand name appears. Researchers have even asked such questions as, "Name all the brands of any kind of product that start with A" to see how often Adidas would appear, along with names such as Audi, Apple, or Acer. The assumption in these tests is that if Adidas appears more often than it should (based on market shares), the ad was successful in bringing the Adidas brand name to mind.

---

## Exhibit 9.4 ▶ Approaches Used to Measure Awareness

**Unaided recall:** Without being given any clues, consumers are asked to recall what advertising they have seen recently. An ad or a brand that can be remembered with no clues at all is presumed to have made a deep impression. As a result, unaided recall represents the highest level of awareness.

Example: What ads for products and brands do you remember seeing?

**Unaided Recall Cue**

**Aided recall:** Consumers are prompted, typically with a category cue. That is, they are asked to remember all ads/brands that they have seen for products and services in a particular product category. Aided recall represents a relatively high level of awareness, but the presence of the cue makes the task easier than unaided recall.

Example: Do you remember recently seeing ads for personal computers?

Personal Computers

**Aided Recall Cue**

**Recognition:** Actual advertisements, brand names, or logos are shown or described to consumers, who are asked whether they remember seeing each one. Because the task is simply to recognize whether or not they have seen an ad, the recognition task is much easier for respondents but represents a lower level of awareness.

Example: Do you remember seeing this ad for Dell?

**Recognition Cue**

## Manager's Focus

"Attitudes" represent a very broad class of variables. Although you might not have recognized it, several of the concepts you have studied in marketing—such as assessments of value, satisfaction, brand image, and quality—resemble attitudes because they are special types of *evaluations* made by consumers. *Value perceptions* are evaluations of a marketing offering in terms of the benefits it provides relative to the costs of acquiring and using it. *Satisfaction*, in contrast, is an evaluation of a marketing offering involving a comparison of benefits actually received with the benefits expected before purchase and use. *Brand image* is an evaluation of the degree to which various characteristics and cultural symbols are associated with a brand as well as the favorability/desirability of those associations. Finally, *quality perceptions* are evaluations of the features and performance of a product or service.

In addition to predicting buyer behavior, marketing managers frequently use measures of attitudinal variables to monitor and control marketing performance. Franchisers in the services sector, for instance, commonly measure the satisfaction of their franchisees' customers. Some require franchisees to maintain satisfaction at or above a specific level. Given the prevalence of attitudinal measurement in marketing, it is essential that you understand what this broad class of variables encompasses and how to appropriately measure each specific type of attitude. As you will learn in later chapters, there are many common pitfalls to avoid when measuring attitudes and other variables.

In addition to ad testing, memory measures are used to assess awareness and knowledge of brands, products, companies, and the like. Marketers are often interested in understanding what different audiences know or believe about their brands and companies. This is the basis of countless brand image or company image studies. In addition, this information, sometimes in combination with attitudes (evaluations of the brand or company based on the knowledge or beliefs held in memory), are key inputs into positioning studies based on perceptual mapping. In general, awareness questions help the marketer assess consumers' knowledge of any element of the consumer experience—advertisements, products, retail stores, and so.

### 9-2f INTENTIONS

A person's **intentions** refer to her anticipated or planned future behavior. Marketers are interested in people's intentions primarily with regard to purchase behavior. Intentions can be measured using a variety of approaches that ask respondents to indicate their likelihood of purchasing a product or service in an upcoming time period. Here is an example of how the response categories might appear on a survey:

- definitely would buy
- probably would buy
- undecided
- probably would not buy
- definitely would not buy

**intentions** Anticipated or planned future behavior.

Imagine responding to this item with respect to your intention to purchase a meal next week at a McDonald's restaurant. If you have eaten at a McDonald's in the past, you probably have a pretty good idea of whether or not you're likely to eat there in the next seven days, and your estimate is likely to be fairly accurate.

Now imagine that you've been asked this question about a new solar-powered iPad that could receive satellite radio broadcasts. How would you respond to this question? Even if we carefully describe the product's features and tell you its selling price, we suspect that your estimates about purchase likelihood might not match up all that well with your future actions. This is the problem with measuring intentions: When dealing with new-to-the-world products or services—especially those that haven't been built yet—consumers usually aren't very accurate about what they'll do in the future.

With purchase intentions, the problem isn't getting people to answer the questions; the problem is getting answers that have meaning to them. Estimating demand for products and services is very difficult to do, but sometimes we simply have no choice if we want an early gauge on the likely success of a product or service. Still, marketing research professionals have learned to discount people's stated intentions in most situations, based on the researchers' past experience in similar situations.

Another concept that researchers are sometimes asked to assess is the price that consumers are willing to pay for a product or service. Although this isn't exactly an intentions measure, it shares some similarities in that respondents are asked to speculate about a future event (i.e., how much they would be willing to pay for a product), as well as the fact that such measures often aren't all that accurate at predicting what consumers will actually pay for the product or service.

## 9-2g  MOTIVATION

A **motive** is a need, a want, a drive, an urge, a wish, a desire, an impulse, or any inner state that directs or channels behavior toward goals. Perhaps you've heard of the *marketing concept*, the idea that companies succeed over the long run by identifying and satisfying customers' needs in a way that is profitable for the company. For organizations that believe in the marketing concept, one of the most important tasks is to uncover the known—and sometimes unknown—needs of their customers. Once uncovered, marketers often appeal to these motives in their communications efforts. For example, the motive that underlies an ad for life insurance may be the desire to make certain that the family has adequate financial resources should something happen to a parent.

> **motive** A need, a want, a drive, a wish, a desire, an impulse, or any inner state that energizes, activates, moves, directs or channels behavior toward goals.

> One of the most important tasks is to uncover the known—and sometimes unknown—needs of the customer.

A marketing researcher's interest in motives typically involves determining *why* people behave as they do. By understanding what drives a person's behavior, it is easier to understand the behavior itself. A desire for status may motivate one car buyer to purchase a Mercedes-Benz; a concern for safety may send another to the local Volvo showroom. If we understand the forces underlying consumer behavior, marketers are in a better position to design and offer products and services that can satisfy the motives driving that behavior.

So, there you have it—the universe of individual-level primary data boiled down to seven categories. There are no doubt other concepts and examples we didn't provide, but almost all of them will fit into one of these categories. These are the things that marketers often want—in fact, need—to know in order to go about the job of delivering products and services that satisfy their customers' needs.

Some of these things are easier to measure than others; asking basic demographic questions is a whole lot easier than assessing true purchase intentions, for example.

If you've been reading closely, you may have noticed that we used several examples of secondary data collected by research companies to demonstrate how primary descriptive data might be measured. We wrote about scanner data and Web analytics as means of gathering behavioral data, and we demonstrated the measurement of attitudes with secondary data from BrandIndex. Each of these different types of data can be collected as primary data by individual companies—and, in fact, thousands of companies collect their own primary data on these things and many more.

These examples allow us to demonstrate a couple of important points, however. First, at some level, data are data, regardless of where they came from. Your task as a marketer is to find or collect data that provide the information you need, whether it is primary or secondary. The second point is closely related to the first: When relevant secondary data are available internally or externally, it's often going to be more efficient to work with those data to obtain the answers you need rather than collecting your own primary data. That's why we organized Exhibit 2.1 as we did: It's really important to look for both internal and external secondary data before undertaking primary data collection. Still, sometimes you won't have any choice, and your next decision is how best to obtain the primary data you need. That's the subject of the next two chapters.

# Summary

## Learning Objective 1

**Cite three major purposes of descriptive research.**
Descriptive research is used when the purpose is to (1) describe the characteristics of certain groups, (2) determine the proportion of people who behave in a certain way, and (3) make specific predictions.

## Learning Objective 2

**List the six specifications of a descriptive study.**
Descriptive studies require a clear specification of the answers to *who*, *what*, *when*, *where*, *why*, and *how* in the research.

## Learning Objective 3

**Discuss the difference between cross-sectional and longitudinal designs.**
A cross-sectional design involves researching a sample of elements from the population of interest. Various characteristics of the elements are measured once. Longitudinal studies involve panels of people or other entities whose responses are measured repeatedly over a span of time.

## Learning Objective 4

**Explain what is meant by a panel in marketing research, and explain the difference between a continuous panel and a discontinuous panel.**
A panel is a fixed sample of elements. In a continuous panel, a fixed sample of subjects is measured repeatedly with respect to the same type of information. In a discontinuous panel, a sample of elements is still selected and maintained, but the information collected from the members varies with the project.

## Learning Objective 5

**Describe the emphasis in sample surveys.**
The sample survey involves the study of a number of cases at the same point in time. The survey attempts to be representative of some known population.

## Learning Objective 6

**List the kinds of demographic and socioeconomic characteristics that interest marketers.**
Marketers are interested in such socioeconomic and demographic characteristics as age, education, occupation, marital status, sex, income, and social class.

## Learning Objective 7

**Cite the three main approaches used to measure awareness.**
The three main approaches used to measure awareness are (1) unaided recall, in which the consumer is given no clues at all; (2) aided recall, in which the consumer is given some prompting; and (3) recognition, in which the consumer is actually shown a stimulus and asked whether or not he or she remembers seeing it.

## Learning Objective 8

**Give an important reason that marketers are interested in people's motives.**
Marketers need to understand individuals' known—and sometimes unknown—needs and what motivates them if they are to develop and deliver products and services that meet those needs.

## Key Terms

cross-sectional study (page 128)
longitudinal study (page 128)
continuous panel (page 128)
discontinuous panel (page 129)
sample survey (page 130)
behavior (page 131)
personality (page 132)
lifestyle (page 132)
attitude (page 133)
awareness/knowledge (page 135)
intentions (page 136)
motive (page 137)

## Review Questions

1. What are the basic uses of descriptive research?

2. What are the six specifications of a descriptive study?

3. What are the main types of descriptive studies, and what do their differences mean?

4. What are the two basic forms of panels? How do they differ?

5. What is a sample survey? What are its advantages and disadvantages?

6. What types of primary data interest marketing researchers most? What are the differences between the types of data?

7. What is an attitude? Why do marketers care about attitudes?

8. What are three ways to assess awareness? What is the basic difference between measures of recall and measures of recognition?

9. What is the basic problem in measuring consumers' intentions about future behaviors?

# Endnote

1. (1996, March 18). Frito-Lay profiles salty snack consumers. *Supermarket News*, 39.

# CHAPTER 10

# Collecting Data by Observation

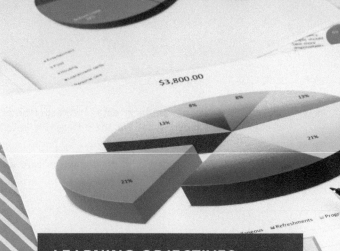

Billion Photos/Shutterstock.com

Rawpixel.com/Shutterstock.com

## [ INTRODUCTION ]

Once you've decided to collect primary data, you have several choices to make about the method to use (see Exhibit 10.1). Your first decision is whether to use communication or observation. **Communication** involves questioning respondents to get the information you need using a questionnaire. The questions may be oral or in writing, and the responses may also be given in either form. **Observation** does not involve questioning. Instead, you'll carefully watch what individuals do in a particular situation and record relevant details and behaviors. A person or a mechanical device can record the observations. For instance, supermarket scanners may be used to determine how many boxes of a particular brand of cereal are sold in a given region in a typical week. And, to complicate things just a little, some studies use both communication and observation to collect primary data.

After choosing a primary method of data collection (communication versus observation), you have more decisions to make. For example, should the questionnaire be administered online, over the phone, in person, or by mail? Should the study's purpose be disguised, or hidden, from respondents?

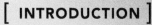

**communication**
A method of data collection involving questioning respondents to secure the desired information using a data collection instrument called a questionnaire.

**observation** A method of data collection in which the situation of interest is watched and the relevant facts, actions, or behaviors are recorded.

**Exhibit 10.1 ▶** Basic Choices Among Means for Collecting Primary Data

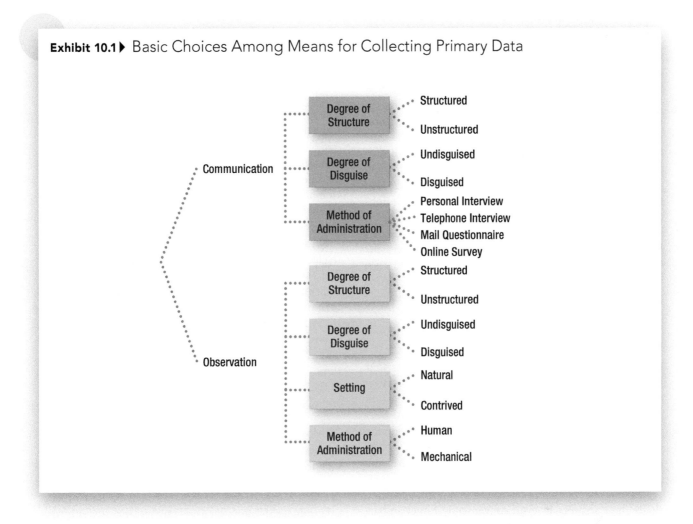

Should the answers to questions be open-ended, or should you ask respondents to choose from a limited set of alternatives? Although Exhibit 10.1 makes it seem that these decisions are independent, they really aren't. For instance, decisions about the method of administration have serious implications about the degree of structure that you can use. We'll return to these issues in later chapters.

Both the communication and observation methods have advantages and disadvantages. In general, the communication method of data collection has the general advantages of versatility, speed, and cost; observational data are typically more objective and accurate.

## VERSATILITY

*Versatility* refers to the ability of a technique to collect information on the different types of primary data (e.g., behaviors, attitudes, motivations, demographics, awareness, intentions, personality). The communication approach can be used for collecting information about all types of primary data from individuals. All we need to do is ask and get people to answer our questions—although the answers aren't necessarily correct.

Observation techniques, however, aren't nearly so versatile: They can provide us with information about behavior and certain demographic/socioeconomic characteristics (e.g., gender—most of the time—and age in very broad categories), but that's about it. And we can only assess current behavior; we can't observe a person's past behavior, and we can't observe his or her intentions about future behavior. If we are interested in past behavior or intentions, we have to ask. The other basic types of primary data can't be measured effectively by observation. We can't observe an attitude or opinion, a person's awareness or knowledge, or motivation. Questioning clearly allows us to gather more types of primary data.

> We can't observe an attitude or opinion, a person's awareness or knowledge, or motivation.

## SPEED AND COST

The speed and cost advantages of the communication method are closely related. Communication is often a faster means of data collection than observation; you don't have to wait for behaviors to occur. In some cases, it is impossible to predict when an event will occur precisely enough to observe it. For other behaviors, the time interval between events can be substantial. If you've drawn a sample of households and want to know which brand of kitchen appliances is purchased most frequently, you might have to wait a long time to get enough observations to be useful.

In some cases, though, observation is faster and costs less than communication. A great example involves the purchase of consumer nondurables. The use of scanners, for example, allows many more purchases to be recorded and at less cost than if purchasers were questioned about what they bought.

## OBJECTIVITY AND ACCURACY

Although the observation method has some serious limitations in terms of scope, time, and cost, it has huge advantages with regard to objectivity and accuracy. You can almost always gather behavioral data more accurately using observation because observation techniques usually don't depend upon the respondent's willingness and ability to provide the information needed. Here's what we mean: Respondents sometimes don't want to cooperate if their replies might make them look bad. They will sometimes shade their answers or even conveniently forget embarrassing events. In other cases, respondents don't even remember events or prior behaviors because they just weren't very important.

Because observation allows the recording of behavior as it occurs, it doesn't depend on the respondent's memory in reporting what occurred and usually produces more objective data than do communication approaches. Sometimes people don't know they are being observed, so they aren't tempted to tell the interviewer what they think he/she wants to hear or to give socially acceptable responses that are not truthful. Because of the increased objectivity and accuracy of observational research, we generally recommend observation techniques when they can be used. In the remainder of this chapter, we'll discuss observation research in detail.

## 10-1   Observation Research

Observation is a fact of everyday life. We are constantly observing other people and events as a means of gaining information about the world around us. When researchers use this approach, however, the observations are systematically planned and carefully recorded. And they often lead to insights that might not be seen in any other way. For example, when researchers watched consumers buy dog food, they found that adults focused on buying dog *food* but that seniors and children bought a bigger proportion of dog *treats*. Unfortunately for these seniors and small children, the treats were usually stocked on the top shelf. The researchers' cameras "witnessed one elderly woman using a box of aluminum foil to knock down her brand of dog biscuits." When the retailer moved the treats to where children and older people could reach them more easily, sales soared.[1] The insights gathered by watching that woman maneuver to get her favorite brand might have taken much longer to obtain—if they could have been uncovered at all—using communication.

Observation is often more useful than surveys in sorting fact from fiction with respect to behaviors, particularly "desirable" behaviors. For example, most people wouldn't want to acknowledge that they spend more on cat food than on baby food, but consumers can be observed doing so. In another study, parents were asked whether the color of a new toy would matter; all the parents said no. At the end of the study, as a small reward for their participation, researchers offered the parents a toy to take home to their child, and all the parents clamored for the purple and blue toys.

### Examples of Observation Research

Observation research involves watching a situation of interest and recording relevant facts and behaviors. Sometimes researchers use *direct observation,* which means watching the actual activity. For example, Hewlett-Packard's medical products division sent its researchers to watch surgeons operate. They noticed that monitors portraying electronic video of scalpel movements were often blocked by other staff members walking between the physician and the monitor, so HP created a surgical helmet that casts images in front of a surgeon's eyes. In other cases, researchers use *indirect observation,* in which the outcomes of the behavior are observed, rather than the behavior itself. For example, one researcher—a "garbologist"—has dug through Tucson trash cans in search of empty toothpaste tubes and used dental floss to see which dental hygiene practices seem to work and which don't, based on correlating what he finds in the garbage with local dental records.[2]

Observation research doesn't have to be sophisticated to be effective. Consider these examples:

- A discount retailer once offered shoppers all the peanuts they could eat while they shopped in the store. The company then could literally follow a trail of peanut shells to discover where shoppers went in the store and which areas of the store were most popular.[3]

- A car dealer in Chicago checked the position of the radio dial of each car brought in for service. The dealer then used this information to decide on which stations to advertise.

- A retailer used a different color of promotional flyer for each zip code to which he mailed. When customers came into the store with the flyers, he could identify which trading areas the store was serving.

- A nonprofit group coded the response forms to be returned with donations with a special code to help it determine which mailing lists were more effective at soliciting donations.

- The number of different fingerprints on a page has been used to assess the readership of various ads in a magazine, and the age and condition of cars in a parking lot have been used to gauge the affluence of those patronizing a particular store.

- Scuff marks on museum floor tile have long been used as a means of measuring the popularity of a display.

- Closely watching real estate company "for sale" and "sold" signs in a geographic area can provide a fairly accurate gauge of company market share and speed of sales.[4]

Sometimes observational research is more sophisticated. Consumers have been watched through one-way mirrors as they try to assemble a computer or use the computer to surf the Web. Many shopping malls determine their trading areas by hiring people to walk the mall parking lot and record every license number they find. These data can then be fed into computers that match the license plates to zip code areas or census tracts and prepare color-coded maps showing customer density from the various areas. And sometimes the degree of sophistication reaches levels that would make James Bond proud. A large sports/convention arena located in the eastern United States once built sensors into its outside walls that could determine which radio stations were tuned on cars driven in its parking lot. This information would be useful for deciding which stations to use for advertising upcoming events at the arena. And Disney recently filed a patent for a foot camera that can unobtrusively capture images of visitors' feet as they travel through its parks to track location and usage—although they claim to have no plans to implement the technology.[5]

Researchers have inventoried or photographed the contents of consumers' refrigerators, medicine cabinets, closets, and garages. Photos of a medicine cabinet's interior will indicate not only what products it contains and what brands and sizes but also their arrangement—items stored front and center are probably used most frequently. Researchers for *Gourmet* magazine have moved right into their readers' homes to "look into their cabinets," "pore over their Visa bills," or "snip labels out of their clothes." *Gourmet* especially wanted to understand its younger readers—readers who were affluent, knowledgeable about food trends, and know hot restaurants and fine wines. A sample of readers were given disposable cameras and asked to take photos of cherished household belongings. Knowing what customers treasure can yield insight into cross-selling opportunities

## Manager's Focus

The marketing research process is often considered the "ears" of an organization because it involves "listening to the voices" of target customers. This is certainly a reasonable depiction, but marketing research can also be considered the "eyes" of the organization. Without a doubt, regularly hearing the voice of the market is an important part of being market-oriented. Some data simply cannot be obtained in any other way. In our view, however, researchers are often too quick to use communication methods (interviews and questionnaires of various types) when observational methods would be more appropriate and helpful. Managers need to reprogram their thinking so their first impulse is not to conduct surveys when information is needed to predict market responses.

As we have emphasized before, consumers can easily tell you what they will do in the future … it's just that what they say they will do and what they actually do are often different. As a result, you are treading on thin ice when you make important decisions based only on what consumers tell you about their likely future purchasing behavior. Consumers' past behavior is almost always a better predictor of their future behavior.

Your effectiveness as a marketing decision maker will be enhanced if you regularly commission research to observe target customers' buying and consumption behavior. For this reason, the methods discussed in this chapter are key to your future success even though they have not traditionally been used as frequently as communication techniques. As the examples in the chapter demonstrate, innovative organizations are increasingly finding clever ways to use technology to gather observational data. You may not always have the resources necessary to perform the more sophisticated forms of observational research, but you should do whatever observation you can to understand how consumers actually behave relative to your offerings and those of your competitors.

or even subtle messages in ads to appeal to this target group's values.[6]

Increasingly, marketing managers, consultants, and researchers have lobbied for observational research over communication research when it comes to assessing consumer behavior. We agree that it is often better to measure consumers' actual behavior and then work backward to determine what led to that behavior than it is to measure their attitudes and intentions and then hope that their future behavior matches their intentions. Doing it this way will almost certainly be more expensive, because the behaviors must be recorded and then connected back to their potential causes, which may mean developing a method of connecting each individual's attitudes, awareness, motivations, and the like, with his or her actual behaviors, but the information will almost always be far more useful.

> We agree that it is often better to measure consumers' actual behavior and then work backward to determine what led to that behavior than it is to measure their attitudes and intentions and then hope that their future behavior matches their intentions.

**structure** The degree of standardization used with the data collection instrument.

**structured observation** Method of observation in which the phenomena to be observed (typically behaviors) can be defined precisely along with the categories used to record the phenomena.

**unstructured observation** Method of observation in which the researcher has a great deal of flexibility in terms of what to note and record.

As indicated in Exhibit 10.1, you'll need to make several important decisions about the design of an observational study. We consider these decisions in the following sections.

### 10-1a STRUCTURED VERSUS UNSTRUCTURED OBSERVATION

The first decision involves how much **structure**, or standardization, to use on the data collection instrument. With **structured observation**, the phenomena to be observed (typically behaviors) can be defined precisely along with the categories used to record the phenomena. With **unstructured observation**, the researcher has a great deal of flexibility in terms of what to note and record. Unstructured observation is much more likely to be used in exploratory research than in descriptive or causal research.

Imagine a study designed to investigate how consumers make decisions about purchasing soup in a grocery store. On the one hand, the observers could be told to stand at one end of a supermarket aisle and record whatever behavior they think is appropriate with respect to each sample customer's deliberation and search. This might produce the following record:

> *Purchaser first paused in front of the Campbell's brand. He glanced at the price on the shelf, picked up a can of Campbell's, glanced at its picture and list of ingredients, and set it back down. He then checked the label and price for Progresso. He set that back down and after a slight pause, picked up a different flavor can of Campbell's than he originally looked at, placed it in his cart, and moved down the aisle.*

On the other hand, you might tell the observers to record a number of specific things—the first soup can examined, the total number of cans picked up by any customer, the brand of soup selected, and the time in seconds that the customer spent in front of the soup shelves—and to record these observations by checking the appropriate boxes on an observation form. This last situation represents a lot more structure than the first:

Record #: _83_
❑ male  ☑ female
First soup can picked up for examination:

☑ Campbell's
❑ Progresso
❑ Lipton
❑ Knorr
❑ other: _____

Total # cans picked up for examination, any brand: _3_
Brand selected:
(leave blank if none selected)

☑ Campbell's
❑ Progresso
❑ Lipton
❑ Knorr
❑ other: _____

Time (in front of soup shelves): _12_ seconds

## Manager's Focus

Imagine for a moment how actively observing consumers, without any preconceived ideas of what behaviors are important or relevant (in an unstructured format), might help you generate new and innovative marketing ideas.

The unexpected behaviors you observe might reveal new uses for your product that could be promoted to prospective new customers. Or the observed behaviors might uncover features that could be redesigned to enhance your product's functionality or convenience. The observed behaviors may even demonstrate how two seemingly unrelated products could effectively be bundled together to augment their overall usefulness to consumers.

The ultimate goal, however, is to identify breakthrough opportunities for new products or services that would satisfy important unmet needs for consumers. For example, by freely watching the actions of consumers and applying creativity, you might identify a remedy for a "problem" consumers do not currently realize exists because they never dreamed of doing something in a new or different way. In such situations, exploratory communication techniques, such as focus groups, depth interviews, or unstructured questions in a survey, would be incapable of generating these insights because it would never occur to consumers to state them.

---

To use the more structured approach, you must decide precisely which behaviors will be observed and which specific categories and units will be used to record the observations. To make these decisions, you'll need to have specific hypotheses in mind. As a result, the structured approach is more appropriate for descriptive and causal studies than for exploratory research.

There are some important advantages and disadvantages to using higher levels of structure in an observational study. On the plus side, structuring the observation reduces the potential for bias and increases the reliability of observations. Another advantage is that the coding and analysis of the data is far simpler (and less costly) when there are a few well-defined behaviors or observable demographic variables to be considered. These advantages come at a cost, however. By structuring the observation, you have necessarily given up additional information that might have been coded, including phenomena that differ from person to person, some of which might be important for understanding purchasing behavior. For instance, in our soup example, the structured observation form isn't going to pick up any effort spent looking at (but not picking up) the cans on the shelf or the discussion between husband and wife about which brand to buy.

### 10-1b DISGUISED VERSUS UNDISGUISED OBSERVATION

**Disguise** refers how much people know about a study in which they are participating. With **undisguised observation,** people know they are being observed; in **disguised observation,** they don't. In the soup purchase study described earlier, observers could stand next to the soup

shelves in the grocery store in plain sight of customers, pencil and clipboard in hand, announcing their purpose to each customer. And they would probably get to watch consumers take much greater care than normal to read the labels for nutrition content, determine the best value, and all the other things that "smart" shoppers do, because the shoppers know they are being observed.

On the other hand, the researchers might find a position where shoppers are less likely to notice them, or, more likely, they might observe the behavior using hidden cameras. Consumers' shopping behavior would be natural, but each consumer's right to be informed has been violated (more on this follows). It is also possible that individuals could be told when they enter the store that their actions would be observed for research purposes and to please shop as they normally would. Most consumers will forget within minutes that they are being observed, that is, unless they see people walking around with white lab coats and clipboards!

Sometimes disguise is accomplished by having observers become part of the shopping scene. This is typically the case when it is a service worker or organization that you're observing, rather than a consumer. For example, some firms use paid observers disguised as shoppers to evaluate important aspects of the shopping process. Mystery shoppers get paid to shop—nice work if you can get it—but there's a lot more to it than just shopping. The "shopping" experience is really used for careful observation, followed by formal written reports to the client company. Mystery shoppers have been used across a wide array of different service and retailing categories.

Krispy Kreme has hired mystery shoppers to visit their stores. Mystery shoppers used tiny cameras to record such things as the evenness

**disguise** The amount of knowledge people have about a study in which they are participating.

**undisguised observation** The subjects are aware that they are being observed.

**disguised observation** The subjects are not aware that they are being observed.

of the jelly in doughnuts and the cleanliness of bathrooms. They often work as independent consultants and sometimes don't even know which client has hired them. One such shopper was hired to negotiate with sellers for luxury watches at a variety of stores on the east and west coasts of the United States, achieving an average discount of 18%. (Unfortunately, she somehow always managed to leave her credit card at home when the "sale" was completed.) Her visits to 26 stores returned about $4,000 for her efforts.[7]

There's an important practical consideration with the use of disguised observation, however. How will you obtain other relevant background information, such as demographic and attitudinal information, if you don't identify yourself as a researcher? This highlights the primary difficulty with observational research in general: Many kinds of data simply cannot be observed. The use of disguise makes it even more difficult to tie data that might be obtained via communication to observational data.

### The Ethics of Disguise

It seems a little strange to suggest that deception can be used to get at the truth in a situation, doesn't it? The use of disguise makes some people and researchers uncomfortable. Any way you look at it, the use of disguise amounts to a conscious effort to deceive the respondent or at least to withhold information. Under the *rights approach* to marketing ethics, using disguise necessarily means a violation of a respondent's right to know that he or she is being observed, how those observations will be used, and/or who will use the information. Researchers almost universally agree, however, that the benefits of true, usable information outweigh the costs of the deception to respondents (note the use of the *utility approach* to marketing ethics), provided that respondents are given appropriate information following the task. This process is known as **debriefing**.

How much information should be shared in the debriefing process? Rarely do researchers offer full disclosure. Most of the time, in fact, there is probably no great need to identify the specific sponsor of a project or the specific purpose of the research. Respondents usually don't care, and sponsors normally prefer to remain anonymous. This recommendation applies to situations in which information has been withheld. When disguise has involved active deception, it is necessary to tell participants that they have been misled, explain why the deception was needed, and provide a general overview of the purpose of the project. On the other hand, employees of an organization should expect that their behaviors on the job will be observed. Thus, there are fewer ethical concerns with mystery shopping than with observing and recording consumer behavior. For the most part, the use of disguise and the amount of debriefing necessary involve judgment calls on the part of the researcher.

**debriefing** The process of providing appropriate information to respondents after data have been collected using disguise.

**natural setting** Subjects are observed in the environment where the behavior normally takes place.

**contrived setting** Subjects are observed in an environment that has been specially designed for recording their behavior.

## 10-1c NATURAL VERSUS CONTRIVED SETTING FOR OBSERVATION

Observations may be obtained in either **natural settings** or **contrived settings**. Sometimes we can alter the natural setting a little for experimental purposes. In the soup study mentioned earlier, researchers might choose to keep the setting completely natural and study only the activities that normally go into the purchase of soup in a normal setting. Alternatively, they might want to examine the effectiveness of point-of-purchase display materials and could include such materials in the stores where observations were taken. One measure of effectiveness might be the amount of time consumers spend reading the display materials or the time they spend looking at the brand being promoted. Objective Experience, a research firm based in Australia and Singapore, does considerable work in natural settings. Research Window 10.1 describes one recent project.

In a contrived setting, you might bring a group of people into a very controlled environment, such as a multiproduct display in a laboratory, and ask them to pretend that they are shopping. This controlled environment might contain, for example, a soup display that would allow researchers to study the degree of search and deliberation that participants go through as they decide what to buy. Taking it a step further, we noted earlier that companies sometimes run virtual test markets as well to observe consumers' behaviors. These approaches allow marketers to display potential new products or product displays without going to the expense of physically building them.

The primary advantage of the laboratory environment is that researchers can control outside influences that might affect the observed behaviors. For example, a shopper in a natural setting might pause to chat with a friend while deciding which soup to buy. If you wanted to measure time spent in deliberation, this interruption could distort the accuracy of the measurement. Another advantage of the contrived setting is that you don't have to wait for events to occur but instead can ask the participants to engage in whatever behavior you want to study. Sometimes an entire study can be completed in a couple of days or a week, which can substantially reduce costs.

As you might guess, the great benefit of natural observation is that the recorded behaviors occur naturally, without prompting. In contrived observation, the prompting from researchers might be direct ("Pretend you are in a grocery store and show us how you would shop for soup") or through the creation of an artificial environment. Either way, the contrived setting may cause differences in

## research window 10.1

### *Observational Research in a Natural Setting: Testing Visa payWave*

Because contactless payment is getting more prevalent, Visa wanted to do a health check on the payment experience to ensure that customers can use their credit or debit cards to pay for their items seamlessly. They commissioned Objective Experience to conduct a study focusing on what customers pay attention to during the payment process of using Visa payWave, including branding on the card, at the merchant checkout and POS (point-of-sale) communications.

Visa payWave is Visa's contactless payment technology. It facilitates fast and convenient transactions at the point of sale and eliminates the requirement for a consumer to make physical contact with the terminal when making a purchase (therefore "contactless").

The study was conducted in both Singapore and Sydney (eight participants per location) at well-known supermarkets like Cold Storage and Woolworths. Participants wore the Tobii Pro Glasses 2—a wearable eye tracker that followed participants' gazes and recorded what they observed while shopping and paying for their purchases. This wearable eye tracker is best used to study human behavior in naturalistic environments. The study used 16 supermarket shoppers between 21 and 54 years old. Participants were instructed to shop for any items they would like to purchase but were told

they had to use the selected Visa payWave credit card to pay.

After the participants finished their task, the video recording was replayed back to them on the spot with the researcher interviewing them about their payment journey based on what the participants saw and did.

Through this study, Objective Experience found several similarities between how customers in Singapore and Sydney pay with the Visa payWave. It helped Visa gain insights into how people use contactless payment via different types of payment terminals, as well as what they really pay attention to when they are at the checkout counter.

Customers generally decide ahead of time on their payment method, even before they start shopping. But the need for, and relevance of, visual prompts varied between customers. This led to rethinking how to best design consumer messaging at checkouts and entrances to strengthen consumers' association between Visa and contactless payment.

**Source:** "Visa uses Tobii Pro Glasses 2 for customer insight." Retrieved and adapted from https://eyetracking.com.sg /2016/04/21/visa-uses-tobii-pro-glasses-2-for-customer -insight/

Courtesy of Tobii AB

behavior and thus raise real questions about the generalizability of the findings. This is much less of a problem with natural observation.

## 10-1d HUMAN VERSUS MECHANICAL OBSERVATION

With **human observation**, one or more people are trained to systematically watch consumers or whatever else is being studied and to record the events that take place. Researchers commonly use written field notes to record their impressions at the time they are observed in the field and later write up summary thoughts back at the office. While some field research still relies on human observation, **mechanical observation** has become increasingly important in marketing research. With mechanical observation, the behaviors of interest are recorded electronically or mechanically for analysis by researchers. (To simplify things, we'll just

> **human observation**
> Individuals are trained to systematically observe a phenomenon and to record on the observational form the specific events that take place.
>
> **mechanical observation** An electrical or mechanical device observes a phenomenon and records the events that take place.

use the traditional term "mechanical observation" to refer to any type of technology used to record data.) New forms of mechanical observation seem to go online each day as more and more pieces of behavioral data are recorded and saved, often as part of the big data revolution. In this section, we'll describe some of the more common forms of mechanical observation—but understand that anything that involves the Internet and connected sensors also falls into this category.

Although some technologies (such as audio recorders and video cameras) have been used for a long time, the development of new and less-expensive technologies is expanding the role of mechanical observation. Observational researchers increasingly rely on technology to assist them, particularly as various tools get smaller in size, which means they are lighter in weight and less intrusive. Research Window 10.2 describes how researchers for PING, the golf club manufacturer,

## research window 10.2

### "Driving" Toward Golfer Insights at PING

How do golfers decide which golf clubs are right for them? An accurate answer to this question is important to makers of golfing equipment. Recently, Don Hein of equipment manufacturer PING and Jon Last of the Sports and Leisure Research Group teamed up to investigate the key factors at play during the moment of truth when a golfer makes a decision about the purchase of a new driver. A driver is a club used to "drive" the golf ball long distances. For example, golfers usually use drivers for their first shots out of the tee box (the starting point for each section of a golf course). Because it is used regularly and because it is normally the most expensive club in a golfer's golf bag, the driver has received a great deal of attention from golfers and the companies that manufacture them. Plus, numerous innovations in the design of drivers, ranging from club face size to adjustable weighting to face shape and depth, have created the need for more information as golfers approach a purchase decision. The research team used a sophisticated observational technique to capture golfers during the key moments when decisions are made at the point of purchase.

Since its founding in 1959, PING has enjoyed a reputation as an innovator. The company is well represented on the PGA Tour by professional golfers,

including Hunter Mahan, Lee Westwood, and Bubba Watson. By 2010, its market share in the driver category has placed the brand near the top with other leading drivers, including Taylor Made and Callaway. Hein and Last believed that a better understanding of the process golfers use when purchasing a new driver would lead to useful insights that could propel future growth in the category.

Prior research conducted by PING, Sports and Leisure Research Group, and others had indicated that golfers go through a decision process that is slightly different from that of shoppers for most other kinds of merchandise. In particular, rather than continuously narrowing the consideration set as information is gathered about various drivers, people shopping for drivers tended to experience more of a two-stage process, during which the consideration set initially narrows, but then widens considerably once the purchaser is in the retail store. Hein and Last knew that golfer shopping behavior within this environment—characterized by rapid proliferation of new products, rampant discounting, and forced obsolescence—was poorly understood. Capturing useful insights could represent a gold mine of opportunity for PING.

## The Research

Based on years of experience in the research industry, the researchers quickly recognized that traditional approaches to gathering data wouldn't produce the kinds of rich data that they needed. So, instead of using a standard communication approach to conduct descriptive research (e.g., surveys, personal interviews), the researchers opted for "retail ethnography," a qualitative observational approach. As Hein put it, "We wanted to observe people, getting as close to the moment of truth as we can." Although this approach would be far more difficult to implement than other approaches, they believed that it was the most straightforward means of getting what they needed.

Not surprisingly, doing something as sophisticated as the research they were proposing takes "buy in" from company decision makers. At the headquarters in Phoenix, Arizona, Hein got PING executives involved early on in the process by helping them recognize what they understood—and especially what they didn't understand—about the retail buying process for their drivers. Those conversations became central for developing discussion guides used to stimulate respondent feedback throughout the research process. Support from the executive team was also important as the research team worked through the legalities of recording video in stores, which required written consent from customers and store employees who would participate in the research. After considerable wrangling to obtain approval from the legal staffs of all the companies involved, Hein and Last were finally ready to implement their research.

**Here's How It Worked:** Retail ethnography involves careful observation of customers as they shop for products, seek information inside a store, touch and examine products, and so on. Working in two different geographic markets and four retail stores selling golfing equipment within each market, the research team set out to carefully observe a total of 50 shoppers as they moved through the store, tried out different drivers, spoke with store salespeople, and—in some cases—made their final selections and purchased a driver. Unlike traditional ethnography, the team added a new wrinkle by using mobile video technology to unobtrusively record as much of the shopping encounter as possible. Later on, they used the 25 hours of in-store video footage to develop and code themes relevant to the shopping experience. They were also able to find specific examples to use to demonstrate the various themes in research presentations to PING executives.

The technique was much more complex than simply taking video of customers in stores, however. For example, it wouldn't have been wise to simply turn on the cameras and record the first 50 customers who showed up. Instead, Hein and Last went to great lengths to ensure that the customers they observed across the eight stores met very specific criteria. In particular, respondents needed to be in the market for a new premium-priced driver from a defined competitive set of leading brands. They secured half of their participants through traditional store intercepts in which they identified potential driver purchasers as they entered the store and then confirmed that they met the screening criteria. The other half of the participants were "seeded": The researchers identified a number of golfers, contacted them in advance to determine if they met the screening criteria, and then encouraged them to participate in the research.

The need to avoid competitors' special promotional events—not to mention dodging inquisitive competitive salespeople—added additional complexity to the research. On top of that, it was paramount that participants remain blind to the fact that PING was sponsoring the research. "It was critical that we derived an unbiased perspective from each respondent. So, we took great care to mask who was sponsoring the research and allowed consumers to shop naturally," said Last. "Only if a respondent did not bring up the PING brand, did we elicit opinions on it, and always incorporated at least one additional brand that they had not mentioned, to keep the dialogue unbiased."

Because observation alone can't get at buyers' motivations and the benefits and features that they believe are important, the research team also communicated with participants before, after, and as they shopped using detailed discussion guides prepared prior to data collection. The goal was to understand, as completely as possible, what shoppers were thinking about as they examined and tried out the different drivers. Finally, about a quarter of the participants received a video camera to use to record guided video diaries in which they reflected on the shopping process and their thoughts and feelings after the conclusion of the shopping event. For example, the researchers were keen to understand the role of

*(continued)*

## research window 10.2   *(continued)*

buyer's remorse in this context as well as other post-purchase reactions.

### *Bringing It to Life—Synthesis*

With data in hand, Hein and Last turned to the task of finding and communicating the meaning held in the videos, interviews, and diaries. The two researchers painstakingly reviewed the material they had collected. In the end, the data led them to identify six different types of shoppers that vary in their level of engagement in the process and the benefits and features that were important to them. For example, some respondents were particularly price sensitive, and that influenced their consideration set.

Now that the data had taken on the form of useful information, the researchers turned their attention to communicating the results to the audiences inside PING most likely to use the information: the executive team and the marketing team.

In addition to a written report, it was critical that the researchers be able to deliver clear oral presentations to both audiences. The core of the presentation was the same for both: an electronic presentation with

embedded video, culled from hours of raw video, illustrating key issues for PING and delivered by both Hein and Last at company headquarters. For PING executives, the presentation also focused on global strategic implications. For the marketing group, however, a more tactical approach was emphasized.

The reaction to the retail ethnography project was extraordinarily positive among both audiences. PING executives and marketers believed that they had uncovered insights that would allow them to better deliver on the aspects that mattered most to people shopping for new drivers. And as is often the case, the research spawned additional questions leading to more research.

Essential Image/Shutterstock.com

---

used portable video technology to learn about the process shoppers use when shopping for golf clubs.

One of the most important methods of mechanical observation is the simple bar-code scanner. Bar codes are scanned billions of times a day; each item scanned is a potential data point for marketing researchers to analyze. Tesco's hugely successful Clubcard program, which allows the UK-based retailer to tie a large percentage of purchases at its stores to particular households, relies on scanner data for its success as do many other companies and research organizations.

Another well-known use of mechanical observation is Nielsen's use of people meters for tracking which family members are watching which television shows and when they are watching them. People meters are far more reliable at measuring viewing behavior compared with surveying viewers or even having them keep detailed diaries.

Mechanical observation is also heavily used in a group of techniques that might be generally categorized under the "neuroscience" label. These tools are used to gauge attention, interest, attitude strength, and emotional response to various

**response latency**
The amount of time a respondent deliberates before answering a question.

**galvanometer** A device used to measure the emotion induced by exposure to a particular stimulus by recording changes in the electrical resistance of the skin associated with the tiny degree of sweating that accompanies emotional arousal; in marketing research, the stimulus is often specific advertising copy.

**voice-pitch analysis** Analysis that examines changes in the relative frequency of the human voice that accompany emotional arousal.

stimuli, including advertisements, web pages, retail displays, and many other things. One of the oldest of these techniques is **response latency**, the amount of time it takes an individual to respond to a stimulus. For example, the amount of time it takes to answer a question is one measure of a respondent's strength of feeling (or the reverse, degree of uncertainty) about her answer. Response latency also helps assess the individual's strength of preference when choosing among alternatives. Measures of response latency can be easily obtained in many online surveys and other tools.

Another method of mechanical observation that falls in this category is galvanic skin response (GSR). A **galvanometer** is used to measure emotional arousal in response to seeing or hearing an advertisement or other stimulus. When a person experiences emotions, slight changes occur in the skin's electrical resistance that aren't under the individual's control. The galvanometer records these changes, which are used to infer the subject's interest or attitude toward the stimulus.

**Voice-pitch analysis** relies on the same basic premise as the galvanometer: Participants experience a number of involuntary physiological reactions, such as changes in blood pressure, rate of per-spiration, or heart rate, when emotionally aroused by external or internal stimuli. Voice-pitch analysis examines changes in the relative vibration frequency of the human voice that accompany emotional arousal. Special audio-adapted computer equipment can measure abnormal frequencies in the voice caused by changes in the nervous system, changes that may not be discernible to the human ear. The more the voice pitch differs from the respondent's normal pitch, the greater the emotional intensity of the consumer's reaction.

An **eye camera** is used to study eye movements while a respondent reads advertising copy or performs any number of other marketing-related activities. Among other things, an eye camera records where a subject's eye is focused: Where did the individual look first? How long did the person linger on any particular place? Did the consumer read the whole ad or just part of it? Which section of a store shelf captured consumers' attention most frequently? Following eye paths has also been used to analyze package designs, billboards, and displays in the aisles of supermarkets. The study described in Research Window 10.1, which we presented earlier, relies upon portable eye camera that can be worn by research participants.

> **eye camera** A device used by researchers to study a subject's eye movements while he or she is reading advertising copy.
>
> **facial coding** A technique for measuring emotions that uses cameras to record small, involuntary movements (microexpressions) in the muscles around a person's mouth and eyes.

There is one additional method of mechanical observation that is growing in popularity. **Facial coding** uses cameras to record small, involuntary movements in the muscles around a person's mouth and eyes. These slight movements, sometimes called microexpressions, have been tied to a number of human emotions. As a result, facial coding offers an advantage that the other mechanical observation techniques cannot: a measure of the type of emotion that the person is experiencing. (The other techniques provide a measure of depth of emotional reaction in addition to focus of attention, but not direct identification of the actual emotion being experienced.) Companies such as Nielsen, through its Nielsen Consumer Neuroscience division, combine facial coding with other forms of mechanical observation to predict consumer response to various marketing stimuli.[8]

Observational research is an incredibly useful tool. As we've noted repeatedly, we think it is often more useful to examine people's behavior than to gather their answers to survey questions, especially when the goal is to predict future behavior. That said, there are many things that researchers need to know that cannot be uncovered by observational research. We turn our attention to communication-based research in the following chapter.

## Manager's Focus

The usefulness of marketing research information is magnified substantially when managers and researchers employ techniques in creative ways. One form of creativity is to use multiple methods simultaneously. An example of this is when highly skilled focus group moderators ask participants to engage in activities during the early stages of the interview process. For example, moderators may ask the participants to collaborate on a task such as sorting various food items into different piles based on their perceptions of the degree to which the items represent ethnic or international cuisine. Certainly, this type of activity is intended to serve as an icebreaker, but it also represents a form of observation in a contrived setting. The participants talk with one another during the process, but they are not responding to questions from the moderator, so their behaviors and their conversations are being "observed." Sometimes their behaviors toward other participants, or the task itself, are more revealing than anything they verbalize.

The research methods you are learning do not necessarily have to be used in isolation or in the same way every time. It is perfectly fine to modify them to meet your needs as long as you are working with a competent researcher who can help you assess the validity of the new approach. Good ideas for blending methods do not emerge exclusively from researchers. As a manager, you should freely share with your research suppliers any ideas you have for creating innovative ways to capture information that addresses your marketing problems.

# Summary

## Learning Objective 1

**Describe the two basic means of obtaining primary data.**
The two basic means of obtaining primary data are communication and observation. Communication involves questioning respondents to secure the desired information using a data collection instrument called a questionnaire. Observation involves scrutinizing the situation of interest and recording the relevant facts, actions, or behaviors.

## Learning Objective 2

**State the specific advantages of each method of data collection.**
In general, the communication method of data collection has the advantages of versatility, speed, and cost, whereas observation data are typically more objective and accurate.

## Learning Objective 3

**List the important considerations in the use of observational methods of data collection.**
Observational data may be gathered using structured or unstructured methods that are either disguised or undisguised. The observations may be made in a contrived or a natural setting and may be secured by a human or an electrical/mechanical observer.

## Learning Objective 4

**Explain the difference between structured and unstructured observation.**
With structured observation, the phenomena to be observed (typically behaviors) and the categories to be used to record the phenomena can be defined precisely. For unstructured observation, the researcher has a great deal of flexibility in terms of what to note and record.

## Learning Objective 5

**Cite the main reason researchers may choose to disguise the presence of an observer in a study.**
Most often, an observer's presence is disguised in order to control the tendency of people to behave differently when they know their actions are being watched.

## Learning Objective 6

**Explain the advantages and disadvantages of conducting an observational experiment in a laboratory setting.**
The advantage of a laboratory environment is that researchers are better able to control outside influences that might affect the observed behavior. The disadvantage of the laboratory setting is that the contrived setting itself may cause differences in behavior and thus threaten the external validity of the findings. A contrived setting, however, usually speeds the data collection process, results in lower-cost research, and allows the use of more objective measurements.

## Learning Objective 7

**List several approaches to mechanical observation.**
The approaches used with mechanical observation range from straightforward things like video cameras, tape recorders, and bar-code scanners to more complex approaches such as response latency, galvanometers, voice-pitch analysis, eye cameras, and facial coding.

## Key Terms

communication (page 140)
observation (page 140)
structure (page 144)
structured observation (page 144)
unstructured observation (page 144)
disguise (page 145)
undisguised observation (page 145)
disguised observation (page 145)
debriefing (page 146)
natural settings (page 146)
contrived settings (page 146)
human observation (page 148)
mechanical observation (page 148)
response latency (page 150)
galvanometer (page 150)
voice-pitch analysis (page 150)
eye camera (page 151)
facial coding (page 151)

## Review Questions

1. What are the general advantages and disadvantages of obtaining data by communication? By observation?

2. What does a high degree of structure look like in an observational study?

3. What are mystery shoppers? What is their purpose?

4. What is the key ethical issue with the use of disguise in observation research? How is this issue typically remedied in disguised marketing research projects?

5. What are the primary advantages and disadvantages of working in a natural setting as contrasted with a contrived setting?

6. What are some of the available types of mechanical observation?

# Endnotes

1. Underhill, P. (2000). *Why we buy: The science*. New York: Touchstone, 18.

2. Becker, B. (1999, Sept. 27). Take direct route when data-gathering. *Marketing News* 33, 29, 31; Kluger, J. (1994, Aug.) Oh, rubbish—A study of garbage in Tucson, Arizona is used to collect dental hygiene statistics. *Discover*. Retrieved from BNET web site at http://findarticles.com

3. SMB Reviews, (2014, May 14) Understanding Marketing Research, Example retrieved from http://www.bizoffice.com/library/files/mktres.txt

4. Observational Research Services, Example retrieved from http://www.pcpmarketresearch.com/services/quantitative-research/observational-research

5. Martin, H. (2016, July 30). What does Disney want to do with photos of your feet? *Los Angeles Times*. Retrieved from www.latimes.com.

6. Case, T. (2000, March 6). Getting personal. *Brandweek* 41, M52–M54.

7. Krispy Kreme example retrieved from the Williams Inference Center web site, http://www.williamsinference.com; Boon, J. (2010, Dec. 13–19). A dance to the music of time. *Bloomberg Businessweek*, 96–97.

8. (2016, June 13). Nielsen consumer neuroscience unveils trailblazing ad testing solution. Retrieved from www.nielsen.com

CHAPTER **11**

# Collecting Data by Communication

## LEARNING OBJECTIVES

▶ Explain the concept of *structure* as it relates to questionnaires.

▶ Cite the drawbacks of using high degrees of structure.

▶ Explain what is meant by *disguise* in a questionnaire context.

▶ Discuss two situations in which disguise might be desirable.

▶ Differentiate among the main methods of administering questionnaires.

▶ Discuss three important aspects used to compare the four different methods of administering questionnaires.

## [ INTRODUCTION ]

Although observational research, including all the new types of big data, usually results in more accurate and objective data about individual behavior, communication techniques in the form of interviews or surveys must be used to capture most other kinds of data from individuals. This is an important point, as illustrated by a leading research professional:

> *But in the age of big data, it's important to remember what surveys are uniquely suited to do. Asking Americans about their values, beliefs and concerns can tease out meaning from mountains of data and uncover the motivations behind the choices we make—providing a path to understanding not just what we do, but why.*[1]

Learning to gather communication-based data well is important: To gain meaningful insights into why customers behave the way that they do, it is almost always necessary to ask questions and let them respond. It helps to think about asking questions in the form of a questionnaire, but you should understand that any systematic effort to gather information from people where they supply the information in response to a prompt of any kind falls in this category (e.g., completing a warranty card; applying for a loan; completing an application for a grocery store discount card). We'll talk a lot about questionnaires in this chapter, but the information applies to any communication-based data collection effort.

In this chapter, we look closely at communication-based approaches. We'll discuss the three key decisions that you'll need to make when using communication: the degree of structure to use, whether to disguise the questionnaire, and which method to use. We end the chapter with a comparison of primary communication techniques across three levels of research control.

## 11-1 Structured Versus Unstructured Communication

The first decision is how much structure to use on the questionnaire. Recall from the previous chapter that structure refers to how much standardization is used with the data collection instrument. In a highly structured questionnaire, the questions to be asked and the response categories provided to respondents are completely standardized. That is, everyone receives the same questions, and everyone responds by choosing from among the same set of possible answers. These are known as **fixed-alternative questions** or closed-ended questions, and they are very commonly used to collect primary data. Consider the following question regarding attitudes toward a U.S.-based retailer.

> **Considering all aspects, what is your overall evaluation of Target, the department store chain?**
>
> ○  Extremely unfavorable
> ○  Unfavorable
> ○  Neither favorable nor unfavorable
> ○  Favorable
> ○  Extremely favorable

Notice that the question itself is standardized, as are the response categories. Everyone asked to answer the question will get the identical question and respond with one of the five possible answers. These questions are similar to multiple-choice questions on an exam.

Now consider another way of asking a similar question, one involving much less structure:

> **Overall, how do you feel about Target, the department store chain? Please type your answer in the box below.**
>
> _____
>
> _____
>
> _____

**fixed-alternative questions** Questions in which the responses are limited to stated alternatives.

**open-ended question** A question in which respondents are free to reply in their own words rather than being limited to choosing from among a set of alternatives.

This is an example of an **open-ended question**, a type of question in which respondents are free to reply using their own words and are not limited to a fixed set of possible answers. Most open-ended questions used for collecting primary data for descriptive research have a standardized question that everyone receives, but people get to answer in any way that they choose. These questions are similar to essay questions on an exam. Questionnaires used for depth interviews, an exploratory research technique, usually have even less structure because the questions and the way they are posed to respondents can change based on answers to previous questions.

### 11-1a ADVANTAGES AND DISADVANTAGES OF HIGH STRUCTURE

Highly structured questions, like the first question above, are relatively simple to administer. No matter what method of administration you choose, once the questionnaire items are written, the questionnaire finalized, and data collected, the analysis is usually easy. There's no need to try to interpret open-ended responses, which saves a lot of time and money and avoids possible interpretation bias. Respondents respond, and that's about it.

Another huge advantage of high structure is that it greatly simplifies data coding and analysis. Open-ended questions are much more difficult to code, which typically means converting answers into code numbers, than are questions with a limited number of possible responses.

Highly structured questions also help improve the consistency of responses across different people because standardized questions and responses provide respondents with an identical frame of reference. Consider the question, "How often do you watch television?" If you don't supply response categories, one respondent might say "every day," another might say "regularly," and still another might respond with the number of hours per day. Responses like that are far more difficult to interpret than those from a highly structured, fixed-alternative question that asks for responses with categories "every day," "at least three times a week," "at least once a week," or "less than once a week."

There are certain disadvantages associated with high degrees of structure, however. Although fixed-alternative questions tend to provide the most reliable responses, they may also encourage misleading answers. For example, fixed alternatives may force an answer to a question on which the respondent has no opinion. Suppose that an individual had never heard of Target or shopped at one of its outlets. When he reads the first question discussed above, is that going to stop him from checking one of the

## Manager's Focus

The degree of structure can differ significantly across the various items included on a questionnaire. As a manager, you play an important role in helping researchers determine how much structure to employ in each area. Your level of knowledge about a marketing situation is the primary driver of the general type of research used (i.e., exploratory, descriptive, or causal). Your input to decisions about structure is quite similar: You must work with the researcher by articulating what you already know about each issue that will be addressed in the questionnaire and how much of this was learned from statements made by individuals in the target population.

Use relatively structured questions in situations where previous research and experience have given you considerable insight into what a particular topic encompasses, from the perspective of the consumer or business buyer. This represents descriptive research in the purest sense because your current purpose is to ask "how large?" types of questions. Use relatively unstructured (open-ended) questions, however, when you believe you need greater insight into the nature or

parameters of a topic. Due to your limited knowledge, you want respondents to reply in their own words so you can learn more about the topic's meaning from their perspective. In a very real sense, whenever you ask open-ended questions, you are performing exploratory research—even when most of the other questions are highly structured and the overall purpose of the study is descriptive in nature.

An example of this type of mixed structure is when respondents are first asked to rate something (such as a brand) using a standardized or structured scale. They are then asked *why* they rated the item that way. The first question is descriptive in nature, and the second is more exploratory in nature. Despite this difference in the focus of the questions, the responses to such open-ended questions are ultimately classified (coded) and tallied and thus presented in a descriptive format. The key point, however, is that it is your responsibility as a manager to highlight for researchers the relevant topic areas where more insight is needed through relatively unstructured questions.

---

boxes? Probably not. Some people will answer the question because they don't want to look dumb. And what if you don't include all of the possible answers to the question? Respondents will probably just choose the one closest to their true feelings, but using high structure in this situation means that you'll be missing out on what is true for some individuals.

High structure is most useful when the possible replies are well known, limited in number, and clear-cut. They work well for obtaining factual information (e.g., age, education, homeownership, amount of rent) and for assessing opinions about issues on which people hold clear opinions. They aren't necessarily very good at getting primary data on motivations, but they could certainly be used to collect data on attitudes, intentions, awareness, demographic /socioeconomic characteristics, and self-reported behavior.

## 11-2 Disguised Versus Undisguised Communication

The second consideration in the use of communication to gather primary data concerns **disguise**. A disguised questionnaire attempts to hide the purpose or the sponsor of the study. An undisguised questionnaire makes the purpose of the research obvious, either in the introduction, the

> **disguise** An activity where a researcher attempts to hide the purpose or the sponsor of the study in order to receive the most objective results possible.

instructions, or the questions themselves. For example, if Ford Motor Co. wanted to determine its customers' satisfaction with its cars and trucks, it could simply send out a survey with a cover letter printed on Ford letterhead stationery and the Ford logo appearing on the questionnaire itself. Doing so, however, means that respondents' answers are very likely biased toward Ford, because the survey's purpose and sponsor are clear. If Ford wants more objective data, it might go without the letterhead, go through an outside marketing research agency, or ask its drivers about Ford, GM, and Honda cars. In this scenario, the target of the research is less clear, and we'd expect customers to answer more truthfully.

There are two general situations in which the use of disguise is often necessary. The Ford example illustrates the first: when knowledge of the sponsor or topic of the survey is likely to cause respondents to change their answers. Here's another example of this: Imagine asking people to "name the first three brands of cars that come to mind" or to "indicate your top two choices among the following brands of cars," when they can clearly see that Ford sponsors the survey. The researcher has "primed" a particular response, and the results will be of little value.

Disguise is also used to help create a more natural environment in which to collect data from individuals. Although this can apply to questionnaires, it more often applies to experimental research. Suppose that Ford wants to compare two television ads to see which could create greater awareness of a new Ford truck. Researchers run a lab study in which two groups of consumers are each shown one of the ads. The ads are imbedded in a 30-minute television show with other ads; consumers are told to watch the show as if they were watching TV at home. Later, they are asked to recall the brands advertised during the show.

> Disguise is also used to help create a more natural environment in which to collect data from individuals.

What will happen if the sponsor and purpose of the study are fully disclosed? The subjects will be watching for anything in the show or ads related to Ford products and, as a result, recall for the test ads will be much higher than it would otherwise have been. In short, the results would be useless.

### 11-2a   THE ETHICS OF DISGUISE

It seems a little strange to suggest that deception can be used to get at the truth in a situation, doesn't it? The use of disguise makes some peo-

**debriefing** A process of informing respondents of the true purpose of a disguised study after respondents have participated in the study itself.

ple and researchers uncomfortable. Any way you look at it, the use of disguise amounts to a conscious effort to deceive the respondent or at least to withhold information. Many people would argue that research participants have a right to know why they are being asked to provide answers, how those answers will be used, and/or who will use the information. On the other hand, as long as people understand the basic motivation for the study (i.e., in order to develop products and services that better meet their needs) and the reason for nondisclosure—so that the results will be more objective—they may not feel as deceived. If the emphasis is on the fact that you want their true response and that is more valuable than any perceived "right answer," they should feel okay with it. Researchers almost universally agree that the benefits of true, usable information outweigh the costs of the deception to respondents, provided that they are given appropriate information following the task. This process is known as **debriefing**.

How much information should be shared in the debriefing process? If all you've done is withhold information from respondents, such as the sponsor or the specific purpose of the research, it's probably not a big deal. Respondents usually don't care, and sponsors normally prefer to remain anonymous. When disguise has involved an active deception, however, it is necessary to tell respondents that they have been misled, explain why the deception was

## Manager's Focus

Sometimes managers or researchers choose not to disguise their research purpose because they hope to influence respondents' answers in a way that will help the managers or their companies look better. Here's an example: A few years ago, one of us bought a new car. When completing the required paperwork, we were informed that a satisfaction survey would soon appear in the mail and to please inform the salesperson if there was any reason that we couldn't give the highest satisfaction rating. They even spelled out what the highest satisfaction rating would be on the scales on the forthcoming survey.

On the one hand, we could conclude that the dealership just wanted to make certain that our needs were met and that the survey would provide confirmation that they had succeeded. On the other hand, let's call it what it really was: a blatant attempt to influence the dealership's satisfaction score at a time when corporate managers and consumers were placing increasingly greater emphasis on satisfaction measures. (See the J. D. Power and Associates customer satisfaction rankings).

It is important to recognize that there are many degrees of disguise. When measuring customers' satisfaction with specific products, services, or companies, it is almost impossible to disguise the purpose of the study. Nevertheless, it is generally good policy to reveal only what is necessary about the purpose of the study to secure cooperation from prospective respondents. You must never reveal your goals as a manager or other underlying purposes for the study if they have any potential to alter how people respond to questions. Similarly, you must resist the temptation to promote your products or services when gathering research data, because doing so is highly likely to influence how current or prospective customers respond to your questions. You may color respondents' views of the issues and/or make respondents skeptical about the integrity of the study. In addition, if you think about it, a questionnaire is an extremely poor promotional platform—it reaches a very limited number of people—so why sacrifice information integrity? Research is research, and promotion is promotion ... and the two functions must *never* be combined in a single effort.

needed, and provide a general overview of the purpose of the project. For the most part, the use of disguise and the amount of debriefing necessary involve judgment calls on your part.

## 11-3 Methods of Administering Questionnaires

The third decision that you must make when collecting primary data via communication is which method(s) to use. The main methods include personal interviews, telephone interviews, paper-based surveys, and online surveys. There are some clear differences in usage rates, as Exhibit 11.1 demonstrates. These data, which were gathered from corporate marketing researchers (i.e., professionals who work for providers or sellers of products and services, not marketing research companies), show the dominance of online surveys (97% of companies use them) compared with the other methods. Current trends show that online surveys are being used even more frequently (about 60% of companies report using online surveys more than they were two years earlier), while telephone and, especially, paper-based surveys, are on the decline.[2]

For each general method, there are three key aspects to consider. *Sampling control* refers to the ability of a particular method to identify and obtain responses from a sample of respondents from the target population. Obtaining lists of population members and likely response rates are key issues in sampling control. *Information control* is concerned primarily with the number and types of questions that can be used and the degree to which researchers and/or respondents might introduce error into the answers or their interpretations. Finally, *administrative control* refers to resource issues, such as the time and monetary costs of the different approaches.

**personal interview**
Direct, face-to-face conversation between a representative of the research organization, the interviewer, and a respondent or interviewee.

**mall intercept**
A method of data collection in which interviewers in a shopping mall stop or interrupt a sample of those passing by to ask them if they would be willing to participate in a research study.

### 11-3a PERSONAL INTERVIEWS

A **personal interview** involves a direct face-to-face conversation between an interviewer and the respondent. Generally, the interviewer asks the questions and records the respondent's answers. Sometimes the interviewer may give all or part of the questionnaire to the respondent and be available to answer questions while the respondent completes it. In still other cases, the researcher gets the respondent to agree to complete the survey, leaves the questionnaire, and returns to pick it up later (or has the respondent return it).

Personal interviews can take place just about anywhere. You can conduct them in a respondent's home or office, at the researcher's office, or at some other location. It depends on the needs of the research and the convenience of the respondents. We've even had a research group do interviews on board rapid transit trains.

**Mall intercepts** are sometimes used to conduct personal interviews among consumers. The technique involves exactly what the name suggests: Interviewers intercept, or stop, people in a shopping mall and ask them to participate in a research study. Mall intercepts place the researcher in a location where people naturally gather together—consumers in their natural habitat. This approach is convenient for finding consumers to answer our questions. There's a cost to this convenience, however. For most purposes, the results cannot be projected to the overall population because the sample is not randomly drawn. Another significant cost is an interviewer who is not properly trained or compensated. It's not uncommon for an interviewer to fill in answers for the respondent in order to speed up the interview process, or to reword open-ended responses for the sake of time instead of accuracy. Still, for exploratory research and situations in which a nonrandom sample will work, mall intercepts can be quite useful.

**Exhibit 11.1** ▶ Percentage of Corporate Marketing Researchers Using Each Method

| | |
|---|---|
| Personal Interviews | 67% |
| Telephone Interviews | 61% |
| Paper-based Surveys | 32% |
| Online Surveys | 97% |

Source: "Quirk's Corporate Research Report," retrieved from www.quirks.com. Although the report is undated, the results represent data from 2014.

## Sampling Control

It's possible to draw some form of random sample when using personal interviews for data collection, but it tends to be a little more difficult than for most other methods. In other ways, however, personal interviews offer more sample control than other approaches. For example, an interviewer can verify the respondent's identity; there is little opportunity for anyone else to reply. Response rates are also higher for personal interviews than most other methods, probably because the direct, personal appeal makes it harder for respondents to say "no" compared with, say, simply tossing a paper-based mail survey into the trash or deleting an e-mail containing a link to a web-based survey.

## Information Control

Personal interviews can be conducted using questionnaires with any degree of structure, from purely open-ended questions to purely fixed-alternative questions. One huge advantage of personal interviews is the ability to explain or rephrase questions and to have respondents explain their answers. In addition, the personal nature of the interaction allows you to see the respondent interact with the product and show pictures, examples of advertisements, lists of words, scales, and so on, as needed. And there's no better approach for gaining a respondent's trust.

You can gather a lot of information in a personal interview, more than with any other approach under normal circumstances. Because of the personal interaction aspect, researchers can usually get respondents to spend more time in a face-to-face interview. Personal interviews also allow the sequence of questions to be changed by the researcher fairly easily in response to the answers provided by respondents. For example, if the answer to a question about homeownership is "no," you can skip questions about length of ownership, satisfaction with the current lender, recent remodels, and so on, and proceed to another point in the survey form, all without the respondent's knowledge.

On the downside, personal interviews are subject to several kinds of error. For example, open-ended responses can be influenced by the biases of the researcher. In the classic form of a personal interview, the researcher asks questions and then records the respondent's answers. This process is full of opportunities for researcher bias to enter (e.g., mishearing the answer, writing it down incorrectly, truncating a written response to keep up with the spoken word and misinterpreting later). And if the researcher changes the wording of questions or even the inflection of his or her voice—more possible error. Add to this the bias from the respondent's side of the equation—in particular the conscious or unconscious desire to appear knowledgeable, socially acceptable, and helpful

> **telephone interview** Telephone conversation between a representative of the research organization, the interviewer, and a respondent or interviewee.

> **random-digit dialing (RDD)** A technique used in studies using telephone interviews, in which the numbers to be called are randomly generated.

to the researcher. Finally, it should be clear that personal interviews must be undertaken with great care and include substantial interviewer training.

## Administrative Control

In most cases, personal interviews cost more to conduct than any other communication method. It's easy to see why: Interviews take place one at a time; interviews tend to last longer; researchers must often travel from one interview to the next (unless all interviews are conducted in a central location, which leads to greater office overhead expense); interviewers must be well trained, which is expensive, and when they are trained, they command higher salaries; and coding and analysis can be much more involved, particularly if open-ended questions have been used. Further, as you might guess, using personal interviews generally takes a great deal of time.

## 11-3b TELEPHONE INTERVIEWS

A **telephone interview** is similar in some ways to a personal interview, except that the conversation between researcher and respondent takes place over the telephone. It is still a social process involving direct interaction between individuals. Telephone surveys used to be very popular because they had fairly high response rates and costs were lower compared with personal interviews. As we'll explain, however, things have changed dramatically with this method over the past couple of decades.

## Sampling Control

Several companies generate and sell lists of consumer or business telephone numbers from which to draw a random sample. These lists can often be selected based on particular geographic or demographic variables, or even on variables representing consumer interests, occupations, lifestyles, hobbies, and so on. If you are calling businesses, it might also be possible to use a telephone directory as a sampling frame.

Although the overall penetration rate of telephones in the United States is quite high, there has been a dramatic shift in the types of telephone service that people use. About half of all adults in the United States now use only mobile phones for which numbers typically are not published. This greatly increases the challenge of sampling control.

With landline telephones, researchers have long used **random-digit dialing (RDD)** to overcome the problem of unlisted telephone numbers. With RDD systems, a computer randomly (or sequentially) generates numbers and automatically dials them, switching over to a live interviewer when someone answers the call. Federal regulations require that wireless numbers must be dialed manually, however, greatly increasing the costs of telephone surveys. For this and other reasons, one estimate places the cost of a completed cell phone survey at 1.5 times the costs of a completed landline survey.[3] The problem isn't likely to get any better, given the trends in cell phone usage.

It's still possible to obtain lists of cell numbers to call, but that's not the end of the problem. Response rates on telephone surveys have dropped precipitously over recent years, mostly as a result of caller ID and other means of screening calls. Despite all this, some companies continue to use telephone surveys (see Exhibit 11.1 on page 158 ).

### Information Control

Most of the time, telephone studies use simple fixed-alternative questions that are easy for the interviewer to explain and easy for the respondent to answer. And it's easy to sequence questions based on the answers to earlier questions, because the interviewer is simply following prompts on the screen. Note that the same technology is available for field interviewers conducting personal interviews if they are using a tablet to record respondents' answers.

Like personal interviews, telephone interviews allow probing and follow-up on respondent answers when necessary. Questions and instructions can be repeated and answers verified. Because of the human contact, a degree of trust can be developed, particularly on longer surveys. Although there's still a chance that bias will enter because of the social interaction, it's less likely than with personal interviews.

One of the biggest disadvantages of telephone interviews is the limited amount of information that can be gathered from any given individual. Unless the topic is of great interest to respondents (or they are either bored enough or nice enough to talk to *anybody*, which actually happens), most are not going to be excited about staying on the phone very long. How long should a telephone interview be? It depends on the likely interest level of the topic, but we recommend trying to keep the interview to 5 to 10 minutes. If you design your survey carefully, you can collect a lot of information in that time frame. The key is to remember that respondents are *listening* to the survey questions—they can't see them.

### Administrative Control

The cost-per-contact on telephone surveys has been rising as telephone response rates drop and costs of data collection from cell phone users rise, making telephone surveys less appealing than in the past compared with personal interviews and online surveys. Interviewers must be recruited and trained, and as with personal interviews, each interviewer can visit with only one respondent at a time. Quality control can be assured by having supervisors periodically listen in on interviews in progress. As a result, data from telephone interviews can be collected in a matter of days, rather than weeks or months.

**paper-based survey** A survey usually administered by mail to designated respondents with an accompanying cover letter. The respondents return the questionnaire by mail to the research organization.

## 11-3c   PAPER-BASED SURVEYS

The **paper-based survey** approach typically involves questionnaires sent by mail to designated respondents with an accompanying cover letter and reply envelope. Respondents complete the questionnaire and mail their replies back to the research organization. Variations to this classic form also exist. For example, a survey might be dropped off at a residence (without direct contact between researcher and respondent), along with instructions to complete it and return it by mail to the researchers. Or you might simply attach questionnaires to products or put them in magazines and newspapers, or even stuff them in shopping bags. Surveys can be e-mailed to respondents as well.

### Sampling Control

If you want to be able to project the results of the survey to the overall population, you'll have to start with an accurate mailing list of the people in the population. This isn't a problem for companies doing customer surveys using customer records from an updated database. In other cases, companies can purchase mailing lists, often for very specific populations, although it isn't always clear how the information was obtained and how complete the list may be. Business-to-business marketing research is usually easier in this regard—contact information for businesses is more stable than that for consumers, and businesses are fewer in number.

When you purchase a mailing list from a list company, you typically are allowed to use it one time. How does the list provider know that you've used the list only once? It's easy: They normally include one or more "dummy" addresses that are delivered back to the list company or its employees. If a company tries to use the list more than once, the owner of the list will soon know about it.

On the downside, paper-based surveys provide little control in getting a response from the intended respondent. You can carefully identify desired respondents and offer them incentives, but you can't control whether the respondents actually complete and return the questionnaires. With no direct contact between researcher and respondent, there is less social pressure to agree to the researcher's request to complete the questionnaire. Although there are circumstances that produce big response rates, this isn't usually the case. On top of that, there's no way to know that the intended respondent really completed a returned questionnaire, or if someone else may have completed it. This is probably more of a problem with questionnaires sent to businesses than with consumer projects.

### Information Control

Paper-based surveys sent by mail offer a couple of nice advantages when it comes to information control. For one thing, with written questions, there is no opportunity for interviewer bias from the wording of questions or the way that the questions are asked. It's also possible to include graphics, images, or other artwork if respondents need to see a stimulus in order to respond effectively. It may also be possible to collect a bit more information with mail surveys than with telephone interviews, but it is usually advisable to keep mail surveys under four pages long. Better yet, keep the survey to two pages (one page, printed on both sides) if at all possible.

One of the biggest advantages of paper-based surveys is that they are the only method that can be truly anonymous. People are likely to be more candid in their responses. If your topic revolves around a sensitive issue (e.g., participation in illegal or socially undesirable activities), the typical recommendation is to send a paper-based survey.

Despite these advantages, these surveys have their shortcomings with respect to information control. Most importantly, they do not allow clarification of questions or response categories, and you can't ask follow-up questions or clarify answers. If open-ended questions are included, individuals must write out their answers, which is more difficult than answering a question orally. All else being equal, more work for respondents translates into fewer surveys returned.

Here's another disadvantage: If they choose, respondents can see the entire survey before answering the questions. This is a real problem if the researcher wants to assess awareness for certain brands and also ask specific questions about those brands in the same survey. If respondents see questions about Target in a survey, don't be surprised if "Target" is one of the most often mentioned answers to the item "list the first three department stores that come to mind." In addition, instructions for question sequencing ("If the answer to the previous question is "no," go to question 7") can quickly become complicated and should be avoided if possible with paper-based surveys.

### Administrative Control

Compared with hiring and training interviewers, it doesn't cost a lot to print surveys, buy a mailing list, and pay postage (outbound and inbound), so paper-based mail surveys have an advantage over personal interviews and telephone questionnaires when it comes to cost. These same cost advantages do not necessarily hold compared to the relative efficiency of online surveys (as noted below). Quality control is also fairly straightforward with paper-based surveys. Supervisory responsibilities are limited to the management of the mailing process, both outgoing and incoming. This also serves to lower costs.

The only administrative disadvantage of sending paper-based surveys via mail is that they take longer than telephone surveys (but they're often faster than personal interviews) because the surveys must go through the postal system going and coming, and respondents respond if and when they want to. As a result, you should budget at least two extra weeks in the timeline of a project using this approach. If you include follow-up mailings, you'll need to budget even more time.

## 11-3d ONLINE SURVEYS

Over the past couple of decades, we've witnessed an explosion in the use of **online surveys**. As indicated in Exhibit 11.1, virtually all corporate researchers use them to gather communication-based data. One estimate placed the dollars spent on online surveys worldwide at $10 billion—that's more than the money spent on personal interviews and telephone surveys combined, as well as more than a quarter of all research expenditures.[4] Online surveys are so attractive that many major research firms use them with respondent panels as their primary point of access to survey data. As we'll show you, online surveys can have serious drawbacks—but their administrative control advantages are large relative to the other options.

> Virtually all corporate researchers use online surveys to gather communication-based data.

As you are probably aware from your own experiences, this approach to data collection involves a survey hosted on a web site. Often, these surveys are created and hosted on commercial sites run by companies such as Qualtrics or SurveyMonkey. Respondents can be recruited in a variety of ways (but often by e-mail) and then linked to the online site to complete the questionnaire using a computer, mobile phone, or any other Internet-connected device. Many of the commercial sites offer assistance with survey design and analysis, along with basic data collection.

### Sampling Control

As with all techniques, the ability to obtain an accurate list of population members' contact information is the first key aspect of sampling control. With most online surveys, this means obtaining lists of e-mail addresses. For some narrowly defined populations this is a real problem; in some cases, researchers turn to a technique using **in-bound surveys** as described in Exhibit 11.2. For other populations, though, reasonable sampling frames of e-mail addresses exist because for many of us, these technologies have been integrated into our everyday lives; as of 2016, 88% of all US adults use the Internet.

Not all categories of US adults are equally accessible online, however. For example, older, lower income, less educated, and rural individuals tend to use the Internet less than other groups. Still, Internet penetration has been growing across all categories of people in the US and is likely to continue growing into the future.[5]

---

**online surveys**
A method of administration that relies on the Web for completing the survey.

**in-bound surveys**
A method of data collection in which respondents access a survey by telephone or online to respond to survey items.

**Exhibit 11.2** ▸ Using In-Bound Surveys to Capture Responses from Difficult-to-Find Populations

Igor kisselev/Alamy Stock Photo

For most of this chapter, we've assumed that a list of population members can be obtained. What happens, however, when the group you need to question is small and can't be identified on a list somewhere? Traditional methods of securing a sample would be as inefficient as hunting for needles in a haystack. In this situation, many researchers have turned to **in-bound surveys.** Originally used with computerized telephone surveys (but now more frequently conducted using online surveys), in-bound survey respondents contact the researcher rather than the other way around (thus, the response is "in-bound").

It's very likely that you've received an invitation to participate in an in-bound telephone or online survey for restaurants or for retailers—these are very common in these environments and usually are generated along with a register receipt. A respondent can complete an in-bound survey at any time, day or night, whenever it is most convenient simply by visiting a web site and providing responses. At the conclusion, respondents typically receive a code number that allows them to obtain a discount or free gift from the survey sponsor.

In-bound surveys make sense for businesses that cater to a unique clientele or that want to measure service quality or satisfaction while the experience is fresh in the consumer's mind. Imagine that a restaurant needed to determine the satisfaction level of customers who only visited the restaurant to pick up "to-go" meals to be eaten elsewhere. No one would offer a list of such customers, and starting with a general sample of residents in the area would be terribly inefficient—it's hard enough to get consumers to respond to surveys in the first place without having to screen out the 95% or so who haven't ordered take-out food from the particular restaurant during the designated time period. In this situation, handing the consumer a receipt at the time of purchase with instructions to visit an online site and the promise of an incentive for doing so may be a cost-effective means of gathering the required data.

**Exhibit 11.3** ▶ SurveyMonkey Panel Sample Selection Attributes (partial list)

- Gender
- Age
- Household income
- Education
- Location
- Race
- Living arrangements
- Marital status
- Parental status
- Exercise habits

- Political affiliation
- Voter status
- Employment status
- Student status
- Small business owner
- Industry
- Job function
- Mobile phones
- Devices owned
- Internet usage

Source: Retrieved from www.surveymonkey.com on January 17, 2017.

Lists of e-mail addresses are available from numerous sources. Much like mailing lists, these lists can often be selected based on respondent demographics, interests, and so on. Several companies have developed panels of respondents that have agreed to answer survey questions. As an example, SurveyMonkey boasts a panel of millions of people around the world who have been profiled along more than 30 attributes. Exhibit 11.3 includes some of the variables available for fine-tuning sample selection using the panel.

You should note, however, that many panels are developed by encouraging individuals to participate in exchange for gifts and/or other incentives. This practice encourages "professional" panelists whose only interest may be in completing as many studies as possible to maximize rewards. Lying about interests, experiences, demographics, and so on, can often increase the number of surveys they can complete—and adds error to the results. Well run online panels or e-mail samples will employ techniques for validating unique e-mail respondents and their devices, limit the number of surveys panel members are allowed to complete in a given period, and may use nonmonetary incentives, such as lotteries or charitable gifts, to reward panel participants. The best run online panels routinely reject panelists because they are either not who they said they were, they completed multiple surveys under different names, or they simply were not thinking about their answers (responding too quickly or selecting the same response for each item). All of this means that obtaining a quality online sample that is at least reasonably representative of some population—which was often very difficult in the past—is now possible. Keep in mind, however, that obtaining a representative sample is not the same thing as obtaining a truly probabilistic sample that can be used

to project sample results to the overall population. We'll address this issue in a later chapter.

As with any technique, we must get people to respond to the questionnaire. Sometimes online studies produce very respectable response rates. Studies using purchased e-mail lists or online panels, however, often have *very* low response rates, often lower than other communication methods. The key is to do the necessary background work to distinguish the good panel that is managed properly from the one populated with "professional" panelists. The anonymity of the Internet makes this an issue of greater concern and a focal point of panel management relative to traditional mail panels, for instance.

A quick word of warning before we move on: Some companies who provide access to online panels are quick to tout the "completion rate" for a study (the percentage of respondents who complete a survey once they've started it). Although this value can give an indication of the quality of the questionnaire, the completion rate is not the same thing as the overall response rate (the percentage of people who were given the opportunity to respond and completed the survey). The response rate is a much better indicator of the quality of the research effort and, in particular, of how concerned you should be about differences between those who responded and those who didn't.

## Information Control

Online surveys are very effective if you need to include pictures and/or other graphics with the questionnaire—assuming that respondents are sitting at a computer to respond to your survey. Increasingly, however, people read their e-mail (and, thus, online survey recruiting messages) on much smaller mobile phone screens, limiting the ability to take advantage of graphics on surveys. At the very least, you'll want to develop your online survey so that it can be completed easily on a mobile device.

As with paper-based surveys, you can collect more information compared with telephone interviews. In addition, there is essentially no interviewer bias in the way questions are asked, and any type of question can be used. This approach also shares a disadvantage with paper-based surveys, however: There is no ability to probe, explain questions, or ask for respondents to explain their answers.

With online surveys, question sequencing can be programmed into the survey, ensuring that the appropriate next question appears on the screen for the respondent. This feature offers greater flexibility compared with paper-based mail surveys. Another potential benefit is the reaction to open-ended questions. It is likely people will take more time and care responding to open-ended questions than is the case with nonelectronic formats. Many people are concerned about privacy when it comes to online activity, however, believing that their answers could be traced back to them if someone wanted to do so. Still, the comfort level of respondents is likely higher with online surveys than with any other approach except paper-based surveys.

### Administrative Control

Online surveys offer two tremendous advantages in terms of administrative control, and these advantages explain their rapid growth in popularity: Compared with other options, they are quite inexpensive and they provide rapid turnaround. In terms of cost, most companies already operate Internet servers, so the necessary hardware is probably already available if you want to host an online questionnaire on your own, and the services of online survey providers are relatively inexpensive if you choose that route. Even better, because responses are automatically recorded in data files (and only valid responses are accepted), respondents effectively code their own responses when they reply to the questions on the survey. This eliminates one step where error can enter into the data set, not to mention a great deal of potential cost.

Online surveys can be distributed to many thousands of people more or less simultaneously and instantaneously—and people can respond to them almost immediately. Most responses to online surveys come within hours, not days or weeks as is usually the case with other approaches. As a result, a survey can be put into the field and data retrieved from respondents and analyzed much more quickly than with any other method.

### 11-3e COMPARING METHODS OF ADMINISTERING QUESTIONNAIRES

Each of these methods of communication possesses advantages and disadvantages. We've summarized our thoughts in Exhibit 11.4. The specific situation surrounding a project often dictates the actual approach chosen. For example, no matter how much you may want to use personal interviews, the budget may not support that option, and you'll have to do the best you can with the budget allocated, even if the final approach is suboptimal. Similarly, you'll need to endure the disadvantages of paper-based surveys if this is the only reasonable method of reaching the designated population. All else being equal, it's easy to see why online surveys are so popular.

### Combining Administration Methods

Although none of the methods we have described for collecting communication data is superior in all situations, the research problem itself will often suggest one approach over the others. It's also possible that a combination of

## Manager's Focus

Sampling control, information control, and administrative control may appear to be primarily concerns for researchers. After all, it is generally the researcher's responsibility to propose a method by which to administer the data collection instrument. Nevertheless, it isn't wise to assume that researchers always propose an administration method after carefully weighing these issues.

Always remember that one of your central responsibilities as a manager is to evaluate research proposals for ways to gather the information *you* need to make marketing decisions. As a result, it is critical that *you* carefully consider the control factors described above when evaluating a research provider's proposal.

You should ask yourself whether it appears the proposed method of questionnaire administration is well justified through a discussion of these control issues or if it was likely selected as a matter of cost or convenience to the researcher. It is not uncommon for research providers to have a "preferred" method of administration (the one they use in most research studies), and the preference may or may not correspond with your organization's specific needs. If it is not clear to you why a particular method has been proposed, you should probe for the research supplier's motivation by asking a series of questions concerning the various control considerations.

**Exhibit 11.4** ▶ Primary Communication Methods of Data Collection: Relative Advantages (+) and Disadvantages (–)

| | PERSONAL INTERVIEWS | TELEPHONE INTERVIEWS | PAPER-BASED SURVEYS | ONLINE SURVEYS |
|---|---|---|---|---|
| **SAMPLING CONTROL** | | | | |
| Ability to secure list of population members | | + | + | – |
| Ability to secure correct respondent | + | + | – | – |
| Response rate | + | | | |
| **INFORMATION CONTROL** | | | | |
| Ability to probe for detailed answers | + + | + | – | – |
| Ability to handle complex information | + | | – | + |
| Ability to clarify questions | + + | + | – | – |
| Amount of information obtained | + | – | | |
| Flexibility of question sequencing | + | + | – | + |
| Protection from interviewer bias | | – | + | + |
| Ability to obtain personal information | – | – | + + | + |
| Ability to show visual displays | + | – | + | |
| Ability to offer anonymity | – | – | + + | + |
| **ADMINISTRATIVE CONTROL** | | | | |
| Time requirements | | + | – | + + |
| Cost requirements | – | | + | + + |
| Quality control/supervisory requirements | | – | + | + |
| Computer support | | + | – | + + |

**Note:** ++ represents greatest relative advantage; — represents greatest relative disadvantage.

approaches may work well in a given situation. For example, a business manager could receive a letter, an e-mail, or a phone call asking for her help in a study, and after this notification a paper-based survey could be sent to her place of business. Online surveys can be initiated either by sending an e-mail to the sample of potential respondents that links them to an online survey, or by a cooperative relationship with another Internet vendor by placing a banner at its site. The respondent then just clicks through the survey. Paper-based questionnaires can be hand delivered to respondents along with product samples, and telephone interviews can be used for follow-up. The best approach depends upon the objectives of the study and the characteristics of the population being studied.

# Summary

## Learning Objective 1

**Explain the concept of *structure* as it relates to questionnaires.**

The degree of structure in a questionnaire is the degree of standardization imposed on it. In a highly structured questionnaire, the questions to be asked and the responses permitted by the subjects are completely predetermined. In a questionnaire with less structure, the response categories are not provided; sometimes even the questions can vary.

## Learning Objective 2

**Cite the drawbacks of using high degrees of structure.**

Fixed-alternative questions may force a subject to respond to a question on which she or he does not really have an opinion. They may also prove inaccurate if none of the response categories allows the accurate expression of the respondent's opinion.

## Learning Objective 3

**Explain what is meant by *disguise* in a questionnaire context.**

The amount of disguise in a questionnaire is the amount of knowledge hidden from the respondent as to the purpose and/or sponsor of the study. An undisguised questionnaire makes the purpose of the research obvious by the questions posed; a disguised questionnaire attempts to hide the purpose of the study.

## Learning Objective 4

**Discuss two situations in which disguise might be desirable.**

Disguise is useful when knowledge of the purpose of the study or its sponsor would cause respondents to change their answers. Disguise is also used to help recreate a more natural environment for those participating in research, especially experimental research.

## Learning Objective 5

**Differentiate among the main methods of administering questionnaires.**

*Personal interviews* imply a direct, face-to-face conversation between the interviewer and the respondent, as opposed to *telephone interviews*. In both types, the interviewer asks the questions and records the respondents' answers, either while the interview is in progress or immediately afterward. *Paper-based surveys* are usually sent by mail to designated respondents with an accompanying cover letter. The respondents complete the questionnaire at their leisure and mail their replies back to the

research organization. *Online surveys* involve surveys that are completed by respondents via the Web.

## Learning Objective 6

**Discuss three important aspects used to compare the four different methods of administering questionnaires.**

Sampling control concerns the ability to identify, reach, and receive answers from population members. Information control involves the amount, type, and quality of information that can be retrieved from respondents. Administrative control is concerned with the degree of quality control possible and time and cost requirements.

## Key Terms

fixed-alternative questions (page 155)

open-ended question (page 155)

disguise (page 156)

debriefing (page 157)

personal interview (page 158)

mall intercepts (page 158)

telephone interview (page 159)

random-digit dialing (RDD) (page 159)

paper-based survey (page 160)

online surveys (page 161)

in-bound surveys (page 161)

## Review Questions

1. What are the advantages of higher degrees of structure? What do researchers gain through the use of lower structure?

2. What is a disguised questionnaire? What are the ethical considerations in using disguise?

3. What are two situations in which the use of disguise would be advisable?

4. How do in-bound surveys work? When are they especially useful?

5. Why are online surveys such a popular choice for collecting communication data?

6. How do personal interviews, telephone interviews, paper-based surveys, and online surveys differ with respect to the following:

   a. sampling control
   b. information control
   c. administrative control

7. How might a researcher combine different methods of communication in the same project? Give an example.

# Endnotes

1. Dimock, M. (2016, June 6). In defense of public-opinion polling, *The Wall Street Journal*. Retrieved from www.wsj.com
2. Data reported in Quirk's Corporate Research Report (n.d., but data collected in 2014), retrieved from www.quirks.com; and Quirk's Marketing Research Review 2016 Corporate Research Report, (report undated). Retrieved from www.quirks.com
3. Cell Phone Surveys, n.d., Pew Research Center. Retrieved from http://www.people-press.org/methodology/collecting-survey -data/cell-phone-surveys/
4. Rao, L. (2015, Sept. 16). The next frontier for online survey companies: Law firms. Retrieved from http://fortune.com /2015/09/16/onlinesurveycompanieslawfirms/
5. Internet/Broadband Fact Sheet. (2017, Jan. 12). Pew Research Center. Retrieved from http://www.pewinternet.org/fact-sheet /internet-broadband/

# CHAPTER 12

# Asking Good Questions

Billion Photos/Shutterstock.com

Rawpixel.com/Shutterstock.com

## LEARNING OBJECTIVES

▶ Define the term *measurement* as it is used in marketing research.

▶ List the four scales (levels) of measurement.

▶ Name some widely used attitude scaling techniques in marketing research.

▶ List some other key decisions to be made when designing scales.

▶ Explain the concept of validity as it relates to survey items.

## [ INTRODUCTION ]

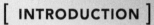

Whether we ask questions—or observe behaviors, for that matter—marketing researchers are always attempting to measure things. Measurement is common to all aspects of life; most of us spend our days doing it, whether it's using a clock to measure time, bathroom scales to measure weight, scores to measure the outcomes of sporting events, stock prices to measure the value of investments, or so on.

Most things we measure are fairly concrete: pounds on a scale, teaspoons of coffee, gallons of gas in a tank. But how can we measure a person's attitude toward a company or the likelihood that a teenager will buy a ticket for a particular new movie? What about the degree of satisfaction with a new laptop computer? Marketers are interested in measuring many qualities that most people rarely think of in terms of numbers.

All of the questions on a survey or marks on an observation form are attempts at measuring important attributes or behaviors of some group or situation that is of interest to marketing managers. In this chapter, we discuss how marketing researchers go about measuring attributes and behaviors. A quick warning: This chapter is a little long, but the material is really important for gathering high-quality data.

## 12-1 **Scales of Measurement**

**Measurement** is the process of assigning numbers to represent properties of an object's attributes. For some attributes, numbers are assigned to represent quantities of the attribute (e.g., a family's income or number of family members), while for other attributes the numbers simply represent category membership (e.g., an individual's gender or ethnicity).

There are a couple of important things to note about this definition. First, we measure the attributes of objects and not the objects themselves. We don't measure a person, for example, but we can measure his or her income, education, height, weight, attitudes, and so forth. Second, the definition is broad; it doesn't specify how the numbers will be assigned. This is because different attributes have different qualities that dictate the rules for how numbers can be assigned. (As a quick example, the attribute *gender* can't be measured using a 1 to 5 rating scale; it doesn't make any sense, and it can't support measurement at that level.)

**measurement** The process of assigning numbers to represent properties of an object's attributes.

So, the first step in measuring some attribute is to determine its properties. Only then can we assign numbers that accurately reflect those properties. The numbering system is simply a tool that must be used correctly so that we don't mislead ourselves or our clients.

There are four types of scales used to measure attributes of objects: nominal, ordinal, interval, and ratio. Exhibit 12.1 summarizes some important features of these scales and provides some examples. These are often referred to as four *levels* of measurement because measures at higher levels of measurement (e.g., ratio scales) have more properties and can be used for more kinds of analyses than can measures at lower levels of measurement (e.g., nominal scales). That's why you should use the highest level of measurement possible when developing a measure for some attribute. Just remember, however, that the properties of the attribute itself determine which levels of measurement are possible. And it's important to understand the level of measurement because, as we'll show you later on, level of measurement dictates the kinds of analyses that are possible.

## Manager's Focus

In many ways, designing and conducting a marketing research study is similar to building a house. Just as you wouldn't begin constructing your future home without a good blueprint, proper planning is necessary before creating and using a measurement instrument such as a questionnaire. The development of a good blueprint for a house requires an understanding of the science of architectural engineering, an ability to discern the necessary relationships between the planned structure and the surrounding environment, and an eye for what will be functional and aesthetically pleasing for those who actually experience the home. Likewise, designing a good questionnaire requires an understanding of the science of measurement theory, an ability to discern the necessary relationships between the measurement instrument and the subjects being measured, and an eye for what will be useful and appropriate when interviewing future respondents.

Most of us do not have the expertise necessary to draw up a set of blueprints or the skills required to follow them in order to build a house. Because houses require a substantial investment, we want the job done right and would hire a professional architect and general contractor. All too often, unfortunately, managers do not exercise similar prudence when it comes to

designing and creating questionnaires, despite the significant investment necessary to conduct the survey and the even larger investment required to implement marketing actions based on the research information. Some managers assume "anyone can ask questions" and create their own questionnaires or have their subordinates do so. The result is generally a questionnaire with very weak measurement properties.

This chapter focuses on some of the fundamental principles of measurement theory (or more formally, the scientific field of psychometrics). However, after reading this chapter, you still won't have the expertise necessary to design a good measurement instrument yourself (there are much more extensive works on these topics that you would need to master first). Instead, you should have enough of an appreciation of the properties of good measurement and the complexity of the measurement process to recognize why it's worth the investment to have a professional researcher do this work for you. Equally important, you will have enough of an understanding to ask prospective researchers meaningful questions to help you determine whether they truly understand the measurement process or if they are more inclined to simply ask questions clients say they want to ask. You should never hire researchers of the latter persuasion.

## Manager's Focus

The different levels of measurement may seem like esoteric abstractions for which only researchers would have any genuine concern. But that's not the case. Having an understanding of the different levels of measurement is extremely important and practical to you as a manager. Without this understanding, you are quite likely to attribute inappropriate meanings to numbers generated in research studies or to readily accept misinterpretations made by others who do research for you. Equipped with an understanding of measurement levels, you will be able to properly interpret the meaning of research findings and assess the appropriateness of techniques researchers propose using to analyze the data generated by the measurement instrument.

In addition, by understanding that there are different levels of measurement, you will be more discerning about the amount of information certain questions and scales can provide. Managers in particular have a propensity to be satisfied with "yes/no" questions or similar ones that also produce nominal data—the lowest level of measurement. Generally, these same questions can easily be recast to produce ordinal, interval, or ratio levels of measurement. Given that higher levels of measurement provide greater information and more analysis options, variables should be measured at the highest levels permitted by the underlying concept and the willingness of respondents to disclose the desired information.

**Exhibit 12.1** ▶ Scales of Measurement

| | Scale | Basic Comparison[a] | Examples | Average[b] |
|---|---|---|---|---|
| **HIGHER** ↑ LEVEL OF MEASUREMENT ↓ **LOWER** | *RATIO* | Comparison of absolute magnitudes | Units sold Income | Geometric mean Harmonic mean |
| | *INTERVAL* | Comparison of intervals | Customer satisfaction Brand attitude | Mean |
| | *ORDINAL* | Order | Brand preference Income (in categories) | Median |
| | *NOMINAL* | Identity | Gender Brand purchase (yes/no) | Mode |

[a]A scale at any given level possesses all the comparison properties of all scales below it in the table. For example, the ratio scale allows the comparison of intervals and the investigation of order and identity, in addition to the comparison of absolute magnitudes.

[b]A scale at any given level can be used to calculate any of the measures of average associated with any of the scales below it in the table. For example, with an interval level measure, the mean, median, and mode are all appropriate measures of average."

## 12-1a  NOMINAL SCALE

One of the most basic uses of numbers is to *identify* or categorize particular objects. A person's social security number is a **nominal scale**, as are the numbers on football jerseys, lockers, and so on. These numbers simply identify the individual or object that has been assigned the number. In these examples, the numbers are used to *uniquely* identify individuals, but nominal scales can also be used to categorize people or things into groups based on

> **nominal scale**
> Measurement in which numbers are assigned to objects or classes of objects solely for the purpose of identification.

their attributes. For example, if we assign the number 1 to represent female respondents to a survey and the number 2 to represent male respondents, we've used a nominal scale that allows us to identify the gender of a particular respondent and to determine the relative proportions of each gender in our sample.

With nominal scales, the numbers don't mean anything other than simple individual or category identification. A basketball player wearing uniform number 15 isn't necessarily taller or a better shooter than a player wearing the number 14. Assigning 1 to represent women and 2 to represent men indicates nothing at all about men versus women on any attribute other than identification. As a result, the numbers we assign to represent the groups don't have any meaning beyond identification. We could actually use any numbers we want, because the numbers don't matter.

With a nominal scale, all you can do is count the number of people that fall into the various categories. As a result, the *mode* (the most frequently occurring category) is the only legitimate summary measure of central tendency or average. It doesn't make sense in a sample consisting of 60 women and 40 men to say that the average gender is 1.4, if females were coded 1 and males 2, even though the computer will calculate the mean *if you tell it to do so*. This is an incredibly important point: The numbers have been assigned by the researcher, and the researcher must be aware of what kinds of analyses are possible with different scales of measurement. In this example, all you can say is that there were more females in the sample than males or that 60% of the sample was female. If you want to say more than that, you'll need to take additional measures.

> The researcher must be aware of what kinds of analyses are possible with different scales of measurement.

Take a look at the first example in Exhibit 12.2; we'll use this exhibit as an ongoing example of the different types of scales. We might choose to score the individual responses as 1 if they check a particular soft drink on the list and as 0 if they don't. If a respondent puts a check mark next to Mountain Dew brand (a score of 1), what do we know? Only that she or he claims to like the brand. Taking all respondents, we can report the proportion who like Mountain Dew (and the proportion who don't). In terms of a summary response, we can report only the mode. Suppose 68% of the people said they liked Mountain Dew; the modal response for this brand, based on the number of times marked, would be "like Mountain Dew" (because the majority said they liked the brand).

## 12-1b  ORDINAL SCALE

With a nominal scale, the numbers assigned to individuals or categories are arbitrary. They can be changed or reversed—it doesn't matter as long as we know which number represents each category. This works because the numbers don't imply any order to the attributes you're trying to measure.

Many of the attributes that marketing researchers want to measure, however, are things that respondents can place in a certain order, and the numbers assigned can reflect this order. Consider the next example in Exhibit 12.2 that deals with preference for soft drinks. Can you put these soft drinks in order from least preferred to most preferred? Having a preference implies that you can order objects. As a result, with an **ordinal scale**, we could say that the number 2 is greater than the number 1, that 3 is greater than both 2 and 1, and that 4 is greater than all three of these numbers. The numbers 1, 2, 3, and 4 are ordered, and in this case the larger the number, the greater the property. You could also set up your ordinal scale so that lower numbers reflect more of the property; the important point is that there is a consistent order in whatever numbers you assign (the numbers are arbitrary except for order). If you assign the number 6 to identify the least preferred brand, 5 to identify the next-least-preferred brand, and so on, until 1 represents the most preferred brand, the numbers will reflect the *relative standing* of the different options for that particular individual. With an ordinal scale, the numbers have more meaning in that they represent this relative standing. But they don't go further than that; we know that one option has more of some attribute than some other option, but we don't know how much more.

**ordinal scale**
Measurement in which numbers are assigned to data on the basis of some order (for example, more than, greater than) of the objects.

Imagine that you've used the ranking task in Exhibit 12.2 with 1,000 college students because you're a brand manager for Mountain Dew and you want to see how your brand stacks up against the competition. Here's how it did: 172 people assigned Mountain Dew a ranking of 6 (last), 163 ranked it fifth, 301 ranked it fourth, 259 ranked it third, 65 ranked it second, and 40 ranked it first. So, the modal ranking for Mountain Dew was fourth out of six brands. Although that's interesting, we can go further: Because there is an order for the responses (i.e., first choice is better than second choice, and so on), we can also calculate an additional measure of central tendency, the *median*. Suppose you could line up the 1,000 student respondents according to their ranking of Mountain Dew. First would come the 172 who ranked it last, then would come the 163 who ranked it next to last, followed by the 301 who ranked it their fourth favorite brand, and so on. The median ranking for the soft drink would be the ranking provided by the person in the center of our lineup (with an even number of respondents, we would consider the scores of the two people in the center). In our example, the median ranking would thus be "fourth choice." If you wanted to see how the competing brands did, you could do the same analysis for each.

Whether we can use the ordinal scale to assign numbers to objects depends on the attribute in question. The attribute itself must possess the ordinal property to allow ordinal scaling that is meaningful. Note that it is impossible to say how much any individual respondent preferred one object to another; all we can say is that one is preferred

**Exhibit 12.2** ▶ Assessing a Respondent's Preference for Soft Drinks with Nominal, Ordinal, Interval, and Ratio Scales

### Nominal Scale

**Which of the soft drinks on the following list do you like? Check all that apply.**

_____ Coke
_____ Dr. Pepper
_____ Mountain Dew
_____ Pepsi
_____ 7 Up
_____ Sprite

### Ordinal Scale

**Please rank the soft drinks on the following list according to your degree of liking for each, assigning your most preferred drink rank = 1 and your least preferred drink rank = 6.**

_____ Coke
_____ Dr. Pepper
_____ Mountain Dew
_____ Pepsi
_____ 7 Up
_____ Sprite

### Interval Scale

**Please indicate your liking for each of the following soft drinks by circling the number that best reflects your opinion.**

|  | Extremely Unfavorable |  |  |  |  |  | Extremely Favorable |
|---|---|---|---|---|---|---|---|
| Coke | 1 | 2 | 3 | 4 | 5 | 6 | 7 |
| Dr. Pepper | 1 | 2 | 3 | 4 | 5 | 6 | 7 |
| Mountain Dew | 1 | 2 | 3 | 4 | 5 | 6 | 7 |
| Pepsi | 1 | 2 | 3 | 4 | 5 | 6 | 7 |
| 7 Up | 1 | 2 | 3 | 4 | 5 | 6 | 7 |
| Sprite | 1 | 2 | 3 | 4 | 5 | 6 | 7 |

### Ratio Scale

**In the past seven days, approximately how many 12 ounce servings of each of the following soft drinks have you consumed?**

_____ Coke
_____ Dr. Pepper
_____ Mountain Dew
_____ Pepsi
_____ 7 Up
_____ Sprite

over the other. In our example, one respondent might like all six brands, ranking them in the following order: first—Dr Pepper; second—Coke; third—Pepsi; fourth—Sprite; fifth—Mountain Dew; and sixth—7-Up. Another respondent might really dislike all six brands, yet still rank them in the same order. Still another student may like Dr Pepper, Coke, and Pepsi a lot, but dislike the others—and once again rank them in the same order. In each case, rank order is the same, but the underlying feelings about the brands are quite different. Representing those feelings requires a higher level of measurement.

### 12-1c INTERVAL SCALE

Some scales possess the following useful property: The *intervals* between the numbers tell us how far apart the objects are with respect to the attribute. This tells us that the differences can be compared. The difference between 1 and 2 is equal to the difference between 2 and 3.

Rating scales for measuring consumer attitudes are commonly used in marketing research. They are great examples of **interval scales**. Consider the soft drink example again and take a look at the third example in Exhibit 12.2. Here we're asking the respondents to rate their attitudes toward the brands, using 1 through 7 scales where 1 equals "extremely unfavorable" and 7 equals "extremely favorable." This interval scale will allow us to see the relative strength of a respondent's feelings toward each of the soft drinks. A respondent who really likes all six brands might assign each of them high scores, such as a 6 or 7. Someone who dislikes each brand might assign low scores to each. Respondents can indicate the full range of possible attitudes (extremely unfavorable to extremely favorable) toward each brand, a big step forward from simply knowing the order of preference.

Thus, interval scales allow us to say that one brand is preferred over another by comparing scores and, even better, to say whether the brand is generally liked or disliked. Further, if we have measures on at least three brands, we can compare the intervals. That is, we can say that the difference in attitude between a brand with a score of 6 and a brand with a score of 4 is the same as the difference in attitude between brands with scores of 3 and 1. Or we could say that the difference between scores of 2 and 6 is twice as great as the difference between scores of 3 and 5.

What if one person rates Pepsi as a 6 on the 1 through 7 favorability scale, and another person rates Pepsi a 3; can we say that the first person's attitude is twice as favorable as the second? The answer is *no*. We can't compare the absolute magnitude of numbers when measurement is made on the basis of an interval scale. The reason is that on an interval scale, the zero point is established arbitrarily. Is there such a thing as having zero attitude toward some object? Attitudes may be negative or positive or neutral (or nonexistent for unknown objects), but there is no obvious point at which attitude is equal to zero.

With an interval scale, you can calculate *mean* scores in addition to median and modal scores. The mean is "meaningful" for interval scales because of the equal intervals between scale positions. So, if Mountain Dew achieves a mean score of 3.4 on the 1 through 7 favorability scale, compared with mean scores of 6.2 and 5.9 for Coke and Pepsi, respectively, we have much stronger information about the relative attitude toward Mountain Dew compared with what was available using only an ordinal measurement scale.

### 12-1d RATIO SCALE

A **ratio scale** differs from an interval scale in that it possesses a natural, or absolute, zero point that reflects the complete absence of the attribute being assessed. Height and weight are examples. Because there is an absolute zero, comparison of the *absolute magnitude* of the numbers is legitimate. Thus,

if a person were completing the final item in Exhibit 12.2 and reported consuming 20 servings of Mountain Dew and only five servings of Sprite, he or she has consumed four times as much Mountain Dew, an indication of a strong preference for Mountain Dew versus Sprite. (Note that this is a communication-based measure of behavior.)

We've already observed that the more powerful scales include the properties possessed by the less powerful ones. So with a ratio scale we can compare intervals, rank objects according to magnitude, or use the numbers to identify the objects (everything that interval, ordinal, and nominal scales can do). And the *geometric mean* (scores are multiplied and then the *n*th root is taken), as well as the more usual arithmetic mean, median, and mode, are meaningful measures of average when attributes are measured on a ratio scale.

A variety of attributes can be measured using ratio scales, including age in years, income in dollars (or other monetary unit), units purchased or consumed, frequency of shopping behavior, and so on. Researchers should use ratio scales for measuring these sorts of attributes whenever possible, unless there is a compelling reason not to do so. (For instance, maybe some people are more likely to accurately provide their age if you let them select age categories—an ordinal measure—rather than ask for age in years.) As we will see later when we discuss data analysis, using the ratio scale will allow us to compute a mean age across a sample of respondents; compute correlations between age and other variables, such as product ratings, satisfaction scores, and the like; and perform other statistical techniques. Although there are analyses that can be performed with ordinal measures, they are less powerful.

**interval scale**
Measurement in which the assigned numbers legitimately allow the comparison of the size of the differences among and between members.

**ratio scale**
Measurement that has a natural, or absolute, zero and therefore allows the comparison of absolute magnitudes of the numbers.

## 12-2 Measuring Attitudes and Other Unobservable Concepts

Some things we measure in marketing research are pretty straightforward. For instance, the fact that a company sold a certain number of units of a new product in a particular store in a test-market city can be confirmed relatively easily. The age, gender, ethnic background, zip code, and purchasing behavior for a particular consumer are real properties, although we often have to depend on the consumer to provide accurate responses to our measures.

Many of the qualities that we measure, however, can't be seen or touched. Have you ever seen someone's attitudes, motivations, or purchase intentions? You may have seen their expressions, heard their words, or observed the behaviors that might result from these qualities, but you haven't seen the characteristics themselves. And that's the dilemma that researchers face when it comes to measuring attitudes and other unobservable concepts. In this section, we'll show you some of the more popular ways of measuring people's attitudes. The ideas apply equally well to other types of unobservable attributes.

> Have you ever seen someone's attitudes, motivations, or purchase intentions?

By far, the most common approach to measuring attitudes is to obtain respondents' **self-reports**, in which people are asked directly for their beliefs or feelings about something. For example, at customerservicescoreboard.com, consumers can self-report ratings of their experiences with companies such as Zappos.com and many, many more. Exhibit 12.3 presents a self-report measure that might be used to assess customer response to the service offered by some company.

It won't surprise you that researchers have developed a number of different self-report methods to measure attitudes. Most approaches use itemized-ratings scales (a form

**self-report** A method of assessing attitudes in which individuals are asked directly for their beliefs about or feelings toward an object or class of objects.

**itemized-ratings scales** A scale on which individuals must indicate their ratings of an attribute or object by selecting the response category that best describes their position on the attribute or object.

of fixed-alternative response scales), but we'll describe a couple of other approaches as well.

12-2a   **ITEMIZED-RATINGS SCALE**

With **itemized-ratings scales**, the respondent selects from a limited number of response categories that typically reflect increasing amounts of the attribute (e.g., attitudes, satisfaction) being measured. So, if you wanted to measure an attitude toward a brand, you might develop a rating scale like that shown in Exhibit 12.2 to assess attitudes toward different brands of soft drinks: a 1 through 7 interval scale where 1 equals "extremely unfavorable" and 7 equals "extremely favorable." In general, five to nine categories work best; they permit fine distinctions but are easily understood by respondents.

There are many different variations of itemized-ratings scales. Two of the most commonly used scales are summated-ratings scales and semantic-differential scales, which we'll describe next.

**Exhibit 12.3** ▶ Using Rating Scales to Assess Unobservable Concepts

Compared to the level of service you should receive, how does your cell phone service provider perform on the following aspects?

|  | Much worse than it ought to be |  | About what it ought to be |  | Much better than it ought to be |
|---|:---:|:---:|:---:|:---:|:---:|
| overall value of service | ☐ | ☐ | ☐ | ☐ | ☐ |
| quality of basic service provided | ☐ | ☐ | ☐ | ☐ | ☐ |
| efficient problem solving when something goes wrong | ☐ | ☐ | ☐ | ☐ | ☐ |
| variety of services offered | ☐ | ☐ | ☐ | ☐ | ☐ |
| friendliness of employees | ☐ | ☐ | ☐ | ☐ | ☐ |
| employee ability to communicate with me | ☐ | ☐ | ☐ | ☐ | ☐ |
| pleasant interactions with employees | ☐ | ☐ | ☐ | ☐ | ☐ |

NEXT

## Manager's Focus

We recognize the tendency of managers, and others who are relatively unfamiliar with the measurement process, to ask questions at the nominal (lowest) level of measurement. For example, they may ask consumers "Are you satisfied with our service?" or "Did you like or dislike your experience in our store?" Think about these questions and try to identify (a) the managerially useful information they fail to generate and (b) how you could change them to provide more useful information.

As you are aware, some consumers may have mildly positive or negative evaluations of your marketing efforts; others may have very strong positive or negative assessments. Yes/No or Like/Dislike questions may provide a crude indication of whether an attitude is favorable or unfavorable, but they fail to capture the relative strength of attitudes across respondents. The self-report attitude scales discussed in this chapter provide ways of converting nominal (e.g., Yes/No or Like/Dislike) scales into interval scales. Rather than ask "Are you satisfied with our service?" you could ask: "Using the five-point scale provided, please indicate how satisfied you are with our service." In other words, the self-report scales can help you follow our recommendation to always employ the highest level of measurement permitted by the subject matter as long as respondents are willing and able to provide the desired information.

### Summated-Ratings (Likert) Scale

The **summated-ratings scale**, also called a *Likert scale* after the name of the scholar who developed it, is one of the most widely used attitude-scaling techniques in marketing research. With the summated-ratings scale, researchers write a number of statements that relate to the issue or object in question and then have respondents express how much they agree or disagree with each statement. Exhibit 12.4 is an example of a scale that you might use to compare the image of one bank with that of its competitors. The response categories represent varying degrees of agreement and are assigned scale values. Let's assume the values 1, 2, 3, 4, and 5 are assigned to the respective response categories shown in Exhibit 12.3. Then it's easy to calculate a total score for each respondent by adding (thus the name "summated-ratings") or averaging the scores across the items.

Suppose that one customer of the bank checked "agree" on items 1 and 4 and "strongly agree" on items 2 and 3.

> **summated-ratings scale** A self-report technique for attitude measurement in which respondents indicate their degree of agreement or disagreement with each of a number of statements.

This customer's total attitude score toward the bank would thus be 18 if we add the scores or 4.5 if we calculate the mean score.

Researchers often use variations of the scale we've shown in Exhibit 12.4, which is considered the classic version of a summated-ratings scale. For example, the version shown includes verbal descriptors, or *anchors,* for each scale position (i.e., "strongly disagree," "disagree," and so forth). Some researchers will anchor only the endpoints of the scale. Another variation asks respondents to select a number representing the level of agreement rather than check the appropriate category. And some researchers use more response categories than the traditional five categories. Regardless of how the particular scale is designed, the key features of the summated-ratings scale remain the same: a set of statements with which respondents indicate their level of agreement.

**Exhibit 12.4 ▶** Example of Likert Summated-Ratings Scale

| | Strongly Disagree | Disagree | Neither Agree nor Disagree | Agree | Strongly Agree |
|---|---|---|---|---|---|
| 1. The bank offers courteous service. | —— | —— | —— | —— | —— |
| 2. The bank has a convenient location. | —— | —— | —— | —— | —— |
| 3. The bank has convenient hours. | —— | —— | —— | —— | —— |
| 4. The bank offers low-interest-rate loans. | —— | —— | —— | —— | —— |

## Semantic-Differential Scale

Another very popular technique for measuring attitudes in marketing research is the **semantic-differential scale**. It is particularly useful in corporate, brand, and product image studies. The scale grew out of research concerning the underlying structure of words but has since been adapted to make it suitable for measuring attitudes.

Semantic-differential scales consist of pairs of bipolar words or phrases that can be used to describe the attitude object. Let's look again at measuring attitude toward a bank. Using the semantic-differential approach, you would first generate a list of bipolar adjectives or phrases. Exhibit 12.5 is similar to Exhibit 12.4 in terms of the attributes used to describe the bank, but it is arranged in semantic-differential format. Respondents are instructed to read each set of phrases and to check the space that best represents their opinions. A respondent who believed that the hours were terribly inconvenient might check the space closest to the phrase "Hours are inconvenient"; someone who was fairly neutral on this issue would select the middle position on the scale.

**semantic-differential scale** A self-report technique for attitude measurement in which the subjects are asked to check which cell between a set of bipolar adjectives or phrases best describes their feelings toward the object.

**snake diagram** A diagram that connects the average responses to a series of semantic-differential statements, thereby depicting the profile of the object or objects being evaluated.

Semantic-differential scales are popular in marketing for several reasons. They're flexible and easy to use for both researchers and respondents (although they don't work as well over the telephone). They are also effective when it comes to presenting the results of a study. For example, suppose that respondents were asked to evaluate two or more banks, using the same scale. When several banks are rated, the different bank profiles can be compared. Exhibit 12.6 presents a **snake diagram** (notice its shape), which illustrates that Bank A is perceived as having more courteous service and a more convenient location and as offering lower interest rates on loans, but as having less convenient hours than Bank B. The values on the chart represent the average score of all respondents on each item.

If you don't want to develop a profile, you can also total the scores on a semantic-differential scale in order to compare attitudes toward different objects. This score is computed by summing or averaging the scores for the individual scales. As was true for summated-ratings scales, variations in scale design are common. Numbers are sometimes substituted for blanks, and different numbers of scale positions can be used.

---

**Exhibit 12.5** ▶ Example of Semantic-Differential Scaling Form

Service is discourteous.     :——:——:——:——:——:——:  Service is courteous.

Location is inconvenient.    :——:——:——:——:——:——:  Location is convenient.

Hours are inconvenient.      :——:——:——:——:——:——:  Hours are convenient.

Loan interest rates are high. :——:——:——:——:——:——:  Loan interest rates are low.

---

**Exhibit 12.6** ▶ Snake Diagram Showing Contrasting Profiles of Banks A and B

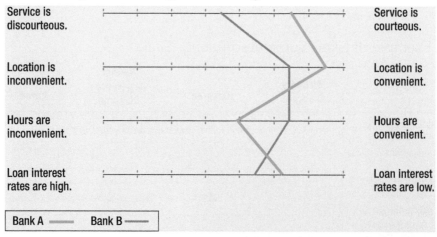

## Other Itemized-Ratings Scales

There are endless possible varieties of itemized-ratings scales. The response categories for this type of scale are always limited in number, however, and they are almost always used to capture interval-level data. Beyond that, it's up to the creativity of the researcher and the demands of the situation. Thus, a set of faces, varying systematically in terms of whether they are frowning or smiling, used to capture a person's satisfaction or preference (appropriately called a *faces scale*) are itemized-rating scales. Faces can also be useful when conducting marketing research with children.

## 12-2b GRAPHIC-RATINGS SCALES

**Graphic-ratings scales** are similar in most respects to itemized-ratings scales except for one very important difference: Instead of a limited set of response categories, there are a large number of possible response categories. For example, one common form of graphic-ratings scale asks people to indicate their ratings by placing a check at the appropriate point on a line that runs from one extreme of the attribute to the other (see Exhibit 12.7). Then, measuring the length of the line from one end to the marked position scores the attribute being assessed. A *slider scale*, in which respondents move a virtual slider until it represents their feelings about the object for a particular attribute, works almost the same way for online surveys. A *thermometer scale* is another common example of a graphics rating scale: Respondents raise the level of a thermometer to represent their responses (or mark a thermometer at the appropriate height on paper-based surveys).

These scales offer respondents the greatest degree of freedom in providing answers because, in theory, there are an infinite number of possible response positions along the continuous scale. Just how useful such fine differences

**graphic-ratings scales** A scale in which individuals indicate their ratings of an attribute typically by placing a check at the appropriate point on a line that runs from one extreme of the attribute to the other.

**comparative-ratings scales** A scale requiring subjects to make their ratings as a series of relative judgments or comparisons rather than as independent assessments.

**constant-sum method** A comparative-ratings scale in which an individual divides some given sum among two or more attributes on a basis such as importance or favorability.

in responses are is questionable, however. Moreover, although there are an infinite number of points along graphic rating scales, in reality, the position along the line (or slider, or thermometer) must be converted to finite numbers. For these reasons, itemized-ratings scales have proven to be much more popular with researchers.

## 12-2c COMPARATIVE-RATINGS SCALE

In graphic and itemized scales, respondents are asked to consider attributes of an entity independently. For example, you might ask respondents to indicate how important a convenient location is to them in choosing a bank. You might also ask how important other attributes are to them. With **comparative-ratings scales**, however, respondents are asked to judge each attribute with direct reference to the other attributes being evaluated. This is an important difference.

The constant-sum scaling method is a common example of a comparative-ratings scale. In the **constant-sum method**, the individual divides some given sum (often, 100 points) among two or more attributes on the basis of importance, favorability, purchase likelihood, or something else. (Note that limiting the number of attributes to be assessed is important. The respondent should not need a calculator to divide the points.) Take a look at Exhibit 12.8, for example. If a respondent gave 25 points to each of the attributes, they would be judged to be equally important. If he assigned 50 points to courteous service, 25 points to convenient location, 15 points to convenient hours, and 10 points to low-interest-rate loans, it's clear that courteous service is most important, low-interest-rate loans are least important, with the other attributes falling in between. Again, we note the important difference in emphasis with this method: All judgments are made in comparison to the other alternatives, not independently.

**Exhibit 12.7 ▶** Graphic-Ratings Scale

Please evaluate each attribute, in terms of how important the attribute is to you personally, by placing an "X" at the position on the horizontal line that most reflects your feelings.

| Attribute | Not Important | Very Important |
|---|---|---|
| Courteous service | | |
| Convenient location | | |
| Convenient hours | | |
| Low-interest-rate loans | | |

**Exhibit 12.8** ▶ Constant-Sum Comparative-Ratings Scale

Please divide 100 points between the following attributes in terms of the relative importance of each attribute to you.

| | |
|---|---|
| Courteous service | _____ |
| Convenient location | _____ |
| Convenient hours | _____ |
| Low-interest-rate loans | _____ |

Comparative-ratings scales (such as the constant-sum scale) are effective for eliminating the *halo effect* that is common in scaling. A halo effect occurs when there is carryover from one judgment to another. For example, suppose you were concerned about two key issues in a survey of department store customers: satisfaction with the service provided and satisfaction with store location. If you ask these questions back-to-back on the survey, a respondent with strong positive feelings about the service provided is likely to provide more positive assessments of store location than he or she might normally provide. Comparative-ratings scales help control this problem by requiring respondents to consider two or more attributes in combination.

Another problem that you might encounter when using graphic- or itemized-ratings scales to measure importance values is that respondents may be inclined to indicate that all, or nearly all, of the attributes are important. The comparative scaling methods allow more insight into the relative ranking, if not the absolute importance, of the attributes.

## 12-3 Other Considerations in Designing Scales

You will need to consider a number of other issues when designing scales for measuring concepts such as attitudes. In this section, we'll deal with some of them.

### 12-3a NUMBER OF ITEMS IN A SCALE

One consideration involves exactly how many items are needed to measure the concept you are trying to assess. Should attitude toward a company be assessed using a single item, three items, 10 items, or 35 items? The answer depends on the purpose of the measure. If an overall summary judgment of how consumers feel about the company is needed, then a single-item **global measure** of attitude on a "very unfavorable–very favorable" scale may be enough. The goal of a global measure is to provide an overall assessment of the attribute. Consider the following global measure of corporate reputation.

**What is your overall evaluation of Amazon.com? (Circle a number)**

| Very Unfavorable | | Neither Favorable nor Unfavorable | | Very Favorable |
|---|---|---|---|---|
| 1 | 2 | 3 | 4 | 5 |

Sometimes, however, you might need a more comprehensive measure that will provide more information about how respondents view various aspects of the phenomenon being studied. These types of measures, often called **composite measures**, are more diagnostic in the sense that they provide more information for identifying strong or weak areas, particularly when aspects can be compared with one another or with measures for other entities. Suppose that marketing managers for a major retail chain are concerned about customer satisfaction. A global measure of satisfaction would provide an overall indication of how things are going, but a composite measure, consisting of measures of satisfaction with the location, product selection, prices, employees, and so on, would allow the managers to more easily diagnose any problem area.

How many items should be used with a composite measure? As many as it takes to fully capture the concept being measured. You'll have to use your best judgment to see that all important aspects of the concept are represented in the measure, but you don't want the survey to end up so long that nobody wants to complete it. Or worse, respondents get tired and start providing "garbage" data just to finish.

### 12-3b NUMBER OF SCALE POSITIONS

You also must decide how many response categories to include when designing measures. For most purposes, a minimum of five response categories should be included. What's the upper limit on the number of response categories? With itemized-ratings scales, there's really no need

**global measure** A measure designed to provide an overall assessment of an object or phenomenon, typically using one or two items.

**composite measures** A measure designed to provide a comprehensive assessment of an object or phenomenon with items to assess all relevant aspects or dimensions.

to go beyond nine or 10 scale positions. Scales with five to nine positions work quite well and are used routinely in marketing research.

There's a related decision that you also get to make: Should you include an even or an odd number of response categories? An odd number allows for a center position, often interpreted as "neutral" by respondents. Sometimes it's easier for a respondent to choose the center position than to actually think about the right answer, so some researchers use an even number of scale positions (i.e., no middle position). On the other hand, there are plenty of issues on which a perfectly well-thought-out answer may be "neutral." As a result, some researchers routinely use an odd number of scale positions. Both even and odd numbers are used regularly in practice.

## 12-3c INCLUDING A "DON'T KNOW" OR "NOT APPLICABLE" RESPONSE CATEGORY

Sometimes researchers choose to include a "don't know" or "no opinion" option along with the regular scale positions for an item. The same is true with a "not applicable" option. This may be a good idea if a fairly sizable percentage of respondents are likely not to have encountered or thought about the object or issue being addressed in the study. Otherwise, any answers that they provide will probably have little meaning, and, as a result, will simply add error to the study. Your exploratory research or pilot studies should shed some light on this issue.

If you believe that most respondents should have an opinion, we advise against including a "don't know" category. If you include the "don't know" option, some respondents will choose it—including some who are simply looking for the easiest way to get through the survey. In fact, research has indicated that "no opinion" options are more frequently chosen (1) by individuals with lower levels of education, (2) by those answering anonymously, (3) for questions that appear later in a survey, and (4) by respondents who indicated that they had devoted less effort to the task of completing a survey.[1] As a result, including a "don't know" option sometimes does more harm than good.

**systematic error**
Error in measurement that is also known as constant error since it affects the measurement in a constant way.

## 12-4 Establishing the Validity and Reliability of Measures

Almost nothing in marketing research can be measured without error. Observation of behavior usually produces the most accurate measures—but most of the things we want to measure in marketing research simply can't be observed. How can we ever have much faith in our measures for things like attitudes, intentions, motivations, and so on?

Try this: Respond to the following question as you would if you saw it on a survey:

> **Taking everything you know about General Electric into consideration, how favorable are you toward the company? Please select a response on the following scale:**
>
> | Very Unfavorable | | Neither Favorable nor Unfavorable | | Very Favorable |
> |---|---|---|---|---|
> | 1 | 2 | 3 | 4 | 5 |

Your observed response (i.e., the response you selected) is a combination of your true position on the issue plus any kinds of error that have influenced your response. We'll call these *response errors*. These errors fall into two general categories: systematic error and random error. Exhibit 12.9 provides an illustration of these ideas. Our goal, of course, is to minimize error. As systematic and random errors decrease, the validity of the measure increases.

**Systematic error**, which is also called *constant error*, is error that affects the measurement in a constant way. Some of these may have influenced how you responded to the question about General Electric. Sometimes personality traits or other stable characteristics of individuals add systematic error to the measurement process. For example, maybe you are more willing to express negative feelings than most other people; some people seem to be systematically negative in all their responses. On the other hand, maybe you tend toward more positive

**Exhibit 12.9 ▶** Components of an Observed Response

Observed Response = Truth + Systematic Error + Random Error

answers—which can introduce systematic error on the positive side. As another example, consumers sometimes have a hard time accurately reporting how frequently they perform behaviors. Those who perform behaviors frequently tend to underreport the level of behavior, and those who perform those behaviors less frequently tend to over report the level of behavior.

Differences in how surveys are administered can also introduce systematic error into a project. Researchers at Silver Dollar City, a theme park located near Branson, Missouri, discovered that responses to the same satisfaction question were consistently higher when obtained via telephone compared with e-mail. Because there were no differences in answers for virtually all other questions, the researchers concluded that the telephone survey respondents were likely inflating satisfaction scores because of the social context: They were talking directly to someone else. With e-mail, there was less social pressure to say nice things.

The other general type of error, **random error**, is due to temporary aspects of the person or measurement situation; this can affect the measurement in irregular ways. Random error is present when we repeat a measurement on an individual and don't get the same scores as the first time we did the measurement, even though the characteristic being measured hasn't changed.

Your mood, state of health, fatigue, and so forth, might have affected your response to the question about General Electric, yet these factors are temporary. So, if you've had a hard day, your answer (assuming you chose to think about it at all) was probably more negative than if you'd had an easy day. And it works the other way, too. Maybe you answered the question after finding out you did really well on a test; everything and everybody looks a little better than it did before, and your answer was a little more positive than it might otherwise have been.

The situation surrounding the measurement also affects the score in random ways. Maybe the room temperature was too hot or too cold when you answered the question. Maybe you had a long list of other things to do, just didn't want to think about it very hard, and fell into **response set bias** (sometimes called *straightlining*). Response set bias is an error that occurs when respondents answer questionnaire items in a similar way without thinking about the items. And it's common for people to interpret questions—especially ambiguous ones—differently. Differences in the resulting scores may have more to do with interpretation than with true differences in the characteristic we wanted to measure. One of your main tasks is to

**random error** Error in measurement due to temporary aspects of the person or measurement situation and affects the measurement in irregular ways.

**response set bias** A problem that arises when respondents answer questionnaire items in a similar way without thinking about the items.

**validity** The extent to which differences in scores on a measuring instrument reflect true differences among individuals, groups, or situations in the characteristic that it seeks to measure or true differences in the same individual, group, or situation from one occasion to another, rather than systematic or random errors.

**reliability** Ability of a measure to obtain similar scores for the same object, trait, or construct across time, across different evaluators, or across the items forming the measure.

write items or questions that mean the same thing to all respondents. If you don't do this, you've added random error.

All of this matters, because the higher the levels of systematic and random error, the lower the **validity**, or correctness, of a measure. Any scale or other measure that accurately assesses what it was intended to assess is said to have validity. Although both types of error lower a measure's validity, in some ways systematic error is less troublesome than random error. If we know the source of the systematic error, sometimes we can adjust for it. For example, researchers know that consumers tend to overestimate their future purchasing behaviors, so they can adjust for this as they analyze survey results. Random error, on the other hand, is just that—random—and we can't hold it constant or account for it statistically. The best we can hope is that random errors cancel themselves out across respondents.

## 12-4a RELIABILITY

**Reliability** refers to the ability of a measure to obtain consistent scores for the same variable or concept across time, across different evaluators, or across the items forming the measure. *Consistency* is the hallmark of reliability; as a result, improving reliability requires decreasing random error. A reliable measure isn't heavily influenced by transitory factors that cause random errors. However, a measure could be reliable but not necessarily valid because of systematic error. A reliable measure is just consistent—it may not be measuring the right thing, but it returns consistent scores.

> Consistency is the hallmark of reliability.

Suppose that you are comparing three different rifles—an old rifle and two new ones. After lining up each rifle's sights perfectly with the center of a target, you fire each one several times. Exhibit 12.10 illustrates the results for the three different rifles. The old rifle is unreliable; despite the fact that the sights are set on the center of the target, the shots go off in random directions. The first new rifle is relatively reliable—it hits about the same spot on the target each time—but its sights are set incorrectly in the center diagram. The error is systematic and not random, but the rifle still misses the mark. The right-hand diagram shows a new rifle with its sights set correctly. Only in the right-hand diagram could a user of any of the rifles be expected to hit the center of the target with regularity. This represents a measure that is both reliable *and* valid.

**Exhibit 12.10** ▶ Illustration of Difference Between Random and Systematic Error

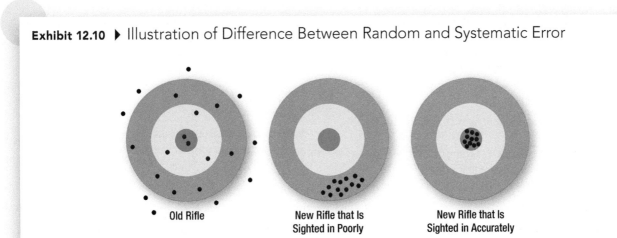

Old Rifle

New Rifle that Is
Sighted in Poorly

New Rifle that Is
Sighted in Accurately

## Manager's Focus

Measuring virtually anything in any field of study involves some degree of measurement error. In marketing, we are often interested in quantifying intangible psychological variables, such as attitudes, motives, satisfaction, or perceptions of a brand's image or position because we believe doing so will ultimately help us understand and predict behavior in the marketplace. However, there will almost always be a higher degree of measurement error when we endeavor to measure what we cannot directly experience with our senses. Stated differently, we are always less certain we have truly measured what we set out to measure when the variable of interest is intangible. Validity is harder to establish with these sorts of concepts.

For these reasons, objectivity and accuracy are much greater for observational studies (in which behavior or physiological responses to marketing stimuli are measured) than for communication studies (in which people are asked to respond to questions pertaining to unobservable psychological variables). As a manager, then, it should be clear that the integrity of the market intelligence you have available to you will be greater if you commission observational studies, rather than surveys, whenever the variables of interest can be directly observed.

That's what asking good questions is all about. We need measures that display both reliability and validity. The goal is to develop measures that produce meaningful results.

This chapter's appendix discusses the importance of developing norms to help interpret the true meaning of rating scale responses.

# Summary

## Learning Objective 1

**Define the term *measurement* as it is used in marketing research.**

Measurement is the process of assigning numbers to represent properties of an object's attributes.

## Learning Objective 2

**List the four scales (levels) of measurement.**

The four types of scales on which an attribute can be measured are nominal, ordinal, interval, and ratio scales.

## Learning Objective 3

**Name some widely used attitude scaling techniques in marketing research.**

The Likert scale, or summated-ratings scale, and the semantic-differential scale are commonly used attitude scaling techniques in marketing research. Researchers also use other types of itemized-rating scales, along with graphic-rating scales and comparative-rating scales.

## Learning Objective 4

**List some other key decisions to be made when designing scales.**

Other key considerations include whether to use a global or a composite scale, how many scale positions to use (and whether to use an even number or an odd number of scale positions), and whether or not to include a "don't know" response category.

## Learning Objective 5

**Explain the concept of validity as it relates to survey items.**

Any scale or other measurement instrument that actually measures what it was intended to measure is said to have validity. As systematic and/or random error increases, the validity of a measure decreases.

## Key Terms

measurement (page 169)
nominal scale (page 170)
ordinal scale (page 171)
interval scale (page 173)
ratio scale (page 173)
self-report (page 174)
itemized-ratings scales (page 174)
summated-ratings scale (page 175)
semantic-differential scale (page 176)
snake diagram (page 176)
graphic-ratings scales (page 177)
comparative-ratings scales (page 177)
constant-sum method (page 177)
global measure (page 178)
composite measures (page 178)
systematic error (page 179)
random error (page 180)
response set bias (page 180)
validity (page 180)
reliability (page 180)

## Review Questions

1. **What are the scales of measurement? What comparisons among scores can be made with each?**

2. **What are the major ways that have been used to measure attitudes? How do they differ?**

3. **What are some factors that may produce systematic errors? What factors may produce random errors?**

4. **What is reliability? What information does it contribute to determining if a measure is accurate?**

5. **What is validity? What are two contributing factors to decreases in validity?**

# Endnote

1. Jon A. Krosnick, et al. (2002, Fall). "The impact of 'no opinion' response options on data quality: Nonattitude reduction or an invitation to satisfice?" *Public Opinion Quarterly* 66, 371–403.

# Interpreting Rating Scales: Raw Scores versus Norms

One of the biggest difficulties with rating scales is trying to interpret what the scores obtained using the scales actually mean. Some time ago, we were asked to develop a scale for measuring patients' perceptions of the quality of service they received from endodontists, dentists who provide specialized dental services such as root canals and oral surgery. We developed a composite scale consisting of 23 items covering two primary dimensions: (a) the procedure and service provided by the endodontist and (b) the service provided by the endodontist's staff. Each of the items described an aspect of the service and asked patients how performance on each aspect compared with their

## Manager's Focus

Marketing research studies are born out of a need to understand your marketing situation better. Measurement scales help answer the important "how much?" questions you face as a manager. How satisfied are your customers? How strong are consumer reactions to your products, marketing communications messages, prices, and so on? How attractive are various product features or benefits? How strongly is your brand positioned on a set of attributes? All of these types of questions, and many others, can be answered in descriptive studies employing self-report attitude scales.

If all marketing variables were measured on ratio scales, managers could look at the numbers and draw relatively clear and unambiguous conclusions about where they stand with consumers. This is because ratio scales represent direct levels of the variables measured. Unfortunately, about the only marketing variables for which ratio measurement is possible are observable behaviors (e.g., the number of purchases made in a particular time frame) and some demographic variables. As we have emphasized throughout this chapter, however, most marketing variables are not directly observable, which means they cannot be measured on scales representing absolute levels. The self-report scales presented in this chapter typically represent the interval level of measurement, and the numbers produced are less precise than ratio scales in terms of the meaning

they convey. For this reason, managers need to be more careful when they interpret the implications of interval scales.

Norms can help in the interpretation of ratio scales and are particularly important when identifying the managerial implications of interval scales. By definition, interval scales represent "relative" values or differences. If something is "relative," then its meaning can be determined only through some type of comparison. One solution is to invest the money necessary to produce norms within a specific study. The primary way of doing this is to obtain ratings of your competitors that serve as norms for the ratings of your brand or company. However, in some situations, it is difficult to produce these sorts of norms. For example, a restaurant or hotel may measure satisfaction levels among customers who just experienced their services. In order to identify the actual implications of such ratings, managers should invest in tracking studies that assess the construct of interest from respondents at regular time intervals. With tracking studies, the managerial implications of the ratings can be determined by examining changes or differences in ratings across time periods. The bottom line is that you should not take unnecessary risks by attempting to directly interpret the meaning of scale values that are inescapably "relative" in nature—you need to establish and use appropriate norms.

expectations using a seven-point scale anchored by "much less than I expected" and "much more than I expected" (the center position was anchored by "about what I expected"). Scores were averaged across the items in each dimension to get a composite rating for each dimension, and the composite scores for the two dimensions were averaged to get an overall service quality score. A total of 95 endodontists and 7,479 of their patients participated in the project.

One endodontist earned an overall service quality score of 5.13. How would you interpret his performance? Is this good, average, or poor performance? The score is well above the middle position on the 1 to 7 scale, so most people would probably conclude that his performance was above average based only on the raw score. To do so without a point of comparison, however, would be a mistake. What if 5.40 were the lowest score achieved by any of the other 94 endodontists? If that were the case, his performance was nothing short of awful. What if the highest score achieved by other endodontists was a 4.88? In this case, a score of 5.13 would represent an outstanding achievement. Here's the point: *It is very difficult to interpret a rating scale score using only the score itself and the scale on which it was obtained to provide meaning.*

When we compare the one endodontist's score against those of the others in the study, it turns out that 75% of the endodontists posted higher scores than he did. Armed with this knowledge, we can say with more confidence that this level of performance was relatively poor, even though the raw score suggested otherwise. In psychological scaling, researchers need to develop *normative standards,* or norms, for use in interpreting raw scores. In this case, norms also come in handy for diagnosing the likely causes of the poor performance. While the overall score was 5.13, the average score for the first dimension (covering aspects of the procedure and the endodontist) was 5.26 and that for the second dimension (covering the staff) was 5.00,

suggesting that the endodontist should focus attention on improving the quality of service provided by the staff. Right? Unfortunately for the endodontist, the comparison of raw scores against norms again points to another conclusion. The staff score was actually much stronger, ranking at the 42nd percentile (meaning that his staff outperformed 41% of the others in the study). The endodontist's score, even though it was higher, placed him only at the 17th percentile when compared to scores for other endodontists on this dimension.[1]

There are two general kinds of norms that can be used, population-based and time-based norms. *Population-based norms,* such as the example we've been using, give meaning to scores by comparing them to scores obtained by similar entities. For example, a department store chain might choose to compare the satisfaction score for a particular store with those of all other stores in the chain. Similarly, a researcher investigating consumer perceptions of a particular producer, service provider, product, or brand should also measure consumer perceptions of competing producers, service providers, and so on, in order to gain a better understanding of what the raw scores mean.

*Time-based norms* track scores for an entity over time. For example, suppose that the endodontist in our example decided to implement changes in the way service was delivered. To monitor the effectiveness of the changes, he decided to collect service quality information from patients on an annual basis. The ratings from earlier time periods serve as norms for ratings in future time periods. Although time-based norms are less informative than population-based norms (because there is no way to tell how scores at any given time compare against similar entities), they are still very useful for tracking progress and identifying problem areas. And they are certainly better than relying on raw scores alone for meaning.

# Endnote

1.   Tom J. Brown. (1997). "Using norms to improve the interpretation of service quality measures," *Journal of Services Marketing* 11, 1, 66–80.

# CHAPTER 13

# Designing the Data Collection Form for Communication Data

## LEARNING OBJECTIVES

▸ Define telescoping error and recall loss and explain how they affect a respondent's ability to answer questions accurately.

▸ List some of the techniques researchers use to secure respondents' cooperation in answering sensitive questions.

▸ List some of the primary rules researchers should keep in mind in trying to develop bias-free questions.

▸ Explain what the funnel approach to question sequencing is.

▸ Explain what a branching question is and discuss when it is used.

▸ Explain the difference between target information and classification information and tell which should be asked first in a questionnaire.

▸ Explain the role of pretesting in the questionnaire development process.

## [ INTRODUCTION ]

Most beginning researchers have no idea how difficult it is to develop an effective questionnaire. You may be saying to yourself: "How hard can it be to write a few questions?" It doesn't matter how perfectly data collection goes if the questions themselves are lousy and introduce error into the data set. As you read this chapter, we hope that you'll gain an appreciation for designing data collection forms carefully.

Exhibit 13.1 offers a method for developing an effective questionnaire.[1] A process with 10 steps may seem a little extreme, especially if you think that 10 minutes is more than enough time to write a few questions. As we describe these steps, however, we think you'll understand why each is important.

**Exhibit 13.1** ▶ Procedure for Developing a Questionnaire

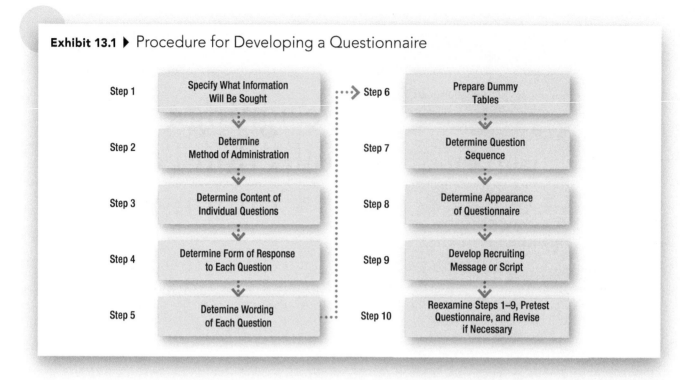

## STEP 1: SPECIFY WHAT INFORMATION WILL BE SOUGHT

With descriptive and causal research, researchers should have enough knowledge about the decision problem and research problem(s) to know what information they need to collect, at least in general terms. Sometimes they even have specific hypotheses to guide the research. As a result, with these kinds of studies, specifying the information to be sought is fairly straightforward.

Here's an important note before you move on to the next step, however: Sometimes you'll think of other things you'd like to include on the survey. Be careful here—if the information is truly important for the research problem you're studying, then go ahead and include the necessary questions. If it simply represents something that might be "nice to know" but isn't central to the purpose of the study, *forget about it*. Including extra questions makes the survey longer, which often causes response rates to drop.

## STEP 2: DETERMINE THE METHOD OF ADMINISTRATION

Once you know the basic information you need to collect, it's time to consider (again) the method of administration. There are four primary methods of collecting data via communication: personal interviews, telephone interviews, paper-based surveys, and online surveys. You'll want to consider the specific circumstances of your project in light of the different methods' advantages and disadvantages and verify that you've chosen the overall best method of administration. The trick is to choose the method that best

fits your information needs, time frame, budget, and the like. It's important to decide on a method as early as possible, because choice of method will influence the number and types of questions, wording of questions and response categories, question sequencing, and so forth.

The type of data you need to collect will naturally have an important effect on the method of data collection. For example, a few years ago, a research firm had a client who wanted to know what proportion of Internet users had various multimedia plug-ins for downloading and playing multimedia files. From experience, the researchers knew that many Internet users don't know which plug-ins they have, especially with respect to which version of the software it might be. It would have been a waste of time to call or write to computer users and pose such questions. Instead, they set up an ingenious online survey that simply asked respondents whether or not they could see a downloaded image. If they clicked "yes," the researchers knew, by the format used to create the image, precisely what plug-in they were using.[2]

## STEP 3: DETERMINE CONTENT OF INDIVIDUAL QUESTIONS

Now it's time to begin thinking about the actual questions that should be asked. We'll deal with the words to use and the response categories to include in later stages—for now, we need to think about the general issues we're addressing and how many questions might be needed to deliver the required information. We also have to consider whether our respondents are likely to have the information and if they'll be willing to share it.

## Manager's Focus

Although the first step in designing a data collection form is to "specify what information will be sought," you should have worked with your research provider much earlier in the project to complete the bulk of this step. As we like to point out, having a strong understanding of the later stages of the research process will help you collaborate more effectively with researchers in the earlier stages. We have urged you to invest time in helping your researchers specify the decision and research problems and formulate research hypotheses. If you follow our advice in these early stages, when it is time to design the data collection form, all that should be necessary is to visit with your researchers to make certain that none of your information needs have changed or been overlooked and that they pursue any additional relevant issues that were discovered through the exploratory research they completed (e.g., literature searches, depth interviews, focus groups). In other words, being thorough at the beginning of the study will facilitate and guide all subsequent stages. Once you have done this, however, you should refrain from micromanaging the design of the data collection form and allow the research professionals to do their jobs without too much interference. Ask questions, provide ideas—but please don't be like some managers who believe that they can do a better job developing the data collection forms than can the professionals who have the experience and training to do it effectively.

In general, we want to capture the needed data using as few questions as possible. So, if your concern is whether there are young children living in a household, it would be better to ask for the age of the youngest child living at home rather than to ask for the ages of all the residents in the household. Sure, it would be great to have the additional information, but if it isn't necessary, don't ask for it. On the flip side, lots of researchers try to get too much information using a single question, which often leads to confusion and unnecessary error in the results. Sometimes you'll need to ask several questions instead of just one.

Here's an example. Consider the question: "Why do you use Crest toothpaste?" One consumer might reply, "To reduce cavities"; another may say, "Because our dentist recommended it." The respondents are using two different frames of reference: the first replying in terms of why he is using it now and the second in terms of how she started using it. A better way is to break the question down into two separate questions, like this:

**filter question**
A question used to determine if a respondent is likely to possess the knowledge being sought; also used to determine if an individual qualifies as a member of the defined population.

How did you first happen to use Crest?
_____

What is your primary reason for using it?
_____

If you wanted one or the other frame of reference, you could include response categories, which would quickly let respondents know the information you want from them. Many times, you'll miss important things like this until you pretest the questionnaire with actual members of the population being studied. That's one reason that pretesting is so important—to make sure that a question won't be interpreted in different ways by different people.

Sometimes people don't know the answers to the questions we'd like to ask. Unfortunately, that probably won't stop them from answering. Most questions will get answers, but we need answers that are meaningful. For that to happen, the questions need to mean something to the respondent. This means that (1) the respondent needs to know something about the issue addressed by the question and (2) the respondent must remember the information.

So how do we improve our chances that a respondent knows the answers to our questions? Many times, it's helpful to ask a **filter question** (sometimes called a *screening* or *qualifying question*) to determine whether the individual is likely to have the information. If we want to understand something about grocery store shopping behaviors and attitudes, a filter question like this might help: "Have you shopped for groceries for your family in the past 30 days?" Filter questions are regularly used at the start of interviews or questionnaires to determine whether the respondent is actually a member of the population being studied, particularly when names have been drawn from general lists.

Obtaining useful data from respondents also requires them to remember the information we need. We often ask people about their purchase and/or use of products and services. No one goes through life trying to remember this sort of stuff, yet we have to depend on the respondent's ability to do so. (Note that observation data using scanner data and the like don't have this problem.) And as you might suspect, for a variety of reasons, an individual's memory for such things just isn't all that good. Returning to our toothpaste example, many people won't be able to recall the first brand they ever used, when they switched to their current brand, or why they switched.

There are two kinds of error, telescoping error and recall loss, that affect a respondent's ability to provide accurate answers to questions about their prior behavior. **Telescoping error** is the tendency to remember an event as having occurred more recently than it did. Suppose that you needed to determine how much Diet Coke had been purchased among a sample of consumers over the prior week. The estimates provided by your respondents will almost always be too high as they recall purchases made prior to the focal seven-day period. Telescoping error gets worse as the time periods respondents are asked to consider get shorter, believe it or not.

**Recall loss** is the tendency to forget an event entirely. As time passes, people simply forget things. As a result, problems with recall loss are reduced as the time period respondents are asked to consider gets shorter. Because recall loss and telescoping error work in opposite directions, in theory there will be an optimal time frame to use with a particular question. For many events and behaviors, the best time frame seems to be between two weeks and one month.[3]

Even if respondents remember the information we want, there is always a question of whether they will share it. Unwillingness to respond to a question (or the whole questionnaire, for that matter) may be a function of the amount of work involved in producing an answer or the sensitivity of the issue. Although a purchasing agent might be able to determine to the penny how much the company spent on a particular brand of janitorial supplies last year, why would she want to take the time to look it up to answer a survey question? Would you? If you ask for something that requires a lot of effort, the respondent is likely to give an approximate answer, ignore the question, or refuse to complete the survey at all.

When an issue is embarrassing or otherwise threatening to respondents, they are naturally less likely to cooperate. Here is the rule about asking sensitive questions: Avoid them unless they are absolutely essential to your project. If you must ask one or more sensitive questions, do so with care. Respect the privacy of your respondents by maintaining the security of the information you collect and by fulfilling any promises of anonymity or confidentiality you have given. Exhibit 13.2 offers several techniques that can be used to more effectively handle sensitive issues.

**telescoping error** A type of error resulting from the fact that most people remember an event as having occurred more recently than it did.

**recall loss** A type of error caused by a respondent's forgetting that an event happened at all.

**randomized-response model** An interviewing technique in which potentially embarrassing and relatively innocuous questions are paired, and the question the respondent answers is randomly determined but is unknown to the interviewer.

## STEP 4: DETERMINE THE FORM OF RESPONSE TO EACH QUESTION

Once you've determined the content of the individual questions, you must decide whether to use closed-ended questions or questions that allow for open-ended responses. Let's look at each in a little more detail.

### Open-Ended Questions

Respondents are free to reply to open-ended questions in their own words rather than being limited to choosing from a set of alternatives. Here are some examples:

1. How old are you? _____ years
2. How would you feel about laws requiring motorcycle riders to wear helmets?
   _____
   _____
3. Can you name three sponsors of the Monday night football games?
   _____
   _____
4. Do you intend to purchase an automobile this year?
   _____
5. Why did you purchase an LG brand HD television?
   _____
   _____
6. In the past month, how many times have you purchased gasoline from a Shell convenience store? _____ times

As these questions demonstrate, just about any kind of information can be gathered using open-ended questions. Open-ended questions are quite versatile.

For example, open-ended questions are often used to begin a survey. An opening question such as, "When you think of flat-screen TVs, which brands come to mind?" gives some insight into the respondent's frame of reference and provides an easy way for the respondent to begin to focus on the topic at hand. And, of course, this particular question also delivers information about a respondent's ability to recall various types of flat-screen TVs.

You may have noticed that some of the open-ended questions we presented seemed very straightforward; others were more subjective. There are two general classes of open-ended questions. One type seeks factual information from a respondent. For example, look back at questions

**Exhibit 13.2 ▶** Handling Sensitive Questions

Here are some tips and techniques for obtaining sensitive information from respondents. We've already given you the most important tip: *Don't include sensitive questions unless you absolutely have to.* Here are some other ideas.

**Tip:**     **Guarantee respondents that their answers will be completely anonymous**—but only if you will actually carry through on your promise. Anonymity is possible with any method of data collection, but with anything other than mail questionnaires, the respondent must rely on you to remove his or her name or other identifying information from the data record. If you cannot promise anonymity, at least promise that respondents' answers will be held in confidence and that information specific to them will not be given to anyone else. Then keep your word.

**Tip:**     **Put any sensitive questions near the end of the questionnaire.** This will allow the researcher and the respondent a little time to develop trust and rapport, especially with personal interviews and telephone interviews. There's another practical advantage too: If the respondent decides to stop answering questions at that point, at least he or she has already completed most of the questionnaire.

**Tip:**     **Use a counter-biasing statement that indicates that the behavior or attitude in question is not unusual.** For example, the following statement might precede a question about household financial difficulties: "Recent studies show that one of every four households has trouble meeting its monthly financial obligations." Doing it this way makes it easier for a respondent to admit the potentially embarrassing information.

**Tip:**     **Phrase the question in terms of other people and how they might feel or act.** For example, "Do you think most people cheat on their income taxes? Why?" Respondents are more likely to reveal their attitudes and behaviors in sensitive areas when asked about other people than if you ask them directly about their own attitudes and behaviors.

**Tip:**     **Ask for general answers, rather than specific answers, when seeking sensitive information.** One frequently used approach is to measure the response by having respondents check one of several categories instead of providing the precise answer. If you need to know a respondent's age, for example, rather than ask for his actual age in years, let him or her check one of the following boxes:

- Less than 20
- 20–29
- 30–39
- 40–49
- 50–59
- 60–69
- 70 or older

Although you won't be able to calculate the precise average age for the sample respondents, it usually isn't necessary to do so anyway.

**Tip:**     **Use the randomized-response model.** With this technique, the respondent is typically given two questions, either of which can be answered "yes" or "no." One question deals with a simple, nonsensitive issue; the other specifically addresses the sensitive issue being studied. Using some random approach, such as flipping a coin, respondents are instructed to answer one or the other question, but the researcher never knows which question they actually answered. That's what makes the approach work: Respondents feel free to answer truthfully because they know that the interviewer will never know if "yes" is in reference to the sensitive or nonsensitive question. The rest is easy. Because we have chosen an innocent question for which we already know the probability of a "yes" answer (e.g., "Were you born in January?") and we know the probability that the respondent is answering the sensitive question (50% based on the coin flip), we can back our way into the proportion of the sample that answered "yes" to the sensitive question. Here's the only catch: Because we can never know specifically which respondents have admitted to the sensitive issue, there is no way for us to look at the relationship between their behavior and other variables such as demographic characteristics.

1, 3, 4, and 6. These questions seek direct answers from the respondent. Each question has a correct answer, and the researcher assumes that the respondent can provide those answers (questions 1, 4, and 6) or is testing to see if the respondent is capable of providing the answers (question 3).

The other type of open-ended question is more exploratory (see questions 2 and 5). Questions designed to uncover motivations and rich descriptions of feelings and attitudes (you might think of these as "touchy-feely" questions) are terrific for exploratory research. You can use them with descriptive research, but they're usually a lot more difficult to code.

## Closed-Ended Questions

With closed-ended questions, respondents choose their answers from a predetermined number of responses, using fixed-alternative response scales. Many times, they respond using rating scales. In this section, we'll present several key issues with using closed-ended questions. Consider the examples below in which we've reframed some of the open-ended questions from the preceding list as fixed-alternative questions. Respondents would be instructed to indicate the response (or responses) that apply.

| Age | HD Television Purchase |
|---|---|
| How old are you? | Why did you purchase an LG brand HD television (check all that apply)? |
| ○ Less than 20 | ○ Price was lower than other alternatives |
| ○ 20–29 | ○ Feel it represents the highest quality |
| ○ 30–39 | ○ Availability of local service |
| ○ 40–49 | ○ Availability of a service contract |
| ○ 50–59 | ○ Picture is better |
| ○ 60 or over | ○ Warranty is better |
| | ○ Other |

| Motorcycle Helmet Use Legislation | Gasoline Purchase Frequency |
|---|---|
| How would you feel about laws requiring motorcycle riders to wear helmets? | In the past month, how many times have you purchased gasoline from a Shell convenience store? |
| ○ Definitely needed | ○ 0 |
| ○ Probably needed | ○ 1–2 |
| ○ Probably not needed | ○ 3 or more |
| ○ Definitely not needed | |
| ○ No opinion | |

These examples highlight some of the difficulties associated with closed-ended questions. None of the alternatives in the motorcycle helmet law question, for example, may capture the respondent's true beliefs on the issue. What if he believes that helmets should be required when riding on highways and streets, but not on private land or dirt tracks? The fixed-alternative question doesn't permit individuals to explain their true position.

The helmet law question also illustrates an issue we discussed in a previous chapter: Should respondents be provided with a "don't know" or "no opinion" option? The general rule is that if a sizable portion of respondents truly don't know an answer or hold an opinion on an issue, they ought to be allowed to say so. How do we define "sizable portion"? If exploratory research or questionnaire pretesting reveals that more than about 20–25% of respondents either don't know or don't hold an opinion, it's probably a good idea to include appropriate response categories to capture this. Another option is to use a filter question (e.g., "Have you ridden on a motorcycle within the last six months?") and avoid asking the question of the respondents who probably don't know or don't have a well-formed opinion.

The HDTV purchase question illustrates another problem with fixed-alternative questions. The list of reasons provided for purchasing an LG brand HDTV may not include all the reasons that could have been used by the respondent. Maybe a respondent purchased an LG television out of loyalty to a friend who owns the local electronics store or for some other reason not included on the list of possible reasons. *Response categories must be exhaustive;* that is, all reasonable possible responses must be included. The "other" response category attempts to solve this problem, but if many people are forced to check this response, the results for that question aren't worth much. How do you know that you've included all necessary responses? Through exploratory research and questionnaire pretesting.

Here's another thing to consider when determining the form of response for each question. If a respondent is supposed to select only one response category, then there must be only one response category that contains her answer. In addition to being exhaustive, *response categories must also be mutually exclusive.* Consider the age question above. What would happen if the response categories were "less than 20," "20–30," "30–40," and so on, and the respondent was 30 years old? Which category should she check? Unless it's a "check all that apply" question, researchers must be very careful that a respondent's answer will fall into only one category. Notice that the television purchase question includes the instruction to "check all that apply" because there might be several legitimate reasons for purchasing the LG brand. On the

Response categories must be mutually exclusive.

other hand, if the instructions had said, "check the most important reason," the categories would have been mutually exclusive because each represents a different reason.

Response categories are also susceptible to response order bias. **Response order bias** occurs when responses are likely to be affected by the order in which the alternatives are presented. Generally speaking, response options presented earlier in a list of options are often more likely to be selected than options appearing later in the list.

There are two general approaches for dealing with response order bias. Under most circumstances, the use of a randomized presentation of response options is preferred. With this approach, the computer randomly selects the order in which the options appear so that any response order biases should balance out across respondents. Randomized response options should be possible with virtually any computerized survey application, whether administered in person, on the telephone, or online. Note, however, that randomizing response options is a bad idea once scale position has meaning (e.g., itemized rating scales).

What do you do about potential response order bias, however, if you are using a paper-based survey? In this case, we recommend the split-ballot technique. In this approach, multiple versions of the questionnaire are produced and distributed. Each version varies the order of the response categories so that each response category will appear in each position (e.g., first, in the middle positions, last) about equally across the sample. Again, the idea is that any order biases will be averaged out across all respondents.

**response order bias** An error that occurs when the response to a question is influenced by the order in which the alternatives are presented.

**split-ballot technique** A technique for combatting response bias in which researchers use multiple versions of a survey, with different wordings of an item or different orders of response options.

## STEP 5: DETERMINE THE WORDING OF EACH QUESTION

Step 5 in the questionnaire development process involves the phrasing—word by word—of each question. This is a critical task because a poorly worded question can cause respondents to refuse to answer it. This is known as *item nonresponse,* and it creates problems for data analysis. Even worse, poorly worded questions introduce error when people do respond, because people may misunderstand the question or interpret it in different ways.

Writing good questions is difficult. Here are some general rules that you can follow to avoid some of the more obvious problems. There is no substitute, however, for careful thought—and a

## Manager's Focus

The process of designing a questionnaire should be guided by the science of measurement theory and the art of asking effective questions. Once again, these are areas in which your research provider should have extensive training and experience. Determining the wording of questions is a step when the input of managers can be very helpful, but it can also be detrimental. You can provide valuable assistance if you are able to give insight to the researcher about the terms used by people within your target population. Through your interactions with customers or prospects, previous research findings (particularly exploratory interviews), and other sources, you may have learned how the population communicates about key issues. However, management staffs have a tendency to develop their own vernacular about market-related issues. To the extent that these expressions diverge from how the target population communicates, they can be detrimental if they are used in the wording of questions.

For example, one of us had the embarrassing experience of working on a research project in which the client managers regularly used an acronym when referring to a competitor's brand. It was the first time our research firm had worked in this industry, and we assumed the acronym was how consumers also referred to the brand. At several points in the questionnaire, we used the acronym instead of the full brand name, and our clients approved this wording when reviewing our proposed questionnaire. Moreover, when we pretested the questionnaire, none of the respondents indicated they were unfamiliar with the acronym. We implemented the questionnaire only to notice after a full day of data collection that while none of the respondents objected to the acronym, most of them provided ratings that were more consistent with an unfamiliar brand than for one with a relatively strong market share. When we expressed concern to our clients, they acknowledged that they had made up the acronym and consumers would never have heard of it. We then had to revise the questionnaire and restart the data collection process. Without question, the mistake was ours, but our clients could have enabled us to avoid this embarrassing outcome by helping us understand the distinction between the way they communicated and the manner in which their target consumers communicated.

good deal of pretesting to ensure that your respondents understand and can accurately respond to your questions.

> Writing good questions is difficult.

### Use Simple Words

Most researchers are more highly educated than the typical survey respondent, and sometimes they use words that they are familiar with but that are not understood by many respondents. A significant proportion of the US population, for example, does not understand the word *Caucasian*, although most researchers do, and determining the best method of assessing ethnic background is an important issue in many projects. Your task is to use words that are precise enough to get the answers you need, but that will be understood by virtually everyone in the designated population. Technical language on a survey is fine and may even be desired for its precision with a technically oriented research topic and population. When seeking answers from the general public, however, it would be wise to remember that the average person in the United States has a high school, not a college, education.

Even though we want you to use simple words when writing survey questions, keep in mind that the words must be precise enough to avoid ambiguity (see next section). Some simple words can cause difficulty on surveys, as Research Window 13.1 indicates.

### Avoid Ambiguous Words and Questions

Not only should the words and questions be simple but they should also be unambiguous. Consider this question:

---

**How often do you watch movies online using the Netflix online service?**

_____ Never
_____ Rarely
_____ Occasionally
_____ Sometimes
_____ Often
_____ Regularly
_____ Frequently
_____ Always

---

For all practical purposes, the replies to this question would be worthless. The words *rarely, occasionally, sometimes, often, regularly,* and *frequently* are ambiguous. For example, to one respondent, the word "often" might mean "almost everyday." To another it might mean "Yes, I use it about once a week when I want to watch a movie." Even the words *never* and *always,* which are more concrete than the others on the list, can cause problems. To one person, "never" means "absolutely, positively, I have never, ever watched a movie online using Netflix"; to another, it may mean "Well, I *used* to use Netflix to watch movies online, but I never do anymore."

## research window 13.1

### *Some Problem Words and Possible Solutions*

| Word | Potential Problem | Possible Solutions |
|---|---|---|
| All | Potentially imprecise; for many respondents, "all" means "almost all" | (1) Avoid use; (2) carefully word question so that meaning is clear; (3) use clearly defined response categories (can help clarify meaning of question) |
| Always | Potentially imprecise; for many respondents, "always" means "almost always" or a goal they want to obtain—"I always do this" | (1) Avoid use, especially when trying to assess behaviors understood as socially desirable; (2) carefully word question so that meaning is clear; (3) use clearly defined response categories (can help clarify meaning of question); (4) allow respondents to provide open-ended count. |
| And | Possibly a double-barreled question | (1) Check carefully to see whether multiple thoughts are included in single question; (2) if so, divide the question into multiple items. |
| Dinner | Potentially ambiguous: for some, this is the midday meal, for others, it is the evening meal | (1) Avoid use and refer to the time of day of the meal (i.e., morning, midday, evening). |
| Feel | Potentially ambiguous; could mean mood or emotion or could mean attitude | (1) Avoid use and use more precise terminology (e.g., "emotions experienced," "evaluation"); (2) use clearly defined response categories (can help clarify meaning of question). |

| | | |
|---|---|---|
| Government | "Loaded" term for many people; potentially ambiguous—does this mean "government in general" or a specific branch or agency of local, state, or federal government? | (1) Avoid use, referring instead to the specific entity. |
| If | Might signal a branching question; be careful that these are easy to understand for respondents | (1) Avoid branching questions if possible; (2) if necessary, carefully design them so that route through questionnaire is clear; (3) if possible, branch at end of questionnaire so that some respondents will complete the questionnaire at that point, whereas others will move to additional questions. |
| Never | Potentially imprecise; for many respondents, "never" likely means "almost never" or a goal they want to obtain—"I never do this" | (1) Avoid use, especially when trying to assess behaviors understood as socially desirable; (2) carefully word question so that meaning is clear; (3) use clearly defined response categories (can help clarify meaning of question); (4) allow respondents to provide open-ended count. |
| Occasionally | Imprecise | (1) Avoid use; (2) allow respondents to provide open-ended count. |
| Often | Imprecise | (1) Avoid use; (2) allow respondents to provide open-ended count. |
| Or | Possibly a double-barreled question | (1) Check carefully to see whether multiple thoughts are included in single question; (2) if so, divide the question into multiple items. |
| Rarely | Imprecise | (1) Avoid use; (2) allow respondents to provide open-ended count. |
| Regularly | Imprecise | (1) Avoid use; (2) allow respondents to provide open-ended count. |
| Sometimes | Imprecise | (1) Avoid use; (2) allow respondents to provide open-ended count. |
| Usually | Imprecise | (1) Avoid use; (2) allow respondents to provide open-ended count. |
| Where | Potentially ambiguous: "Where do you plan to work after graduation?" could refer to geography, industry, department within a company, etc. | (1) Avoid use; (2) carefully word question so that meaning is clear; (3) use clearly defined response categories (can help clarify meaning of question). |
| You | Potentially ambiguous: Does this refer to the specific person, his household, etc.? | (1) Avoid use; (2) carefully word question so that meaning is clear. |

**Source:** For additional information, see Bradburn, N., Sudman, S., & Wansink, B. (2004). *Asking questions.* San Francisco, CA: Jossey-Bass, 324–325, and Payne, S. L. (1979). *The art of asking questions.* Princeton, NJ: Princeton University Press, 158–176.

Here's a better way to ask about the frequency of behaviors using a fixed-alternative scale:

> **leading question** A question framed so as to give the respondent a clue as to how he or she should answer.

Another—maybe even better—approach might be to just let respondents provide the actual number:

**Over the past two weeks, how many movies have you watched online using the Netflix online service?**

- ○ None
- ○ 1
- ○ 2
- ○ 3
- ○ 4
- ○ 5
- ○ more than 5

**Over the past two weeks, how many movies have you watched online using the Netflix online service?**
_____ movies

## Avoid Leading Questions

Sometimes questions are written in such a way that they basically tell respondents what answer they ought to provide. A **leading question** might have been an accident by a careless researcher. Sometimes, though, it's an intentional attempt to manipulate the study's results. Remember that manipulating results produces *advocacy research* and is blatantly unethical. Under no circumstances should leading questions be used intentionally. Here's a question that appeared on a paper-based survey that one of us, a lifelong Republican, received a few years ago from the Republican National Committee:

> **Are you committed to helping ensure that in 2012, the Obama-era of radical liberalism, reckless spending, and embarrassing foreign policy comes to an end?**
>
> ○ Yes
>
> ○ No

This was one of 30-plus questions appearing on survey, many of which were written in much the same fashion. The survey itself had the look and feel of a voting ballot, complete with a verification number and the note that the document "must be accounted for during tabulation." It's clear that the survey writers had little interest in uncovering the truth of how people felt about the direction of the country or their intentions to vote in the upcoming election. Instead, some other agenda was leading the effort. This is also an example of *sugging* (i.e., sales disguised as research), because the survey concluded with the opportunity to support the cause with a donation. (And lest you take this example as a political statement, we could easily have found similar examples from the Democratic Party as well. Advocacy research has no party affiliation.)

Leading questions like this have become commonplace, unfortunately. The words that you use in a question can have a great deal of influence on the results. Here are some words that can easily lead to biased results (please avoid using them):

> *allege, allude, arbitrary, blame, claim, demand, error, failure, fault, ignore, ill-advised, ill-informed, incompetence, ineptness, insist, just, maintain, misinformed, must, neglected, one-sided, only, overreact, peremptory, purport, questionable, rejection, rigid, so-called, unfortunately, unilateral, unreasonable*[4]

One final tip: When you see the results of surveys and public opinion polls presented in the news media, pay no attention whatsoever to any results that aren't accompanied by (a) the actual questions asked, (b) a description of how the study was conducted, and (c) what group was surveyed. Reputable media outlets will provide this information.

**unstated alternative** An alternative answer that is not expressed in a question's options.

**assumed consequences** A problem that occurs when a question is not framed so as to clearly state the consequences, and thus it generates different responses from individuals who assume different consequences.

## Avoid Unstated Alternatives

A response alternative that is not expressed in the options is an **unstated alternative**. Here's what can happen when unstated alternatives are made clear to respondents. Let's say researchers wanted to know employee reactions to end-of-year bonuses. They asked two random samples of employees the following two questions:[5]

> **Would you like to have an end-of-year bonus, if this were possible?** _____
> **Would you prefer to have an end-of-year bonus, or do you prefer to increase your individual retirement contribution for next year?** _____
> _____
> _____

While the two questions appear similar, it would stand to reason that they would produce dramatically different responses. In the first version, an extremely high number of "yes" responses would be expected as the employees get immediate personal gain for their hard work on the job. In the second version, the responses would be decidedly more mixed. Is it better to get money today or plan for one's financial future? The difference in the two questions is that the second version makes explicit an important alternative: Planning for long-term financial benefit is important, too. As a general rule, you should avoid unstated alternatives; in this example, the second version of the question is better than the first. In many ways, this is consistent with our earlier advice that response categories must be exhaustive. Thorough exploratory research and questionnaire pretesting will help identify unstated alternatives.

## Avoid Assumed Consequences

A question should be framed so that all respondents will consider all relevant information as they respond. Unfortunately, it's easy to ask questions that don't spell out what might happen as a consequence of certain actions. These questions leave **assumed consequences**. Consider the following example from the Pew Research Center:

> *An example of a wording difference that had a significant impact on responses comes from a January 2003 Pew Research survey. When people were asked whether they would: "favor or oppose taking military action in Iraq to end Saddam Hussein's rule," 68% said they favored military action while 25% said they opposed military action. However, when asked whether they would "favor or oppose taking military action in Iraq to end Saddam Hussein's rule even if it*

*meant that U.S. forces might suffer thousands of casualties," responses were dramatically different; only 43% said they favored military action while 48% said they opposed it. The introduction of U.S. casualties altered the context of the question and influenced whether people favored or opposed military action in Iraq.*[6]

Exhibit 13.3 shows that respondents can assume a wide range of possible alternatives if consequences are assumed instead of explicitly stated. The favorable or unfavorable nature of these consequences can also vary greatly. While some may view repairing aging bridges as justification of a state tax increase, others may not feel as positively if the consequence is salary increases for state legislators. The key point is that it's important to ask questions that are precise and that don't require respondents to make assumptions.

## Avoid Generalizations and Estimates

Questions should always be asked in specific, rather than general, terms. Imagine that you asked purchasing agents, "How many salespeople did you see last year?" To answer the question, the agent would probably estimate how many salespeople call in a typical week and would multiply this estimate by 52. Don't make your respondents work this hard. Instead, ask about a shorter time frame that won't force a respondent to provide an estimate. For this question, how about asking "How many representatives have you personally seen in the last two weeks?" If you need an estimate for the year, you can multiply the answer by 26. The important point is to choose the appropriate time frame, one that avoids both telescoping error and recall loss. The best time frame will differ depending upon what you want to know.

## Avoid Double-Barreled Questions

Try to answer the following question:

> **Think back to the last meal you purchased at a fast-food restaurant. How satisfied were you with the price and the quality of service that you received?**
>
> ○ Very Dissatisfied
>
> ○ Dissatisfied
>
> ○ Neutral
>
> ○ Satisfied
>
> ○ Very Satisfied

**Exhibit 13.3 ▶** Illustration of Assumed Consequences

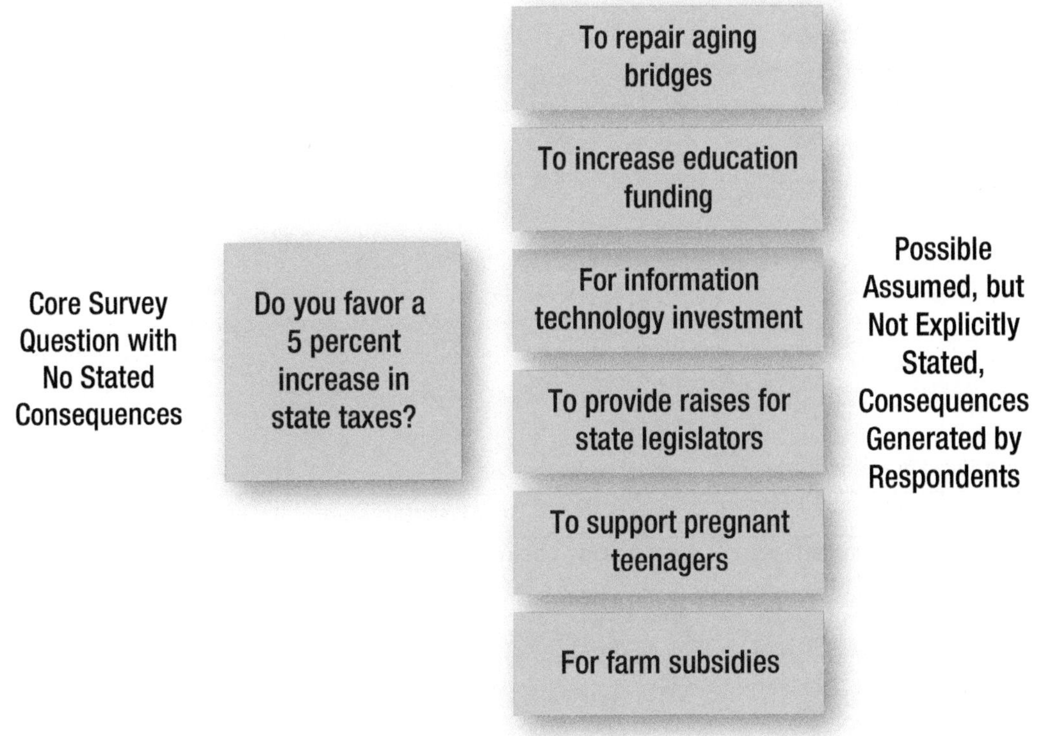

Core Survey Question with No Stated Consequences

Do you favor a 5 percent increase in state taxes?

- To repair aging bridges
- To increase education funding
- For information technology investment
- To provide raises for state legislators
- To support pregnant teenagers
- For farm subsidies

Possible Assumed, but Not Explicitly Stated, Consequences Generated by Respondents

Was it difficult to answer the question? Maybe not, if you felt the same way about both the price and the service quality. But what if the service was great but the price was too high? Now how should you answer the question? With **double-barreled questions**, two questions are rolled into one, leading to confusion for respondents.

Most of the time double-barreled questions are fairly easy to spot. Just look over your survey closely, circling the words *and* and *or*. Finding one of these words doesn't necessarily mean you've written a double-barreled question, but it often does. Usually, a double-barreled question (or a *triple-barreled question,* for that matter) can easily be fixed by splitting the question into two or more separate questions.

**double-barreled question** A question that calls for two responses and creates confusion for the respondent.

**dummy table** A table (or figure) used to show how the results of an analysis will be presented.

## STEP 6: PREPARE DUMMY TABLES

Once you've written all of the items and response categories for your survey, you should prepare a set of dummy tables before beginning the data collection process. A

**dummy table** is simply a table (or figure) used to show how the results of an analysis will be presented. It is a "dummy" table because there are no actual data in the table (they haven't been collected yet). Preparing a complete set of dummy tables forces you to think carefully about each piece of information to be collected. It also takes the guesswork out of the analysis phase of the project. Some will be simple tables or figures that show the results of individual items; others may show relationships between important variables. Exhibit 13.4 shows two dummy tables that might be used by an athletic shoe retailer as it prepares to investigate store awareness and preference in a particular geographic market.

Notice a couple of things about the dummy tables. Before awareness data are collected, we don't know all of the stores that respondents might recall; that's why the researchers left several open spots on the awareness table. By the way, this is a very useful

**Exhibit 13.4 ▶** Dummy Table Examples

Athletic Shoe Store Awareness

| | OVERALL RECALL PERCENTAGE | T.O.M. RECALL PERCENTAGE | RECALL INTENSITY RATIO | OVERALL RECOGNITION PERCENTAGE |
|---|---|---|---|---|
| Finish Line | XX% | XX% | 0.XX | XX% |
| Foot Locker | XX% | XX% | 0.XX | XX% |
| The Athlete's Foot | XX% | XX% | 0.XX | XX% |
| Champ Sports | XX% | XX% | 0.XX | XX% |
| Academy | XX% | XX% | 0.XX | XX% |
| _____ | | | | |
| _____ | | | | |
| _____ | XX% | XX% | 0.XX | XX% |

Athletic Shoe Store Preference by Age

| | Store Preference | | | |
|---|---|---|---|---|
| AGE | FINISH LINE | FOOT LOCKER | THE ATHLETE'S FOOT | TOTAL |
| Less than 18 | XX% | XX% | XX% | 100% |
| 18–29 | XX% | XX% | XX% | 100% |
| 30–39 | XX% | XX% | XX% | 100% |
| 40 or over | XX% | XX% | XX% | 100% |

(Sample size = XX)

table for reporting awareness. The columns represent *overall recall percentage* (the percentage of respondents that recalled each store), *top-of-mind recall percentage* (the percentage of people who recalled each store in the first position on the recall task), *recall intensity ratio* (top-of-mind recall percentage divided by overall recall percentage, which provides an assessment of how dominant in memory an object is among people who are aware of the object), and the *recognition percentage* (the percentage of people who recognized each store when presented with the store name or logo in a recognition task).

The other thing we want you to notice is that the preference dummy table lists the age segments the company managers want to compare. It is crucial that the exact variables and categories to be investigated, as well as the necessary statistical tests, are specified before you begin to collect the data. Once data are collected and analysis is underway, it's too late to say "Oops!" and start over. Dummy tables provide a check for connecting the information that needs to be collected to the data collection form you have just prepared. If you've prepared your dummy tables but haven't used some of the questions that you placed on the survey, it's time to reconsider whether or not you really need those questions.

## STEP 7: DETERMINE QUESTION SEQUENCE

Once you've developed the questions and responses, you're ready to begin putting them together into a questionnaire. The order in which the questions are presented can be crucial to the success of the research effort. There are no hard-and-fast rules, but we can offer a few rules of thumb.

### Use Simple and Interesting Opening Questions

The first questions asked are really important. If respondents can't answer them easily—or if they find them uninteresting or threatening in any way—they may refuse to cooperate at all. As a result, it's essential that the first few questions be simple, interesting, and nonthreatening. Questions that ask respondents for their opinions on some issue are often good openers if they help get the respondent engaged.

### Use the Funnel Approach

One approach to question sequencing is the **funnel approach**, which gets its name from its shape: Start with broad questions and progressively narrow down the scope. For example, if you wanted to measure customer satisfaction, it's best to start with the overall satisfaction questions first before getting down to satisfaction with individual

**funnel approach** An approach to question sequencing that gets its name from its shape, starting with broad questions and progressively narrowing down the scope.

**question order bias** The tendency for earlier questions on a questionnaire to influence respondents' answers to later questions.

**branching question** A question that routes people to different survey items based on their responses to the question.

attributes of the products and services provided. If you start with some of the particular attributes, the later overall satisfaction question may be strongly influenced by answers to one or more of the particular attributes selected. This is an example of **question order bias**, the tendency for earlier questions to affect respondents' answers to later questions. In general, the funnel approach helps prevent problems with question order bias.

When measuring awareness, the sequence of the questions is a very important concern. Recall questions ("Please name the first three athletic shoe stores located in Martinsville that come to mind first") must always be asked before recognition questions ("Tell me whether or not each of the following athletic shoe stores is located in Martinsville") if the results of the recall question are to be meaningful. (These questions might be used to gather the data needed to complete the first dummy table shown in Exhibit 13.4.)

There should also be some logical order to the questions. It's best not to make sudden changes in topics or to jump around from topic to topic. When it's time to change the topic, most researchers simply insert a brief explanation as a way of moving to the new topic.

### Design Branching Questions With Care

It's not uncommon for researchers to design surveys on which some respondents answer different or additional questions depending upon their answers to a question in the survey. For example, suppose an initial question was: "Have you bought a car within the last six months?" If the respondent answers "yes," she next gets questions about specific details of the purchase. If she responds "no," she never gets those additional questions and instead moves on in the survey. A **branching question** is a question that routes people to different survey items based on their responses. Some companies use the term *skip pattern* for the sequencing of respondents through different questions on a survey; a branching question serves as the starting point for a skip pattern. The advantage to branching questions and skip patterns is that respondents for whom a question is irrelevant are simply directed around it.

As you might guess, using computer technology makes skip patterns much easier to use with telephone interviews, personal interviews, and online surveys than they are for paper-based surveys. With paper-based surveys, it's certainly possible to use branching questions, but you must be careful to not let respondents become confused. If possible, it's best to place branching questions near the end of the survey so that those who need to continue do so, but those who don't are simply done with the survey.

## Ask for Classification Information Last

The typical questionnaire aims to collect two types of information: target information and classification information. **Target information** refers to the key issues being studied-for example, the intentions or attitudes of respondents toward a new product or service. **Classification information** refers to the other data we collect to classify respondents, typically for demographic breakdowns. For instance, we might be interested in determining whether a respondent's attitudes toward a new product or service are affected by the person's income. In this case, income would be a classification variable. Demographic/socioeconomic characteristics of respondents are often used as classification variables for understanding the results.

> **target information**
> The basic information that addresses the subject of the study.
>
> **classification information** Information used to classify respondents, typically for demographic breakdowns.

Except under rare circumstances, *target information should be obtained first,* followed by classification information. There is a logical reason for this. The target information is most critical. Without it, there is no study. The researcher shouldn't risk alienating the respondent by asking a number of personal questions before getting to the heart of the study. Respondents who readily offer their opinions about television programming may balk when asked about their income.

## Place Difficult or Sensitive Questions Late in the Questionnaire

The target information itself can also present some sequence problems. Some of the questions may be sensitive. Early questions should not be sensitive for the reasons we mentioned earlier. If respondents feel threatened, they may refuse to participate in the study. Thus, sensitive questions should be placed near the end of the questionnaire. Once respondents have become involved in the study, they are less likely to react negatively or refuse to answer when delicate questions are posed.

## STEP 8: DETERMINE APPEARANCE OF THE QUESTIONNAIRE

For paper-based surveys and online studies, the appearance of the questionnaire can influence respondents' cooperation. If the survey looks sloppy, respondents are likely to feel the study is unimportant or unprofessional and refuse to cooperate no matter how important the researcher says it is. If the study is important—and why would you be conducting it if it isn't?—make the questionnaire reflect that importance.

If you are fielding an online survey, don't forget that most people who respond will use their mobile phones. This creates real issues with how the survey appears on the smaller mobile screens. Fortunately, the better online survey companies include standard templates for surveys that are "mobile-friendly," producing surveys that are functional and attractive on mobile phones.

There's one other thing to consider. Don't bother with long, drawn-out sets of instructions unless you are doing something new and different and they are absolutely necessary. Most people have completed enough surveys to know how to respond to them, so a sentence or two ought to be enough. We learned this the hard way. Years ago, one of us included a set of instructions that took up roughly a quarter of the first page of a survey. About 25% of our respondents didn't answer the first question that closely followed the instructions (and was a little wordy itself). We suspect that in their haste to skip over our burdensome instructions, most of these people never even saw the first question. Learn from our experience; keep instructions simple and short.

## STEP 9: DEVELOP A RECRUITING MESSAGE OR SCRIPT

The introduction to the research can also affect acceptance of the questionnaire. With personal interviews and telephone interviews, the opening script used to recruit potential respondents is probably your only chance to secure their participation, so put some thought into what you'll say. In fact, your "script" needs to be carefully developed and pretested to ensure that it is effective in getting people to agree to participate. Then you must make certain that the people making the contacts actually follow the script. Note that it is important for recruiters to practice the script until it sounds as natural as possible; nobody likes to hear someone reading or reciting a "canned" presentation to them.

With paper-based and online surveys, the questionnaire is typically introduced with a written message, either a cover letter or an e-mail recruiting message. Because there's no direct social connection between you and the potential respondent, the task of introducing the survey and gaining cooperation is even more difficult.

Good recruiting messages and scripts are rarely written in a hurry. Like the questionnaire itself, they usually require a series of painstaking rewrites to get the wording just right. The most important things to communicate are (1) who you are, (2) why you are contacting them, (3) your request for their help in providing information, (4) how long it will take, (5) that their responses will be anonymous and/or confidential (if this is true), and (6) any incentives they will receive for participating. Regardless of how you administer the survey, the recruiting message needs to convince potential respondents about the importance of the research and why you need their help.

## STEP 10: REEXAMINE STEPS 1 THROUGH 9, PRETEST QUESTIONNAIRE, AND REVISE IF NECESSARY

You should never expect the first draft of a survey to be the one that is ultimately used. Questionnaire development is an iterative process, even for professional researchers. Each question should be reviewed to ensure that it is easy to answer and not confusing, ambiguous, or potentially offensive to the respondent. Questions must not be leading or likely to bias respondents' answers. How can you tell? An extremely critical attitude and good common sense should help. You need to examine each word in each question. When a potential problem is discovered, the question should be revised. After examining each question and each word in each question for its potential meanings and implications, test the questionnaire by having different members of the research team answer the questions using the method of administration to be used in the actual study. Call them on the telephone, send them an e-mail, walk up and ask for their participation, or let them find the questionnaire with their mail. This sort of role playing should reveal some of the most serious shortcomings and should lead to further revision of the questionnaire.

The real test of a questionnaire, however, is how it performs under actual conditions of data collection. That's what makes a questionnaire **pretest** so vital. The pretest serves the same role in survey design that test marketing serves in new product development. While the product concept, different advertising appeals, alternative

**pretest** Use of a questionnaire (or observation form) on a trial basis in a small pilot study to determine how well the questionnaire (or observation form) works.

packages, and so on, may all have been tested previously in the product development process, test marketing is the first place where they all come together. Similarly, the pretest provides the real test of the questionnaire and the mode of administration.

*Data collection should never begin until you have pretested the survey.* Better yet, use two pretests. Do the first as a personal interview, no matter how you actually plan to administer the actual survey. Watch your respondents to see whether they actually remember the data requested of them or whether some questions seem confusing or produce resistance or hesitancy for whatever reason. The pretest interviews should be conducted among respondents similar to those who will be used in the actual study by the firm's most experienced interviewers. Then make any necessary changes and do a second pretest, using the chosen method of administration for the project.

There are no strict guidelines for how many respondents to include in a pretest. We recommend using at least five people with the face-to-face pretest and probably five to 10 more with the actual pretest. If changes are still necessary—and they usually are—it will be important to make the changes and then roll in more pretest participants.

If you don't pretest your data collection forms, you're asking for trouble. The pretest is the most inexpensive insurance you can buy to ensure the success of the project. A careful pretest along with proper attention to the dos and don'ts presented in this chapter and summarized in Exhibit 13.5 should make the questionnaire development process successful.

## Manager's Focus

Pretesting does not guarantee a questionnaire will have no problems. Proper pretesting, however, will help researchers discover most problems. We all tend to believe we communicate far more clearly and effectively than is usually the case. The pretesting process quickly reveals how instructions, questions, and response formats we thought were perfectly clear can be easily misunderstood or misinterpreted by respondents. If these problems are not corrected, there will be a significant amount of unnecessary measurement error in our research findings.

Managers often do not appreciate the importance of pretesting, and unfortunately, some researchers don't

either. By this point in the research process, deadlines are becoming more pressing, and it is tempting to conserve time by beginning the actual data collection process. But neglecting the pretest would be a major mistake that would probably lower the quality of the information obtained. It is quite rare that a pretest does not reveal one or more problems with how a questionnaire was originally designed. For this reason, pretesting is absolutely critical, and under no conditions should you ever allow researchers to proceed without pretesting and revising a questionnaire. In fact, if your research provider does not suggest a pretest or objects to the pretesting process, you probably need to find a different provider.

**Exhibit 13.5** ▶ Questionnaire Preparation Checklist

**Step 1: Specify What Information Will Be Sought**

☐ Make sure that you have a clear understanding of the issue and what you want to know. Frame your research questions, but don't write the actual questions just yet.

☐ Write the research problem(s) you're addressing on a card and keep it in front of you. Review it often as you are working on the questionnaire.

☐ Conduct a search for existing questions on the issue and revise to meet your current purposes.

**Step 2: Determine Method of Administration**

☐ Use the type of data to be collected as a basis for deciding on the type of questionnaire.

☐ Use the desired degree of structure and disguise to guide selection of method of administration.

☐ Compare your situation against the advantages and disadvantages of the different approaches.

**Step 3: Determine Content of Individual Questions**

☐ For each possible question, ask yourself, "Why do I want to know this?" Answer it in terms of how it will help your research. "It would be interesting to know" is not an acceptable answer.

☐ Make sure each question is specific and addresses only one important issue.

☐ Ask yourself whether the question applies to all people who receive the questionnaire; if it doesn't, either the population must be redefined, or you need a filter question and/or a branching question.

☐ Split questions that can be answered from different frames of reference into multiple questions, one corresponding to each frame of reference. If you don't need each frame of reference, carefully rephrase the question to provide only the perspective you need.

☐ Ask yourself whether respondents will be informed about, and can remember, the issue that the question is dealing with.

☐ Make sure the time period of the question is appropriate for the topic.

☐ Avoid questions that require excessive effort or that deal with sensitive (embarrassing or threatening) issues.

☐ If sensitive questions must be asked,
   (a)   guarantee respondent anonymity or confidentiality.
   (b)   use a counter-biasing statement.
   (c)   phrase the question in terms of others and how they might feel or act.
   (d)   put sensitive questions near the end.
   (e)   use categories or ranges rather than specific numbers.
   (f)   use the randomized-response model.

**Step 4: Determine Form of Response to Each Question**

☐ Determine which type of question—open-ended or closed-ended—provides data that fit the information needs of the project.

☐ Use structured questions whenever possible.

☐ Consider using open-ended questions that require short answers to begin a questionnaire.

☐ Try to convert open-ended questions to fixed-response questions to reduce respondent work load and coding effort for descriptive and causal studies.

☐ If open-ended questions are necessary, make the questions fairly specific to give respondents a frame of reference when answering.

☐ Provide for "don't know" and "no opinion" responses, if these are likely to apply to a significant proportion of the population.

☐ When using fixed-alternative questions, be sure the choices are exhaustive and mutually exclusive.

☐ If multiple responses are possible, use "check all that apply" in the instructions.

☐ Watch out for response order bias when using closed-ended questions. Consider the use of a split-ballot procedure to reduce order bias.

☐ Use the highest level of measurement possible for each question unless there is a solid reason to do otherwise.

**Step 5: Determine Wording of Each Question**

☐ Use simple words.

☐ Avoid ambiguous words and questions.

**Exhibit 13.5** ▶ Questionnaire Preparation Checklist

☐ Avoid leading questions.

☐ Avoid unstated alternatives.

☐ Avoid assumed consequences.

☐ Avoid generalizations and estimates.

☐ Avoid double-barreled questions.

☐ Make sure each question is as specific as possible.

### Step 6: Prepare Dummy Tables

☐ Adopt the manager's perspective to think through the analyses necessary to present the results.

☐ Consider which variables will be analyzed in isolation and which will be analyzed in combination with other variables.

☐ Make certain that every variable has a purpose and will be used in the analysis.

### Step 7: Determine Question Sequence

☐ Use simple, interesting questions for openers.

☐ Use the funnel approach, first asking broad questions and then narrowing them down.

☐ Design branching questions with care.

☐ Ask for target information first and classification information last.

☐ Ask for classification information last so that if respondent refuses, the other data are still usable.

☐ Watch out for question order bias; use a split-ballot procedure if necessary.

### Step 8: Determine Appearance of Questionnaire

☐ Make sure the questionnaire looks professional and is relatively easy to answer.

☐ Be sure that all online surveys will be optimized for mobile phones.

☐ Use quality paper and printing for paper-based surveys.

☐ Attempt to make the survey as short as possible while avoiding a crowded appearance.

☐ List the name of the organization conducting the survey on the first page or screen; a fictitious name may be necessary if disguise is used.

☐ Use concise, clear instructions.

☐ Be certain that branching questions are easy to follow when using paper-based surveys.

☐ Use appropriate graphics to improve the appearance of the questionnaire.

### Step 9: Develop Recruiting Message or Script

☐ Keep the message as brief as possible, especially with personal and telephone interview scripts, but include the following information at a minimum:
  - (a) Who you are
  - (b) Why you are contacting the respondent
  - (c) Your request for his or her help in providing information
  - (d) Approximately how long it will take to participate
  - (e) That responses will be anonymous or confidential (if this is true)
  - (f) Any incentives the respondent will be given

☐ Practice the script until it sounds natural, rather than "canned" or memorized.

### Step 10: Reexamine Steps 1–9, Pretest Questionnaire, and Revise if Necessary

• Examine each word of every question to ensure that the question is not confusing, ambiguous, offensive, or leading.

• Have members of the research team complete the surveys using the method of administration selected.

• Pretest the questionnaire first by personal interviews among respondents similar to those to be used in the actual study.

• Obtain comments from the interviewers and respondents to discover any problems with the questionnaire, and revise it if necessary.

• Pretest the questionnaire using the method chosen for the study.

# Summary

## Learning Objective 1

**Define telescoping error and recall loss and explain how they affect a respondent's ability to answer questions accurately.**

Telescoping error refers to people's tendency to remember an event as having occurred more recently than it did. Recall loss means they forget it happened at all. The two types of error work in opposite directions, which means that finding the optimal time frame for recalling prior behaviors is important.

## Learning Objective 2

**List some of the techniques researchers use to secure respondents' cooperation in answering sensitive questions.**

When asking sensitive questions, researchers may find it helpful to (a) guarantee respondent anonymity or confidentiality; (b) make use of a counter-biasing statement; (c) phrase the question in terms of others and how they might feel or act; (d) put sensitive questions near the end; (e) use categories or ranges rather than specific numbers; or (f) use the randomized-response model.

## Learning Objective 3

**List some of the primary rules researchers should keep in mind in trying to develop bias-free questions.**

Among the rules that researchers should keep in mind in developing bias-free questions are (1) use simple words, (2) avoid ambiguous words and questions, (3) avoid leading questions, (4) avoid unstated alternatives, (5) avoid assumed consequences, (6) avoid generalizations and estimates, and (7) avoid double-barreled questions.

## Learning Objective 4

**Explain what the funnel approach to question sequencing is.**

The funnel approach to question sequencing gets its name from its shape, starting with broad questions and progressively narrowing down the scope. This is important for question sequencing, because asking for specific information early in a questionnaire will often influence respondents' answers to later questions, a source of error known as question order bias.

## Learning Objective 5

**Explain what a branching question is and discuss when it is used.**

A branching question is one that initiates a skip pattern in a survey. Respondents are "branched" to different questions in a survey based on their answer to the branding question. Among other things, this allows respondents who (should) have information about a topic to provide that information, while those who don't have the information to skip those questions altogether.

## Learning Objective 6

**Explain the difference between target information and classification information and tell which should be asked first in a questionnaire.**

Target information refers to the subject of the study; classification information refers to the other data we collect to classify respondents in hopes of gathering more insights about the phenomenon of interest. The proper questionnaire sequence is to obtain target information first and classification information last on the data collection form.

## Learning Objective 7

**Explain the role of pretesting in the questionnaire development process.**

Questionnaire pretesting is the final step in the survey development process. It is the last chance that the researcher has to ensure that the data collection form is working properly prior to data collection; pretesting must not be overlooked.

## Key Terms

filter question (page 187)
telescoping error (page 188)
recall loss (page 188)
randomized-response model (page 188)
response order bias (page 191)
split-ballot technique (page 191)
leading question (page 193)
unstated alternative (page 194)
assumed consequences (page 194)
double-barreled questions (page 196)
dummy table (page 196)
funnel approach (page 197)
question order bias (page 197)
branching question (page 197)
target information (page 198)
classification information (page 198)
pretest (page 199)

## Review Questions

1. Suppose you wanted to determine the proportion of men in a geographic area who dye their hair. How could the information be obtained by open-ended questions and by closed-ended questions? Which would be preferable?

2. What criteria can a researcher use to determine whether a specific question should be included in a questionnaire?

3. What is telescoping error? What does it suggest about the period to be used when asking respondents to recall past experiences?

4. What are some recommended ways for asking for sensitive information?

5. What is a split-ballot, and why is it used?

6. What is an ambiguous question? A leading question? A question with unstated alternatives? A question with assumed consequences? A double-barreled question?

7. What is the proper sequence when asking for target information and classification information? Why?

8. What is the funnel approach to question sequencing?

9. What is a branching question? Why are such questions used?

10. What is a cover letter? What key things should be included in a cover letter?

11. What is a questionnaire pre-test? Why should researchers pre-test surveys?

# Endnotes

1. This procedure is adapted from one suggested by Arthur Kornhauser and Paul B. Sheatsley, Questionnaire construction and interview procedure, in Selltiz, C., Lawrence S. Wrightsman, L. W., & Stuart W Cook. (1976). *Research methods in social relations,* 3rd ed. New York: Holt, Rinehart and Winston, pp. 541–573.

2. Grecco , C., & King, H. (1999, July). Of browsers and plug-ins: Researching Web surfers' technological capabilities. *Quirk's Marketing Research Review,* 58–62.

3. Bradburn, N., Sudman, S., & Wansink, B. (2004). *Asking Questions,* rev. ed. San Francisco: Jossey-Bass, 66.

4. Guide to writing survey questions, *Management Analysis and Development.* Retrieved from http://www.mad.state.mn.us/

5. Noelle-Neumann, E. (1970, Summer). Wanted: Rules for wording structural questionnaires. *Public Opinion Quarterly* 34, 200; Gendall, P., & Hoek, J. (1990, May). A question of wording, *Marketing Bulletin* 1, 25–36.

6. Question Wording, Pew Research Center for the People and the Press, retrieved from http://www.people-press.org /methodology/questionnaire-design/question-wording/

# CHAPTER 14

# Developing the Sampling Plan

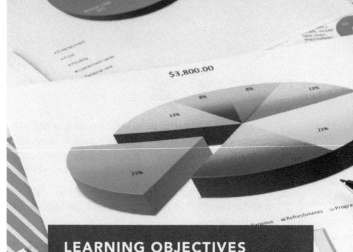

Billion Photos/Shutterstock.com

## [ INTRODUCTION ]

Once you've specified the problem, made important decisions about the type of research to pursue, and carefully crafted your data collection instrument, it's time to think about the people (or other units) from which you'll collect data. If you collect information from (or about) each member of the relevant population, you are conducting a **census**. When the overall population is limited in size, it is usually smart to attempt a census, even if you can't get information from everyone. Most of the time, however, we develop a sampling plan, the process of selecting the people or objects (i.e., companies, products, and so forth) to be surveyed, interviewed, or observed. With a sampling plan, we collect information from a **sample**, or subset, of elements from the larger group, with the goal of making projections about what would be true for the population. As we'll see, the ability to make inferences about the overall population from a sample of population members depends on how we select the sample. Exhibit 14.1 lays out a six-step process for drawing a sample and collecting data.

Rawpixel.com/Shutterstock.com

**census** A type of sampling plan in which data are collected from or about each member of a population.

**sample** Selection of a subset of elements from a larger group of objects.

**Exhibit 14.1** ▶ Six-Step Procedure for Drawing a Sample

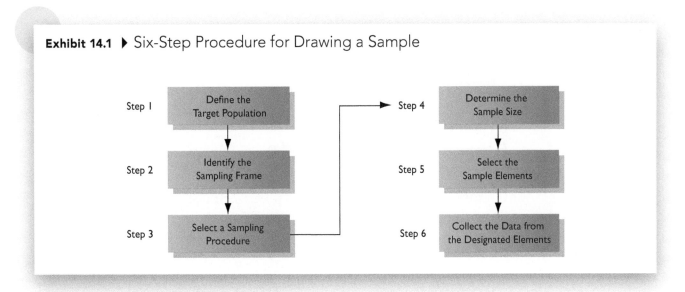

## 14-1 Defining the Target Population

The first step in the process outlined in Exhibit 14.1 is to define the target population. By **population**, we mean all the individuals or objects that meet specific requirements for membership in the overall group. We often refer to those who qualify as *population elements*. You must be very clear and precise in defining the population. For example, does the population consist of individuals, households, business firms, other institutions, credit card transactions, lightbulbs on an assembly line, or something else? When the elements are individuals, the relevant target population might be defined as all those over 18 years of age, or females only, or those with a high school education only, or those who have visited a certain restaurant within the last 30 days. The point is that you must be painfully explicit about who or what qualifies to be a member of the population.

In general, the simpler the definition of the target population, the easier (and less costly) it will be to find the sample. Alternatively, as the number of criteria for population membership increases, so do the cost and time necessary to find them. But ease and cost don't outweigh the importance of defining the population that is relevant to your study, even if it means adding criteria. If you need the opinions of left-handed women between the ages of 65 and 75 located in Southern California, then you'll just have to find a way to locate them.

In general, populations that are larger in number are easier to locate. Exhibit 14.2 details the percentage of people in the United States who reported participating in various categories of sports during 2016. You'll likely find

> **population** All cases that meet designated specifications for membership in the group.
>
> **parameter** A characteristic or measure of a population.

that it's more difficult and costly to conduct a study with people who participate in winter sports (7% of population) than with people who participate in fitness-related sports (62%).

### 14-1a PARAMETERS VERSUS STATISTICS

Before we go on, let's revisit why we are drawing a sample in the first place. Our goal with a sample is to determine what is likely to be true for a population based on data obtained from only a subset of that population. When seeking customer insights, we almost always work with a sample rather than a census, because a sample is often easier and less costly to obtain than is a census. Note, however, that sampling isn't an issue at all if data are available for all members of the population. This would be the case, for example, for many types of mechanically collected behavioral data (e.g., number of online purchases tied to a particular account or credit card number in a 30-day period; number of times an employee identification card is swiped for entry into a building). When data are available for all members of the population, it's easy to work with the population—and there's no real reason to work with a sample. Still, for most of the kinds of individual data that researchers routinely obtain, sampling is an important issue.

Any population has certain characteristics; these characteristics are called **parameters**, and we assume that if we could take measurements of these characteristics from all population elements, without any kind of error getting into our data, then we would know what is true about the population on these parameters. For example,

**Exhibit 14.2** ▸ 2016 Participation Rate in Various Sports Categories

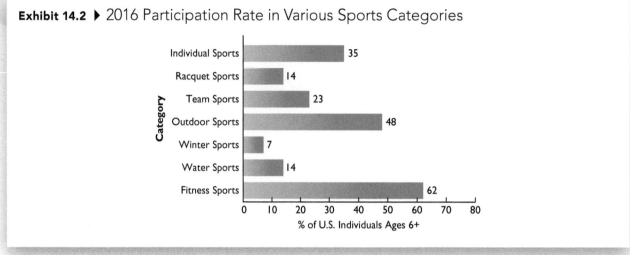

Source: "2016 Participation Report," Physical Activity Council, downloaded from http://www.physicalactivitycouncil.com/pdfs/current .pdf on January 27, 2017.

suppose the population for a study consists of all adults living in Phoenix, Arizona. We could describe this population on a number of parameters, including average age, proportion with a college degree, range of incomes, attitude toward a new service offering, awareness of a new retail store that has just opened, and so on. Note that within the population, there is a real quantity or value for each of these parameters, even though we'll never know for sure what these true values are (because, as a practical matter, we can never measure something without error).

When we work with a sample drawn from a population, we are attempting to describe the population parameters based on the measures we take from the sample members. That is, we calculate the average age, range of income, or awareness level for the sample as a means of gaining insights into what likely would be true for the whole population. In short, we work with **statistics**, which are characteristics or measures of a sample, to draw inferences about the larger population's parameters (see Exhibit 14.3). When we work with a sample instead of a census, it is likely that our results will be at least a little different than they would have been had we gathered information from every member of the population. This difference is known as **sampling error**.

How big a problem is sampling error? Well, it's something that you'll want to take into account, but unless you're working with a really small sample, it's probably not as much a problem as are other kinds of errors. Fortunately, you can

**statistic** A characteristic or measure of a sample.

**sampling error** The difference between results obtained from a sample and results that would have been obtained had information been gathered from or about every member of the population.

**sampling frame** The list of population elements from which a sample will be drawn; the list might consist of geographic areas, institutions, individuals, or other units.

estimate sampling error fairly easily—provided that you've drawn the right kind of sample. We'll get to this shortly.

## 14-2 Identifying the Sampling Frame

Once you've carefully defined the population, the next step is to find an adequate **sampling frame**, a listing of population elements from which you'll draw the sample. Unfortunately, perfect sampling frames often don't exist except in unusual circumstances. That makes developing an acceptable sampling frame one of your most important and creative tasks. For instance, trying to survey individuals who have visited a specific department store in the last 60 days is very challenging. No list exists of this group. Thus, the sampling frame is used like a fisherman uses a large net. Not every fish caught will be kept but casting a wide net is necessary to find qualified individuals.

Sometimes you'll work with sampling frames that have been developed by companies that specialize in compiling databases and then selling the names, addresses, phone numbers, and/or e-mail addresses. For example, infoUSA, a database company located near Omaha, Nebraska, employs over 350 researchers who gather information from a broad range of sources; they call businesses to verify the accuracy of the information (over 24 million phone calls per year). As a result, you can easily develop a sampling frame for a fairly specific population of businesses based on the variables coded

**Exhibit 14.3** ▶ The Relationship Between Populations and Samples

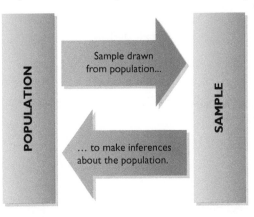

in the company's database. The company also maintains lists of consumers that can be selected using a variety of different characteristics.

## 14-3 Selecting a Sampling Procedure

Once you've made the decision to pursue a sample (rather than a census), defined the population, and identified a sampling frame, your next task is to choose a particular sampling procedure. Because your client will be interested in what would likely be true for the whole population rather than just the sample, it's important to draw the right kind of sample. Sampling techniques can be divided into two broad categories: probability and nonprobability samples. Exhibit 14.4 shows the basic types of samples.

### 14-3a NONPROBABILITY SAMPLES

**Nonprobability samples** involve personal judgment somewhere in the selection process. Not all elements have an opportunity to be included so we can't estimate the probability that any particular element will be included in the sample. As a result, it's impossible to assess the degree of sampling error. And that means that we can't say anything at all about what would have been true for the overall population—we're stuck with sample statistics and don't know whether they apply to the population as a whole. Managers may still choose to use the results from nonprobability samples, but they are taking risks when they do so. Foremost among these risks is attempting to apply the outcomes of the research to the population in total. This is not advisable as we can only talk about the sample, not the population.

**nonprobability sample** A sample that relies on personal judgment in the element selection process.

**convenience sample** A nonprobability sample in which population elements are included in the sample because they were readily available.

Three common types of nonprobability samples are convenience samples, judgment samples, and quota samples.

**Convenience Samples** With **convenience samples**, the name says it all: Being included in the sample is a matter of convenience. People or objects are selected for the sample because they happen to be in the right place at the right time to be included. Convenience samples are easy—just go out and find a location where lots of people who are likely to be members of the population are located and do interviews or pass out surveys. Lots of organizations put surveys on web sites so that people who visit the sites can respond electronically—but what about people who don't visit the web site? Still, sometimes convenience samples are just fine. For instance, convenience samples are commonly used with exploratory research, when the goal is to generate insights or to develop hypotheses.

> Managers may still choose to use the results from nonprobability samples, but they are taking risks when they do so.

Problems arise, however, when people begin to draw important conclusions based on data from convenience samples. The main problem is that we have no way of knowing if those included in a convenience sample are representative of the larger target population. As a simple example, passing out surveys to passersby at the corner of Manvel Avenue and Tenth Street in a certain city during business hours on a Tuesday means that anyone who happened *not* to be at that corner during that time period had no chance of participating. It's very likely that important points of view may have been missed.

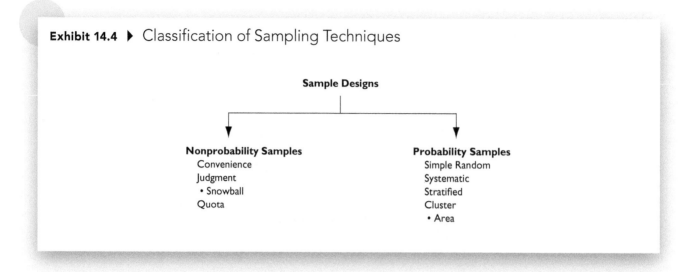

**Exhibit 14.4** ▶ Classification of Sampling Techniques

## Judgment Samples

With **judgment samples**, the sample elements are hand-picked by the researcher because she believes that they can serve the research purpose. Procter & Gamble (P&G) used this method once when it advertised for interns ages 13 to 17 from the area around its Cincinnati headquarters. The company selected a group of teenagers to serve as a kind of consumer panel. Working 10 hours a week in exchange for $1,000 and a trip to a concert, they reviewed television commercials, visited the mall with P&G managers to study retail displays, tested new products, and discussed their purchasing behavior. By selecting the panel members through a hiring process rather than randomly, the company could focus on traits it considered helpful—for example, the teenagers' ability to articulate their views clearly—but with the risk that their views might not be representative of their age group.[1]

A **snowball sample** is a judgment sample that is sometimes used to sample special populations, in particular those that are difficult to find and identify. This type of judgment sample relies on the researcher's ability to locate an initial set of respondents with the desired characteristics. These individuals are then asked to help identify others with the desired characteristics. When the overall number of people who qualify as members of the population is relatively small and there isn't a valid list of these people, a snowball sample might be the most efficient way to draw a sample.

As long as the researcher is at the early stages of research when ideas or insights are being sought—and when the researcher realizes its limitations—the judgment sample is perfectly appropriate. In some cases, it may be about the only way to develop a sample of people who meet specific criteria that don't occur frequently and/or cannot easily be observed. A judgment sample becomes dangerous, however, when it is used in descriptive or causal studies and its weaknesses are ignored.

## Quota Samples

Researchers sometimes use a **quota sample** that mirrors the population on one or more important aspects. For example, if you are asked to draw a quota sample of 1,000 undergraduate students, you'll make sure that your sample contains the right proportions of freshmen, sophomores, juniors, and seniors. You might also want to ensure that you have the right proportions of men and women in the sample, or maybe you'd want to have the right proportions of students from the various colleges or majors across campus. The goal would be to build a sample that looks like the larger population of students. And once you've identified the kinds of students that you need—that is, you've developed a quota for different types of people to be included—you're ready to go.

Many online panels in use today are essentially large quota samples. The better panels are constructed by asking a potential panel member to opt in and then comparing her data against U.S. Census demographic characteristics. These panels are widely used in both consumer and business research and often contain millions of panel members.

Note, however, that the specific sample elements to be used in a quota sample are left to the discretion of the researcher. That's what makes a

**judgment sample**
A nonprobability sample in which the sample elements are handpicked because they are expected to serve the research purpose.

**snowball sample**
A judgment sample that relies on the researcher's ability to locate an initial set of respondents with the desired characteristics.

**quota sample** A nonprobability sample chosen so that the proportion of sample elements with certain characteristics is about the same as the proportion of the elements with the characteristics in the target population.

## Manager's Focus

Each of the sampling methods discussed in this chapter can be useful in the right circumstances. What you need to understand, then, are the situations in which each is appropriate. You have just learned that for each type of nonprobability sample there is no way to know or estimate the likelihood of selecting or not selecting specific population members for inclusion in the sample. As a result, you have no way of assessing sampling error. This does not mean nonprobability samples are unrepresentative. It is possible for them to be highly representative, but the likelihood of this occurring is lower, and there is simply no way to assess this likelihood.

As a result, nonprobability samples are most useful when it is not necessary to assume responses came from a representative sample. This is only the case when we are conducting exploratory research when our primary aim is to gain tentative insights about what might be happening or important in a market situation. Nonprobability samples should be avoided when the purpose is to describe or profile a population or to identify cause-and-effect relationships between variables. In order to be confident in our descriptions of a population or in our inferences about what marketing variables cause specific outcomes, we need information about the

probability of population members being included in the sample. This means probability samples are more useful when conducting descriptive or causal studies.

Much too commonly, nonprobability samples, particularly convenience samples, are used in descriptive and causal studies in an effort to save time and money. If a sampling frame is available from which a probability sample can be drawn, it isn't smart to trade off information about sample representativeness in favor of time or monetary savings. It is dangerous to make inferences about a population based on data from a nonprobability sample. If you choose to do so, you should understand that the little bit of money saved by employing a nonprobability sample may be offset by the costs of taking inappropriate marketing actions based on imprecise statistical estimates. In the long run, it is in your organization's best interest to invest in a quality probability sample to facilitate effective decision making. If you face a situation where it is very difficult or impossible to generate a probability sample, you should at least invest the time and money necessary to compare your nonprobability sample's characteristics against external information sources (such as census data) to determine how representative it is on key demographic or other characteristics.

---

quota sample a nonprobability sampling plan. And even though the resulting sample *looks* like the overall population on certain key aspects, it may not accurately represent other aspects of the population.

### 14-3b PROBABILITY SAMPLES

In a **probability sample**, each member of the target population has a *known, nonzero* chance of being included in the sample. The chances of each member of the target population being included in the sample may not be equal, but everyone has some chance of being included. Plus, there is a random component in how population elements are selected for the sample to ensure that they are selected objectively and not according to the whims of the researcher or fieldworker. Because of this objectivity, we can make inferences to the larger population based on the results from the sample and estimate the likely amount of sampling error.

Probability samples depend on the sampling distribution of the particular statistic being

**probability sample** A sample in which each target population element has a known, nonzero chance of being included in the sample.

**simple random sample** A probability sampling plan in which each unit included in the population has a known and equal chance of being selected for the sample.

considered for the ability to draw inferences about the larger population. That is, we'll be able to project the range within which the population parameter is likely to fall in the population based on the sample statistic. (This range is known as the *confidence interval*; we'll discuss the calculation of confidence intervals later on in the book.) We discuss the basics of the sampling distribution in much more detail in Appendix 14A. In this section, we'll introduce several different types of probability samples.

### Simple Random Samples

Most people have had experience with **simple random samples** either in beginning statistics courses or in reading about results from such samples in newspapers or magazines. In a simple random sample, each unit included in the sample has a known and equal chance of being selected for study, and every combination of population elements is a sample possibility. For example, if we wanted a simple random sample of all students enrolled in a particular college, we might have a computer pick a sample randomly from a list of students in that college.

Drawing a simple random sample depends mainly on having a good sampling frame. For some populations, this isn't a problem—a list of population members is readily available. For many target populations, however, a list of population elements simply doesn't exist, and you'll need to resort to other sampling methods. If the population is moderate to large in size, you'll normally use a computer to randomly select the sample from the sampling frame, so having a digital version of the sampling frame is a real advantage.

## Systematic Samples

Suppose you were asked to conduct telephone interviews with 250 college students at a particular school and that the university published a directory that contained the names and telephone numbers of all 5,000 of its students. If you had access to a computer file containing the information, it would be a relatively easy matter to draw a simple random sample from the list. If you don't have such a computer file, however, drawing a simple random sample isn't so simple. It is difficult to randomly select each sample member.

A **systematic sample** offers an easy, but very effective, solution in situations like this. With a systematic sample, you'll randomly select the first population element to be included in the sample and then select every $k$th element following it in the sampling frame. In our example, let's assume for a moment that we'll be able to interview all 250 college students who are selected for the sample. We'll end up interviewing one out of every 20 students on campus (5,000/250 = 20). So, you would randomly select one of the first 20 names in the student directory, then count down 20 names on the list and select that name, count down 20 more names and select that name, and so on, until you have gone through the entire directory. (It may not sound like it, but this is *much* easier than trying to randomly select each member of the sample by hand.)

So what makes this a probabilistic sampling plan? It's because the first element is randomly selected, and every other element selected for the sample is a function of the first element, which makes them all randomly selected, in effect.

Calculating the **sampling interval** (i.e., $k$, the number of names to count when selecting the sample members) is easy—sort of. In general, we simply divide the number of population elements in the sampling frame by the number of elements that we need to draw to obtain the sample size we want. In the previous example, $k = 5,000/250$, so our sampling interval was 20. Here's where it gets a little tricky, though. Remember how we

**systematic sample**
A probability sampling plan in which every $k$th element in the population is selected for the sample pool after a random start.

**sampling interval**
The number of population elements to count ($k$) when selecting the sample members in a systematic sample.

**total sampling elements (TSE)** The number of population elements that must be drawn from the population and included in the initial sample pool in order to end up with the desired sample size.

assumed that we could conduct telephone interviews with all 250 students selected for the sample? For lots of reasons, it almost never works out that way.

If we selected only 250 students for our sample, it is almost a certainty that we'll end up with fewer than 250 respondents—maybe a whole lot fewer. Why? Some people won't be home to answer their telephones, even if we try multiple times to reach them. Others will have changed telephone numbers since the directory was published. A few people will refuse to answer our questions because they are too busy or just don't care to help. As a result, in almost all cases, we need to start with a larger number of population elements in our initial sample pool in order to end up with the desired sample size. We refer to the total number of elements to be selected for inclusion in the initial sample pool as **total sampling elements (TSE)**.

The notion of TSE is general and applies to any type of sample, not just systematic samples. Anytime it is necessary to select a larger initial sample in order to reach the necessary sample size, the calculation of TSE becomes important. Calculating TSE typically requires making predictions about the proportion of sample elements that (1) have incorrect contact information (telephone number, e-mail address, or mailing address); (2) are ineligible because they don't meet criteria for inclusion in the sample; (3) refuse to participate; and (4) cannot be contacted, even after multiple tries.

The formula for TSE looks like this:

$$\text{total sample elements} = (TSE) = \frac{\text{sample size}}{(1 - BCI)(1 - I)(1 - R)(1 - NC)}$$

where $BCI$ = the estimated proportion of bad contact information (wrong telephone numbers, mailing or e-mail addresses), $I$ = the estimated proportion of ineligible elements in the sampling frame (i.e., people or entities that don't meet the criteria to be population members but were included in the sampling frame anyway), $R$ = the estimated proportion of refusals, and $NC$ = the estimated proportion of elements that cannot be contacted after repeated attempts.

Returning to the current problem, we need a sample of 250 respondents from the 5,000 students in the directory. Even if the directory is updated annually, we should assume that some of the telephone numbers won't be working because some people may have left school and others will have changed telephone numbers. Let's assume that percentage is 15%; thus, $BCI = 0.15$. Because some of the people who left school (and are no longer eligible to be included in the population) might still have working telephone numbers, we also need to include an ineligibility proportion. That proportion is likely to be low, however, so we'll set it at 2% ($I = 0.02$). Refusal rates vary from study to study, but we'll assume a refusal rate of 20%

($R = 0.20$) for this study. Finally, and this is often the biggest issue of all for telephone studies—we'll assume that we won't be able to reach 30% of the people selected for the sample; thus, $NC = 0.30$. Putting it all together, we need to draw a total of 536 students from the population in order to obtain a sample size of 250:

$$\text{total sample elements} = (TSE) = \frac{250}{(1 - 0.15)(1 - 0.02)(1 - 0.20)(1 - 0.30)}$$

Once we know how many elements we need to draw from the population, it's a simple matter to determine the sampling interval:

$$\text{sampling interval} = \frac{\text{number of elements in the sampling frame}}{\text{total sampling elements}}$$

$$= \frac{5,000}{536} = 9.3$$

To draw the sample, you would randomly select one of the first nine names in the directory, maybe using a random-number generator on a computer or even something as simple as pulling a number out of a hat. Once that name is selected, you'll draw every ninth name following the first one. Because drawing every ninth name will result in a list of 556 students instead of the 536 that you want, you might choose to count down nine names to get the second sample element and another nine names to get the third sample element—and then count down 10 names to get the fourth. It doesn't matter, provided that you follow the same pattern throughout the whole sampling frame (i.e., down nine, down nine, down 10, down nine, down nine, down 10, and so on); each name after the first is still a function of the position of the randomly selected first sample element.

## Stratified Samples

Our goal in drawing a probabilistic sample from a population is to describe the population's characteristics, or parameters, based on statistics calculated from the sample. Stratified samples sometimes allow researchers to do this more efficiently. A **stratified sample** is a probability sample in which (1) the population is divided into mutually exclusive and exhaustive subgroups (i.e., each population element fits into one—and only one—subgroup), and (2) samples are chosen from each of the subgroups.

Stratified samples take advantage of the fact that, all else being equal, smaller samples are required to estimate a population parameter if there is little variation on the characteristic in the group being sampled. (If everyone's opinion is exactly the same about some issue, we only need to ask one person to be able to project to the population.) So, if we can find a way to group together

**stratified sample**
A probability sample in which (1) the population is divided into mutually exclusive and exhaustive subsets, and (2) a probabilistic sample of elements is chosen independently from each subset.

**cluster sample** A probability sampling plan in which (1) the parent population is divided into mutually exclusive and exhaustive subsets, and (2) a random sample of one or more subsets (clusters) is selected.

population elements that are similar on some characteristic we're trying to study, we can be more efficient by drawing a smaller sample within that subgroup. We can use the extra efficiency in a couple of ways: either by increasing sample size in subgroups that have greater variation on the characteristic to get greater precision or confidence (we'll discuss these notions later) or by saving money thanks to the overall lower sample size.

To make this work, you'll have to be able to group population elements that are likely to be similar to one another on the parameter of interest into subgroups. That is, the subgroups should be *homogenous within* the groups. Once the subgroups have been formed, samples are taken from each of them so that all subgroups are represented in the final sample.

There is one other reason that stratified samples might be used, and this has more to do with effectiveness than efficiency. Sometimes it's necessary to work with stratified samples as a means of ensuring that particular categories of respondents are included in the final sample. Suppose, for example, that a manufacturer of diamond rings wants to conduct a study of sales of the product by social class. Unless special precautions are taken, it's possible that the upper class—which represents only a small percentage of the total population—won't be represented at all or will be represented by too few cases. Yet this may be an extremely important segment to the ring manufacturer. Stratified sampling is one way of ensuring adequate representation from each subgroup of interest.

## Cluster Samples

Sometimes researchers use **cluster samples**, another type of probability sampling. Cluster sampling is similar to stratified sampling in that the population is divided into mutually exclusive and exhaustive subgroups, but the similarities stop there. With cluster sampling, you'll randomly select one or more subgroups and then either select all the elements included in those subgroups for the sample (*one-stage cluster sampling*) or a probabilistic sample of elements from the randomly selected subgroups for the sample (*two-stage cluster sampling*).

Notice the difference here. With stratified sampling, a sample of elements is selected from each subgroup, but with cluster sampling a sample is selected only from the randomly selected subgroups. Because of this, it is important that each cluster reflect the diversity of the whole population. The goal with cluster sampling is thus to have clusters that are as heterogeneous as possible on the key issues. That way, no matter which cluster(s) are randomly selected, the full range is represented. (Recall that we wanted the subgroups to be as homogeneous within each subgroup as possible with stratified sampling.)

An **area sample** is a special form of cluster sample in which geographic areas (city blocks, neighborhoods, housing additions, etc.) serve as the clusters. With area samples, you'll randomly select one or more geographic clusters and then take population elements from these clusters for the sample. This approach is particularly useful when no good sampling frame is available. Suppose, for example, that you needed to draw a sample of households in Chicago, Illinois. One approach would be to identify the residential areas throughout the city and then randomly identify one or more of these areas. The next step would be to contact a probabilistic sample (two-stage sampling) or all (one-stage sampling) of the households in the selected areas, maybe by knocking on doors, gathering addresses for paper-based mail surveys, or some other method. Nielsen has used two-stage area sampling to collect its television viewership data.

The difficulty with area samples is that the people who live in the same area often share many characteristics. As a result, the area clusters often don't represent the full variability on important parameters that we'd like to see. Still, unless the degree of homogeneity is very high within areas, we can often reduce (but not eliminate) the problem by drawing from a larger number of clusters.

**area sample** A form of cluster sampling in which areas (e.g., census tracts, blocks) serve as the primary sampling units. Using maps, the population is divided into mutually exclusive and exhaustive areas, and a random sample of areas is selected.

**precision** The degree of error in an estimate of a population parameter.

**confidence** The degree to which one can feel confident that an estimate approximates the true value.

## 14-4 Determining How Big a Sample You Need

The next step of the process is to determine the necessary sample size for your study. You might be tempted to assume that the sample should be as large as the client can afford, but there's more to it than that—and in many cases the advantages of a larger sample (i.e., lowered sampling error) don't outweigh the costs of gathering it.

Computer programs are routinely used to calculate the needed sample size in a given situation, but in case you really, really want the formulas, we've included them in Appendix 14B. It's important, though, that you understand the simple factors that influence the size of the sample you need. Looking at the formulas in Appendix 14B is a good way to understand how these factors influence sample size.

### 14-4a BASIC CONSIDERATIONS IN DETERMINING SAMPLE SIZE

Three basic factors affect the size of sample needed when working with a probabilistic sample. The first of these, the amount of diversity or variation of the parameter in question within the population, is beyond your control. As we noted earlier, when there is very little variation across elements on some characteristic, it doesn't take a very large sample to estimate the value of that characteristic.

As variation increases, larger samples are required, all else being equal.

A second consideration is how precise the estimate must be. This depends on the importance of the issue. For example, suppose that you were asked to develop a profile of the "average" diner in a particular restaurant. One thing the client will probably want to know is the mean income of the restaurant's diners. Should your estimate be within $100, high or low, of the true population value? Or can you get by with a less precise estimate—say, within $500 or $1,000 of the true value? The closer we need the estimate to be to the true value in the population (i.e., the more **precision** we need), the larger the sample that will be required, all else being equal.

The other factor that affects sample size is the degree of confidence you'd like to have in the estimate. By **confidence**, we mean the degree of certainty that the true value of the parameter that we are estimating falls within the precision range that we have established. For example, suppose that you have decided that in describing the average diner in the restaurant, an acceptable precision range for mean income is ±$500 and that the mean income in the sample is $45,300. Does mean income *necessarily* fall between $44,800 and $45,800 in the population? No, it doesn't. Because we are working with the sampling distribution of the sample means, however, we can have a certain level of confidence that the population parameter does fall within the precision range that we have established. How much confidence? With a given precision range, the amount of confidence is directly related to the size of the sample. The bigger the sample, the more certain we can be that the true value in the population falls within the precision range, which is calculated based on the sample estimate.

At any given sample size, there is a trade-off between the degree of confidence and the degree of precision. The most precise measure of mean income for our restaurant diners would be a *point estimate* of the mean, which is an estimate that involves a single value with no associated bounds of error. In our study, the sample mean income was $45,300. This point estimate is our best guess about the overall population mean, but it is almost certain to be off by at least a little bit, and thus, we can have virtually no confidence in it despite its preciseness. On the other hand, we might have complete confidence in an estimate that the population mean income is between zero and $10 billion—but that estimate is too imprecise to be of any practical value. The desire for precision and confidence must be balanced. It might be entirely reasonable, for example, to end up being 95% confident that the population parameter lies between $44,800 and $45,800.

In sum, in order to determine the necessary sample size, you need three basic pieces of information: (1) how

## Manager's Focus

Let's assume that your company initiated an annual national tracking study 2 years ago. The proportion of your customers who were "Dissatisfied" or "Very Dissatisfied" (the bottom two points on a five-point scale) with your services was 0.23 the first year and 0.28 the second year. You have since implemented some service changes with the goal of reducing this proportion to 0.15 this year.

The sample size was set at 400 for each of the first two tracking surveys simply because that was as large as your research budget would allow. This year, there is more money available, and you would like to determine the appropriate sample size for the tracking study using a statistical approach. You talked with the manager of the field research firm that administered the survey last year. She said it was somewhat difficult to reach the designated respondents in the sample, and on average each telephone interviewer was able to obtain only 2.13 completed questionnaires per hour. Assuming the same response rate this year, she indicated it would cost $32.00 per completed questionnaire.

You decide to use the formula presented in Appendix 14B to help you determine the appropriate sample size. After reflecting a while, you decide you definitely want the degree of confidence to be 95%. You also conclude it would be fine to have a precision level of ±0.04.

Using 0.15 (the level to which you are trying to reduce dissatisfaction) as the estimate of the population proportion, you calculate you should have a sample size of 306. This means the data collection expenses would be $9,792 (roughly $3,000 less than last year).

These calculations were much lower than you were expecting, so you decide it would be nice to increase the level of precision to ±0.02. The other specs are kept the same, and you calculate the sample size should be 1,225. This would cause the data collection costs to jump to $39,200. Staggered by this increase in sample size and data collection expenses, you slightly decrease the precision level to ±0.03. Keeping the other specs unchanged, you calculate a new sample size of 544 with associated data collection expenses of $17,408.

You may be surprised to see how such small changes in your specifications can produce such large changes in the sample size and corresponding data collection costs. Which sample size should you ask your researchers to generate? There is a tendency among managers to believe that larger sample sizes are always preferable. But, you should ask yourself if a small increase in precision is worth paying substantially more for data collection. If the increased precision is unlikely to change how you will respond to the market information, then it is poor financial management to pay for a substantially larger sample.

---

homogeneous or similar the population is on the characteristic to be estimated, (2) how much precision is needed in the estimate, and (3) how confident you need to be that the true value falls within the precision range you've established. Increases in desired precision, confidence, or the variation of the characteristic in the population lead to increases in the necessary sample size. Armed with this information, it is relatively easy to calculate a desired sample size using a computer program.

### 14-4b MULTIPLE ESTIMATES IN A SINGLE PROJECT

You might have noticed that our discussion of precision, confidence, and variation referred to determining sample size for a single parameter. Most projects, however, ask questions about lots of characteristics, not just a single one. A natural question, then, is "How do I calculate sample size if I'm asking more than one question on a survey?"

Because sample size is calculated based on individual items, you will usually end up with different sample size requirements for many of the items when you are measuring multiple characteristics in a study. Somehow you'll have to come up with an overall sample size for the project. The best approach is to focus on the variables that are the most critical and select a sample that is big enough to estimate them with the required precision and confidence.

### 14-4c POPULATION SIZE AND SAMPLE SIZE

You may not have noticed it before, but so far we haven't talked at all about the size of the population as we've discussed determining the necessary sample size. It may seem odd, but the size of the population has no direct effect on the size of the sample (with one exception that we'll discuss shortly).

As we've noted before, if all population elements have exactly the same value of the characteristic, then a sample of one is all that is needed to represent the population. This is true whether there are 1,000, 10,000, or 100,000 elements in the population. As a result, it is desired precision, confidence, and variation of the characteristic in the population that drive sample size, not the size of the population itself. Many managers have a hard time accepting this because it isn't intuitive.

> It is desired precision, confidence, and variation of the characteristic in the population that drive sample size, not the size of the population itself.

The exception to this rule occurs when the calculated sample size is more than about 5–10% of the population. In this case, the calculated sample size can safely be reduced using the finite population correction factor. If, for example, the population contained 100 elements and you needed a sample of 20 elements, fewer than 20 observations would, in fact, be taken if the finite population correction factor were used. The good news is that computer programs can also handle this calculation in practice.

## 14-4d  OTHER APPROACHES TO DETERMINING SAMPLE SIZE

So far, we've taken a statistical approach to calculating sample size. Researchers and companies often use other approaches to determine sample size. We'll discuss a few of these in this section.

Marketing research can be an expensive proposition. For the most part, data collection is a variable cost; the bigger the sample size, the greater the cost. Because it takes about the same amount of money to design a data collection form for a project with 100 respondents as it does for a project with 10,000 respondents, when the research budget is limited, sample size is often a function of the amount of money "left over" after taking other research costs into consideration. So, one common method of determining sample size, unfortunately, is to take the remaining budget and divide it by the expected cost per contact of the method of administration.

Another consideration is the type of analysis to be conducted on the data. One very common type of analysis (cross-tab analysis) requires that a minimum number of respondents (say, 10 to 20) fall into each of the different categories based on the variables used in the analysis (this will make more sense once you've read the analysis chapters). As a result, the sample size must be big enough to ensure that the minimum requirements are met for the particular type of analysis to be conducted.

One final method used by some researchers to determine the size of the sample is to use the size that others have used for similar studies in the past. Although this may be different from the ideal size in a given problem, the fact that the sample size is in line with that used for similar studies is psychologically comforting, particularly to inexperienced researchers. One of us once had a client who had just taken a marketing research position with an organization. When asked about the sample size that she had selected on a particular project, the client responded with a particular number of paper-based surveys that were going to be sent by mail. When asked how she had arrived at that number, she said, "Because we always send out that many." Many companies operate in a similar fashion.

Using history as a guide might not be a bad strategy. At some point in time, someone may have determined that a certain number of mail surveys sent will deliver enough confidence and precision for the types of assessment needed by the client company. Until things change—more confidence or precision is needed, response rates decrease significantly, or a parameter with much wider variation in the population is estimated—the necessary sample size probably won't change much.

# Summary

## Learning Objective 1

**Explain the difference between a parameter and a statistic.**

A parameter is a characteristic of the population; if it were possible to take measures from all population members without error, we could arrive at the true value of a parameter. A statistic is a characteristic or measure of a sample; statistics are used to estimate population parameters.

## Learning Objective 2

**Explain the difference between a probability sample and a nonprobability sample.**

In a probability sample, each member of the target population has a known, nonzero chance of being included in the sample. The chances of each member of the target population being included in the sample may not be equal, but everyone has a known probability of inclusion. With nonprobability samples, on the other hand, there is no way of estimating the probability that any population element will be included in the sample. Thus, there is no way of ensuring that the sample is representative of the target population. All nonprobability samples rely on personal judgment at some point in the sample-selection process.

## Learning Objective 3

**List the primary types of nonprobability samples.**

The primary types of nonprobability samples include convenience samples, judgment samples (including snowball samples), and quota samples.

## Learning Objective 4

**List the primary types of probability samples.**

The primary types of probability samples include simple random samples, systematic samples, stratified samples, and cluster samples (including area samples).

## Learning Objective 5

**Discuss the concept of total sampling elements (TSE).**

Because it is rare that all of the people who have been selected to participate in a study will do so, it is usually necessary to draw a larger pool of sample elements from the sampling frame than is actually needed in the study. The larger set drawn from the sampling frame is referred to as total sampling elements.

## Learning Objective 6

**Cite three factors that influence the necessary sample size.**

The three factors that influence sample size are the desired degree of precision, the desired degree of confidence, and the degree of variability in the population on the parameter in question.

## Learning Objective 7

**Explain the relationship between population size and sample size.**

In most instances, the size of the population has no direct effect on the size of the sample.

## Key Terms

census (page 204)
sample (page 204)
population (page 205)
parameters (page 206)
statistics (page 206)
sampling error (page 206)
sampling frame (page 206)
nonprobability sample (page 207)
convenience sample (page 207)
judgment sample (page 209)
snowball sample (page 209)
quota sample (page 209)
probability sample (page 209)
simple random sample (page 209)
systematic sample (page 210)
sampling interval (page 210)
total sampling elements (TSE) (page 210)
stratified sample (page 211)
cluster sample (page 211)
area sample (page 212)
precision (page 212)
confidence (page 212)

## Review Questions

1. What is a census? What is a sample?

2. Why is it important to carefully define the population?

3. What is the difference between a parameter and a statistic? How are they related?

4. What distinguishes a probability sample from a nonprobability sample?

5. What are the main types of nonprobability samples? What are their differences?

6. What are the main types of probability samples? What are their differences?

7. How do cluster samples differ from stratified samples?

8. What is the notion of total sampling elements (TSE)? Why is TSE calculated?

9. In determining sample size, what three basic factors must you consider?

10. What effect would relaxing the precision with which a population mean or proportion is estimated have on sample size? What about decreasing the degree of confidence from 95% to 90%?

11. What is the relationship between population size and sample size?

12. What are some other methods of determining sample size?

# Endnote

1. Neff, J. (1999, June 28). P&G enlists 13-year-olds in summer intern jobs. *Advertising Age*, 20.

# Basics of the Sampling Distribution

In this appendix, we'll share a few of the statistical principles that make it possible to make projections to the population based on results obtained from a sample. We'll spare you many of the details, but these concepts are so important that they merit more attention than we gave them in the chapter.

Consider the hypothetical population of 20 individuals shown in Exhibit 14A.1. Now, most of the populations that marketers work with are much larger than this, but a small population allows us to calculate the true population parameter (mean monthly gross income in this example) and compare it to the estimates we would obtain from various samples drawn from the population.

For the population included in Exhibit 14A.1, the population mean ($\mu$) is calculated as follows:

$$\text{population mean } (\mu) = \frac{\text{sum of population elements}}{\text{number of population elements}}$$

$$= \frac{\$5,600 + \$6,000 + \ldots \$13,200}{20} = \$9,400$$

Next, let's see how well we can estimate this value based on samples drawn from the population.

## A-1 Derived Population

The *derived population* consists of all the possible samples that can be drawn from the population under a given sampling plan. As discussed in the chapter, a statistic is a characteristic or measure of a sample; we use sample statistics to estimate population parameters. The value of a statistic used to estimate a particular parameter depends on the particular sample selected from the parent population under the sampling plan specified. Different samples yield different statistics and different estimates of the same population parameter.

Consider the derived population of all possible samples that could be drawn from our population using a sample size of $n = 2$ and a simple random sample. Suppose that the information for each population element—in this case, the person's name and gross monthly income—is written on a disk, placed in a jar, and shaken thoroughly. The researcher then reaches into the jar, pulls out one

**Exhibit 14A.1 ▶ Population**

| POPULATION ELEMENT | MONTHLY INCOME (DOLLARS) |
|---|---|
| 1 A | $ 5,600 |
| 2 B | 6,000 |
| 3 C | 6,400 |
| 4 D | 6,800 |
| 5 E | 7,200 |
| 6 F | 7,600 |
| 7 G | 8,000 |
| 8 H | 8,400 |
| 9 I | 8,800 |
| 10 J | 9,200 |
| 11 K | 9,600 |
| 12 L | 10,000 |
| 13 M | 10,400 |
| 14 N | 10,800 |
| 15 O | 11,200 |
| 16 P | 11,600 |
| 17 Q | 12,000 |
| 18 R | 12,400 |
| 19 S | 12,800 |
| 20 T | 13,200 |

disk, records the information on it, and puts it aside. She does the same with a second disk. Then she places both disks back in the jar and repeats the process. Exhibit 14A.2 shows the many possible results—190 combinations—of following this procedure. In addition, the exhibit includes the mean income for each sample combination. So, for sample number 1, which includes population elements A and B, the sample mean $\bar{x}$ is calculated as follows:

$$\text{sample mean } (\bar{x}) = \frac{\text{sum of sample elements}}{\text{number of elements in sample}}$$
$$= \frac{\$5,600 + \$6,000}{2} = \$5,800$$

Exhibit 14A.3 displays the sample mean monthly income for samples 25, 62, 108, 147, and 189. It also indicates the amount of error that would occur if each of the samples was used to estimate the population parameter.

There are a couple of things to keep in mind about the derived population. Although we demonstrated the concept by drawing all possible samples under our sampling plan (see Exhibit 14A.2), it is not necessary to do so in practice. Instead, we draw a single sample and rely on

**Exhibit 14A.2** ▶ Derived Population of All Possible Samples of Size $n = 2$ With Simple Random Selection

| SAMPLE | ELEMENTS | MEAN | SAMPLE | ELEMENTS | MEAN | SAMPLE | ELEMENTS | MEAN | SAMPLE | ELEMENTS | MEAN |
|---|---|---|---|---|---|---|---|---|---|---|---|
| 1 | AB | 5,800 | 49 | CO | 8,800 | 97 | FR | 10,000 | 145 | JT | 11,200 |
| 2 | AC | 6,000 | 50 | CP | 9,000 | 98 | FS | 10,200 | 146 | KL | 9,800 |
| 3 | AD | 6,200 | 51 | CQ | 9,200 | 99 | FT | 10,400 | 147 | KM | 10,000 |
| 4 | AE | 6,400 | 52 | CR | 9,400 | 100 | GH | 8,200 | 148 | KN | 10,200 |
| 5 | AF | 6,600 | 53 | CS | 9,600 | 101 | GI | 8,400 | 149 | KO | 10,400 |
| 6 | AG | 6,800 | 54 | CT | 9,800 | 102 | GJ | 8,600 | 150 | KP | 10,600 |
| 7 | AH | 7,000 | 55 | DE | 7,000 | 103 | GK | 8,800 | 151 | KQ | 10,800 |
| 8 | AI | 7,200 | 56 | DF | 7,200 | 104 | GL | 9,000 | 152 | KR | 11,000 |
| 9 | AJ | 7,400 | 57 | DG | 7,400 | 105 | GM | 9,200 | 153 | KS | 11,200 |
| 10 | AK | 7,600 | 58 | DH | 7,600 | 106 | GN | 9,400 | 154 | KT | 11,400 |
| 11 | AL | 7,800 | 59 | DI | 7,800 | 107 | GO | 9,600 | 155 | LM | 10,200 |
| 12 | AM | 8,000 | 60 | DJ | 8,000 | 108 | GP | 9,800 | 156 | LN | 10,400 |
| 13 | AN | 8,200 | 61 | DK | 8,200 | 109 | GQ | 10,000 | 157 | LO | 10,600 |
| 14 | AO | 8,400 | 62 | DL | 8,400 | P10 | GR | 10,200 | 158 | LP | 10,800 |
| 15 | AP | 8,600 | 63 | DM | 8,600 | 111 | GS | 10,400 | 159 | LQ | 11,000 |
| 16 | AQ | 8,800 | 64 | DN | 8,800 | 112 | GT | 10,600 | 160 | LR | 11,200 |
| 17 | AR | 9,000 | 65 | DO | 9,000 | 113 | HI | 8,600 | 161 | LS | 11,400 |
| 18 | AS | 9,200 | 66 | DP | 9,200 | 114 | HJ | 8,800 | 162 | LT | 11,600 |
| 19 | AT | 9,400 | 67 | DQ | 9,400 | 115 | HK | 9,000 | 163 | MN | 10,600 |
| 20 | BC | 6,200 | 68 | DR | 9,600 | 116 | HL | 9,200 | 164 | MO | 10,800 |
| 21 | BD | 6,400 | 69 | DS | 9,800 | 117 | HM | 9,400 | 165 | MP | 11,000 |
| 22 | BE | 6,600 | 70 | DT | 10,000 | 118 | HN | 9,600 | 166 | MQ | 11,200 |
| 23 | BF | 6,800 | 71 | EF | 7,400 | 119 | HO | 9,800 | 167 | MR | 11,400 |
| 24 | BG | 7,000 | 72 | EG | 7,600 | 120 | HP | 10,000 | 168 | MS | 11,600 |
| 25 | BH | 7,200 | 73 | EH | 7,800 | 121 | HQ | 10,200 | 169 | MT | 11,800 |
| 26 | BI | 7,400 | 74 | EI | 8,000 | 122 | HR | 10,400 | 170 | NO | 11,000 |
| 27 | BJ | 7,600 | 75 | EJ | 8,200 | 123 | HS | 10,600 | 171 | NP | 11,200 |
| 28 | BK | 7,800 | 76 | EK | 8,400 | 124 | HT | 10,800 | 172 | NQ | 11,400 |
| 29 | BL | 8,000 | 77 | EL | 8,600 | 125 | IJ | 9,000 | 173 | NR | 11,600 |
| 30 | BM | 8,200 | 78 | EM | 8,800 | 126 | IK | 9,200 | 174 | NS | 11,800 |
| 31 | BN | 8,400 | 79 | EN | 9,000 | 127 | IL | 9,400 | 175 | NT | 12,000 |
| 32 | BO | 8,600 | 80 | EO | 9,200 | 128 | IM | 9,600 | 176 | OP | 11,400 |
| 33 | BP | 8,800 | 81 | EP | 9,400 | 129 | IN | 9,800 | 177 | OQ | 11,600 |

| SAMPLE | ELEMENTS | MEAN | SAMPLE | ELEMENTS | MEAN | SAMPLE | ELEMENTS | MEAN | SAMPLE | ELEMENTS | MEAN |
|---|---|---|---|---|---|---|---|---|---|---|---|
| 34 | BQ | 9,000 | 82 | EQ | 9,600 | 130 | IO | 10,000 | 178 | OR | 11,800 |
| 35 | BR | 9,200 | 83 | ER | 9,800 | 131 | IP | 10,200 | 179 | OS | 12,000 |
| 36 | BS | 9,400 | 84 | ES | 10,000 | 132 | IQ | 10,400 | 180 | OT | 12,200 |
| 37 | BT | 9,600 | 85 | ET | 10,200 | 133 | IR | 10,600 | 181 | PQ | 11,800 |
| 38 | CD | 6,600 | 86 | FG | 7,800 | 134 | IS | 10,800 | 182 | PR | 12,000 |
| 39 | CE | 6,800 | 87 | FH | 8,000 | 135 | IT | 11,000 | 183 | PS | 12,200 |
| 40 | CF | 7,000 | 88 | FI | 8,200 | 136 | JK | 9,400 | 184 | PT | 12,400 |
| 41 | CG | 7,200 | 89 | FJ | 8,400 | 137 | JL | 9,600 | 185 | QR | 12,200 |
| 42 | CH | 7,400 | 90 | FK | 8,600 | 138 | JM | 9,800 | 186 | QS | 12,400 |
| 43 | CI | 7,600 | 91 | FL | 8,800 | 139 | JN | 10,000 | 187 | QT | 12,600 |
| 44 | CJ | 7,800 | 92 | FM | 9,000 | 140 | JO | 10,200 | 188 | RS | 12,600 |
| 45 | CK | 8,000 | 93 | FN | 9,200 | 141 | JP | 10,400 | 189 | RT | 12,800 |
| 46 | CL | 8,200 | 94 | FO | 9,400 | 142 | JQ | 10,600 | 190 | ST | 13,000 |
| 47 | CM | 8,400 | 95 | FP | 9,600 | 143 | JR | 10,800 | | | |
| 48 | CN | 8,600 | 96 | FQ | 9,800 | 144 | JS | 11,000 | | | |

**Exhibit 14A.3 ▶** Several Possible Samples and Their Respective Errors When Estimating the Population Mean

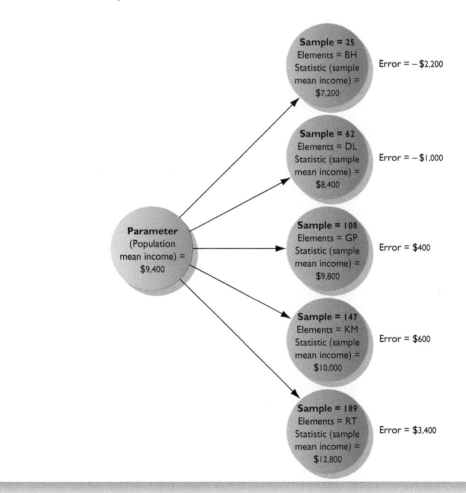

the *concept* of the derived population and the related sampling distribution to make inferences about the population based on the sample. Picking a sample of size = 2 from the population is equivalent to picking one of the 190 possible combinations out of the derived population. This fact is basic in making statistical inferences.

A second thing to note is that the derived population is defined as the population of all possible distinguishable samples that can be drawn under a *given sampling plan.* Change any part of the sampling plan and the derived population will also change. For example, with samples of size 3 instead of 2, *ABC* is a sample possibility, and there are a number of additional possibilities as well: 1,140 versus the 190 with samples of size 2. Change the method of selecting elements by using something other than simple random sampling, and the derived population will also change.

## A-2 Sample Mean Versus Population Mean

If we want to evaluate the income of those in a simple random sample, can we assume that the sample mean will equal the parent population mean? No, it's not especially likely that any particular sample will produce a sample mean that equals the population mean, but if we have drawn a probabilistic sample, certain statistical principles allow us to assume a relationship between the sample mean and population mean. But how much error is there likely to be in using the sample to estimate something about the population?

Suppose we added up all the sample means in Exhibit 14A.2 and divided by the number of samples; that is, suppose we were to average the averages. Doing this, we would get the following:

$$\frac{\$5,800 + \$6,000 + \cdots \$13,000}{190} = \$9,400$$

This is the mean of the parent population that we calculated earlier. Thus, *the mean of all possible sample means is equal to the population mean.* Note, however, that any particular estimate may be very far from the true population value—for example, the sample means for sample 1 or sample 190 provide very poor estimates of the population mean. In some cases, the true population value may even be impossible to achieve with any possible sample; this is not true in our example, however, since a number of sample possibilities—for example, sample 19—yield a sample mean that equals the population average.

Next, it is useful to look at the spread of these sample estimates, and particularly the relationship between this spread of estimates and the dispersion of incomes in the population. A very useful measure of spread is the population variance. To compute the population variance, we calculate the deviation of each value from the mean, square these deviations, sum them, and divide by the number of

values making up the sum. Letting $\sigma^2$ denote the population variance, the calculation yields:

population variance ($\sigma^2$)

$$= \frac{\text{sum of squared differences of each population element from the population mean}}{\text{number of population elements}}$$

$$= \frac{(5,600 - 9,400)^2 + (6,000 - 9,000)^2 + \cdots + (13,200 - 9,400)^2}{20}$$

$$= 5,320,000$$

The variance of *mean incomes* could be calculated similarly. That is, we could calculate the variance of mean incomes by taking the deviation of each mean around its overall mean, squaring and summing these deviations, and then dividing by the number of cases. Alternatively, we could determine the variance of mean incomes indirectly by using the variance of incomes in the population, since there is a direct relationship between the two quantities. When the sample is only a small part of the population, the variance of sample mean incomes is equal to the population variance divided by the sample size. In symbols, this means that

$$\sigma^2_x = \frac{\sigma^2}{n}$$

where $\sigma^2_x$ is the variance of sample mean incomes, while $\sigma^2$ is the variance of incomes in the population, and $n$ is the sample size. So, *the variance of sample means is related to the population variance.*

Finally, consider the distribution of the estimates from the derived population in contrast to the distribution of the mean monthly incomes in the population. Exhibit 14A.4 indicates that the population distribution, depicted by Panel A, is flat—each of the 20 values occurs once—and is symmetrical around the population mean value of $9,400. The distribution of estimates from the derived population, displayed in Panel B, was constructed by grouping the sample means from Exhibit 14A.2 into categories ($6,000 or less; $6,100 to $6,600; and so on) and then counting the number contained in each category. Panel B presents a simple bar chart, known as a histogram, showing the number of sample means that fell into each category. This is the *sampling distribution* of the statistic. Notice that *the sampling distribution is mound shaped,* even though the population distribution is flat.

The notion of sampling distribution is the single most important notion in statistics; it is the cornerstone of statistical inference procedures. If you know the sampling distribution for the statistic in question, you can make inferences about the corresponding population parameter. If, on the other hand, you only know that a particular sample

**Exhibit 14A.4** ▶ Population Distribution Versus Sampling Distribution

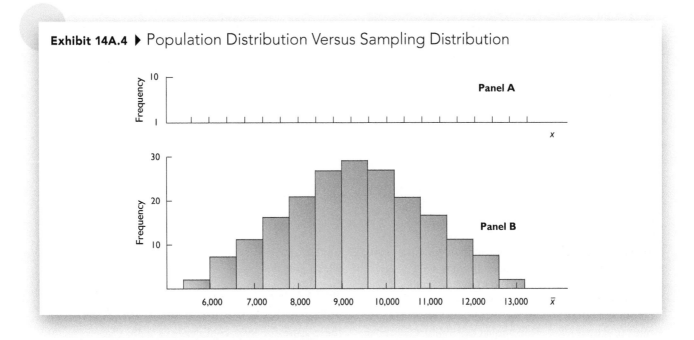

estimate will vary with repeated sampling but you have no information about *how* it will vary, then it is impossible to estimate sampling error. Because the sampling distribution of an estimate describes how that estimate will vary with repeated sampling, it provides a basis for determining the reliability of the sample estimate. This is why probability sampling plans are so important to statistical inference. When we know the probability that any population element will be included in the sample, we can derive the sampling distribution of various statistics. Researchers then rely on the sampling distributions to make inferences from single samples to population values.

## A-3 Central-Limit Theorem

The mound-shaped sampling distribution provides initial evidence that the *central-limit theorem* is in operation. The central-limit theorem holds that if simple random samples of a given size $n$ are drawn from a parent population, with mean equal to $\mu$, and variance equal to $s^2$, then when the sample size $n$ is large, the *distribution of sample means* will be approximately normally distributed with its mean equal to the population mean and its variance equal to the parent population variance divided by the sample size; that is,

$$\sigma\frac{2}{x} = \frac{\sigma^2}{n}$$

The approximation will become more and more accurate as $n$ becomes larger. Note what this means: Regardless of the shape of the parent population, the distribution of *sample means will be normal* if the sample is large enough. How large is large enough? If the distribution of the variable in the parent population is normal, then the distribution of means of samples of size $n = 1$ will be normal. If the distribution of the variable is symmetrical but not normal, then samples of very small size will produce a distribution in which the means are normally distributed. If the distribution of the variable is highly skewed in the population, then samples of a larger size will be needed.

Here's the bottom line: We can assume that the sampling distribution of sample means is normal as long as we work with a sample of sufficient size. We don't have to assume that the variable is normally distributed in the population in order to make inferences using the normal curve. Instead, we rely on the central-limit theorem and adjust the sample size according to the population distribution so that the normal curve can be assumed to hold. Fortunately, the normal distribution of the statistic occurs with samples of relatively small size—the normal standard is a sample size of 30, and sometimes even fewer are required. (You will usually need more cases than this to achieve reasonable levels of precision and confidence, but the sampling distribution becomes approximately normally distributed with around 30 cases.)

# Calculating Sample Size

Imagine that your state's department of tourism wants to know two things about hunters in your state: (1) how much do they spend on average each year for food and lodging while on hunting trips, and (2) what proportion are from out of state? Your job is to use a simple random sample to estimate the mean annual expenditures of those people and their state of residence, using a list of all those who applied for hunting licenses in the prior year.

In estimating the amount of money spent, the director of tourism wants the estimate to be within ±$25 of the population mean. She also wants to be 95% confident that the precision interval you construct will contain the true population mean. So, you already have two of the three pieces of information you need. The remaining piece of information, an estimate of the variance of money spent by the hunters, is a little tougher to come up with. We might get an estimate by looking at prior research studies on this topic, so secondary data would be a good place to start. Another option is to conduct a pretest study; because it's always a good idea to conduct a pilot study prior to implementing a study (to check measures, data collection forms, and so on), this is an attractive option. And when all else fails, researchers sometimes just guess. In this case, prior studies indicate that the variance in annual spending is about $125.

The formulas used to calculate sample sizes differ depending on the level of measurement used to estimate a particular parameter. If the attribute is assessed on a nominal or ordinal scale, the result will be expressed as a proportion of the sample that falls into a certain category. If the attribute is assessed on an interval or ratio scale, it is appropriate to calculate a mean score. In this case, the average amount of money spent on hunting trips for the year, we'll use the formula for sample size when estimating a population mean (amount spent is taken on a ratio measure):

$$n \frac{z^2}{H^2} (\text{est } \sigma^2)$$

where $n$ = required sample size, $z$ = z-score corresponding to the desired degree of confidence, $H$ = half-precision

(or how far off the estimate can be in either direction, which would represent half of the full precision range), and $\sigma^2$ = the variance in expenditures in the population.

As you might recall from a basic statistics course, the z-score corresponding to 95% confidence is equal to 1.96; the z-score for 99% confidence is 2.58. (Take a second and look at the sample size formula and notice what will happen to the required sample size $(n)$ if you increase the desired degree of confidence from 95% to 99%. If you want greater confidence that the precision interval captures the true value in the population, the required sample size increases.)

As noted, the director of tourism wants your estimate to be within $25 (in either direction); as a result, the full precision range is $50 and half-precision $(H)$ equals $25. (Once again, look at the formula to see what would happen if you wanted to increase the precision of the answer. Because increased precision means decreasing the precision interval, $H$ gets smaller in the formula, and the necessary sample size increases.) Putting it all together, the calculation of sample size for estimating the amount of money spent looks like this:

$$n \frac{z^2}{H^2} (\text{est } \sigma^2) = \frac{(1.96)^2}{(25)^2} (125)^2 = 96$$

You would need a sample of 96 respondents. The next step would be to determine the number of total sampling elements (TSE; see Chapter 14) to be drawn randomly from the sampling frame. The goal is to achieve a sample size of at least 96 to reach the level of precision (and/or confidence) that we desire.

The other population parameter you need to estimate, the proportion of hunters who come from out of state, requires you to use a slightly different formula, but all the same principles are involved. The director of tourism wants your estimate to be within ±2 percentage points and again wants to be 95% confident that your precision interval has captured the true value of the parameter in the population. But how do you estimate the degree of variability on this parameter in the population? *Think about it this way:* What would a completely homogeneous population look like on a particular nominal or ordinal characteristic? Everyone (100%) would possess the particular characteristic, or no one (0%) would possess the characteristic. Either way, everyone is exactly alike on the parameter in question. As the population becomes more heterogeneous, the percentage who possess (or do not possess) the characteristic moves away from the extremes toward 50%, the level representing the most heterogeneity on the characteristic within the population. So, your (advance) estimate of the proportion of hunters who come from out of state will serve as your estimate of the variation in the population on this characteristic. Because a similar study, conducted 2 years ago, had found that 25% of hunters had come from out of state, that's the estimate of variability you'll use for the current study.

Sample size for estimating proportions is given by the formula

$$n\frac{z^2}{H^2}\pi(1-\pi)$$

where $n$ = required sample size, $z$ = z-score corresponding to the desired degree of confidence, $H$ = half-precision (or how far off the estimate can be in either direction), and $p$ = the population proportion.

Substituting the appropriate values in the formula yields

$$n\frac{z^2}{H^2}\pi(1-\pi) = \frac{(1.96)^2}{(0.02)^2}0.25(1-0.25) = 1,800$$

As before, you would then determine the number of total sampling elements to be randomly drawn from the sampling frame of people who had applied for hunting licenses in the past year. The goal is to draw enough so that you would end up with the 1,800 you need.

You probably noticed that in the first example you ended up with a sample size of 96 and in the second you need 1,800. Why such a large difference? Sample size is calculated for a particular parameter based on the needs of the research situation. It is possible that there would be different sample sizes for each parameter that might be estimated in a study. In the current situation, there must have been differences in confidence level, precision, or variability of the characteristic being estimated in the population. (In this case, the difference is mostly because the required precision was much greater in estimating the proportion of the population that traveled from out of state.)

CHAPTER

# Data Collection: Types of Error and Response Rate Calculation

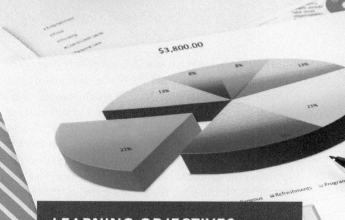

## LEARNING OBJECTIVES

▶ Describe the six types of error that can enter a study.

▶ Give the general definition for response rate.

▶ Discuss several ways in which response rates might be improved.

Billion Photos/Shutterstock.com

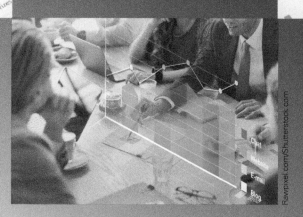

Rawpixel.com/Shutterstock.com

## [ INTRODUCTION ]

Once you've designed an observation- or communication-based study, it's time to collect the data. In this chapter, we focus on the different kinds of error that can bias a project's results. We'll also show you how to calculate the response rate for a communication-based study, an important consideration for assessing the overall quality of the data collection effort. Finally, we offer several suggestions for improving response rates.

## 15-1 Types of Error

Exhibit 15.1 presents the different errors that can enter a project and illustrates how these errors can bias results away from the truth about a population. You'll notice that this illustration is similar to one we showed you earlier in which an individual's response to a survey item is a combination of truth, systematic error, and random error. Exhibit 15.1, however, shows that the results of any study are some combination of truth, sampling error, noncoverage error, nonresponse error, response error, recording error, or office error.

**Exhibit 15.1 ▶** Six Types of Error

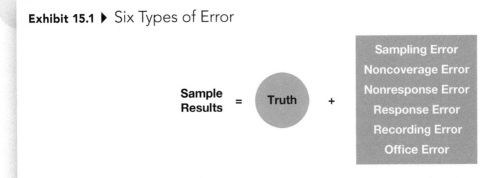

## 15-1a SAMPLING ERROR

We've already mentioned one kind of error—sampling error—that affects projects that rely on samples drawn from a population. Recall that sampling error is the difference between results obtained for a sample and the results we would have obtained had we gathered information from the whole population. Sampling error often is less troubling than the other sorts of errors that can find their way into your study—there are easy ways to reduce it (increase the sample size) or account for it statistically (calculate the margin of sampling error). If you don't use a probability sampling technique, however, it is impossible to estimate the degree of sampling error.

**noncoverage error**
Error that arises because of failure to include qualified elements of the defined population in the sampling frame.

> If you don't use a probability sampling technique, it is impossible to estimate the degree of sampling error.

As an example of the impact of sampling error versus other kinds of errors, consider how a probabilistically drawn sample of consumers might respond to the following question on a survey: "On average, how many times per week do you brush your teeth?" Suppose that the mean response was 21 brushings per week. Further, we could be 95% confident that had we talked with all consumers in the population, the answer would fall between 19 and 23. In our analysis, we have fully accounted for possible sampling error. That doesn't really buy us all that much, however, because many of our respondents probably overstated their brushing behavior in order to be seen as socially acceptable. Estimating sampling error can't correct for errors caused by the questions themselves, the manner in which they were asked, or a host of other factors.

So, if sampling error isn't really that big of a deal, what kinds of errors should you be watching for? We'll talk about those next. Unfortunately, these other kinds of errors aren't as manageable as sampling errors. They don't

necessarily decrease with increases in sample size and may, in fact, increase. And in many cases, it's difficult to even estimate the size and effects of these errors.

## 15-1b NONCOVERAGE ERROR

**Noncoverage error** enters a study when we fail to include qualified elements of our defined population in the sampling frame. That is, one or more consumers, households, and so on, which met the criteria for membership in the population weren't included in the list of population members—and thus they had no chance of being included in the sample. Noncoverage error, then, is essentially a sampling frame problem.

It is common to conduct projects with populations for which no lists of members exist. In these cases, one of your key tasks is to develop a reasonable sampling frame so that the project can proceed … and most of the time it's going to be nearly impossible to get it completely right. Even if a list of population members is available, it is often dated and inaccurate. As a result, noncoverage error enters the project.

Noncoverage error isn't a problem in every survey. For some studies, clear, convenient, and complete sampling frames exist. For example, a furniture store that wants to survey its past customers should have little trouble with noncoverage error, assuming that it kept accurate records. Still, accurate sampling frames seem to be the exception.

Given that noncoverage bias is likely, how can you reduce its effect? The most obvious step is to improve the quality of the sampling frame. This may mean taking the time to bring available city maps up to date (for area samples) or taking a sample to check the quality and representativeness of a mailing list with respect to a target population. Telephone surveys can take advantage of computerized dialing approaches to handle unlisted numbers, but this won't help with households that don't have phones.

We should mention one other potential problem with many sampling frames. Overcoverage error occurs when the same name or household ends up on the sampling frame more than once, giving them an increased likelihood of being included in the project. Most of the time, though, noncoverage error is a much bigger problem than is overcoverage error.

## 15-1c NONRESPONSE ERROR

**Nonresponse error** can occur when you fail to obtain information from elements of the population that were selected for the sample. Suppose that 5 years from now a university conducts a survey of this year's senior class to determine how "successful" the school's graduates were based on their current salary. Who would be most likely to respond to the survey? (Those who were happy about their salaries.) Who would be least likely? (Those who weren't happy with their salaries.) As a result, those who responded to the survey would likely be systematically different from those who didn't respond, and the results would be biased upward in this case. This upward bias reflects nonresponse error.

Nonresponse error is a potential problem in any communication-based project for which data are not collected from all respondents selected for the sample. It is a *potential* problem, because it only occurs when those who respond are systematically different in some important way from those who do not respond. The degree of nonresponse error, however, is difficult to assess because we obviously don't have answers from those who didn't

**nonresponse error** Error from failing to obtain information from some elements of the population that were selected and designated for the sample.

**refusals** Nonresponse error resulting because some designated respondents refuse to participate in the study.

respond. Exhibit 15.2 presents two possible methods of determining if nonresponse error is likely to be a problem in a particular study. Neither of these approaches is foolproof, however.

Nonresponse bias mostly comes about because some people simply refuse to participate in the study. As a result, this is a potential problem for all types of communication-based studies. The rate of **refusals** depends on many factors. Different methods typically produce different response rates.

All else being equal, personal interviews seem to be the most effective at generating responses, with the other methods trailing behind. The most obvious reason for the superiority of personal interviews over other methods is the social nature of the contact: A respondent doesn't run the risk of hurting someone's feelings by deleting an e-mail message or throwing a mail survey in a trash can. And it's become so difficult to contact people on the phone that interviewers can't use the interpersonal nature of telephone conversations to their advantage as much as in the past.

Overcoming refusals is an important issue with any method of communications-based data collection—and we offer a number of suggestions in the final section of this chapter. In almost all cases, one important (and maybe obvious) tactic is to make multiple requests. For example, if the initial e-mail recruitment message goes unanswered, try again at least a couple more times before counting that sampling element as a refusal.

**Exhibit 15.2 ▶** Two (Imperfect) Methods for Diagnosing Nonresponse Error

**Method 1 Contact a sample of nonrespondents.** If a researcher can identify persons who have not responded to a survey (perhaps after several attempts), it is sometimes possible to select a sample of the nonrespondents and contact them again, typically using a different method of contact. This time, however, the goal is not to get the respondent to complete the entire survey, but instead to simply answer one or two questions that focus on the key issue in the project. The answers from the "nonrespondents" sample on these items are then compared with those from the initial sample. If the responses from the two samples are not different on the key items, then nonresponse error is probably not an issue in the project. This is the preferred method of diagnosing nonresponse bias, but it is also the most difficult under normal circumstances.

**Method 2 Compare respondent demographics against known demographics of the population.** Sometimes researchers conduct sample surveys among populations for which data about the population are available from other sources. For example, suppose that you were conducting a survey among the residents of a particular state in the United States and that when you completed the data collection process you computed the various demographic characteristics of your sample (e.g., gender, age, education). These sample statistics could then be compared to statistics from other sources, such as U.S. census data, to determine if certain demographic groups are over- or underrepresented in the sample, which would indicate the possibility of nonresponse error. Note, however, that this result might also be an indication of noncoverage error if the sampling frame is less than adequate. Further, even if the sample demographic statistics match perfectly with the known population parameters, we haven't eliminated the possibility of nonresponse error, because the key issues being addressed may be completely unrelated to the demographic variables we are considering. In that case, those who respond may be systematically different from those who don't respond, yet still have the same demographic characteristics on average. Despite its shortcomings, however, this approach is much better than simply assuming that those who don't respond are no different than those who do respond.

Another type of potential nonresponse error applies mostly to telephone studies (and sometimes to personal interviews). People who never answered the telephone when the researcher called (or answered a knock at the door with some forms of personal interviews), even after several attempts, are classified as **not-at-homes**. Maybe the individual is screening calls by caller ID, or sends all unknown calls to voicemail—or maybe he simply wasn't available when the researcher attempted to call. In any case, the researcher attempted to reach a sample element but never succeeded. It's not exactly a refusal, because the potential respondent was never actually asked to participate, but it does need to be taken into account when calculating response rates as we'll see in a later section.

The nonresponse problem is so important to the accuracy of most communication-based projects that it is almost always better to work diligently to get a higher response rate from a smaller sampling pool (i.e., lower total sampling elements or TSE) than to start with a larger sampling pool to get the same number of respondents (and lower response rate).[1] This is an important takeaway: Be careful about any data collection tool that offers thousands of respondents but must send surveys to millions of people to accomplish it. Unless the 99% who do not respond are similar to the 1% who do respond on the key issues, the risk of nonresponse error is probably too great.

**not-at-homes** Nonresponse error that arises when respondents are not at home when the interviewer calls.

**response error** Error that occurs when an individual provides an inaccurate response, consciously or subconsciously, to a survey item.

15-1d **RESPONSE ERROR**

**Response error** occurs when an individual provides a response to an item, but the response is inaccurate for some reason. There are many factors that can cause response error, ranging from poorly written items that respondents misinterpret, to characteristics of the respondent that subconsciously influence his or her responses, to a variety of other things. In any case, it's the researcher's responsibility to do everything in her power to minimize the presence of response error in the data.

The following questions are useful for considering the different ways response errors can affect individuals' responses.[2] You might also use these questions to anticipate possible problems when developing questionnaire items in the first place.

### Does the respondent understand the question?

Survey items must be written using simple, direct language, especially when a general audience is being surveyed. If respondents don't understand a question, one of three things is likely to happen: They will either skip the question, stop completing the survey, or answer the question based on their interpretation, which may not match your intentions. None of these are good outcomes. Pretesting

the questionnaire with members of the relevant population can usually eliminate this source of error.

Several years ago, we conducted a satisfaction study among patients of a number of healthcare providers. The questionnaire included items assessing patient expectations and perceptions of service-provider performance across a range of relevant dimensions. One respondent appeared to have read the directions and (we presume) accurately responded to the first of the items on the rating scale, then proceeded to provide open-ended responses to most of the other items. The respondent, a 92-year-old woman, was doing her best to answer our questions. It was clear that she understood the questions, for the most part, but she didn't understand how we wanted her to respond. Was this her fault? No; it was our job to make sure that the instructions were clear.

### Does the respondent know the answer to the question?

Just because a respondent understands a question doesn't mean that he actually knows the answer to the question. The problem is that many people will answer the question anyway. This is especially common with closed-ended questions for which respondents simply choose a response category. Dealing with this issue is a bit trickier. Providing a "don't know" response category is one option, but this strategy will often create difficulties in data analysis (i.e., lots of missing cases). People will sometimes select the "don't know" option as a way of not having to think about a particular item, even when they do know the answer to the question. A preferred strategy is to perform sufficient exploratory research and questionnaire pretesting to understand what population members are likely—and not likely—to know.

### Is the respondent willing to provide the true answer to the question?

Respondents who understand a question don't always provide a truthful answer. There are lots of reasons for this. Respondents may consciously lie because they want to make themselves look better or to avoid appearing "dumb" when they don't know the answer to a question. Sometimes respondents are angry or in a bad mood and they knowingly provide inaccurate answers. Some respondents just don't care, even though they could understand the questions and provide accurate responses if they wanted to. Others simply don't want to say something negative about a product, store, or service provider.

Here's another kind of response error: Respondents' current attitudes and emotions sometimes influence their responses. We once conducted a study with dental patients that included a question about patient moods prior to treatment. One elderly respondent was less than thrilled with our questionnaire, writing on the data collection form that he was "crotchety enough without seeing questionnaires like this!" His attitude toward the questionnaire also seemed to influence his response to the mood item: He checked the category nearest "good" (on a "bad" to "good" semantic differential scale) and added, "I always experience absolute euphoria at the prospect of going to the endodontist. I sing the 'Ode to Joy' at the top of my lungs all the way."

What can you do about these sorts of response errors? Once again, the key is thorough exploratory research and questionnaire pretesting. Questions that might cause respondents to be even slightly defensive—especially sensitive questions—must be carefully designed and tested. When the data collection forms are designed, careful attention must be given to the questions (and the order in which they are asked) so as to hold the respondent's attention.

### Is the wording of the question or the situation in which it is asked likely to bias the response?

As noted, the wording of a question and its response categories has a strong influence on individuals' responses. For example, leading questions must be avoided, and researchers must be careful not to accidentally use "loaded" words if they are to uncover the truth about an issue.

Personal interviews and telephone interviews create an opportunity for interviewers to influence, or bias, the results of the study. Interviewers must be trained not to let the tone of their voice or inflections in their speech vary from one interview to the next. You'll probably guess that interviewer bias is worse with open-ended questions because interviewers both ask the questions and record the answers, creating lots of opportunities for bias. Closed-ended questions aren't immune from the problem, though, because interviewers sometimes emphasize one of the response categories, and changes in emphasis or tone can change the meaning of the question entirely. As a result, interviewer training—and clear instructions—are very important.

> Interviewers must be trained not to let the tone of their voice or inflections in their speech vary from one interview to the next.

This next point is a bit obvious, but it's important: A respondent's answers to questions may change depending on who else is in the room when the questions are asked, especially with personal interviews. It's not just that some questions (and answers) might be embarrassing for a respondent; answers to even simple questions can differ based on the situational context. For example, imagine asking a husband about who makes decisions about important household purchases when his wife is—or is not—in the room when the question is asked. Maybe the answer is the same in either case. Or maybe it isn't.

## 15-1e RECORDING ERRORS

**Recording errors** refer to mistakes made by humans or machines in the process of recording respondents' communication- or observation-based data. Personal interviews and telephone surveys rely on the accuracy of the interviewer in recording the actual responses of the subjects. This isn't always as easy as it sounds. One of the interviewer's main tasks is to keep the respondent interested and motivated. At the same time, the interviewer must try to record what the respondent says by carefully writing down the person's answers to open-ended questions or selecting the appropriate answers with closed-ended questions. That's a tough job, and sometimes interviewers make mistakes.

In addition, it's also possible for online data collection systems to experience hardware or software glitches. A more common issue is the online survey that was simply programmed incorrectly by the researcher. Once the answers are recorded—correctly or not—there's usually no going back to the respondents to fix the problem. Instead, the problematic data are scrapped and more data collected.

Observational data can also contain recording errors. With human observation, one obvious form occurs when observers fail to record important behaviors, or manage to record them incorrectly. Training the observers—and letting them practice before the actual data collection—is the key to limiting this form of recording error.

The increased availability of machine-recorded behavioral data (e.g., scanner data, video data, online search or purchase data, and many other varieties) has also heightened the possibility of recording errors. Computers and software can be miscalibrated or programmed to record the wrong behaviors. Sometimes equipment malfunctions, or maybe a power outage or other glitch prevents behaviors from being recorded at all. Regardless of the specific problem, when relevant data are not recorded accurately, a recording error has occurred.

## 15-1f OFFICE ERRORS

Unfortunately, error can enter a project even after the data are collected. **Office error** can show up during the process of editing, coding, and analyzing the data. In many ways, office error is the most frustrating kind

> **recording error** Mistakes made by humans or machines in the process of recording respondents' communication- or observation-based data.
>
> **office error** Error due to data editing, coding, or analysis errors.

of error. Here's a simple example with communication-based data: Suppose that a survey question has been carefully designed for a mail survey, a respondent understands it and provides the true response—and then someone makes a simple keystroke error during data entry that transforms the true response into something else. The efforts of all involved have been wasted, at least for that question and that respondent. (By the way, one of the advantages of online data collection is that respondents enter their own data, leaving little opportunity for office error of this type.)

One type of office error that is growing in importance concerns the aggregation of data from or about a population member from multiple sources, a type of error we refer to as **data merger error**. As companies learn to gather and use data about their customers, products, employees, and the like from all kinds of sources—often as part of marketing analytics—a key issue is the creation of a combined dataset that includes data from multiple sources. As you might imagine, merging multiple types of data (purchase data, location data, responses to survey questions, and so on, for example) from different sources can be quite complicated and often results in data that are lost, combined with the wrong cases, not readable because they are in the wrong format, or a host of other potential problems. Careful use of case identifiers, used consistently and embedded in each of the individual datasets

**data merger error**
Error resulting from the aggregation of data from or about a population element from multiple sources.

to identify data associated with a particular analytic unit (e.g., customer, employee, brand) is key to merging the data from the various sources.

## 15-1g TOTAL ERROR IS THE KEY

Each of these potential sources of error is important. We want to make sure you understand an important point, though. Controlling the overall amount of error, rather than any single type of error, is the key in a research project. We think that far too many researchers focus too much on decreasing sampling error in communications-based studies when they should be focusing more closely on other potential sources of error. Managers, students (especially those with a course in statistics behind them), and some researchers often argue for the "largest possible sample," reasoning that a large sample is much more likely to produce a "valid" result than a small sample is. Increasing the sample size will certainly help you decrease sampling error, but it can also increase other types of errors. If you want to be an effective researcher, try to manage total error, not just one particular kind of error.

Exhibit 15.3 attempts to summarize the sources of errors and how they can be reduced and controlled. You could use this table as a checklist for evaluating the quality of research prior to making important decisions based on the research results.

## Manager's Focus

Sampling error is certainly a concern, but as we've noted it's only one of several sources of error, and every type of error keeps you from accurately understanding your market. During election cycles, for example, we regularly hear claims that poll results have a margin of error of plus or minus a small number of percentage points. Yet many political polls prove to be poor predictors of what actually occurs in the electoral "marketplace." Why? Because in addition to sampling error (which the margin of sampling error accounts for), the findings are also subject to the other types of error discussed in this chapter. These types of error can be much more dangerous than sampling error, and they're hard to estimate—and many survey sponsors are either unaware of them or simply do not publicly acknowledge them.

The same is true in marketing research studies. Managers are much more aware of sampling error

than the other types of error. What they don't realize is that their own behavior can lead to a tremendous increase in total error. For example, they may require researchers to generate large sample sizes believing the error in the study will be minimized—but then insist that the study be completed within a short time period. The larger sample may decrease sampling error (assuming an appropriate probability sampling plan is employed), but racing to complete a larger study may cause an exponential increase in other sorts of error. Our main point is that managers need to allocate ample time to generate samples and provide resources for the various approaches we discuss later in this chapter for reducing error. We urge you to have a candid discussion with your research supplier about all of the types of error that are likely to occur in a study and to offer support for all reasonable efforts to reduce each type of error.

**Exhibit 15.3** ▶ Types of Errors and Methods for Handling Them

| TYPE | DEFINITION | METHODS FOR HANDLING |
|---|---|---|
| Sampling | Difference between results for the sample and what would be true for the population. | 1. Increase sample size. |
| Noncoverage | Error that arises because of failure to include qualified elements of the defined population in the sampling frame. | 1. Improve sampling frame using other sources.<br>2. Adjust the results by appropriately weighting subsample results (assuming weighting scheme is known). |
| Nonresponse | Failure to obtain information from some elements of the population that were selected for the sample. | 1. Attempt to convince the respondent of the importance of his or her participation.<br>2. Frame the study to enhance respondent interest.<br>3. Keep the survey as short as possible.<br>4. Guarantee confidentiality or anonymity.<br>5. Train interviewers well and match their characteristics to those of the subject pool.<br>6. Personalize the recruiting message/script when possible.<br>7. Use an incentive.<br>8. Send follow-up surveys. |
| Response | Although the individual participates in the study, he or she provides an inaccurate response, consciously or subconsciously, to a survey item. | 1. Match the background characteristics of interviewer and respondent as closely as possible.<br>2. Make sure interviewer instructions are clear and written down.<br>3. Conduct practice training sessions with interviewers.<br>4. Avoid using ambiguous words and questions.<br>5. Avoid the use of leading questions.<br>6. Avoid unstated alternatives; include all reasonable response options.<br>7. Avoid assumed consequences; write clear questions.<br>8. Don't ask respondents for generalizations or estimates.<br>9. Don't include double-barreled questions. |
| Recording | Errors that arise when recording observational data manually or mechanically. | 1. With manual observation, make sure that observer instructions about what is to be observed and recorded are clear and written down.<br>2. With manual observation, conduct practice observation sessions with observers using "live" or recorded subject actions.<br>3. With mechanical observation, ensure that observation technologies and connected computer systems are properly calibrated and functioning correctly. |

| TYPE | DEFINITION | METHODS FOR HANDLING |
|---|---|---|
| Office[a] | Errors that arise when coding, tabulating, or analyzing the data. | 1. Use a field edit to detect the most glaring omissions and inaccuracies in the data. |
| | | 2. Use a second edit in the office to decide how data collection instruments containing incomplete answers, obviously wrong answers, and answers that reflect a lack of interest are to be handled. |
| | | 3. Use closed-ended questions to simplify the coding process, if possible, but when open-ended questions need to be used, specify the appropriate codes that will be allowed before collecting the data. |
| | | 4. When open-ended questions are being coded and multiple coders are being used, divide the task by questions and not by data collection forms. |
| | | 5. Have each coder code a sample of the other's work to ensure that a consistent set of coding criteria is being used. |
| | | 6. Follow established conventions; for example, use numeric codes and not letters of the alphabet when coding the data for computer analysis. |
| | | 7. Prepare a codebook that lists the codes for each variable and the categories included in each code. |
| | | 8. When merging data from multiple sources, ensure that the identification number used to represent an element is identical in each of the different data sources. |
| | | 9. After merging data from multiple sources, draw a sample of elements and check to see that data were merged properly. |
| | | 10. Use appropriate methods to analyze the data. |

[a]Steps to reduce the incidence of office errors are discussed in more detail in the analysis chapters.

## 15-2 Calculating Response Rates

With communication-based studies, once data have been collected, the researcher must calculate the **response rate** for the project. The response rate—the number of completed interviews with responding units divided by the number of eligible responding units in the sample—serves two important functions. First, it allows an assessment of the potential influence of nonresponse error on the study's results. Although this assessment is qualitative in nature (because even if you've obtained responses from 90% of those chosen for the sample, the other 10% could have been very different on the issue in question), higher response rates generally suggest fewer problems with nonresponse bias. Second, the response rate serves as an indicator of the overall quality of a data collection effort. Very low response rates may indicate poor questionnaire design, lack of interest among respondents, and so on. Unless

**response rate** The number of completed interviews with responding units divided by the number of eligible responding units in the sample.

the client is willing to collect more data, however, it's too late to do anything about these problems. To avoid this outcome, use enough exploratory research and questionnaire pretesting in advance to be comfortable about what will happen when you collect your data.

The following general formula is used to calculate a project's response rate:

$$\text{Response Rate } (RR) = \frac{\text{number of completed interviews with responding units}}{\text{number of eligible responding units in the sample}}$$

How this formula is applied depends upon the data collection method used. "Completed interviews" includes completed survey forms for methods that don't include an actual interview. We show how this formula is applied with the most common methods of administration in the following sections.

## 15-2a ONLINE AND MAIL SURVEYS (NO ELIGIBILITY REQUIREMENT)

With these methods of data collection, response rate calculation is usually straightforward when there is no eligibility requirement (i.e., everyone who receives the survey is eligible to complete it). The first step is to determine the number of usable questionnaires completed. Not every completed questionnaire is usable—and you'll need to exclude the bad ones. Common reasons for excluding a questionnaire include evidence that a respondent wasn't really paying attention to the questions or a large percentage of items weren't answered by the respondent.

Once the number of usable questionnaires is known, you need to determine the number of eligible response units. With mail surveys and online surveys distributed by electronic media to specific individuals, we usually assume that all sampling elements or people in the sampling frame meet the criteria for membership in the population and sample, which makes calculating the number of eligible response units quite simple. All you have to do is take the number of sample elements that you attempted to contact and subtract the number of invalid addresses. With either approach, you'll normally know very soon which addresses weren't valid because the surveys will be returned to you in the mail or in your e-mail system. Thus, for these methods of data collection, response rate (RR) is calculated as:

$$RR = \frac{\text{number of usable questionnaires}}{\text{number of contacts attempted} - \text{number of wrong addresses}}$$

Suppose that an online retailer decided to conduct an online survey among its past customers. A sample of 1,000 customers is randomly selected to receive an e-mail survey. A total of 202 customers respond to the survey; 58 of the e-mail addresses are no longer valid. Here's how to calculate the response rate:

$$RR = \frac{202}{1,000 - 58} = 21\%$$

## 15-2b TELEPHONE INTERVIEWS (NO ELIGIBILITY REQUIREMENT)

Things get a little more complicated with telephone interviews—but not much. In cases where there is no eligibility requirement (i.e., everyone in the sample pool meets the criteria for being included in the sample), we can categorize the attempted contacts into three groups: completed interviews, refusals, and not-at-homes (which includes when no one answers as well as when someone who isn't the correct respondent answers the telephone). The response rate formula looks like this:

$$RR = \frac{\text{number of completed interviews}}{\text{number of completed interviews} + \text{number of refusals} + \text{number of not-at-homes}}$$

Notice that wrong numbers or nonworking numbers are automatically excluded from the formula and thus don't lower the calculated response rate. You'll want to keep track of the number of incorrect telephone numbers (along with completed interviews, refusals, and not-at-homes), however, as an indication of the quality of the sampling frame.

Consider the following scenario: A researcher has designed a project using a telephone survey as the method of data collection. The respondents are current members of a health club. Using the membership roster as a sampling frame, the researcher has randomly selected 200 members. At the conclusion of the data collection phase, 112 interviews have successfully been conducted, 27 people refused to participate in the study, 57 people could not be reached after at least three tries, and 4 telephone numbers were no longer in service. What is the response rate for this project?

$$RR = \frac{112}{112 + 27 + 57} = 57\%$$

In addition, the quality of the sampling frame appears to be very good, with only 4 nonworking numbers, or $4/200 = 2\%$.

Before moving on, there's an important issue we need to address, and it applies to all methods of administration. What exactly counts as a "completed" interview? Once in a while respondents hang up the phone before they have completed the telephone interview (or they will only answer some of the questions on a mail or online survey). In these cases, you need to use good judgment. Usually, a response that is nearly complete should be included in the data set and counted as a completed interview. At the other extreme, a respondent who answers only one or two questions should probably not be included. The troubling cases are those lying between these extremes. Our general recommendation is to count any interview (or survey) as completed if the respondent provides answers for most of the survey items.

## 15-2c ONLINE SURVEYS AND TELEPHONE INTERVIEWS (WITH ELIGIBILITY REQUIREMENTS)

Sometimes researchers are forced to work with sampling frames that include response units that are not members of the population being studied. Suppose, for example, that a department store wants to know shoppers' opinions of a new store layout. Unfortunately, the store can't keep records on who has shopped at the store and who hasn't (because not all shoppers actually buy something and get into its database). Store managers believe that at least half of the households in a test market city contain at least one adult who has visited the store since the new layout was introduced. To conduct a telephone interview, researchers working with the company might use random digit dialing to contact local households. They might also purchase access to an online panel with members located in the local area. Regardless of how they are contacted, the problem is that some of the households won't include anyone who has shopped at the store during the relevant time frame and is ineligible to complete the survey. To identify these households, a screening question will be included ("Has any adult in this household visited Smart's Department Store in the previous 3 months?"); the surveys will end at that point for those that haven't visited the store.

Because some households are ineligible, how would you calculate the response rate? The first step is to count the number of completed interviews, refusals, not-at-homes—*and* the number of ineligible response units. If you're wondering why you must keep track of the number of ineligibles, we need them to help adjust for the fact that some proportion of the people who refused to take the survey or who weren't at home wouldn't have qualified anyway. (By the way, with e-mail recruitment for online studies, any household that doesn't respond is considered a refusal.) We need to adjust the response rate to account for this; otherwise, the response rate will be lower than it really was. The *eligibility percentage (E%)* is computed as follows:

$$E\% = \frac{\text{number of completed interviews}}{\text{number of completed interviews + number of ineligibles}}$$

The eligibility percentage is then used to adjust the number of refusals and not-at-homes to reflect the fact that many of them would not have qualified to participate in the survey even if we had successfully contacted them and gotten them to agree to participate. The response rate is calculated as follows:

$$RR = \frac{\text{number of completed interviews}}{\text{number of completed interviews + } (E\%)(\text{number of refusals + number of not-at-homes})}$$

Imagine that researchers working with the department store had purchased a list of 1,000 telephone numbers and had attempted to contact each household. Here are the final results of the calls, along with the correct response rate calculation:

| | |
|---|---|
| Completed interviews | 338 |
| Refusals | 89 |
| Not-at-homes | 169 |
| Ineligibles | 292 |
| Nonworking numbers | 112 |
| | 1,000 telephone numbers |

$$E\% = \frac{338}{338 + 292} = 54\%$$

$$RR = \frac{338}{338 + (0.54)(89 + 169)} = 71\%$$

Without adjusting for ineligibles, the calculated response rate would have been only 57%, so it is important to keep track of the number of response units that don't qualify for the survey. A similar approach is taken for online studies with an eligibility requirement except that there are no not-at-homes (everyone is assumed to have received the request, even if they didn't read it). The number of refusals equals the number of contacts attempted *minus* the nonworking e-mail addresses *minus* the completed surveys *minus* the ineligibles. Otherwise, you apply the formula shown above, which will adjust the number of refusals by the eligibility percentage.

## 15-2d OTHER METHODS OF DATA COLLECTION

So far, we've talked about calculating response rates for most of the major types of data collection. What about other types, such as personal interviews or the residential "drop-off" surveys common with area samples? Regardless of the type of data collection, the same logic is applied: The response rate equals the number of completed interviews with responding units divided by the number of eligible responding units in the sample. Regardless of the circumstances, the researcher can usually use common sense and the basic formulas we've discussed to arrive at the appropriate response rate.

## 15-3 Improving Response Rates

As noted, the lower the response rate, the more likely it is that nonresponse error will affect research results. Because of this potential problem, researchers have suggested lots of techniques over the years for improving response rates on communication-based projects of various types. In this section, we briefly discuss a few of the most promising techniques. The trick is to figure out which ones are likely to be most influential in a particular study. Because of its growing popularity, we pay special attention to improving online survey response rates in Exhibit 15.4.

**Exhibit 15.4** ▶ Tips for Increasing Response Rates on Online Surveys

**Recruiting Messages on E-mail**

- Use a personal "From" name.
- Keep the subject line simple, but interesting.
- Avoid language that will get caught in spam filters (using all caps, exclamation points, money symbols, "free," "important message," and so on).
- Personalize the message by using recipient's name.
- Include short, effective message to capture attention containing information about: (a) who you are, (b) purpose of study, (c) request for help, (d) length/time of survey, (e) confidentiality, and (f) incentives.
- If offering incentives, make them meaningful.
- Consider timing of e-mail—know your audience.
- Send reminder e-mails—but no more than two.
- Pretest the recruiting message.

**The Online Survey**

- Keep it as short as possible, including instructions.
- Optimize the survey for use with mobile phones.
- Begin with a question likely to engage the respondent's attention.
- Keep questions as simple as possible.
- Use visuals/graphics if they help, but don't make the survey complex or difficult to navigate.
- Remind respondents about incentives, and explain how to obtain them.
- For long surveys (rarely a good idea), let respondents see progression through the survey and how much remains.
- Pretest the online survey.

There is one factor that probably has more effect than any other on response rates: how interested the sample pool is in the topic. Unfortunately, this factor isn't really under the control of the researcher. Some topics are inherently more interesting than other topics to particular respondents. Although you can't change the topic of a research project, you might consider different approaches for introducing and framing the issue under study. Use exploratory research for gauging respondent interest in the topic. It would also be wise to give trial runs to different introductory scripts so that you can choose the one that seems to work the best.

## Manager's Focus

All other things being equal, total error will be reduced if you employ a *probability sampling plan* that achieves the highest possible response rate from the people in the target population. In other words, you are much more likely to obtain an accurate portrayal of the market situation if your research supplier probabilistically samples a smaller number of target population members and does whatever it can to maximize the response rate. Conversely, your assessment of the market situation will likely be less precise if your research provider generates the desired sample size by contacting a large number of prospective respondents through a low response mode of administration. The latter situation should be avoided if the research objective is important because the risk is simply too high that those who respond will not be representative of those who do not.

## 15-3a SURVEY LENGTH

Although there are exceptions, respondents typically do not respond well to long surveys. As surveys get longer, respondents get tired, lose focus, become inattentive, and start speeding through the survey just to finish … or maybe they just stop responding. None of these are good things, especially in terms of response quality. All else being equal, short surveys are more likely to be completed than are long surveys. This is one reason that you should only include questions that are truly important and that will be used in the analysis.

## 15-3b GUARANTEE OF CONFIDENTIALITY OR ANONYMITY

It is routine practice to promise respondents that their answers will be held in confidence by the researcher. This is especially important when the topic or specific questions are likely to be sensitive to the respondent. With mail surveys, you can also guarantee that responses will be anonymous, providing an even greater sense of security to the respondent. By the way, if you promise confidentiality or anonymity, you are ethically bound to keep the promise. Sometimes managers will want access to respondent names, addresses, or telephone numbers—particularly those who have expressed interest in a proposed product or service. Even if you made no promises at all, you shouldn't share this information with managers because it blurs the line between research and sales.

## 15-3c INTERVIEWER CHARACTERISTICS AND TRAINING

With personal interviews (and telephone interviews to an extent), an interviewer is likely to get better cooperation and more information from a respondent when the two share similar backgrounds. This is especially true for characteristics like race, age, and gender. Sufficient training is also important so that interviewers can learn to quickly convince potential respondents of the value of the research and the importance of their participation. So, you'll want to develop an effective recruiting script and train your interviewers to follow the script. To the extent possible, the script should also communicate information about the content and purpose of the study so that respondents may develop greater involvement and interest in the topic.

## 15-3d PERSONALIZATION

Anything you can do to make the data collection process seem more personalized will improve response rates. With online surveys, for example, a personalized e-mail message ("Hello, Amjad") is always better than a generic greeting ("Hello"). Sending a recruitment e-mail from a personal or company e-mail account is a lot more personal than sending it from a "do not reply" type of account from the online survey provider. With mail surveys, hand-addressed envelopes, handwritten signatures on cover letters, and the use of actual stamps should increase the odds that a respondent opens a mail survey (and they need to open it before they can respond to it!). Again, anything you can do to make things more personal is probably a good idea.

## 15-3e RESPONSE INCENTIVES

Considerable research has shown that offering an incentive to respondents usually increases response rates on a project. Response incentives can take several forms ranging from money to lotteries to donations for charity. Monetary incentives often have the greatest influence on response rates. Including a reasonable amount of money as a token of appreciation is often a good idea—but it obviously raises the cost of data collection.

Many researchers use lotteries as a means of generating response. By participating in the survey, the respondent is typically entered into a drawing for a prize. The difficulty, if there is one, lies in the amount of trust that the respondent must place in the researcher. From the respondent's perspective, there may or may not be an actual lottery; they may or may not actually be entered in such a lottery; and their responses may not be confidential or anonymous if contact information is kept for contact purposes (in order to notify the winner). Be careful here; remind respondents that the information will be held in confidence, and don't do anything to violate that trust.

## 15-3f FOLLOW-UP SURVEYS AND REMINDERS

In some cases, the circumstances surrounding a contact are responsible for a respondent's refusal to participate. Because these circumstances may be temporary or changeable, follow-up reminder contacts are sometimes useful for generating a response. With online surveys, it's not uncommon at all to receive additional responses with second and third recruitment messages; the same applies to mail surveys, although the expense is greater.

The timing of the follow-up contact is important with email recruitment on online surveys. For one thing, unlike with mail surveys, delivery is instantaneous (more or less)—but if the potential respondent doesn't participate right away, the recruitment message quickly slides down the e-mail inbox (if it wasn't already deleted). As a result, it might be reasonable to send a follow-up recruiting message within a day or two rather than the week or two that you'd normally wait to send a second wave of mail surveys. Here's another issue about the timing of a follow-up e-mail: Choose a different time of day to send the recruiting message. If you send the first recruiting message on a Monday afternoon, consider following up on Wednesday morning. In this case, a respondent who only checks e-mail in the morning is more likely to see the message that arrives on Wednesday than the one you sent on Monday because it is less likely to be buried deep in the inbox.

## Manager's Focus

Marketing research studies are often expensive endeavors and managers understandably look for ways to reduce costs. Before you dismiss the idea of offering response incentives because you believe they will increase the study's cost, you should first run the numbers. In an earlier chapter, we stressed how important it is to pretest your data collection instrument. When completing this important step, we recommend testing alternative incentives (including having no incentive) and calculating the differences in response rates. If you do this, you will find that paying for incentives can sometimes decrease the overall cost of the study by reducing the amount of interviewer time or other expenses that would be necessary to get the study completed without an incentive. Plus, as we've advised elsewhere, it's always better to get a stronger response rate from a smaller sampling pool; incentives can help with this objective.

# Summary

## Learning Objective 1

**Describe the six types of error that can enter a study.**

There are six basic types of errors: sampling errors, noncoverage errors, nonresponse errors, response errors, recording errors, and office errors. Sampling error occurs anytime that we work with a subset of the population instead of the population itself. Noncoverage errors occur because part of the population of interest was not included in the sampling frame. Nonresponse errors are possible when some elements designated for inclusion in the sample did not respond and were systematically different from those who did respond on key characteristics. Response errors occur because inaccurate information was secured from the sample elements. Recording errors occur when researchers or the technology they employ fail to accurately record observational data. Office errors occur when errors are introduced in the processing of the data or in reporting the findings.

## Learning Objective 2

**Give the general definition for response rate.**

Response rate may be defined as the number of completed interviews with responding units divided by the number of eligible responding units in the sample.

## Learning Objective 3

**Discuss several ways in which response rates might be improved.**

There are several approaches for improving response rates, including framing the study to enhance respondent interest, keeping the survey as short as possible, guaranteeing confidentiality or anonymity, training interviewers well and matching their characteristics to those of the subject pool, personalizing the recruiting message when possible, using an incentive, and sending follow-up surveys.

## Key Terms

noncoverage error (page 225)

nonresponse error (page 226)

refusals (page 226)

not-at-homes (page 227)

response error (page 227)

recording error (page 228)

office error (page 228)

data merger error (page 229)

response rate (page 231)

## Review Questions

1. What are the six general types of error that can enter a research project? How do they differ?

2. Why is sampling error potentially less troubling than the other kinds of error?

3. Why is noncoverage error considered to be a sampling frame problem?

4. Why is nonresponse error a "potential" source of error?

5. What are the two primary sources of nonresponse error? Describe how each source could result in nonresponse error.

6. Why might it be better to work with a smaller total sampling elements (TSE) and work diligently to get responses than to start with a much larger TSE but obtain a lower response rate?

7. What are the basic considerations underlying response error?

8. What is recording error? How might it apply to both communication- and observation-based studies?

9. Why can office error be described as the most frustrating kind of error?

10. What causes data merger errors?

11. What is a response rate?

12. How should response rates be calculated for the different methods of data collection?

13. What are some of the techniques for improving response rates?

# Endnotes

1. Deming, W. E. (1953, December). On a probability mechanism to attain an economic balance between the resultant error of response and the bias of nonresponse. *Journal of the American Statistical Association, 48*, 766–767. See also Lipstein, B. (1975, February). In defense of small samples. *Journal of Advertising Research, 15*, 33–40; Dunkelburg, W. C., & Day, G. S. (1973, May). Nonresponse bias and callbacks in sample surveys. *Journal of Marketing Research, 10*, 160–168; Opatow, L. (1991, February/March). Some thoughts about how interview attempts affect survey results." *Journal of Advertising Research, 31*, RC6–RC9.

2. Weiers, R. M. (1988). *Marketing Research*, 2nd ed. Englewood Cliffs, NJ: Prentice Hall, 213–217.

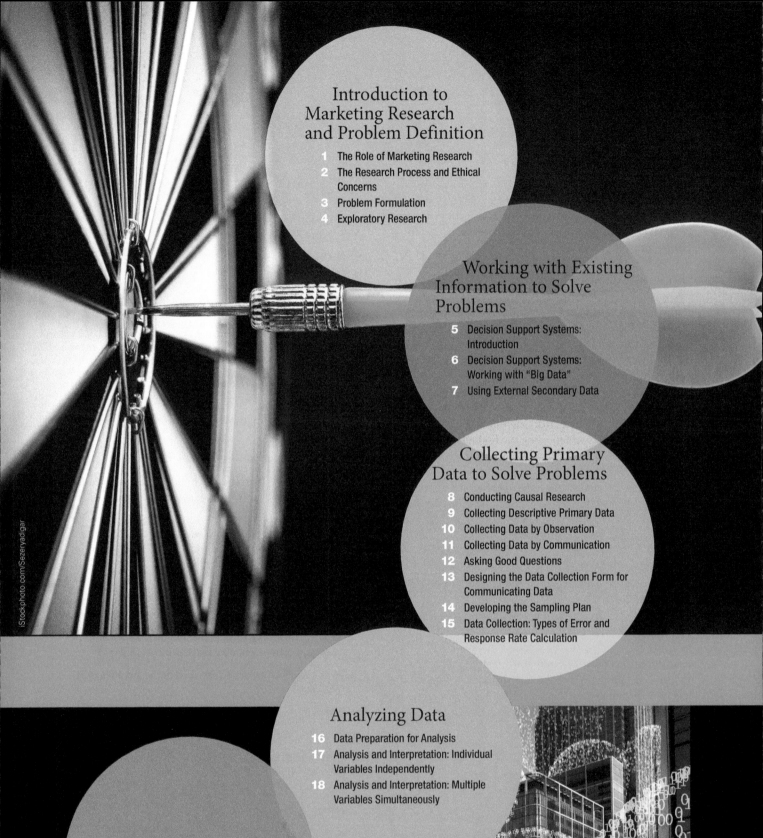

iStockphoto.com/Sezeryadigar

iStockphoto.com/peterhowell

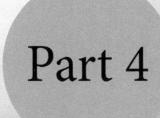

# Part 4

# Analyzing Data

iStockphoto.com/mrcmos

239

# Data Preparation for Analysis

## LEARNING OBJECTIVES

▶ Explain the purpose of the editing process.

▶ Define coding.

▶ Explain why data must sometimes be aggregated.

▶ Discuss the merging of data.

▶ Describe the kinds of information contained in a codebook.

▶ Describe common methods for cleaning the data file.

▶ Discuss options for dealing with missing data.

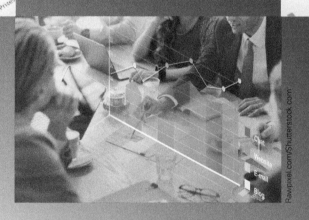

## [ INTRODUCTION ]

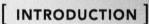

If you've ever tried to impress someone by preparing a really nice meal for them, then you know that the process is a lot more involved than simply going to the store, buying some groceries, and returning home to throw the meal on the table. Instead, there is a fairly complex process of preparing each of the dishes, often following somewhat complicated recipes. The table must be set with dishes, silverware, flowers and/or anything else appropriate for the occasion. And then there's the process of arranging for everything—the entrée, the side dishes, breads, and desserts—to be ready, at the right temperatures, when the meal is served. Only when all of the preliminary steps are completed can the actual meal begin.

It's much the same with the analysis stage in the marketing research process. Even though you have the raw materials needed for the analysis (i.e., data from new or existing sources, computer hardware, and analysis software), the analysis can't begin until a number of preliminary steps have been completed.

With marketing research (and analytics involving behavioral data), the preliminary steps include editing and coding the raw data, aggregating behavioral data to usable units, merging data from different sources, building the data set (which may include merging data from different sources), creating a codebook, cleaning the data, and handling missing data. Handling these steps with great care prior to analysis can prevent great confusion and errors once analysis begins in earnest. With that in mind, we turn our attention to the editing process.

## 16-1 Editing Data

The basic purpose of editing is to make certain that the raw data meet minimum quality standards. **Editing** involves the inspection and, if necessary, correction of the data received from or about each case to be included in the analysis. Editing is primarily a concern for communication-based studies.

Here's an example of the kinds of things you're watching for in the editing process: Suppose that you have used an open-ended question to ask a company's customers how many years they have been shopping at a particular retail outlet. What if someone wrote in "8 months"? You'll have to convert this answer to one that can be used in the analysis (in this case, probably "1 year"); the units must be consistent.

At this stage, you also must decide what to do about cases with incomplete data. Unless you are using an online survey that forces respondents to complete each item before they can move on in the survey (and we don't usually recommend using such a strategy), it's very likely that many respondents won't complete all of the items on a survey. Some surveys will have complete sections omitted. In the case of forced response in an online context, the respondent could break off her participation midway through the survey. It's not a formal rule, but if half or more of the responses are missing on a survey, we usually recommend dropping that case entirely. Questionnaires containing only isolated instances of item nonresponse should be kept.

> It's not a formal rule, but if half or more of the responses are missing on a survey, we usually recommend dropping that case entirely.

Sometimes data are simply incorrect. The problem might have been mechanical or human recording errors (often relatively easy to identify—but not always easy to correct), or it might have resulted from response error in all its various forms. Poorly worded questions lead to inaccurate answers—and sometimes respondents simply don't tell the truth. It's not always possible to catch these sorts of things in the editing process, but you'll certainly want to pay close attention to catch inaccuracies when you can.

Consider, for example, a respondent who checked the "5" position on a five-point scale for each of 20 items in an attitude questionnaire. This sort of response error (typically called *response set bias*) occurs fairly frequently and

**editing** The inspection and correction of the data received from each element of the sample (or census).

**coding** The process of transforming raw data into symbols (usually numbers).

is relatively easy to detect with a hard-copy survey—but it's not as obvious with an online survey, unless you are looking closely or are testing for lack of variation across items. We've also seen returned surveys on which respondents created patterns out of their responses, for example, selecting the numbers 1, 2, 3, 4, 5, 6, 7, 6, 5, 4, 3, 2, 1, and so on, for successive items. When it's obvious that a respondent hasn't taken the study seriously, his or her answers should be deleted, at least for that section of the survey.

Finally, any additional codes that need to be placed on the data collection forms should be added during the editing process. For example, a unique identifying number of some type should be added unless one already exists. This number will be coded in the data file along with the answers provided by the respondent and will be used to look up the data record or original questionnaire if necessary. Exhibit 16.1 provides a list of the primary tasks involved in the editing process.

## 16-2 Coding Data

**Coding** is the process of transforming raw data into symbols. Most often, the symbols are numerals because computers can handle them easily. The task is to transform the information to be coded (often respondents' answers or human observations) into numbers representing the answers. Sometimes the transformation is extremely straightforward (e.g., when respondents or observers have circled numbers on rating scales); sometimes, however, the coding process involves considerable effort on the part of the coder (e.g., when respondents or observers provide open-ended data).

### 16-2a CODING CLOSED-ENDED ITEMS

In descriptive research, most of the items included in a questionnaire are likely to be closed-ended. That is, most questions will provide a limited number of response categories and will ask the respondent to choose the best response or, sometimes, all responses that apply. These types of items are generally quite simple to code. When there is a single possible answer to a question (e.g., male or female), the researcher uses one variable for the question and simply assigns a number to each possible response (e.g., 1 = female, 2 = male). The appropriate code number is then recorded in the data file. If you ask respondents to check boxes or to provide some other form of response, it's usually easy to assign a number to represent each particular response. For example, the following semantic differential item to measure attitude toward a service provider

**Exhibit 16.1** ▶ Primary Tasks in the Editing Process

1. *Convert all responses to consistent units.* For example, if income is to be measured in thousands of dollars, convert the response "46,350" to 46.

2. *Assess degree of nonresponse. If limited, keep the available data*; if excessive, eliminate the remaining data for that case.

3. *Where possible, check for consistency across responses.* For example, if the respondent indicates in one part of a survey that he has never been seen by a particular health care provider but later reports that he was "very satisfied" with the service received from that health care provider, the editor must decide whether to correct one or the other answer or to treat both responses as if they were missing.

4. *Look for evidence that the respondent wasn't really thinking about his or her answers.* This typically takes the form of response set bias in which the respondent provides the same answer to a series of rating scale items. Responses that are clearly due to response set bias should be treated as missing. If this creates an excessive degree of nonresponse, eliminate the survey.

5. *Verify that branching questions were followed correctly.* From time to time, sections are only to be answered based upon answers to earlier questions. For instance, survey instructions might say, "If yes, continue to Question 3; if no, skip to Question 12." It is important to verify that respondents followed directions properly. Respondents answering "yes" in this example should have answered Questions 3 through 11, whereas "no" responses should not. If those answering "no" did answer Questions 3 through 11, this data should be omitted.

6. *Add any needed codes.* For example, each completed survey must have an identification number. For telephone surveys and personal interviews, it's also important to add a code representing which interviewer conducted the survey.

can easily be coded with the numbers 1 through 7, where 1 represents the box nearest "unfavorable," and 7 represents the box nearest "favorable":

| Unfavorable | 1 | 2 | 3 | 4 | 5 | 6 | 7 | Favorable |
|---|---|---|---|---|---|---|---|---|

For the purposes of analysis, there will be a single variable representing this item, with possible codes 1 through 7 representing increasing levels of favorability.

The coding process for closed-ended items becomes a bit more complex when respondents can indicate more than one answer for a given question, as with "check all that apply" types of items. For example, consider the following question:

**How did you learn about Brown Furniture Company? (check all that apply)**

○ billboard advertising

○ newspaper advertising

○ radio advertising

○ recommended by others

○ drove by the store

○ other

In this situation, using a single variable coded 1 through 6, representing the different options, won't work very well. How would you code responses for someone who checked

both "billboard advertising" and "newspaper advertising"? A simple solution is to create six variables to represent the six possible answers and to indicate for each whether the option was selected. An easy coding scheme is to record a "1" if a respondent selected a response and to record a "0" if she didn't. For the respondent who checked "billboard advertising" and "newspaper advertising," the variables representing these two responses would be coded "1," and each remaining variable would be coded "0."

16-2b **CODING OPEN-ENDED ITEMS**

Open-ended items don't provide response categories for respondents; respondents answer them using their own words. Coding open-ended responses is typically much more difficult than coding closed-ended responses.

**Coding Factual Open-Ended Items**

There are two general classes of open-ended questions. One type seeks factual information from a respondent. For example, consider the following open-ended questions:

In what year were you born? _____

How many times have you eaten at Streeter's Grill in the last month? _____

Each of these questions seeks a factual answer from the respondent. There is a correct answer to each question, and the researcher assumes that the respondent can provide that answer. This type of open-ended question is easy to code by simply coding the actual response (or, if the actual responses aren't numeric, converting the responses to numbers). Numerical data should be recorded as they were reported on the data collection form, rather than being collapsed into smaller categories. For example, don't code age as 1 = under 20 years, 2 = 20 through 29, 3 = 30 through 39, and so on, if actual ages of the people were provided. Instead, record the age in years so that information isn't sacrificed. If you need the information in categories, it's easy to do the conversion later. (Remember our earlier advice: Always use the highest level of measurement possible. In this case, recording the actual age results in ratio-level measurement; recording age in categories would result in ordinal-level measurement.)

## Coding Exploratory Open-Ended Items

The other type of open-ended question is often more exploratory in nature and, as a result, usually much more difficult and expensive to code. For many open-ended questions, there are multiple legitimate responses, some of which you might not anticipate in advance. Suppose that you wanted to determine the causes of so-called brain drain, the migration of college graduates from one state to another after graduation. In response to the question, **"In your own words, give us two or three reasons why you prefer to leave the state after graduation,"** students might provide answers such as "my family lives in another state," "want to try something different," "going to graduate school in another state," and so on. Some might provide a single reason to leave, while others might provide multiple reasons to leave. The process of coding the answers to this sort of question involves a number of steps, as shown in Exhibit 16.2.

**Exhibit 16.2** ▶ Steps in Coding Exploratory Open-Ended Items

**Step 1**

The first step is to go through each questionnaire and highlight each separate response given by each individual. Some respondents can provide multiple answers in only a few words, but others can write whole paragraphs and communicate only one answer, so be careful at this stage. Normally, at least two coders should review all of the responses separately and then compare results to ensure that all responses are considered.

**Step 2**

The next step in coding is specifying the categories or classes into which the responses are to be placed. The goal is to reduce the great number of individual responses into a much smaller set of general categories so that insights may be drawn from the results. The categories must be mutually exclusive and exhaustive, so that every open-ended response logically falls into one and only one category. Usually, a researcher can anticipate some or most of the categories in advance—but don't become "locked in" on those categories alone. Respondents' actual answers will often reveal categories that were initially overlooked or anticipated categories that turn out to have very few responses.

For example, the brain drain researcher (see example in text) might not anticipate that some graduates want to leave just to try something new. To make the categories exhaustive, it is often necessary to include an "other" category for responses that simply don't fit anywhere else. However, if the number of responses in the "other" category rises to more than 5%–10% of the total number of responses, the researcher should consider whether additional categories are needed.

**Step 3**

After an appropriate set of categories is identified, the actual coding of responses into the categories begins. Each response identified during the first step must be given the code number for one, and only one, of the categories developed in the second step. Unless the questions (and responses) are very straightforward (rarely the case for this type of open-ended question), at least two coders who have been trained to understand the types of responses that should be placed in each category should code the responses. Multiple coders help reduce bias in interpreting different responses, a form of office error. Each coder will individually decide which category is appropriate for a response and then assign the numerical code for that category to the response.

**Step 4**

When each coder has coded all responses, the coders meet to compare results, discuss differences in the codes assigned to particular responses, and assign a final code for each response. The coders must keep careful records of the number of disagreements so that a summary measure of percentage agreement (or other measure of reliability) can be computed. The lower the overall level of agreement, the greater the possibility that either the categories aren't mutually exclusive or that one or more coders didn't do a thorough job.

## Manager's Focus

Coding open-ended items is a time-consuming process that involves a significant amount of subjective interpretation of respondents' comments. There are several reasons why open-ended questions in descriptive surveys generally produce relatively imprecise findings. Respondents are not always capable of clearly expressing their precise thoughts, interviewers do not always probe properly to clarify what is meant, and responses do not always get recorded accurately. And different respondents may attempt to communicate the same ideas using very different language.

All of this means that it is a daunting task for a coder to produce a set of categories that captures what respondents were thinking or trying to convey. Although quite useful in exploratory research where the purpose is to obtain insights and new ideas that can be further tested, these types of open-ended questions generally should be avoided in descriptive research.

## 16-3 Aggregating Data

Editing and coding data are important processes that apply to all kinds of data. The process of **data aggregation**, however, applies almost exclusively to longitudinal behavioral data collected by mechanical observation (e.g., scanner data, purchase behavior tied to an online account). Data aggregation is the process of creating summary data (e.g., count, sum, mean) for a particular repeated behavior over a specified period of time. Decisions about data aggregation are important for many types of marketing analytics.

For example, if purchase behavior is tracked at the individual level, you'll have to decide how to combine the purchase data into something meaningful for analysis. Do you want number of purchases per day, per week, or per month—or something else? Or do you need the dollar amount of purchases in some time frame? Or is a simple "yes" or "no" that someone has purchased at all in a certain period of time good enough? This is an important issue that must be addressed during the data aggregation process to ensure that the right kind of information is available when analysis begins. Also note that data aggregation must be accompanied by careful data coding so that analysts understand exactly what the numbers represent when they proceed with their analyses.

> **data aggregation**
> The process of creating summary data for a particular repeated behavior over a specified period of time.
>
> **merging** The process of combining data from different data sources into a single database.

### 16-3a BUILDING THE DATA FILE

To use a computer to analyze the data, the codes representing respondents' answers to questions or behavioral data about them must be placed in a data file that the computer can read. Communication data are often collected using online data collection tools, making the process more or less automatic; data are normally stored in spreadsheet format and can be downloaded for further analysis. Behavioral data that have been mechanically recorded can usually be downloaded into spreadsheets as well; data

aggregation issues and other factors may make the process more involved.

In some cases, however, you may need to manually enter the data yourself. There are numerous methods, including creating text data files in word processing software, using spreadsheet software, using database software, entering data directly into statistical software packages, such as SPSS, or using optical scanning. Regardless of how the data input process will be handled, it helps to visualize the input in terms of a multiple-column record, where columns represent different variables and rows represent different cases.

If the data you intend to analyze have been drawn from different sources, there is an additional preliminary task to be performed. The process of **merging** data involves combining data from different data sources into a single database. Sometimes this will be a fairly straightforward process, as when survey data from an individual are combined with other information about the individual that are already held in a company's databases and a consistent identification number is used to connect the data in the data file. The merger process can quickly become more complicated; however, if data come from multiple sources (perhaps both inside and outside the organization) in different software formats with different identifiers (e.g., names can be misspelled, written with or without middle initials; identification numbers can be mistyped or include extra spaces or zeros), and so on. Although the actual merger process goes beyond the scope of this book, we hope you understand our point: It sometimes takes a great deal of time and other resources to produce a combined data file that is ready for analysis.

### 16-3b BUILDING A CODEBOOK

A data file that is ready for analysis usually consists of row after row of numbers and, occasionally, alphabetic text, taken from one or more sources. As we noted, the rows represent population or sample elements (e.g., customers, households, stores, or some other unit of analysis) and the columns contain data about the variables (e.g., survey responses, purchase data, demographic data) included in the data set. If you were to open a data file and examine it, you would be completely lost about what each number or other character might mean. Researchers solve this dilemma by creating codebooks.

A **codebook** contains explicit directions about how raw data for each case are coded in the data file. At a minimum, the codebook must provide (1) the variable name to be used in statistical analyses for each variable included in the data file (e.g., "gender"); (2) a description of how each variable and how the variable is coded (e.g., "What is your gender?" [1=female, 2=male]); (3) the source of the data when multiple sources are used (e.g., "Member Survey, April 2017"), and (4) an explanation of how missing data are treated in the data file (e.g., "missing=blank"). In a very real sense, the codebook is a map to help the researcher navigate from completed questionnaires or other sources of data to the data file. (If you want to look ahead a little, Exhibit 16.6 provides a nice example of a codebook.)

Although there are numerous ways to code and enter data into the data file, we suggest the following standards:

- When a question allows multiple responses, assign separate variables for each response option. Look ahead at Question 1 on the Avery Fitness Center survey (Exhibit 16.5). Because this question allows multiple answers ("please check all that apply"), the researchers have assigned separate variables for each option in the data file.

- Use only numeric codes, not letters of the alphabet or special characters, like @. Follow this suggestion for open-ended responses if possible. For instance, note that Question 4 is open-ended. The EVENT variable associated with this question in the codebook (see

Exhibit 16.6) shows five common, general responses provided as answers to this question: "1 = general health/exercise, 2 = pool/facilities," and so on, plus a "6 = other" category.

- Use standard codes for "no information." Thus, all "don't know" responses might be coded as 8, "no answers" as 9, and "does not apply" as 0. It is best if the same code is used throughout the study for each of these types of "no information." If "don't know" and "does not apply" are not response options (and thus there is no distinction between different types of "no information"), it is often best to just leave the column(s) blank.

## 16-4 Cleaning the Data

**Blunders** are office errors that occur during editing, coding, or data entry (especially when done by hand). Of all possible sources of error in a marketing research project, blunders are among the most frustrating because they are usually caused by simple carelessness. In this section, we will talk about how to identify blunders and discuss several data entry options that might limit this source of error. One of the advantages of online data collection is that when respondents answer questions, they automatically enter their responses into the data file, reducing the number of potential blunders.

Sometimes blunders are relatively easy to find. For example, suppose that you were coding a 1 through 5 Likert scale and accidentally entered a 7 instead of the 4 that the respondent circled on the questionnaire. The blunder can be seen by performing a simple univariate analysis known as a frequency count (which we will introduce in the next chapter). A frequency count tells us all of the different responses coded for a variable along with how many cases responded in each way. In our example, the miscoded 7 will turn up as a response in the frequency analysis, and we will immediately know that a mistake has been made (remember that only the

> **codebook** A document that contains explicit directions about how data from data collection forms are coded in the data file.
>
> **blunder** An office error that arises during editing, coding, or data entry.

## Manager's Focus

As a manager, it is not your responsibility to "clean the data" or "handle missing data." However, you should verify that these tasks are completed in an appropriate way by your research provider. These two pre-analysis steps may not seem as important as the final analyses, but if they are not handled properly, the findings produced by the final analyses will be compromised.

Prior to a study, it might be a good idea to ask all of the prospective research suppliers how they generally handle these tasks. If a research firm doesn't give a direct and convincing response, choose a different provider. Once the data collection process is underway, you should revisit these two topics with your research provider to ensure there is an appropriate plan in place to handle each step prior to completing the final analyses.

numbers 1 through 5 are valid responses to the question). At this point, it's only a matter of identifying which questionnaire was coded 7 for that variable, pulling the actual questionnaire to find the correct response (i.e., 4), and correcting the mistake in the data file. On most projects, frequencies should initially be run on all variables to help identify blunders.

Other blunders are more difficult to detect. In the previous example, suppose that you accidentally entered a 1 instead of the 4 circled by the respondent. Because a 1 is one of the possible valid responses to this item (i.e., a 1 through 5 scale), a frequency analysis won't uncover this blunder; more involved types of examination are required. One possibility, which is similar to quality control in manufacturing processes, is to select a sample of questionnaires that have been coded and entered and compare the data file against the original questionnaires to find discrepancies. If no blunders are found, there is less concern about data entry error. If several blunders are identified, it may be necessary to check additional records or even examine all records.

A better option, known as **double-entry** of data, requires that the data be entered by two separate people in two separate data files and then the data files be compared for discrepancies. The differences are resolved by referring to the original questionnaires. Because it's unlikely that two different people would make the same blunders during data entry, this approach is likely to produce the "cleanest" data file possible with manual data entry. Using modern word processing software packages, the file comparison process is quite straightforward. Note, however, that this technique requires greater resources (i.e., time, effort, money).

Finally, **optical scanning** of data collection forms takes information directly from the data collection form and reads it into a data file. Numerous companies offer optical scanning services, which are especially useful for mail or other self-administered questionnaires.

**double-entry** Data entry procedure in which data are entered separately by two people in two data files, and the data files are compared for discrepancies.

**optical scanning** The use of scanner technology to "read" responses on paper surveys and to store these responses in a data file.

**item nonresponse** A source of error that arises when a respondent agrees to an interview but refuses, or is unable, to answer specific questions.

## 16-5 Handling Missing Data

As we noted earlier, **item nonresponse** is often a significant problem when collecting communication-based primary data. Unless you "force" respondents to complete each item before continuing an online survey, it's almost a sure thing that some respondents will skip questions or even whole sections. Although forcing answers is convenient for the researcher (i.e., it eliminates missing data), it will likely lead to (1) response error when respondents simply choose a response so that they can get on with the survey, or (2) nonresponse error when individuals become frustrated and simply terminate the process. If you want to use this approach, ensure that all or most potential respondents know the answers to the questions and that all potential responses are represented (i.e., the response categories are exhaustive). As always, we advise careful exploratory research and pretesting in order to avoid problems.

The degree of item nonresponse often serves as a useful indicator of research quality. When there are lots of missing items, you should question the whole research effort and critically review your objectives and procedures. Even when there's not a lot of missing information, you still must decide what to do about it before you analyze the data. Here are several possible strategies:

**Eliminate the case with the missing item(s) from all further analyses.** This extreme strategy results in a "pure" data set with no missing information at all. In the extreme, you might throw out a questionnaire from which only a single piece of information was missing. Given that data are so valuable and sometimes difficult to collect, we rarely recommend this strategy. Any case with a significant amount of missing information should have been eliminated during the editing process.

**Eliminate the case with the missing item only in analyses using the variable.** When using this approach, you'll

## Manager's Focus

We strongly encourage you to have the results of each research study entered into your organization's marketing information system (MIS) or corporate library so that other managers can also benefit from what was learned. As part of this process, we would advise you to develop a system for archiving copies of the (a) final report, (b) blank questionnaire, (c) data file, and (d) codebook.

These materials will enable research personnel (or even managers) to understand the nature of the original data and will enhance their ability to conduct appropriate new analyses at future points in time. This ability will dramatically enhance the value of the research findings when managers use them as secondary data with which to address new marketing problems.

need to continually report the number of cases on which an analysis is based, because the sample size won't be constant across analyses. The obvious advantage to this strategy is that all available data are used for each analysis.

**Substitute values for the missing items.** Sometimes you can estimate a value for the missing item based on responses to other related items on the respondent's questionnaire, perhaps using a statistical technique known as regression analysis, which measures the relationship between two or more variables. Or you can use the values from other respondents' questionnaires to determine the mean, median, or mode for the variable and substitute that value for the missing item. The substitution of values makes maximum use of the data because all the reasonably good cases are used. At the same time, it requires more work from the analyst, and it contains some potential for bias, because the analyst has "created" values where none previously existed.

**Contact the respondent again.** If the missing information is critical to the study and responses were not anonymous, it is sometimes possible to contact the respondent again to obtain the information. This approach is especially applicable if it appears that the respondent simply missed the item altogether or if the respondent tried to answer the question but didn't follow the instructions.

There is no "right" or simple answer as to how missing items should be handled. It all depends on the purposes of the study, the incidence of missing items, and the methods that will be used to analyze the data.

> There is no "right" or simple answer as to how missing items should be handled.

## 16-6 Avery Fitness Center Project

Many of the key points in this chapter, as well as the following data analysis chapters, can best be illustrated using an example. The Avery Fitness Center (AFC) is located in a midsized city in the southeastern United States. The company offers a variety of exercise programs to its members under the supervision of personal trainers. The company was founded 15 years ago and operates from a single location in an old shopping center near a large university. AFC primarily targets "prime-timers"—men and women aged 55 years and older, some of whom are struggling with health issues. Many customers are attracted to the large indoor therapy pool that allows them to exercise using water resistance, which is much easier on bones and joints than traditional exercise options. Individuals

become members of the fitness center by completing an application form (see Exhibit 16.3) and paying a monthly fee; they pay additional fees for special classes, use of personal trainers, and so forth.

Although business has been steady, AFC managers believe that the company could grow substantially without adding additional facilities. As a result, AFC managers were interested in better understanding the kinds of individuals that are attracted to AFC and how best to recruit more of these kinds of people. More specifically, the AFC researchers began to address two research problems: (1) discover existing member demographics and usage patterns (including fees paid) and (2) investigate how members initially learn about AFC and their motivations for using the center.

To address these research problems, researchers decided to gather the appropriate data from a variety of sources. As a review of Exhibit 16.4 will confirm, the company is quite forward-thinking in terms of the data that it gathers (and would like to gather in the future) about its customers. In addition to communication data gathered on the initial application and from periodic surveys sent to members, the company tracks a wide variety of other data based on member behaviors ranging from data from location-enabled mobile phones to fees paid.

For the current project, the company gathered primary data by sending a mail survey designed to determine member motivations for using AFC, among other things (see Exhibit 16.5). Researchers sent surveys to 400 members drawn using a simple, random sample; respondents completed and returned 231 usable surveys for a response rate of 58%. For the purposes of the analysis, the sample was limited to members who had visited AFC at least once in the previous 12 months. Note that the survey was administered via regular mail because many of the members are elderly and not responsive to online surveys.

Researchers used the member number to match the survey data to other data about the members obtained from their original application forms (refer to Exhibit 16.3), accounting records (i.e., revenues aggregated over the prior 12 months), and digital facility entry records (i.e., total number of visits over a 30-day period; modal time of entry aggregated into three parts of the day over the 30-day period). Thus, the data to be analyzed came from four different sources, (1) application forms for joining AFC, (2) a member survey, (3) AFC accounting records, and (4) stored computer records on time and date of facility entry.

During the editing and coding process, the researchers added code numbers for the open-ended responses for question 4 on the survey. The codebook for the project is presented in Exhibit 16.6. We'll take a look at what these multi-source data can tell us about AFC members in the following chapters.

**Exhibit 16.3** ▶ Avery Fitness Center Application Form

# Avery Fitness Center
## MEMBERSHIP APPLICATION

### CONTACT INFORMATION

Your Name _____

Address Street _____ Apt _____

City _____ State _____ Zip _____

Preferred Telephone _____ Alternate Telephone _____

Email Address _____

Emergency Contact _____

Relationship _____ Telephone _____ Email address _____

### FAMILY MEMBERS Include your name on line 1.

| Name (Last, if Different) | Birth Date | Gender | Employer (if applicable) |
|---|---|---|---|
| 1. | | ☐ M ☐ F | |
| 2. | | ☐ M ☐ F | |
| 3. | | ☐ M ☐ F | |
| 4. | | ☐ M ☐ F | |
| 5. | | ☐ M ☐ F | |
| 6. | | ☐ M ☐ F | |
| 7. | | ☐ M ☐ F | |
| 8. | | ☐ M ☐ F | |

### MEMBERSHIP TYPE

Please select one of the following:
Membership

How did you learn about AFC? (Please check all that apply)

☐ Adult  ☐ Youth  ☐ Program Member
☐ Senior  ☐ Teen
☐ Family I  ☐ Student
☐ Family II

☐ Recommendation from Doctor

☐ Recommendation from Friend of Acquaintance

☐ Advertising (including Yellow Pages)

☐ Heard AFC director speak

☐ Drove by location

☐ Article in Paper

☐ Other

Signature _____

Date ____ _____ _____

For Office Use Only

Staff Name _____

Membership Number
☐☐☐☐☐☐☐☐☐☐☐☐

**Exhibit 16.4 ▶** Data Sources on Avery Fitness Center Project

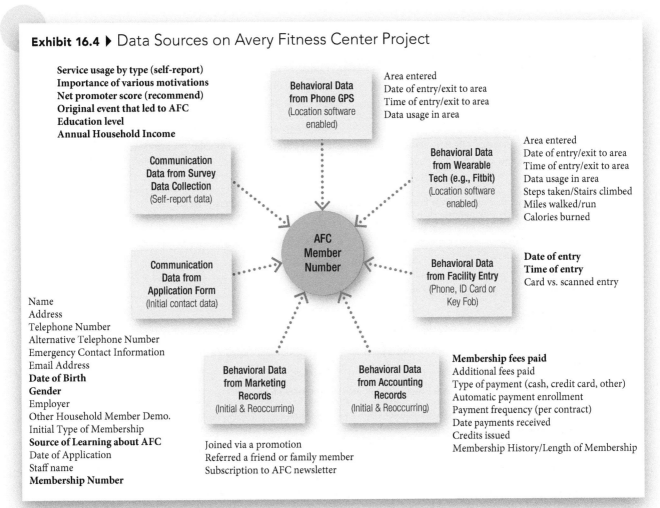

Service usage by type (self-report)
Importance of various motivations
Net promoter score (recommend)
Original event that led to AFC
Education level
**Annual Household Income**

**Behavioral Data from Phone GPS** (Location software enabled)

Area entered
Date of entry/exit to area
Time of entry/exit to area
Data usage in area

**Communication Data from Survey Data Collection** (Self-report data)

**Behavioral Data from Wearable Tech (e.g., Fitbit)** (Location software enabled)

Area entered
Date of entry/exit to area
Time of entry/exit to area
Data usage in area
Steps taken/Stairs climbed
Miles walked/run
Calories burned

**AFC Member Number**

**Communication Data from Application Form** (Initial contact data)

**Behavioral Data from Facility Entry** (Phone, ID Card or Key Fob)

**Date of entry**
**Time of entry**
Card vs. scanned entry

Name
Address
Telephone Number
Alternative Telephone Number
Emergency Contact Information
Email Address
**Date of Birth**
**Gender**
Employer
Other Household Member Demo.
Initial Type of Membership
**Source of Learning about AFC**
Date of Application
Staff name
**Membership Number**

**Behavioral Data from Marketing Records** (Initial & Reoccurring)

**Behavioral Data from Accounting Records** (Initial & Reoccurring)

**Membership fees paid**
Additional fees paid
Type of payment (cash, credit card, other)
Automatic payment enrollment
Payment frequency (per contract)
Date payments received
Credits issued
Membership History/Length of Membership

Joined via a promotion
Referred a friend or family member
Subscription to AFC newsletter

Note: Types of data noted in bold are available for the current project.

**Exhibit 16.5** ▶ Avery Fitness Center Questionnaire

### AVERY FITNESS CENTER SURVEY

Thank you for taking time to provide important feedback about *Avery Fitness Center* (AFC) on this short survey. Please answer the following questions. Your candid responses will help us provide better services in the future. We have included your membership number so that we can include this informtion in your file. Please note that we do not share your information with anyone else.

**(1) Which of the following AFC services have you utilized at least once in the last 30 days? (Please check all that apply)**

☐ Weight Training      ☐ Exercise Circuit      ☐ Therapy Pool

☐ Classes      ☐ Circulation Station

**(2) How important to you personally is each of the following reasons for participating in AFC programs? (Circle a number on each scale)**

| | not at all important | | | | very important |
|---|---|---|---|---|---|
| General Health and Fitness | 1 | 2 | 3 | 4 | 5 |
| Social Aspects | 1 | 2 | 3 | 4 | 5 |
| Physical Enjoyment | 1 | 2 | 3 | 4 | 5 |
| Specific Medical Concerns | 1 | 2 | 3 | 4 | 5 |

**(3) How likely is it that you would recommend AFC to a friend or colleague?**

| not at all likely | | | | | neutral | | | | | extremely likely |
|---|---|---|---|---|---|---|---|---|---|---|
| 0 | 1 | 2 | 3 | 4 | 5 | 6 | 7 | 8 | 9 | 10 |

**(4) What was the original event that caused you to begin using services from AFC?**

_____

**(5) Highest Level of Education Achieved:**

☐ Less than High School      ☐ Some College      ☐ Four-year College Degree

☐ High School Degree      ☐ Associates Degree      ☐ Advanced Degree

**(6) What is your approximate annual household income from all sources before taxes? (Please check the appropriate category & employment status):**

☐ $0-15,000      ☐ $45,001-$60,000      ☐ $90,001-105,000

☐ $15,001-30,000      ☐ $60,001-75,000      ☐ $105,001-120,000

☐ $30,001-45,000      ☐ $75,001-90,000      ☐ more than $120,000

Membership Number:
**072612**

***THANK YOU!***

**Exhibit 16.6** ▶ Codebook for Avery Fitness Center Project

| Variable Name | Data Source | Description | Data Code |
|---|---|---|---|
| MEMBERNUM | Application Form | Questionnaire identification number | (record number) |
| WEIGHT | Member Survey, April 2017 | Utilized weight training in previous 30 days? | 0 = no  1 = yes |
| CLASSES | Member Survey, April 2017 | Utilized classes in previous 30 days? | 0 = no  1 = yes |
| CIRCUIT | Member Survey, April 2017 | Utilized exercise circuit in previous 30 days? | 0 = no  1 = yes |
| STATION | Member Survey, April 2017 | Utilized circulation station in previous 30 days? | 0 = no  1 = yes |
| POOL | Member Survey, April 2017 | Utilized therapy pool in previous 30 days? | 0 = no  1 = yes |
| FITNESS | Member Survey, April 2017 | Importance for participation: General Health and Fitness | (1-5, "not at all important–very important") |
| SOCIAL | Member Survey, April 2017 | Social Aspects | (1-5, "not at all important–very important") |
| ENJOY | Member Survey, April 2017 | Physical Enjoyment | (1-5, "not at all important–very important") |
| MEDICAL | Member Survey, April 2017 | Specific Medical Concerns | (1-5, "not at all important–very important") |
| RECOM | Member Survey, April 2017 | How likely to recommend? (NPS) | (0–10, "not at all likely–extremely likely") |
| EVENT | Member Survey, April 2017 | What original event caused you to begin using services at AFC? | 1 = general health / exercise; 2 = pool/facilities; 3 = rehab / specific medical needs; 4 = social considerations; 5 = transfer from another center; 6 = other |
| EDUCAT | Member Survey, April 2017 | Highest level of education achieved? | 1 = less than high school; 2 = high school degree; 3 = some college; 4 = associates degree; 5 = four-year college degree; 6 = advanced degree |
| INCOME | Member Survey, April 2017 | Annual household income before taxes | 1 = $0–15,000; 2 = $15,001–30,000; 3 = $30,001–45,000; 4 = $45,001–60,000; 5 = $60,001–75,000; 6 = $75,001–90,000; 7 = $90,001–105,000; 8 = $105,001–120,000; 9 = more than $120,000 |
| DOCTOR | Application Form | How learned about AFC? Doctor Rec. | 0 = no  1 = yes |
| WOM | Application Form | How learned about AFC? Friend Rec. | 0 = no  1 = yes |
| ADVERT | Application Form | How learned about AFC? Advertising | 0 = no  1 = yes |
| SPEAKER | Application Form | How learned about AFC? Heard director speak | 0 = no  1 = yes |
| LOCATION | Application Form | How learned about AFC? Drove bv location | 0 = no  1 = yes |
| ARTICLE | Application Form | How learned about AFC? Article in newspaper | 0 = no  1 = yes |
| OTHER | Application Form | How learned about AFC? Other | 0 = no  1 = yes |
| AGE | Application Form | Current Age | (current year minus birth year) |
| GENDER | Application Form | Gender | 1 = male; 2 = female |
| REVENUE | Accounting Records | Previous year Revenue from Respondent | (record aggregated amount) |
| VISITS30 | Facility Entry Data | Number of visits to AFC in previous 30 days | (record aggregated number) |
| DAYPART | Facility Entry Data | Modal time of day to visit AFC (prior 30 days) | 1 = morning; 2 = afternoon; 3 = evening |

MISSING = BLANK

# Summary

## Learning Objective 1

**Explain the purpose of the editing process.**
The purpose of editing is to detect and correct obvious errors in the data collection process.

## Learning Objective 2

**Define coding.**
Coding is the technical procedure by which data are categorized. Through coding, the raw data are transformed into symbols—usually numerals—that may be tabulated and counted. The transformation involves judgment on the part of the coder.

## Learning Objective 3

**Explain why data must sometimes be aggregated.**
When data are collected over time, decisions must be made about how to produce summary measures representing specific time periods before analyses can begin.

## Learning Objective 4

**Discuss the merging of data.**
For many projects, data are gathered from multiple sources. Merging the different data sets can be a complicated process that requires very careful attention.

## Learning Objective 5

**Describe the kinds of information contained in a codebook.**
The codebook contains the general instructions indicating how each item of data was coded. It contains the variable names, sources of the data (if the data came from multiple sources), a description of how each variable is coded, and an explanation of how missing data are treated in the data file.

## Learning Objective 6

**Describe common methods for cleaning the data file.**
Blunders may be located by examining frequency distributions for all variables to identify obviously incorrect codings, by sampling records from the data file and comparing them with the original questionnaires, or by using double-entry of data in which data are entered into two separate data files and then compared for discrepancies.

## Learning Objective 7

**Discuss options for dealing with missing data in analyses.**
Several options exist, including (a) eliminating the case with missing information from all analyses, (b) eliminating the case with missing information from only analyses using variables with missing information, (c) substituting values for the missing items, and (d) contacting the respondent again.

## Key Terms

editing (page 241)
coding (page 241)
data aggregation (page 244)
merging (page 244)
codebook (page 245)
blunders (page 245)
double-entry (page 246)
optical scanning (page 246)
item nonresponse (page 246)

## Review Questions

1. What should a researcher do with incomplete answers? Obviously wrong answers? Answers that reflect a lack of interest?
2. How might a researcher best code "please check all that apply" questions?
3. What are the two kinds of open-ended questions, and why is one more difficult to code than the other?
4. Why should multiple coders be used to establish categories and code responses for open-ended questions? Does this apply to all open-ended questions?
5. What methods are available for building a data file?
6. What is the purpose of the codebook?
7. What is a blunder?
8. What is double-entry of data?
9. What are the possible ways for dealing with missing data? Which strategy would you recommend?

# Endnote

1. Shulman, War stories: True-life tales in marketing research, *Quirk's Marketing Research Review*, 16.

# CHAPTER 17

# Analysis and Interpretation: Individual Variables Independently

## LEARNING OBJECTIVES

▸ Distinguish between univariate and multivariate analyses.

▸ Describe frequency analysis.

▸ Describe descriptive statistics.

▸ Discuss confidence intervals for proportions and means.

▸ Overview the basic purpose of hypothesis testing.

## [ INTRODUCTION ]

There are some aspects of marketing research that are fairly difficult. Fortunately, data analysis usually isn't one of them, despite what you may have heard. Data analysis hinges on two questions about the variable(s) to be analyzed. First, will the variable be analyzed in isolation (univariate analysis) or in relationship to one or more other variables (multivariate analysis)? Second, what level of measurement (nominal, ordinal, interval, ratio) was used to measure the variable? If you can answer those questions, data analysis usually isn't that difficult—especially because a computer can do the analysis for you.

In this chapter, we present some common types of univariate data analysis techniques and introduce the concept of hypothesis testing. Many analyses in applied marketing research involve simple univariate analyses. For example, a magazine publisher might want to know the proportion of the magazine's readers who are male; a restaurant might like to know the average income of its typical diner; a service provider might need to know her customers' average level of satisfaction with the services provided. In each of these cases, a single variable is analyzed in isolation—gender, income, satisfaction.

## 17-1 Basic Univariate Statistics: Categorical Measures

Because both nominal and ordinal measures are easily used to group respondents or objects into groups or categories, researchers often refer to these types of measures as **categorical measures**. To illustrate, recall the Avery Fitness Center (AFC) project that we introduced in the previous chapter. For this project, researchers merged data from several sources to create a data set for analysis. One of the research problems on that

> **categorical measures** A commonly used expression for nominal and ordinal measures.
>
> **frequency analysis** A count of the number of cases that fall into each of the possible response categories.

project involved discovering member demographics. The AFC member database includes measures of the (1) gender (from the initial application) and (2) highest level of education achieved (from the survey) of the population of AFC members, among other things.

The first of these measures is clearly at the nominal level of measurement: Each individual belongs to either the "male" or "female" category. The second measure was assessed at the ordinal level of measurement. Respondents indicated the highest level of education they had achieved by choosing one of six categories ordered from low ("less than high school") to high ("advanced degree"). Results for both items are easily obtained through frequency analysis.

### 17-1a FREQUENCY ANALYSIS

A **frequency analysis** consists of counting the number of cases that fall into the various response categories. This is a very simple analytic tool, yet it is incredibly important and commonly used to report the overall results of marketing research studies. You can produce frequencies for any of the variables in a study; any packaged statistical program, such as SPSS, and even spreadsheet programs, such as Excel, can perform frequency analysis. Some programs will calculate summary statistics and plot a histogram of the values (discussed later) in addition to reporting the number of cases in each category. Additionally, many of the current online survey tools will provide summary statistics in the form of frequency analyses.

Exhibit 17.1 presents a frequency analysis for the gender of the individuals in the AFC study data set (SPSS Menu Sequence: Analyze > Descriptive Statistics > Frequencies). As indicated, 177 of the 222 individuals who provided their gender on the initial application (nine people in the data set did not provide this information) were women. The second column in Exhibit 17.1 includes percentages calculated using all cases, including those who didn't provide the information. The third column pres-

### Manager's Focus

Managers depend upon researchers to perform data analysis. Why, then, should they know something about data analysis techniques? Technology has developed to the point where data analysis software is very user friendly, even for nonresearchers. You may find yourself in a position of wanting or needing to quickly analyze data for yourself. Being able to easily run software is not the same thing, though, as running and understanding the analyses properly. You need to be able to determine which analyses are appropriate given such considerations as the level of measurement (i.e., nominal, ordinal, interval, or ratio) and the nature of the research objectives. In addition, you need to know how to properly interpret the results of each test. Even when researchers do the data analysis, you will be less reliant on the judgment of others and better able to independently interpret the marketing relevance of the findings if you understand the nature of the statistical tests performed for you.

**Exhibit 17.1** ▶ Avery Fitness Center: Gender

| GENDER | NUMBER | PERCENT | VALID PERCENT | VALID CUMULATIVE PERCENT |
|---|---|---|---|---|
| Male | 45 | 19% | 20% | 20% |
| Female | 177 | 77% | 80% | 100% |
| Total | 222 | 96% | 100% | |
| Missing | 9 | 4% | | |
| Overall total | 231 | 100% | | |

ents "valid" percentages (the missing cases are excluded). Although the number of missing cases in a frequency analysis should be indicated, valid percentages are normally reported along with the count. The final column in Exhibit 17.1 reports the cumulative valid percent associated with each level of the variable. This is the percentage of observations with a value less than or equal to the level indicated.[1]

Exhibit 17.2 presents frequency results for the highest level of education reported by the AFC members. As you can see, 15% of respondents reported a high school degree as the highest level of education achieved. Working with the cumulative percentages, however, it is probably more informative to report that 83% of respondents indicated having taken courses beyond the high school level. The results in Exhibit 17.2 indicate that AFC members tend to be well educated (60% have at least a 4-year college degree).

### About Percentages

Before going further, let's think about using percentages for reporting results. First, you'll almost always want to include percentages along with the raw count for frequency analyses—percentages help readers interpret results. (Which do you think is more informative—that "80% were women" or that "177 of 222 were women"?) Second, percentages should be rounded off to whole numbers because whole numbers are easier to read and because decimals might make the results look more accurate or "scientific" than they really are, especially in a small sample. In some cases, it might be reasonable to report percentages to one decimal place (rarely two decimal places), but the general rule is to use whole numbers.[2]

**outlier** An observation so different in magnitude from the rest of the observations that the analyst chooses to treat it as a special case.

**histogram** A form of column chart on which the values of the variable are placed along the *x*-axis and the absolute or relative frequency of the values is shown on the *y*-axis.

17-1b **OTHER USES FOR FREQUENCIES**

In addition to communicating study results, frequency analysis is useful for other things as well. For example, frequencies can help determine the degree of item non-response for a variable as well as help locate blunders, as we discussed in the previous chapter. As a general rule, you should run frequencies for all the variables in a study before you do anything else.

Another use of frequency analysis is to locate **outliers**, valid observations that are so different from the rest of the observations that they ought to be treated as special cases. This may mean eliminating the observation from the analysis or trying to determine why this case is so different from the others. For instance, consider the histogram of AFC members' ages presented in Exhibit 17.3. A **histogram** is a form of bar chart that is based on information from a frequency count. The values of a variable—age, in this example—are placed along the *x*-axis, and the raw count or proportion of cases that occur at each level is plotted on the *y*-axis.

A quick look at the histogram shows that one AFC member in the merged data set is considerably younger than all the other cases. The SPSS frequency analysis output (see Exhibit 17.4) shows that this particular person is 18 years old; the next youngest AFC member among the respondents was 35 years old. This case is clearly out of line with the rest of the sample—it should be considered an outlier. What you choose to do with this observation depends on the objectives of the study. In this case, it's reasonable for an AFC member to be 18 years old (although unusual), so we'll keep it in the data file for now.

**Exhibit 17.2** ▶ Avery Fitness Center: Level of Education

| LEVEL OF EDUCATION ACHIEVED | NUMBER | VALID PERCENT | CUMULATIVE PERCENT |
|---|---|---|---|
| Less than high school | 4 | 2% | 2% |
| High school degree | 34 | 15% | 17% |
| Some college | 46 | 20% | 37% |
| Associate's degree | 7 | 3% | 40% |
| Four-year college degree | 52 | 23% | 64% |
| Advanced degree | 82 | 36% | 100% |
| Total | 225 | 100% | |

(number of missing cases = 6)

**Exhibit 17.3** ▶ Avery Fitness Center: Histogram of Respondent Age (SPSS Output)

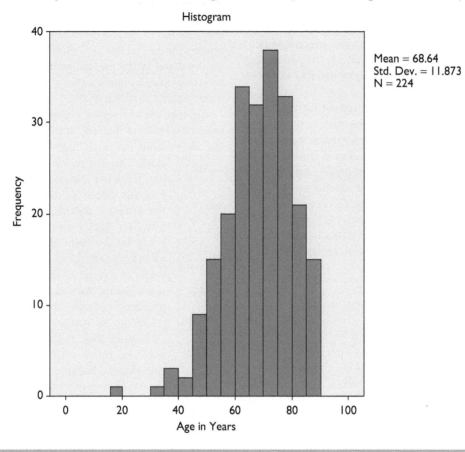

**Exhibit 17.4** ▶ Avery Fitness Center: Age (SPSS Output)

| | AGE | FREQUENCY | PERCENT | VALID PERCENT | CUMULATIVE PERCENT |
|---|---|---|---|---|---|
| Valid | 18 | 1 | 0.4 | 0.4 | 0.4 |
| | 35 | 1 | 0.4 | 0.4 | 0.9 |
| | 36 | 1 | 0.4 | 0.4 | 1.3 |
| | 38 | 1 | 0.4 | 0.4 | 1.8 |
| | 40 | 1 | 0.4 | 0.4 | 2.2 |
| | 43 | 1 | 0.4 | 0.4 | 2.7 |
| | 45 | 1 | 0.4 | 0.4 | 3.1 |
| | 46 | 1 | 0.4 | 0.4 | 3.6 |
| | 47 | 1 | 0.4 | 0.4 | 4.0 |
| | 48 | 2 | 0.9 | 0.9 | 4.9 |

AGE IN YEARS

| | AGE IN YEARS | | | |
| --- | --- | --- | --- | --- |
| AGE | FREQUENCY | PERCENT | VALID PERCENT | CUMULATIVE PERCENT |
| 49 | 2 | 0.9 | 0.9 | 5.8 |
| 50 | 3 | 1.3 | 1.3 | 7.1 |
| 51 | 2 | 0.9 | 0.9 | 8.0 |
| 52 | 1 | 0.4 | 0.4 | 8.5 |
| 53 | 4 | 1.7 | 1.8 | 10.3 |
| 54 | 4 | 1.7 | 1.8 | 12.1 |
| 55 | 4 | 1.7 | 1.8 | 13.8 |
| 56 | 1 | 0.4 | 0.4 | 14.3 |
| 57 | 3 | 1.3 | 1.3 | 15.6 |
| 58 | 3 | 1.3 | 1.3 | 17.0 |
| 59 | 7 | 3.0 | 3.1 | 20.1 |
| 60 | 6 | 2.6 | 2.7 | 22.8 |
| 61 | 7 | 3.0 | 3.1 | 25.9 |
| 62 | 3 | 1.3 | 1.3 | 27.2 |
| 63 | 13 | 5.6 | 5.8 | 33.0 |
| 64 | 6 | 2.6 | 2.7 | 35.7 |
| 65 | 5 | 2.2 | 2.2 | 37.9 |
| 66 | 8 | 3.5 | 3.6 | 41.5 |
| 67 | 8 | 3.5 | 3.6 | 45.1 |
| 68 | 4 | 1.7 | 1.8 | 46.9 |
| 69 | 6 | 2.6 | 2.7 | 49.6 |
| 70 | 6 | 2.6 | 2.7 | 52.2 |
| 71 | 11 | 4.8 | 4.9 | 57.1 |
| 72 | 4 | 1.7 | 1.8 | 58.9 |
| 73 | 6 | 2.6 | 2.7 | 61.6 |
| 74 | 9 | 3.9 | 4.0 | 65.6 |
| 75 | 8 | 3.5 | 3.6 | 69.2 |
| 76 | 6 | 2.6 | 2.7 | 71.9 |
| 77 | 7 | 3.0 | 3.1 | 75.0 |
| 78 | 7 | 3.0 | 3.1 | 78.1 |
| 79 | 8 | 3.5 | 3.6 | 81.7 |
| 80 | 5 | 2.2 | 2.2 | 83.9 |

*(Continued)*

**Exhibit 17.4 ▶** Avery Fitness Center: Age (SPSS Output) (Continued)

### AGE IN YEARS

| AGE | FREQUENCY | PERCENT | VALID PERCENT | CUMULATIVE PERCENT |
|---|---|---|---|---|
| 81 | 2 | 0.9 | 0.9 | 84.8 |
| 82 | 11 | 4.8 | 4.9 | 89.7 |
| 83 | 1 | 0.4 | 0.4 | 90.2 |
| 84 | 3 | 1.3 | 1.3 | 91.5 |
| 85 | 4 | 1.7 | 1.8 | 93.3 |
| 86 | 4 | 1.7 | 1.8 | 95.1 |
| 87 | 5 | 2.2 | 2.2 | 97.3 |
| 88 | 2 | 0.9 | 0.9 | 98.2 |
| 89 | 3 | 1.3 | 1.3 | 99.6 |
| 90 | 1 | 0.4 | 0.4 | 100.0 |
| Total | 224 | 97.0 | 100.0 | |
| Missing System | 7 | 3.0 | | |
| Total | 231 | 100.0 | | |

The frequency count for age presented in Exhibit 17.4 also allows us to point out one final use of frequency analysis. With ordinal-, interval-, or ratio-level measures, it is often useful to identify the median point as a measure of "average" for the distribution. It is a simple matter to locate the value of age at which the 50th percentile (the observation in the middle of the distribution when ordered from low to high) lands; in this case, the median age is seventy. (And, if it matters, the first quartile falls at age 61 and the third quartile at age 77.)

So, what have we learned so far about AFC members from frequency analysis? They are mostly female, well-educated, and older. An additional analysis indicated that 70% reported household incomes above $45,000 (you can try this one on your own using the data file located at www.cengagebrain.com). Finally, Exhibit 17.5 presents information about AFC service usage behavior—all of these results were obtained using simple frequency analysis.

**confidence interval**
A projection of the range within which a population parameter will lie at a given level of confidence, based on a statistic obtained from a probabilistic sample.

### 17-1c CONFIDENCE INTERVALS FOR PROPORTIONS

We learned from the results presented in Exhibit 17.2 that 60% of the respondents in the sample had earned, at minimum, a 4-year college degree. Although this sample statistic is interesting, AFC managers care more about the entire population of AFC customers than they do about a particular sample. Recall that we draw a sample to represent the population. In this case, our best guess is that 60% of the members in the population have at least a 4-year degree, but because of sampling error (not to mention the other types of error, but let's not worry about those right now), we can't be confident that this estimate is precisely true for the population.

Fortunately, because the researchers drew a sample using a probabilistic sampling plan, we can account for sampling error and make inferences about the population as a whole based on the results from the sample. A **confidence interval** is a projection of the range within which a population parameter will lie at a given level of confidence based on a statistic obtained from an appropriately drawn sample.[3] To produce a confidence interval, all we need to do is calculate the degree of sampling error for the particular statistic. To calculate sampling error for a proportion, we need three pieces of information: (1) $z$, the $z$ score representing the desired degree of confidence (usually 95% confidence, where $z = 1.96$); (2) $n$, the number of valid cases overall for the proportion; and (3) $p$, the relevant proportion obtained from the sample. The sample size and the proportion are easily obtained

**Exhibit 17.5▸** Avery Fitness Center: Services Used Within the Past 30 Days

| SERVICE | NUMBER | PERCENT OF RESPONDENTS USING |
|---|---|---|
| Weight training | 73 | 32% |
| Classes | 61 | 26% |
| Exercise circuit | 51 | 22% |
| Circulation station | 28 | 12% |
| Therapy pool | 104 | 45% |

($n$ = 231; no missing cases)

from the frequency analysis output. These pieces of information are entered into the following formula for sampling error for a proportion:

$$\text{sampling error for proportion} = z\sqrt{\frac{p(1-p)}{n}}$$

The resulting value is also frequently called the *margin of sampling error.* Using the information in Exhibit 17.2, the margin of sampling error for the proportion of AFC members with at least a 4-year college degree in the population is calculated as follows:

$$\text{sampling error} = 1.96\sqrt{\frac{0.60(1-0.60)}{225}} - 0.06$$

You calculate the confidence interval itself like this:

$$(p - \text{sampling error} \leq \pi \leq p + \text{sampling error})$$
$$(0.60 - 0.06 \leq \pi \leq 0.60 + 0.06)$$
$$or\ (0.54, 0.66)$$

Here's how to interpret the confidence interval: We can be 95% confident that the actual percentage of AFC members with at least a 4-year college degree in the population ($\pi$) lies between 54% and 66%, inclusive. This is a strong statement that highlights the beauty of probabilistic sampling. Even though the AFC researchers had responses from only 225 individuals, they have a strong notion of what the answer would have been had they taken measures from all the customers in the population. If they want a narrower confidence interval (i.e., greater precision), they can decrease the degree of confidence desired (e.g., at 90% confidence, $z$ = 1.65) or increase the sample size.

**continuous measures** A commonly used expression for interval and ratio measures.

**descriptive statistics** Statistics that describe the distribution of responses on a variable. The most commonly used descriptive statistics are the mean and standard deviation.

### A Word of Caution

Before we start letting the numbers do the thinking for us, recognize that the confidence interval only takes sampling error into account. To the extent that other types of error have entered the study—and you can be sure that they have to some degree—the confidence interval is less likely to have "captured" the population parameter within its bounds. Unfortunately, there is no quantitative way of adjusting the confidence interval to reflect these types of errors.

## 17-2 Basic Univariate Statistics: Continuous Measures

Because interval- and ratio-level measures are similar when it comes to analysis (the mean is the most commonly calculated statistic for both types), many researchers refer to them as **continuous measures,** even though the label is not technically correct, especially for interval measures such as rating scales.

### 17-2a DESCRIPTIVE STATISTICS

For continuous measures, numerous types of descriptive statistics can be calculated. **Descriptive statistics** describe the distribution of responses on a variable, including measures of central tendency (mean, median, and mode), measures of the spread, or variation, in the distribution (range, variance, standard deviation), and various measures of the shape of the distribution (e.g., skewness, kurtosis). In this section, we discuss the calculation and interpretation of two commonly used descriptive statistics, mean and standard deviation. These descriptive statistics are easily obtained from any statistical software package (SPSS Menu Sequence: Analyze > Descriptive Statistics > Descriptives).

The **sample mean** ($\bar{x}$) is simply the arithmetic mean value across all responses for a variable and is found using the following formula:

$$\bar{x} = \frac{\sum\limits_{i=1}^{n} x_i}{n}$$

where $x_i$ is the value of the variable for the $i$th respondent and $n$ is the total number of responses. In the AFC member project, mean age is found by summing the age values across members and dividing by 224, the total number of valid cases in the merged data set. In this example, the computed mean age turns out to be 68.6 years.

Although means are easy to calculate or obtain from computer output, there are several issues to keep in mind. First, although mean values can be calculated for any variable in a data set, they are only meaningful for continuous (i.e., interval, ratio) measures. Thus, knowing that the mean level of education is 4.4 is of little value at best—and misleading at worst—because this variable is at the ordinal level of measurement (i.e., "1 = less than high school, 2 = high school degree," and so on; not years of education or some other continuous measure). The mean is only useful with equal-interval scales, one of the common characteristics of interval and ratio measures.

A second issue with respect to interpreting mean values concerns spurious precision. Just as we warned you about the use of decimals with percentages, you'll need to be careful about just how precise a mean value can be. Although we captured respondent age by asking for date of birth on the initial application form, imagine that we had simply asked for age in years. If that were the case, would it be reasonable to report that the mean age was 68.6437261 years? No, it wouldn't. Instead, you would round off the result to a whole number (69 years) or use a single decimal (68.6 years) at the most. Anything more suggests a level of precision that simply isn't justified or necessary.

The third issue about mean values concerns their use with variables with one or more extreme cases, or outliers. As noted earlier, one AFC member was only 18 years old, while most members were 60 years or older. In this case, leaving the respondent in the data set has only a slight effect on the mean age calculated for the sample, so it really isn't much of an issue. There are situations, however, where outliers can have a very strong influence on the sample mean. In general, it is better to report the median value when there are outliers in a distribution because it more accurately represents the vast majority of cases. Another option is to temporarily ignore the extreme cases and calculate the mean across the remaining cases.[4]

The **sample standard deviation**(s) provides a measure of the variation in responses for continuous measures. If everyone were basically the same on some characteristic or felt the same way about some topic or object, then the standard deviation would be very small. If, on the other hand, responses were different—some high, some low—then the standard deviation for the variable would be larger.

If you don't take the variation of responses into account, you'll sometimes end up making bad decisions. Consider the classic case of a new sauce product:

*On the average, consumers wanted it neither really hot nor really mild. The mean rating of the test participants was quite close to the middle of the scale, which had "very mild" and "very hot" as its bipolar adjectives. This happened to fit the client's preconceived notion.*

*However, examination of the distribution of the ratings revealed the existence of a large proportion of consumers who wanted the sauce to be mild and an equally large proportion who wanted it to be hot. Relatively few wanted the in-between product, which would have been suggested by looking at the mean rating alone.[5]*

The following formula is used to calculate the sample standard deviation:

$$s = \sqrt{\frac{\sum\limits_{i=1}^{n} (x_i - \bar{x})^2}{n-1}}$$

where $x_i$ is the value of the variable for the $i$th respondent, $\bar{x}$ is the mean value of the variable, and $n$ is the total number of responses. Again, statistical software packages easily calculate descriptive statistics, including the standard deviation. For the age of the AFC members, the sample standard deviation turns out to be 11.9 years, providing evidence of a considerable spread in ages around the sample mean. As demonstrated by the sauce product example above, this could have important implications for AFC managers if different marketing mix elements are found to be more or less effective among different age groups, for example.

In almost all cases, it's important to report standard deviations along with mean values. Be careful, however: Issues related to spurious precision and the presence of outlier cases apply to standard deviations as well as to means. And remember, the standard deviation is meaningful only for interval- and ratio-level measures.

**sample mean** The arithmetic average value of the responses on a variable.

**sample standard deviation** A measure of the variation of responses on a variable. The standard deviation is the square root of the calculated variance on a variable.

> In almost all cases, it's important to report standard deviations along with mean values.

## 17-2b CONVERTING CONTINUOUS MEASURES TO CATEGORICAL MEASURES

Sometimes it is helpful to convert interval- or ratio-level measures to categorical measures. Because higher levels of measurement have all the properties of lower levels of measurement, this conversion is perfectly acceptable—and, in many cases, it's really useful for interpreting the results. Exhibit 17.3 was created by converting member age (aggregated into years based on date of birth provided on the membership application), a ratio-level measure, into a number of age categories (an ordinal-level measure) and plotting the results on the graph. Was this conversion necessary for describing the sample with respect to age? No. Researchers could simply have reported descriptive statistics for age in years ($\bar{x}$ = 68.6 years, $s$ = 11.9 years, median = 70 years) without the columns of data histograms provide. On the other hand, Exhibit 17.3 allows a condensed picture of the distribution that should be easy for managers or other readers to grasp, particularly when presented in combination with the descriptive statistics.

There aren't a lot of rules for the actual conversion process. Sometimes, you'll just use your best judgment to determine relevant categories. Occasionally, a client will have a predetermined structure for categories. In other cases, the data themselves determine category divisions. For example, if you want to convert a continuous measure into two approximately equal-sized groups, you'll probably create the categories based on a **median split**. That is, the cumulative percent column of the frequency analysis output will identify a value at the 50th percentile, and values up to and including this value will form one group (typically the "low" group for ratio measures) and values above the median value will form the second group (the "high" group).

**median split** A technique for converting a continuous measure into a categorical measure with two approximately equal-sized groups. The groups are formed by "splitting" the continuous measure at its median value.

**cumulative percentage breakdown** A technique for converting a continuous measure into a categorical measure. The categories are formed based on the cumulative percentages obtained in a frequency analysis.

**two-box technique** A technique for converting an interval-level rating scale into a categorical measure, usually used for presentation purposes. The percentage of respondents choosing one of the top two positions on a rating scale is reported.

The median split is actually just one case of the **cumulative percentage breakdown**, a technique in which groups are created using cumulative percentages. For example, look again at the age data in Exhibit 17.4. If we wanted to convert these data into three approximately equal-sized groups, which categories would be combined? Based on the cumulative percentage breakdown, the three groups would be as follows:

Less than 64 years

64 to 74 years

More than 74 years

When using statistical software for analyses—which is almost always—we strongly recommend that you create a new variable whose values are initially identical to the original continuous variable. Then you can recode the new variable into the desired categories, using data manipulation commands. This way, both the original variable and the new categorical variable are available for analyses (SPSS Menu Sequence: Transform > Recode Into Different Variables).

### Two-Box Technique

Here's another example of converting continuous measures into categories: Analysts often report the results of rating scale questions by presenting the percentage of respondents who checked one of the top two positions on a rating scale. This is known as the **two-box technique**. As an example, look at the response frequencies (and percentages) presented in Exhibit 17.6. The AFC researchers wanted to understand the importance of various reasons for participating in AFC programs. The researchers could correctly report that the mean rating score for the importance of physical enjoyment was 3.9 on a 5-point importance scale. To make this result easier to grasp, they might also report that 70% of respondents selected one

**Exhibit 17.6** ▶ Avery Fitness Center: Reasons for Participation "How important to you personally is each of the following reasons for participating in AFC programs?" *Number (Percentage) of Respondents Selecting Each Response Category*

| | NOT AT ALL IMPORTANT | | | | VERY IMPORTANT |
|---|---|---|---|---|---|
| General health and fitness | 5 (2) | 2 (1) | 4 (2) | 26 (11) | 192 (84) |
| Social aspects | 27 (13) | 34 (17) | 59 (29) | 48 (24) | 35 (17) |
| Physical enjoyment | 8 (4) | 10 (5) | 43 (21) | 67 (33) | 74 (37) |
| Specific medical concerns | 17 (8) | 8 (4) | 22 (11) | 62 (30) | 100 (48) |

of the top two levels of importance on the 5-point scale. Responses for the other reasons for participation are interpreted in the same way. The next table, Exhibit 17.7, presents two-box results and descriptive statistics as they might appear in the research report.

You need to understand that converting from continuous to categorical measures results in the loss of information about a variable. Most of the time, conclusions drawn using categorical approaches will roughly parallel those drawn using the full information from the continuous measure, but this isn't always the case. To be safe, always perform data analysis using the continuous version of a variable. Then, if it will help managers interpret the results, use the categorical version to present the results. A simple solution for many univariate analyses is to provide both types of results (see Exhibit 17.7).

### 17-2c CONFIDENCE INTERVALS FOR MEANS

The sample mean ($\bar{x}$) is an important piece of information about a variable, but as we noted earlier, managers care more about the population than they do any particular sample. Our job, as a result, is to make projections about where the population mean ($\mu$) is likely to fall, rather than to be satisfied with the sample mean. One important piece of information that the fitness center researchers gathered with respect to usage was the number of times that the respondents had visited AFC over the previous 30 days. Note that the number of visits is a ratio-level measure produced by electronically counting the number of times that the membership card was logged into the system upon entering the facility. For the 231 AFC members in the analysis dataset, the mean number of visits was 8.6, with a standard deviation of 7.6. So, 8.6 visits per month on average per individual is our best point estimate (based on the sample) about the mean value of the population parameter ($\mu$), but we have so little confidence that this point estimate is correct that we need to construct an interval that will allow us greater confidence that we have actually "captured" the parameter within its bounds. As with proportions, to establish the confidence interval, we must estimate the degree of sampling error for the sample mean. The following formula is used:

$$\text{sampling error} = z\frac{s}{\sqrt{n}}$$

where $z = z$ score associated with confidence level (for 95% confidence, $z = 1.96$), $s =$ sample standard deviation, and $n =$ total number of cases (standard deviation and number of cases are part of the standard output for descriptive analysis). Thus, at the 95% confidence level,

$$\text{sampling error} = 1.96\frac{7.6}{\sqrt{231}} = 0.98$$

Thus, the margin of sampling error for this estimate is approximately 1.0. Substituting this value and the sample mean ($\bar{x} = 8.6$) into the following formula

$$(\bar{x} = \text{sampling error} \leq \mu \leq \bar{x} + \text{sampling error}$$
$$(8.6 - 1.0 \leq \mu \leq 8.6 + 1.0)$$
$$\textit{or } (7.6, 9.6)$$

results in a 95% confidence interval ranging from 7.6 to 9.6. We can therefore be 95% confident that the mean number of visits to the fitness center in the past 30 days in the population lies somewhere between 7.6 and 9.6, inclusive.

## 17-3 Hypothesis Testing

The fact that marketing researchers are almost always working with a sample rather than full information from all population members creates something of a dilemma for managers who must make decisions based on research results. *How can we tell whether a particular result obtained from a sample would be true for the population as a whole and not just for the particular sample?* In truth, we can never know for sure that a sample result is true for the population. Through hypothesis testing, however, we can establish standards for making decisions about whether to

---

**Exhibit 17.7 ▶** Avery Fitness Center: Two-Box Results, With Descriptive Statistics

| | TWO-BOX | MEAN | (S.D.) | N |
|---|---|---|---|---|
| General health and fitness | 95% | 4.7 | (0.7) | 229 |
| Social aspects | 41% | 3.2 | (1.3) | 203 |
| Physical enjoyment | 70% | 3.9 | (1.1) | 202 |
| Specific medical concerns | 78% | 4.1 | (1.2) | 209 |

accept sample results as valid for the overall population. We introduce hypothesis testing at this point because it applies to both univariate analyses (this chapter) and multivariate analyses (the next chapter).

> Through hypothesis testing we can establish standards about whether to accept sample results as valid for the overall population.

When marketers prepare to launch a research study, they generally begin with a hypothesis. "I'll bet," the advertising manager might say to the marketing director, "that if we hired an attractive actor to promote our shampoo, sales would increase." Using inferential statistics, we are often able to determine whether there is empirical evidence from a sample to confirm that a **hypothesis** like this may be true for the population.

### 17-3a NULL AND ALTERNATIVE HYPOTHESES

Marketing research studies can't "prove" results. At best, we can indicate which of two mutually exclusive hypotheses is more likely to be true, based on the results of the study. The general forms of these two hypotheses and the symbols attached to them are as follows:

$H_0$, the hypothesis that a proposed result is not true for the population.

$H_a$, the alternate hypothesis that a proposed result is true for the population.

The first of these hypotheses, $H_0$, is known as the **null hypothesis**. The typical goal is to reject the null hypothesis in favor of the **alternative hypothesis**. (Note, however, that we can't prove that the alternative hypothesis is true even if we can reject the null. A hypothesis can be rejected, but it can never be accepted completely because further evidence may prove it wrong.) You should frame the null hypothesis so that its rejection leads to the tentative acceptance of the alternative hypothesis.

As a brief example, suppose your company wanted to introduce a new product if more than 20% of the population could be expected to prefer it to the competing products. Here's the way to frame this sort of hypothesis.

$$H_0: \pi \leq 0.20$$
$$H_a: \pi > 0.20$$

If the results of the study lead you to reject $H_0$, you would tentatively accept the alternative hypothesis and the product

**hypothesis** Unproven propositions about some phenomenon of interest.

**null hypothesis** The hypothesis that a proposed result is not true for the population. Researchers typically attempt to reject the null hypothesis in favor of some alternative hypothesis.

**alternative hypothesis** The hypothesis that a proposed result is true for the population.

**significance level** ($\alpha$) The acceptable level of error selected by the researcher, usually set at 0.05. The level of error refers to the probability of rejecting the null hypothesis when it is actually true for the population

**p-value** The probability of obtaining a given result if in fact the null hypothesis were true in the population. A result is regarded as statistically significant if the p-value is less than the chosen significance level of the test.

would be introduced because such a result would have been unlikely to occur if the null were really true. If $H_0$ could not be rejected, however, the product wouldn't be introduced.

### 17-3b HYPOTHESIS TESTING IN PRACTICE

In a technical sense, hypothesis testing involves a number of steps, ranging from specifying hypotheses to calculating the appropriate inferential statistics to specifying the significance level for the test. In practice, researchers learn very quickly to let the computer run the basic analyses as well as handle the more technical aspects of hypothesis testing.

With any type of hypothesis testing, you'll need to select an appropriate level of error related to the probability of rejecting the null hypothesis ($H_0$) when it is actually true for the population. This is usually referred to as the **significance level** or alpha level of the test and is symbolized by alpha ($\alpha$). We prefer, not surprisingly, that the probability of this type of error be as small as possible. By convention, most social scientists have decided that an $\alpha$ level of 0.05 is an acceptable level, which means that we'll end up rejecting a true null hypothesis 5% of the time. If the consequences of an error are particularly bad, it's appropriate to lower the $\alpha$ level, maybe to 0.01 or 0.001.

As noted, when you conduct an analysis, statistical software is usually used to calculate the appropriate inferential statistic that allows you to decide whether a sample result can reasonably be projected to the overall population. Actually, the software also takes it a step further by calculating the **p-value** associated with the test statistic. (Some statistical software packages place p-values in a column labeled "significance.") The p-value represents the likelihood of obtaining the particular value of a test statistic if the null hypothesis were true. Once you have the p-value, it's a simple matter to compare it with the significance level of the test to determine whether the result can be considered "statistically significant" (i.e., the sample results can be projected to the population). If the p-value is less than the significance level established, you can reject the null hypothesis and tentatively accept the alternative hypothesis.

Think about the logic of this for a second and it will make sense. A statistically significant result simply means that the probability that you could have obtained a particular result if the null hypothesis were really true (the p-value) is less than the level of error that you're willing to tolerate (the significance level). So, researchers virtually always want to obtain low p-values, and, as long as the p-value is lower than the significance level (typically $\alpha = 0.05$), the results can be applied to the population. If the p-value isn't lower than the established significance level, then there's just too much risk that the results were a fluke produced by chance.

## 17-3c ISSUES IN INTERPRETING STATISTICAL SIGNIFICANCE

When the $p$-value associated with a test statistic is lower than the level of $\alpha$ set by the researcher, we refer to the result as a statistically significant result. However, there are several common misinterpretations of $p$-values and the associated phrase "statistically significant." One of the most frequent is to view a $p$-value as representing the probability that the null hypothesis is true. Thus, a $p$-value of 0.04 might be mistakenly interpreted to mean that there is a probability of only 0.04 that the results were caused by chance. Instead, a $p$-value of 0.04 means that if—and this is a big if—the null hypothesis is true, the odds are only one in 25 of getting a sample result of the magnitude that was observed.

Another very frequent misinterpretation is the belief that the $\alpha$ level set by the researcher or the $p$-value obtained in the analysis is related to the probability that the alternative hypothesis is true. For example, some people might incorrectly interpret a $p$-value of 0.07 to mean that the probability that the alternative hypothesis is true is $1 - 0.07$, or 0.93. This interpretation is wrong. The $p$-value simply represents the probability that the result from the sample could have been obtained if the null hypothesis is true.

As a result, you have to be careful when interpreting the results of your analyses so that you don't mislead yourself or others. In particular, you need to make sure that you do not misinterpret what a test of significance reveals. It represents no more than a test against the null hypothesis.

## 17-4 Testing Hypotheses About Individual Variables

There are numerous occasions when you'll want to compare univariate sample statistics against preconceived standards. Maybe, for instance, you'll need to compare the mean customer satisfaction score for a particular department

## Manager's Focus

During presentations, researchers frequently stress the findings that are statistically significant, and when they do not, managers commonly inquire, "Are those differences significant?" (meaning statistically significant). The emphasis placed on statistical significance by both managers and researchers would appear to suggest that it is the primary consideration when interpreting the results of a study. However, other factors should be given equal—if not more—attention.

Throughout this book, we have been highlighting the role that you as a manager can play in helping a research project generate actionable findings. That is, the goal is to generate information that is relevant to the marketing decisions you face and gives you clear guidance on how to respond to your market situation. Therefore, it is crucial that you understand that statistical significance is not the same thing as managerial relevance or actionability.

We do not mean to suggest that knowing whether or not specific findings are statistically significant is unimportant. What we are saying, though, is that your search for the meaning of findings must go beyond this one consideration. Why? One reason is that data patterns can be of practical importance and yet not be statistically significant. This commonly occurs when sample sizes are small. If sample sizes are not sufficiently large, the power of a statistical test is lower, and the chances of finding statistically significant results (i.e., rejecting

a false null hypothesis) are lower. In such a situation, a marketing researcher might find that average attitude scores (measured on a seven-point favorability scale) are much higher for men (mean = 6.2) than for women (mean = 4.4), but the differences are not statistically significant. This pattern of findings, nonetheless, may suggest the need for different marketing actions for men versus women (or, perhaps, a larger sample size to determine whether or not this apparent difference is real).

Conversely, results can be statistically significant and yet have little managerial relevance. This can occur when sample sizes are very large, resulting in a high level of statistical power (i.e., a much greater chance of rejecting a false null hypothesis). In such situations, very small differences in proportions or means can be statistically significant. For example, a marketing researcher might find that attitude scores (using the same seven-point favorability scale) are higher for men (mean = 6.2) than for women (mean = 6.1) and that the difference is statistically significant. Do these "statistically significant" results suggest that the company should forget about marketing the product to women or develop separate marketing strategies for men versus women? Your managerial sensibilities should be telling you that such a conclusion would be ill-founded, given both genders had very similar and relatively high mean ratings. You should employ these same managerial sensibilities whenever you form conclusions about how to respond to a set of research findings.

store against the overall mean satisfaction score for all department stores in the chain or to determine whether the characteristics of sample respondents match those of the overall population from which the sample was drawn. Each of these examples calls for a researcher to test a hypothesis about a univariate measure.

## 17-4a TESTING STATISTICAL SIGNIFICANCE WITH CATEGORICAL VARIABLES

Suppose that AFC managers wanted to know whether their current customers were different from the overall population of people who lived in their trading area. Although you could make this comparison on several different classification variables, the managers are especially interested in whether their customers have higher or lower levels of education than the population in general. To determine whether this is the case, you need to compare the results from the sample (see Exhibit 17.2) with those for the overall population in the trade area. In this case, we'll compare the sample results with the results of a larger general opinion survey conducted at about the same time that included a similar measure of respondent education.

Exhibit 17.8 presents data from the general opinion survey alongside the data from the AFC study. You'll notice quickly that a bigger proportion of AFC customers fall in the highest education category (and lower proportions fall in the lower categories). But is this enough evidence to reject the null hypothesis that the education levels are the same? This is the type of problem for which the **chi-square goodness-of-fit test** is ideally suited. Using SPSS (SPSS Menu Sequence: Analyze > Nonparametric Tests > Legacy Dialogs > Chi-square), we obtained $X^2 = 118.38$, on 5 degrees of freedom and the associated $p$-value, $p < 0.001$.[6] Because the $p$-value is lower than the significance level we established for the test ($\alpha = 0.05$), we have evidence to suggest that AFC customers are different in terms of education level

**chi-square goodness-of-fit test** A statistical test to determine whether some observed pattern of frequencies corresponds to an expected pattern.

from the general population in the city. In particular, they appear to be considerably more highly educated.

The chi-square test can also be applied when there are only two levels for a variable, for example, gender. An alternative approach is the binomial test (SPSS Menu Sequence: Analyze > Nonparametric Tests > Legacy Dialogs > Binomial).

## 17-4b TESTING STATISTICAL SIGNIFICANCE WITH CONTINUOUS VARIABLES

When the variable to be compared against a standard is a continuous measure, the approach is a little different and allows us to take advantage of increased statistical power. As an example, AFC managers learned from a trade association that, nationwide, members of fitness centers visit a center six times per month on average. For years, AFC trainers had been encouraging clients to come to the center more frequently, even if they stayed less time per visit. The results of the current study suggest that clients do visit the center more frequently per month compared with fitness center clients overall (recall that mean visits in the prior 30 days for the sample was 8.6), but can we say with any certainty that the population of AFC members does, in fact, visit the center more frequently than the national average? In this situation, we'll use SPSS (or another software package) to compare the sample mean against an external standard. The analysis (SPSS Menu Sequence: Analyze > Compare Means > One-Sample T Test) returns the following results—$t$-value = 5.11, on 230 degrees of freedom, $p < 0.001$. So, the probability that we could have obtained a difference this large (a mean of 8.6 visits vs. 6.0 visits) if there truly were no difference between the mean visits for AFC members and the standard is less than one in 1,000. The $p$-value is lower than the conventional standard for significance level ($\alpha = 0.05$), and we would conclude that AFC members visit the center more frequently per month than the national average.

**Exhibit 17.8** ▶ AFC Customer Education Level Versus Education Level in Trade Area

| LEVEL OF EDUCATION ACHIEVED | AFC NUMBER | AFC VALID PERCENT | TRADE AREA NUMBER | TRADE AREA VALID PERCENT |
|---|---|---|---|---|
| Less than high school | 4 | 2% | 147 | 10% |
| High school degree | 34 | 15% | 294 | 20% |
| Some college | 46 | 20% | 412 | 28% |
| Associate's degree | 7 | 3% | 59 | 4% |
| Four-year college degree | 52 | 23% | 368 | 25% |
| Advanced degree | 82 | 36% | 191 | 13% |
| Total | 225 | 100% | 1,471 | 100% |

# Summary

## Learning Objective 1

**Distinguish between univariate and multivariate analyses.**
Univariate analyses are conducted on individual variables; multivariate analyses involve multiple variables.

## Learning Objective 2

**Describe frequency analysis.**
A frequency analysis is a univariate technique that involves counting the number of responses that fall into various response categories.

## Learning Objective 3

**Describe commonly used descriptive statistics.**
The most commonly used descriptive statistics for continuous measures (interval- or ratio-level measures) are the mean, or arithmetic average, and the standard deviation. The mean is a measure of central tendency; the standard deviation provides a convenient measure of the dispersion of responses.

## Learning Objective 4

**Discuss confidence intervals for proportions and means.**
A confidence interval is the range within which the true proportion or mean for the population will fall, with a given level of confidence (usually 95%). For means, the confidence interval is equal to the sample mean ($\bar{x}$) plus or minus the estimated sampling error. For proportions, the confidence interval equals the sample proportion (p) plus or minus the estimated sampling error.

## Learning Objective 5

**Overview the basic purpose of hypothesis testing.**
Hypothesis testing is used to establish whether or not to accept study results based on a sample as being true for the overall population from which the sample was drawn. The goal normally is to determine whether or not the null hypothesis (i.e., the result isn't true for the population) can be rejected in favor of the alternative hypothesis (i.e., the particular result holds for the population).

## Key Terms

categorical measures (page 254)
frequency analysis (page 254)
outliers (page 255)
histogram (page 255)
confidence interval (page 258)
continuous measures (page 259)

descriptive statistics (page 259)
sample mean (page 260)
sample standard deviation (page 260)
median split (page 261)
cumulative percentage breakdown (page 261)
two-box technique (page 261)
hypothesis (page 263)
null hypothesis (page 263)
alternative hypothesis (page 263)
significance level ($\alpha$) (page 263)
$p$-value (page 263)
chi-square goodness-of-fit test (page 265)

## Review Questions

1. What types of variables might be analyzed with frequency analysis?

2. What is an outlier?

3. How many decimal places should normally be reported with percentages?

4. What is a histogram? What information does it provide?

5. Why do analysts often construct confidence intervals? What is their purpose?

6. What type of error do confidence intervals take into account?

7. What are the most commonly used descriptive statistics?

8. Why must the distribution of responses be taken into account when deciding which type of "average" to present?

9. Why might an analyst choose to convert a continuous measure to a categorical measure?

10. What is a two-box technique? A median split? A cumulative percentage breakdown?

11. What is the difference between the null and alternative hypotheses?

12. Why can a hypothesis be rejected, but never fully accepted?

13. What is a $p$-value? Do researchers typically want to obtain higher or lower $p$-values?

14. What is the basic use of a chi-square goodness-of-fit test?

15. How would you compare a sample mean against a standard?

# Endnotes

1. We could get a more accurate picture of the gender of the population by including all of the individuals in the population in the analysis (because gender data came from the initial application, not the survey). For presentation purposes, however, we are only including individuals for whom we could match survey responses with data from the other sources ($n = 231$). This is true for all of the analyses in this chapter.

2. See the classic book by Hans Zeisel, *Say It with Figures*, 5th ed. (New York: Harper and Row, 1968), pp. 16–17, for conditions that would support reporting percentages with decimal-place accuracy.

3. Earlier, we referred to this range as the precision range. After data have been collected and analyzed, it is more appropriate to refer to this range as a confidence interval, because the range itself, which represents the margin of sampling error, is established for a given level of confidence. If we change the level of confidence, the confidence interval itself will also change.

4. See the classic book by Darrell Huff, *How to Lie With Statistics* (New York: Norton, 1954).

5. Robert J. Lavidge. (1984, January 6). How to Keep Well-Intentioned Research From Misleading New-Product Planners. *Marketing News, 18*, 8.

6. The term "degrees of freedom" refers to the number of things that can vary independently, and for the chi-square test, degrees of freedom is one less than the number of categories. If we know the total number of respondents and the number of respondents in five of the six categories of education level, the number of respondents in the remaining education category is fixed and cannot vary independently.

# CHAPTER 18

# Analysis and Interpretation: Multiple Variables Simultaneously

Billion Photos/Shutterstock.com

## LEARNING OBJECTIVES

▶ Discuss why a researcher might conduct a multivariate analysis.

▶ Explain the purpose and importance of cross tabulation.

▶ Describe a technique for comparing groups on a continuous dependent variable.

▶ Explain the difference between an independent sample $t$-test for means and a paired sample $t$-test for means.

▶ Discuss the Pearson product-moment correlation coefficient.

▶ Discuss a technique for examining the influence of one or more predictor variables on an outcome variable.

Rawpixel.com/Shutterstock.com

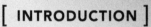

## [ INTRODUCTION ]

Sometimes univariate analyses are enough for providing answers for a research problem. Lots of times, however, you'll need to use multivariate analyses to get the information you need. In many cases, adding one or more additional variables to an analysis can provide a much deeper understanding of the situation.

Here's an example: In an awareness test for an ice-cream shop, 58% of survey respondents could name the shop in a recall task. Closer analysis revealed several insights, however. For one thing, gender seemed to be related to the awareness level: Only 45% of male respondents could name the shop, compared with 71% of female respondents. And age also seemed to be related to awareness: 69% of respondents 20 years old and younger could name the shop, but only 54% of those who were 21 to 40 years old and 39% of those over 40 years old could do so. If you stopped with the univariate analysis result (i.e., 58% correct in recall task), you would miss important managerial insights about gender and age. Exhibit 18.1 presents the information graphically; note how conclusions change when we consider the additional variables.

In this chapter, we present some commonly used multivariate analysis techniques. Although we'll barely scratch the surface of the full range of techniques that are available and used in industry, we'll provide enough detail to get you started on the most common analyses. As with the univariate analyses presented in the previous

**Exhibit 18.1** ▶ Univariate Versus Multivariate Analysis: Enhanced Meaning

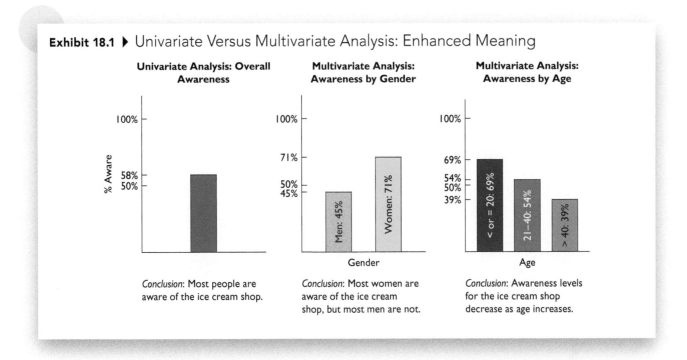

*Conclusion:* Most people are aware of the ice cream shop.

*Conclusion:* Most women are aware of the ice cream shop, but most men are not.

*Conclusion:* Awareness levels for the ice cream shop decrease as age increases.

chapter, the computer does most of the work—including providing tests of statistical significance—but you'll need to know when to use each of the approaches and how to interpret the results. Interpretation is the key !

## 18-1 Cross Tabulation

**Cross tabulation** is an important tool for studying the relationships between two (or more) categorical variables. It's among the most used multivariate data analysis techniques in applied marketing research, with many marketing research studies going no further than simple cross tabulations between two variables at a time. Because they are so commonly used, you'll want to take the time to fully understand how cross tabulations are developed and interpreted.

In most multivariate analyses, you'll determine whether one variable (the independent or predictor variable) has an influence on another variable (the dependent or outcome variable). With cross tabulations, the respondents are divided into groups based on the independent variable in order to see how the dependent variable varies from group to group. For example, consider again the Avery Fitness Center project discussed in previous chapters. AFC researchers wanted to know whether being referred by a doctor to the fitness center led to greater usage of the therapy pool. A quick univariate analysis reveals that the therapy pool was the service used by the highest percentage (45%) of AFC members in the past 30 days based on survey responses. Does this percentage differ for people who were recommended by a doctor compared with

> **cross tabulation**
> A multivariate technique used for studying the relationship between two or more categorical variables. The technique considers the joint distribution of sample elements across variables.

people who were not? Cross tabulation is the right kind of analysis because both pool usage ("yes" or "no") and learning about AFC from a doctor ("yes" or "no") are measured on categorical scales.

Exhibit 18.2 presents SPSS output for the two-way classification of the sample respondents by pool usage and whether they learned about AFC from a doctor (SPSS Menu Sequence: Analyze > Descriptive Statistics > Crosstabs). There's a lot going on in this table, so take some time to look it over carefully. First, note the *marginal totals* for each variable: 104 (45%) respondents had used the therapy pool (127, or 55%, had not), and 54 (23%) respondents had learned about AFC from a doctor (177, or 77%, did not). The marginal totals represent the frequency counts for each of the variables independently.

With cross-tab analysis, however, you can also examine the joint distribution of the two variables. This allows us to see whether the outcome (percentage of people using the pool) is different for those who learned about AFC from a doctor versus those who did not. Because there are two levels for each of the variables being considered, there are four possible combinations when both variables are considered together (2 × 2 = 4). These combinations are represented by four *cells* in the cross tabulation. For example, of the 54 respondents who had learned about AFC from a doctor, 34 of them had used the therapy pool in the past 30 days and 20 of them had not. Of 177 who did not learn about AFC from a doctor, 70 had used the pool and 107 had not. But what does this mean for AFC managers? Does it appear that there is some connection between doctors' recommendations and therapy-pool usage?

iStockphoto.com/Ana Abejon

AFC researchers wanted to know if being referred by a doctor to the fitness center led to greater usage of the therapy pool.

**Exhibit 18.2 ▶** Avery Fitness Center: Therapy Pool Usage by Doctor's Recommendation (SPSS Output)

**DOCTOR * POOL CROSSTABULATION**

| | | | POOL | | TOTAL |
|---|---|---|---|---|---|
| | | | 0 | 1 | |
| **DOCTOR** | 0 | Count | 107 | 70 | 177 |
| | | % within doctor | 60.5% | 39.5% | 100.0% |
| | | % within pool | 84.3% | 67.3% | 76.6% |
| | 1 | Count | 20 | 34 | 54 |
| | | % within doctor | 37.0% | 63.0% | 100.0% |
| | | % within pool | 15.7% | 32.7% | 23.4% |
| **TOTAL** | | Count | 127 | 104 | 231 |
| | | % within doctor | 55.0% | 45.0% | 100.0% |
| | | % within pool | 100.0% | 100.0% | 100.0% |

We've noted before that percentages are incredibly useful for interpreting results. Each of the cells in Exhibit 18.2 contains two different percentages (because we asked for them as part of the analysis in SPSS) that differ depending on what number is used as the denominator in the calculation of the percentage. The first percentage in each cell, sometimes called the "row percentage," is calculated using the row total as the denominator. For example,

consider the cell representing respondents who neither used the pool nor learned about AFC from a doctor. The row percentage is 61% (i.e., 107/177 = 0.605). The next percentage in each cell is the "column percentage" and is calculated using the column total as the denominator. Thus, for those who neither used the pool nor learned about AFC from a doctor, the column percentage is 84% (i.e., 107/127 = 0.843).

# Manager's Focus

This chapter will help you become familiar with some analytical techniques that are a bit more sophisticated than the basic analyses discussed in Chapter 17. Your primary role in this process is to accurately and comprehensively describe your information needs to your research provider. It is the researcher's responsibility to develop an analysis plan that will fill those needs. As the client, though, you will ultimately have to approve the proposed plan. If you select highly competent and trustworthy research suppliers, you will likely rely heavily on their judgment.

One benefit of having a basic understanding of the various analyses presented in this chapter, however, is that when your provider believes techniques other than conventional cross tabulations will better meet your information needs, you may be more understanding and receptive of more advanced or innovative methods. Like everyone else, managers tend to fear what they do not understand. The objective of data analysis is not to simply do what is conventional or comfortable. The goal is to employ the techniques that will most directly address your marketing problem. In other words, the material in this chapter will help you become an informed consumer of research services and make you less likely to block the path that will best answer the questions you have about your market situation.

---

Which of these percentages should you use? To answer this question, think about which of the variables being studied is likely to be the independent variable (cause) and which is likely to be the dependent variable (effect). *Percentages are always calculated in the direction of the causal variable.* That is, the marginal totals for the causal variable are always used as the denominator when calculating percentages in cross tabulations. We've already theorized that a doctor's recommendation might have caused respondents to use the therapy pool; because the different levels of the causal variable are represented by the rows in the cross tabulation (see Exhibit 18.2), the row percentages should be used.

> Percentages are always calculated in the direction of the causal variable (in cross-tabs).

Now back to the original question: Does it appear that people who are recommended by doctors are more or less likely to use the therapy pool? Looking only at the row percentages, can you detect a different pattern of responses for the two groups (i.e., those who learned about AFC from doctors versus those who did not)? From the sample results, it looks as though people who learn about AFC from doctors are more likely to use the therapy pool than people who don't learn about it from a doctor (63% versus 40%, respectively). Thus, from a manager's perspective, it appears that if the proportion of AFC customers who come because of a doctor's recommendation increases (perhaps through increased promotion to doctors), use of the therapy pool may go up.

**Pearson chi-square ($X^2$) test of independence** A commonly used statistic for testing the null hypothesis that categorical variables are independent of one another.

**Cramer's *V*** A statistic used to measure the strength of the relationship between categorical variables.

Before you race off to build promotions for doctors (assuming you wanted to increase the use of the therapy pool), however, it's important to slow down long enough to consider whether this sample result is likely to be true for the whole population. There's always some degree of chance that the sample result was just a fluke. The **Pearson chi-square ($X^2$) test of independence** assesses the degree to which the variables in a cross-tab analysis are independent of one another. The value can range from zero to some upper value limited by sample size and the distribution of cases across the cells. The chi-square value, degrees of freedom for the chi-square test, and the $p$-value are provided in the output for standard statistical analysis software packages.

For the analysis presented in Exhibit 18.2, the Pearson chi-square value is 9.17, on 1 degree of freedom (df), and the associated $p$-value is 0.002; we obtained this value by selecting the appropriate statistics option in the cross-tabs analysis in SPSS. Thus, if these variables are truly independent of one another in the population, the probability that we could have obtained a chi-square value this large is less than 0.002, and we can reject the null hypothesis that the variables are independent. (Recall that for most purposes, $p$-values have to be under 0.05 for a result to be "statistically significant"; this is the case for the analysis in Exhibit 18.2.)

Although the chi-square test indicates whether two variables are independent, it doesn't measure the strength of association when they are dependent. One popular approach for measuring the strength of the relationship between two categorical variables is **Cramer's *V***, which is scaled to range between 0 and 1, with higher values representing a stronger relationship between the variables. For our analysis, Cramer's *V* is equal to 0.199, an indication of a modest degree of association between the variables.

# Manager's Focus

Sometimes managers request that every question on a questionnaire be cross tabulated against every other question. What's wrong with that? First, seldom do all of the questions address the same marketing issues. Conducting every conceivable analysis represents little more than an aimless fishing expedition. The primary purpose of a descriptive (or causal) study is not to explore the data for unanticipated relationships, but to test hypothesized relationships (which might have come from previous exploratory research).

The second reason this approach might be problematic is statistical in nature. The more analyses that are performed, particularly those that are not guided by a set of meaningful hypotheses, the greater the likelihood of obtaining results that are "statistically significant" due to chance rather than real relationships between the variables in the target population(s). Remember, when you set the significance level (a) at 0.05, there is 1 chance in 20 of drawing the wrong conclusion about the null hypothesis. Accordingly, as more and more

analyses are performed, roughly 5% of the statistically significant findings you obtain will suggest relationships or differences that really do not exist. This, in turn, can lead to bad marketing decisions.

Having extended this caution, we should note that there are times when managers or researchers identify legitimate unplanned new tests to run. In other words, if guided by the original purpose of the study and logic, rather than mere availability of data, there is nothing wrong with searching for additional insights that your data may offer. However, when exploring your data beyond the primary purpose of your study, it would be best to treat any "interesting" or "surprising" findings as tentative in nature. In other words, you should avoid automatically concluding that these findings represent something meaningful about your market situation. Instead, you should view these findings as representing new hypotheses that should be confirmed or disconfirmed through additional research designed for that specific purpose.

## 18-1a PRESENTING CROSS-TAB RESULTS: BANNER TABLES

Cross-tab results for commercial marketing research studies are often presented using banners. A **banner** is a series of cross tabulations between an outcome (dependent) variable and several possible causal variables in a single table

**banner** A series of cross tabulations between an outcome, or dependent variable, and several (sometimes many) explanatory variables in a single table.

on a single page. The outcome variable usually serves as the row variable, which is also known as the stub. The causal variables serve as the column variables, with each category of these variables serving as a banner point. Exhibit 18.3 shows what the banner format might look like for part of the fitness center analysis. In this

**Exhibit 18.3 ▶** Avery Fitness Center: Banner Table

| USED THERAPY POOL? | GENDER | | DID RESPONDENT LEARN ABOUT AFC FROM DOCTOR? | | IMPORTANCE OF "SPECIFIC MEDICAL CONCERNS" | |
|---|---|---|---|---|---|---|
| | MALE | FEMALE | NO | YES | LESS | VERY |
| NO | 36 | 86 | 107 | 20 | 73 | 40 |
| | (80)* | (49) | (61) | (37) | (67) | (40) |
| YES | 9 | 91 | 70 | 34 | 36 | 60 |
| | (20) | (51) | (40) | (63) | (33) | (60) |
| | (n = 222) | | (n = 231) | | (n = 209) | |

*Percentages shown in parentheses

example, three variables that are statistically significantly related to whether or not respondents use the therapy pool are included. The top line in each row of the table indicates the absolute number possessing the characteristic; the second line indicates the percentage. Banner tables allow a lot of information to be presented using very little space, and they are easy for managers to understand.

## 18-2 Independent Samples *T*-Test for Means

Researchers commonly encounter situations in which a continuous outcome measure needs to be compared across groups. For instance, imagine that a brand manager wanted to know whether men and women held different attitudes toward her brand, where attitudes are measured on rating scales. Or maybe a manager for a small hospital chain wanted to compare patient satisfaction rating scores across two different hospitals in the chain. In these and many other cases, the task is to test for differences across groups (i.e., men versus. women; hospital A patients versus hospital B patients) on some important variable assessed using a continuous measure (i.e., attitude toward the brand; perceptions of satisfaction). In situations like this, the **independent samples *t*-test for means** is the correct method of analysis.

The AFC managers had begun to wonder if the space within the facility might be better used. They were especially concerned that a great deal of floor space—not to mention equipment—was currently dedicated to circuit training, a form of exercise in which participants move fairly rapidly from one exercise to another. The goal of the exercise circuit is to provide a workout for all muscle groups in the body. It wasn't clear, however, whether they could continue to justify the amount of space dedicated to circuit training.

The managers knew that about 22% of AFC members had used circuit training in the past month based on survey results, but that alone wasn't enough to justify the space requirements. If there were evidence, however, that participants who used circuit training were more involved in the center, as evidenced by visiting AFC more frequently than those who don't use the circuit, they decided that they would leave the status quo. Otherwise, they intended to use the space for activities that might be more appealing. Because of the importance of the decision, they decided to consider only the responses of AFC members who had actually visited the center during the previous 30 days. (In the SPSS analysis, this is easily accomplished using the following SPSS Menu Sequence: Data > Select Cases.)

Do the data obtained from AFC members verify that those who used circuit training visited the fitness center more regularly than those who didn't? Given that the outcome variable is continuous (number of visits, based on facility entry data) and the independent variable is categorical (use of circuit training, based on responses to

the member survey), this is an ideal situation to use the independent samples *t-test* to determine whether the two groups (i.e., those who used circuit training versus those who did not) truly differ with respect to how frequently they visit the fitness center.

Just about any statistical software package can be used to easily perform the analysis. Exhibit 18.4 presents the output from an SPSS analysis (SPSS Menu Sequence: Analyze > Compare Means > Independent-Samples *T*-Test). First, notice that the mean number of visits over the 30-day period does appear to be different for members who used circuit training (mean = 14.2 visits) compared with those who did not (mean = 11.8 visits). Can we conclude, however, that this is the case? Not yet.

As usual, we must test to determine how likely it is that we could have obtained these *sample* results (a difference of 2.4 visits per month) if there really were no difference in the overall *population* from which the samples were drawn. The test statistic, *t*, is found in the SPSS output in Exhibit 18.4. In this case, the calculated *t* -value is –2.31 with 156 degrees of freedom. The associated *p*-value is less than 0.05. Thus, if there really were no difference in number of visits for those who used circuit training versus those who didn't, the probability that we could have obtained the results we did in our sample is less than the conventional standard for achieving statistical significance ($p < 0.05$). As a result, we can conclude that members who use the exercise circuit do, in fact, visit the fitness center more frequently than those who don't. The managers decided to keep the exercise circuit.

## 18-3 Paired Sample *T*-Test for Means

The independent samples *t*-test for means always compares mean scores for the same variable measured in two groups (e.g., people who have used circuit training versus those who haven't). What happens when you need to compare two means when both measures are provided by the same people? In that case, you'll use the **paired sample *t*-test** for means.

As with the independent samples *t*-test, the paired sample *t*-test is common in marketing research. For example, the AFC researchers wanted to understand what motivates people to participate in AFC programs and asked about four different motivations on the member survey (i.e., general health and fitness; social aspects; physical enjoyment; specific medical concerns). If the results indicated that the social benefits of meeting with other people were especially important, managers planned to develop additional social activities for members and were even considering rearranging the layout of the center to encourage greater interaction among members while they exercise.

Exhibit 18.5 presents the mean importance scores for four possible reasons for participating in AFC programs. (Because we are comparing the mean scores to one

**independent samples *t*-test for means** A technique commonly used to determine whether two groups differ on some characteristic assessed on a continuous measure.

**paired sample *t*-test** A technique for comparing two means when scores for both variables are provided by the same sample.

**Exhibit 18.4** ▶ Avery Fitness Center: Number of Visits (Past 30 Days) by Exercise Circuit Usage

**GROUP STATISTICS**

|  | CIRCUIT | N | MEAN | STD. DEVIATION | STD. ERROR MEAN |
|---|---|---|---|---|---|
| Visits 30 | 0 | 114 | 11.83 | 5.782 | 0.542 |
|  | 1 | 44 | 14.2 | 5.773 | 0.87 |

**INDEPENDENT SAMPLES TEST**

|  |  | LEVENE'S TEST FOR EQUALITY OF VARIANCES | | T-TEST FOR EQUALITY OF MEANS | | | | |
|---|---|---|---|---|---|---|---|---|
|  |  | F | SIG. | T | DF | SIG (2-TAILED) | MEAN DIFFERENCE | STD. ERROR DIFFERENCE |
| Visits 30 | Equal variances assumed | 0.196 | 0.658 | −2.312 | 156 | 0.22 | −2.371 | 1.026 |
|  | Equal variances not assumed |  |  | −2.313 | 78.276 | 0.23 | −2.371 | 1.025 |

| | T-TEST FOR EQUALITY OF MEANS | |
|---|---|---|
| | **95% CONFIDENCE INTERVAL OF THE DIFFERENCE** | |
| | LOWER | UPPER |
| Visits 30 Equal variances assumed | −4.397 | −0.345 |
| Equal variances not assumed | −4.412 | −0.331 |

**Exhibit 18.5** ▶ Avery Fitness Center: Importance of Various Reasons for Participating

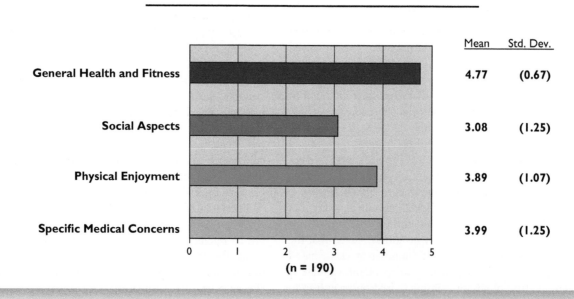

**IMPORTANCE LEVEL**

| REASON | | Mean | Std. Dev. |
|---|---|---|---|
| General Health and Fitness | | 4.77 | (0.67) |
| Social Aspects | | 3.08 | (1.25) |
| Physical Enjoyment | | 3.89 | (1.07) |
| Specific Medical Concerns | | 3.99 | (1.25) |

(n = 190)

another, we've limited the sample to only those respondents that provided answers to each of the questions.) The results indicate that social aspects are the least important of all the possible reasons for participating in AFC programs. Managers wanted to be sure, however, before giving up their plans. Is there evidence in the sample data to support the conclusion that social aspects are least important to population members?

Exhibit 18.6 presents SPSS output for three different paired sample $t$-tests, one each for comparing the importance of social aspects with the importance of the other three possible reasons for participating in AFC

programs (SPSS Menu Sequence: Analyze > Compare Means > Paired-Samples $T$-Test). As an example, the paired sample $t$-value comparing the importance of social aspects with the importance of general health and fitness is $t = -18.05$, on 189 degrees of freedom, and the associated $p$-value is well under 0.05, so we can conclude that AFC members place greater importance on general health and fitness than social considerations when it comes to program participation. Now, take a close look at Exhibit 18.6 and see whether there is evidence that the members think that the other reasons are also more important.

**Exhibit 18.6** ▶ Avery Fitness Center: Paired Sample $t$-Tests (SPSS Output)

**PAIRED SAMPLES STATISTICS**

| | | MEAN | N | STD. DEVIATION | STD. ERROR MEAN |
|---|---|---|---|---|---|
| PAIR 1 | social | 3.08 | 190 | 1.253 | 0.091 |
| | fitness | 4.77 | 190 | 0.672 | 0.049 |
| PAIR 2 | social | 3.08 | 190 | 1.253 | 0.091 |
| | enjoy | 3.89 | 190 | 1.074 | 0.078 |
| PAIR 3 | social | 3.08 | 190 | 1.253 | 0.091 |
| | medical | 3.99 | 190 | 1.249 | 0.091 |

**PAIRED SAMPLES CORRELATIONS**

| | | N | CORRELATIONS | SIG. |
|---|---|---|---|---|
| PAIR 1 | social & fitness | 190 | 0.211 | 0.003 |
| PAIR 2 | social & enjoy | 190 | 0.553 | 0.000 |
| PAIR 3 | social & medical | 190 | 0.230 | 0.001 |

**PAIRED SAMPLES TEST**

| | | PAIRED DIFFERENCES | | | | | | | |
|---|---|---|---|---|---|---|---|---|---|
| | | | | | 95% CONFIDENCE INTEVAL OF THE DIFFERENCE | | | | |
| | | MEAN | STD. DEVIATION | STD. ERROR MEAN | LOWER | UPPER | T | DF | SIG. (2-TAILED) |
| PAIR 1 | social - fitness | −1.689 | 1.290 | 0.094 | −1.874 | −1.505 | −18.048 | 189 | 0.000 |
| PAIR 2 | social - enjoy | −0.811 | 1.111 | 0.081 | −0.969 | −0.652 | −10.058 | 189 | 0.000 |
| PAIR 3 | Social - medical | −0.911 | 1.552 | 0.113 | −1.133 | −0.688 | −8.085 | 189 | 0.000 |

## 18-4 Pearson Product-Moment Correlation Coefficient

So far, we've looked at relationships in which the causal, or independent, variable was a categorical measure. What happens when both the independent variable(s) and the dependent variable are measured on continuous scales? One option is to calculate the degree of correlation between the two continuous variables.

The correlation coefficient is a fundamental building block of data analysis. You probably have a basic understanding of what it means when someone says that two things are "correlated." You might not know the technical details, but you have an intuitive understanding that the two concepts, events, or ideas somehow "go together," that there is some sort of association or even relationship between them. As one thing changes, so does the other.

> The correlation coefficient is a fundamental building block of data analysis.

The **Pearson product-moment correlation coefficient** provides a means of quantifying the degree of association between two continuous variables. Essentially, the Pearson product-moment correlation coefficient assesses the degree to which two continuous variables change consistently across cases. That is, are higher or lower scores on one variable associated with higher or lower scores on the second variable as we go across cases? The correlation coefficient can range from –1 (representing perfect negative linear correlation) to + 1 (representing perfect positive linear correlation). In practice, correlations rarely approach –1 or +1.

Is there a relationship between an AFC member's age and the total fees that he or she pays the center? Managers thought that there might be—and if so, they planned to pay a little closer attention to their older customers. To find out, they used SPSS (SPSS Menu Sequence: Analyze > Correlate > Bivariate) to obtain the Pearson product-moment correlation coefficient. Exhibit 18.7 presents the output for the correlation between age and 1-year revenues for AFC members in the analysis data set. Notice that the output provides the correlation coefficient, the corresponding p-value (Sig.), and the number of cases in the analysis (N). In this case, the correlation coefficient equals 0.25, which is evidence of a modest relationship between the two variables in the sample data. As always, though, the first question to consider is whether there is an association between the variables in the *population* of all AFC members, not just within the *sample*. The p-value for the analysis is below the usual significance level (i.e., 0.05), and we can conclude that there is a statistically significant relationship between age and revenue.

> **Pearson product-moment correlation coefficient** A statistic that indicates the degree of linear association between two continuous variables. The correlation coefficient can range from –1 to +1

### 18-4a CAUTION IN THE INTERPRETATION OF CORRELATIONS

Before going further, we need to offer a quick caution about interpreting correlation coefficients (and this also applies to other multivariate analyses as well). Sometimes you'll be tempted to assume that one variable caused the other one when you obtain a statistically significant correlation coefficient between two variables. Just because two variables are correlated doesn't mean that one necessarily caused the other, however. There is nothing in correlation analysis, or any other mathematical procedure, that can be used to establish causality. All these procedures can do is measure the nature and degree of association between variables. Statements of causality must come from underlying knowledge and theories about the phenomena under investigation. They do not come from the mathematics.

**Exhibit 18.7 ▶** Avery Fitness Center: Correlation Between Age and Revenues (SPSS Output)

**CORRELATIONS**

|  |  | AGE | REVENUE |
|---|---|---|---|
| AGE | Pearson Correlation | 1 | 0.246** |
|  | Sig. (2-tailed) |  | 0.000 |
|  | N | 224 | 224 |
| REVENUE | Pearson Correlation | 0.246** | 1 |
|  | Sig. (2-tailed) | 0.000 |  |
|  | N | 224 | 231 |

** Correlation is significant at the 0.01 level (2-tailed).

Here's an example: If we did the math, we would discover that ice cream purchases are positively correlated with murder rates. *What?* Does this mean that purchasing ice cream can cause someone to commit a murder? Of course not. What we know is that people purchase more ice cream when the weather is warmer and the days are longer. And murder rates tend to be higher when more people are outside. So, what do these two activities have in common? If you said they both happen during the summer, you are correct. Ice cream sales and murder rates are higher during summer months, so the relationship between the two is due to a third variable (i.e., time of year, which itself reflects temperature). Yes, ice cream purchases and murder rates are correlated, but this in no way provides evidence that one causes the other.

So, in the AFC case, managers can theorize that growing older causes members to spend more money with AFC, but the correlational data alone cannot prove this to be true. The available evidence is consistent with this theory, but not sufficient to establish causality.

## 18-5 Regression Analysis

**Regression analysis** provides a means for getting at the nature of the relationship between one or more predictor variables and an outcome variable. If there is a single predictor variable, the technique is referred to as *simple regression*; with multiple predictors, it's called *multiple regression*. Usually, you'll have reason to believe that the predictor variable(s) somehow influence the dependent variable (keeping in mind that the mathematics alone cannot prove causation), although this doesn't have to be the case.

We've already established that there is a correlational relationship between age and revenues for AFC members. Managers also wanted to see whether they could pinpoint any basic motivations that were associated with spending more money at the fitness center. Recall that respondents provided importance ratings for four different reasons for participating in AFC programs (see Question 5 in Exhibit 16.2). Is it possible that the importance of visiting the center for (1) general health and fitness, (2) social aspects, (3) physical enjoyment, and/or (4) specific medical concerns leads to spending more money with AFC? If so, managers might try to attract new members by appealing to those needs in their promotional efforts.

In regression analysis, the dependent variable (revenues) is "regressed" on the set of predictor, or independent, variables (SPSS Menu Sequence: Analyze > Regression > Linear). Mathematically, an equation is produced that represents the best fit between the predictors and the outcome. As shown in Exhibit 18.8, the analysis produces

> **regression analysis**
> A statistical technique used to derive an equation representing the influence of a single (simple regression) or multiple (multiple regression) independent variables on a continuous dependent, or outcome, variable.
>
> **coefficient of multiple determination ($R^2$)** A measure representing the relative proportion of the total variation in the dependent variable that can be explained or accounted for by the fitted regression equation. When there is only one predictor variable, this value is referred to as the *coefficient of determination.*

regression coefficients for each of the predictor variables. These coefficients represent the average change in the outcome variable per unit change in the associated predictor variable, holding all other predictor variables constant. For example, the sample results indicate that for each additional year in age we can expect an average increase in yearly revenues of about \$4 (i.e., \$4.33 rounded to a whole number, which is how revenues were measured). Similarly, increasing the importance of social aspects one position on the rating scale (say, from 3 to 4) is associated with an increase of about \$37 in annual revenue. But we're getting ahead of ourselves.

Before we try to interpret the individual regression coefficients, it's important to check a couple of things first. Start by looking to see whether there is an overall statistically significant relationship between the set of predictors and the outcome variable; if there isn't, there's no point in looking at any of the individual predictors. In Exhibit 18.8 you'll see a section of SPSS output labeled "ANOVA" (which stands for "analysis of variance"). The overall model is tested on the basis of the amount of variance in the dependent variable that can be explained by the combination of predictor variables relative to the variation in the dependent variable that cannot be explained. In this case, the $F$-statistic equals 7.06 and the corresponding $p$-value is less than 0.001, so there is a statistically significant relationship between the amount of fees members pay and the predictor variables (age plus the four importance ratings).

We also need to verify that our set of predictors can explain (or predict) a meaningful portion of the variation in the outcome variable. (If you work with a large enough sample, almost any relationship at all between variables will become statistically significant, even if the effects are trivial from a managerial standpoint.) If some or all of our predictor variables are causing changes in the outcome variable, then there has to be some degree of association between changes in the predictors and changes in the outcome variable. The **coefficient of multiple determination** calculates the closeness of the relationship between the predictor variables and the outcome variable in a multiple regression analysis and is symbolized by $R$. (In simple regression, this is called the *coefficient of determination.*) The AFC researchers found this value in the "Model Summary" section (see Exhibit 18.8); $R$ was equal to 0.17. This means that the predictors have a small-to-modest association with the outcome variable; together they can account for 17% of the variation in revenues for the 1-year period. We'd like the coefficient of multiple determination to be higher, but considering all of the many other things that might influence how much a member spends at the center, this result was meaningful to AFC managers.

**Exhibit 18.8 ▶** Avery Fitness Center: Regression of Revenues on Several Predictors (SPSS Output)

### MODEL SUMMARY

| MODEL | R | R SQUARE | ADJUSTED R SQUARE | STD. ERROR OF THE ESTIMATE |
|---|---|---|---|---|
| 1 | 0.408[a] | 0.166 | 0.143 | 156.241 |

[a] Predictors: (Constant), Importance: Specific Medical Concerns, Age in Years, Importance: Physical Enjoyment, Importance: General Health and Fitness, Importance: Social Aspects

### ANOVA[b]

| MODEL | | SUM OF SQUARES | DF | MEAN SQUARE | F | SIG. |
|---|---|---|---|---|---|---|
| 1 | Regression | 861276.227 | 5 | 172255.245 | 7.056 | 0.000[a] |
| | Residual | 4320770.289 | 177 | 24411.132 | | |
| | Total | 5182046.516 | 182 | | | |

[a] Predictors: (Constant), Importance: Specific Medical Concerns, Age in Years, Importance: Physical Enjoyment, Importance: General Health and Fitness, Importance: Social Aspects
[b] Dependent Variable: Previous Year Revenue ($)

### COEFFICIENTS[a]

| MODEL | | UNSTANDARDIZED COEFFICIENTS | | STANDARDIZED COEFFICIENTS | | |
|---|---|---|---|---|---|---|
| | | B | STD. ERROR | BETA | T | SIG. |
| 1 | (Constant) | −88.819 | 108.633 | | −0.818 | 0.415 |
| Age in Years | Age in Years | 4.334 | 0.996 | 0.304 | 4.351 | 0.000 |
| | Importance: General Health and Fitness | 14.850 | 18.769 | 0.060 | 0.791 | 0.430 |
| | Importance: Social Aspects | 36.637 | 11.224 | 0.273 | 3.264 | 0.001 |
| | Importance: Physical Enjoyment | −29.639 | 13.609 | −0.188 | −2.178 | 0.031 |
| | Importance: Specific Medical Concerns | 2.486 | 9.828 | 0.018 | 0.253 | 0.801 |

[a] Dependent Variable: Previous Year Revenue ($)

Now we'll shift our attention back to the individual predictors. Looking at the $t$-values associated with the five predictors (see Exhibit 18.8), we see that age ($t = 4.35$), the importance of social aspects ($t = 3.26$), and the importance of physical enjoyment ($t = -2.18$) are statistically significant predictors of revenues. However, we also see that the importance of attending the center for general health and fitness and the importance of attending because of specific medical concerns do not seem to influence the amount of money people spent over the year at AFC. (For the latter two predictor variables, the $p$-value, the probability that we could have seen an effect of this magnitude if there truly

were no relationship between the predictor and revenues, is greater than 0.05.)

So, what do these results mean? First, it appears that older people spend more money each year at the center compared with younger people. Managers might want to adjust their promotional efforts to appeal to older customers. And, more importantly, maybe they could spend more time determining what this important market really needs with respect to fitness and how to satisfy these needs.

Second, people who place greater importance on social aspects as a reason for going to AFC seem to spend more money than those who place less importance on social aspects. Interestingly, we saw earlier that this is the least important reason for attending the center on average across all respondents, which suggests that there is an opportunity for growth in this area. Specifically, managers might want to promote the importance of social interaction as an ingredient in maintaining health and fitness as people grow older.

Finally, look closely at the coefficient that represents the influence of the perceived importance of physical enjoyment as a reason for visiting AFC on revenues. This value (−29.64) indicates that for every 1-unit increase in the importance rating for this aspect, 1-year revenues decrease by about $30. In effect, if physical enjoyment is an important reason for a member to visit the center, then he or she ultimately seems to spend less money. AFC managers may need to put some thought into what this means for the organization.

As a final note to our discussion of regression, we should point out that regression is a robust analytic tool that can also be used when one or more independent variables are categorical as opposed to continuous variables. You can learn more about this—and many other multivariate analysis techniques—by reading a good multivariate statistics text. We hope, however, that you now have a better understanding of the value of analyzing variables in combination.

# Summary

### Learning Objective 1

**Discuss why a researcher might conduct a multivariate analysis.**
Multivariate analysis often provides a much deeper understanding of the data. Univariate analyses produce broad, overall results. Multivariate analyses look for differences across groups or associations among variables.

### Learning Objective 2

**Explain the purpose and importance of cross tabulation.**
Cross tabulation is a commonly used multivariate technique. Its purpose is to study the relationships among and between categorical variables.

### Learning Objective 3

**Describe a technique for comparing groups on a continuous dependent variable.**
When comparing two groups, the independent samples $t$-test is used to determine whether the mean score on the dependent variable for one group is significantly different from the mean score for the second group.

### Learning Objective 4

**Explain the difference between an independent sample $t$-test for means and a paired sample $t$-test for means.**
In the independent samples $t$-test, mean scores on the dependent variable are compared for different groups of respondents. In a paired sample $t$-test, mean scores on two different variables (measured on similar scales) are compared across a single group (i.e., all respondents provide scores on both variables).

### Learning Objective 5

**Discuss the Pearson product-moment correlation coefficient.**
The Pearson product-moment correlation coefficient assesses the degree of linear association between two continuous variables.

### Learning Objective 6

**Discuss a technique for examining the influence of one or more predictor variables on an outcome variable.**
With regression analysis, a mathematical equation is derived that relates a dependent variable to one or more independent, or predictor, variables. The predictor variables can be either categorical or continuous.

## Key Terms

cross tabulation (page 269)

Pearson chi-square ($X^2$) test of independence (page 271)

Cramer's $V$ (page 271)

banner (page 272)

independent samples $t$-test for means (page 273)

paired sample $t$-test (page 273)

Pearson product-moment correlation coefficient (page 276)

regression analysis (page 277)

coefficient of multiple determination ($R^2$) (page 277)

## Review Questions

1. Why would a researcher consider conducting multivariate analyses? Why not just conduct overall univariate analyses?

2. What technique is typically used to investigate relationships between two categorical variables?

3. How do you determine which set of percentages (i.e., row versus column percentages) to use on a cross-tab analysis?

4. What would be the appropriate test to determine if men differed from women in their satisfaction with a meal served in a fast-food restaurant?

5. How do you test for differences between scores on two continuous measures when each respondent provides both measures? Explain.

6. What does the Pearson product-moment correlation coefficient measure? When is it appropriate to use?

7. If two continuous measures are positively correlated with one another, does that mean that one of them caused the other? Why or why not?

8. What is the proper procedure for testing the influences of two different independent variables on a single continuous dependent variable simultaneously?

9. What is the difference between regression analysis and correlation analysis?

10. What is the coefficient of multiple determination, and what does it measure?

# Endnote

1. Using current demographic and importance ratings to predict revenues from a prior time period is technically not correct, because effects should follow causes in time. Note, however, that this approach (1) is reasonable with the assumption that immediate past behavior is the best predictor of behavior in a following time period and (2) greatly increased the timeliness of the report (the alternative would have been to collect revenue data over the following 12 months, delaying presentation of results by 1 year).

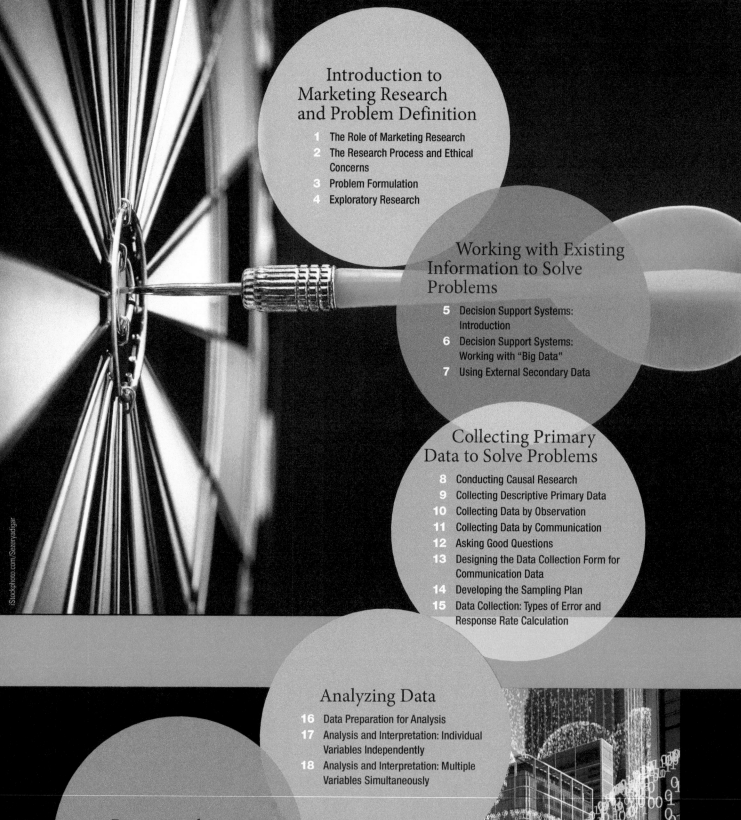

# Part 5

# Reporting the Results

iStockphoto.com/nrcmos

# The Oral Research Presentation

## LEARNING OBJECTIVES

▶ Discuss two fundamental rules for making good oral presentations.

▶ Explain how the time allotted for an oral presentation should be organized.

▶ List some of the different kinds of charts that can be used in presenting study results.

## [ INTRODUCTION ]

It doesn't help much to conduct a flawless research project—as if that were possible—if you can't communicate the results of the study. Creating an effective report, whether oral or written, is a challenging process that takes a lot more time that most researchers budget for the process. It isn't easy to do. In this chapter, we'll provide some "best practice" suggestions for preparing a strong oral presentation. In addition, we'll describe quite a few different types of charts that you might find useful for presenting your results. In Chapter 20, we address written reports.

## 19-1 The Oral Research Presentation

Most marketing research projects require one or more oral presentations. A recent study found that 95% of respondents do small-group presentations (with 78% doing large-group presentations) to report results inside organizations.[1] And sometimes clients or managers want progress reports during the course of the project. Bottom line, if you are responsible for a marketing research study, it is likely you will be asked to share the results of that study in an oral presentation format.

As you design your presentation, keep in mind that many of your listeners won't fully understand the technical aspects of your research and, as a result, may not be able to accurately judge its quality. They

**Exhibit 19.1 ▶** OPEN UP! Exceptional Presentation Skills

OPEN UP! is an acronym representing the six characteristics shared by exceptional presenters. The secret is not just knowing the characteristics, but understanding how to incorporate them into your presentation style.

**THE EXCEPTIONAL PRESENTER IS:**

**ORGANIZED** Exceptional presenters take charge! They look poised and polished. They sound prepared. You get the sense that they are not there to waste time. Their goal is not to overwhelm, but to inform, persuade, influence, entertain, or enlighten. Their message is well structured and clearly defined.

**PASSIONATE** Exceptional presenters exude enthusiasm and conviction. If the presenter doesn't look and sound passionate about his or her topic, why would anyone else be passionate about it? Exceptional presenters speak from the heart and leave no doubt as to where they stand. Their energy is persuasive and contagious.

**ENGAGING** Exceptional presenters do everything in their power to engage each audience member. They build rapport quickly and involve the audience early and often. If you want their respect, you must first connect.

**NATURAL** Exceptional presenters have a natural style. Their delivery has a conversational feel. Natural presenters make it look easy. They appear comfortable with any audience. A presenter who appears natural appears confident.

**AS AN EXCEPTIONAL PRESENTER, YOU MUST:**

**UNDERSTAND YOUR AUDIENCE** Exceptional presenters learn as much as they can about their audience before presenting to them. The more they know about the audience, the easier it will be to connect and engage.

**PRACTICE** Those who practice improve. Those who don't practice don't improve. Exceptional skills must become second nature. Practice is the most important part of the improvement process. If your delivery skills are second nature, they will not fail under pressure.

Source: Excerpted from Timothy J. Koegel, *The Exceptional Presenter* (Austin, TX: Greenleaf Book Group, 2007), pp. 4–5.

## Manager's Focus

In case you're thinking, "I can coast a little bit here and let the researchers be responsible for this final stage of the research process"—hold on a minute. Researchers begin the process of disseminating research findings by writing reports and giving oral presentations, but ultimately it is marketing managers that are responsible for transmitting relevant market research findings to key decision makers throughout the organization. There will likely be times when you create abbreviated reports that are passed along to others on the management team, and you will probably need to tailor the report differently for the different types of managers who will receive it. You might even need to give oral presentations to managers higher in the chain of command about what has been learned from research studies. For these reasons, the material in these final two chapters is just as relevant to you as it is to researchers.

can, however, judge whether you present the research in a professional, confidence-inspiring manner or in a disorganized, uninformed one. A quality presentation can disguise poor research to some extent, but quality research cannot improve a poor presentation. Exhibit 19.1 contains some excellent ideas about becoming an effective presenter by being organized, passionate, engaging, and natural when you present. It also highlights the importance of understanding your audience and of practicing in advance.

### 19-1a PREPARING THE ORAL REPORT

As noted, preparing a successful oral report requires advance knowledge of the audience. What is their technical level of sophistication? Their involvement in the project? Their interest? You may want to present more detailed reports to those who are deeply involved in the project or who have a high level of technical sophistication. In general, though, it is better to have too little technical detail than too much. Executives want to hear and see what the information means to them as managers of marketing activities. What do the data suggest with respect to marketing actions? They can ask for the necessary clarification with respect to the technical details if they want it.

You also need to decide in advance how the presentation will be organized. There are two popular forms of

**Exhibit 19.2 ▶** 10 Tips for Preparing Effective Presentation Slides

1. **Keep them simple.** Present one point per slide, with as few words and lines as possible.

2. **Use lots of slides as you talk,** rather than lots of talk per slide. Less is more when you are speaking.

3. **Aim for one minute per slide,** then move on. Visuals should make their impact quickly.

4. **Highlight and emphasize significant points,** using bullets, font sizes or styles, color, animation, or by some other means.

5. **Make the slides easy to read.** Use large, legible fonts. Limit fonts to one or two typefaces and no more than three sizes. Make certain that the color of the text or exhibits shows up well against the background color.

6. **Be careful with the use of color.** Color can add interest and emphasis; it can also distract the audience if not used carefully. Plan your color scheme and use it faithfully throughout.

7. **Be careful with the use of slide backgrounds.** A consistent background (figure, logo, borders, etc.) can help the visual display, but not if it gets in the way of communicating the content of the slide.

8. **Build complex thoughts sequentially.** If you have a complicated concept to communicate, start with the ground level and use three or four slides (or add elements to a single slide one by one) to complete the picture.

9. **Prepare copies of slides.** Hand them to the audience before or after your presentation. If people have to take notes, they won't be watching or listening closely.

10. **Number the slides or pages in the handout.** You will have a better reference for discussion or a question-and-answer period.

organization. Both begin by stating the general purpose of the study and the specific research problems that were addressed. They differ, however, with respect to when the conclusions are introduced. In the more common structure, you state the conclusions after you have presented the results, the evidence supporting the conclusions. This allows you to build a logical case.

The other approach is to present conclusions immediately after you state the research problems. This is an immediate attention grabber, especially if the conclusions are surprising. It not only gets managers to think about what actions the results suggest but also causes them to pay close attention to the evidence supporting the conclusions.

Another important aspect of preparing the oral report is the development of effective visual aids. Even if you can avoid the technical aspects of the research in your presentation, it's all but impossible to communicate results without the use of tables and figures. Presentation software (e.g., PowerPoint, Keynote, Prezi) makes it relatively easy to prepare many different kinds of exhibits ranging from definitions, to bulleted lists, to maps, to various types of charts. Presentation software also allows the use of special effects such as the addition of sound or video in the presentation or the use of animation, fading, dissolving, progressively adding or deleting items in an exhibit—all of which can also create some desired emphasis. Exhibit 19.2 offers some advice for preparing effective presentations. In addition, Appendix 19A includes a set of slides prepared to present some of the results of the Avery Fitness Center project.

Regardless of how the visuals are prepared or which types are used, it's important to make sure they can be read by everyone in the room. We have endured far too many presentations in which the words are too small or are so close in color to the slide background that they can't be read. It's also important that visuals be kept simple so that they can be understood at a glance.

### 19-1b DELIVERING THE ORAL REPORT

You probably already know that speaking in front of people is quite stressful for most people. We've experienced that fear too, whether teaching a new group of students for the first time, speaking at church, giving speeches, making research presentations, or on other occasions. Delivering an oral marketing research report is no different; it can be an anxious process, especially for researchers with little experience. It turns out, however, that most of the fear can be eliminated with a little preparation prior to the presentation. You're still likely to experience a little anxiety, but that's okay—if you feel no stress at all, it probably means that you aren't taking it seriously and may be about to embarrass yourself.

There are two fundamental rules for delivering good oral presentations. Carefully following these rules will also alleviate much of the fear of speaking in front of people for most presenters. Here's the first rule: *Know your stuff.* It's amazing how much fear is caused by uncertainty. In an oral presentation of a marketing research project, there are many potential sources of uncertainty: the nature of the problem, the processes involved with data collection, what the results really mean, whether decision makers want recommendations in addition to conclusions, what objectives need to be accomplished in the oral report, and so on. If you know what you're talking about, it's much easier to stand up and tell your audience what they need to know. And don't forget to practice. Presenting an oral report without practicing it, maybe several times, is foolhardy; you're asking for trouble.

> Presenting an oral report without practicing it is foolhardy.

The second rule for delivering a quality presentation is going to sound familiar: *Know your audience*. The audience is likely to be composed of marketing managers, executives, or others. You need to know your audience at the group and individual levels. If possible, find out in advance who will be attending the oral presentation. Always keep in mind the purpose of the research and the general answers your audience is interested in learning about. And you'll also need to understand the level of technical sophistication of the overall audience. For example, if most people listening to you would understand the notions of sampling error or statistical significance, then feel free to talk about these issues if needed. If you're not sure, go with the lower level of technical sophistication but have more detailed slides ready to go if you need them.

There are a few other things to keep in mind about the oral presentation. Honor the time limit set for the meeting; use no more than half of the time for the formal presentation, saving the rest for questions and answers. But be careful not to rush the presentation of the information contained in the visuals. Remember, the audience is seeing them for the first time. Run the presentation so that you'll have enough time to both present and discuss the most critical findings.

One benefit of an oral presentation is that it allows interaction. The question-and-answer period may be the most important part of your presentation. It allows you to clear up any confusion that may have arisen during your talk, emphasize points that deserve special attention, and get a feeling for the issues that are of particular concern to the audience. Although it's impossible to know in advance what issues may come up, if you'll follow the two rules given—that is, know your stuff and know your audience—you should be able to handle anything your audience can throw at you.

Finally, it's always smart to get into the presentation room well before the actual presentation. This allows you to get a feel for the room and to make absolutely certain that the presentation equipment and software are working correctly. Nothing kills a great presentation faster than technical problems. And if you have to rely on others to run the audiovisual aspects of the presentation, be there when *they* test the system. Trust no one; you want firsthand knowledge that the presentation software is working the way it is supposed to work.

## 19-2 Graphic Presentation of Results

The old adage that a picture is worth a thousand words is also true for marketing research reports and presentations, provided that you do it right. Sometimes, however, the graphics can get in the way of effective communication. An inappropriate, inaccurate, or poorly designed chart can easily cause confusion or be misinterpreted. In this section, we briefly consider some of the more popular forms of charts. To be effective, an illustration must give your audience—whether they are reading a report or watching an oral presentation—an accurate understanding of comparisons or relationships that they would have to "hunt through the numbers" to get otherwise. If you do it right, a chart will allow greater understanding more quickly, forcefully, completely, and accurately than any other way.

Graphic presentation isn't the only way to present quantitative information, nor is it always the best. Sometimes text and tables are more effective. Over the years, we've seen lots of beginning researchers get a little bit carried away with charts—and we understand that temptation. But not every result needs to be illustrated graphically. In fact, tables are often more than enough to effectively present results from a project. Graphics should be used only to illustrate key findings and when they allow insights into data that might not be seen otherwise. If you use too many charts, you'll dilute the value of the really important ones.

To help demonstrate some different types of charts, we pulled 12 years' worth of personal consumption expenditures (see Exhibit 19.3) from a government report. We'll use these data for many of the examples in this section.

### 19-2a PIE CHART

A **pie chart** is simply a circle divided into sections, with each of the sections representing a portion of the total. Because the sections are presented as part of a whole, pie charts are really effective for depicting relative size, for one variable, at one point in time. Exhibit 19.4, for instance, shows the breakdown of personal consumption expenditures by major category for a particular year (Year 12). The conclusion is obvious. Expenditures for services account for the largest proportion of total consumption expenditures. If there are more than five or six levels, though, the pie chart can quickly get confusing; maybe a table would work better. The sections of a pie chart normally are organized clockwise in decreasing order of size—be sure to include exact percentages (but remember, no decimal places) on the chart.

**pie chart** A circle representing a total quantity that is divided into sectors, with each sector showing the size of the segment in relation to that total.

**Exhibit 19.3** ▸ Personal Consumption Expenditures for a Recent 12-Year Period (Billions of Dollars)

| YEAR | TOTAL PERSONAL CONSUMPTION EXPENDITURES | DURABLE GOODS | NONDURABLE GOODS | SERVICES |
|---|---|---|---|---|
| Year 1 | $3,659.3 | $480.3 | $1,193.7 | $1,983.3 |
| Year 2 | 3,887.7 | 446.1 | 1,251.5 | 2,190.1 |
| Year 3 | 4,095.8 | 480.4 | 1,290.7 | 2,324.7 |
| Year 4 | 4,378.2 | 538.0 | 1,339.2 | 2,501.0 |
| Year 5 | 4,628.4 | 591.5 | 1,394.3 | 2,642.7 |
| Year 6 | 4,957.7 | 608.5 | 1,475.8 | 2,873.4 |
| Year 7 | 5,207.6 | 634.5 | 1,534.7 | 3,038.4 |
| Year 8 | 5,433.7 | 657.4 | 1,619.9 | 3,156.7 |
| Year 9 | 5,856.0 | 693.2 | 1,708.5 | 3,454.3 |
| Year 10 | 6,246.5 | 755.9 | 1,830.1 | 3,660.5 |
| Year 11 | 6,683.7 | 803.9 | 1,972.9 | 3,906.9 |
| Year 12 | 6,987.0 | 835.9 | 2,041.3 | 4,109.9 |

**Exhibit 19.4** ▸ Pie Chart: Personal Consumption Expenditures by Major Category (One Year)

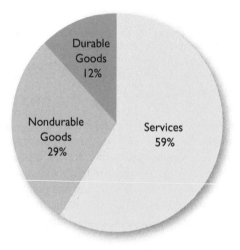

## 19-2b LINE CHART

The **line chart** is a two-dimensional chart that is particularly useful in depicting relationships over time. For example, Exhibit 19.5 has the same information about personal expenditures for Year 12 as the pie chart in Exhibit 19.4—but it also contains information for the other 11 years as well.

The line chart is probably used even more often than the pie chart. The x-axis normally represents time, and the y-axis represents values of the variable or variables. When

**Exhibit 19.5** ▶ Line Chart: Personal Consumption Expenditures by Major Category (12 Years)

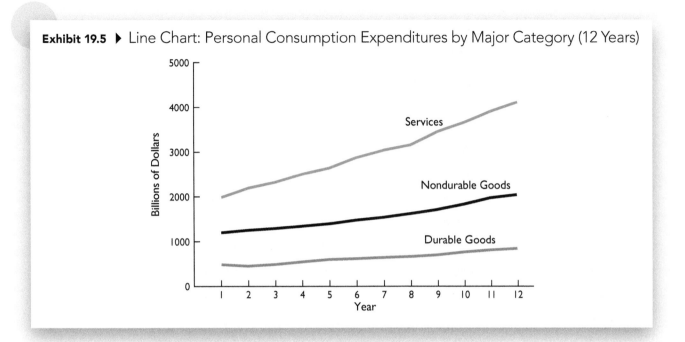

more than one variable is presented, use different colors or types of lines (dots and dashes in various combinations) to represent the different variables. Also, be sure to identify the different variables, using a key, or legend.

## 19-2c STRATUM CHART

The **stratum chart** is like a dynamic pie chart, in that it can be used to show relative emphasis by sector (e.g., quantity consumed by user class) at any one point in time. It goes further, however, to also show changes in relative emphasis over time. The stratum chart consists of a set of line charts whose quantities are grouped together (or a total that is broken into its components). It is also called a *stacked line chart*. For example, Exhibit 19.6 again shows personal consumption expenditures by category for the 12-year period. The lowest line shows the expenditures just for services; the second-lowest line shows the total expenditures for services plus nondurable goods; the top line shows the total of all three expenditures. We would need multiple pie charts (one for each year) to capture the same information, and the message wouldn't be as obvious.

## 19-2d BAR CHART

The **bar chart** is a widely used chart that can take several different forms. Exhibit 19.7, for example, is a simple bar chart that shows personal consumption expenditures by major category at a

**line chart** A two-dimensional chart with the *x*-axis representing one variable (typically time) and the *y*-axis representing another variable.

**stratum chart** A set of line charts in which quantities are aggregated or a total is disaggregated so that the distance between two lines represents the amount of some variable.

**bar chart** A chart in which the relative lengths of the bars show relative amounts of variables or objects.

**pictograms** A bar chart in which pictures represent amounts—for example, piles of dollars for income, pictures of cars for automobile production, people in a row for population.

single point in time. This is pretty much the same information as shown in the earlier pie chart (Exhibit 19.4), but it's a little more revealing because it offers information about the size of the expenditures by category. Bar charts can be drawn either vertically or horizontally, but if you're going to show change in a variable over time, standard procedure is to use a vertical chart and to track time along the horizontal axis.

### Bar Chart Variations

Bar charts are flexible and can be used in many ways. You can use bar charts to present the same information we included earlier with our line chart (called a grouped bar chart) and our stratum chart (called a stacked bar chart). Another interesting variation is to convert a bar chart to a **pictogram**. Instead of using the length of the bar to capture quantity, amounts are shown by piles of dollars for income, pictures of cars for automobile production, people in a row for population, and so on. Pictograms can be really effective, but be careful because they can easily mislead an audience. Exhibit 19.8 shows two different pictograms, both of which are supposed to communicate the same thing (i.e., a doubling of taxes paid over a two-year period). The first chart makes the tax burden seem much greater, don't you think? The proper form for the pictogram is the second version. Be careful when reading pictograms because it's easy to draw the wrong conclusion (which is exactly what people who practice advocacy research are hoping).

**Exhibit 19.6**  ▶  Stratum Chart: Personal Consumption Expenditures by Major Category (12 Years)

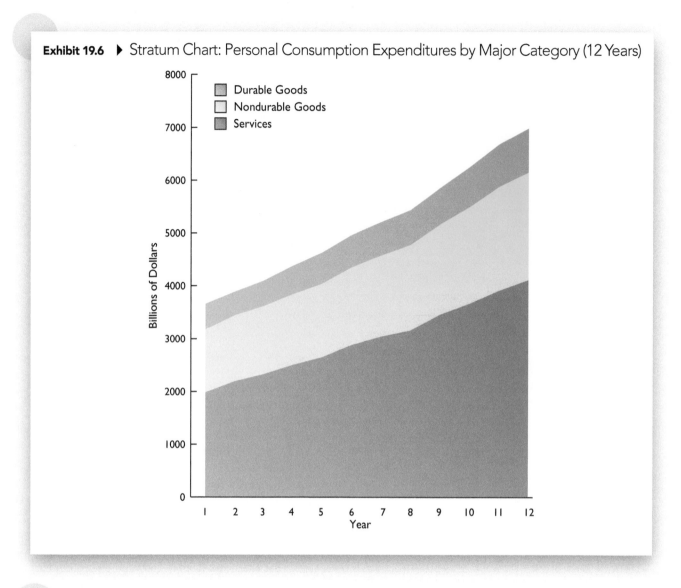

**Exhibit 19.7**  ▶  Bar Chart: Personal Consumption Expenditures by Major Category (Year 12)

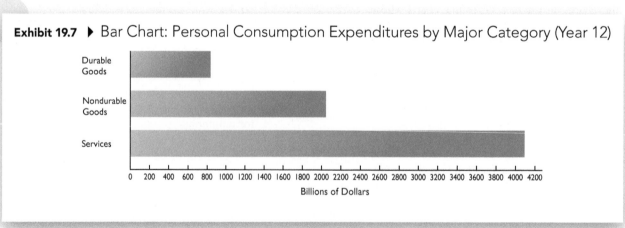

**Exhibit 19.8** ▶ Two Versions of a Pictogram

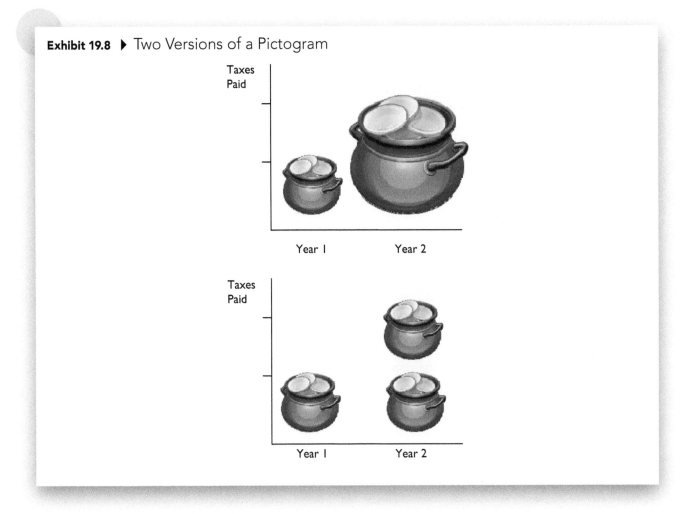

## 19-2e OTHER CHARTS

The charts we've presented so far are great when working with a single variable (broken into categories), sometimes tracked over time. Things get a bit more complicated (and sometimes a lot more interesting) when data about multiple variables and/or multiple objects are presented simultaneously. Charts to accomplish these purposes are useful, but if they become too complicated, they lose much of their effectiveness as a communications tool.

Recent decades have seen a remarkable number of tools become available for **data visualization**, which we define simply as the process of using graphic illustrations to understand and communicate important relationships in large data sets. Not surprisingly, many of the tools have been developed to try to deal with—and take advantage of—the rapid increase in sources and types of data available to companies. A wide variety of charts, ranging from simple two-dimensional scatterplots that plot objects along two continuous variables to more complex diagrams are used to "see" what the data are saying. Regardless of the type of chart, when it comes to oral and/or written research presentations, the key point is the degree to which the chart helps communicate the important results.

**data visualization**
The process of using graphic illustrations to understand and communicate important relationships in large data sets.

## Manager's Focus

As the client, there are essentially two routes you can take. You can follow the conventional path and passively wait to see if your research supplier's written report and oral presentation meet your expectations and needs. Or you can be proactive and provide concrete guidelines in advance that your research provider can follow when writing the report and developing the oral presentation.

To illustrate this proactive approach, when a researcher we know was beginning a relationship with a particular client, a manager from the marketing department came to the researcher's office for a one-day orientation/training session. He had developed a standards manual that outlined the company's expectations and standards for each phase of a marketing research project (not simply the report and presentation). Because the client took this initiative, the researcher

did not have to assume what his company expected and desired—he knew with certainty. It provided a sound start to what proved to be a long-term, mutually beneficial relationship.

We highly recommend that you follow a similar approach. By developing a standards manual, you and your colleagues will become clearer in your own minds as to what your specific expectations are. When you develop a clear understanding of your own expectations and needs (which would be very difficult without the knowledge of marketing research you have acquired from this book, research providers, or your own experience), you will be able to communicate those expectations and needs clearly to your research suppliers. This will dramatically increase the likelihood you will be satisfied with the services they provide.

# Summary

## Learning Objective 1

**Discuss two fundamental rules for making good oral presentations.**

When presenting oral reports, the two fundamental rules are (1) know your stuff and (2) know your audience.

## Learning Objective 2

**Explain how the time allotted for an oral presentation should be organized.**

Honor the time limit set for the meeting. Use no more than half of the time for the formal presentation. Reserve the remaining time for questions and discussion.

## Learning Objective 3

**List some of the different kinds of charts that can be used in presenting study results.**

A number of different charts can be used. Some of these include (1) pie charts, (2) line charts, (3) stratum charts, (4) bar charts, and (5) pictograms.

## Key Terms

pie chart (page 287)
line chart (page 289)
stratum chart (page 289)
bar chart (page 289)
pictograms (page 289)
data visualization (page 292)

## Review Questions

1. What are the key considerations in preparing an oral report?

2. What are the two rules for presenting the oral report?

3. What is a pie chart? For what kinds of information is it particularly effective?

4. What is a line chart? For what kinds of information is it generally used?

5. What is a stratum chart? For what kinds of information is it particularly appropriate?

6. What is a bar chart? For what kinds of problems is it effective?

7. What is a pictogram?

# Endnote

1. "Corporate Research Report," undated, downloaded from www.quirks.com, p. 12.

# Oral Research Presentation, Avery Fitness Center

## A Deeper Understanding of Avery Fitness Center Customers

○

SUTER AND BROWN RESEARCH

## Presentation Outline

○

- Introduction
- Method
- Results
  - ○ Section One – Overall Demographics and Usage Statistics
  - ○ Section Two – How Members Initially Learn about AFC
  - ○ Limitations
- Conclusions and Recommendations

## Introduction

- How can we increase revenues at our current location?
- To answer this question, the research was approached with two perspectives in mind
  - Determine member demographics and usage patterns
  - Investigate how members learn about AFC

## Method

- **Exploratory Research**
  - Literature Search
    - AFC's role in the community was consistent with other organizations and programs across the country
    - Older adults seek community programs and facilities that help them to be more active
  - AFC Employee Depth Interviews
    - The goal was to gain insights about AFC members who attend regularly
  - AFC Member Depth Interviews
    - The goal was to gain understanding about motivations for AFC attendance and methods for initially learning about the facility

## Method

- **Descriptive Research**
  - Mail surveys were sent to a simple random sample of current and former AFC members who had utilized the Center at least once in the past 12 months
  - 231 usable surveys were returned over a two week period from the 400 members contacted
    - 58% response rate
  - Data from member surveys were matched with internal data from (1) facility entry records, (2) initial application forms, and (3) accounting records
  - All analyses based on 231 matched cases (although where possible we confirmed the results with all available cases; there were no meaningful differences)

## Results
### Section One – Overall Demographics and Usage Statistics

- **The average AFC member can be described as**
  - Female (80%)
  - Older (mean age 69, with 50% between the ages of 60-77)
  - Well educated (60% with a four-year or advanced college degree)
  - Comfortable income (29% with annual household income greater than $75,000)

## Results
### Section One – Overall Demographics and Usage Statistics

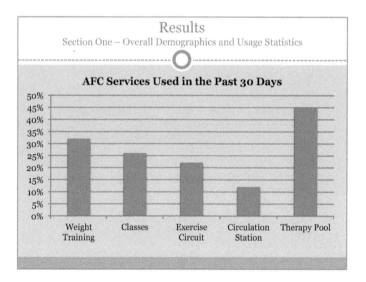

**AFC Services Used in the Past 30 Days**

## Results
### Section One – Overall Demographics and Usage Statistics

- **Weight Training (32% usage)**
  - Men (51% compared to 27% women)
  - Higher education (37% compared to 23% with less education)
  - Higher incomes (41% compared to 27% with lower incomes)
- **Classes (26% usage)**
  - Women (30% compared to 9% men)
- **Exercise Circuit (22% usage)**
  - No statistical differences among demographic categories
- **Circulation Station (12% usage)**
  - Lower incomes (17% compared to 5% with higher incomes)

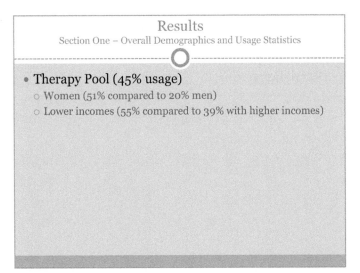

Results
Section One – Overall Demographics and Usage Statistics

- **Therapy Pool (45% usage)**
  - Women (51% compared to 20% men)
  - Lower incomes (55% compared to 39% with higher incomes)

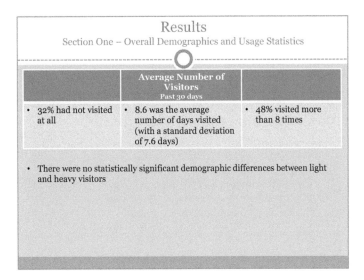

Results
Section One – Overall Demographics and Usage Statistics

| | Average Number of Visitors Past 30 days | |
|---|---|---|
| • 32% had not visited at all | • 8.6 was the average number of days visited (with a standard deviation of 7.6 days) | • 48% visited more than 8 times |

- There were no statistically significant demographic differences between light and heavy visitors

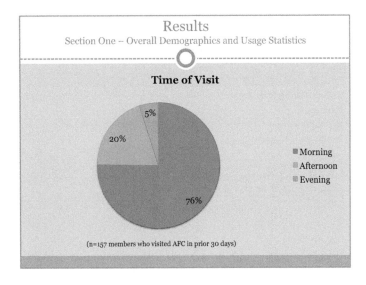

Results
Section One – Overall Demographics and Usage Statistics

**Time of Visit**

- Morning
- Afternoon
- Evening

5%
20%
76%

(n=157 members who visited AFC in prior 30 days)

## Results
### Section One – Overall Demographics and Usage Statistics

- **Overall Revenue**
  - Annual average of $282/member (standard deviation of $166)
    - 25% paid $155 or less per member
    - 25% paid $400 or more per member
- **Revenue by Demographics**
  - $\geq$ 70 years = Annual average of $324
  - < 70 years = Annual average of $246

## Results
### Section One – Overall Demographics and Usage Statistics

- **Revenue by Usage**
  - Those who visited more frequently = Annual average of $318
  - Those who visited less frequently = Annual average of $248
  - Class Participants = Annual average of $320
  - Class Non-participants = Annual average of $268
  - No statistically significant differences for
    - Weight Training Participants/Non-participants
    - Exercise Circuit Participants/Non-participants
    - Circulation Station Participants/Non-participants
    - Therapy Pool Participants/Non-participants

## Results
### Section One – Overall Demographics and Usage Statistics

| | Not at All Important (1) | | | | Very Important (5) |
|---|---|---|---|---|---|
| General Health & Fitness | | | | | 4.7 |
| Social Aspects | | | 3.2 | | |
| Physical Enjoyment | | | | 3.9 | |
| Specific Medical Concerns | | | | 4.1 | |

- Further analysis indicated that the more strongly people were motivated by "Social Aspects," the higher the fees they paid over the course of the year (i.e., $40 more for every point higher on the 1-5 importance scale)
- A respondent scoring "Social Aspects" a "5" would have paid $120 more in fees than a respondent who scored it a "2," on average

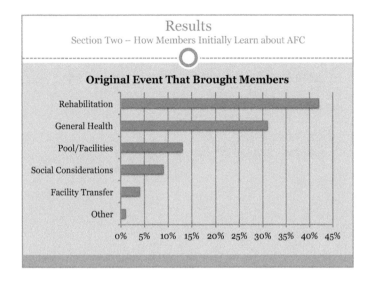

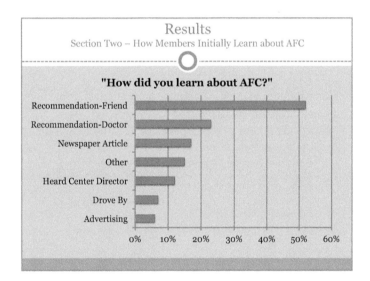

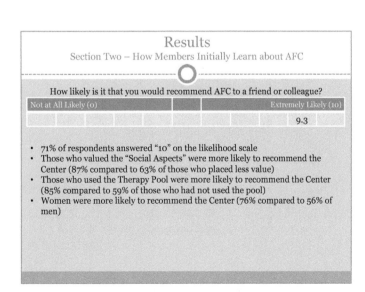

## Limitations

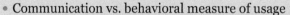

- Communication vs. behavioral measure of usage
  - Can track by GPS location, but current members not using smartphones or wearable technology

## Conclusions and Recommendations

- How can we increase revenues at our current location?
- To answer this question, the research was approached with two perspectives in mind
  - Determine member demographics and usage patterns
    - Older, well educated, females with a comfortable income
    - The Therapy Pool is the most frequently used service followed by Weight Training and Classes
    - AFC members visit an average of 8.6 days per month primarily in the mornings
  - Investigate how members learn about AFC

## Conclusions and Recommendations

- How can we increase revenues at our current location?
- To answer this question, the research was approached with two perspectives in mind
  - Determine member demographics and usage patterns
  - Investigate how members learn about AFC
    - Respondents first came to AFC for rehabilitation purposes or to address specific medical needs or general health and exercise
    - Word-of-mouth communication from friends and doctors was the most common way in which members first learned about the Center

## Conclusions and Recommendations

- How can we increase revenues at our current location?
  - Speak at senior citizen centers and living groups whenever possible
  - Focus on delivering the highest quality experience possible for existing members to promote word-of-mouth
    - This is especially true for members motivated by social considerations
  - Make information materials available for existing members
    - Allows them to learn more about the under-utilized services
    - Gives them something to pass along to friends and their doctors
    - Materials could also be "leave behinds" at speaking engagements

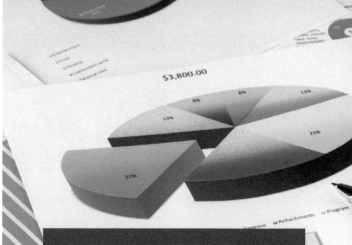

CHAPTER

# The Written Research Report

Billion Photos/Shutterstock.com

## LEARNING OBJECTIVES

▸ Discuss three writing standards that a report should meet if it is to communicate effectively with readers.

▸ Outline the main elements that make up a standard research report.

▸ Explain the kind of information contained in the executive summary.

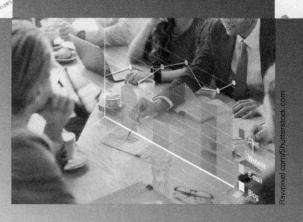

Rawpixel.com/Shutterstock.com

## [ INTRODUCTION ]

At the conclusion of a project, you will almost always be expected to prepare a written research report. And you need to put in the time to get it right—the project is a failure if you can't communicate the results effectively. The written report has a huge impact on whether the information generated by the research is actually used. This makes sense when you consider that the reports are all that most executives—the people who needed answers in the first place and who can make decisions based on the results—will see of the project. A solid written report sends an important signal about the likely quality of the overall project.

In this chapter, we offer some simple guidelines for developing successful written research reports. We'll also give you an example that you can use when developing your own written reports.

## 20-1 The Written Research Report

Share prices for Apple, Inc., dropped 3% back in 2006 after reports surfaced in the media about a sharp drop in revenues from the iTunes music download service offered by the company. An article in Britain's *The Register*, for example, described iTunes's monthly revenues as "collapsing" by 65% since January of that year, citing a marketing research report prepared by Forrester Research. Given that iTunes went on to be hugely successful with many billions of song downloads, somebody missed the mark badly in this case.

It turns out that the data in the report released by Forrester had been misunderstood. What the study actually revealed was a leveling off of iTunes downloads, certainly nothing coming close to a collapse in sales. Not surprisingly, with Apple's market value on the line, the research company received a call from a "clearly upset" Apple, and analysts quickly set the record straight.[1]

As this example illustrates, only one thing really matters with written research reports—how well they communicate with the reader. Research reports must be tailor-made for their readers, paying attention to their technical sophistication, their interest in the subject area, the circumstances under which they will read the report, and how they are likely to use it. Some readers understand technical issues—and some don't. As a general rule, it is not a good idea to try to impress the boss with big, scientific-sounding words in the written report. (That strategy can backfire because the use of technical language can make managers suspicious of whoever wrote the report.) Take the time to make the report understandable to your readers.

> Some readers understand technical issues—and some don't.

Sometimes managers prefer less information. They only want the results, not a discussion of how the results were obtained or any conclusions or recommendations. Other executives prefer just the opposite. They not only want a discussion of the results but also detailed information on how the results were obtained, as well as your conclusions, reasoning, and recommendations. In a nutshell, your audience determines the report type, and you need to learn their specific preferences.

## 20-1a RESEARCH REPORT WRITING STANDARDS

To communicate effectively, a written report must be complete, accurate, and clear.[2]

### Complete

A report is **complete** when it provides all the information readers need in language they understand. This means that you must continually ask whether every question in the original assignment has been addressed. An incomplete report probably means that you'll soon be writing supplementary reports, which are annoying and potentially deadly to your credibility as a researcher.

When it comes to completeness, there's a bit of a paradox. A written report must be complete, without being too complete. You need to include all relevant information—

**complete** The degree to which the report provides all the information readers need in language they understand.

**accuracy** The degree to which the reasoning in the report is logical and the information correct.

**clarity** The degree to which the phrasing in the report is precise.

but if you include too much information, the report quickly becomes less usable (see the section on clarity). You certainly don't want to force the reader to sift through page after page of nonessential results looking for the things that really matter. The trick is to determine what really matters and what ought to be included in appendices to the report or left out entirely. This isn't always easy. Think carefully about the reader.

### Accuracy

Imagine that you've done an amazing job of collecting and analyzing data that are perfectly appropriate for making a key decision, but you hurried as you prepared the research report and made mistakes. **Accuracy** in report development is another important consideration. Exhibit 20.1 illustrates some examples of sources of inaccuracy in report writing.

Problems with accuracy are hard to correct after the written report has been distributed. As a result, it's an extremely wise idea to ask several people to review the report for accuracy before it's sent to managers. And, much like a pretest of a survey, it wouldn't hurt to have a manager review a preliminary version of the written report.

### Clarity

**Clarity** of writing is one of the most difficult standards to achieve. Clarity comes from clear and logical thinking and precision of expression. When the underlying logic is fuzzy or the language imprecise, readers won't understand what they've read. If they have to guess what you meant, bad things can happen. Achieving clarity, however, requires effort.

The first, and most important, rule is that the report be well organized. For this to happen, you must first clarify for yourself the purpose of your report and how you intend to accomplish writing it. Make an outline of your major points. Put the points in logical order and place the supporting details in their proper position. Tell the reader what you are going to cover in the report and then do what you said you were going to do.

When it comes to the actual writing of the report, you should use short paragraphs and short sentences. Don't be evasive or ambiguous; once you decide what you want to say, come right out and say it. Choose your words carefully, making them as precise and understandable as possible. Research Window 20.1 offers a warning about the pitfalls of using "pompous" writing; the example is old, but the lesson is just as important today. Research Window 20.2 provides some specific suggestions about choosing words.

Don't expect your first draft to be satisfactory. First drafts are never good enough. Expect to rewrite—or at least severely edit—the written research report several times. When rewriting, attempt to reduce the length by half. That forces you to simplify and remove the clutter.

**Exhibit 20.1** ▶ Some Examples of Sources of Inaccuracy in Report Writing

**A. Simple Errors in Addition or Subtraction**

"In the past 30 days, 76% of AFC members usually visited the Center in the morning, 15% visited during the afternoon hours, and 5% visited during evening hours."

An oversight such as this (76 + 15 + 5 does not equal 100%) can easily be corrected by the author, but not so easily by the reader, because she may not know whether one or more of the percentage values is incorrect or whether a category (e.g., overnight hours?) might have been left out of the tally.

**B. Confusion Between Percentages and Percentage Points**

"Avery Fitness Center profits as a percentage of sales were 6.0% in 2011 and 8.0% in 2016. Therefore, they increased only 2.0% in five years."

In this example, the increase is 2.0 percentage points, or 33%.

**C. Inaccuracy Caused by Grammatical Errors**

"Increasing labor costs have reduced AFC net income $6,000 to $8,000 per year."

To express a range of reduction, the author should have written, "Increasing labor costs have reduced AFC net income between $6,000 and $8,000 per year."

**D. Confused Terminology, Resulting in Faulty Conclusions**

"Avery Fitness Center annual revenues increased from $80,000 in 2006 to $162,000 in 2016, thereby doubling the company's market power."

Although the company's annual revenues may have doubled over the time frame, we need a lot more information about the company (e.g., how much did costs increase in the same time period) and market (e.g., how well did competitors perform over the same time frame; growth of market size) before making meaningful comments about market power.

## research window 20.1

### How to Write Your Way out of a Job

Jock Elliott, a former executive with the Ogilvy & Mather advertising agency, offered this example of the importance of clear writing:

"Last month I got a letter from a vice president of a major management consulting firm. Let me read you two paragraphs. The first:

Recently, the companies of our Marketing Services Group were purchased by one of the largest consumer research firms in the United States. While this move well fits the basic business purpose and focus of the acquired MSG units, it is personally restrictive. I will rather choose to expand my management opportunities with a career move into industry.

"What he meant was: The deal works fine for my company, but not so fine for me. I'm looking for another job.

"Second paragraph:

The base of managerial and technical accomplishment reflected in my enclosed resume may suggest an opportunity to meet a management need for one of your clients. Certainly my experience promises a most productive pace to understand the demands and details of any new situation I would choose.

"What he meant was: As you can see in my resume, I've had a lot of good experience. I am a quick study. Do you think any of your clients might be interested in me?

"At least, that's what I think he meant.

"This fellow's letter reveals him as pompous. He may not be pompous. He may only be a terrible writer. But I haven't the interest or time to find out which. ... Bad writing done him in—with me, at any rate."

**Source:** Jock Elliott, "How Hard It Is to Write Easily," *Viewpoint: By, For, and About Ogilvy & Mather*, 2, 1980, p. 18.

# research window 20.2

## Some Suggestions When Choosing Words for Marketing Research Reports

1. **Use short words.** Always use short words in preference to long words that mean the same thing.

| Use this | Not this |
| --- | --- |
| Now | Currently |
| Start | Initiate |
| Show | Indicate |
| Finish | Finalize |
| Use | Utilize |
| Place | Position |
| So | Accordingly |
| Help | Facilitate |
| After | Subsequently |

2. **Avoid vague modifiers.** Avoid lazy adjectives and adverbs and use vigorous ones. Lazy modifiers are so overused in some contexts that they have become clichés. Select only those adjectives and adverbs that make your meaning precise.

| Lazy modifiers | Vigorous modifiers |
| --- | --- |
| Very good | Short meeting |
| Awfully nice | Crisp presentation |
| Basically accurate | Baffling instructions |
| Great success | Tiny raise |
| Richly deserved | Moist handshake |
| Vitally important | Lucid recommendation |

3. **Use specific, concrete language.** Avoid technical jargon. There is always a simple, down-to-earth word that says the same thing as the show-off fad word or the vague abstraction.

| Jargon | Down-to-Earth English |
| --- | --- |
| Implement | Carry out |
| Viable | Practical, workable |
| Suboptimal | Less than ideal |
| Proactive | Active |
| Bottom line | Outcome |

4. **Write simply and naturally—the way you talk.** Use only those words, phrases, and sentences that you might actually say to your reader if you were face to face. If you wouldn't say it, if it doesn't sound like you, don't write it.

| Stiff | Natural |
| --- | --- |
| The reasons are fourfold | There are four reasons |
| Importantly | The important point is |
| Visitation | Visit |
| As a means of | To |
| At this point in time | Now |
| In regard to | About |
| In the event that | If |
| With the exception of | Except |
| Due to the fact that | Because |

5. **Strike out words you don't need.** Certain commonly used expressions contain redundant phrasing. Cut out the extra words.

| Don't write | Write |
| --- | --- |
| Advance plan | Plan |
| Take action | Act |
| Study in depth | Study |
| Consensus of opinion | Consensus |
| Until such time as | Until |

**Source:** Table adapted from Chapter 2 of *Writing That Works* by Kenneth Roman and Joel Raphaelson. Copyright © 1981 by Kenneth Roman and Joel Raphaelson, Harper-Collins Publishers, Inc. Additional table entries from Laura Hale Brockway, "20 Phrases You Can Replace with One Word," *Ragan's PR Daily*, downloaded from www.prdaily.com/Main/Articles/11285.aspx on November 1, 2012; and "Long Words," *Garbl's Writing Center*, downloaded from http://home.comcast.net/~garbl/stylemanual/words.htm on November 1, 2012.

might also include tables and figures and the pages on which they will be found. For most reports, exhibits will be labeled as either tables or figures, with maps, diagrams, and charts falling into the latter category.

## Executive Summary

This might surprise you, but the executive summary is the most important part of the report—because this is the only part that many executives will read. So, it needs to contain the most essential information in the report. A good strategy when writing the executive summary is to think about what you would most want to communicate about the project if you had only 60 seconds to do so. The executive summary should fit on a single page if at all possible.

The summary begins with a statement of who authorized the research and the specific research problems or hypotheses that guided it. Next comes a brief statement about how the data were collected, including the response rate. The most important results obtained in the study are included next, often in "bullet" format, followed by conclusions (and maybe recommendations, depending upon what managers want to see). Invest the time necessary to produce a strong executive summary.

## Introduction

The introduction provides the background information readers need to appreciate the discussion in the remainder of the report. A little bit of background about the nature of the issue being studied is a good idea. The introduction should always state the specific research problems being addressed by the research (and include hypotheses where appropriate). In addition, this is the best place to define unfamiliar terms or terms that are used in a specific way in the report. For instance, in a study of market penetration of a new product, the introduction might define the market and name the products and companies considered "competitors" in calculating the new product's market share.

## Method

The methods section is one of the most difficult sections of the report to write. You face a real dilemma here. You need to provide enough information so that readers can appreciate the research design, data collection methods, sampling procedures, and analysis techniques that were used—but you don't want to bore or overwhelm the reader. Don't include a lot of technical jargon, because many of your readers won't understand it (nor should they be expected to).

Readers should be told in general terms about the types of research used (that is, exploratory, descriptive, and/or causal). If your project involved multiple stages (e.g., a descriptive survey followed by an online experiment), you should present the method and results of the stages sequentially. In some ways, your methods section is a summary—

---

**Exhibit 20.2 ▶** Written Research Report Outline

(A) Title page
(B) Table of contents
(C) Executive summary
(D) Introduction
(E) Method
(F) Results
    a. Research Findings
    b. Limitations
(G) Conclusions and recommendations
(H) Appendices
    a. Copies of data collection forms
    b. Data collection forms with univariate results
    c. Codebook
    d. Technical appendix (if necessary)
    e. Exhibits not included in the body (if necessary)
    f. Data file for archival storage
    g. Bibliography

---

It also forces you to think about every word and its purpose, to evaluate whether each word is helping you say what you want to say. Good reports tend to be concise.

## 20-1b RESEARCH REPORT OUTLINE

Research reports can be organized in different ways. In this section, we'll offer some advice about the key components that need to be in the report, regardless of the specific way that you choose to organize them. Using a good outline can help you achieve clarity, accuracy, and completeness in your report. Don't forget that the report format should be guided by the nature and needs of your audience. As a result, the general format presented in Exhibit 20.2 should be considered flexible.

### Title Page

The title page shows the subject/title of the report; the name of the organization, department, or individual for whom the report was written; the name of the organization, department, or individual submitting it; and the date. It is especially important to include the name and contact information of the researcher responsible for the project.

### Table of Contents

The table of contents lists the headings and subheadings of the report, with page references. The table of contents enough detail, but not too much—of the research proposal we discussed earlier. Readers should also be told whether the results are based on existing data or new primary data. If primary, are they based on observation or questionnaires? And, if the latter, how were the questionnaires administered (online, in person, mail, telephone)?

Sampling can be a technical subject, but you need to convey how it was approached. If you've used a particularly complicated approach, place the details in a technical appendix. At a minimum, you need to include the following aspects of the sampling plan in the methods section: (1) explicit population definition, including unit of analysis (e.g., individuals, households, businesses); (2) sampling frame and its source; (3) type of sample drawn; (4) size of sample; and (5) response rate.

### Results

The results section presents the findings of the study in some detail, often including supporting tables and figures. This section usually makes up the bulk of the report. The results need to address the specific research problems posed and must be presented with some logical structure. Results that are interesting but irrelevant in terms of the specific research problems should be omitted. A word of advice: Very few managers have any interest in seeing computer output or page after page of charts and tables. It is crucial that you think about how to best organize and present your research findings.

One effective approach is to organize the results section around the questions to be answered by the research. There are typically one or two key issues that are central to the manager's decision problem. Organize the results to provide information and answers to these issues. For example, if target market awareness is a central issue, then present the results for the questions used to assess awareness (e.g., overall recall, recognition, location recall) in a single section. If you have useful breakdowns on these variables (perhaps by gender or zip code or some other relevant variable), present these results in the same section. If another issue driving the research was target market perceptions of the company, organize these results in another section.

At the end of this chapter, we've included a written research report based on the Avery Fitness Center project (see Appendix 20A). The report is organized around the two research problems driving the project: (1) discover existing member demographics and usage patterns (including fees paid) and (2) investigate how members initially learn about AFC.

Tables and figures are sometimes more effective than plain text for communicating results. Note something, however: Tables, charts, and exhibits of other kinds can't replace text completely. You'll need to explain what the tables and charts mean. Still, clients will expect to see key points illustrated clearly. Tables and charts that appear in this section of the report should be easy to understand and focused around a single issue. More complex exhibits should appear in the technical appendix. And note that not every result requires a table or chart. Tables are often the better choice for presenting results, compared with charts. It's often smart to use charts only for those key findings that need extra emphasis because having too many of charts can quickly become a distraction.

## Manager's Focus

As we emphasized in the early parts of this book, marketing managers are responsible for evaluating the quality of marketing research studies before using the information they provide. Written research reports are the primary and most comprehensive sources of evidence for this purpose and should, therefore, be carefully scrutinized.

Things to think about: Were the research objectives made explicit, and does the report demonstrate they were actually attained? Is the communication throughout the report clear, complete, and accurate? Was a sound research design employed, and were all of the procedures employed equally sound? Are all of the insights offered in the conclusions and recommendations based directly on the research information (or data)? Is the report openly honest about what was done, and was the research conducted in an objective manner? Are the numerical data (or qualitative findings) reliable and trustworthy?

As you assess the degree to which these criteria were met, you must finally answer the big question: Does the report provide clear suggestions for appropriate **action** given my marketing situation, and am I willing to risk my reputation and career by acting on this information? Thus, the ACTION acronym presented below:

- **A**ttained research objectives
- **C**ommunication is clear, complete, and accurate
- **T**echnically sound design and procedures
- **I**nformation-based insights in conclusions and recommendations
- **O**bjective and open
- **N**umerically (or qualitatively) reliable and trustworthy

It is impossible to conduct a "perfect" study because every study has limitations. As the researcher, you know what the limitations are, and it is in your interest to point them out to the reader (many of them are beyond your control). Stating the limitations allows you to discuss whether, and by how much, the limitations might bias the results. So after you've provided the results, include a short section that highlights any limitations that need to be mentioned.

## Conclusions and Recommendations

The results lead to the conclusions and recommendations. Conclusions are based on an interpretation of the results; recommendations are suggestions about what managers should do next. There should be a conclusion for each of the research problems that motivated the study. One good strategy is to link research problems and conclusions so closely that the reader—after reviewing the research problems—can turn directly to the conclusions to find a specific conclusion for each objective. If the study does not provide enough evidence to draw a conclusion about a research problem, you need to make that clear.

Researchers' recommendations should follow the conclusions. With strategy-oriented research, recommendations should be straightforward; after all, the whole point of the project was to make a decision. Recommendations are less straightforward—and probably more important—with discovery-oriented research. You've collected information and now have some answers; how should the manager use this information? Note, however, that some managers may not want you to offer recommendations. Others will, because they recognize that you're the one who is closest to the research (and results), and they'll value your input.

## Appendices

The appendices to the report contain material that is too complex, too detailed, too specialized, or not absolutely necessary for the text. The appendices will typically include a copy of the questionnaire or observation form used to collect the data. If there are more detailed calculations for such things as sample size justification or test statistics, these will often appear in a technical appendix. It's also a good idea to compute univariate results for each of the measures in the study and include them on a second copy of the data collection form. Or sometimes researchers simply include data tables that present all of the univariate results. Either way, if all else fails, a manager can at least get an overall look at how respondents answered the questions. And be sure to include a bibliography if you've used references in the body of the report.

The research report will probably be the only document that eventually remains of the research project. As a result, it serves an important archival function. In addition to the copy of the data collection form, we suggest that you also include a copy of the codebook along with the actual data file containing the raw data of the project. This usually means including the electronic data file in some format, or at least including instructions about where the data are archived in the company's databases. With the data collection form, the codebook, and the data file, any competent researcher ought to be able to recreate your results—or conduct additional analyses. Remember that your current project might become a useful piece of secondary data for some later project.

# Summary

## Learning Objective 1

**Discuss three writing standards that a report should meet if it is to communicate effectively with readers.**
A report that achieves the goal of communicating effectively with readers is generally one that meets the standards of completeness, accuracy, and clarity.

## Learning Objective 2

**Outline the main elements that make up a standard research report.**
A standard report generally contains the following elements: title page, table of contents, executive summary, introduction, method, results, conclusions and recommendations, and appendices.

## Learning Objective 3

**Explain the kind of information contained in the executive summary.**
A good executive summary gives the most important points of the report, especially focusing on key results, conclusions, and recommendations.

### Key Terms

complete (page 303)
accuracy (page 303)
clarity (page 303)

### REVIEW QUESTIONS

1. What is the most important goal of a research report? Explain.

2. What is meant by the written report standards of completeness, accuracy, and clarity?

3. On the one hand, we argued that the research report must be complete and, on the other hand, that it must be clear. Are these two objectives incompatible? If so, how do you reconcile them?

4. What content appears in each of the following parts of the research report?
   a. Title page
   b. Table of contents
   c. Executive summary
   d. Introduction
   e. Method
   f. Results
   g. Conclusions and recommendations
   h. Appendices

# Endnotes

1. Kahn, J., (2014, May 28). "Eddy Cue: Apple passed 35 billion songs sold on iTunes last week, 40 million iTunes Radio listeners." Retrieved from https://9to5mac.com; Orlowski, A., (2006, December 11). "iTune's sales 'collapsing.'" Retrieved from www.theregister.co.uk/2006/12/11/digital_downloads_flatline/; and Gonsalves, A., (2006, December 13). "Research firm clarifies: iTunes sales are not collapsing," *Information-Week*. Retrieved from www.informationweek.com.

2. Gallagher, W. J. (1969) *Report Writing for Management* Reading, MA: Addison-Wesley, p. 78. Much of this introductory section is also taken from this excellent book. See also Sageev, P. (1995) *Helping Researchers Write, So Managers Can Understand* (Columbus, OH: Batelle Press).

# Written Research Report, Avery Fitness Center

## A Deeper Understanding of Avery Fitness Center Customers

Who Are They, What Services Do They Use, and What Draws Them to the Center?

Final Report

Prepared for:

## Avery Fitness Center

Prepared by:

## Suter and Brown Research

1

# Table of Contents

# Executive Summary

Suter and Brown Research was contracted by Avery Fitness Center (AFC) to examine opportunities for revenue enhancement utilizing existing facilities and equipment. In particular, we conducted research (1) to discover existing member demographics and usage patterns (including fees paid) and (2) to investigate how members initially learn about AFC. The purpose of the research is to provide AFC managers a valid understanding of who their customers are and how they use the center, including insights about how use may differ depending upon demographics, so that growth opportunities may be identified. In addition, understanding how AFC members are initially attracted to the center will assist managers in planning communication efforts.

**About the Research.** We used mail surveys to reach a simple random sample of the population of all current and former AFC members who had utilized the center at least once in the previous 12 months. We received 231 usable mail surveys, for a response rate of 58%. We matched the survey data to existing data in the company's data base that were relevant to the research questions.

**Key Results.**

- The typical AFC member is female (80%), older (mean age 69, with 50% between the ages of 60 and 77), well educated (60% with a four-year or advanced college degree), and has a comfortable income (29% with annual household income greater than $75K).
- The most frequently used service at AFC is the therapy pool, with 45% of respondents having used the pool at least once in the 30 days prior to the survey. Weight training (32%) and classes (26%) were the next most frequently used services.
- On average, AFC members visit the Center 8.6 times per month (based on facility entry data), usually attending in the morning (76%). There were no demographic differences between heavy and light users.
- Respondents paid an average of $282 each in fees during the 12 months prior to the survey. The results indicate that being older, placing greater importance on social aspects as a reason to participate at AFC, and visiting the Center more frequently are associated with paying higher fees to the Center over the course of the year.
- 42% of respondents first came to AFC for rehab purposes or to address specific medical needs; 31% reported joining the Center for general health and exercise purposes. Word-of-mouth communication from friends and acquaintances (52%) or from doctors (23%) was the most common way in which members first learned about the Center.

**Recommendations.** We offer a number of recommendations based on these results:

1. Focus external marketing efforts on older individuals with greater social needs.
2. Implement programs for the identified target market to be held during morning hours. Alternatively, there is facility capacity in the afternoon and evening hours

3

when AFC is less populated. Opportunities exist to use this presently unused capacity or to consider cutting back hours to lower costs.

3. Speak at senior citizen centers and living groups whenever possible.

4. Focus on delivering the highest quality experience possible for existing members to promote word-of-mouth. It is especially important to encourage members who are motivated by social considerations to refer others to the Center.

5. Make informational brochures available for existing members to (a) allow them to learn more about the services available beyond those currently utilized and (b) pass along to their friends and acquaintances. Brochures can also be distributed during visits to senior citizen centers and living groups during speaking engagements.

6. Track the sources of medical referrals and develop a recognition system for those doctors who are referring the most patients.

7. Visit each of the medical offices regularly to supply informational brochures regarding the rehabilitation equipment and services available at the Center.

# Introduction

The owners and managers of Avery Fitness Center (AFC) are interested in growing the company at its current location. Founded 15 years ago, the company operates a single location in an older shopping center near a large university. AFC targets men and women ages 55 years and older, some of whom struggle with health issues. Many customers are attracted to the large indoor therapy pool that allows exercise using water resistance. Individuals become members of the Center by paying a monthly fee; they pay additional fees for special classes, use of personal trainers, etc.

Over the first 10 years of the company's existence, revenues grew steadily. Since that time, however, revenues have reached a plateau. Managers believe that AFC could easily support a 20-30% increase in membership without harming service quality utilizing its existing facility and current staffing level. Despite some initial efforts at advertising the Center, however, the number of members and total fees paid has remained about the same. Simply stated, the decision facing managers and guiding this research effort is **"How can we increase revenues at our current location?"**

AFC staff and managers can describe their clientele in general terms based on information provided on members' initial application forms. In addition, they have accurate data about when specific members are at the facility based on facility entry data, as well as accurate accounting records for each member. They have little information, however, about what motivates people to use AFC, what specific services they use, or basic education and household income data. As a result, we advised AFC to conduct a discovery-oriented project to collect communication-based survey data to match with the existing data held in their member data files. The resulting data were used to address two specific research problems: **(1) Determine member demographics and usage patterns, and (2) Investigate how members learn about AFC.**

On the following pages, we describe the method used, detail the results of our analyses, and offer recommendations based on our conclusions.

5

# Method

**Exploratory Research.** As we worked with AFC managers to define the problem to be addressed (see previous section), we conducted several types of **exploratory research**. We initially collected and read a variety of resources on fitness centers that cater to the mature target market in order to provide background information. The American Association of Retired Persons (AARP) and the International Council on Active Aging (ICAA) provided excellent insights.  The same was true of specific programs like Healthways' SilverSneakers Fitness Program and YMCA's Active Older Adults program.  Cheryl Matheis, AARP's senior vice president of health strategies stated, "Many older adults want to find community programs or facilities that can help them be more active."  This information was consistent with AFC's role in the community. Next, we conducted depth interviews with three company employees (one manager, two fitness trainers) to gain insights into the kinds of members who seem to attend AFC more regularly than others and their perceptions of the goals of the members with whom they most frequently interact.

In addition, we conducted depth interviews with six AFC members (four women, two men; three who use the facility daily, three who use the facility only occasionally). The goal was to begin to understand motivations to attend the Center and methods by which members initially learn about the Center. As a result of the exploratory research, we identified several motivations for attending and a variety of methods by which members might learn about the Center; these insights served to guide the development of the data collection form used in the next stage of our research.

**Descriptive research.** We collected primary data using a mail survey from a random sample of AFC members. We chose a mail survey over personal interviews or telephone surveys to keep costs as low as possible and because we anticipated a reasonable response rate due to the population and interest in the topic of the survey. Although an online survey would have been less expensive, we were concerned about the ability to reach the population, many of whom are elderly.

We matched the cross-sectional primary data from AFC members with existing data in the company's member database, including data from the initial application form, facility entry data, and accounting records (i.e., revenues paid by members in the 12 months prior to data collection). Thus, the project used data from four sources (i.e., the member survey, the initial application form, facility entry data, and accounting records). **Appendix A** presents the member survey, which contained several closed-ended questions along with an open-ended question that asked the respondent about the event that triggered the initial use of the Center. The initial application form, included

6

here as **Appendix B**, collects a variety of information about the applicant, including a closed-ended question about how they learned about the Center. We note that date-of-birth data was used to compute the age of the member in years. Facility entry data were aggregated across the 30-day period prior to distribution of the member survey to count number of visits to the Center and determine modal time period of entry (i.e., morning, afternoon, evening). Membership fees paid were aggregated across the 12 months prior to distribution of the member survey. Finally, we include the codebook for the project as **Appendix C**.

Based on input from AFC managers, we defined the population for the study as any AFC member who had utilized the Center at least once in the prior 12 months. Using the membership roster as a sampling frame and facility entry data to confirm membership in the defined population, we drew a simple random sample of 400 members, with a goal of receiving 200 usable responses. When we cut off the data collection period two weeks after distributing the mail surveys, we had received 231 surveys that could be matched to the other data sources for a <u>response rate of 58%</u>.

<u>Note:</u> We have constrained all analyses to the 231 matched cases for consistency purposes, even though we could have used data for the entire population from some analyses. Follow-up analyses using all available data showed no meaningful differences with the results included in this report.

# Results

## SECTION ONE: Determine member demographics and usage patterns.

<u>Overall Demographics.</u> To get a picture of the typical AFC member, we examined basic demographic data. An average AFC member can be described as:

- Female (80%)
- Older (mean age 69, with 50% between the ages of 60 and 77)
- Well educated (60% with a four-year or advanced college degree)
- Comfortable Income[1] (16% with annual household income of $30K or less; 29% greater than $75K)

---

[1] Note that 23% of respondents did not respond to the income item, leaving open the possibility of nonresponse error if those who did not respond are systematically different from those that did respond with respect to income. The high response rate to the survey (58%) lessens the potential impact of such error, however. In addition, it is reasonable to expect higher levels of income given the higher levels of education represented in the sample.

The data tables in **Appendix D** include complete information on these demographic variables.

Because increasing revenues is important to AFC managers as they plan future growth of the facility, investigating member income levels is an important determinant in their ability to pay both monthly and service-specific fees. We calculated the 95% confidence interval on the estimate of members with household incomes greater than $75,000 per year. We are 95% confident that the percentage of members with incomes above $75,000 in the population of all AFC members lies between 22% and 36%, inclusive. Given that AFC currently has 962 members, we can project that between 212 and 346 have incomes exceeding $75,000.

**Usage Statistics.** In this section, we present usage information for the Center and its services. Where appropriate, we indicate differences in usage based on various demographic variables; the differences are statistically significant at traditional levels ($p < .05$). To simplify the analysis and its presentation, we created combined response categories for age (younger: 70 years or less; older: 70+), level of education (less: some college or less; more: associates degree or above), and household income (lower: $60,000 or less; higher: more than $60,000).

(A) Services Used in Prior 30 Days

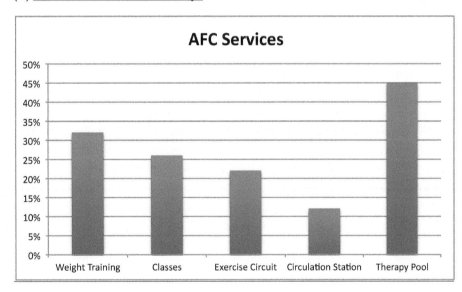

(1) **Weight Training:** Overall, **32%** of respondents reported using weight training at the Center in the prior month. Further analyses revealed that (a) men (51% vs. 27% for women), (2) those with higher levels of education (37% vs. 23% with less education), and (3) those with higher incomes (41% vs. 27% for those with lower levels of income) are more likely to have used weight training.

(2) **Classes: 26%** of respondents reported participating in classes at AFC in the prior month. The only demographic difference on use of classes occurred with gender. A higher proportion of women (30%) had participated in classes than had men (9%).

(3) **Exercise Circuit: 22%** of respondents utilized the exercise circuit during the prior 30 day period. There were no statistically significant differences in usage based on demographic variables.

(4) **Circulation Station:** Only **12%** of respondents overall had used the circulation station in the prior month. Respondents reporting lower income categories were more likely to have utilized the circulation station (17%) compared with those in higher income categories (5%).

(5) **Therapy Pool: 45%** of respondents reported using the therapy pool in the prior month, making it the most frequently mentioned service. Women (51%) were more likely than men (20%) to have used the therapy pool. In addition, those in lower income categories (55%) were more likely to have used the pool than those in higher categories (39%).

(B) Number of Visits to Center in Prior 30 Days

Across all respondents, the mean number of visits to AFC in the prior month was **8.6** (standard deviation = 7.6). Thirty-two percent (32%) of respondents had not visited the Center at all in the time frame; 48% had visited more than 8 times.

To determine if there were differences between those who visit AFC more frequently or less frequently, we performed a median split to convert number of visits from a continuous measure into two categories representing lower usage (8 visits or fewer) and higher usage (9 or more visits).[2] The results

---

[2] Normally, independent samples t-tests would be used to take advantage of the full information held in the ratio-level measure of number of visits. In this case, however, number of visits is not normally distributed (the modal response was "0") and we have opted to use cross-tab analyses.

9

indicate that there are no demographic differences between heavy half and light half users.

(C) Usual Time of Visit to AFC

Using actual time of facility entry we determined that the majority of AFC members visit the Center during the morning hours, as reported in the following pie chart and table:

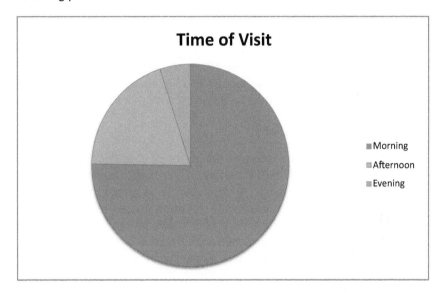

### Time of Visit

| Time of Visit | # Respondents | % Respondents |
|---|---|---|
| Morning | 119 | 76% |
| Afternoon | 31 | 20 |
| Evening | 7 | 5 |

(n = 157 AFC members who visited Center in prior 30 days)

As a result, about three-fourths of member activity at AFC occurs during morning hours. As a validity check on these results, Center employees confirmed that the majority of customers utilize the facility before noon.

Follow-up analyses revealed that the vast majority (81%) of those over the age of 70 attended the Center during morning hours and all of those visiting the facility during the evening were 70 years old or younger.

**Usage Statistics: Revenues.** In this section, we present overall revenues per customer along with breakdowns based on (1) demographic variables and (2) other usage variables.[3]

(A) Overall Revenue

The mean revenues amounted to **$282 per member** (std. dev. = $166). Twenty-five percent (25%) of respondents paid $155 or less in fees; 25% paid $400 or more.

(B) Revenues by Demographic Variables

Respondents aged more than 70 years spent an average of $324 per year at the Center; those below that age spent $246 per year. No other demographic characteristics were statistically significantly related to annual revenues.

(C) Revenues by Usage Variables

Next, we compared revenues per customer based on usage characteristics to determine if use of certain services (i.e., weight training, classes, exercise circuit, circulation station, therapy pool) or frequency of visits was associated with higher revenue streams. Two of these usage variables were associated with higher revenues: (1) Heavy-half users (those who visited nine or more times in the prior 30 days) paid annual fees of $318; light-half users paid annual fees of only $248, and (2) members that had participated in a class paid annual fees of $320, while those who had not taken a class paid fees of only $268.

(D) Revenues by Motivation to Attend

We asked respondents to rate the importance of four possible reasons to attend AFC on five-point scales. The most important reason was "general health and fitness" (4.7), followed by "specific medical concerns" (4.1), "physical enjoyment" (3.9), and "social aspects" (3.2). We performed a linear regression analysis to determine if the importance of any of these motivators was associated with greater revenues.

The results indicated that the more strongly people were motivated by "social aspects," the higher the fees they paid at the Center over the course of the

---

[3] Using current demographic and usage data to predict revenues from a prior time period is not ideal. Note, however, that this approach (1) is reasonable with the assumption that immediate past behavior is the best predictor of behavior in a following time period and (2) greatly increased the timeliness of the report (the alternative would have been to collect revenue data over the following 12 months, delaying presentation of results by one year).

11

year (i.e., $40 more for every point higher on the 1-5 importance scale; a respondent who scored the importance of social aspects as a "5" would have paid $120 more in fees than a respondent who scored the importance of social aspects as a "2," on average[4]).[5]

(D) <u>Revenues by All Statistically Significant Predictors</u>

Finally, because of the potential for interrelationships among the different statistically significant predictors of revenue (i.e., age, having taken classes, number of visits in the past 30 days, and the felt importance of social aspects for participating), we ran an overall analysis to confirm the important predictors of revenue. **The results indicate that being older, placing greater importance on social aspects as a reason to participate at AFC, and visiting the Center more frequently (p < .10) are associated with paying higher fees to the Center over the course of a year**. When considered simultaneously with the other predictors, taking classes at the Center does not lead to greater revenue. Overall, the model explained a modest amount of the variation in annual revenues; the coefficient of multiple determination ($R^2$) equaled 0.14.

---

**SECTION TWO: Investigate how members initially learn about AFC.**

A key outcome of the research for AFC managers is to discover the factors associated with bringing members to the Center in the first place. Two variables addressed this issue.

**"What was the original event that caused you to begin using services from AFC?"** Although we received a variety of responses to this open-ended question on the member survey, we were able to identify six basic categories, as shown below:

---

[4] The amount of increase is subject to change if additional predictors are added to the regression model, so the amount shown should be used with caution.

[5] The results also indicated that those more strongly motivated by "physical enjoyment" paid lower fees over the year (i.e., $36 less for every point higher on the scale). Follow-up analyses, however, revealed a robust positive correlation between the importance of physical enjoyment and the importance of social aspects, which, in effect, neutralizes the negative influence of "physical enjoyment" motivation on revenues. In fact, there is no bivariate correlation between "physical enjoyment" motivation and revenues. As a result, we see no net gain from attempting to influence AFC members' felt importance of physical enjoyment for participation. Increases in the importance of physical enjoyment will increase the importance of social aspects (which positively influences revenues) while at the same time exerting a direct negative influence on revenues.

12

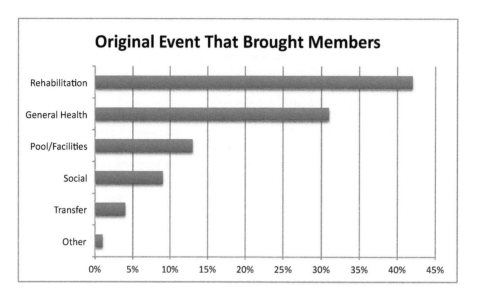

| Event | Percent |
|---|---|
| Rehabilitation or specific medical needs | 42% |
| General health and exercise | 31 |
| Pool / facilities | 13 |
| Social considerations | 9 |
| Transfer from another center | 4 |
| Other | 1 |

(n = 224)

As indicated in the table, the vast majority of AFC members originally came to the Center for rehabilitation purposes or to address specific medical needs (42%) or they came to the Center simply to pursue general health/exercise needs (31%).

Follow-up analyses found no differences in annual revenues across the categories of events leading members to the Center.

**"How did you learn about AFC?"** This closed-ended, check-all-that-apply question was included on the application form. Respondents considered seven possible responses about how they might have learned about the Center.

13

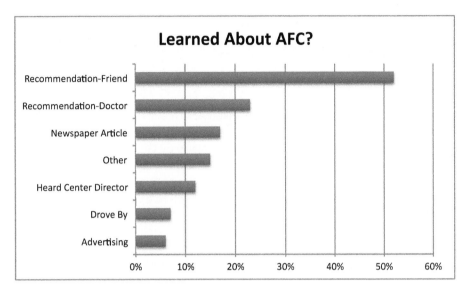

| Response | Percent |
| --- | --- |
| Recommendation from friend or acquaintance | 52% |
| Recommendation from doctor | 23 |
| Article in paper | 17 |
| Other | 15 |
| Heard AFC director speak | 12 |
| Drove by location | 7 |
| Advertising (including Yellow Pages) | 6 |

(n = 231)

It is clear that word-of-mouth recommendations provide the majority of AFC members initial information about the Center.[6]

To gain insight into future word-of-mouth behavior, we also asked respondents how likely they were to recommend AFC to others. Overall, the mean score on the 0-10 rating scale was 9.3 (std. dev. = 1.5) and fully 71% of respondents provided the highest score possible; AFC members have very strong intentions about telling others about the Center. Further analyses indicated that (1) those who place greater importance on social aspects as a motivation to visit the Center were more likely to recommend compared with those who placed lesser importance on the social aspect (87% vs. 63% provided the highest possible score on likelihood of recommending); (2) those who had

---

[6] Follow-up analyses found no differences in annual revenues across the different methods of learning about AFC, except that revenues for those who fell in the "other" category were higher on average ($346) than for those who did not ($270).

14

used the therapy pool in the prior 30 days were more likely to recommend the Center (85% vs. 59% for those who had not used the pool); and (3) women were more likely than men to recommend the Center to others (76% vs. 56%).

## Limitations

One potential limitation of the study is that we asked AFC members about their usage of various activities at the Center rather than obtain a behavioral measure of their actual activity. Although the technology exists for tracking activity by GPS location, many of the AFC members do not use the necessary technologies (e.g., smartphone, wearable technology) or simply do not turn on location services. We anticipate a degree of error in the study due to tendencies to over-report positive activities (e.g., working out).

# Conclusions and Recommendations

Because this project involved discovery-oriented research, the research itself does not offer a direct course of action for AFC managers. Instead, the results provide a wealth of background information necessary as building blocks for formulating strategies to address the key issue, **"How can we increase revenues at our current location?"**

The following is a summary of the key findings of the study and initial recommendations organized by the two research problems:

**(1) Determine member demographics and usage patterns.**

- The typical AFC member is female (80%), older (mean age 69, with 50% between the ages of 60 and 77), well educated (60% with a four-year or advanced college degree), and has a comfortable income (29% with annual household income greater than $75K).
- The most frequently used service at AFC is the therapy pool, with 45% of respondents having used the pool at least once in the 30 days prior to the survey. Weight training (32%) and classes (26%) were the next most frequently used services.
- On average, AFC members visit the Center 8.6 times per month, usually attending in the morning (76%). There were no demographic differences between heavy and light users.
- Respondents paid an average of $282 each in fees during the 12 months prior to the survey. The results indicate that being older, placing greater importance on social aspects as a reason to participate at AFC, and visiting the Center more frequently are associated with paying higher fees to the Center over the course of a year.

We offer a number of recommendations based on these results. A reasonable first step is to focus on the characteristics of the higher revenue members so that prospects with similar characteristics might be targeted in future marketing efforts.

As a result, **focusing marketing efforts on older individuals with greater social needs is recommended.** Identifying those with greater need for social interaction might be difficult, but efforts might begin with those who are widowed (or otherwise single). It might also be useful to train employees to inquire of current members about other group activities outside of the Center. Knowing the other interests of this target group and the groups to which they belong might help identify others with similar characteristics that might be interested in becoming members of the Center.

We took the analysis a step further to try and identify how the higher revenue members might differ from other members. As we reported in the results section, older members are more likely to utilize AFC during the morning hours; in fact, none of the older respondents in the dataset utilized the facility during the evening. **It may be possible to implement (and communicate) programs for the identified target market during morning hours** to further build on a strength of the Center. With sustained growth in morning hours, however, at some point it may be important **to shift demand to the afternoon hours**. (On a related note, given that very few members seem to visit AFC during the evening, **it may be advisable to cut costs by closing the facility earlier in the day**.)

**(2) Investigate how members learn about AFC.**

- 42% of respondents first came to AFC for rehab purposes or to address specific medical needs; 31% reported joining the Center for general health and exercise purposes. Word-of-mouth communication from friends and acquaintances (52%) or from doctors (23%) was the most common way in which members first learned about the Center.

It is clear that word-of-mouth communication is the dominant force in reaching new potential members. The primary recommendation we offer is to **focus on delivering the highest quality experience possible for existing members**. The existing members serve, in effect, as the "marketing department" for AFC and they will continue to spread positive recommendations as long as their experiences remain positive.

Given that many individuals first come to the Center for rehab or other medical needs and that many of them first learn about AFC from their doctors, establishing and maintaining relationships with the medical community in the region should also be a key priority. We recommend that the Center begin to **track the sources of medical referrals and to develop a recognition system for those doctors who are referring the most patients**. Recognition might be as simple as a phone call or note to say "thank you" or flowers sent to the office. It is also important to **visit each of the offices regularly to supply informational brochures** to be given to patients

16

needing rehab following medical procedures or who have been advised to pursue an exercise regimen.

Finally, it is important to **make informational brochures available for existing members** so that they have something tangible to give friends and acquaintances who may also be interested in finding a fitness center. It is interesting that AFC members who are motivated by social considerations are associated with both (1) higher revenues and (2) higher levels of intended word-of-mouth. It might be especially advantageous to **promote referrals among these individuals** because they are already motivated to promote the company to others and are more likely to be in contact with other individuals who share similar characteristics.

# References

American Association of Retired Persons (AARP), http://www.aarp.org.

International Council on Active Aging (ICAA), http://www.icaa.cc.

Healthways SilverSneakers Fitness Program, http://www.silversneakers.com.

YMCA, http://www.ymca.net.

Colin Milner, "Find a Fitness Center That Fits You," February 2011, accessed November 2011, http://www.aarp.org/health/fitness/info-02-2011/find_a_fitness_center_that_fits_you.html.

17

# Appendices

### Appendix A
### AFC Member Survey

**AVERY FITNESS CENTER SURVEY**

Thank you for taking time to provide important feedback about **Avery Fitness Center** (AFC) on this short survey. Please answer the following questions. Your candid responses will help us provide better services in the future. We have included your membership number so that we can include this informtion in your file. Please note that we do not share your information with anyone else.

**(1) Which of the following AFC services have you utilized at least once in the last 30 days? (Please check all that apply)**

- ☐ Weight Training
- ☐ Exercise Circuit
- ☐ Therapy Pool
- ☐ Classes
- ☐ Circulation Station

**(2) How important to you personally is each of the following reasons for participating in AFC programs? (Circle a number on each scale)**

| | not at all important | | | very important | |
|---|---|---|---|---|---|
| General Health and Fitness | 1 | 2 | 3 | 4 | 5 |
| Social Aspects | 1 | 2 | 3 | 4 | 5 |
| Physical Enjoyment | 1 | 2 | 3 | 4 | 5 |
| Specific Medical Concerns | 1 | 2 | 3 | 4 | 5 |

**(3) How likely is it that you would recommend AFC to a friend or colleague?**

| not at all likely | | | | neutral | | | | | extremely likely | |
|---|---|---|---|---|---|---|---|---|---|---|
| 0 | 1 | 2 | 3 | 4 | 5 | 6 | 7 | 8 | 9 | 10 |

**(4) What was the original event that caused you to begin using services from AFC?**

_____

**(5) Highest Level of Education Achieved:**

- ☐ Less than High School
- ☐ Some College
- ☐ Four-year College Degree
- ☐ High School Degree
- ☐ Associates Degree
- ☐ Advanced Degree

**(6) What is your approximate annual household income from all sources before taxes? (Please check the appropriate category & employment status):**

- ☐ $0-15,000
- ☐ $45,001-$60,000
- ☐ $90,001-105,000
- ☐ $15,001-30,000
- ☐ $60,001-75,000
- ☐ $105,001-120,000
- ☐ $30,001-45,000
- ☐ $75,001-90,000
- ☐ more than $120,000

Membership Number:
**072612**

*THANK YOU!*

18

**Appendix B**
**AFC Application Form**

# Avery Fitness Center
## MEMBERSHIP APPLICATION

### CONTACT INFORMATION

Your Name _____

Address Street _____ Apt _____

City _____ State _____ Zip _____

Preferred Telephone _____ Alternate Telephone _____

Email Address _____

Emergency Contact _____

Relationship _____ Telephone _____ Email address _____

### FAMILY MEMBERS Include your name on line 1.

| Name (Last, if Different) | Birth Date | Gender | Employer (if applicable) |
|---|---|---|---|
| 1. | | ☐ M  ☐ F | |
| 2. | | ☐ M  ☐ F | |
| 3. | | ☐ M  ☐ F | |
| 4. | | ☐ M  ☐ F | |
| 5. | | ☐ M  ☐ F | |
| 6. | | ☐ M  ☐ F | |
| 7. | | ☐ M  ☐ F | |
| 8. | | ☐ M  ☐ F | |

### MEMBERSHIP TYPE

Please select one of the following:
Membership

☐ Adult     ☐ Youth     ☐ Program Member
☐ Senior    ☐ Teen
☐ Family I  ☐ Student
☐ Family II

How did you learn about AFC? (Please check all that apply)

☐ Recommendation from Doctor                    ☐ Drove by location

☐ Recommendation from Friend of Acquaintance     ☐ Article in Paper

☐ Advertising (including Yellow Pages)           ☐ Other

☐ Heard AFC director speak

Signature _____

Date _____ _____ _____

For Office Use Only

Staff Name _____

Membership Number
☐☐☐☐☐☐☐☐☐☐☐☐☐

19

## Appendix C

## Codebook

| Variable Name | Data Source | Description | Data Code |
|---|---|---|---|
| MEMBERNUM | Application Form | Questionnaire identification number | (record number) |
| WEIGHT | Member Survey, April 2017 | Utilized weight training in previous 30 days? | 0 = no 1 = yes |
| CLASSES | Member Survey, April 2017 | Utilized classes in previous 30 days? | 0 = no 1 = yes |
| CIRCUIT | Member Survey, April 2017 | Utilized exercise circuit in previous 30 days? | 0 = no 1 = yes |
| STATION | Member Survey, April 2017 | Utilized circulation station in previous 30 days? | 0 = no 1 = yes |
| POOL | Member Survey, April 2017 | Utilized therapy pool in previous 30 days? | 0 = no 1 = yes |
| FITNESS | Member Survey, April 2017 | Importance for participation: General Health and Fitness | (1-5, "not at all important–very important") |
| SOCIAL | Member Survey, April 2017 | Social Aspects | (1-5, "not at all important–very important") |
| ENJOY | Member Survey, April 2017 | Physical Enjoyment | (1-5, "not at all important–very important") |
| MEDICAL | Member Survey, April 2017 | Specific Medical Concerns | (1-5, "not at all important–very important") |
| RECOM | Member Survey, April 2017 | How likely to recommend? (NPS) | (0–10, "not at all likely–extremely likely") |
| EVENT | Member Survey, April 2017 | What original event caused you to begin using services at AFC? | 1 = general health / exercise; 2 = pool/facilities; 3 = rehab / specific medical needs; 4 = social considerations; 5 = transfer from another center; 6 = other |
| EDUCAT | Member Survey, April 2017 | Highest level of education achieved? | 1 = less than high school; 2 = high school degree; 3 = some college; 4 = associates degree; 5 = four-year college degree; 6 = advanced degree |
| INCOME | Member Survey, April 2017 | Annual household income before taxes | 1 = $0–15,000; 2 = $15,001–30,000; 3 = $30,001–45,000; 4 = $45,001–60,000; 5 = $60,001–75,000; 6 = $75,001–90,000; 7 = $90,001–105,000; 8 = $105,001–120,000; 9 = more than $120,000 |
| DOCTOR | Application Form | How learned about AFC? Doctor Rec. | 0 = no 1 = yes |
| WOM | Application Form | How learned about AFC? Friend Rec. | 0 = no 1 = yes |
| ADVERT | Application Form | How learned about AFC? Advertising | 0 = no 1 = yes |
| SPEAKER | Application Form | How learned about AFC? Heard director speak | 0 = no 1 = yes |
| LOCATION | Application Form | How learned about AFC? Drove by location | 0 = no 1 = yes |
| ARTICLE | Application Form | How learned about AFC? Article in newspaper | 0 = no 1 = yes |
| OTHER | Application Form | How learned about AFC? Other | 0 = no 1 = yes |
| AGE | Application Form | Current Age | (current year minus birth year) |
| GENDER | Application Form | Gender | 1 = male; 2 = female |
| REVENUE | Accounting Records | Previous year Revenue from Respondent | (record aggregated amount) |
| VISITS30 | Facility Entry Data | Number of visits to AFC in previous 30 days | (record aggregated number) |
| DAYPART | Facility Entry Data | Modal time of day to visit AFC (prior 30 days) | 1 = morning; 2 = afternoon; 3 = evening |

MISSING = BLANK

20

**Appendix D**
**Data Tables**

## PART ONE: ITEMS FROM MEMBER SURVEY

**Which of the following AFC services have you utilized at least once in the last 30 days (Please check all that apply)**

| Service | Count | % Utilized | Sample Size (n) |
|---|---|---|---|
| Weight training | 73 | 32 | 231 |
| Classes | 61 | 26 | 231 |
| Exercise Circuit | 51 | 22 | 231 |
| Circulation Station | 28 | 12 | 231 |
| Therapy Pool | 104 | 45 | 231 |

**How important to you personally is each of the following reasons for participating in AFC programs? (Circle a number on each scale)**
**1 – 7, "not at all important" – "very important"**

| Reason | mean | std. dev. | two-box % | Sample Size (n) |
|---|---|---|---|---|
| General Health and Fitness | 4.7 | 0.7 | 95% | 229 |
| Social Aspects | 3.2 | 1.3 | 41 | 203 |
| Physical Enjoyment | 3.9 | 1.1 | 70 | 202 |
| Specific Medical Concerns | 4.1 | 1.2 | 78 | 209 |

**How likely is it that you would recommend AFC to a friend or colleague?**
**0 – 10, "not at all likely" – "extremely likely"**

mean = 9.3; std. dev. = 1.5; median = 10; n = 231

**What was the original event that caused you to begin using services from AFC? (open-ended)**

| Original Event | Count | % Respondents |
|---|---|---|
| General health / exercise | 70 | 31 |
| Pool / facilities | 28 | 13 |
| Rehab / specific medical needs | 95 | 42 |
| Social considerations | 20 | 9 |
| Transfer from another center | 8 | 4 |
| Other | 3 | 1 |

(n = 224)

**Highest Level of Education Achieved:**

| Education Level | Count | % |
|---|---|---|
| Less than High School | 4 | 2 |
| High School Degree | 34 | 15 |
| Some College | 46 | 20 |
| Associates Degree | 7 | 3 |
| Four-year College Degree | 52 | 23 |
| Advanced Degree | 82 | 36 |

(n = 225)

21

**What is your approximate annual household income from all sources, before taxes? (Please check the appropriate category & employment status)**

| Household Income | Count | % |
|---|---|---|
| $0 – 15,000 | 7 | 4 |
| $15,001 – 30,000 | 22 | 12 |
| $30,001 – 45,000 | 25 | 14 |
| $45,001 – 60,000 | 42 | 24 |
| $60,001 – 75,000 | 31 | 17 |
| $75,001 – 90,000 | 18 | 10 |
| $90,001 – 105,000 | 13 | 7 |
| $105,001 – 120,000 | 12 | 7 |
| More than $120,000 | 9 | 5 |
| (n = 179) | | |

## PART TWO: ITEMS FROM APPLICATION FORM

**How did you learn about AFC? (Please check all that apply)**

| Source | Count | % Utilized | Sample Size (n) |
|---|---|---|---|
| Recommendation from Doctor | 54 | 23 | 231 |
| Recommendation from Friend or Acquaintance | 121 | 52 | 231 |
| Advertising (including Yellow Pages) | 14 | 6 | 231 |
| Heard AFC director speak | 28 | 12 | 231 |
| Drove by Location | 15 | 7 | 231 |
| Article in Paper | 38 | 17 | 231 |
| Other | 35 | 15 | 231 |

**Current Age (computed from date of birth information)**

mean = 68.6; std. dev. = 11.9; (first quartile = 61, median = 70, third quartile = 77); n = 224

**Gender**

| Gender | Count | % |
|---|---|---|
| Male | 45 | 20 |
| Female | 177 | 80 |
| (n = 222) | | |

## PART THREE: ITEMS FROM ACCOUNTING RECORDS

**Previous 12-Month Revenues**

mean = $282; std. dev. = $166; (first quartile = $155; median = $280; third quartile = $400); n = 231

## PART FOUR: ITEMS FROM FACILITY ENTRY DATA

**Visits to AFC in prior 30-day period:**

mean = 8.6; std. dev. = 7.6; (32% did not visit; median = 8); n = 231

**Modal time of day to enter AFC in prior 30-day period:**

| Daypart | Count | % |
|---|---|---|
| Morning | 119 | 76 |
| Afternoon | 31 | 20 |
| Evening | 7 | 5 |
| (n = 231) | | |

23

**Appendix D**
**Data File**

The data file (Avery Fitness Center Data) for this project has been archived at www.cengagebrain.com and is available for download.

24

# Glossary

## A

**A/B test**  A field experiment in which two versions (i.e., A and B) of some marketing element are randomly assigned to subjects and then compared on outcomes of interest.

**accuracy**  The degree to which the reasoning in the report is logical and the information correct.

**advocacy research**  Research conducted to support a position rather than to find the truth about an issue.

**alternative hypothesis**  The hypothesis that a proposed result is true for the population.

**area sample**  A form of cluster sampling in which areas (e.g., census tracts, blocks) serve as the primary sampling units. Using maps, the population is divided into mutually exclusive and exhaustive areas, and a random sample of areas is selected.

**assumed consequences**  A problem that occurs when a question is not framed so as to clearly state the consequences, and thus it generates different responses from individuals who assume different consequences.

**attitude**  An individual's overall evaluation of something.

**awareness/knowledge**  Insight into, or understanding of, facts about, some object or phenomenon.

## B

**banner**  A series of cross tabulations between an outcome, or dependent variable, and several (sometimes many) explanatory variables in a single table.

**bar chart**  A chart in which the relative lengths of the bars show relative amounts of variables or objects.

**behavior**  What subjects have done or are doing.

**big data**  The process of capturing, merging, and analyzing large and varied data sets for the purpose of understanding current business practices and seeking new opportunities to enhance future performance.

**blunder**  An office error that arises during editing, coding, or data entry.

**branching question**  A question that routes people to different survey items based on their responses to the question.

## C

**case analysis**  Intensive study of selected examples of the phenomenon of interest.

**categorical measures**  A commonly used expression for nominal and ordinal measures.

**causal research**  Type of research in which the major emphasis is on determining cause-and-effect relationships.

**census**  A type of sampling plan in which data are collected from or about each member of a population.

**chi-square goodness-of-fit test**  A statistical test to determine whether some observed pattern of frequencies corresponds to an expected pattern.

**clarity**  The degree to which the phrasing in the report is precise.

**classification information**  Information used to classify respondents, typically for demographic breakdowns.

**cluster sample**  A probability sampling plan in which (1) the parent population is divided into mutually exclusive and exhaustive subsets, and (2) a random sample of one or more subsets (clusters) is selected.

**codebook**  A document that contains explicit directions about how data from data collection forms are coded in the data file.

**coding**  The process of transforming raw data into symbols (usually numbers).

**coefficient of multiple determination ($R^2$)**  A measure representing the relative proportion of the total variation in the dependent variable that can be explained or accounted for by the fitted regression equation. When there is only one predictor variable, this value is referred to as the *coefficient of determination*.

**communication**  A method of data collection involving questioning respondents to secure the desired information using a data collection instrument called a questionnaire.

**comparative-ratings scales**  A scale requiring subjects to make their ratings as a series of relative judgments or comparisons rather than as independent assessments.

**complete**  The degree to which the report provides all the information readers need in language they understand.

**composite measures**  A measure designed to provide a comprehensive assessment of an object or phenomenon with items to assess all relevant aspects or dimensions.

**confidence**  The degree to which one can feel confident that an estimate approximates the true value.

**confidence interval**  A projection of the range within which a population parameter will lie at a given level of confidence, based on a statistic obtained from a probabilistic sample.

**constant-sum method**  A comparative- ratings scale in which an individual divides some given sum among two or more attributes on a basis such as importance or favorability.

**continuous measures**  A commonly used expression for interval and ratio measures.

**continuous panel**  A fixed sample of respondents who are measured repeatedly over time with respect to the same variables.

**contrived setting** Subjects are observed in an environment that has been specially designed for recording their behavior.

**controlled test market** An entire test program conducted by an outside service in a market in which it can guarantee distribution.

**convenience sample** A nonprobability sample in which population elements are included in the sample because they were readily available.

**Cramer's *V*** A statistic used to measure the strength of the relationship between categorical variables.

**cross-sectional study** Investigation involving a sample of elements selected from the population of interest that are measured at a single point in time.

**cross tabulation** A multivariate technique used for studying the relationship between two or more categorical variables. The technique considers the joint distribution of sample elements across variables.

**cumulative percentage breakdown** A technique for converting a continuous measure into a categorical measure. The categories are formed based on the cumulative percentages obtained in a frequency analysis.

**customer relationship management (CRM)** A system that gathers all relevant information about a company's customers and makes it available to the employees that interact with the customers.

# D

**data aggregation** The process of creating summary data for a particular repeated behavior over a specified period of time.

**data merger error** Error resulting from the aggregation of data from or about a population element from multiple sources.

**data mining** The use of powerful analytic technologies to quickly and thoroughly explore mountains of data to obtain useful information.

**data system** The part of a decision support system that includes the processes used to capture and the methods used to store data coming from a number of external and internal sources. It is the creation of a database.

**data visualization** The process of using graphic illustrations to understand and communicate important relationships in large data sets.

**debriefing** A process of providing appropriate information, including informing respondents of the true purpose of a disguised study, after respondents have participated in the study itself and data have been collected.

**decision problem** The problem facing the decision maker for which the research is intended to provide answers.

**decision support system (DSS)** A system that combines data, models for guiding decisions, and a user interface that allows users to interact with the system to produce customized information.

**depth interview** Interviews with people knowledgeable about the general subject being investigated.

**descriptive analysis** Designed to enhance understanding of available data to benefit firm performance.

**descriptive research** Research in which the major emphasis is on describing characteristics of a group or the extent to which variables are related.

**descriptive statistics** Statistics that describe the distribution of responses on a variable. The most commonly used descriptive statistics are the mean and standard deviation.

**dialog system** The part of a decision support system that permits users to explore the databases by employing the system models to produce reports that satisfy their particular information needs. It is the user interface of the decision support system, which is also called a language system.

**discontinuous panel** A fixed sample of respondents who are measured repeatedly over time but on variables that change from measurement to measurement.

**discovery-oriented decision problem** A decision problem that typically seeks to answer "what" or "why" questions about a problem/opportunity. The focus is generally on generating useful information.

**disguise** An activity where a researcher attempts to hide the purpose or the sponsor of the study in order to receive the most objective results possible. The amount of knowledge people have about a study in which they are participating is an assessment of the effectiveness of the disguise activity.

**disguised observation** The subjects are not aware that they are being observed.

**double-barreled question** A question that calls for two responses and creates confusion for the respondent.

**double-entry** Data entry procedure in which data are entered separately by two people in two data files, and the data files are compared for discrepancies.

**dummy table** A table (or figure) used to show how the results of an analysis will be presented.

# E

**editing** The inspection and correction of the data received from each element of the sample (or census).

**ethics** Moral principles and values that govern the way an individual or a group conducts its activities.

**ethnography** The detailed observation of consumers during their ordinary daily lives using direct observations, interviews, and video and audio recordings.

**experiment** Scientific investigation in which an investigator manipulates one or more independent variables and observes the degree to which the dependent variables change.

**exploratory research** Research conducted to gain ideas and insights to better define the problem or opportunity confronting a manager.

**external validity**  The degree to which the results of an experiment can be generalized, or extended, to other situations.

**eye camera**  A device used by researchers to study a subject's eye movements while he or she is reading advertising copy.

# F

**facial coding**  A technique for measuring emotions that uses cameras to record small, involuntary movements (microexpressions) in the muscles around a person's mouth and eyes.

**field experiment**  Research study in a realistic situation in which one or more independent variables are manipulated by the experimenter under as carefully controlled conditions as the situation will permit.

**filter question**  A question used to determine if a respondent is likely to possess the knowledge being sought; also used to determine if an individual qualifies as a member of the defined population.

**fixed-alternative questions**  Questions in which the responses are limited to stated alternatives.

**focus group**  An interview conducted among a small number of individuals simultaneously; the interview relies more on group discussion than on directed questions to generate data.

**frequency analysis**  A count of the number of cases that fall into each of the possible response categories.

**funnel approach**  An approach to question sequencing that gets its name from its shape, starting with broad questions and progressively narrowing down the scope.

# G

**galvanometer**  A device used to measure the emotion induced by exposure to a particular stimulus by recording changes in the electrical resistance of the skin associated with the tiny degree of sweating that accompanies emotional arousal; in marketing research, the stimulus is often specific advertising copy.

**geodemography**  The availability of demographic, consumer behavior, and lifestyle data by arbitrary geographic boundaries that are typically quite small.

**global measure**  A measure designed to provide an overall assessment of an object or phenomenon, typically using one or two items.

**graphic-ratings scales**  A scale in which individuals indicate their ratings of an attribute typically by placing a check at the appropriate point on a line that runs from one extreme of the attribute to the other.

# H

**histogram**  A form of column chart on which the values of the variable are placed along the *x*-axis and the absolute or relative frequency of the values is shown on the *y*-axis.

**human observation**  Individuals are trained to systematically observe a phenomenon and to record on the observational form the specific events that take place.

**hypothesis**  A statement of unproven propositions about some phenomenon of interest that specifies how two or more measurable variables are related.

# I

**in-bound surveys**  A method of data collection in which respondents access a survey by telephone or online to respond to survey items.

**independent samples *t*-test for means**  A technique commonly used to determine whether two groups differ on some characteristic assessed on a continuous measure.

**intentions**  Anticipated or planned future behavior.

**internal validity**  The degree to which an outcome can be attributed to an experimental variable and not to other factors.

**interval scale**  Measurement in which the assigned numbers legitimately allow the comparison of the size of the differences among and between members.

**item nonresponse**  A source of error that arises when a respondent agrees to an interview but refuses, or is unable, to answer specific questions.

**itemized-ratings scales**  A scale on which individuals must indicate their ratings of an attribute or object by selecting the response category that best describes their position on the attribute or object.

# J

**judgment sample**  A nonprobability sample in which the sample elements are handpicked because they are expected to serve the research purpose.

**justice approach**  A method of ethical or moral reasoning that focuses on the degree to which benefits and costs are fairly distributed across individuals and groups. If the benefits and costs of a proposed action are fairly distributed, an action is considered to be ethical.

# K

**knowledge management**  The systematic collection of employee knowledge about customers, products and processes, and the marketplace.

# L

**laboratory experiment**  Research investigation in which investigators create a situation with exact conditions in order to control some variables and manipulate others.

**leading question**  A question framed so as to give the respondent a clue as to how he or she should answer.

**lifestyle**  How individuals live, what interests them, their values, and what they like.

**line chart** A two-dimensional chart with the *x*-axis representing one variable (typically time) and the *y*-axis representing another variable.

**literature search** A search of statistics, trade journal articles, other articles, magazines, newspapers, books, and/or online sources for data or insight into the problem at hand.

**longitudinal study** Investigation involving a fixed sample of elements that is measured repeatedly through time.

# M

**mall intercept** A method of data collection in which interviewers in a shopping mall stop or interrupt a sample of those passing by to ask them if they would be willing to participate in a research study.

**market testing (test marketing)** A controlled experiment done in a limited but carefully selected sector of the marketplace.

**marketing dashboard** A visual display of relevant marketing information designed to provide interactive access to a company's key marketing metrics.

**marketing ethics** The principles, values, and standards of conduct followed by marketers. Marketing researchers must make many decisions over the course of a single research project. Throughout the process, researchers must consider the ethics involved in the choices they make.

**marketing information system (MIS)** A set of procedures and methods for the regular, planned collection, analysis, and presentation of information for use in making marketing decisions.

**marketing research** The process of gathering and interpreting data for use in developing, implementing, and monitoring the firm's marketing plans.

**measurement** The process of assigning numbers to represent properties of an object's attributes.

**mechanical observation** An electrical or mechanical device observes a phenomenon and records the events that take place.

**median split** A technique for converting a continuous measure into a categorical measure with two approximately equal-sized groups. The groups are formed by "splitting" the continuous measure at its median value.

**merging** The process of combining data from different data sources into a single database.

**mobile data** Both structured and unstructured data available from mobile telephones, including smartphones and other mobile devices like tablet computers.

**model system** The part of a decision support system that includes all the routines that allow the user to manipulate the data so as to conduct the kind of analysis the individual desires. It is the collection of analytical tools to interpret the database.

**moderator** The individual that meets with focus group participants and guides the session.

**moderator's guidebook** An ordered list of the general (and specific) issues to be addressed during a focus group; the issues normally should move from general to specific.

**motive** A need, a want, a drive, a wish, a desire, an impulse, or any inner state that energizes, activates, moves, directs or channels behavior toward goals.

# N

**natural setting** Subjects are observed in the environment where the behavior normally takes place.

**nominal groups** A group interview technique that initially limits respondent interaction while attempting to maximize input from individual group members.

**nominal scale** Measurement in which numbers are assigned to objects or classes of objects solely for the purpose of identification.

**noncoverage error** Error that arises because of failure to include qualified elements of the defined population in the sampling frame.

**nonprobability sample** A sample that relies on personal judgment in the element selection process.

**nonresponse error** Error from failing to obtain information from some elements of the population that were selected and designated for the sample.

**not-at-homes** Nonresponse error that arises when respondents are not at home when the interviewer calls.

**null hypothesis** The hypothesis that a proposed result is not true for the population. Researchers typically attempt to reject the null hypothesis in favor of some alternative hypothesis.

# O

**observation** A method of data collection in which the situation of interest is watched and the relevant facts, actions, or behaviors are recorded.

**office error** Error due to data editing, coding, or analysis errors.

**Omni-channel Transactional Data** A collective term for all the different purchasing options a consumer has available, including store-based retailers, e-commerce sites, mobile purchasing, in-store pickup, home delivery, and so on.

**online surveys** A method of administration that relies on the Web for completing the survey.

**open-ended question** A question in which respondents are free to reply in their own words rather than being limited to choosing from among a set of alternatives.

**optical scanning** The use of scanner technology to "read" responses on paper surveys and to store these responses in a data file.

**ordinal scale** Measurement in which numbers are assigned to data on the basis of some order (for example, more than, greater than) of the objects.

**outlier** An observation so different in magnitude from the rest of the observations that the analyst chooses to treat it as a special case.

# P

**paired sample *t*-test**  A technique for comparing two means when scores for both variables are provided by the same sample.

**paper-based survey**  A survey usually administered by mail to designated respondents with an accompanying cover letter. The respondents return the questionnaire by mail to the research organization.

**parameter**  A characteristic or measure of a population.

**Pearson chi-square ($X^2$) test of independence**  A commonly used statistic for testing the null hypothesis that categorical variables are independent of one another.

**Pearson product-moment correlation coefficient**  A statistic that indicates the degree of linear association between two continuous variables. The correlation coefficient can range from −1 to +1.

**people meter**  A device used to measure when a television is on, to what channel it is tuned, and who in the household is watching it.

**personal interview**  Direct, face-to-face conversation between a representative of the research organization, the interviewer, and a respondent or interviewee.

**personality**  Normal patterns of behavior exhibited by an individual; the attributes, traits, and mannerisms that distinguish one individual from another.

**pictograms**  A bar chart in which pictures represent amounts — for example, piles of dollars for income, pictures of cars for automobile production, people in a row for population.

**pie chart**  A circle representing a total quantity that is divided into sectors, with each sector showing the size of the segment in relation to that total.

**population**  All cases that meet designated specifications for membership in the group.

**portable people meter**  A pager-like device carried with a person or worn on a person's clothing used to measure when a person is listening to a radio station or watching a television broadcast outside their home.

**precision**  The degree of error in an estimate of a population parameter.

**predictive analysis**  Designed to aid both explanatory and forecasting abilities for the betterment of the firm.

**prescriptive analysis**  Designed to optimize the various courses of action available to enhance firm performance.

**pretest**  Use of a questionnaire (or observation form) on a trial basis in a small pilot study to determine how well the questionnaire (or observation form) works.

**primary data**  Information collected specifically for the investigation at hand.

**primary source**  The originating source of secondary data.

**probability sample**  A sample in which each target population element has a known, nonzero chance of being included in the sample.

**projective methods**  Methods that encourage respondents to reveal their own feelings, thoughts, and behaviors by shifting the focus away from the individual through the use of indirect tasks.

**p-value**  The probability of obtaining a given result if in fact the null hypothesis were true in the population. A result is regarded as statistically significant if the *p*-value is less than the chosen significance level of the test.

# Q

**question order bias**  The tendency for earlier questions on a questionnaire to influence respondents' answers to later questions.

**quota sample**  A nonprobability sample chosen so that the proportion of sample elements with certain characteristics is about the same as the proportion of the elements with the characteristics in the target population.

# R

**random error**  Error in measurement due to temporary aspects of the person or measurement situation and affects the measurement in irregular ways.

**random-digit dialing (RDD)**  A technique used in studies using telephone interviews, in which the numbers to be called are randomly generated.

**randomized-response model**  An interviewing technique in which potentially embarrassing and relatively innocuous questions are paired, and the question the respondent answers is randomly determined but is unknown to the interviewer.

**ratio scale**  Measurement that has a natural, or absolute, zero and therefore allows the comparison of absolute magnitudes of the numbers.

**recall loss**  A type of error caused by a respondent's forgetting that an event happened at all.

**recording error**  Mistakes made by humans or machines in the process of recording respondents' communication- or observation-based data.

**refusals**  Nonresponse error resulting because some designated respondents refuse to participate in the study.

**regression analysis**  A statistical technique used to derive an equation representing the influence of a single (simple regression) or multiple (multiple regression) independent variables on a continuous dependent, or outcome, variable.

**reliability**  Ability of a measure to obtain similar scores for the same object, trait, or construct across time, across different evaluators, or across the items forming the measure.

**request-for-proposal (RFP)**  A document that describes, as specifically as possible, the nature of the problem for which research is sought and that asks providers to offer proposals, including cost estimates, about how they would perform the job.

**research problem**  A restatement of the decision problem in research terms.

**research proposal** A written statement that describes the marketing problem, the purpose of the study, and a detailed outline of the research methodology.

**research request agreement** A document prepared by the researcher after meeting with the decision maker that summarizes the problem and the information that is needed to address it.

**response error** Error that occurs when an individual provides an inaccurate response, consciously or subconsciously, to a survey item.

**response latency** The amount of time a respondent deliberates before answering a question.

**response order bias** An error that occurs when the response to a question is influenced by the order in which the alternatives are presented.

**response rate** The number of completed interviews with responding units divided by the number of eligible responding units in the sample.

**response set bias** A problem that arises when respondents answer questionnaire items in a similar way without thinking about the items.

**rights approach** A method of ethical or moral reasoning that focuses on the welfare of the individual and that uses means, intentions, and features of an act itself in judging its ethicality. If any individual's rights are violated, the act is considered unethical.

**role playing** A projective method in which a researcher will introduce a scenario or context and ask respondents to play the role of a person in the scenario.

# S

**sample** Selection of a subset of elements from a larger group of objects.

**sample mean** The arithmetic average value of the responses on a variable.

**sample standard deviation** A measure of the variation of responses on a variable. The standard deviation is the square root of the calculated variance on a variable.

**sample survey** Cross-sectional study in which the sample is selected to be representative of the target population and in which the emphasis is on the generation of summary statistics, such as averages and percentages.

**sampling error** The difference between results obtained from a sample and results that would have been obtained had information been gathered from or about every member of the population.

**sampling frame** The list of population elements from which a sample will be drawn; the list might consist of geographic areas, institutions, individuals, or other units.

**sampling interval** The number of population elements to count (k) when selecting the sample members in a systematic sample.

**scanner** An electronic device that automatically reads the bar code imprinted on a product, looks up the price in an attached computer, and instantly prints the description and price of the item on the cash register receipt.

**secondary data** Data that have already been collected, often for some other purpose or by some other organization.

**secondary source** A source of secondary data that did not originate the data but rather secured them from another source.

**self-report** A method of assessing attitudes in which individuals are asked directly for their beliefs about or feelings toward an object or class of objects.

**semantic-differential scale** A self-report technique for attitude measurement in which the subjects are asked to check which cell between a set of bipolar adjectives or phrases best describes their feelings toward the object.

**sentence completion** A projective method in which respondents are directed to complete a number of sentences with the first words that come to mind.

**significance level (a)** The acceptable level of error selected by the researcher, usually set at 0.05. The level of error refers to the probability of rejecting the null hypothesis when it is actually true for the population

**simple random sample** A probability sampling plan in which each unit included in the population has a known and equal chance of being selected for the sample.

**simulated test market (STM)** A study in which consumer ratings are obtained along with likely or actual purchase data often obtained in a simulated store environment; the data are fed into computer models to produce sales and market share predictions.

**single-source data** Data that allow researchers to link together purchase behavior, household characteristics, and advertising exposure at the household level.

**snake diagram** A diagram that connects the average responses to a series of semantic-differential statements, thereby depicting the profile of the object or objects being evaluated.

**snowball sample** A judgment sample that relies on the researcher's ability to locate an initial set of respondents with the desired characteristics.

**social data** Unstructured data available from social media and social networking Web-based platforms.

**split-ballot technique** A technique for combatting response bias in which researchers use multiple versions of a survey, with different wordings of an item or different orders of response options.

**standard test market** A test market in which the company sells the product through its normal distribution channels.

**standardized marketing information** Secondary data collected by companies that sell the data to multiple companies, allowing the costs of collecting, editing, coding, and analyzing them to be shared. The data are standardized so that multiple companies can use them rather than customized for a specific company.

**statistic** A characteristic or measure of a sample.

**storytelling** A projective method of data collection relying on a picture stimulus such as a cartoon, photograph, or drawing, about which the subject is asked to tell a story.

**strategy-oriented decision problem**   A decision problem that typically seeks to answer "how" questions about a problem/opportunity. The focus is generally on selecting alternative courses of action.

**stratified sample**   A probability sample in which (1) the population is divided into mutually exclusive and exhaustive subsets, and (2) a probabilistic sample of elements is chosen independently from each subset.

**stratum chart**   A set of line charts in which quantities are aggregated or a total is disaggregated so that the distance between two lines represents the amount of some variable.

**structure**   The degree of standardization used with the data collection instrument.

**structured data**   Data that can be written into rows on a spreadsheet or database based on standard column headings.

**structured observation**   Method of observation in which the phenomena to be observed (typically behaviors) can be defined precisely along with the categories used to record the phenomena.

**sugging**   Attempting to sell products or services or ideas under the guise of marketing research.

**summated-ratings scale**   A self-report technique for attitude measurement in which respondents indicate their degree of agreement or disagreement with each of a number of statements.

**systematic error**   Error in measurement that is also known as constant error since it affects the measurement in a constant way.

**systematic sample**   A probability sampling plan in which every $k$th element in the population is selected for the sample pool after a random start.

## T

**target information**   The basic information that addresses the subject of the study.

**telephone interview**   Telephone conversation between a representative of the research organization, the interviewer, and a respondent or interviewee.

**telescoping error**   A type of error resulting from the fact that most people remember an event as having occurred more recently than it did.

**total sampling elements (TSE)**   The number of population elements that must be drawn from the population and included in the initial sample pool in order to end up with the desired sample size.

**two-box technique**   A technique for converting an interval-level rating scale into a categorical measure, usually used for presentation purposes. The percentage of respondents choosing one of the top two positions on a rating scale is reported.

## U

**undisguised observation**   The subjects are aware that they are being observed.

**unstated alternative**   An alternative answer that is not expressed in a question's options.

**unstructured data**   Data that take the form of social media comments, blog posts, other text-based communication, photos, video, audio, or any other form that is not easily arranged in structured format.

**unstructured observation**   Method of observation in which the researcher has a great deal of flexibility in terms of what to note and record.

**utility approach**   A method of ethical or moral reasoning that focuses on society and the net consequences that an action may have. If the net result of benefits minus costs is positive, the act is considered ethical; if the net result is negative, the act is considered unethical.

## V

**validity**   The extent to which differences in scores on a measuring instrument reflect true differences among individuals, groups, or situations in the characteristic that it seeks to measure or true differences in the same individual, group, or situation from one occasion to another, rather than systematic or random errors.

**variety**   The combination of structured and unstructured data collected in "big data" systems.

**velocity**   The pace of data flow, both into and out of a firm.

**veracity**   The accuracy and trustworthiness of data collected in "big data" systems.

**virtual test market**   A simulated test market in which subjects "interact" with products and stores electronically, rather than physically.

**voice-pitch analysis**   Analysis that examines changes in the relative frequency of the human voice that accompany emotional arousal.

**volume**   The sheer amount of data being collected in "big data" systems.

## W

**word association**   A projective method in which participants are asked to respond to a list of words with the first word that comes to mind.

# Index